Organization Theory
Volume I

The International Library of Critical Writings on Business and Management

For a list of all Edward Elgar published titles visit our site on the World Wide Web at
www.e-elgar.com

Organization Theory
Volume I

Central Topics

Edited by

Barbara Czarniawska

Swedish Research Council and Malmsten Foundation Chair of Management Studies,
Göteborg University, Sweden

THE INTERNATIONAL LIBRARY OF CRITICAL WRITINGS ON BUSINESS AND MANAGEMENT

An Elgar Reference Collection
Cheltenham, UK • Northampton, MA, USA

Published by
Edward Elgar Publishing Limited
Glensanda House
Montpellier Parade
Cheltenham
Glos GL50 1UA
UK

Edward Elgar Publishing, Inc.
136 West Street
Suite 202
Northampton
Massachusetts 01060
USA

A catalogue record for this book is available from the British Library

ISBN-13: 978 1 84376 937 8
ISBN-10: 1 84376 937 9 (2 volume set)

Printed and bound in Great Britain by MPG Books Ltd, Bodmin, Cornwall.

Contents

Acknowledgements

The editor and publishers wish to thank the authors and the following publishers who have kindly given permission for the use of copyright material.

Administrative Science Quarterly for articles: D.J. Hickson, C.R. Hinings, C.A. Lee, R.E. Schneck and J.M. Pennings (1971), 'A Strategic Contingencies' Theory of Intraorganizational Power', *Administrative Science Quarterly*, **16** (2), June, 216–29; Michael D. Cohen, James G. March and Johan P. Olsen (1972), 'A Garbage Can Model of Organizational Choice', *Administrative Science Quarterly*, **17** (1), March, 1–25; Karl E. Weick (1976), 'Educational Organizations as Loosely Coupled Systems', *Administrative Science Quarterly*, **21** (1), March, 1–19; Chris Argyris (1976), 'Single-Loop and Double-Loop Models in Research on Decision Making', *Administrative Science Quarterly*, **21** (3), September, 363–75; Stewart Clegg (1981), 'Organization and Control', *Administrative Science Quarterly*, **26** (4), December, 545–62; Linda Smircich (1983), 'Concepts of Culture and Organizational Analysis', *Administrative Science Quarterly*, **28** (3), September, 339–58.

American Society for Public Administration for article: Dwight Waldo (1961), 'Organization Theory: An Elephantine Problem', *Public Administration Review*, **21** (4), Autumn, 210–25.

Blackwell Publishing Ltd for article: Nils Brunsson (1982), 'The Irrationality of Action and Action Rationality: Decisions, Ideologies and Organizational Actions', *Journal of Management Studies*, **19** (1), 29–44.

Copyright Clearance Center for article: Jeffrey Pfeffer (1977), 'The Ambiguity of Leadership', *Academy of Management Review*, **2** (1), January, 104–12.

Elsevier for articles and excerpt: Gary Yukl (1971), 'Toward A Behavioral Theory of Leadership', *Organizational Behavior and Human Performance*, **6** (4), July, 414–40; Edgar H. Schein (1983), 'The Role of the Founder in Creating Organizational Culture', *Organizational Dynamics*, **12**, Summer, 13–28; John Van Maanen and Stephen R. Barley (1984), 'Occupational Communities: Culture and Control in Organizations', in B.M. Staw and L.L. Cummings (eds), *Research in Organizational Behavior: Volume 6*, 287–365.

Institute for Operations Research and the Management Sciences for article: William G. Ouchi (1979), 'A Conceptual Framework for the Design of Organizational Control Mechanisms', *Management Science*, **25** (9), September, 833–48.

Oxford University Press for excerpt: Bo Hedberg (1981), 'How Organizations Learn and Unlearn', in Paul C. Nystrom and William H. Starbuck (eds), *Handbook of Organizational Design, Volume 1: Adapting Organizations to Their Environments*, Chapter 1, 3–27.

RAND for article: James G. March (1978), 'Bounded Rationality, Ambiguity, and the Engineering of Choice', *Bell Journal of Economics*, **9** (2), Autumn, 587–608.

Sage Publications Inc. for articles: Linda Smircich and Gareth Morgan (1982), 'Leadership: The Management of Meaning', *Journal of Applied Behavioral Science*, **18** (3), 257–73; Scott D.N. Cook and Dvora Yanow (1993), 'Culture and Organizational Learning', *Journal of Management Inquiry*, **2** (4), December, 373–90.

Sage Publications Ltd for excerpt and article: Niklas Luhmann (1986), 'The Autopoiesis of Social Systems', in Felix Geyer and Johannes van der Zouwen (eds), *Sociocybernetic Paradoxes: Observation, Control and Evolution of Self-steering Systems*, Chapter 11, 172–92; Nils Brunsson and Kerstin Sahlin-Andersson (2000), 'Constructing Organizations: The Example of Public Sector Reform', *Organization Studies*, **21** (4), 721–46.

Springer Science and Business Media for article: Charles Perrow (1991), 'A Society of Organizations', *Theory and Society*, **20** (6), December, 725–62.

Every effort has been made to trace all the copyright holders but if any have been inadvertently overlooked the publishers will be pleased to make the necessary arrangement at the first opportunity.

In addition the publishers wish to thank the Marshall Library of Economics, Cambridge University, the Library of the University of Warwick and the Library of Indiana University at Bloomington, USA for their assistance in obtaining these articles.

Introduction

Barbara Czarniawska

As civilized human beings, we are the inheritors neither of an inquiry about ourselves and the world, nor of an accumulating body of information, but of a conversation begun in primeval forest and extended and made more articulate in the course of centuries ... (Michael Oakeshott, [1959] 1991, p. 490)[1]

This collection of texts is not intended to present organization theory as an edifice, constructed from its fundaments upward, on its way to becoming a monument. Its conception has been inspired by Michael Oakeshott's idea of science as a historically situated conversation. The topics of such conversation are shaped by historical contingencies and inserted in place and time by fashion, understood in the way Gabriel Tarde and Georg Simmel suggested: as the central mechanism of collective choice. Accordingly, the topics of today may be influenced by the topics of yesterday, but could just as well deliberately avoid the latter if they seem to have exhausted their promise. This does not mean that the problems of yesterday have been solved, merely that the metaphors of the past have lost their glitter, the turns of phrase are worn out, and a satiation of form has created a satiation of contents, for the two always go together. Later, the same topics may be rediscovered, either because of a contingency external to the conversation that placed them again in the light of day or because their 'antiquity' gives them a new charm, while the recontextualization renders them meaningful once again.

One of the difficulties inherent in the task of portraying the course of any such conversation, however sketchily, is its necessary limitation in time. Situated in a European tradition, as this collection will inevitably be, a collection of texts on organization theory could start with Plato; or, if limited only to modernity, Machiavelli might be chosen as the first interlocutor. Obviously, such an enterprise is beyond my capacity. Therefore, I decided to treat the term literally, and begin at the point when the 'organization theory' label was first applied in the 1960s – at the time when systems theory entered the conversation.

For the end of my reporting, I chose the year 2000 – because it inaugurated a new century, but also because it seems to be the point where this originally theoretical invention has reached, widely and persistently, the practice of organizing. Whether this means that the conversation of theoreticians has had serious impact on the conversation of practitioners or that the emerging practice has been accurately depicted by theory, as suggested by Charles Perrow, is not an issue. I adhere to the circuit model of culture (Johnson, 1986–87),[2] according to which the production, circulation, and consumption of cultural products constitute a loop, not a line.

A loop or a line, the development of organization theory during those 40 years was never smooth and unidirectional. Like all conversations tend to do, it jumped from topic to topic, digressed, ran in circles. I feel justified, however, in omitting topics that enjoyed a faddish popularity for a short time, then vanished from the collective attention. I selected writings that in my opinion – corroborated by citation patterns – continue to influence contemporary thinking about organizations. If they will continue to do so, or if they will make room for dramatically new topics and conversation forms, is more than anybody can say at the moment. Should the latter be the case, the present collection can be treated as a document of its time.

Volume I begins with the witness testimony – a book review from 1961 by Dwight Waldo who, with mixed feelings, observes the emergence of a new entity: an 'organization', which is not, as before, a state of affairs (opposite of disorganization) or an association, but an abstract entity soon to subordinate all others, known earlier as companies, enterprises, associations, or bureaucracies. By 1991, says Charles Perrow with alarm, large organizations invaded modern societies; by 2000, observe Nils Brunsson and Kerstin Sahlin-Andersson, societies are composed of organizations through and through.

In the remaining part of Volume I, the collection addresses topics that are, in fact, older than organization theory, but that have become adapted to it. These themes are classical, although 'organizational culture' is the latest arrival, on its way, as it were, from the second to the first volume. Volume II addresses 'current trends' – current, that is, in the 1990s, and in that sense, the selection is relatively conservative. It ends with reflections on method and on theory writing; even within those topics, the ordering is chronological.

Notes

1. Oakeshott, Michael ([1959] 1991), 'The Voice of Poetry in the Conversation of Mankind', in *Rationalism in Politics*. Indianapolis, IN: LibertyPress, 488–541.
2. Johnson, Richard (1986–87), 'What is Cultural Studies Anyway?', *Social Text*, **16**, 38–80.

Part I
Creating the Object of Organization Theory

In 1961, Dwight Waldo, then a central figure in administration theory, wrote a review essay for *Public Administration Review* (Chapter 1), at that time a leading journal in the field, entitled: 'Organization Theory: An Elephantine Problem.' Waldo's review encompassed six books: *Human Organization Research: Field Relations and Techniques*, edited by Richard N. Adams and Jack J. Preiss, 1960; *Understanding Organizational Behavior*, by Chris Argyris, 1960; *Modern Organization Theory*, edited by Mason Haire, 1959; *General Systems: Yearbook of the Society for General Systems Research*, vol. IV part II, *Contributions to Organization Theory*, edited by Ludwig von Bertalanffy and Anatol Rapoport, 1960; *Comparative Studies in Administration*, edited by the staff of the Administrative Science Center, University of Pittsburgh, 1959; and *Some Theories of Organization*, edited by Albert H. Rubenstein and Chadwick J. Haberstroh, 1960. Most of these works were edited books, and among the most frequent contributors were Herbert Simon, James G. March, Richard Cyert, Chris Argyris, Mason Haire, Anatol Rapoport, Jacob Marshak, Rensis Likert, Peter Blau, William Foote Whyte, James Thompson, and Kurt Lewin. Waldo noted:

> [N]early all the pieces printed or reprinted are the product of the past ten years; and ... a high proportion of the authors are in their early professional years. In short ... there is no doubt that organization theory and research are in a boom period. (1961, p. 212)

Waldo identified the main trends in this boom. One was a transition from administrative theory to organization theory. This shift resulted from an innovation in social science methodology – behaviorism – initiated by following the lead of the natural sciences. Such an approach did not conform with the notion of administration, which was 'an applied science – if it is not indeed a profession, and art, or something less. "Administrative theory" suggests an engagement with the world, a striving after values' (Waldo, 1961, p. 217). Organization theory was, on the other hand, a theory not of action, but of a unit existing 'out there'.

This unit had to be created, and the motive for its creation was a growing fascination with systems theory. The mainstream conceptual apparatus of today's organization theory was created in the 1950s in an attempt to apply systems theory to what used to be the object of administrative theory. 'Organization' was formerly employed as a noun denoting a state of being organized and was rarely, if ever, used in the plural. The application of systems theory required a creation of 'organizations', separate units divided by 'boundaries' from their 'environments' and related to them by 'adaptation'. This conceptual move must have been attractive at the time of its construction, providing a middle ground between mechanistic Taylorism and idealist administration theory, and permitting close bonds with the most attractive branch of science at the time – cybernetics.

Charles Perrow (Chapter 2) sees all of this as a historical process that started in practice long before an organization theory was created to accommodate it, and creates a counter-factual alternative. Nils Brunsson and Kerstin Sahlin-Andersson (Chapter 3) report a society filled with formal organizations, and describe the mechanisms that make it possible. One issue that they fail to raise is the likelihood that when everything becomes organized, it will be no longer possible to continue the process, and some new forms could emerge and dominate. This is a question that can be properly addressed only in another half-century, however.

[1]

Reviews of Books and Documents

Organization Theory: An Elephantine Problem

By DWIGHT WALDO, University of California

HUMAN ORGANIZATION RESEARCH: *Field Relations and Techniques,* edited by Richard N. Adams and Jack J. Preiss. Published for the Society for Applied Anthropology by the Dorsey Press, 1960. Pp. 456. $8.35.

UNDERSTANDING ORGANIZATIONAL BEHAVIOR, by Chris Argyris. The Dorsey Press, 1960. Pp. 179. $6.00.

MODERN ORGANIZATION THEORY: *A Symposium of the Foundation for Research on Human Behavior,* edited by Mason Haire. John Wiley & Sons, 1959. Pp. 324. $6.50.

GENERAL SYSTEMS: *Yearbook of the Society for General Systems Research,* Vol. IV (Part II, Contributions to Organization Theory, pp. 87-185), edited by Ludwig Von Bertalanffy and Anatol Rapoport. Society for General Systems Research, 1960. Pp. 251. $7.50.

COMPARATIVE STUDIES IN ADMINISTRATION, edited by the staff of the Administrative Science Center, University of Pittsburgh. University of Pittsburgh Press, 1959. Pp. 224. $6.00 cloth, $3.95 paper.

SOME THEORIES OF ORGANIZATION, edited by Albert H. Rubenstein and Chadwick J. Haberstroh. The Dorsey Press, 1960. $10.60.

I

TRYING to review these six books is like trying to review a vegetable market. All but one are collections of essays and excerpts, and altogether there is a round hundred of pieces. The purposes and perspectives of the editors vary and the pieces vary in their subjects from steel production in the Ruhr to human fertility interviewing in the Caribbean, from administering Thematic Apperception Tests to Asian peasants to the technical problems of constructing an "artificial organism," from potential relationships of graph theory with or-

ganization theory to techniques proper for research on the social structure of a West African urban community.

It may be well, therefore, to begin with an acknowledgment that perhaps these books should not be reviewed together on the presumption that they are related by virtue of a common subject. Let due weight be given to accidents of scheduling which brought them off the press fairly close together, to the perhaps not very significant fact that the titles seem to "cluster," to a wild and aberrant impulse of the reviewer which led him to request that three books be added to three already accepted for review.

So much admitted, let us get on with an attempt to describe and characterize. What do these books have—or reject—in common? In general, what is the range of their diversity?

All of the six books are concerned with theory of organization and with methods of research on organizations. However, there is a great range in the meaning ascribed to "organization" and what "theory" about it is or might be; and the proportions between "theory" and "research" vary widely. Two books illustrate both points. At one end of the scale is probably *Modern Organization Theory,* which is in large part concerned with various theoretical models for conceptualizing and analyzing organizations. At the other end is undoubtedly *Human Organization Research* which, as the title indicates, is more concerned with methods of research than with general organizational concepts. As to the meaning ascribed to organization, the first has, in general, a harder, sharper view: a meaning given to students of administration by customary associations—a manufacturing company or government bureau, certainly; a labor union or church, perhaps. The latter has a softer, more inclusive view: a meaning given by the broad disciplinary interests of sociolo-

BOOK REVIEWS

gists and anthropologists. So conceived, organization shades on one side into "group," on the other into "institution" or "society."

In general—as the above suggests—the authors and editors are behavioral in orientation. That is to say that they take the name and mission of social science very seriously, that they regard the biological, and especially the physical, sciences as supplying a model for emulation, and that they are deeply engaged with questions of scientific philosophy, logic, and techniques.[1] Conversely, not many are interested in specific practical reforms, fewer with general problems of public policy, none with philosophical concerns in a general or abstract sense. To be sure, there is a wide range of outlook and the opening phrase, "in general," bears repeating. It should be made clear also that certain authors are deeply concerned with the ethical as well as the methodological questions raised by social science research. In fact—though not necessarily by intent—*Human Organization Research* is a rather good "casebook" review of the ethical problems of the social science researcher: relations with colleagues, with informants, with the employing entity, with the subject organization or culture, etc.

The five edited books are more or less interdisciplinary in intent and to a considerable degree in fact. It is usually assumed and sometimes explicitly stated that organizations are complex interactions of phenomena of interest to all the social (or behavioral) sciences; and that therefore all disciplines are or should be concerned, so that the contribution of each may supplement and enrich that of the others. Sometimes it is thought that research should be undertaken by interdisciplinary teams, so that personal and disciplinary interaction will have an immediate "multiplier" effect; and there are some reports on interdisciplinary projects. Sometimes it is thought that, while organizational phenomena cross all the conventional disciplinary boundaries, the researcher to be effective must have mastered several disciplines, transforming himself into a general-purpose social scientist. At the extreme it may be held that organizational research is a multidisciplinary (or somehow unique) field in itself, to be differentiated from other social or behavioral sciences.

While multidisciplinary, the material presented is far from representing all disciplines equally. Sociology, business administration (and industrial management), social psychology, and anthropology are all well represented. Economics is less prominent. About a fourth of the contributions are by writers whose disciplinary background or professional-scientific interest is not to be classified by common academic field; they are multidisciplinary, perhaps, or identified with a research focus that has no clear disciplinary status. A few have clear labels, but outside social science: a mathematical biologist, for example.

Conspicuously absent are writers identified (at least presently and prominently) with public administration, political science, or history. This surely is no accident, but a judgment on the part of the editors that whatever the usefulness of these disciplines they have nothing at present to contribute to sophisticated organization theory or research. Nor for that matter is there any attention given to governmental organizations, excepting a few studies of the military, two slices from Selznick's study of the T.V.A., a piece on the problems of conducting social science research under contract with a Federal agency,[2] a report on patterns of communication in a government agency, and two pieces by one author discussing the problems of doing research in the Japanese Relocation Centers. Since it is generally assumed or asserted that organization has universals regardless of purpose or structure of particular organizations, this neglect of government may not be significant. But, it is at least a bit ironical that an enterprise that aspires for universality in its fruits should be so parochial in its roots.[3] In fact,

---

[1] Altogether there is a considerable amount of mathematical and quasi-mathematical formulation in the six books, and in some selections diagrams and equations bulk larger than prose. I confess that much of this was beyond my competence, and that I was limited to following the trail up to its disappearance into the clouds and picking it up again where it came down, always at about the same place. I accept it on authority that the view is much better at the higher altitudes, and draw what comfort I can from the fact that there is no significant change in latitude.

[2] Having had an experience similar to that related, I advise anyone contemplating such a research contract to read this piece: "Client Structure and the Research Process," by Smith, Sim, and Bealer, in *Human Organization Research*.

[3] For example, Rubenstein and Haberstroh state in their Preface that, "Although the dominant emphasis

excepting the anthropologists, the "organization theorists" smell strongly of the American factory. And students of public administration, after two decades of dispersal around the world, are (despite all their anguished cries about how "culture bound" their discipline is) comparatively cosmopolitan.[4]

Many of the points made in this attempt to characterize the six books will be illustrated or emphasized by indicating the names that occur frequently. The name Chris Argyris is prominent, as there are three of his essays in addition to his *Understanding Organization Behavior*. Without meaning to belittle Argyris, who is certainly one of the more rewarding to read,[5] his prominence is in part due to the "accidental" inclusion of his book. Not accidental, certainly, is the pre-eminence of the name of the unique and all but ubiquitous Herbert Simon, and on the manifest evidence a Simon Admiration Society of respectable size could be formed among the editors and contributors. The names of (at least) Anatol Rapoport, E. Wight Bakke, Jacob Marschak, Rensis Likert, and Richard Cyert appear on essays in more than one book. The names Peter Blau, William Foote Whyte, James Thompson, Kurt Lewin, and Harold Guetzkow will help further to suggest scope and orientation. There are no selections from Mary Parker Follett or Ordway Tead.

---

is on commercial and industrial organizations, the reader will appreciate that the principles discussed apply to any type of organization, including governmental, philanthropic, military, educational, voluntary, or political." The most restrained response I can make to such a statement is that it is presumptuous. There may be universal "principles," but we are a long way from knowing *whether* this is true, and *what* they may be.

[4] On the other hand, Edward H. Litchfield says in his Foreword to the Pittsburgh volume: "More sophisticated public administrators are now giving attention to the developments in business administration, but it has not been my observation that a great deal of interest in or knowledge of such developments has yet permeated to the working levels of public administration throughout the country." (p. viii) The editors of this volume, in their Preface, also feel that they must explain the "omission" of public administration by lamenting that despite their overseas involvement the public administrationists are not interested in "the administrative process involved." I have a suggestion for Fred Riggs' mailing list.

[5] Certainly *I* find him interesting and rewarding. But I cannot forbear observing that I read him with an adventitious interest—in some unusual spelling and syntax.

It may be noted further that nearly all of the pieces printed or reprinted are the product of the past ten years; and that a high proportion of the authors are in their early professional years. In short, while there may be a fortuitous factor in the review of these six books at one time, there is no doubt that organization theory and research are in a boom period, and many signs, including the youth of the participants in the boom, suggest more rather than less of what these books represent.

So much for an attempt to describe and characterize the books as a group. We now look briefly at each. For the most part, we must be content to indicate "what the book is like." Even to indicate the main theme of a hundred selections is impossible. Only a few essays that struck the reviewer as significant or interesting will receive comment. As there is no "natural" order apparent to the reviewer, the order selected is alphabetical, following the listing above.

Human Organization Research

The book edited by Adams and Preiss was published for the Society for Applied Anthropology, and seventeen of the thirty-two articles therein are reprinted from the Society's journal, now titled *Human Organization*. While the anthropological outlook is very strong, two-thirds of the contributors (say the editors) designate themselves sociologists. As the subtitle indicates, the book is focused upon "Field Relations and Techniques," and of the six books we deal with, this is the least concerned with general theory, the most closely concerned with research processes. Having decided upon a book on field research, say the editors, the material they found fell into "two fairly clear-cut areas: human relations, and instruments or techniques" (p. ix), and half the book is given to each.

This is also the book identified above as having the "softest" view of organization. Organization is not defined—certainly not by the editors—and from all that the book contains, "organization" is what exists when any two or more people are gathered together in any name whatsoever; though we are given an orienting observation in a Foreword by the President of the Society for Applied Anthropology, to the effect that the hallmark of the applied anthropologist is that he "tries to

BOOK REVIEWS

see the particular problem with which he is concerned as part of a larger functioning configuration of organizational and behavioral patterns, rather than in isolation." (p. vi)

Since few of the readers of *Public Administration Review* will be faced with the problem of installing a research team in an Indian village, or of translating interviews in Thai into English, this book may seem far afield indeed. The reviewer, however, found it one of the more interesting books that he set himself to read during the past year. It does not irritate with pretentiousness, and the pieces have the concreteness of case materials; indeed, the settings are so varied and exotic that there is some of the appeal of the travelogue. Probably any researcher (academic or "practicing") in public administration who has not finished learning would find something of value in it.

Understanding Organizational Behavior

This work by Argyris ranges widely between very general—but easily read—theoretical formulations to extensive quotations from interviews with factory workers, complete with Plain Talk. One has the impression that Argyris is writing too much, repeating himself —*Understanding Organizational Behavior* repeats the theoretical presentation of his *Personality and Organization* (1957), and there is further repetition in the three essays by his pen in the other books here represented. One also has the impression, however, of an unusual and desirable balance between the theoretical and the concrete, and between the scientific and the normative; of great energy, inquisitiveness, and a capacity for experimentation and growth.

In briefest compass, the theory developed at some length in *Personality and Organization* and repeated briefly in Chapter I of this work is that there is a conflict between the needs of the personality and the needs of the organization, and much of what takes place in organizations is to be understood in terms (a) of the resulting dissatisfactions and frustrations of the employees who react and adapt in various ways, (b) the resulting reactions by management to employee resistances and adaptations, which may actually accentuate the "undesirable" resistances and adaptations, and (c) the continual and intricate feedback and interac-

tion of the system of dynamic tension thus established. Informal organization and activities are the chief manifestations of employees' attempts to satisfy personality needs left unsatisfied or even actively frustrated by formal organization; but precisely these phenomena are the chief aberrations and ills of organization as seen by management.

Much more would have to be said to present the theory properly; and the criticisms that could then be made and the responses to the criticism would only open up the door to ethical and scientific questions that will perplex us as far into the future as we can imagine. If the employee has a thrust toward "self-actualization" that is thwarted by "a pyramid-shaped structure usually called the 'formal organization'," (p. 1) to what extent is his thwarted nature innate, to what extent culturally determined? Assuming that the frustration exists and self-actualization (whatever that is) is desirable, to what extent do alternative and better organizational strategies exist? If they do not exist, can they be created?

We should not leave the impression that this is a book concerned with exploring such questions in general and at length. Chapter II goes on to "Diagnostic Procedures," and the bulk of the book is concerned with the use of the semi-structured interview in organizational diagnosis and prognosis. Nor is it a discussion in abstract; the extensive empirical material, always related to the theoretical framework, concerns research made by Argyris in an unnamed but obviously very real industrial plant.

Modern Organization Theory

The papers that compose this book are the product of a symposium held at the Foundation for Research on Human Behavior at Ann Arbor in February 1959. In addition to the "academic participants" who read the papers, there was present an impressive roster of business executives. Since the papers are hardly light reading and active executives probably are not often operating at this level of abstraction, one wonders what these worthy gentlemen got out of it, apart from the agreeable feeling of contributing to a good cause in elevated surroundings.

The book consists of eleven papers or essays, counting the introductory chapter "Recurrent Themes and General Issues in Organization Theory" by the editor. Chapter Two consists of an essay by E. Wight Bakke, "Concept of Social Organization," which is both a highly general and abstract formulation of theory and a summary statement of presentations he has previously made in *The Bonds of Organization* and *The Fusion Process*. While this is the essay of broadest scope, two or three of the other essays (including one by Argyris) develop a theory of organization in very general terms, and all of the essays proceed at a high level of abstraction, even though their focus may be one particular part or aspect of organizational theory. Perhaps the point is made by noting that the other contributors are Cyert and March, Rapoport, Whyte, Likert, Dubin, Cartwright, and Marschak.

Excepting the *General Systems* volume, this book was the most difficult reading for the reviewer, but also the most rewarding. The feeling of reward for hard work was related, no doubt, to a long-standing if little-cultivated interest in general socio-political theory, and whether or not the book is "worthwhile" for any particular individual is probably to be gauged by his taste for theory.

Of the various essays, the editor found particularly intriguing and suggestive Haire's "Biological Models and Empirical Histories of the Growth of Organizations." This is a report on a study of the patterns of growth of various organizations, using a "biological model" for purposes of reference and comparison. The essay intrigues in part, perhaps, because of its unabashed use of biological analogies in a period in which this is regarded (in the company the editor-author keeps) with disdain and suspicion. Anyhow, the essay centers on the square-cube law "which points out that in normal spacial geometry, as volume increases by a cubic function, the surface inclosing it increases by a square," and dictates that fleas and elephants will be very dissimilar in structure and in actions. And anyone who has ever wondered about organizational efficiency in relation to size, or worried about the excessive growth of staff and auxiliary services in his organization, will find the analogies and hypotheses—whether significant or specious—fascinating.

General Systems: Contributions to Organization Theory

Approximately half of the 1959 *Yearbook* of the Society for General Systems Research consists of Part II, "Contributions to Organization Theory." The first of the eight essays, "Thoughts on Organization Theory and A Review of Two Conferences," by Rapoport and W. J. Horvath, is an interesting essay to which we shall return below. Suffice it here to note that one of the two conferences referred to is the Ann Arbor Conference; and that the three following essays by Bakke, Argyris, and Marschak are the same essays, identically or substantially, as those appearing in the Haire volume. Two of the remaining four, "Artificial Organisms" and "Digital Simulation of an Evolutionary Process," are, in terms of a distinction drawn below, "organization theory" rather than "theory of organization." Indeed, they are Far Out, and a bit frightening to one introduced to the study of administration through White's Second Edition.

"Games, Decisions, and Organizations" by Russell L. Ackoff is a counter-argument, in English prose, against the enthusiasm of the past decade for Game Theory. There has been, he argues, a misconception derived from a failure to distinguish an "exercise" from a "problem," a failure that "has led many scientists to play games while suffering under the illusion that they are conducting theoretical or experimental inquiries." (p. 145) "In a real problem-solving situation the decision maker is not given a game to play, he must extract it out of the situation itself." (p. 146) However: The believer in Experience and Common Sense cannot draw too much solace from this, for some of the most ardent believers in the efficacy of mathematics have long been of opinion that Game Theory, though certainly useful, has been oversold by its devotees.

The final essay, "Explorations in the Realm of Organization Theory," by Richard L. Meier, is a curious, rambling, but interesting and rewarding piece, essentially a series of reflections and observations induced by a review of the works of Herbert Simon, "certainly the most fertile mind intensively investigating the properties of organization at the present time." (p. 185) We note only that, apropos the rise of new management technologies, espe-

BOOK REVIEWS

cially the burgeoning information technology, Meier foresees the rise of a new elite: "A technical elite is already appearing on the scene to handle this apparatus, and it is important to observe that it reports directly to the executive or his immediate staff. We may anticipate that this elite will become isolated from the middle management of the firm so that top men do not work up from the lowest professional ranks, as at present, but enter as organization 'specialists' of one kind or another." (p. 197) This is followed by broader speculation on the social implications of the "Rise of the Meritocracy": "A 'meritocracy' is a Platonic republic embedded in modern Western culture employing late twentieth century technology and behavioral science." (p. 198) There is irony here, for it is the jibe of the behavioralists that their tradition-bound colleagues ought to leave off counting the bones of "those dead men," whose concerns were metaphysics and morality, not social science.

Comparative Studies in Administration

This volume consists of twelve pieces, each a chapter, in addition to a Foreword by Edward H. Litchfield. Part I is an essay by the editors, "On the Study of Administration." To quote from the summary of the essay is an economical way both to indicate its nature, and to suggest the floor of the book: "The objective has been set as a valid theory which will encompass all types of administration and be adaptive to all cultural or historical contexts. A strategy for moving toward that objective has been outlined. The strategy involves focusing on complex organization as the unit of analysis, but to see the organization both in a larger context, in interaction with its environment, and in terms of its parts." (p. 14)

Part II deals with "Organizational Comparisons," Part III with "Environmental Comparisons," Part IV with "Variations in Process," and Part V with "Research Frontiers." Those interested in comparative administration will find this a rewarding volume. There is a conceptual framework—agree with it or not—that gives unity; there is a quality of integrity (given probably by the hand of Thompson, whose name as author or co-author appears on four essays); several of the essays are very stimulating.

In fact, the reviewer found one of the selections the most interesting of the total lot of one hundred. This is a piece reprinted from *The American Anthropologist*, "Two Concepts of Authority," by Walter B. Miller. The essay treats the concept of authority of the Central Algonkian Indians, the Fox, in comparison with the European concept—in both cases in relation to history, language, religion, geography, etc. The Fox, he argues, have not and do not conceive of authority in the way that seems part of the order of nature to a European. The European conception is vertical: power flows downward, from God, Pope, King, owners, and managers. "The vertical authority relationship is a fundamental building block of European society. Without it the phenomenon of 'ranked' authority—where given individuals are permanently empowered to direct others—would be impossible. . . ." (p. 101) In contrast, the Fox conception is horizontal: his gods are earthbound and "manitu power" situational and fluid. "In brief, Fox society lacks 'vertical' authority, and the co-ordination of collective action utilizing the device of role-relationship combining the right to direct, permanent incumbency, differential prestige, differential functions, and differential access to procedural rules." (p. 113) Which is not to say that some kind of Science of Administration or Theory of Organization is impossible; but to speak relevantly, importantly, to ways of approaching them and what their nature might be.

Some Theories of Organization

This book edited by Rubenstein and Haberstroh is the only one of the works under consideration with an avowed pedagogical purpose. It is described in the Preface as a "textbook . . . intended to integrate scientific studies of organization from many of the traditional scholarly disciplines," with "the principal purpose envisioned" as use in senior or graduate courses in curricula in business administration, industrial management, or industrial engineering. Thirty-eight selections (some only two or three pages) are presented, organized under the following headings: "The Nature of Organization Theory," "Organizational Structure and Process," "Leadership and Morale," "Communication," "Control and Evaluation," and "Decision Making." A brief essay by the editors introduces each of six divisions. The selections range widely, from Max Weber and Chester Barnard, the oldest and most "traditional" selections in all of the six books, to, say, a piece "Evaluation of Decisions Written by *Ad Hoc* Groups and Simulated Commanders." Though the selections from Weber and Barnard represent a concession to the past, "inspirational" and "intuitive" pieces are omitted—at least in the editors' intention.

There is much good material in this book, including the introductory essays written by the editors, and it would be pleasant to report it an unqualified success. Unfortunately, however, it must be reported that it is a rather diffuse and confusing book. It is not clear what the editors wished to accomplish, other than represent as many points of view and please as many users as possible. (Of course, they wanted to Be Scientific, but this hardly will do as an answer—nobody in this day sets off to be un-scientific.) The pieces often seem to relate to each other only by editorial fiat and physical proximity, and their usual brevity heightens the reader's sense of discontinuity.

The reviewer hastens to add that while he cannot report that the editors won the game, perhaps they were playing a game impossible to win. As it happens, the reviewer has tried his hand at putting together a book of readings with a pedagogical end in view, and can certainly sympathize with the discomforts entailed. It is rather like trying to do a jig-saw puzzle when some of "your" pieces are missing, and you also have intermixed pieces from other puzzles.

II

Referring to the diversity of approach among his authors, Haire recalls the fable of the blind men describing an elephant: "There is little doubt here that it is a single elephant being discussed, but, by and large, each of the observers begins his description from a different point, and often with a special end in view." (p. 2)

In point of fact it is not clear that all of the contributors to this volume, much less all the contributors to the several volumes, are talking about the same elephant, or even members of the same species. How do we know

that they are not really describing ropes, fans, walls, snakes, trees, and spears—as they often appear to be? In view of the inclusiveness, the diversity, the amorphousness of the materials put under Organization Theory heading nowadays, one must conclude that, if they all concern the same elephant, it is a *very* large elephant with a generalized elephantiasis.

It may be worthwhile, therefore, to try to get some perspective on the currently popular preoccupation with organization theory. How did it arise? What's old and what's new in the movement? What are the ways in which organization is defined, what is a "theory of organization" in the view of the various writers, what are the conceptual schemes that may help to enlighten and clarify? No doubt the "theory of the theories" deserves a book, but a few pages may be better than nothing.

A Look Backward

Writers on theory of organization make much of recent and rapid development—"even ten years ago, it would not have been possible to bring together such a group of papers." Indeed, this sense of recent origins and rapid development tends to be shared widely among the behaviorally oriented who are concerned with the development of "administrative science," whether or not they are identified with organization theory by name or intent. No doubt the self-conscious pioneer always is inclined to deprecate his forerunners so that his own exploits may appear the greater,[6] but there is a sense in which the current writers are quite correct. Volume XI of the *Encyclopedia of the Social Sciences* (1933) contains the entry "Organization, Administrative," by Herman Finer, and the entry "Organization, Economic," by Walton Hamilton (in addition to the piece by L. D. White, "Administration, Public," in Volume I), but there is no entry for Theory of Organization or Organization Theory. It is wholly predictable that the new

---

[6] A study of stock phrases and postures in the opening and concluding portions of social science writings is interesting and, if one is so inclined, amusing: predecessors generally have been stupid, confused, bemused. Now, however, there are Momentous New Developments, we are beginning to Get the Subject Organized, and the present essay hopefully is a Modest Contribution to that end. Hopefully, also, it will soon be superseded by Better Formulations, for All Signs Now Point to Rapid Progress. In any event, Further Research is Necessary.

BOOK REVIEWS

edition of this work, now in the planning, will have a lengthy essay under one of these headings. There *are* new data, new ideas, new interminglings of disciplines, and fresh strong impulses, all in addition to the idea that it is useful to try to theorize about organization "as such."

Nevertheless, there are many themes in the contemporary writings with roots and analogues in the past, more than the contemporary writers would appear to believe; as anyone can verify who will, for example, leaf through the pages of the *Papers on the Science of Administration* (1937). In the study of administration one can find for at least two generations back, firm declarations that what up to this point has been art, experience, guess, and intuition is now about to become Science, that momentous and converging developments now make this possible for the first time, that what has seemed diverse is about to be unified by general, abstract principles or theories, etc. As to theory of organization, specifically, the *Papers* are introduced by Luther Gulick's famous "Notes on the Theory of Organization." In a more general sense much of social science (if I may use the term) through the centuries has dealt with theory of organization. John Gaus once suggested that Plato's *Republic* be viewed as a treatise on personnel administration; alternatively, it might be viewed as a treatise on organizing a government. In short, when one of our writers states that some years ago a discussion of organization theory would have dealt with such things as line and staff and span of control, whereas present writers deal with all manner of different things, he is correct; but it is not yet clear what the new theory *is,* nor how great is the net gain.

From Administrative Theory to Organization Theory

The rise to popularity of organization theory probably can be attributed to various sources, among them the oft-cited fact that ours is an Age of Organization and that this pervasive phenomenon is a natural subject for attention. It is plausible, however, that fashions in social science methodology and philosophy have played a part. In general, among those concerned with the Scientific approach to the study of "cooperative action,"

there has been something of a movement away from the terms "administration," "administrative," and "administrative theory" to the terms "organization," "organizational," and "organization theory." It is hypothesized (to use a favorite expression of our authors) that the mood and methods of behavioralism are responsible for this movement, and my speculation runs as follows.

The behavioralists want above all else, of course, to be Scientific in the study of social phenomena, taking as their model what they conceive to be the outlook and methods of physical science. The general goal is a value-free generalization about how the subject phenomena behave, given specified conditions. "Values" are proper data for scientific generalizations, but the social scientist, as scientist, has no concern for their "intrinsic validity" (if I may be forgiven the term). Technologies and applied sciences take the theories achieved by pure science and use them in the realization of human values. To be sure, this is desirable and gives further importance to the enterprise of pure science; but pure science is higher on the Scientist's value-scale than applied science. Pure science is *purer,* untainted by the humanness of values.

Now, administration, private or public, is an applied science—if it is not indeed a profession, an art, or something less. "Administrative theory" suggests an engagement with the world, a striving after values. One can, to be sure, make a respectable compromise, and seek a "normative science," one in which values are posited but not justified, striven for but not examined; and some would argue that for administrative (or organizational) science this not only is the best approach, but the only feasible one. But even in this case particular organizational values must be dealt with aseptically.

"Organization," on the other hand, suggests something "out there." Organizations are value-saturated, of course, but the researcher can be free not only from the values of particular organizations, but from the administrator's natural involvement with the organization's values. He can become an anthropologist, so to speak, completely detached from the society he observes.[7] Organization theory—

---

[7] I am aware that many anthropologists argue that they must become a part of the society they observe,

PUBLIC ADMINISTRATION REVIEW

"how things are"—suggests, in short, less value-involvement than administrative theory—"how things should be done (at least if you want to achieve such-and-such)."

The Meaning of Theory

Since our undertaking is an examination of theory of organization, with a view to assessing the present status of this theory, a proper next step is to ask: What is theory? *This* is a tangled skein, for certain; but fortunately our involvement can be brief. One or two distinctions will serve our purposes.

As used in this discussion, an organizational theory means simply a conceptual scheme, the aim (but not necessarily the achievement) of which is to enable us to understand, to predict, and to control (if we wish) organizational phenomena. We regard it as quite legitimate to use the term theory in treating of the ethical, the valuational; but we shall not use it here in that connection, except as such considerations are involved in descriptive or causal theories of an "if-then" variety.

On the other hand, we avoid the strict meaning of the term given in the physical sciences (or at least by their interpreters), according to which a theory not only is a tight logical structure with empirical referents, but can be refuted by a single contrary empirical finding. (Presumably, nobody would argue that we have yet achieved much if any organizational theory by *these* criteria.) Most importantly, we shall not distinguish between *theories* and *models*,[8] meaning by the latter conceptual representations of organizational phenomena, the first aim of which is *understanding* as a step toward prediction and control, but which, compared to theories, are generally looser in logical structure and less precisely, and differently, related to their empirical referents. Some would prefer to call "models" many or all of the conceptualizations reviewed below. They may, if they wish!

"About It, and About"

Those who not only do much of their living in organizations but deal with them profes-

sionally, so to speak, may feel that it is very obvious what organization "is," and that attempts to construct theories of organization are at best an unnecessary elaboration, at worst a positive obfuscation. There is, to be sure, a case for knowledge gained from personal experience, for the intuitive, for direct sensual perception; for some purposes such knowledge, not theoretical constructs, is of the essence. However, only the mildest sort of commitment to the position that through study administration can become more scientific (not necessarily A Science) suffices to arouse a concern for organizational theory. What is the "stuff" of organization? How does it move? To have any answer that can be stated in general terms, even if the level of abstraction is not high, is to have a theory of organization.

A definition of organization is a theory of organization—at least a crude sketch of a theory—for it must necessarily try to state in general, more or less abstract, terms what the essentials are and how they relate. Who has not tried his hand at framing a one-sentence (or even one-paragraph) definition of organization has denied himself an educational experience of high value. The abstract nouns and adjectives that are the conventional building blocks will be found to be unbelievably complex, awkward, misshapen.[9] At the end, one may believe he knows less rather than more about organization, but he is likely to have a new respect for semantics and more understanding of the problems of the scientific enterprise in its application to human affairs.

Personally, I am of two minds about the value of taking the problem of definition seriously, head-on, as a part of the scientific enterprise or (and) constructing useful theory. On the one hand it seems cavalier, even outrageously slipshod, to try to proceed to a careful examination of any phenomena without an attempt to define, that is, to understand and agree upon, what the object of examina-

in order to understand it. But some of the students of organization are more anthropological than the anthropologists!

[8] Rubenstein and Haberstroh's introductory essay, "The Nature of Organization Theory," is recommended

reading for those wishing to sharpen their thinking with reference to these distinctions.

[9] To escape the frustrations and to solve the problems of precise statement some social scientists turn from words to a quasi-mathematical notational system. There is undoubtedly significant gain in some areas, but there is inescapably some loss, if only in general understanding; and at worst the result may be only a private language with neither significant empirical referents nor heuristic value.

BOOK REVIEWS

tion is, at least in general terms and as now understood. On the other hand, one can argue persuasively that the scientific enterprise has no close and necessary relationship to conventional definitions, that the verbal difficulties outweigh the scientific gain, that the problem of definition can really only be solved by by-passing it and proceeding to activities that eventually will "define" in meaningful, operational terms.

The first of these positions is best represented among the writers in our six volumes by E. Wight Bakke, whose "Concept of the Social Organization" is an essay in definition. It worries him that, though there is a large and growing literature dealing with organizations and organizational behavior, "seldom does one find a careful and systematic description of the nature of the 'thing' with whose internally and externally directed activity the hypotheses are concerned." (p. 16) After twenty pages of wind-up, Bakke delivers the following one-sentence definition:

> A social organization is a continuing system of differentiated and coordinated human activities utilizing, transforming, and welding together a specific set of human, material, capital, ideational, and natural resources into a unique problem-solving whole engaged in satisfying particular human needs in interaction with other systems of human activities and resources in its environment. (p. 37)

This is followed by thirty-five pages in which the meaning of the definition is explained, its implications explored.[10] To me, the essay is rewarding, but also, eventually, confusing and mystifying. Frankly, I don't understand what The Fusion Process is, unless it consists of phenomena with which, under different names, I have long been familiar.

Various of the other writers in our six volumes attempt definitions,[11] but most of them

---

[10] The "major features essential to a more specific definition of a particular organization," to which the discussion is devoted, are (1) The Organizational Charter (the image of the organization's unique wholeness), (2) The Basic Resources (as listed in the definition), (3) The Activity Processes (by which the resources are acquired and manipulated) and (4) The Bonds of Organization (which integrate into operating systems (1), (2), and (3)).

[11] Most notably, Argyris: "Organizations are grand strategies individuals create to achieve objectives that require the effort of many." (p. 24) Much of Chapter I of *Understanding Organizational Behavior* is an essay in definition.

are content simply to ignore the problem—indeed, given their limited concerns, they are justified in ignoring it. We turn to the recent *Organization* (1958), by James G. March and Herbert A. Simon, to illustrate the other extreme. This work is a presentation of all organization theory, as the authors conceive the subject, in summary, schematic form; and it might be presumed, therefore, to begin with a careful definition of a title stated in one word, no qualifiers, no subtitle. Instead, the book begins simply:

> This book is about the theory of formal organizations. It is easier, and probably more useful, to give examples of formal organizations than to define the term. The United States Steel Corporation is a formal organization; so is the Red Cross, the corner grocery store, the New York Highway Department. . . . But for present purposes we need not trouble ourselves about the precise boundaries to be drawn around an organization. . . . We are dealing with empirical phenomena, and the world has an uncomfortable way of not permitting itself to be fitted into neat classifications.

This reasoning is very appealing to me. But I still find myself wondering about the significance of *"formal"* in the first sentence, about the criteria by which a formal organization is differentiated from a non-formal or un-formal organization, and whether the authors really mean to assert that a corner grocery store is a formal organization (and if so, what would an *in*formal organization look like?).

The Classical Theory

The theory of organization best known to American students of administration, of course, is that developed largely in the Scientific Management movement during the early decades of this century. This theory, designated "classical" by March and Simon, is (for students of public administration) closely associated with the noted *Papers on the Science of Administration*, which contains the well-known essays by Gulick, Urwick, Fayol, Mooney, and others. It is the theory that, taking efficiency as the objective, views administration as a technical problem concerned basically with the division of labor and the specialization of function. It is the theory which (in Gulick's famous essay) distinguishes four organizational bases: purpose, process, clientele or materiel, and place; and designates the work of the executive as concerned

220   PUBLIC ADMINISTRATION REVIEW

with POSDCORB—Planning, Organizing, Staffing, Directing, Co-ordinating, Reporting, and Budgeting. Its symbol is the organization chart.

For the readers of this *Review* no more need be said in explanation or elaboration. But what should be said in trying to see such theory in perspective?

Since publication of the *Papers* in 1937, a generation of younger students have demolished the classical theory, again and again; they have uprooted it, threshed it, thrown most of it away. By and large, the criticisms of the new generation have been well-founded. In many ways the classical theory was crude, presumptuous, incomplete—wrong in some of its conclusions, naive in its scientific methodology, parochial in its outlook. In many ways it was the End of a Movement, not the foundation for a science.

Nevertheless, not only is the classical theory still today the formal working theory of large numbers of persons technically concerned with administrative-organizational matters, both in the public and the private spheres, but I expect that it will be around a long, long time. This not necessarily because it is "true," though I should say that it has much truth in it, both descriptively and prescriptively; that is to say, both as a description of organizations as we find them in our society and as a prescription for achieving the goals of these organizations "efficiently." But in any event a social theory widely held by the actors has a self-confirming tendency and the classical theory now is deeply ingrained in our culture. Granted, the new girl in the typing pool may know little of it but, on the other hand, she very certainly would not even have heard of a Feedback Loop or a Bavelas Communication Net. Not only is the simplicity and wide diffusion of the classical theory in its favor, we have made cultural adjustments to it: at every level from the heights of Pittsburgh to the new girl in the typing pool, we know when to take it seriously, when to charge it with error or injustice, when to acknowledge it formally while we ignore it informally.

Bureaucracy

The map of the organizational world associated with the term bureaucracy and the name Max Weber is also "classical," in the

sense that it has been with us for some time and has had many "believers," much attention. It, too, has been much subject to criticism during the past decade, both on scientific and moralistic grounds. As to the former, March and Simon treat such theory rather peremptorily, placing it in effect in their "paleolithic" period.[12]

Bureaucratic theory enjoyed a vogue in this country following the publication of two translations of Weber's relevant writings immediately after World War II. In general, Weber's description of bureaucracy as one type of organization merely puts in formal terms what most of us are familiar with in working for or dealing with government bureaus or business corporations: it is the familiar picture of a hierarchy of authority organizing and in turn shaped by the division of labor and the specialization of function, with full-time positions filled in principle on merit, regular career ladders, etc. But it was the frame in which this familiar picture was placed that made it exciting to some. Speaking for myself, not only was I greatly stimulated on first reading, I am sure I could now read Weber on bureaucracy for the tenth time with fresh insights.

The point is that Weber related what is "natural" for us by deep inculturation, to history, to economic life, to technological development, to political philosophy, to social structure and processes. Bureaucratic-type organization as *the* most efficient way of doing things develops, he argued, in conjunction with certain other developments in a society, and it acts upon and in turn is shaped by these environing factors.

Though the Weber vogue has subsided, he inspired and continues, even if indirectly, to inspire considerable scholarship—I venture to call it scientific inquiry—from various students, particularly and naturally from the sociologists. Much of what is written "refutes" some aspect of Weber; much more "qualifies" some aspect of Weber. But this is the natural pattern of the scientific enterprise, and that there continues to be need to refute or qualify this or that bureaucratic hypothesis is a tribute to

---

[12] Just above Frederick Taylor. In point of fact, it would be arbitrary to place Weber any place in the schema of the book; but in view of the fact that his central concern was rationality, he might with more aptness have been treated in that connection.

BOOK REVIEWS

the strength and vitality of the theory. Certainly any striving toward a general organizational theory through the comparative route cannot ignore bureaucratic theory; nor until a more accurate and revealing picture of the total organizational world is created, can anyone ignore bureaucratic theory if the objective is the central one of a liberal education: to understand one's world in relation to oneself.

Simon's Three-Fold Schemata

Simon, and March and Simon, have set forth two more or less complementary conceptualizations—theories, schemata, maps, or models, I am not sure what is the proper term —for viewing, classifying, and understanding organizations and organization theory.

The first of these, chronologically, is set forth in Simon's essay "Comments on the Theory of Organizations," published in 1954 in the *American Political Science Review* and reprinted in the volume by Rubenstein and Haberstroh. Here we begin with a definition:

Human organizations are systems of interdependent activity, encompassing at least several primary groups and usually characterized, at the level of consciousness of participants, by a high degree of rational direction of behavior toward ends that are objects of common acknowledgement and expectation. (p. 157)

As an empirical matter, Simon feels that organizational phenomena are different from those of institutions on the one hand, and primary groups on the other;[18] and while the differentiation on either side is far from sharp, he feels that the organizational "level" meets appropriate tests for scientific study and theory construction—tests of internal cohesion and differentiation from the next level.

Addressing himself to the organizational level, so to speak, he then discusses "Major Problem Areas." He makes clear that he does not purport to be presenting finished theory: "Until we know what frames of reference are going to be the most useful for organization theory, it will surely be desirable to retain alternative frameworks, and to take considerable pains to develop means for translating

---

[18] "We will restrict the term 'organization' to systems that are larger than primary groups, smaller than institutions. Clearly, the lower boundary is sharper than the upper." (p. 158) I *thought* "institutions" was explained or characterized by "economic institution," but on a hurried re-reading cannot find this phrase.

from one framework to another." (p. 159) The major problem areas he conceives as: (1) the process of decision making in an organization, (2) the phenomena of power in organizations, (3) rational and non-rational aspects of behavior in organization, (4) the organizational environment and the social environment, (5) stability and change in organizations, and (6) specialization and the division of work.

Returning in conclusion to a justification of his focus, Simon states:

The characteristics of this level that give it its particular flavor are the following: (a) its focus on relations among interlocking or non-interlocking primary groups rather than on relations within primary groups; (b) it is largely concerned with situations where *zweckrationalität* plays a large role relative to *wertrationalität* (as compared with the study either of small groups or of cultures); (c) in these situations the scheme of social interaction becomes itself partly a resultant of the rational contriving of means and the conscious construction and acting out of "artificial" roles; and (d) explanation of phenomena at this level requires the closest attention to the fluid boundaries of rational adaptation, including the important boundaries imposed by group frames of reference, perceptual frameworks, and symbolic techniques.

There is no ostensible attempt to relate *Organizations* to this earlier "Comments on the Theories of Organizations," but the two fit together, after a fashion, to form a larger schema. That is, we can assume that the three-fold distinction between institutions, organizations, and primary groups remains; and that a new three-fold distinction introduced in *Organizations* is theory of organization, i.e., theory about the organization "layer." This does not seem too arbitrary, despite the fact that organizations are now designated "social institutions" (p. 2) and that the book contains considerable summary of the theory of primary groups.

Be that as it may, there is a new three-fold schema introduced. Three "models" are discerned, each concentrating on a partial aspect of the human organism, and, though overlapping, coming in chronological sequence:

Thus, the model of the employee as instrument is prominent in the writings of the scientific management movement. In the last several decades the second model, emphasizing attitudes and motivations, has gained the greater prominence in research in bureaucracy, human relations, leadership and supervision, and power phenomena. The third model, emphasizing the rational and intellective aspects of organizational behavior, has been less extensively used than the other two, but is represented particularly by the work of the economists and others on the planning process, and by the work of psychologists on organizational communication and problem-solving. (p. 7)

Though *Organizations* is not organized in three distinct "parts," as this language suggests, nevertheless the theory summarized in the book is ranged along a scale, beginning with the "classical" and ending with the planners. The schema is obviously one of large scope, great adaptability, and considerable usefulness.

Theory of Organization and/or Organization Theory

In their essay in the General Systems *Yearbook,* "Thoughts on Organization Theory and a Review of Two Conferences," Rapoport and Horvath present a sharp distinction between organization theory and theory of organization:

We see organization theory as dealing with general and abstract organizational principles; it applies to any system exhibiting organized complexity. As such, organization theory is seen as an extension of mathematical physics or, even more generally, of mathematics designed to deal with organized systems. The theory of organizations, on the other hand, purports to be a social science. It puts real human organizations at the center of interest. It may study the social structure of organizations and so can be viewed as a branch of sociology; it can study the behavior of individuals or groups as members of organizations and so can be viewed as a part of social psychology; it can study power relations and principles of control in organizations and so fits into political science. (p. 90)

As to organization theory, the authors perceive three important lines of development that had no important part in classical physics but which show promise of providing its theoretical underpinnings, and then of extension, hopefully, to theory of organization, namely, (1) cybernetics, the theory of complex interlocking "chains of causation," from which goal seeking and self-controlling forms of behavior emerge, (2) topology or relational mathematics, and (3) decision theory, including such branches as game theory. However, they warn against "premature application" and observe that " 'Scientism' is still a predominant childhood disease of organization theory as it is applied in social science." (p. 91) They foresee, and urge, a diversity of approaches applied under the headings both of organization theory and theory of organiza-

tion, sound a warning on over-optimism and premature cross-applications, but express a hope that eventually "the two streams of ideas will actually merge."

For me, this conceptualization does much to put order into the present blooming, buzzing confusion of "theory concerned with organization(s)." To be sure, it doesn't tuck in all loose ends, doesn't point a solution to all the riddles; but it helps. In terms of the introductory metaphor we know that, for the present at least, there are a minimum of two elephants, not one. It would help if the writers would be very clear as to which one they are addressing themselves, and observe the cautions enjoined by Rapoport and Horvath about relating the one to the other.

And Back to Administration

To the generalization above that there is a movement from *administration* to *organization* there is a significant exception among the six books for review, namely, the presentation by Thompson and associates, which is in fact titled *Comparative Studies in Administration* —not organization. This is the more significant and interesting because, though the movement from administration to organization is associated with behavioralism, the editors of the Pittsburgh volume are strongly behavioral. They yield to none in their respect and hope for Science, but it is "administrative science" or "science of administration," not organization theory or science, that is the ostensible goal: "We firmly believe that there is in the making a rigorous science of administration, which can account for events in particular times and places and for the ethical or normative content of those events without itself incorporating the particular conditions and values of those events." (p. 4) Their introductory essay, "On the Study of Administration," deserves a look, both because it is a distinctly different and perhaps significant conceptualization of the world on which we seek perspectives, and for its interesting combination of the old dream and even the old term with the latest behavioral thought.

The focus, say the authors, should be on what administration *does* rather than what it *is.* This avoids semantic traps and methodological dead ends. They note that there is "reasonable consensus" that administration is

BOOK REVIEWS

found in such entities as corporations, trade unions, and philanthropic foundations, but not importantly in "mobs, crowds, or publics." What differentiates the one from the other? "In seeking to answer these questions, we have identified four characteristics among those collectivities which clearly have administration." (p. 5) These four are: (1) Administered organizations exhibit sustained collective action. (2) Administered organizations are integral parts of a larger system. (3) Administered organizations have specialized, delimited goals. (4) Administered organizations are dependent upon interchange with the larger system.

There is some sleight of hand here, as "collectivities," "organizations," "societies," and "systems" are all referred to but not defined or explained. But the end product, "administered organizations" is perhaps clear enough. In any event it is *administered* organizations that are the subject of their study, they are interested in administration as a *process*, and they wish to distinguish between "administrative action" and a broader "organizational action."

However, they recognize that "without an organization to be administered, administrative activity has no meaning or significance," and state that "administrative activity may be defined as activity related to the creation, maintenance, or operation of an organization as an organization." (p. 7) From the four characteristics "posited" as distinguishing administered organizations, they derive three "organizational requirements and administrative functions," namely: (1) structuring of the organization as an administrative function, (2) definition of purpose as an administrative function, and (3) management of the organization-environment exchange system as a function of administration.

These are, hopefully, the essentials. The essay as a whole deserves reading, however, by anyone seeking ways of structuring the administrative-organizational world with which he deals as practitioner or student. The authors deserve a chance to explain how they propose to relate substantive disciplines and process disciplines (their name for cybernetics, etc.) to their grand scheme. The reader may not be convinced, but at least he will be impressed with the stated goal: "a valid theory which will encompass all types of administration and

be adaptive to all cultural or historical contexts."

Hopefully, I have sketched a fairly large variety and range of the ways in which theory of organization can be conceptualized, though I am painfully aware that the treatment is neither exhaustive nor systematic. What observations can we make? What reasonable conclusions are possible to the question: Where are we now?

That there has been a tremendous increase in the number of theories; of theories about the theories; of the number of interested persons; of interdisciplinary connections and borrowings; of the volume of the literature—this is the first and firmest fact. Probably there has also been "progress," and I am optimistic enough to think that there has been a great deal of it since the *Papers*.

Obviously also, however, we are a long, long way from the goal of *a* theory of organization, in whatever way or ways one might choose to define the term "theory"; and there is no reason to believe that agreement, unification, simplification, and systematization lie in the immediate future. It is clear that, even if we take any one conceptualization, it is fortunate if we get a reasonably clear idea of what the "thing" is in the writer's opinion; and if we take several writers together the answers to the questions of definition of subject, of the type of inquiry that is proper, and of the conclusions that are warranted, become vague, obscure, confused. Of the various writers dealing with theory of organization, Herbert Simon enjoys the highest reputation, and his "maps" are undoubtedly useful. But others also aspire to be the Newton of this science, and the claims of some warrant examination. And it should be re-stated that Simon's "maps," as I called them, are not theory in any strict scientific sense. In fact, Simon (while always confident of present and, especially, future progress) emphasizes often that so far we have achieved little that meets his own high standards for scientific theory.

Fortunately, there does not have to be a single firm, agreed theory in a field before "progress" is possible and demonstrable. The physical sciences have sometimes thrived when within the same field alternative and seemingly incompatible theories flourished,[14] and even, perhaps, we can designate as stagnant periods in which a single theory was unquestioned. It is at least possible that at this stage of exploration and expansion the heuristic[15] value of a variety of theories or models is desirable.

While I am personally optimistic for progress in many directions (my "scientific" standards are much lower than Simon's), it strikes me that the eventual achievement of any general Theory of Organization is as problematical as the achievement of any kind of Unified Social Science. Indeed, I think the two are related. According to all the definitions and schemes we reviewed (except perhaps the "classical"), organizations exist in a larger social environment and interact with it,[16] and a theory of this interaction when firm and finished should mesh with a theory of the milieu.

Reductionism Versus Holism

I am far from certain what the central problem or issue is in the further development of theory of organization, and in fact the idea of "a" central problem or issue may be specious. Forced to guess, however, I should state the central problem to be that of reductionism versus holism. This is by implication related to the vexing problem of defining the "thing" we are talking about and differentiating it from and relating it to other phenomena.

By reductionism I mean a disposition to explain phenomena by analyzing them into their constituent parts, and these constituent parts in turn into their constituent parts, and so forth, presuming that understanding of the original phenomena can be arrived at by "adding" the understandings of the parts. This is the classical strategy of physical science, and its success in that area hardly

needs underscoring. The basic metaphor of reductionism is mechanical. Machines are understood through their parts; a machine *is* a combination of parts with determinate "causal" relations.

By holism is meant the theory that phenomena—certain kinds of phenomena at least —can be understood only in terms of the *whole* phenomenon involved, that in some sense the whole is greater than or different from the sum of its parts. Though expounded by such respectable figures as Alfred North Whitehead, holism tends to be suspect because it suggests an "unscientific" metaphysic. It is much more congenial to biology than to physics, and its basic metaphor is organic: a living (at least *higher*) organism must be understood at the level of the living whole. That is to say, there must be a theory appropriate to this level, or the whole is not understood, accounted for, comprehended.

Now perhaps I have some constitutional disposition toward holistic explanations, but I do not wish to be interpreted as arguing that The Holistic Way Is The Way Forward. I do have doubts about the value, the "payoff," of some of the reductionist efforts in the study of organization. But I also have doubts about the scientific (though not pedagogical) value of the holistic "case study," as pursued by the Inter-University Case Program.

My point is rather that the analytic-holistic dichotomy provides an interesting perspective on these works on theory of organization. By and large the reductionist tendency is foremost, indeed decidedly so. But a holistic theory or metaphor occasionally occurs. Some of the writers introduce a decided holistic strain of thought, and there are at least two explicit discussions of some of the issues.

As to metaphor, Haire's biological analogy is the most prominent example, but even Simon, who certainly takes "hard" science as his inspiration and model, occasionally uses a biological analogy after taking care that it has been thoroughly disinfected. As to writers who make some attempt to balance the holistic against the analytic, I cite Argyris as outstanding, as he probes the psyche on the one hand but seeks also on the other hand to understand it in relation to an entire organizational (even cultural) *gestalt*.

---

[14] It could be argued with some force, to be sure, that at least it was clear that the theories were incompatible; whereas in social science the alternative theories are so diverse and shapeless that often one theory cannot be clearly or meaningfully posed against another.

[15] Very good word in social science writings the past few years. I hope I'm not too late with it.

[16] The Pittsburgh group observe (p. 15) that totalitarian governments may be interpreted as attempts to make government (i.e., organization) and society coterminous. But this is a footnote to their own theory and in a sense proves my point.

BOOK REVIEWS

The two explicit discussions to which I refer are both in the *General Systems* volume. Rapoport and Horvath introduce their "Thoughts on Organization Theory" with a discussion of the two viewpoints, and then proceed with a hope—and theory—that the two points of view are becoming synthesized, largely through "naturalizing" teleology (i.e., in cybernetics). Richard L. Meier in his "Explorations in the Realm of Organization Theory" has a section titled "March and Simon on 'Organizations'" (pp. 194-95) which is essentially a statement of the holistic elements missing in that review. (The word holistic is mine, not his, but I do not think I do violence to his meaning.) This is the more interesting because Meier yields to nobody in his admiration of Simon.

The argument deserves brief summary: Meier fully agrees that "any science still in its swaddling clothes must concentrate upon phenomena associated with small deviations from equilibrium conditions, not the catastrophes and revolutions. . . ." Equilibrium analysis "provides by far the best foundation for creating a propositional framework that will predict the consequences of events for the system being studied." Yet the failure to observe and study other important factors worries him: "The dynamics of inception, growth, decline, disintegration, salvage, and amalgamation fall outside the range of equilibrium analysis of organizations. What is left is the endless mottled gray of the bureaucratic steady state." Particularly he is concerned with the "missing ingredients" of history, spatial distribution, and the "design of artifacts."

To repeat, I am not arguing that all research be turned in holistic directions. I am merely observing that the choice of one direction or another is obviously important, and may be the central consideration in answering the question: Where do we go from here? Per- haps we need to go in both directions, separately or in some deliberately chosen "mix."

It Didn't Begin Yesterday

I close on an old theme—related to the argument of the preceding paragraph—namely, that those concerned with organization theory are denying themselves a source of insight and even, I venture to think, of scientific conclusions and hypotheses when they scorn the traditional literature of social and political theory. March and Simon remark that their review of the literature on organization conveyed the impression that "not a great deal has been said about organizations, but it has been said over and over in a variety of languages." (p. 5) As to the first, I feel quite differently: a great deal has indeed been said, diverse and important. We "know" more, I submit, about organizations and indeed about societies than about some things that have a firm scientific theory.

But one of my frequent feelings in reading the organizational literature is that indeed I have read it before in another language: the language of political theory. When, for example, Bakke writes of the "Organizational Charter" he is (if I understand him at all) writing about something close to the center of the interests of Plato and Aristotle, namely, a group's conception of self-identity and differentiation. Or when Cyert and March talk about "organization as a coalition," the giving of "side payments," and so forth, I think not only of Robert Dahl and David Truman (who are acknowledged), but of a range of names from Machiavelli to George Washington Plunkitt.

Do not mistake me. I do not argue that everything was known by the ancients. Only that anyone who thinks theory of organization began with Fayol or Taylor owes himself a look at the frontispiece of Hobbes' *Leviathan*. Now *there's* an organization chart!

[2]

A society of organizations

CHARLES PERROW
Department of Sociology, Yale University

It is a commonplace today that organizations are a key element of U.S. society and those of other industrialized nations. I argue here that the importance of *large* organizations in the United States is still insufficiently appreciated. The nineteenth-century industrial revolution, much of our politics and social structure, and many of the crises of the 1980s and 1990s must be reinterpreted in the light of "organizational variables." I cannot do all of this in an essay, but I lay out the argument and lightly illustrate it.

The importance in history of organizations as such, as distinct from individual leaders, economic exchanges, social classes etc., is increasingly recognized. Others have made valuable and extended observations along these lines. Robert Presthus announced it on a grand scale with his 1962 volume, *The Organizational Society*; Henry Jacoby was even grander in his *The Bureaucratization of the World*. The power of the modern corporation, another theme of my work, is also widely discussed, as in Christopher Stone's *Where the Law Ends* and James Coleman's *The Asymmetric Society*, and in the organizational analysis literature.[1] The topic, however, is so commodious, as exemplified by The Source himself, Max Weber, that no apology is needed for yet another inquiry.

My own inquiry is frankly imperialistic. I argue that the appearance of large organizations in the United States makes organizations the key phenomenon of our time, and thus politics, social class, economics, technology, religion, the family, and even social psychology take on the character of dependent variables. Their subject matter is conditioned by the presence of organizations to such a degree that, increasingly, since about 1820 in the United States at least, the study of organizations must precede their own inquiries. Politics changes drastically

Theory and Society 20: 725–762, 1991.

726

when large organizations appear. Politicians come from them, work through them, and are beholden to them. Our class structure was remade by organizations, and stratification within organizations and between them becomes the central determinant of our class system. Economics, increasingly grounded in assumptions about individual self-interest, flags in predictive power and relevance as organizations become the important interests and actors. The techniques of producing goods and services – technology – has no life of its own without organizations. For example, the first factories gathered people together for control reasons, and then the machinery we associate with factories, the technology, was invented to maximize the utility of controlling a collection of docile workers. Technology today is more the product of organizations than just the motor of them. The social infrastructure of society, including religion and the family, has been shaped to cope with the new phenomenon and has less independent reality. Finally, our social psychology, that is, our ways of constructing reality, is more and more forged by and accommodative to organizations.

To make everyone else's subject matter a dependent variable of one's own requires a fair bit of presumptuousness.[2] But I expect political scientists, class theorists, and other claimants to do the same. The limits of our perspectives and disciplines best become evident when we exceed them. Only then will there be occasion for the judicious synthesis for which we always yearn. A fair bit of imperialism should precede attempts at synthesis.

But my organizational imperialism pushes me to an extremity that may evoke ridicule, so I had better warn the reader at the outset: in my grandest proposition I argue that organizations are the key to society because *large organizations have absorbed society*. They have vacuumed up a good part of what we have always thought of as society, and made organizations, once a part of society, into a surrogate of society.

By "large organizations absorbing society" I mean that activities that once were performed by relatively autonomous and usually small informal groups (e.g. family, neighborhood) and small autonomous organizations (small businesses, local government, local church) are now performed by large bureaucracies. This is the "pure" case of absorption – the large organization with many employees. As a result, the organization that employs many people can shape their lives in many ways, most of which are quite unobtrusive and subtle, and alternative sources of shaping in the community decline. But shaping through organizational

727

processes can also occur in two other respects that are still important, though less so: shaping through "satellites" of economic organizations and through "branches" of non-economic organizations.

Large employing organizations: The societal functions that are absorbed are performed within organizations employing large numbers of people instead of being performed by small independent organizations or informal groups. For example, for their employees, the corporation, school district, voluntary association or whatever is the source of friends and marriage partners, counseling, medical care, recreation facilities and opportunities, apprenticeship training, food services, and retirement options. All of these could be, and once were, performed by small, relatively autonomous groups and organizations in society or left to individual choice. I include in this category the branches, franchises, subsidiaries and so on of economic organizations; these dependent units have little autonomy with respect to the services provided.

Satellites: Societal functions are performed by those small organizations that are quite dependent upon one or a few large employing organizations. Instead of being brought into the large organization, the functions are left outside and the satellites cluster about the large organization, dependent upon it for their existence. Examples are small organizations that provide travel, food, and medical services if the employing organization does not, entertainment and recreation facilities tuned to the large organization, and specialized education and welfare functions dependent upon the problems generated by, or at least not met by, the large organization. Absorption takes place because the large organizations dictates the policies of these nominally independent firms and agencies.

Branches: These are chapters of national non-profit organizations such as Mothers Against Drunk Drivers, the Red Cross, ACLU, political parties, and fraternal and religious denominational groups. Absorption takes place insofar as the headquarters, which may itself be a large employer providing services similar to large corporations, controls or shapes the service policies of the branches. This is a less powerful and linear development than the two described above, since local affiliates can retain much independence at times, and even if they do not, small independent groups keep springing up outside the bureaucratic headquarters. But arguably, compared to nineteenth-century America, religious groups are more tightly tied into centralized denominational headquarters; voluntary services are more tied into national groups or

728

spawned by them; and political party organizations are less autonomous and less frequently survive outside the major parties.

In all three cases, small groups or small formal organizations lose their
autonomy or actually disappear, their functions surviving under the
control or auspices of centralized bureaucracies and shaped by the
needs of those formal organizations. The process of absorption is both
deliberate and unwitting; the consequences bring some kinds of benefits and some kinds of costs. (Part of the cost is organizationally generated problems, which give rise to more small organizations trying to
deal with them. Thus, while absorption is taking place, the number of
organizations can actually increase.)

First I outline three phenomena that constitute the basis of my argument; next, discuss some objections to my position; and then outline
the historical development of a society of organizations. The three phenomena are wage dependency, which made citizens available for organizations; the externalization of the social costs of extensive organized
activity, which hid the costs from citizens; and the development and
spread of a novel form of bureaucracy, "factory bureaucracy," which
made controls unobtrusive.

The importance of the first, wage dependency, is that for a good part of
society to disappear into organizations it was important that a high proportion of the economically active have no other economic opportunities than employment in an organization. In a society of organizations,
the self-employed had to decline as a category, and wage dependency
insured this.

The importance of the second, externalization of social costs, was two-
fold. First, the costs of "bigness," of economic activity on a grand scale,
had to be disguised and dispersed to the weaker parts of society to
insure the legitimacy of large organizations. Second, the "society of
organizations" theme is not limited to large factories or distributors,
but includes government, services, and voluntary organizations. A
good part of their growth is concerned with dealing with the externalized social costs of, say, unemployment, overcrowding, disputes, alienation, social pathology, and even the necessity of mass recreation.

The importance of the third, bureaucracy, was that organizations are
above all devices for controlling and coordinating the activities of many
more or less unwilling employees. Wage dependency brought them to

729

the organization, but for a society of organizations to exist, organizational control had to be efficient and, above all, relatively unobtrusive, accepted, and legitimated. Factory bureaucracy first made this possible, and it spread until today the term "bureaucracy" is virtually synonymous with organizations.

My three phenomena have more conventional terms when a society of organizations is being assumed and uncritically accepted: labor supply, infrastructure, and administration. Add to these capital and technology, and a wholly conventional and benign history of our times can be written, ignoring, I believe, the real meaning that emerges when wage dependency, externalization, and unobtrusive controls are used instead, and capital and technology are seen as dependent upon them.

Wage dependency

Wage dependency means that in order to survive one must depend upon a wage income, that is, working for someone else (and their profit) and receiving compensation in the form of money. Both the percent of the population involved and the size of the employing organizations are important. Wage dependency covered about 20 percent of the population in 1820, and 80 to 90 percent by 1950. The size of the units increased as well, going from a few employees in any one business or government office who could know each other well and relate to one another on non-organizational criteria to hundreds or thousands in any one organization, where the organizational relationship would be the only thing they had in common. In 1820 it was important that, even for the 20 percent or so who were dependent upon wages for all or most of their lives, they worked in small rather than large organizations and were surrounded by an 80 percent who did not work for anyone else.

Those outside of the wage-dependent population were mostly farmers. In addition, a small segment consisted of craftsmen or small-business people; another farmed part of the time and worked part of the time for others; and still others moved back and forth between the wage labor market and subsistence farming, or crafts and trades.

Lack of permanent wage dependency in what was, for the early part of the 19th century, a bountiful society, meant a great deal of individual discretion. Even the temporary laborer had the resources to secure

730

food and fuel through hunting, fishing, a bit of farming, woodcutting, and had time for handicrafts, all of which prevented dependency upon employers.[3] Permanent wage dependency cut off all alternatives and increased dependency upon employing organizations.[4]

Though a non-wage dependent economy had been the traditional situation since the first colonies (feudalism never existed in the United States) it was rapidly becoming an inefficient system for all concerned. Why the change? The abundant resources of the North American continent allowed substantial economic surpluses and thus fostered a large potential market for goods and services that required continuous feeding. A farmer would find it inefficient to make his own clothing and implements if an organization could produce it more efficiently, through specialized labor working long hours, and distribute it through a state subsidized transport system. A low price required new technologies that could take advantage of large-volume production. Large-volume production meant continuous production, but existing producers were part-time in many cases, farming in some seasons and working at production in others, for example. Or, production was in the hands of small craftsmen and the "putting-out" system, where parts of the production process were carried out in private homes. As Alfred DuPont Chandler argues at length, the production system could not meet the demands of the growing market once transportation improved and population density increased.[5]

The capitalists emerging from the merchant class required continuous reliable production if customers were to become dependent upon "store-bought goods," capital goods, and other durables. The appearance of an all-weather power source, the steam engine, made year-round production possible, and electric lighting made the 10 or 12 hours of work a day more efficient, solving one part of the problem. The other part was a tractable labor force. It had to be one that had no other source of income or wealth and thus would work longer hours on a more regular basis than they were accustomed to working.

The hours, and the repetitive tasks, made this source of income unpopular. Initially, it was hard to recruit for the factories. In England owners initially relied on paupers, orphans, and criminals, since few would voluntarily work in the "dark, Satanic mills." This source was not as important in the United States; the first factories (the textile mills) drew on the daughters of New England farmers, who were in plentiful supply. Then, as agriculture moved west, the factories drew on the displaced New England farmers themselves. As these supplies dwindled, the U.S. industrialists drew upon the impoverished, overpopulated sections of Europe, whose waves of immigrants left for the comparative plenty of the United States. About 60 percent of them stayed rather than returned with the money they saved, almost all becoming a permanent wage-dependent class.

Both organizations and the wage-dependent population had a steady increase and produced bountiful goods that enriched the nation and especially enriched the new capitalist class. Inequality of wealth in the United States grew steadily in the nineteenth century,[6] but the nation as a whole prospered too, heedlessly consuming the abundant resources and herding the remaining natives into "reservations." Despite rising standards of living and the demand for labor in the new factories, the spread of the wage system was a fearful change for the society. It was chronicled as "wage slavery" until the last quarter of the century and after that the workers were referred to as the "industrial army." Slavery and the military were the only institutions people could conceive of that had such control over human beings.

One might want to escape the idiocy of rural life and the hardships of farming by going to the city, but going to the city was supposed to mean going into business for oneself, learning or working at a craft, joining a business of a relative, or temporary wage labor until one could be self-employed. To go into a factory and be a wage slave was something else. By the last quarter of the century it was clear that few could escape wage dependency through sufficient savings that would allow them to be independent craftspersons, businessmen, or farmers, with the autonomy it implied. Nor could many gain managerial positions in the new organizations that gave them some autonomy in work to offset their income dependency.

But wage dependency had other consequences than longer hours, a reduction in personal autonomy, and limited mobility. A bit of society disappeared: the traditional obligation that the farm owner or master craftsman or the merchant had for the welfare of his "hands" was not a part of the new wage system. As limited as that obligation might be, it was perceptible, and could include economic support when sickness, hard economic conditions, or natural disasters had to be confronted; personal attention in family or community crises; concern with employment of employees' offspring, and so on. This was help based upon one's membership in a society or community, not an organization.

732

The helping relationship extended beyond the wage contract and entailed local community standards and values, rather than being limited to the formalized large-scale organizational help that uses the organization as the referent.

The obligation under the wage system could be non-existent until gradually and inexorably the large organizations of the twentieth century replaced the reciprocity of the small owner/employee/community relationship with society-absorbing formal programs. With an unskilled mobile labor force, reciprocity was of no economic benefit to the master. A century later the unskilled no longer dominated the factory wage group; retention became important and bargaining produced contract-specific fringe benefits. But that was later; from the 1820s to the end of the century, the appearance of large organizations meant that a buffer against hard times, accidents, or deaths, was removed. Moreover, the consequences of uncontrolled business cycles of boom and bust were greater with wage dependency.[7]

There was another part of society that was absorbed: more of the hours in the day that had been spent in recreation, religious activities, and socialization of children now were spent in the factory. The new factory workers spent 12 hours a day for 6 or 7 days a week away from the home. The generation of profits and of industrial and business expansion also required considerably more effort as well as more hours from the "wage slaves."

But beyond the efforts and hours, the major effect of the new system of wage dependency was (1) to insure that labor would have to move to where it was needed, and (2) to reduce reciprocal obligations. Leaving one's employer merely meant another had to be found, if blacklisting by employers did not prevent that; and being laid off meant that the obligations of the employer ended, whether the departure was "for cause" or because of business conditions. Blacklisting was extensively used in the first factories, the textile mills of New England where rural recruits from the Northeast, then migrants from Ireland and then Canada were virtually indentured servants for their first year. It continued to be used in the mining industry and possibly others. It is an expression of enforced wage dependency. Since the economic system now produced violent business cycles, wage dependency was a very serious condition.

733

Externalities

The second important transformation stemmed from the increasing amount of economic activity controlled by ever larger organizations and involved the displacement of social costs onto non-owners, principally workers and communities. These are referred to here as *externalities*, social costs of activity that are not included in the price of the goods or services, but absorbed by non-owners. This makes rational pricing and thus rational choices by citizens difficult. The price of the good does not reflect its true cost, and those who subsidize the cost are generally the poorer and weaker parts of the population.

For example, citizens cannot say to manufacturers with huge factories, "while economies of scale may make your product a bit cheaper for you and thus for us, if you had to reimburse the city for the costs of public transportation that large factories required, for the spread of contagious diseases, the crime rates attendant upon crowding, and the high cost of sanitary services in crowded urban areas, the price of goods manufactured in huge factories would be higher than those manufactured in small ones spread about the urban area, and our purchases would favor the goods of the latter."

Managers and owners may not be aware of the externalities, of course. They may deplore increasing crime rates but not see how their need for a population of surplus labor, to accommodate periods of boom and bust, contributes to crime. But even if they are aware of this, capitalism as a system will not pursue the "public good" of steady employment unless some external mechanism, such as the federal government, requires contributions or restraints from each organization. Otherwise, those who tried to even out the rate of production would be less profitable in boom times because they did not expand, and less profitable in bust times because they were carrying excess personnel. They would lose out to those whose expansion and contraction policies produced the externalities they sought to mitigate.

But it is also possible that capitalists were quite aware of the effects of their actions, yet in the face of the extraordinary profits available, disregarded the effects or rationalized them away. It seems that the owners of the New England textile mills were quite aware, in the 1820s and 1830s, of how industrial activity was responsible for such slums and depravity that existed in the old textile towns of England. A reference I have unfortunately lost reports the minutes of a board meeting where

734

the Directors of one large firm explicitly resolved not to repeat the mistakes of Manchester, England, and established dormitories and other amenities for the young women and children they employed. Business boomed, profits were enormous, and ever larger numbers of employees were required. However, for this and other firms the fear of creating industrial slums appears to have abated. The amenities were not extended to employees in new facilities, and were reduced, then eliminated in old ones; coercive practices such as blacklisting expanded even in profitable times, and so did the employment of young children. The mill towns began to resemble the slums of their English competitors even though the English were no longer serious competitors.

In a system that emphasizes maximizing stockholder gain, and thus organizational self-interest, a central authority is required to address the issue of costs that are displaced on those parts of the population who are not organized to defend their interests. In Europe, this was the state, and Germany, for example, led the way in social welfare legislation that addressed the externalities. Even England did not allow capitalism the free reign that it had in the United States. The United States however, deliberately lacked a strong central government, resolved as it was to avoid the feudal aspects of Europe, and thus capitalists were relatively unchecked.[8] Competitive capitalism that maximized the self-interest of the owner or controller had its purest form of growth in this new land, unchecked by labor unions or labor parties. From the beginning the colonial settlers *knowingly* destroyed and wasted non-renewable resources, leaving the bill to be paid by the next generation.[9] With industrialization, the bill frequently had to be paid by workers and communities immediately. The very power and productivity of industrialization meant that externalities extended to more areas of society and did so more quickly.

The United States was fortunate that there were no feudal interests or an aristocracy made up of land holders, merchants, and manufacturers to hold up our industrial progress and democratic development, but this also meant free reign for the power and interests of the industrialists that eventually became known as the robber barons. It was an environment most congenial among the developing industrial nations for absorbing society and delaying the payment. This was because of two effects that followed the appearance of externalities. First, the externalities were so large that they overwhelmed the existing institutions that had traditionally absorbed similar but smaller externalities. Second, new organizations, usually sponsored by or supported by local or national governments, but large in their own right, were created to cope with the externalities. This only increased the rush to an organizational society, and these new organizations generated their own externalities.

Some of the externalities that were disguised or neglected by firms were pollution, crowded cities, transportation costs once workers could no longer live near their workplace, industrial accidents, violent business cycles leading to unemployment, and the exhaustion of easily available natural resources. In the long run they could not be neglected, and their costs were evident, so they became either new business opportunities or were handled through taxation. Thus, more organizations were required to cope with them, from welfare institutions such as prisons, asylums, and the related court system, to public health departments, hospitals, and associated training institutions, on to pollution clean-up organizations concerned with sewage and toxic wastes, and more intensive resource extraction organizations as the easily available resources were exhausted.

The problems exceeded the capacity of social groups that traditionally handled them. These groups were the small, kin-oriented organizations, the local craft associations, the churches, town governments, extended families, and even informal neighborhood groups that made up so much of society in the first half of the nineteenth century. They were a vital part of what we think of as society, making adjustments and easing hardships in a local, somewhat representative way. From our vantage point in the United States today, prizing individualism, competition, and private gratifications, they were particularistic, paternalistic, suffocating at times, and limited in efficiency. But for the scope of problems with which they had to deal, before large organizations appeared, and considering the expectations and values of the time, they were adequate.

Overwhelmed by the problems, these groups became more irrelevant; their functions were replaced by larger, centralized bureaucracies controlled by more distant authorities, and financed by general taxation of the very recipients of the externalities. Much of industrialization, even the triumphs we celebrate, is concerned with coping with the problems industrialization itself generates. Traditional groups were disappearing, their functions becoming encapsulated into new organizations. Non-bureaucratic society was being whittled away throughout the nineteenth century.

736

Factory bureaucracy

I refer to the third major change as the development of "factory bureau-cracy" rather than simply as bureaucracy, because I want to highlight its novelty and the role of factories in developing the bureaucratic form. After around 1920, it is so widespread and firmly grounded that bureaucracy, or even just "organization" will suffice.

Large-scale organizations have been around for centuries, building the pyramids or Venetian ships, establishing religions, fighting wars, ad-ministering kingdoms. Some had a core of permanent employees – that is wage-dependent individuals – or were institutions such as the Catho-lic Church. But only with industrialization, and initially with the facto-ry, did the elements of factory bureaucracy come together in a large number of organizations, enough of them for the organizational pattern to be readily and easily adopted by new organizations in the growing economy.

The principal problem for entrepreneurs and capitalists producing goods and services was continuous, predictable production. As wage dependency made clear, if the work force had to work for someone else in order to eat, they would show up for work. But more is required. To get them to work hard, and to do exactly what they are told, *centralized control* is required. The putting-out system, craft production, inside contracting, and other practices did not provide centralized control such that one person at the top could reach directly into all processes. These older forms required a good deal of negotiation, bargaining, and even trust. Interactions could be complex and time-consuming, pre-sumably, but they forced a degree of network cooperation and a sense of shared fate. By contrast, factory bureaucracy established centralized control where all processes were either brought together under one roof or otherwise controlled by the owner. Trust was no longer as important; the failure to follow orders led to dismissal, and under wage dependency did not make one independent; it merely meant one had to find another employer to obey. Since production was complex, central-ization also meant that *hierarchy* had to be established, making it quite clear to whom each person in turn reported. By establishing hierarchy as a principle, persons such as foremen or supervisors filled roles or job slots that were independent of the person, and obedience was given to the position, an aspect of formalization.

Formalization meant establishing not only hierarchical chains, but standard operating procedures, rules, and regulations. When fully implemented (it took F. W. Taylor to see the need for full implementation, but it was emerging before he conceptualized it), it meant that superiors would know what skills the subordinate used (the better to control him or her), could control and change those skills as needed, and subdivide the work so that wages could be closely matched to the level of skill, thus paying the minimum possible. Finally, *standardization* and *specialization* of as many tasks as possible were necessary. Standardizing tasks reduced the necessary training time and simplified the work so that more people would be qualified for the job, lowering employee power. (It also probably meant more even-quality levels, necessary for mass production, and lower materials costs.) Specialization could take place once tasks were standardized, raising output. Specialization is normally thought to mean raising skill levels, and it can mean that. But is can also mean narrowing them, or what has come to be called "deskilling." The growth of bureaucracy entailed both skilling and deskilling.

Factory bureaucracy does not require large organizations, but it certainly permits them, and that is one of its advantages. At the end of the nineteenth century, most firms had less than 250 employees; perhaps a third had less than 100. The situation is not vastly different now with respect to the continuing presence of many small firms. What has changed is that we now have enough enormously large and reasonably large ones to dominate employment, and to dominate the smaller firms, many of which are only nominally autonomous. But bureaucracy is not restricted to the large firm. For a firm of, say, 20 employees, the control elements of bureaucracy could still be important. Our negative image of bureaucracy and modern organizations includes the perception of great size, which presumably leads to impersonality. But while bureaucracy makes it possible to put together huge organizations, it is not masses of people that account for the control. A firm of 20 can exercise a great deal of centralization, hierarchy, standardization, and specialization. Furthermore, in today's economy, all of these can be evident in a branch location with no more than five employees, or even in a franchised operation with five. A huge bank with many offices, or a fast food operation with many outlets, is not significantly decentralized and certainly not debureaucratized because the employee size of the modal outlet is, for example, only five. In the technical terms of the census, establishment size may be small, but firm size can be very large indeed. And it is the firm that can establish the elements of factory bureaucracy.[10] These elements, which constitute the definition of the modern

738

form of bureaucracy – centralization, hierarchy, formalization, stand-ardization, and specialization – were only gradually introduced. One of the biggest impediments to full bureaucratization during much of the nineteenth century was the inside contracting system, and it had to be eliminated before factory bureaucracy could triumph. It was used in the most technologically advanced and most mass production indus-tries, and it prevented full-fledged bureaucracy from appearing in these organizations. In this system the owner provided the building, supplies, power source, and major pieces of machinery, and the contractor hired, fired, paid, and directed the work of his crew, which could be as large as 100. He worked on the basis of annual contracts for so many trigger assemblies, rifle stocks, sewing machine treadles, or whatever.

Inside contracting, though very efficient and responsible for continu-ous innovations, violated most of the emerging principles of bureaucra-cy to some extent. The *hierarchy* was truncated since the inside con-tractor hired his own workers and the owner had no control over them; thus *centralized control* was limited. *Formalization, standardization,* and *specialization* were all limited since the contractor could set his own production rules, etc. He was bound by the contract to deliver a certain number and quality of rifle barrels or sewing machine chains or whatever, and the delivery date was formalized, but this concerned his contract with the owner, not his more informal and particularistic agreement with his own employees.

The system was remarkably efficient since it was in the interests of the contractor to innovate continually, thus making more profit on his yearly contract, and the owner did not incur the many "transaction costs" of hiring, paying, and especially, supervising workers. But it also meant that profits were diffused among the autonomous contractors, spreading the wealth, and some of the contractors made as much as the owners did; there was a significant "income stream" that remained to be appropriated by the capitalist. It also fostered group loyalty because contractors utilized personalistic bases of hiring and often boarded with or lived close to their workers. The loyalty was to the contractor, not the capitalist. In fact, this highly decentralized, profit sharing, "human relations-oriented" system is being rediscovered today mini-mally by "job enlargement," somewhat by profit centers, and maximally by flexible production systems of small autonomous firms.[11] It disap-peared in the late nineteenth century, I believe, for two reasons. The profits of the contractors could be appropriated by owners if contrac-tors became foremen, and it fostered too much labor solidarity.[12]

Exploitation

In the swelling, humming new society, daily unloading boat loads of people seeking freedom and prosperity, we tend to ignore several forms of labor exploitation, or treat it as an unfortunate and inevitable side effect of industrialization. But it was substantial, unnecessary, and important for our argument. Wage cuts, long hours, industrial accidents, and child labor made it difficult for indigenous forms of association, such as guilds, craft and industrial unions, and ethnic and religious groups, to survive and protest. They disappeared, fell silent, or were absorbed by the corporations.

Exploitation might be seen as a fairly benign derivative of the logic of capitalism: wages would be cut only when profits fell, reestablishing the equilibrium; 12-hour days and 6- or 7-day weeks were necessary because of labor shortages; safety costs money, and would be addressed only when the costs of downtime and medical or death payments made it worthwhile; only firms faced with fierce competition would resort to child labor in order to survive, until the state finally equalized the burden of paying adult wages. By this reasoning, exploitation is to be expected only when firm survival is at stake; prosperous industries do not require it, and no organizations have a "taste" for exploitation. The equilibrium account is not inconsistent with the thesis of absorption, but it does not particularly strengthen it.

More relevant to our thesis, and more menacing, is the explanation of "class warfare." In this view, wages were cut when labor was weak, regardless of profits, and deplorable working conditions made protests difficult and signalled a strong class distinction that grew in force through the nineteenth century. Destruction of independent bases of identity and class cohesion through corporate absorption followed, with appeals to (Protestant) religion, Americanization, city managers, company unions, and charities. The following supports the class rather than the equilibrium view:

In 11 mills in Lowell, Massachusetts, from 1844 to 1845, the invested capital, number of spindles, output of cloth, and dividends increased markedly. Dividends went from $4\frac{1}{2}$ to $12\frac{1}{2}$ percent. In these years of great prosperity wages were cut by $12\frac{1}{2}$ percent. The actual profit of the mills in 1846 was estimated to be 40 percent per year.[13] A strike occurred at a Lawrence, Massachusetts mill in 1882 over a reduction of wages from 85 cents a day to 67 cents a day. The mill dividends on its

740

capital stock had averaged over 20 percent per year for 19 years and were presumably high at the time of wage cut.[14]

A Massachusetts Senate document reports "A Holyoke manager found his hands 'languorous' in the early morning because they had breakfast-ed. He tried working them without breakfast and got 3,000 more yards of cloth a week made."[15] The years 1845–46, a period of unprecedented profits, corresponded with a tightening up of regulations, including the one that an operative must serve 12 months at the same factory or not be employed by any factory.[16]

Wages were low and hours long in many industries. Though I do not have poverty-level figures for the following instances, it appears that exploitation may have been an appropriate term. In 1853 a woman binding shoes worked 80 hours a week, and after the cost of light and fire were deducted, received $1.60 a week.[17] Journeymen dressmakers made from $1.25 to $2.50 a week and worked 14–16 hours a day. Weavers experienced a decline in wages of about 50 percent in 10 years without any change in technology.[18]

Wages at Western Union had been systematically reduced since 1871 and the work week extended. Telegraph operators in 1885 were work-ing 7 days a week with nothing extra for Sunday work, a 12-hour day, and were paid about $54 a month. The company had profits of $7 mil-lion on sales of only $17 million about this time. The wage rate figures out to about $1.80 a day.[19]

Carroll Wright, the first head of the U.S. Bureau of Labor Statistics and a great fan of the factory system, testified that in Massachusetts the average annual wage of each employee was $364 and the average profit of the employer on each employee was $98,[20] a *very* good return. Wright may have even been underestimating the degree of surplus prof-it. Another person testified that, using census data for the total United States, the profit to the factory owner was "nearly as much as each man, woman, and child receives," with all expenses taken into account.[21]

The Carnegie Steel Company was making net profits of 17.2 percent in 1891 when it proposed a severe reduction in wages and sustained a strike. The strike in 1892 reduced its profits to only 16 percent for that year.[22] Wages continued to go down after the strike, and in some mills, in order to keep the same wage, those working only 8 hours had to work 12 hours. In 1907, a year of "unexampled prosperity" in the industry, one plant that was surveyed showed 71 percent of the workers receiving $2.50 a day or less. (It was generally agreed that a family of four needed nearly twice that much to survive.[23]) After Carnegie broke the union in 1892, he "thereafter began to introduce the 12-hour day wherever possible." Other mills followed more slowly, but after the strike, the 8-hour day, which some operations had, disappeared. Sunday work came in after the strikes, where it wasn't before.[24] (Incidently, a 12-hour day means that every other week there is one 24-hour day worked.) Most plants and most men worked a 7-day week. There were two holidays a year and even these were denied to the blast furnace crews.

In 1907 at the Homestead Mill in Pittsburgh, a southern European immigrant made $12 for an 84-hour week with no lunch break. Pittsburgh iron and steel mills killed approximately 15 workmen a month outright at this time.[25] The industry was highly profitable in this decade.

It was not until after World War I, despite endless public outcries, that the steel industry abandoned the 12-hour day. There was even evidence that 8-hour shifts cost management very little since output went up. For most of the workers it was not only a 12-hour day, but a 7-day week.[26]

The death and injury toll was substantial and assuredly unnecessary. Daniel Nelson, a rather conservative historian, concludes that before World War I manufacturers paid almost no attention to industrial accidents, blamed them on the men, and paid little if any compensation.[27] As late as 1910 nearly one-quarter of the full-time workers in the iron and steel industry suffered some type of injury in one year, Gutman notes. "Nearly 25% of the recent immigrants employed at the Carnegie South Works were injured or killed each year between 1907 and 1910, 3,723 in all."[28] Not surprisingly, and in marked contrast to conventional belief, "44 south and east Europeans left the United States for every 100 that arrived between 1908 and 1910."[29]

Finally, a few large firms, suffering from suits by workers as the courts gradually changed their position regarding employer liability, undertook safety programs that reduced accidents by 50 to 75 percent, with comparatively little effort on their part. But most companies did little or nothing. After World War I, the Progressive movement and the high cost of a number of individual suits led industry leaders to "socialize"

742

the cost, and workman's compensation legislation was passed. It forced all managers to consider the benefits of accident prevention.

The railroad strikes of 1873–74 were over withholding earned wages for weeks and *even months*. The workers generally lost. Buying outside the company store in many communities where these existed was grounds for dismissal and upheld by the courts. Excess charges of around 25 percent were commonplace. Companies in remote areas advertised for large families to move there and work, because the children could be employed at very low wages (and the adults found they were unemployed). Child labor was not restricted until quite late in the nineteenth century. It was very economical for employers until production processes changed in many industries. (It still exists in the United States, but on the fringes of the economy rather than at the center of it.) Think of a child of 10 or 11 whom you know, working a 10-hour day in a mine or factory.

As Gutman notes, "In the 1880 manuscript census 49.3% of all Paterson boys and 52.1% of all girls aged *11–14* had occupations listed by their names."[30] Child labor rose as the prosperity of industry rose, until the technology made children inefficient. The reduction of child labor appears to have not been steady as capitalism "matured" or softened. There were twice as many children under 12 working in Rhode Island in 1875 as there had been in 1851.[31]

It is hard to reconcile this litany of wage cutting during times of record profits, of long hours, company stores, and withheld wages, needless accidents, and child labor, with the conventional equilibrium models where competition and declining profits force wages down, or with accounts of labor scarcity and high wages; the latter dominate today and bring widespread endorsement of the capitalist system. Elites in a land of abundant natural resources and famine-driven immigrants practiced exploitation upon a wage-dependent population under increasing bureaucratic control. Obviously the production figures had to soar to Chandlerian heights.

Discussion

The principles of factory bureaucracy I have outlined were noted, of course, by Max Weber just after the turn of the century, but his focus was more upon the problem of control of staff rather than of workers, and less with control than with efficiency. The five principles, centralization, hierarchy, etc., were distilled out of survey data by the "Aston" researchers in the 1960s in one of the first large-scale comparative studies of organizations.[32] However, insofar as they interpreted the principles, it was in terms of a functionalist view of organizational efficiency and a celebration of the Weberian model, rather than a view of bureaucracy as a control device.

Bureaucracy means efficiency for most organizational theorists, but for me it means primarily an unobtrusive control device of unprecedented power, so efficient and effective that it could supplant many of the controls that had non-workplace sources, such as those related to the family, church, neighborhood and community, removing the need for them from non-organizational society and weakening these institutions. "Habits of the heart" were being installed, often at the age of 10 or 12; certainly by 16, and then 18 later in our century.

I do not claim that elites planned the transformation of society and conspired to absorb it into their organizations. The process took place gradually over more than a century, and the motivations for each small step were more prosaic than grand – controlling "ruinous" competition, keeping the work force in good condition, appropriating the profits of successful contractors by incorporating them, responding to community concerns about externalities, etc. Bureaucracy was not a demonic invention of evil elites; it simply offered elites an assist that gave them unprecedented (but unanticipated) control over the society, given the scope and complexity of that society, since it provided such exquisite control over the institutions that were absorbing society – the bureaucracies they were establishing.

For owners in the private sector and managers in the public and nonprofit sectors, indirect and unobtrusive controls are far less costly than direct controls, where orders have to be given and performance observed. Factory bureaucracy replaced direct controls with rules and procedures, which are always in existence and quite impersonal, and with machinery, which in essence is a bundle of rules built into a machine. The factory preceded large machines. Workers were brought into factories for surveillance and for long work hours; the machinery came later to make use of this convenient agglomeration of hands.[33] The factory structure delegated any necessary surveillance to lower levels in the hierarchy. It standardized inputs and outputs as much as possible to reduce the need for many controls. The result was not just

744

mass production, but a much more impersonal and remote control system, and a vastly more effective one.[34] It served to legitimize factory bureaucracy in society, since it was a vast improvement over direct controls.

But since so much of one's daily time and, indeed, one's fate now lay with the organization, the society outside the organization had to prepare and socialize its members for these bureaucratic structures. Citizenship came to emphasize punctuality, obedience, respect, patience in service to another, and patience about moving up, and the necessary literacy and numerical skills. The unobtrusive controls of *society* that were irrelevant to the workplace, to the organization, such as reciprocity, ethnic and religious culture, and the extended family, withered in importance.

An alternative path?

The importance of factory bureaucracy can be seen in its swift adoption by almost all organizations in the United States in the latter part of the nineteenth century and into the first third of the next century. Schools, colleges, hospitals, prisons, state and private welfare agencies, foundations, voluntary associations of all types, and government itself "bureaucratized." The founders of organizations of all types and reformers of existing ones repeatedly held the industrial organization model – factories, by and large – as the important social innovation of the times. And indeed it was. As Max Weber put it at the time, all else is dilettantism, and he cited speed, precision, calculation, predictability, impersonality, and accountability as its virtues.

But was the spread of factory bureaucracy the only or the best way to achieve these efficiencies? Max Weber and his contemporaries appeared to think so, and so do the vast majority of social scientists today. Weber and social scientists today have acknowledged a few externalities – cogs in the machine and so on – but Weber and we read the development of bureaucracy as virtually inevitable. I believe two alternative paths were conceivable: a craft orientation, that would have slowed economic development somewhat by limiting the volume of goods, but in turn raising their quality and reducing the social costs, and a fully Taylorist approach as was enthusiastically adopted in Lenin's U.S.S.R.

Regarding the first, forms of production that emphasized craft control,

745

extensive inside contracting, producer cooperatives, and networks of small firms did survive the competition from mass production in a few parts of Europe and even are thought to be the basis for some extra-ordinary regional booms today (see Sabel and Zeitlin for the evidence[35]). But capitalism in the United States was relatively unencumbered compared to Europe, and thus self-interest maximizing forms of behavior were at a peak. A very weak state ignored social costs; community mindedness and cohesion were less robust than in Europe; and an easy political franchise did not favor class consciousness and radical parties that might have checked the destruction of crafts and the rise of huge corporations. (The origins of our form of capitalism had much to do with politics and culture, but once it began its society-consuming growth, capitalist organizations became the key "independent variable.") Externalizing the social costs and gulping down the natural resources and the dependent labor supply, the successful firms extracted more profits than those with fewer self-regarding and more other-regarding orientations (cooperatives, small firms built around a craft, firms that did not aggressively grow), and thus could get cheaper investment capital for expansion and even generate more surplus for corrupting public authorities (a widespread practice).

The following structural characteristics favor self-regarding behavior, and all were emphasized by factory bureaucracy and other capitalist organizational structures (and then spread to public and non-profit organizations): individual rather than collective rewards; storage of rewards allowing accumulation rather than distribution; structures favoring notions of omnicompetent and permanent leadership, rather than task-specific and rotating leadership; behavior surveillance rather than output surveillance for as much of the work force as possible. (These are characteristics of the "agency" model of organizations so much in current favor.)[36]

Alternatively, factory and industrial organizations in the United States could have pursued the self-interest model even more assiduously than they did. While crafts suffered extensive declines, cooperatives failed, and the inside contracting system was destroyed, the change across industries was uneven; there were some survivals, and some checks upon the power of large bureaucracies were installed, as we shall see. More of a "society" independent of large organizations survived than was the case in the U.S.S.R., where Taylorism installed precise control over a deskilled labor force through a swollen management system, and the lack of an independent citizenry left state power unchecked. Of

746

course, the United States had far richer resources available to elites, and this made it easier to consent to a less than fully Taylorized system. But both the more "liberal" and the more reactionary paths were possible. The liberal one survived in enclaves in Europe and the reactionary one was installed in Russia and its satellites.

The efficiency argument

Of course, this argument runs counter to most respected interpretations, which all claim that it was efficiency that brought about modern bureaucracy. The efficiency argument is accepted without much comment in economics, history, and even functionalist versions of sociology (and, I am ashamed to admit, in the first, 1971 edition of my own work, *Complex Organizations: A Critical Essay*). Chandler is at least explicit about the efficiency of "throughput coordination" and economies of scale in his frequent celebrations of giant firms, and after him Oliver Williamson argued that it was the efficiency of reductions in "transactions costs" that brought about modern bureaucracy.[37] But both scholars had a very narrow view of efficiency. They excluded all externalities and assumed that survival, growth, and profits signified efficiency. But if one raised profits by externalizing many costs to the community, exploiting the workforce, evading government controls by corrupting officials, manipulating stock values, and controlling the market by forming quasi-cartels or other predatory practices – all common practices in the nineteenth and twentieth century – then profits will not reflect the efficient use of labor, capital, and natural resources. Chandler, Williamson, and other celebrants admit these practices existed, of course, but think they played a minor role. Some of us think the role was major.[38]

Moreover, Chandler, Williamson, and other conventional economic historians see a linear, implicitly inevitable development with few dysfunctions. They also discount many externalities as inevitable requirements of the marketplace, or temporary evils that were rectified by Progressivism or whatever. I would argue that they were far from inevitable and that it took a surprisingly long time and amount of struggle to mitigate the evils. In a democratic society with such abundant resources what needs explanation is the scope and persistence of these externalities.

I have already referred to child labor, wage cuts when profits were high, and the unnecessary accident rate. Even those events that so hearten conventional historians as examples of industry's progressivism are questionable – for example, company welfare programs, including community experiments, and workman's compensation. For the great majority of the few firms that established them, company welfare programs appeared in times of labor shortage and were abandoned at the first sign of labor surplus. This suggests that nothing but obtaining sufficient labor at the lowest cost was involved, despite the rationalizations that owners offered and current researchers accept.

The externality of industrial accidents was addressed in a fashion, under pressure, and with a distinctively bureaucratic solution: Workman's compensation was enacted because the contingent fee system allowed lawyers to represent poor workers, and the law suits being won were beginning to cost industry dearly. The solution was to set up a bureaucracy to adjudicate cases and control the benefits. Benefits were set at a minimal level, far below those awarded in courts to individuals, all firms were taxed, thus spreading the resulting price increase extremely widely, and effectively minimizing the incentive of the individual firm to follow safe practices. The conservative A.F. of L. union supported workman's compensation, but most other unions saw its implications and opposed it.

I do not want to idealize the nineteenth century. Certainly life was nastier, more brutish, and rather short. But in terms of the opportunity we had as a nation unencumbered by a rigid class structure, with immense resources on a sparsely settled continent whose owners died like flies of our diseases, a country with a growing market that would soon become huge, and in the early stage of the industrial revolution, it is hard to ignore the costs and instead preach the efficiency. Generally speaking, the historiography of industrialization has *not* been one of wage dependency, externalities, the control consequences of bureaucracy, and alternative paths that might have been taken, for better or worse. Instead, it assumes linear development, inevitable "stages," is concerned with efficiency for the few, assumes that benefits can be measured by output statistics, and is, withall, relentlessly celebratory. I believe a focus upon organizations as instruments of unobtrusive control will redress that deficiency.

Furthermore, the long-run costs to our society were high, and are generally unremarked. The increase in standard of living is hardly a matter for unalloyed celebration since it was based in considerable part on the

748

rapid consumption of the vast natural resources available in the new land, the increased hours of labor of the wage dependent citizenry, the geographical mobility of labor, and the exploitation of Latin America.

In fact, it was *necessary* for the standard of living to rise because it had to compensate for the new degradations and the new necessities that industrialization and bureaucracy required, such as more health facilities because of more accidents and pollution, or better transportation because people could no longer live close to their source of livelihood. The most important change in the standard of living was better nutrition, and industrialization's contribution to better nutrition was rather indirect – improved transportation and refrigeration.

Inequality in wealth and income increased markedly up to about the turn of the century, the time of rising prosperity and the great industrial gains. Thus, while life for all improved, life for the poor improved far less. Inequality of wealth stabilized at the end of the century, but remained high; to this day, it is the highest of all industrialized nations except, I believe, France and South Africa, despite 80 years of social movements and progressive legislation.[39] Indeed, inequality seems far more responsive to political decisions than to the "efficiency" of capitalist organizations. In less than a decade, from 1980 to 1989, the top 1 percent of the U.S. population increased its share of wealth by over 20 percent (from 9 to 11 percent); the top 20 percent by 6 percent; and the poorest 20 percent absorbed the losses. These changes were deliberately induced by the Reagan administration.

Most of industrialization's triumphs were concerned with itself, coping with the fouling of its own nest. The triumphs involved such matters as facilitating the growth of the organizations that industrialization needed by moving people and goods about more quickly and to more distant places, by enabling more crowded cities to appear and survive so that organizational efficiency could be higher, and with the improvement of weapons and warriors for acquiring territory and protecting overseas markets. A society of organizations began to appear when feeding the organizations became the criteria for efficiency, productivity, and progress.

The infrastructure

I have argued that economic organizations, and particularly the factories, were largely responsible for the absorption of society by organizations in the nineteenth century. Wage dependency provided the labor force, factory bureaucracy the control, and the social costs were externalized to the poorer parts of society and future generations. This was accompanied by a fair degree of exploitation, given the national resources and other advantages the U.S. corporate class had, and many inefficiencies if we broaden the term to include impacts upon workers, communities, and future generations. Non-economic organizations (government at all levels, and voluntary and non-profit organizations) dealt with the externalities, I noted. But we should look a bit more closely at non-economic organizations in a society of organizations. These are the infrastructure of the new system, not only picking up the pieces, but moderating conflict, developing the resources, and shaping the culture in ways consistent with a society of organizations, including providing the cognitive categories, or ways of thinking, that legitimate it. I will note that the process was not always smooth, and citizens and employees struck back at times and still do.

Consider a landscape dotted with many small organizations, loosely clustered around ports and rivers, with few and slow interactions. A disturbance, economic, social, or political, does not radiate far, and thus is not likely to interact with other disturbances. This might be the U.S. eastern seaboard in 1820. By 1900 we have a continent with many large organizations and large cities among the small groups and settlements, with externalities pouring out of them, creating new organizations. The large organizations also have increasingly complex interactions, requiring new organizations to deal with the interactions, such as government bureaus and trade associations. The panic of 1893 might have been such an unexpected interaction among increasingly coupled organizations and interests. (Its consequences were quite unexpected; massive investments shifted from the railroads to industry, permitting mergers; within a decade most of the giant corporations that have survived as giants today were created.[40])

By 1950 the small groups and organizations continue to exist and expand, but they increasingly exist as satellites of large economic ones, or branches of large non-economic ones. Meanwhile the large organizations of both types, economic and non-economic, have expanded in both number and size, filling the landscape and bumping into each other. Between 1950 and 1990 the density of large employing organizations, satellites, and branches increases only gradually (there seems to be a limit upon organizational size, at least under our form of capi-

750

talism, even with the multidivisional and conglomerate control devices), but the problem of the unexpected interactions of failures in disparate parts of the system increases. The large organizations have no
choice but to feed off of one another, and the interdependencies are
sometimes unexpected, as was the case of the October, 1987 stock
market crash.[41] These are the themes we now take up – the growth of
non-economic organizations and their stabilizing functions, and the
related growth of unmanageable interdependencies.

A growing economy can produce more organizations, increase the size
of existing organizations, or both. The United States did both, but the
more mature the sector, the more it emphasized hierarchy and concentration (a few dominant organizations) rather than markets fed by
numerous small firms. The problem for both individual firms and for
sectors or industries was to maintain control in the face of increasing
size. (Increasing the number of organizations but not their size would
spread the wealth, reduce hierarchy, and reduce the concentration of
power; elites were not likely to favor these and become lesser elites.[42])
Mature sectors (steel, railroads, flour, etc.) tried trusts and cartels, and
when these were outlawed, price leadership and administered prices,
and then mergers and acquisitions.[43] The individual firms followed suit,
moving to the multidivisional form, and then conglomerates (the
organization of organizations). Only new areas, and then only briefly,
had large numbers of small firms. With increasing concentration of
power within sectors and within individual firms, the problem of regulating this power arose for both the competing firms and their customers, and for the citizens. Competition might end up producing only one
firm with monopoly profits, and both competitors and the public would
object.

The solution, of course, was more organizations, either trade association or other self-regulatory bodies in business and industry, or government bureaus such as the Interstate Commerce Commission. These
were fairly direct attempts to regulate an industry. Less direct were the
attempts to control the interactions between sectors or industries. Here
where such things as Judge Gary's dinners or those of J. P. Morgan (the
temporary organization of organizations), the Civic Federation, the
present-day Business Roundtable, or, on the government side, the
Council of Economic Advisors and even the Bureau of Management
and Budget. We should also include a fair proportion of the legal trade,
and management consulting firms. These organizations of course are
not examples of big employing organizations that are sucking in socie-

ty; instead, they should be seen as the "ball bearings" that reduce the frictions of huge organizations working and colliding with one another.

Though they are not big employing organizations, it is still important that they are organizations – that the legal firm, the Chambers of Commerce, the Department of Commerce, and so on will develop interests of their own as organizations, as bureaucracies with careers and managerial powers and extra-organizational interests available for pursuit. Until now I have been using a simplified model of organizations – clear interests, single goal. For economic organizations that is sufficient for accounting for wage dependency, bureaucratic control, and externalization, but for infrastructure organizations, as we shall see, the notion that organizations are tools that can be used by many for many purposes becomes important.

As economic organizations grew, so of course did society, the labor force, communities, and the infrastructure. But business and industry grew faster than the infrastructure, and pretty much dominated local and national government at the turn of the century. The power of individual capitalists, families, and alliances peaked about 1920; their control over government and communities was unprecedented. But internal divisions and contradiction within business and industry made control of the expanding economy more and more difficult, and the tycoons faded. Nevertheless, their organizational empires continued to grow, bumping into each other, merging and dissolving, increasingly reacting to organizational rather than class or family dynamics. They not only became more complexly interactive among themselves, but new sources of interactions arose from the state, labor, and the communities.

All three, the federal government, labor, and communities, presented challenges to the hegemony of the large financial, industrial, and business bureaucracies. The challenge was somewhat successful. Most important, the degree of inequality of wealth in society no longer increased, but was stabilized. (One might have wished for, even expected, a reduction of inequality with so much new national wealth, the reforms of the progressive movement and the New Deal, the taxes on corporations and the progressive income tax, the extended franchise, the union movement, and the growth of government. Alas, all these heroic efforts did was to stabilize the degree of inequality, of which the Reagan administration brought about a further increase.)[44] A web of federal and local laws was passed to restrain the power of the corpora-

752

tion, to address the issue of externalities, and unions extracted conces-
sions in the 1920s and again in the 1940s. But while this was going on,
and the power of corporations was being somewhat checked, another
significant transformation was taking place. The countervailing forces
were becoming indistinguishable from their targets with respect to
bureaucratization and the absorption of what once was considered the
rest of society.

The local community was swallowed by the urban area, and the social
costs of industrialization had to be dealt with by ever larger governmental units or more consolidated and federated voluntary associations. The bureaucratic model was the only possible organizational
form, with its centralization, hierarchy, specialization, standardization,
and formalization. But bureaucracy in the federal government, local
government, unions, and voluntary associations created its own externalities, just as industry had done, and required still more organizations
to cope with them. A major social cost was increased wage dependency
as a result of organizational growth; it went from about 65 percent of
the economically active population at the turn of the century to 80
percent in 1950. The independent professions became increasingly tied
to large bureaucracies, whether business, government, or voluntary
associations; small businesses came and went at the margins, ever vulnerable to and dependent upon big business. Economic prosperity and
consumption became the dominant criteria by which the effectiveness
of the infrastructure of the economy, represented by non-economic
organizations, was to be judged.

From 1900 on schooling was standardized, with the boards of consolidated districts exercising more remote and universalistic control and
reducing cultural diversity in the process. Cultural diversity as reflected
in small organizations hangs on today, an authentic representative of
society in a nation of organizations, but it is diminished. The most
important source of diversity now is immigration. The centralized
school system seeks to eliminate the diversity, only grudgingly allowing
bilingual teaching. The charities movement, starting at the end of the
nineteenth century, succeeded in *reducing* decentralized municipal aid
and the role of religious and voluntary associations, in an open drive to
blame the victims of unemployment and accidents for their plight. The
social work profession divorced itself from charity and devoted itself to
intrapsychic problems of the non-poor, rationalizing and organizing the
self.[45] Medicine transformed the hospices and withdrew into them. All
professions became preoccupied with credentialing and state protec-

753

tion, and bureaucratized and grew. Government professionalized at all levels. Locally the city manager movement was supported by imperial business. Nationally there was the growth of staff colleges and civil services at the federal level.

Everywhere the example of rational industry was cited as the model, and detachment from citizens and their particularistic needs paralleled the impersonality of wage dependency upon which industry had flourished. The infrastructure that supported the economy – welfare, education, medical care, and local governance – not only began to resemble the economic organizations; the infrastructure interacted more directly with them and less with what remained independent of bureaucracies, that is, the remnants of society. The infrastructure organizations pulled their very charges, the needy, the young, the sick, and the citizens seeking redress from externalities, into their bureaucracies, recasting their needs in organizationally appropriate terms.[46] Less and less remained outside that was untouched by the organizations.

The movement toward the society of organization came in two distinct forms. As I have just suggested, the organization redefines the needs of citizens in organizationally convenient forms, including the convenience of easy control. The person becomes a "case" or his or her needs are unattended; the worker either becomes a party to the wage contract or is without income. This entails the stripping of the society from the person to meet the needs of the organization. The central authority, the boss, uses standardization, specialization, and placement in an organizationally defined hierarchy to change the social citizen into an organizational member. Of course, the difficulty is that this cannot be complete, and people track in the mud of the social identity achieved outside of the organization into the organization, but the organization works assiduously to counteract this pollution.

The second form is akin to the reproduction of the working class, but now it is better to call it the employed class. The organization undertakes the socialization process that it has just denied society. It replaces the social entity that it finds in the new employee with its own version of socialization. It does this more or less unwittingly, piecemeal, often at the employee's behest, through union contracts or employee benefits that appear to attract and retain workers. The first expression of this was the company town – the organizational provision of education, religion, stores, housing, recreation. When labor was scarce these towns flourished; they were abandoned when labor was plentiful. The

754

more scarce the labor, the more of society has to be provided by the organization to attract labor, and the more intense the socialization into the society of organizations must be. Organizations are forced to insure a labor supply to reproduce the working class.

It is important to recognize that this is not a witting, planned accomplishment on the part of power elites. The logic of factory bureaucracy, mass production, the prevention of "ruinous competition" etc. simply creates the conditions for the absorption. As society disappeared through the processes I have described, more and more employees ceased protesting and became witting accomplices in the process of having through these centralized organizations. Since 1950 the absorption of society into the organizations has accelerated as less and less of societal reproduction is either available in what remains outside of the large employing organization, and because managing the ever more tightly coupled and complexly interactive network of organizations requires ever more control over the employees.

What kind of a society is being created within the large employing organizations or through the smaller organizations that are largely dependent upon the large ones for their existence? It is a rationalized, controlled, surrogate society (but one that may be given to dangerous outbursts reflecting old oppressions and community fears – a topic for which there is no space to explore here). For employees of the large organizations, the bureaucracy has increasingly become more than a source of wages and salaries that can then be freely spent on the products that other bureaucracies chose to produce. Increasingly, up to 45 percent of labor costs are paid in fringe benefits, many of which are not freely chosen and if not used, are lost to employees.

I think it makes a difference in the relative strength of society as opposed to organizations if the organization is the source of the following social functions, or the arbiter of their availability: counseling, educational opportunities, sex therapy, days off for Christmas shopping, tax and investment advice, sports facilities, comprehensive medical care, maternal and paternal medical leave, vacation planning and vacation resorts, travel services, relocation services, formal training programs, retirement counseling and planning, religious facilities and funeral services, and if you are really lucky, even child care.

We applaud these; we count as a progressive employer the firm or university that supplies our needs through these services, some of them tax-avoiding devices that are thus financed by the less fortunate employees in marginal organizations. But they shape our behavior and our consciousness in unobtrusive ways, taking a bit of choice that once was outside the employment contract and putting it into that context. Our choice is less subject to family and kin, neighbors, peer groups, and religious or ethnic ties. It may even be a compassionate organizational gesture, to be welcomed in a society where compassion, some feel, is harder and harder to find. But that is just the point. What happened to the source of that compassion? The groups that had provided it are too weak to carry the burden or have disappeared.

I know my long list of services that the enlightened employer provides was poorly performed in 1820, if at all. But most of these services now exist to redress externalities that hardly existed then, and with the wealth of this nation we might expect these and more services to be now available as a right of citizenship rather than as a condition of employment at a progressive organization. Then the issue would be more tractable: whether these services were to come from a large central government, with all the dangers of centralization, or from small, local and more or less autonomous groups and organizations, what we once thought of as community. If they are a condition of employment, rather than citizenship, the logic of profit maximization is likely to make the issue of small, independent, versus large organizations quite intractable. There will be no reasonable choice.

Concluding comments

There are many dangling ends that I do not have the space to weave into the argument or to clip off. These include (1) comparisons with the capitalism and society of Europe and with pre-1988 command economies of the U.S.S.R. and Eastern Europe – in some respects both groups are more "organizational" societies than our own; (2) contrasting dense, resilient webs, such as we think of in connection with Gemeinschaft, with the rigid, hard-wired nets with dedicated nodal functions that characterize deliberate attempts by infrastructure organizations to control interactions; (3) a possibility that a retreat to isolated, functionless "havens in a heartless world," with the "fall of public man" nursing solisiptic "habits of the heart" may bring outburst and subcultures that do not reverse the trend but destabilize further the unmangeable complexity, and (4) the possibilities of "deconstruction"; of society gradually and peacefully flowing back out of the large

756

employing organization into small, autonomous organizations and informal groups. I would like to expand briefly on the last.

Figure 1 summarizes a part of the argument and the problem. The first column indicates the possibilities for vertical de-integration; obviously, horizontal de-integration is also possible since scale economies are less relevant for the vast majority of public and private organizations than they have ever been. One vertically and horizontally integrated organization could dissolve into dozens or hundreds of smaller ones, just in terms of the through-put activities of column 1. The second column lists some of the support activities that large economic organizations provide internally. These, and many others, could be provided by autonomous organizations that could easily be small if the integrated organization had dissolved, since the units served would be small. Governmental regulation could easily keep their size from exceeding the maximum needed for economies of scale (not economies of market control). The third column lists just a few of the social services the large organization is likely to provide, and in doing so, control, however unobtrusively. These all present opportunities for small, autonomous

Some production stages	Business functions	Corporate services
Raw materials	Transportation	Medical and dental services
Raw materials processing	Food service	
Initial production	Legal services	Fitness facilities
Final production	Accounting	Sports programs
Final assembly	Advertising	Off-site recreational facilities
Wholesale distribution	Research and development	Vacation planning, sites
Retail distribution		
	Purchasing	Child care
	Training	Retirement counseling
	Business travel services	Career counseling
		Legal services
		Drug and alcohol abuse programs
		Psychological counseling

Fig. 1. Activities that could be performed in separate organizations.

organizations and informal groups. All told, then, the large organization is large because it has embraced dozens of activities that other organizations (or family, neighborhood, and peer groups) could perform, in through-put production, in business services, and in social services.

The elements of such a model of "small firm networks" are: small organizations that are autonomous because they have multiple customers and multiple suppliers; a strong regulatory system at the local and national level to prevent labor exploitation, pollution, and other externalities, including those born by future generations; and trade associations and unions to control wages and prices in the industry and the region. Obviously, these would be difficult to establish and controversial in any case. I hope to discuss them, and to document the argument of this article in a future book.

Acknowledgments

I have been getting valuable comments at seminars where I have presented this material at the University of Arizona, University of California at Los Angeles and Santa Barbara, Stanford, Oregon, MIT, Duke, North Carolina, North Carolina State, Yale, Fundacion Juan March (Madrid), Uppsala, Stockholm and European universities, and the Stockholm School of Economics. Numerous individual colleagues have provided detailed critiques. The project has been so drawn out, starting in the State University of New York-Stony Brook in 1979, that I have long since lost the ability to list the individual scholars who made early contributions. Needless to say, their help and the comments at the numerous seminars have been invaluable, and I have taken them seriously. Throughout the period, the comments and encouragement of Paul DiMaggio and Walter Powell must be singled out, and Robert K. Merton was particularly helpful during my stay as a visiting scholar at the Russell Sage Foundation, a most enjoyable experience.

Notes

1. Louis Galambos was the first historian to discuss explicitly the work of historians concerned with organizational analysis, and a recent article of his is an excellent bibliographic source. His striking formulation of the organizational synthesis has been influential. See his "The Emerging Organizational Synthesis in Modern Amer-

758

ican History," *History Review* 44 (1970), 279–290; and "Technology, Political Economy, and Professionalization: Central Themes of the Organizational Synthesis," *History Review* 57 (1983), 471–493. The other references are: Robert Presthus, *The Organizational Society* (New York: Knopf, 1962); Henry Jacoby, *The Bureaucratization of the World* (Berkeley: University of California Press, 1973); Christopher Stone, *Where the Law Ends* (New York: Harper and Row, 1975); James Coleman, *The Asymmetric Society* (Syracuse: Syracuse University Press, 1982).

2. "Everyone else" excludes much of demography and anthropology. The dynamics of demographic change, based minimally on culture, more on social structure, and even more on epidemics, diseases, and public health practices, is such a pervasive element of social change that it constitutes the major independent variable in history. Though increasingly subject to organizational factors, it remains substantially independent even today.

3. I am ignoring slavery, of course, an extreme form of dependency, but also the variety of forms of contract labor and indentured labor that flourished in the 1700s in New England, and well into the 1800s in the American West. For an excellent survey see Howard Lamar's "From Bondage to Contract: Ethnic Labor in the American West, 1600–1890," in Steven Hahn and Jonathan Prude, editors, *The Countryside in the Age of Capitalist Transformation* (Chapel Hill: University of North Carolina Press, 1985), 293–326. Despite all the rhetoric about the freedom of the frontier, Lamar points out that it is precisely on frontiers that bondage is most desirable because of the shortage of labor. The question must be asked, he says, "Was the American West and the Western frontier more properly a symbol of bondage than of freedom when it comes to labor systems?" (294). He concludes that it was a mixture, with a significant and unrecognized element of bondage along with freedom.

4. Lewis Coser called the monarchies of pre-industrial Europe "greedy organizations" because they chose for their key officials slaves, stigmatized groups such as Jews, or eunuchs. These could have no existence outside the court and thus had to be loyal. In the nineteenth century the social equivalent, wage dependency, extended that social condition to most citizens; life was with the employer. See his *Greedy Institutions* (New York: Free Press, 1974).

5. Alfred DuPont Chandler, *The Visible Hand* (Cambridge: Cambridge University Press, 1977).

6. Jeffrey G. Williamson and Peter H. Lindert, *American Inequality: a Macro-Economic History* (New York: Academic Press, 1980).

7. The trials of wage dependency are well illustrated in Alexander Keyssar's *Out of Work: The First Century of Unemployment in Massachusetts* (New York: Cambridge University Press, 1986).

8. Contrast, for example, the experience of municipal electric lighting systems in three countries described by Hughes. In New York City and Chicago, Thomas Edison (and Samuel Insull) sought monopolistic positions that required customers to buy equipment from them down to lights and toasters, received valuable franchises and rights-of-way to support a luxury item for the rich, and sought monopolistic control over all adjacent systems. In London, authorities forbade any control over the appliances to be used, would not give franchises for luxury lighting for the rich when there was a substantial public investment in an efficient gas lighting system, were satisfied with efficient, localized power stations for trolleys and railways, and feared that local authorities would be weakened if a private monopoly emerged. In

Berlin, a powerful state-aided private economic enterprise, through enabling legislation and infusions of capital, carefully regulated private enterprise in the public interest and cross-subsidized mass transport, thus helping the working class. In contrast to Hughes's account, I would argue that the technological imperatives and problems were quite secondary to the political and economic ones, which involved the distribution of externalities, or of the non-obvious costs and benefits. These resided with, and were framed by, the powerful organizations of the day. See Thomas Hughes, *Networks of Power: Electrification in Western Society, 1810–1930* (Baltimore: Johns Hopkins University Press, 1983), and Charles Perrow, "The Power of Capitalist Networks: A Critique of Hughes," (Conference on the Development of Large Technical Systems, Max Planck Institute, Cologne, November, 1987), unpublished manuscript, Yale University.

9. William Cronon, *Changes in the Land: Indians, Colonists, and the Ecology of New England* (New York: Hill and Wang, 1983).

10. For a brief discussion of this and a criticism of the "small is bountiful" argument of Mark Granovetter, see Charles Perrow, *Complex Organizations: A Critical Essay*, 3rd ed. (New York: Random House, 1986), 211. Small is beautiful when we consider a network of small firms versus one or two large ones. It reduces the degree of hierarchy and thus of centralized control, spreads the wealth, and promotes trust and cooperation between the firms rather than the imperative coordination within the large firm, and allows society to "flow back out" of the giant organization into the relatively autonomous small groups where it once belonged. For an elaboration of these points see C. Perrow, "Small Firm Networks," presented at "Networks and Organizations" conference, Harvard University, August, 1990, to be published by Harvard Business School Press.

11. Chandler, Williamson, and others cite the exploitation of workers by contractors as a principal reason for the disappearance of the system, but the evidence is thin and never weighed against the overwhelming evidence of exploitation by capitalists. In fact, the only time Chandler mentions exploitation in his vast account, *The Visible Hand*, is in connection with inside contractors (226). Exploitation by *owners* was, of course, extensive, but does not call for comment by Chandler. Some inside contractors in the nineteenth century surely exploited workers as much as many owners did, but the system had safeguards and cannot be compared to today's labor boss in agriculture. Exploitation was limited, I suspect, because of the close ethnic, religious, and neighborhood ties of contractors and their workers. The owner of a firm large enough to use contractors was distant from the workers in status, living area and living conditions, and generally, religion and ethnicity. While some contractors no doubt moved away when they became affluent, it is likely that most remained close to their labor supply. A contractor's profits depended more directly upon the work of his subordinates than did the owner's. Thus, it would have been in the interests of the contractor to treat his crew well to increase their productivity, and the effect of this would have been more directly apparent than for the owner.

12. The most important work on the inside contractor is Daniel Clawson's excellent *Bureaucracy and the Labor Process* (New York: *Monthly Review* Press, 1980), but the implications for social bonding and nonbureaucratic social control need still more exploration. Though it does not deal explicitly with inside contracting, similar issues are raised in the debate between Oliver Williamson and S. H. R. Jones over early labor processes and "transaction costs." See Oliver Williamson, "The Organization of Work: A Comparative Institutional Assessment," *Journal of Economic*

760

Behavior and Organizations 1 (1980), 5–38 and his "Reply to Jones," in the same journal, 4 (1983), 57–68, and S. H. R. Jones's "The Organization of Work: A Historical Dimension," same journal, 3, no. 2–3 (1982), 117–137, a quite brilliant essay too curtly dismissed by Williamson.

13. Norman Ware, *The Industrial Worker 1840–1860* (Chicago: Quadrangle Books, 1964, first published in 1924 by Houghton Mifflin Co., Boston), 8.
14. United States Education and Labor Committee (Senate 1885), "Report on the Relations between Labor and Capital," Vol. I, 80.
15. Ibid., Vol. I, 77.
16. Ibid., Vol. I, 150.
17. Ibid., Vol. I, 48.
18. Ibid., Vol. I, 64.
19. Ibid., Vol. I, 188.
20. Ibid., Vol. III, 422.
21. Ibid., Vol. I, 80.
22. John A. Fitch, *The Steel Workers*, New York Charities Publication, 1911 (reprint Arno Press, 1969), 127.
23. Ibid., 165.
24. Ibid., 169.
25. Robert L. Heilbroner, *The Economic Transformation of America* (New York: Harcourt Brace Jovanovich, Inc., 1977), 129.
26. David Brody, *Steelworkers in America* (New York: Harper & Row, 1960).
27. Daniel Nelson, *Managers and Workers* (The University of Wisconsin Press, 1975).
28. Herbert G. Gutman, *Work, Culture & Society* (New York: Vintage Books, 1977), 30.
29. Ibid.
30. Ibid., emphasis added, 47.
31. Norman Ware, *The Industrial Worker 1840–1860*, 76.
32. For their discussion of structure, see D. S. Pugh, D. J. Hickson, C. R. Hinings, and C. Turner, "Dimension of Organization Structure," *Administrative Science Quarterly* (1968) 65–105.
33. See Clawson, *Bureaucracy and The Labor Process*, Ch. 2, and his references to Pollard, Ure, and others who made this observation that has been so neglected and indeed, is counter-intuitive given our linear view of industrialization as Pareto-optimal in its social consequences.
34. For managers and professionals, rules cannot be as specific, machinery is less evident, and standardization is reduced. It is more efficient to control the *premises* under which they make their decisions than to try to control the decisions themselves. Premise control is the ultimate non-reactive, unobtrusive control, but requires considerable socialization, as in college and university professional programs, and greater financial and status rewards. It also has the effect of absorbing the citizen into the organization more thoroughly, contributing at this elite, policy-setting level to a more effective absorption of society by the organization. For a discussion of the movement from direct to bureaucratic, and then premise controls, see Charles Perrow, "The Bureaucratic Paradox: The Centralized Decentralized Organization," *Organizational Dynamics*, Spring 1977, 2–14, and *Complex Organizations: A Critical Essay* (New York: Random House, 3rd. edition, 1986), 128–136. See also Richard Edwards, *Contested Terrain* (New York: Basic Books, 1979), for a related discussion.

35. Charles Sabel and Jonathan Zeitlin, "Historical Alternatives to Mass Production," *Past and Present* 108 (August, 1985) 133–167.

36. For a discussion of self-interest versus other-regarding organizational models, and a critique of agency theory, see my *Complex Organizations: A Critical Essay*, (3rd ed.), Ch. 7, especially 231–234, which deals with the structural conditions in organizations that promote one rather than the other. (The chapter is reprinted in part in "Economic Theories of Organization," *Theory and Society* 15, 1986, reprinted in *Structures of Capital*, Sharon Zukin and Paul DiMaggio, editors (New York: Cambridge University Press, 1990)).

37. Chandler, *The Visible Hand*, Oliver E. Williamson, *Markets and Hierarchies: Analyses and Antitrust Implications* (New York: The Free Press, 1975); and Oliver E. Williamson, *The Economic Institutions of Capitalism* (New York: The Free Press, 1985).

38. For an excellent critique, one of the few, of Chandler, see Richard DuBoff and Edward Herman, a historian and an economist, "Alfred Chandler's New Business History: A Review," *Politics and Society* 10, 1 (1980), 87–110. For another early critique of Chandler and of Williamson see Charles Perrow, "Markets, Hierarchy and Hegemony: A Critique of Chandler and Williamson," in *Perspectives on Organizational Design and Behavior*, Andrew Van de Ven and William Joyce, editors (New York: Wiley Interscience, 1981), 371–386, 403–404, with replies by Chandler, and Charles Perrow, *Complex Organizations*, Ch. 9. Historians are beginning to qualify and question the efficiency argument. See, for example, Naomi Lamoreaux, *The Great Merger Movement in American Business, 1885–1904* (Boston: Cambridge University Press, 1985), where she finds that market control rather than efficiency was the motivation or at least the consequence, in the short term, of the merger movement. In the long run, competition and what the Marxists would call the contradictions of capitalism weakened the market control of the majors. The most ambitious attempt to deal with the state vs. capitalist power issue is Neil Fligstein, *The Transformation of Corporate Control* (Cambridge: Harvard University Press, 1990). Fligstein interprets the very form and structure of capitalist organizations (all consistent with the form "factory bureaucracy" outlined here) as major attempts to subvert state attempts to regulate them and to address the externality issues. This is, however, only a duel between capitalist and elite political or governmental groups; the role of labor, protest groups, and citizens in general is ignored. In this respect it is as ghostly as Chandler's *Visible Hand*.

39. Williamson and Lindert, *American Inequality*. For the recent increase in inequality see Lester Thurow, "A Surge in Inequality," *Scientific American* 256: 5 (May 1987), 30–36; and Frank Levy, "Changes in the Distribution of American Family Income, 1947 to 1984," *Science* 236 (May 1987), 923–927.

40. William Roy, "Functional and Historical Logics," Department of Sociology, UCLA, September 22, 1986.

41. As the Presidential Commission investigating the 500-point drop concluded, three markets were more tightly coupled than anyone realized, the computers were overloaded or broke down in trying to handle the complex interactions, exacerbated by the unanticipated demands of program trading, and the automatonistic virtue of programmed trading introduced irreversible and instantaneous processes into the linkages. The crash probably had more to do with the unexpected interactions of these failures than with the inability of the economy to reduce the trade deficit and job deficit, and add jobs that were not low-paid and low-skilled. The notion of unexpected interaction of multiple failures is the subject of Charles Perrow,

762

Normal Accidents: Living with High Risk Technologies (New York: Basic Books, 1984). I had just started work on the "society of organizations" topic when I was asked to prepare a background paper on the accident at Three Mile Island for the presidential commission. I utilized the emerging notions of complexity and coupling in our society to analyze TMI and other risky system accidents in that book, and subsequently, with Mauro Guillén, to analyze the organizational response to AIDS in the U.S. See Charles Perrow and Mauro Guillén, *The Aids Disaster: The Failure of Organizations in New York and the Nation* (New Haven: Yale University Press, 1990).

42. For the welfare functions of small firms see Charles Perrow, "Small Firm Networks."

43. Fligstein, *The Transformation of Corporate Control.*

44. See Thurow, "A Surge in Inequality," and Kevin Phillips, *The Politics of Rich and Poor* (New York: Random House, 1990).

45. Roy Lubove, *The Professional Altruist* (New York: Atheneum, 1980, Harvard University Press, 1965).

46. John Mohr, unpublished ms., "Poverty Relief in the Progressive Era: The Duality of Cultural and Organizational Forms."

[3]

Constructing Organizations: The Example of Public Sector Reform

Nils Brunsson, Kerstin Sahlin-Andersson

Abstract

Nils Brunsson
Stockholm School
of Economics,
Sweden

Kerstin Sahlin-Andersson
Uppsala
University, and
Stockholm Centre
for Organizational
Research, Sweden

Organizations are socially constructed phenomena. A crucial task for organizational research is to analyze how and why people construct organizations rather than other social forms. In this paper, it is argued that recent public-sector reforms can be interpreted as attempts at constructing organizations. Public-sector entities that could formerly be described as agents or arenas have been transformed into 'more complete' organizations by installing or reinforcing local identity, hierarchy and rationality. This interpretation helps to explain important aspects of the reform process.

Descriptors: constructing organizations, reform, public sector, new public management, agent, arena

Introduction

Social science has a tendency to take its objects of study as given, seeing them as natural entities of some kind. Individuals, organizations, states and other basic social units just seem to be there, waiting for the social scientist to study them (Strang and Meyer 1993). Alternatively, however, phenomena such as these can be regarded as highly problematic: why, we might ask, do people believe in them; what meanings do they assume in various social settings; and under what circumstances do they become perceived as real and important aspects of reality? In other words, we can ask questions about the social construction of reality (Berger and Luckmann 1966). Social theorists' constructions may not always coincide with those of other people; what the theorist sees as a certain type of entity, may be interpreted differently by the practitioner.

In other situations, the abstract and general concepts of theorists have a considerable practical impact. Theoretical concepts are based on the study of the actions, descriptions and interpretations of practitioners. Once formulated, they are often reintroduced later into the world of practice. There they are compared with current practices and used to determine what is good or bad, what is lacking and what needs to be done. Concepts travelling back and forth in this way, between theory and practice, are a com-

Organization
Studies
2000, 21/4
721–746
© 2000 EGOS
0170-8406/00
0021–0030 $3.00

mon feature of late modernity (Giddens 1990). Theoretical concepts are used for developing practice as well as theory.

In this paper, we discuss the social construction of organizations and the way in which this is influenced by the theoretical concept of organization. The examples will be taken from recent public-sector reforms in several European countries, including Denmark, France, Germany, Great Britain and Sweden, as well as in Australia and New Zealand.

Constructing organizations involves the setting up or changing of entities in such a way that they come to resemble the general and abstract concept of organization. We will argue that traditional public services in many countries have lacked some of the key aspects of organization. They can be described, at the most, as conspicuously 'incomplete' organizations. When existing services have been compared with the organization concept, their incompleteness in organizational terms has become obvious, and they have seemed to call for reforms to render them — in this sense — more complete. In fact, many public-sector reforms can be interpreted as attempts at constructing organizations. This interpretation provides some clues as to why the reforms occurred at all, why they acquired their particular content, and how they were received. In other words, our present focus is on the origins and reception of reforms, rather than on their implementation or their possible direct or indirect effects on the services offered by the public sector.

The next section will be mainly descriptive. We will show how popular reforms can be interpreted as ways of constructing organizations. In the third section, we will discuss the extent to which the concept of organization, as revealed in the reforms, deviates from previous forms adopted by public-sector services, and how it deviates. This helps to explain the content of reforms, i.e. what had been seen as calling for change. In the fourth section, we discuss whether the constructive nature of the reforms can explain why they were launched on such a massive scale and why they gained acceptance so easily.

A more fundamental question is why the concept of organization came up at all as a model in contemporary public sectors. In the fifth section, we will offer some speculations on this topic.

Reforms that Construct Organizations

Over the last twenty years or so it has been possible to observe a great number of public-sector reforms in several OECD countries (Hood 1991; Olsen and Peters 1996; Olson et al. 1998). In many cases, the reforms were not aimed at the products of the public sector, at health care or education for example. Rather, they have represented attempts at changing the modes of managing, controlling and accounting for the actual production of such services. Many of the reforms have met astonishingly little resistance and have been introduced at great speed by governments of various political shades (Hood 1991; Olsen and Peters 1996; Brunsson and Olsen 1997).

Public services have themselves taken the initiative in reforming and adopting new management techniques.

Students of these trends have described them in various ways: as the result of new or liberal ideas and policies (Fry 1984; Aucoin 1990; Pollitt 1990); as part of a shift in ideals away from hierarchy and the state and towards the market and the business firm (Czarniawska 1985; Brunsson 1994; Czarniawska-Joerges 1994; Humphrey and Olson 1995; Boston et al. 1996; Forssell and Jansson 1996; Easton 1997): as the expression of a growing tendency for rationalization (McSweeney 1994; Power 1994, 1997) or for putting a numerical value on, and accounting for, more aspects of human life (Preston 1992; Preston et al. 1992; Mouritsen 1997; Power 1997); and as a fashion (Abrahamson 1996; Røvik 1996). In this section, we will argue that the reforms can also, or alternatively, be interpreted as attempts at constructing organizations. The reforms can thus be described as a way of turning public services into organizations, or at least into something closer to this than before.

Organization literature has been concerned with organization in the general sense of co-ordinating actors and activities: it has also dealt with the specific, social entities known as formal organizations, or simply organizations, such as companies, labour unions or voluntary associations (Friedberg 1993; Sorge 1996; Brunsson and Olsen 1998). Here we focus on organization in this second sense. The literature on formal organizations tends towards exemplification rather than definition (Thompson 1967; Scott 1992; for examples see Barnard 1938; March and Simon 1958), but seems, nonetheless, to provide a fair degree of consensus on some of the important aspects that constitute organizations. In this section, we will describe these aspects under the general labels of identity, hierarchy and rationality and will examine public-sector reforms in relation to them.

Constructing Identity

Seeing something as an organization means endowing it with an identity. This, in turn, means emphasizing its autonomy, and defining its boundaries and collective resources. Organizational identity also involves the idea of being special, of possessing special characteristics, at the same time as being part of a highly general category, the organization. Many reforms represent an attempt to install or reinforce such features of identity in the public services.

Autonomy

An organization has a certain degree of autonomy. It is hierarchically subordinate to only a small part of its environment, for instance its owners. Its autonomy implies that it can own, or at any rate control, resources, as well as controlling its own boundaries, by commanding the opportunities for entering or exiting (Weber 1968; Ahrne 1994).

In many countries, attempts have been made to increase the local autonomy of public services, such as schools (Schick 1996), universities (Colado

1996; Easton 1997; Musselin 1997), hospitals (Freddi and Björkman 1989; Harrison and Pollitt 1994; Schick 1996; Ham 1997; Lapsley 1997), local governments (Boston et al. 1996; Fernler 1996; Forssell and Jansson 1996) or state authorities (Martin 1995; Hood 1996).

Rules emanating from the centre have become fewer and less specific (OECD 1995); instead, decisions are taken in the relevant local unit. The task of the central bodies is now more frequently framed in terms of giving advice and follow-up rather than imposing directives on local units (Jacobsson and Sahlin-Andersson 1995). Staff is employed by the local school, the local university, the particular authority and so on, rather than by the state or the local government, as was usual in the past. Conditions of employment, and to a large extent the division of labour, among professional groups are determined locally, rather than by central or professional regulations (OECD 1995; Boston et al. 1996; Schick 1996). Local entities engage in setting the boundaries for their own activities (Åkerstrøm Andersen 1995).

Changes in budget procedures have aimed at giving local units and their managements greater control over resource allocations and operations. Integrated funding has been introduced: how the budget is to be divided among various items such as rent, personnel and technical equipment is not specified from above, but is assumed to be decided by the local management (Easton 1997; Olson and Sahlin-Andersson 1998). Some public services have even been allowed to acquire and dispose of income from sources other than central funding, at their own discretion (Schick 1996). In other cases, units have been transformed into organizations that are also legally independent, becoming publicly owned companies or even being privatized (Boston 1995; Svedberg-Nilsson 1999).

Collective Resources

An organization is held together by its members and by the collective resources that it controls (Ahrne 1994). However, an organization is something more than its members and its present resources: such things can be exchanged, while the organization itself continues to exist. Barnard (1938) described organizations in this context by comparing them to human life. Organization theories have often designated life and the ambition to survive as a purpose and an intrinsic value for organizations (Selznick 1957). In the course of the 1980s and 1990s, public-sector accounting was reformed and accrual accounting was introduced in many places (Olson et al. 1998). Result centres were defined, and assets and debts attributed to them were presented on a balance sheet. The asset side of the balance sheet confirms that a public service is more than just its members. Result centres are treated as the owners of resources, such as buildings or equipment, and are assumed to bear the full costs for these resources and for their own personnel.

Constructing Boundaries

An organization is defined by boundaries between itself and its environment. A distinction is made between what is happening inside and outside the organization, and these things are evaluated differently (Selznick 1957). This also means that internal and external relations are assumed to be different in kind; customers are treated differently from organization members, for instance. Organizations are 'controlled' and 'managed' internally, but they 'adapt to', 'influence' or 'handle' their environment (Pfeffer and Salancik 1978).

In connection with the recent public-sector reforms, local entities have been asked to define their environments and their boundaries in policy documents. Under extended accounting systems, boundaries are constructed and maintained between the organization and its environment, thus defining costs, revenues, assets or results as internal or external (Miller and O'Leary 1987; Miller 1992, 1994). Public services used to have pupils, patients or colleagues, i.e. people belonging at least in certain respects to the individual service. These services now define their own environments in terms of customers and competitors, i.e. actors clearly external to themselves (Forssell and Jansson 1996).

More autonomous local bodies have changed their relations with each other and with the central government. They have become providers and customers: they sell services to other public bodies, or buy from them (Boston et al. 1996; Easton 1997). They face competition from others. They may even 'sponsor' activities — the Swedish Foreign Office 'sponsors' the state-owned Royal Opera. Rather than following orders emanating from higher levels, local entities negotiate with such levels and sometimes enter into contracts with them. Swedish universities have established a private co-operative organization to work for their common interests *vis-à-vis* the central state.

Being an Organization

An organization is also defined by conceptual boundaries: it is likely to be presented as belonging to the category 'organization', rather than just to some other category such as school, hospital, etc. This has occurred in the case of many schools and hospitals, as well as in various state authorities (Sahlin-Andersson 1996; Schick 1996; Mouritsen 1997; SOU 1997). In some British and New Zealand policy statements, it has even been stated explicitly that public services should be regarded as organizations no different from any others (McSweeney, 1994; Boston et al. 1996).

The base for recruiting leaders and personnel has become increasingly defined according to this broad concept of organization. New leaders for schools, hospitals, libraries, and so on, are not recruited exclusively from other schools, hospitals, etc. Explicit policies have been designed for recruiting public-service managers from other types of organization (Hood 1996; Rombach 1997), and the fact that there are so few leaders in the public sector with experience from non-public organizations has been seen as a problem (McSweeney 1994; OECD 1995). The experience of leading and managing organizations in general has come to be regarded as an important career qualification, more valuable than experience within the practical field of the public service concerned.

726   Nils Brunsson, Kerstin Sahlin-Andersson

Being Special

Identity also involves the idea of being special — the idea that one entity
is different from others, that it has certain characteristics or combinations
of characteristics that are different from those of the others. The organization has a special task or purpose. It possesses certain features, such as a
special competence, special resources, a special structure or a special way
of working; or it represents special ideas. It has its own history or even its
own organizational culture.

Public services have been asked to formulate their own particular objectives and to produce policy statements and performance reports (Boston et
al. 1996; Hood 1996; Power 1997) in which they emphasize the differences
between themselves and other services. Individual schools (Jacobsson and
Sahlin-Andersson 1995), maternity wards (Rothstein 1994) and universities (Musselin 1997), for example, have developed and projected their own
profiles. Some have actively marketed themselves with the help of these
profiles, with logos of their own and sometimes even with new names
emphasizing their special identity in order to attract more 'customers' (Berg
and Jonsson 1991; Rombach 1997).

Constructing Hierarchy

Organizations co-ordinate activities. In fact, the ability to co-ordinate action
is often seen as the very point of creating organizations (Thompson 1967;
Mintzberg 1979). Members of organizations should act in a way that contributes to certain common co-ordinated actions. Co-ordination is achieved
by an authorative centre that directs the actions of the organization members. In other words, there is an element of hierarchy within the organization. With the help of this hierarchy, the special identity of the organization
is to be transformed into organizational action. The authoritative centre
should have some freedom of choice when it comes both to forming the
organizational identity and to shaping organizational action. The centre is
responsible for the organization and its actions. Constructing such local
hierarchies is the objective of many public-sector reforms.

Co-ordination and Control

Reformers have tried to strengthen the co-ordination within the local unit
by creating teams drawn from various personnel categories. Co-ordination
and co-operation within hospital clinics, municipal offices or state authorities have been reinforced, while spontaneous co-operation among individual professionals representing different units is no longer encouraged
(Czarniawska-Joerges 1994; Sahlin-Andersson 1994). The idea is that the
internal teams should be guided by organizational policies rather than by
central rules or professional norms. This also means that any achievements
are attributed to the unit as a whole. Achievements at many universities,
for instance, are increasingly attributed not only to the individual
researchers, but to the unit, the university or the research institute. At these
universities, management has consequently come to be regarded as an

important factor, and university presidents have been given more responsibility (Berrivin and Musselin 1996; Colado 1996).

Constructing Management

The authoritative centre of an organization should consist of 'managers'
who are asssumed to exert control and bear responsibility for the organization, its actions and results (Fayol 1916; Selznick 1957). It is often
assumed that, internally, managers are organized hierarchically in layers of
leaders and led, whereby the led are leaders of the next layer down (Weber
1968). A board can give general directions to an executive, but the executive is then responsible for organizational activities and results.

Several recent public-service reforms have aimed at 'letting managers manage' or at 'freeing managers to manage' (OECD 1995; Schick 1996). Chief
executives are defined as managers enjoying freedom of choice, rather than
as civil servants following and implementing central directives. These managers are expected to launch their own initiatives, to design activities and
to transform the entity concerned so that it becomes something special,
with its own special characteristics. In order to strengthen local co-ordination and control, many public services have established management teams,
and a number of new middle management positions have been created
(Humphrey and Olson 1995). As managers have been allowed greater discretion, their leadership role has been emphasized and consequently also
the need for training in leadership and strategic management (OECD 1995).
Top management is expected to achieve control with the help of management accounting techniques, whereby people or units are made accountable for certain activities and results.

Constructing Rationality

Another aspect of organization is rationality. Organizations are assumed to
be 'intentional', in the sense that they work towards specific goals or purposes (Thompson 1967; Weber 1968). Intentionality represents a kind of
process hierarchy, whereby organizational policy is transformed into action.
Organizations are also assumed to be rational: executives are expected
systematically to forecast goals, objectives and preferences as well as action
alternatives and their consequences, and then to allow comparisons between
these factors to determine their choice of action. The individual organization, rather than organizational sub-units, or society as a whole, is the relevant subject for organizational rational analysis; the relevant objectives,
alternatives and consequences are those related to the organization as a unit.
In many organization theories, it has been assumed that organizational
actions are governed by decisions under a norm of rationality — a norm
that, in practice, is difficult to satisfy. Thus we find a lack of rationality
being treated in much organization theory as a deviation that calls for a
special explanation (Simon 1945; Cyert and March 1963; March 1981).

Setting Objectives

Public-service reformers have tried to install various systems of management-by-objectives (Christensen 1991; Rombach 1991). The idea is that
objectives specific to the individual entity should replace rules, so that the
objectives then control the action, and that the achievement or otherwise
of the objectives can then be registered accordingly.

Rationality is easier to achieve if the organization has a single, possibly a
few, but not too many objectives. Too many objectives make it more difficult to determine what action is the best. Consequently, the demand for
rationality in the organization often leads to attempts at simplification,
reducing the number of objectives, possibly even to one — a single abstract
goal perhaps, or a clear hierarchy of one overarching goal and several sub-
goals (Cyert and March 1963).

A recurrent complaint in recent reviews of public-sector services is that
they embrace several tasks and objectives, which to some extent contradict
one another. A number of public-sector reforms have been intended to break
services down into smaller units, so that each unit could have one clear
objective. For example, inspection and service-supplying units or purchasing and providing units, or inspecting and advising bodies have been separated from one another (OECD 1995; Boston et al. 1996; Fernler 1996;
Laughlin 1996; Schick 1996).

Measuring Results and Allocating Responsibility

The demands for rationality in organizations call for the rational justification of past actions. Objectives and action are thus assumed to be connected
in a systematic way. Organizations are expected to account for their actions
with the help of the pre-set objectives; and they are expected to be efficient and to achieve their objectives at minimal cost (Thompson 1967;
Ahrne 1994). Accounts are presented to higher levels in the hierarchy, or
to external stakeholders with a legitimate interest in the organization. These
statements describe the activities and results of the organization in recognized terms, that permit comparison with other organizations (Hopwood
and Miller 1994).

The results of public-service operations are being increasingly controlled
by means of the accounting system or by specific evaluations comparing
results with objectives (Power 1997). Whereas accounting in the public sector was previously regarded largely as a way of reporting revenues and
expenses, it is now seen as a device for controlling results (Roberts 1991;
Mouritsen 1997; Olson et al. 1998). A disappointing result is expected to
trigger some reaction from the top.

In some cases, the required results are assigned numerical values and are
specified in such detail that they actually control things as much as the earlier rules ever did (Lindström 1997). Unlike rules, though, a focus on results
passes responsibility to the local leadership, since it is their job to decide
the means whereby the results are to be achieved. Managers who are free
to choose the means are also responsible for the results of their choices,
or, to put it the other way round, if they are to be held responsible, they

must have freedom of choice. In the British public sector, the concept of the 'accountable manager' is often cited (McSweeney 1994). The accounting system has helped to construct the idea of the rational organization, in which specific individuals can be identified as being in control and bearing the responsibility (Miller 1992; Roberts and Scapens 1985).

In France, contracts or contract-like agreements have been drawn up between central government and the universities, in which specific objectives and expected results are given for each individual university (Berrivin and Musselin 1996; Musselin 1997). In Germany, the focus of local government budgeting has shifted away from the input side and is now based on the performance achieved by clearly defined result-centres (Lüder 1998). In New Zealand, performance agreements covering the performance of the individual manager, as well as the unit as a whole, are made between chief executives and their ministers (Boston et al. 1996). Managers and the units they manage are then monitored every year in light of these agreements, and the chief executive's pay is set accordingly. In the British public administration system, performance-related pay was introduced in 1985, following what was known as the 'financial management initiative', whereby aims, costs and performance indicators were set for the various departments, which thus became cost centres (Hood 1996).

Reforms in Packages or in Strings

Reforms in the public sector do not usually proceed by introducing various aspects of organization one by one, as described above. Rather they tend to come in packages, or in strings: a particular reform focuses on several aspects of organization at the same time; or reforms focusing on one or a small number of aspects are followed by other reforms focusing on other aspects. Packages or strings of public-sector reforms like this have sometimes even been given their own collective labels. 'The New Public Management' is such a tag (Hood 1995).

For example, when Swedish pupils were given more opportunity to choose their own school and each school's revenue was made contingent on its pupil numbers, the pupils and their parents began to take an interest in the special qualities offered by individual schools and, in turn, each school began to invent and emphasize its own particular profile. There was to be more co-operation across professional borders within each school, but there was less co-operation with other professionals outside it; other schools came to be seen as competitors rather than as parts of the same local authority, while teachers and certain kinds of resources became clearly associated with specific schools (Sahlin-Andersson 1994). Similarly, French universities used to be governed by several ministries and experts associated with various disciplines (Berrivin and Musselin 1996). Budgets were allocated to specific curricula. After a budget reform in 1989, this was changed, and resources were allocated to each university as a lump sum. The universities were asked to analyze their own situation and define 4-year plans, setting priorities between the various curricula and other activities. They acquired a new interest in providing information about their situation, and spotlighting their specific qualities, all of which served to strengthen the power of the university presidency (Musselin 1997).

Constructing Organizations

Constructing organizations means introducing certain aspects of organization — labelled above as identity, hierarchy and rationality — that are constitutive of organizations. The constitutive character means that were these aspects to be lacking in a certain setting, it is doubtful whether that setting would be called an organization at all. Reforms aimed at installing these aspects can be interpreted as a way of constructing an organization, as organizatory reforms. If the reforms appear to be successful, then a reformed entity is more likely to be perceived by many people as a 'real' or fully-fledged organization, possessing the standard organizational attributes.

We have given examples of recent reforms in the public sector and have shown how they assign various aspects of the concept of organization to individual public services. Public services such as schools, hospitals or state authorities have been constructed as organizations by means of organizatory reforms. Whereas before, the state could perhaps be described as a single organization, albeit consisting of many sub-units (Ahrne 1998), its construction is now a kind of polycentric network consisting of many separate organizations (Steward and Walsch 1992; Martin 1995; Åkerstrøm Andersen 1995; Hood 1996). Also, whereas relations between public entities used to be characterized by many of the typical attributes of large hierarchies, such as setting rules, giving orders, inspecting and providing information, their interaction now includes features that are more typical of the relations between autonomous organizations, such as competition, collaboration, negotiation, advising, contracting, selling and buying.

These organizatory reforms are similar to other attempts at constructing organizations, for instance the creation of a single new business firm out of two or more previously independent companies through merger or acquisition, although this time, it is a question of creating one organization out of several, rather than the other way round. In such cases, an attempt is made to replace separate identities, hierarchies and rationalities by new, common, versions (Nahavandi and Malekzadeh 1988). New organizations are also created by splitting up larger ones, for instance when the vast hierarchies of big corporations are divided over separate business units, or are sold off as part of an 'outsourcing' strategy. The recent interest in such measures in the business world represents a slightly delayed parallel to the public-sector reforms, and, in particular, to the more radical examples such as privatizations.

In both the public and private sectors, the practical effects of constructing organizations can vary. In merged corporations it is often very difficult, in reality, to get employees to behave as though there were now only one new company (Sales and Mirvis 1984). Likewise, reforms in the public sector often make little impact on the products and services provided, or the impact they make is quite different from what was intended (Pressman and Wildavsky 1973; Brunsson and Olsen 1997). In the organizatory reforms described here, the practical effects are equally uncertain.

Degrees of Organization: Actors, Agents and Arenas

Despite their constitutive character, the aspects of organization described above should be regarded as variables rather than constants; they can occur to a varying extent and in a variety of combinations in different organizations.

The Actor

When an organization clearly exhibits all the aspects of organization, it is likely to be regarded as a fully-fledged, 'complete' or 'real' organization. Corporations and independent companies in contemporary market economies are often viewed in this way. They can also be regarded as social actors, an actor being an entity with a clear and strong identity, hierarchy and rationality. Alternatively, using the terminology adopted in Meyer et al. (1987), an actor is an entity possessing independence and sovereignty, with autonomous or self-interested goals, with rational means and qualities, commanding independent resources and having clear boundaries. In our own culture, these attributes are also attached to individuals. Like the actor-organization, the actor-individual is also assumed to exhibit a high degree of identity, hierarchy (between soul and body) and rationality. An actor is able to act. Both actor-organizations and actor-individuals can perform actions: they can invest, produce, sell and buy, and they can make statements, and since autonomous actors choose and control their own actions, they also become responsible for them (Brunsson 1996).

The fact that an organization is perceived as an actor possessing all aspects of organization, is no obstacle to the launching of organizatory reforms. Management may want to make minor or even major changes in what constitutes the organization's identity, hierarchy or rationality. They are also likely to perceive any contradiction between norm and practice: although the organization is constructed as an actor, it may not function in exactly the same way (Brunsson and Olsen 1997). As a long tradition in organization studies tells us, practice in large organizations seldom lives up to the ideal image: deviations from a strong identity, hierarchy or rationality are common in practice, which provides an argument for reform, for trying to make the organization actually work in the way it should.

Thus, although business corporations are often seen as actor-organizations, they are frequently the subject of organizatory reforms. Attempts are made to reformulate, reinforce or implement the current business ideas; or to reinforce or abandon what is regarded as established organizational culture; or to reinforce hierarchy by introducing new leadership principles or more intricate management techniques. Reforms intended to increase rationality

may involve trying to formulate clearer objectives, to improve the systems
for gathering and utilizing information or, in the old days, to introduce better planning techniques.

In fact, such reforms reconstruct an existing organization rather than constructing a new one. In other cases, organizatory reforms are more radical,
involving the introduction of a new way of conceiving reality. This is obviously true in the case of trying to create an organization from scratch or
by outsourcing, and to some extent in trying to create a single organization out of many, as in mergers. Organizatory reforms are also radical in
many public services, i.e. in services that have hitherto lacked many aspects
of organization, not only in practice, but even in principle. We will now
describe two ideal types, namely the agent and the arena, that can usefully
capture some of the characteristics commonly found in many traditional
public services.

The Agent

Organizations can be seen as instruments for other actors, for organizations
or for individuals. Companies can be seen as instruments for their owners,
subsidiaries as instruments for their parent companies, departments as
instruments for head office, or public services as instruments for the politicians. Entities of this instrumental kind, working on behalf of others, can
be described as agents: they act as agents for their principals. They form
an administration or *verwaltung*. Agents are not complete actors in themselves; the principal is supposed, at least indirectly, to control the action
and to be responsible for it.

If we regard something as an agent, we attribute qualities to it other than
those we ascribe to an actor-organization. An agent has an unclear or weak
identity. Resources are controlled by the higher level and are typically allocated through a budget process, where the formal decision is taken about
who gets money, and how much. In addition, the higher level may control
employment or the terms of employment.

An agent also has unclear boundaries. The results which an agent is to
achieve may actually occur outside its own borders. The results of an R&D
department, for instance, ultimately show up in the sales figures for the
company as a whole. The police are expected to reduce criminality in society at large. Moreover, in order to achieve results, agents often have to co-
operate with others. Schools, for example, have to co-operate with the social
services and with parents in order to achieve good results. Even an agent's
clients sometimes have to co-operate, and it is not clear whether they should
be regarded as internal or external to the agent: e.g. are the pupils part of
a school, or not?

There may be detailed rules that apply to many agents. In many countries,
the police departments, the prisons or the tax authorities have been assumed
to have the same structure and to work along the same lines all over the
country. Opportunities for the local officers are restricted when it comes to
influencing goals, structure, working procedures or results, which means
that their responsibility is also very limited. Responsibility resides mainly

with the principal, with the politicians at the top of the state structure, for instance, or with top managers at the corporate level.

The survival of an agent is not a legitimate interest. Agents are instruments for solving certain tasks, and have no value in their own right (Weber 1968). Nor is an agent expected to have interests of its own. If an agent actually strives for survival and growth, it is considered to be dysfunctional (Crozier 1964).

Agents are supposed to fulfil centrally given tasks or to follow centrally given rules, which leave little room for local intentions or rationality. Agents may have to try to fulfil several inconsistent objectives at once. The chances of achieving rationality are then likely to be small. The results achieved by an agent are difficult to identify, if the agent is able to make a partial contribution only to the achievement of a particular general goal. It is notoriously difficult, for instance, to single out the contribution of the accounting department to the common result achieved by a corporation. Things are even more problematic if the connection between means and ends is ambiguous. The interventions of social workers may help their clients to a better life, for example, but they could also make these clients more helpless and dependent than they were before. Such an uncertainty in the connection between means and ends makes it difficult to use rationalizing models, or to measure the effectiveness and efficiency of an individual agent. When results are difficult to measure, rules rather than objectives are more appropriate as a way of controlling agents (Ouchi 1977).

Although agents are weak as regards identity, hierarchy and rationality, most organization theorists would probably still refer to entities of the agent type as 'organizations'. However, the agent's status as an organization is fragile, and is sometimes threatened: many people would prefer to treat a principal and its agent as a single organization, i.e. to consider the combination — the more complete actor — as the organization (Ahrne 1994). A department is often regarded as being part of an overall organization, rather than an organization in its own right. The same is often said of subsidiaries or state authorities too, such that the parent-company-plus-subsidiaries, or the state-as-a-whole are seen as the relevant organizations.

For an agent to become a complete organization, it should exhibit all the aspects of organization: local identity, hierarchy and rationality. It has to be assigned clear boundaries and to be given greater autonomy and more control over recruitment, members and resources. It has to have a local management which is granted fairly wide discretion. Within reasonable limits, management should be able to set its own objectives and to be free to make its own decisions, rather than just following centrally imposed rules.

On the other hand, the agent may already possess some organizational features, such as systems for auditing and accounting, or professional managers as opposed to leaders representing the professions involved in its operations. However, in the new organization, the accounting systems would be more firmly focused on controlling and measuring the results of the organization's activities, and the local management would be held responsible for these results. This type of management is likely to have a personal interest in the local results itself, and will probably prefer to work towards a few consistent objectives rather than several conflicting goals. Management may seek to motivate organization members to contribute to results by raising their awareness of, and interest in, their organization, producing mission statements and generally emphasizing the great importance of the organization as a unit.

In agents, the organizatory type of reform involves more radical attempts at change, than in the more complete organizations. They not only try to infuse new content into existing organizational features, or to bring practice in line with principles, but mainly suggest new principles that imply a major change for the former agent. The content of organizatory reforms contrasts sharply with the classic conceptions of bureaucracy and with what are regarded as the traditional problems in such bureaucratic set-ups. In that world, the tendency for agents to become autonomous and self-serving has been regarded as one of the main practical problems of the bureaucracy, calling for reform in the opposite direction (Crozier 1964).

The Arena

An entity can also be 'incomplete' in terms of organization because its members, and what they do, are legitimately guided by external interests, values, norms and standards, rather than by an internally generated organizational policy. Entities may be set up to represent and handle conflicting interests (Brunsson 1989): parliaments provide an example of this. Other entities may represent specific competencies, so that entry into the entity and the activities of its members is controlled by professional norms and standards. Hospitals, for instance, must recruit registered doctors, whose professional activities are governed by their common education and the explicit norms of their profession. In some countries, universities have not had the right to choose their own professors; recruitment has been controlled by external experts such as professors from other universities.

Such entities can be described as arenas, whose members perform their tasks relatively free from control by the local leadership. Instead, they represent, or are controlled by, external parties. An arena may enjoy considerable autonomy *vis-à-vis* higher bureaucratic levels, but far less in relation to relevant external ideologies, interests, standards or norms. The boundaries between a parliament and the political parties are weak and vague, as are the boundaries between a professionally dominated arena and the relevant professions. Values and rules created outside the arena are crucial. Professional norms and standards make units associated with a particular profession similar to each other: it is difficult for a hospital or a university to define a clear profile or create an obvious niche for itself, except in relatively simple terms, perhaps by advertizing the generous resources it receives for certain specialities, or by claiming a higher quality compared with its fellow organizations.

The arena may include some of the elements of organization. It may have considerable control over material resources, and there may be a fair degree of internal co-ordination, but its external governance often leads to blurred hierarchial arrangements. Traditional hospital and university managements, for instance, are restricted in their control over activities. Arenas may contain more than one hierarchy. For instance, some professionals may control activities, while bureaucrats have the economic and administrative responsibility for them. Hierarchies within the professions, on the other hand, may be very clear, but they do not coincide with the boundaries of the arena.

In arenas built up round professional activities, the individual professionals — doctors or teachers, for example — generally bear a good deal of the responsibility for their own work and are often the main target for external inspection or complaints from clients. It is the professionals who act, rather than the arena as such.

The external parties associated with arenas, such as political parties, interest groups and the professions, tend to have their own distinctive rules regarding appropriate behaviour. Members of these external groupings learn how to rationalize the rules they represent, but their rationalizations are based on general, political, partisan or professional objectives, rather than on local, organizational ones (Abbott 1988). For instance, values about being economical or even efficient seldom loom large among the professionals, which can easily mean that what managers regard as good results and what professionals strive to achieve are by no means the same thing (Abernethy and Stoelswinder 1995).

For an arena to become a more complete organization, it therefore needs clear organizational boundaries, local hierarchical control over recruitment and over the activities of its members, a clear idea of its own special mission and characteristics relative to other organizations (in particular those with similar tasks), goals for the organization as such rather than general external objectives, and a local management responsible for achieving organizational results.

Entities that are perceived as arenas are often referred to by relatively narrow categories — such as parliament, university or hospital, for instance. Most organization theorists would subsume such entities under the general category of organizations, but they are marked out by certain peculiarities. In the case of agents, whenever the organization concept becomes the norm, arenas' weaknesses as regards identity, hierachy and rationality, i.e. their incompleteness in terms of organization, can provide reason for reform. Here, too, reforms that transform an arena in the direction of the organization concept imply an attempt at radical change. Recent public-sector reforms have included attempts at transforming services with some of the characteristics of the arena into something more resembling the complete organization. The targets for such reforms have usually been services with strong professional affiliations.

Organizatory Reform as Completion

We have argued that many public-sector reforms have introduced more aspects of organization into public services, thus turning them into more complete organizations. In other words, aspects of organization constitute the content of the reforms described above.

In some cases, the content of these reforms may have been designed without giving a thought to the concept of organization as such. Reformers and reformees may have been attracted by a certain feature of organization without relating it in any way to the general organization idea. In other cases, reformers have explicitly referred to the concept of organization in arguing for their reforms, as was illustrated in the second section.

In yet other cases, the concept of organization may have been the underlying mental image or frame of reference for reformers and reformees, without there being any explicit reference to it. Well-established institutions, such as the organization, may represent 'knowledge without concepts' (Bourdieu 1984: 470): institutions affect people's way of thinking, talking and acting, without being directly referred to. The content of the reforms may have been inspired by a line of thought built on the concept of organization, and the content may have inspired this line of thought. The concept of organization is thus invoked, but not mentioned. The explicit or implicit role of the concept of organization would explain why so many and such extensive organizatory reforms have been initiated, and why they have been so widely accepted. There are several indications that this may be the case.

First, the concept of organization may create a problem and thus the need for reform. There is nothing intrinsically problematic about being an agent or an arena. The agent and the arena are both modern, rationalized institutions, well embedded in established systems such as the state or the various professions. It is only when such entities are measured against the organization concept that their weakness as regards identity, hierarchy and rationality emerges as a problem. In a comparison with the general and abstract concept of organization, entities like agents and arenas seem incomplete — they lack certain aspects that the complete organization possesses. This incompleteness stimulates a desire for reforms that construct an organization. Just what aspects should be added to an entity will depend on the initial state, as described in the preceding section. An entity may lack the same organizational characteristics as the agent or the arena do, or perhaps a combination of both.

Second, many of the reforms we have described above have been launched smoothly during a relatively short period of time, and have met little resistance. With the possible exception of the most radical reforms, such as attempts at privatization — which in many countries have been a sensitive political issue — the need for reforms has often appeared self-evident, and the reforms themselves have not required much in the way of supporting arguments (Brunsson and Olsen 1997). This could be due to the invocation and acceptance of the organization concept, the introduction of which represents a switch to a different institution: when people find themselves in a different type of institution than they have been in before, they tend to change their norms, beliefs and behaviour much more quickly and more dramatically than they usually manage to do within a given institutional setting (March and Olsen 1989). Change also proceeds more easily if the new institution — as is the case with the organization — is a well-known one. Once people recognize this institution, they are likely to have similar ideas about what should be done, and this facilitates collective change.

Third, the organization concept may explain why reformers have often suggested packages of change, or why reforms of individual aspects have come in strings, in both cases projecting an image of a complete or almost complete organization. The various aspects of organization are likely to appear together or to follow quickly upon one another, because they all belong to the organization concept, and this concept and its particular logic determine what should be done: a strong local hierarchy, for example, presupposes a certain degree of autonomy; the measuring and accounting for collective results presuppose clear boundaries and a certain degree of co-ordination; accounting demonstrates results and allocates responsibility; rationality presupposes objectives. It is not necessary to wait to acquire practical experience of one organizational aspect before introducing another one; different aspects succeed each other by the dictates of logic (and therefore quickly) rather than awaiting practice. Even the suggestion of introducing one aspect may be enough to trigger the suggestion of others.

In this way the organization concept can also expand and reinforce attempts at reform by creating more reformers: if reformees accept the idea that their entity is, or should become, an organization, they may become reformers themselves. Reforms can also be demanded and initiated by others: the discrepancy between a public service and the organization concept may be perceived by rank-and-file members or by external parties, who will then generate a demand for reform. When the funding of Swedish schools was made dependent on pupil numbers, local managers asked for more autonomy; when parents were able to choose schools for their children, they asked for information about the specific profiles of the different schools.

Sometimes ideas about particular features of organization may trigger the idea of organization, rather than the other way round. Policy makers or local managers may have been attracted by certain popular ideas about leadership or management accounting techniques, and later have found out that these ideas or techniques actually presuppose the existence of a complete organization. In arguing for the favoured techniques, they have then found it necessary to claim organizational status, and the concept of organization has then inspired further organizatory reforms. For example, people may have wanted to increase quality and may have thus been attracted by quality standards. The advocates of such standards often emphasize that they are useful for 'organizations' (Henning 2000), and the standards are indeed based on the organization concept (Furusten 2000). In implementing such standards, the entity concerned easily comes to be seen as an organization that also needs other completing reforms. Hence, even if no explicit reference was made to the concept of organization, when people were first attracted by a specific organizational aspect, nor was it present even as an implicit frame of reference, it may have been brought to mind by the aspect that had first aroused people's interest, thus triggering further organizatory reforms.

Finally, the concept of organization as a frame of reference may also explain a certain element of imitation in public-sector reforms. Once something has been constructed as an organization, it becomes vulnerable to further reforms of a kind common in organizations. The idea of being an organization may lead to reforms inspired not only by the abstract concept of organization, but also by the example of other more complete organizations. Once a public service has come to be regarded as an organization, it seems natural to compare it with other organizations, and in looking for improvement, it is tempting to compare it with organizations that are believed to be more 'real' or complete. When modern corporations are viewed in this way, we can expect an increasing 'company-ization' of the public sector (Brunsson 1994; Forssell and Jansson 1996): the introduction into public services of whatever specific ways of displaying organizational aspects as happen to be popular among companies at the time.

Some of the reforms discussed here have sometimes been described as organizational fashions, and reformers as the followers of fashion (Abrahamson 1996; Røvik 1996). This interpretation on its own does not explain the content of the reforms — there are, after all, many fashions around. We suggest, instead, that following a fashion is more likely to be the effect, rather than the cause of the organizatory type of reform. Organizations are the entities most likely to be vulnerable to organizational fashions. It is not until an entity has been envisaged as an organization, that organizational fashions become positively and routinely attractive, or even difficult to resist. Reforms that construct the organization make organizational fashions spread more widely. New fashionable models for organizational leadership will be more readily adopted, for instance, if there is already an organizational leadership possessing a certain autonomy and authority. Once organizational status has been envisaged, it is easier to argue for the use of experts, consultants or training of a kind that target organizations and that tend to reinforce the organization concept.

Hence reforms that construct organizations may trigger more reforms of the same kind, and all these reforms tend to be repeated. Introducing the idea of organization does not guarantee that practice will be fully consistent with this concept, and the discrepancies between principle and practice tend to stimulate recurring reforms, just as they do in organizations that have long appeared complete.

Incentives for Constructing Organizations

We have argued that entities like agents or arenas are likely to be perceived as requiring complementary reforms, if they are supposed to be — or to be becoming — complete organizations. We have also noted that the very notion of the organization may trigger or reinforce organizatory reforms.

This brings us to the difficult task of explaining why people invoke the idea of organization, why they can become convinced that what was formerly accepted as an agent or an arena is, or should now be, a complete organization.

On a very general level, it can be argued that the recognition of certain entities as complete organizations is consistent with a current tendency to perceive individual people or organizations as actors, highly autonomous and self-interested, who interact with other actors on markets or in various negotiations (Meyer et al. 1987). If we wanted to explain more fully and in process terms why the concept of organization is invoked, we would need detailed empirical studies of the way the organization concept and the organizatory reforms have spread into various settings. In this section, we will merely indicate a few directions in which such explanations may be sought.

First, explanations can be based on the assumption that intentions, strategies and plans do matter. Perhaps policy-makers and reformers have consciously chosen a strategy aimed at constructing organizations. During the eighties public sectors were growing rapidly in many countries, and in doing so they came under strong political attack and were criticized for a number of alleged shortcomings. There was also widespread agreement that their expansion should be restricted, or their size even reduced. Attempts along these lines then produced further complaints. The very size of the sector makes it difficult to control from the top, and bearing responsibility for all this while not having much control over it, cannot be a very attractive task.

In a traditional state bureaucracy the main responsibility resides with the policy makers, since they are perceived as the only real actors. Whether or not they agreed with the criticisms, policy makers may have found the responsibility difficult to bear and the imbalance between power and responsibility awkward to deal with. It may have seemed wise to share this responsibility with others, for instance with a large number of organizations and their managers.

Second, the policy-makers may have planned to generate something new, but not organizations as such. They may have planned to introduce markets, and acquired organizations as a side-effect. The market was a popular model at the time, and markets or market-like conditions were introduced into various parts of the public sector. This may have stimulated the rise of organizations.

A market requires actors (individuals or organizations), who can supply or demand goods and services. For the market to function well, it is important that the boundaries between the actors are clearly perceptible; it is necessary to know who owns what, and how property rights are transferred between actors. Market actors must have a certain degree of autonomy — they should be able to choose what to buy and sell, and who to deal with. It is also assumed that market actors are intentional and rational — that they act in accordance with their own intentions and interests (Brunsson and Hägg 1992).

Thus, complete organizations constructed as actors fit better with markets than either agents or arenas. If markets are introduced, we can expect more organizations to emerge. The example of Swedish schools, mentioned above, provides a case in point. Markets may constitute an alternative to a strongly coherent state bureaucracy (Lindblom 1977), but they accord well with state organizations.

Third, events that were not part of any grand plan, or that were not planned at all, may have helped to reinforce the organization concept. Fairly small changes in views or practices may have created or supported the need felt for more complete organizations. The customer concept, for instance, could have been such a trigger. It was a concept that was enjoying some popularity at the time of our observations (Forssell and Jansson 1996; Sahlin-Anderssson 1996), and it obviously agrees better with a powerful modern conception of the individual than the notion of the client or even the citizen. Customers, like the modern individual, enjoy autonomy, have preferences, and possess the right and ability to choose what is right for themselves (Brunsson 1996; Meyer and Jepperson 2000). A customer normally operates on a market. If public entities start seeing an important part of their environment as customers, or if people in the environment start seeing themselves as customers, then people may also start seeing markets and organizations where there were none before.

Another factor which may have helped to give prominence to the organization concept could be the popularity of evaluations and auditing. Evaluations have become common in the public sector, typically targeting individual services (Power 1994, 1997; Rombach and Sahlin-Andersson 1995). An evaluation defines the unit to be evaluated in organizational terms — its boundaries, results and responsibilities. It also compares results with objectives. Hence the absence of clear objectives is seen as a major problem. When results are difficult to measure, evaluations often come to focus on the administrative systems, which are expected to reflect the organization concept. In recent Swedish evaluations, for instance, good social care has been equated with the existence of written policy documents and the presence of well-qualified managers (Socialstyrelsen 1992; Olsson 1995).

Finally, directives appear to have become less popular and less acceptable in the public sector, as in many other social settings, and advice now tends to be more popular. Several national boards in Sweden have become advisory rather than directive: their authority is based on expertise rather than on any right to issue orders or binding rules (Jacobsson and Sahlin-Andersson 1995). In the European Union, much co-ordination and control is supposed to be effected by way of voluntary standards rather than binding directives (Vad 1998). The substitution of advice and standards for directives can be seen as something that creates more autonomy at the local level, but the very act of providing advice and standards also assumes that the recipient already enjoys some autonomy. Directives can be issued to subordinates and agents, whereas there can only be any point in offering advice and standards to actors possessing a certain autonomy, who can evaluate and act upon them if they meet with their approval (Brunsson and Jacobsson, Chap. 9, 2000).

Clearly, all these factors can be both causes and effects: they may reinforce the idea of organization, and they may be reinforced by it. The various factors may also directly reinforce each other. The idea of organization in public-sector reforms did not appear all by itself: in fact, it appeared together with a package of other ideas and practices. In the fourth section, we argued that organizatory reforms themselves come in the shape of a package, not as a number of isolated ideas, or that one idea may bring a whole package in its wake. The same may well apply to the explanations mentioned here, i.e. the factors cited can also appear as packages or strings, whereby one idea or activity is accompanied by — or quickly leads to — the next.

Conclusions

Students of social life and the people they study often share common conceptual frameworks, which means that. to a great extent, they interpret or construct the social world with the help of the same or similar concepts. They learn from each other. Students of organizations have often usurped the privilege of deciding when the organization concept should be applied, without consulting those who are acting within, or in association with, these putative organizations. There may, in fact, be a discrepancy between how the people observed define their own situation and the researcher's definition of the same situation. People's definitions may vary considerably; they may change either quickly or slowly; and they may not be very predictable, given the present state of our knowledge. None the less, the concepts used by people to construct and make sense of their own reality do have important consequences. For instance, people will behave differently if they see themselves as acting in an organization rather than in some other context. and their beliefs and norms will differ accordingly. Every major concept, such as the organization. the market, the family. and so on, can be expected to arrive bearing a whole set of beliefs, norms and practices.

We have sought to illustrate this thesis by demonstrating the way in which aspects of the concept of organization have come to be applied to new areas. and some of the consequences that this has had. We have argued that even seemingly minor changes in the way something is understood — viewing it as an agent, an arena or an organization — have important implications: certain aspects. issues or problems emerge as more important than before, for example, and this, in turn, can affect the kind of changes that are seen as desirable and acceptable.

Two issues call for further exploration by researchers in the organizational field: we need to ask what it is that makes people liable to construct the organization rather than any other social form, and we need to know more about the consequences of being an organization. Indeed, these issues are fundamental to the field.

References

Abbott, Andrew
1988 *The systems of professions*. Chicago: University of Chicago Press.

Abernethy, Margaret A., and Johannes U. Stoelwinder
1995 'The role of professional control in the management of complex organizations'. *Accounting, Organizations and Society* 20/1: 1–17.

Abrahamson, Eric
1996 'Technical and aestetic fashion' in *Translating organizational change*. B. Czarniawska and G. Sevón (eds.), 117–138. Berlin: Walter de Gruyter.

Ahrne, Göran
1994 *Social organizations*. London: Sage.

Ahrne, Göran
1998 'Stater och andra organisationer' in *Stater som organisationer*. G. Ahrne (ed.), 123–156. Stockholm: Nerenius och Santérus förlag.

Åkerstrøm Andersen, Niels
1995 *Selvskabt forvaltning: forvaltnings-politikkens og centralforvaltningens udvikling i Danmark fra 1900–1994.* Copenhagen: Nyt Fra Samfundsvidenskaberne.

Aucoin, Peter
1990 'Administrative reform in public management: Paradigms, principles, paradoxes and pendulums'. *Governance* 3/2: 115–137.

Barnard, Chester
1938 *The functions of the executive*. Cambridge, MA: Harvard University Press.

Berg, Per Olof, and Christer Jonsson
1991 *Strategisk ledning på politiska marknader*. Lund: Studentlitteratur.

Berger, Peter L., and Thomas Luckmann
1966 *The social construction of reality: A*

treatise in the sociology of knowledge. New York: Doubleday.

Berrevin, Renaud, and Christine Musselin
1996 'Les politiques de contractualisation entre centralisation et décentralisation: Les cas de l'équipement et de l'enseignement supérieur'. *Sociologie du Travail* 4/96: 575–596.

Boston, Jonathan, *editor*
1995 *The state under contract*. Wellington: Bridget Williams Books.

Boston, Jonathan, John Martin, June Pallot, and Pat Walsh
1996 *Public management: The New Zealand model*. Oxford: Oxford University Press.

Bourdieu, Pierre
1984 *Distinction: A social critique of the judgement of taste*. Cambridge, MA: Harvard University Press.

Brunsson, Nils
1989 *The organization of hypocrisy: Talk, decision and actions in organizations.* Chichester: Wiley.

Brunsson, Nils
1994 'Politicization and 'company-ization': On institutional affiliation and confusion in the organizational world'. *Management Accounting Research* 5: 323–335.

Brunsson, Nils
1996 'Institutional beliefs and practices: The case of markets and organizations'. Stockholm: Stockholm School of Economics and Stockholm University, SCORE Report 1996: 6.

Brunsson, Nils, and Ingemund Hägg, *editors*
1992 *Marknadens makt*. Stockholm: SNS förlag.

Brunsson, Nils, and Johan P. Olsen
1997 *The reforming organization*, 2nd. Ed.. Bergen: Fagbokforlaget. (1st. Ed. published in 1993 by Routledge).

Brunsson, Nils, and Johan P. Olsen
1998 *Organizations*. Oslo: Fagbokforlaget.

Brunsson, Nils, and Bengt Jacobsson *et al.*
2000 *A world of standards*. Oxford: Oxford University Press.

Christensen, Tom
1991 *Virksomhetsplanlegging*. Oslo: Tano.

Colado, Eduardo, I.
1996 'Excellence at large: Power, knowledge and organizational forms in Mexican universities' in *The politics of management knowledge*. Stewart R. Clegg and G. Palmer (eds.), 99–120. London: Sage.

Crozier, Michel
1964 *The bureaucratic phenomenon*. Chicago, IL: University of Chicago Press.

Cyert, Richard M., and James G. March
1963 *A behavioral theory of the firm*. Englewood Cliffs, NJ: Prentice Hall.

Czarniawska, Barbara
1985 'The ugly sister: On relationships between the private and the public sectors in Sweden'. *Scandinavian Journal of Management Studies* 2/2: 83–103.

Czarniawska-Joerges, Barbara
1994 'Narratives of individual and organizational identities' in *Communication yearbook*, Vol. 17. S. A. Deetz (ed.), 193–221. Thousand Oaks, CA: Sage.

Easton, Brian
1997 *The commercialisation of New Zealand*. Auckland: Auckland University Press.

Fayol Henri
1916 'Administration industrielle et générale. Prévoyance. Organisation. Commandement. Coordination. Contrôle.' in *Bulletin de la societé de l'industrie minérale Paris*.

Fernler, Karin
1996 *Mångfald och likriktning*. Stockholm: Nerenius och Santérus förlag.

Forssell, Anders, and David Jansson
1996 'The logic of organizational transformation: On the conversion of non-business organizations' in *Translating organizational change*. B. Czarniawska and G. Sevón (eds.), 93–115. Berlin: Walter de Gruyter.

Freddi, Giorgio, and James W. Björkman
1989 *Controlling medical professionals. The comparative politics of health governance*. London: Sage.

Friedberg, Erhard
1993 *Le pouvoir et la règle. Dynamiques de l'action organisée*. Paris: Seuil.

Fry, Geoffrey K.
1984 'The development of the Thatcher government's "grand strategy" for the civil service: A public policy perspective'. *Public Administration* 62 (Autumn): 322–335.

Furusten, Staffan
2000 'The knowledge base of standards' in *A world of standards*. N. Brunsson and B. Jacobsson et al. Oxford: Oxford University Press.

Giddens, Anthony
1990 *The consequenses of modernity*. Stanford: Stanford University Press.

Ham, Christopher
1997 *Health care reform. Learning from international experience*. Buckingham: Open University Press.

Harrison, Stephen, and Christopher Pollitt
1994 *Controlling health professionals*. Buckingham: Open University Press.

Henning, Roger
2000 'Selling standards' in *A world of standards*. N. Brunsson and B. Jacobsson et al. Oxford: Oxford University Press.

Hood, Christopher
1991 'A public management for all seasons'. *Public Administration* 69: 3–19.

Hood, Christopher
1995 'The new public management in the 1980's: Variations on a theme'. *Accounting, Organizations and Society* 20/2–3: 93–110.

Hood, Christopher
1996 'United Kingdom: From second chance to near-miss learning' in *Lessons from experience: Experiential learning in administrative reforms in eight democracies*. J. P. Olsen and B. G. Peters (eds.), 36–112. Oslo: Scandinavian University Press.

Hopwood, Anthony G., and Peter B. Miller, editors
1994 *Accounting as social and institutional practice*. Cambridge: Cambridge University Press.

Humphrey, Christopher, and Olov Olson
1995 'Caught in the act: Public services disappearing in the world of 'accountable' management?' in *Issues in management accounting*. D. Ashton, T. Hopper and R. Scapens (eds.), 347–370. Exeter: Prentice Hall.

Jacobsson, Bengt, and Kerstin Sahlin-Andersson
1995 *Skolan och det nya verket*. Stockholm: Nerenius och Santérus förlag.

Lapsley, Irvine
1997 'The new public management diaspora: The health care experiment'. *International Association of Management Journal* 9/2: 1–14.

Laughlin, Richard
1996 'Principals and higher principals: accounting for accountability in the caring professions' in *Accountability: Power, ethos and the technologies of managing*. R. Munro and J. Mouritsen (eds.), 225–244. London: International Thomson Business Press.

Lindblom, Charles E.
1977 *Politics and markets. The world's political–economical systems*. New York: Basic Books.

Lindström, Stefan
1997 *Det svåra samspelet*. SOU 1997: 15. Stockholm.

Lüder, Klaus
1998 'Towards a new financial management for Germany's public sector: Local governments lead the way' in *Global warning! Debating international developments in new public*

financial management. O. Olson, J. Guthrie and C. Humphrey (eds.), 114–129. Oslo: Cappelen Akademisk forlag.

March, James G.
1981 'Decisions in organizations and theories of choice' in *Perspectives on organization design and behavior*. A. H. Van de Ven and W. F. Joyce (eds.), 205–244. New York: Wiley.

March, James G., and Johan P. Olsen
1989 *Rediscovering institutions*. New York: Free Press.

March, James G. and Herbert A. Simon
1958 *Organizations*. New York: Wiley.

Martin, John
1995 'Contracting and accountability' in *The state under contract*. J. Boston (ed.), 36–55. Wellington: Bridget Williams Books.

McSweeney, Brendan
1994 'Management by accounting' in *Accounting as social and institutional practice*. A. G. Hopwood and P. Miller (eds.), 237–269. Cambridge: Cambridge University Press.

Meyer, John W., John Boli, and George M. Thomas
1987 'Ontology and rationalization in the western account' in *Institutional structure: Constituting state, society and the individual*. G. M. Thomas, J. W. Meyer, F. O. Ramirez and J. Boli (eds.), 12–37. Newbury Park, CA: Sage.

Meyer, John W., and Ronald L. Jepperson
2000 'The "actors" of modern society: The cultural construction of social agency'. *Sociological Theory* 18: 100–120.

Miller, Peter
1992 'Accounting and objectivity: The invention of calculating selves and calculable spaces'. *Annals of Scholarship* 9/1–2: 61–86.

Miller, Peter
1994 'Accounting as social and institutional practice: An introduction' in *Accounting as social and institutional practice*. A. G. Hopwood and P. Miller (eds.), 1–39. Cambridge: Cambridge University Press.

Miller, Peter, and Ted O'Leary
1987 'Accounting and the construction of the governable person'. *Accounting, Organizations and Society* 12/3: 235–265.

Mintzberg, Henry
1979 *The structure of organizations.* Englewood Cliffs, NJ: Prentice-Hall.

Mouritsen, Jan
1997 *Taellelighedens Regime.* Copenhagen: Jurist och økonomforbundets forlag.

Musselin, Christine
1997 'State/university relations and how to change them: the case of France and Germany'. *European Journal of Education* 32/2: 145–164.

Nahavandi, Afsaneh, and Ali R. Malekzadeh
1988 'Acculturation in mergers and acquisitions'. *Academy of Management Review* 13/1: 79–90.

OECD
1995 *Governance in transition.* Paris: OECD.

Olsen, Johan P., and B. Guy Peters
1996 *Lessons from experience.* Oslo: Scandinavian University Press.

Olson, Olov, James Guthrie, and Christopher Humphrey, editors
1998 *Global warning: Debating international developments in new public financial management.* Oslo: Cappelen Akademisk forlag.

Olson, Olov, and Kerstin Sahlin-Andersson
1998 'Accounting transformation in an advanced welfare state: the case of Sweden' in *Global warning! Debating international developments in new public financial management.* O. Olson, J. Guthrie and C. Humphrey (eds.), 241–275. Oslo: Cappelen Akademisk forlag.

Olsson, Lena
1995 *Styra med kvalitet.* Fou-rapport 1995:16, Stockholms socialtjänst.

Ouchi, William G.
1977 'The relationship between organization structure and organizational control'. *Administrative Science Quarterly* 32/1: 264–289.

Pfeffer, Jeffrey, and Gerald R. Salancik
1978 *The external control of organizations.* New York: Harper and Row.

Pollitt, Christoffer
1990 *Managerialism and the public services.* Oxford: Blackwell.

Power, Michael
1994 'The audit society' in *Accounting as social and institutional practice.* A.G. Hopwood and P. Miller (eds.), 219–316. Cambridge: Cambridge University Press.

Power, Michael
1997 *The audit society: Rituals of verification.* Oxford: Oxford University Press.

Pressman, Jeffrey, and A. Wildawsky
1973 *Implementation.* Berkeley, CA: University of California Press.

Preston, Alistair M.
1992 'The birth of clinical accounting: A study of the emergence and transformations of discourses on costs and practices of accounting in U.S. hospitals'. *Accounting, Organizations and Society* 17/1: 63–100.

Preston, Alistair M., David J. Cooper, and Rod W. Coombs
1992 'Fabricating budgets: A study of the production of management budgeting in the National Health Service'. *Accounting, Organizations and Society* 17/6: 561–593.

Roberts, John
1991 'The possiblities of accountability'. *Accounting, Organizations and Society* 16/4: 355–368.

Roberts, John, and Robert W. Scapens
1985 'Accounting systems and systems of accountability: Understanding accounting practices in their organisational contexts'. *Accounting, Organizations and Society* 10/4: 443–456.

Rombach, Björn
1991 *Det går inte att styra med mål.* Lund: Studentlitteratur.

Rombach, Björn
1997 *Den marknadslika kommunen.* Stockholm: Nerenius och Santérus förlag.

Rombach, Björn, and Kerstin Sahlin-Andersson
1995 *Från sanningssökande till styrmedel*. Stockholm: Nerenius och Santérus förlag.

Rothstein, Bo
1994 *Vad bör staten göra? Om välfärdsstatens moraliska och politiska logik*. Stockholm: SNS förlag.

Røvik, Kjell-Arne
1996 'Deinstitutionalization and the logic of fashion' in *Translating organizational change*. B. Czarnaiwska and G. Sevón (eds.), 139–172. Berlin: Walter de Gruyter.

Sahlin-Andersson, Kerstin
1994 'Varför låter sig organisationer omvandlas?' in *Organisationsexperiment i kommuner och landsting*. B. Jacobsson (ed.), 170–200. Stockholm: Nerenius och Santérus förlag.

Sahlin-Andersson, Kerstin
1996 'Imitating by editing success' in *Translating organizational change*. B. Czarnaiwska and G. Sevón (eds.), 69–92. Berlin: Walter de Gruyter.

Sales, Arnold L., and Philip H. Mirvis
1984 'When cultures collide: Issues in acquisition' in *Managing organizational transitions*. J.R. Kimberley and R.E. Quinn (eds.), 107–133. Homewood, IL: R.D. Irwin.

Schick, Allen
1996 'The spirit of reform: Managing the New Zealand state sector in a time of change'. A report prepared for the State Services Commission and The Treasury, New Zealand.

Scott, W. Richard
1992 *Organizations: Rational, natural and open systems*. Englewood Cliffs: Prentice Hall.

Selznick, Philip
1957 *Leadership in administration*. New York: Harper and Row.

Simon, Herbert
1945 *Administrative behavior*. New York: Free Press.

Socialstyrelsen
1992 *Vad menar man med kvalitet och hur bedömer man kvalitet i barnomsorgen?*. Report.

Sorge, Arndt
1996 'Organizational behaviour' in *International encyclopedia of business and management*, Vol. 4. M. Warner (ed.) 3793–3820. London: International Thompson Publishing.

SOU
1997 *I medborgarnas tjänst*. Betänkande från förvaltningspolitiska kommissionen. Stockholm.

Stewart, John, and Kieron Walsch
1992 'Change in the management of public services'. *Public Administration* 70: 499–518.

Strang, David, and John W. Meyer
1993 'Institutional conditions for diffusion'. *Theory and Society* 22: 487–511.

Svedberg-Nilsson, Karin
1999 *Effektiva företag*. Stockholm: EFI.

Thompson, James D.
1967 *Organizations in action*. New York: McGraw-Hill.

Vad, Torben B. P.
1998 *Europeanisation of standardisation*. Institute of Political Science, University of Copenhagen.

Weber, Max
1968 *Economy and society*. Berkeley, CA: University of California Press.

Part II
Systems: Open, Loosely Coupled or Autopoietic?

Among those works that attempted to make a massive loan from systems theory, one was especially prominent: Daniel Katz and Robert L. Kahn's *The Social Psychology of Organizations* (1966). Rather than an original contribution, it was a summary of all the work inspired by systems theory and therefore an enormously popular textbook. Its three sources of inspiration were the works of Floyd Henry Allport, Talcott Parsons, and James Grier Miller, the author of the theory of living systems. I have chosen Allport's work (Chapter 4) because, although not a system theorist in the strict sense, he has been influential in later developments in organization theory in the way the two other authors have not. His influence is especially visible in the work of Karl E. Weick, whose *The Social Psychology of Organizing* ([1969] 1979) clearly announced its links to the open systems theory, but also an intention to advance beyond this perspective. The concept of open systems became the mainstay of organizational analysis, but remained underdeveloped. Weick (Chapter 5) undertook its development while simultaneously transcending it with the adoption of concepts related to the autopoietic – i.e. self-regulating and self-reproducing systems. In this way, he bridged the open system approach with the autopoietic systems approach, best represented by Niklas Luhmann (Chapter 6). An important element of this bridging was the concept of loosely coupled systems, adopted simultaneously by James G. March and his collaborators (see Volume I, Part III).

References

Katz, D. and Kahn, R.L. (1966), *The Social Psychology of Organizations*, New York: John Wiley.
Weick, K.E. ([1969] 1979), *The Social Psychology of Organizing*, Reading, MA: Addison-Wesley.

[4]

Journal of Abnormal and Social Psychology
1962, Vol. 64, No. 1, 3–30

A STRUCTURONOMIC CONCEPTION OF BEHAVIOR:

INDIVIDUAL AND COLLECTIVE

I. STRUCTURAL THEORY AND THE MASTER PROBLEM OF SOCIAL PSYCHOLOGY [1]

FLOYD H. ALLPORT [2]

Syracuse University

It is probably unwise to regard any broad problem of science as a subject that can be irrevocably closed. Though the past is strewn with errors we have learned to discard, there is always the chance that somewhere along the way certain significant but controversial issues have, like sleeping dogs, been merely allowed to lie. Sooner or later these issues may rise again to challenge us. There is one such question which, though it has been bypassed and largely forgotten in the main trend of social thinking, has never been laid aside so far as the writer is concerned.

GROUP VERSUS INDIVIDUAL AGENCY: SEMANTIC AND LOGICAL CONFUSIONS

The story began for the writer on the day when Hugo Münsterberg assigned to him as a problem for his doctoral dissertation the investigation of the possible "influence of the group upon the mental processes of the individual." The exact details of this investigation, which were carried out in due course, are not important in the present context; but that such an influence was unmistakably shown, that it was measurable, that the results have been confirmed by others, and finally that a "group" influence has been taken for

granted as the basis for so many social theories, are facts which have posed for the writer a searching question. In what terms should the "social influence" actually be understood and explained?

There had been much writing upon the subject in an earlier day that seemed nebulous. The older theorists were often inclined toward a heavyhanded social determinism. In some instances they hypostatized a plane of "collective reality" quite distinct from the plane of the individuals. One recalls the superindividual doctrine of Durkheim, and at a later date the cultural determinism and "superorganic" theories of Kroeber and other anthropologists. There was also Le Bon's crowd consciousness and the "crowd mind," and Ross' "planes and currents" in a society. From a somewhat different point of view we had the old "social organism" metaphor, elaborated in modern times by Spencer and others, as well as the "group mind" concept of McDougall. Though strangely endowed with human qualities, the "collective" reality in most of these theories was nevertheless supposed to be above the individuals and somehow to control or direct their actions.

With respect to everyday parlance that is still current even among social scientists, it has seemed to the writer that there is also something unfortunate in the practice of employing psychological (that is, individually oriented) concepts as personifications applying to groups. If, for example, it is said that a "group convenes," "thinks," "feels," "decides," "achieves solidarity," "becomes organized," "legislates," or "adjourns," either the expression is a tautology, a borrowing for the group of a term that has meaning only at the level of the individual organism, or else it refers to some kind of "concerted doing"

[1] Editor's Note. As originally written, this critique of systems of social psychology included a structurally oriented examination, also, of network theories, open systems, and theory of social roles. A second article, continuing this series in the journal, will take a different course and will proceed more directly with the exposition and testing of the writer's theory of event-structure, the collective aspects of which are foreshadowed in the present analysis.

[2] Grateful acknowledgement is made to the administrative officers of Syracuse University for financial assistance in the preparation of this article.
The author is now Professor of Social and Political Psychology Emeritus of Syracuse University.

3

4   Floyd H. Allport

performed by an alleged agent for which we can find no unique referent. An *individual* can be said to "think" or "feel"; but to say that a group does these things has no ascertainable meaning beyond saying that so many individuals do them. On the other hand, an individual can walk into a room with others and sit down with them, he can arrange to do certain things with them, and he may answer "Aye" when his name is called in order to express his agreement. But the individual does not "convene," "become organized," "legislate," or "achieve solidarity." Such expressions have meaning only as designations of action at the "group" level. But here we run into a difficulty. No matter how closely we look, we can never actually experience any group agent who is performing such actions. If we point to, or try to touch, the group, we are doing nothing that can be distinguished from pointing to or touching individuals. Hence we must realize either that the description we give of the act makes it appropriate for individuals (but only figurative for a group), or else that it is appropriate for groups, but whenever we allude to any particular group that does it we are using a term (and concept) that has no unambiguously denotable referent. In this latter case the group as such, if it exists at all, must be always an unencounterable "something" of which we have no direct or sensible evidence. We have "constructed" a singular, nondenotational, group *concept* out of a plurum of experiences of elements (individuals) each of whom, separately, can be actually encountered.

This sort of usage seemed to the writer to reflect a vagueness in the social sciences with respect to important matters that contrasted strangely with ideals of precision in other disciplines. Did it represent an imprecision not only in terms, but in the very meanings the terms were supposed to express? Could it be that when one tries to put into language his thoughts and observations about what a group actually "does" (as, for example, when some cooperative act is performed), he really does not know *what* he means because he has never seriously tried to think the matter out?

There are no doubt many persons, even in the social disciplines, to whom such matters are not of vital consequence—who will say

that so long as we get useful results out of "group action" there is no real need to define it. This, of course, is a legitimate position, since the choice of methods and problems is always likely to be in part a matter of individual values. Such a view, however, is different from the evaluation here implied, and if the reader should happen to hold strongly to the opinion expressed above, he would probably find the present article pointless and might do well to lay it aside. For the conviction here expressed is that in using language to refer to "social" action it *is* important to know what we mean.

A social scientist or a social psychologist who has been prone to the usage we are criticizing might reply that he certainly knows what *he* means. He uses such terms, he may say, only as convenient "fictions." If, for example, we had to observe (and go through a statement of) all the hundreds of acts of individuals which are involved in a piece of legislation, we should never get anywhere in the social scene. We can sum it all up with great economy by saying "Congress" legislates. Is this not, he might ask, the way all scientists work? The physicist cannot observe atoms directly. He sets up the concept of an atom as a useful "construct" inferable from "results" or from other forms of evidence. In the same way the molar concepts of learning in psychology are hypothetical constructs, used not as clear-cut realities, but only to aid our thinking.

In answer to this argument the writer would raise the following question. Is our knowledge of what the phrase "Congress legislates" means gained from observing *acts of Congress* in the same (empirical) way that the physicist's knowledge of what interionic attraction means is gained by observing (even though indirectly) the *behavior of atoms*, or in the same way that the psychologist's description of the learning of the rat is gained by watching the *rat* as it runs the maze? *Or*, is the word "Congress" in the phrase "Congress legislates" a term whose meaning is established only on the basis of evidence from *other sorts* of things, such, for example, as acts that *individuals* are seen to do? To make the cases comparable would we not have to assume that the physicist had had no techniques whatever that had revealed to him (through a chain of observable physical happenings) encounters with "atoms," that he had first known, by direct or indirect encounter, only electrons, protons, and neutrons, and their behavior, and that he had *then* proceeded to construct the atom *conceptually* out of these particles? These assumptions, which might have justified the social scientist's analogy, are all contrary to the actual sequence of discoveries in the physical science. The psychologist, similarly, does not construct the learning phenomenon, in the first instance, out of neurons and their properties; he begins by the molar observation of "the rat" and its macroscopically observed movements. In both of these cases observation of what happens properly begins at a level which is at the time available to denotational (that is, encountering) procedures.

The word "Congress," in contradistinction to these instances, has *actual* denotational reference only at a step that is lower down in the natural hierarchy than the level to which it is presumed to refer. Its referent is encounterable only at the level of *individuals* and their actions. Ought we not, therefore, to observe *the acts of the individuals* and base our generalizations upon *them* (that is, upon the experiences actually obtained from the phenomenon through our senses) rather than attempt to describe what *Congress* is said to do? If we were to set ourselves to study Congress and "its" actions, would we not be starting our investigation by choosing as its object something that cannot check us to tell us whether, in experiencing it, we are actually experiencing *something,* and that cannot tell us where this "something" leaves off and some other object begins? How, with such criteria omitted at the very start, could it be claimed that the social sciences are empirical? [3]

---

[3] A social scientist might reply that it is only the accident of our "smaller" size relative to the group that renders the group, unlike the objects of the physicist and psychologist, incapable of encounter as such. If we had much duller senses, or were far out in space looking down, the "group" would then appear "as an object" and would be available denotationally for experiments, just as the "atom" now is. Though the logic of this argument seems sound, it really betrays its originator. For the group as *then* experienced would certainly *not* be the group

THE INDIVIDUALISTIC POSITION: ATTACK ON "GROUP FALLACIES"—THE SOCIOLOGISTS' REPLY

It was near the beginning of such reflections that the writer decided to make a clean sweep, and concluded that although the individual behaves differently in a "group" than when alone, this fact offered no evidence of the existence of a "social" as distinct from an "individual" entity. The explanation of the so-called social influence *lay only in the psychology of the individual as he operated in situations with others.* The writer (1924b) presented this viewpoint systematically in his *Social Psychology* and followed it with numerous theoretical and experimental studies extending the same thought to such topics as conformity, customs, culture, public opinion, political organization, and collective action generally (Allport, 1924a, 1924b, 1927a, 1927b, 1933, 1934a, 1934b, 1937, 1939, 1940, 1942; Allport & Hartman, 1924, 1931). His *Institutional Behavior* (1933) documented, in addition, the psychological and ethical consequences of the indiscriminate use of group and institutional fictions in collective or social living. This program of "debunking" sociodeterministic conceptions made up in vigor all that it lacked in tact.

On the scenes that followed, the writer would like to draw the curtain. To say the least, it was scarcely a love feast. Some stoutly denied that sociologists were to any serious extent guilty of such a confusion of language as the writer had charged. The usual reaction seemed to be that it was only a matter of figurative or terminological convenience, and that of course they did not mean any of these terms literally. The implication was that in using group-agency terminology they knew exactly what they were talking about, or else that no one should require a phenomenon so familiar as a "group" or "group action" to be further defined; but if they *were* pressed for a statement, they could readily translate

---

phenomenon as the social scientist now conceives and studies it. The hope of a useful theoretical or practical approach to the *social* scene would seem to lie rather in our ability to construct some sort of model that will show both the individual and the collective levels *simultaneously*—that will describe, in other words, how the latter *is made up of the former.*

these matters into language that would satisfy the most meticulous. A more deliberate answer was that although some sociologists might have erred through the "group fallacy" in borrowing the psychologists' terms to apply to collective entities, their error was only skin deep. It was due to their slowness in developing a proper vocabulary for group reference. In the course of time they would be able to devise their own terminology and the problem would disappear.

Still others, like the psychologist Asch (1952b), maintained that although it was true that "group facts" have their foundation in "individual facts," and group consciousness, group purposes, and group goals are found only in individuals, "social fields" must be recognized as existing cognitively *within the individual*. Even if the group is not a separate entity, the fact that the individual often conceives it as such makes all the difference in his behavior.[4] To sociologists in general it did not seem that the writer's program of ascribing all causality to individual motivation could provide much enlightenment concerning social control, social institutions, culture, or similar topics which were their own primary interests.

DEFINING THE ISSUE

The writer readily concedes that in 1924 he did not realize the full implications of the problem. He was worrying only about the *personification* involved in the "group mind" and about the usage that he called the "institutional *fallacy*," when he should have been worrying also about groups and institutions themselves. That is to say, he should have been trying to examine and learn *what sort* of reality the referents of these words might actually have. Regardless of the adequacy of their own conceptual equipment, in doubting that the writer's treatment of social psychology as a purely "individual" discipline could solve their problem sociologists certainly had a point. One can, of course, discount as illogical the familiar argument that because individuals behave in a crowd as they would not behave alone, the crowd is therefore a mental entity that "embraces" or "descends upon" its members. But even if we got rid of the *crowd mind*, the problem of describing the differential of crowd-like behavior, that is, the phenomenon of a crowd as such, would remain. Granting that the individual is the only referent to which the terms of psychology can be applied, there remains the problem of stating in unambiguous terms, and not merely for this collectivity or that, but for collectivities in general, just what is occurring in the phenomena to which *we allude* when we say that the group "has solidarity," "is organized," "decides," or "controls its members."

Though such expressions cannot lead us to an unambiguous referent for the term "group," nor can they themselves be useful starting points for an empirically oriented investigation, one cannot for a moment deny that certain sets of happenings referred to by these terms do occur. Such happenings are important in social science and in daily life. It is also clear that an individual determinist who, in describing the individual as the agent, isolates him from acting "collectively" with others, will be equally unable to cope with them.

But unfortunately these realizations at once place us in a dilemma. Granted that there are realities that can be seen only by looking at individuals as such, and also realities that can be experienced or demonstrated only when individuals are taken together, how can these realities, in both cases, be stated in terms that are explicit, clear, and general? If we cannot be anthropomorphic in referring to groups for fear of running into a group tautology or fallacy, how then *can* we describe them? If thoroughgoing individual causality and group determinisms are either inadequate or illogical, what then is left? What sort of agency *can* be invoked? Or, if these two antithetical determinants are to be combined, who can provide the magic formula by which it is to be done?

Nothing that has been said above should be construed as a lessening of the *need* for a solution of this problem. We are merely pointing out the difficulties. It is not conceded that

---

[4] This position, though relevant to the problem of the group and individual in the broader sense, was not a definitive answer to the question of whether or in what sense, a "group" really exists. Nor did it render any less appropriate the attack upon terminological laxity and confusion which the writer was making.

social scientists' intent in the use of group fictions has been trivial, or that such fictions were used "merely" for convenience, or that the remedy could have lain in a mere change of terminology. Suppose we had gotten rid of the group fallacy by refusing to assign to the group any of the terms of description that belong to individuals. Our logic would then have become impeccable; but of what would our discourse have consisted? What *are* social phenomena if they are not the behaviors of individuals? Or, if social realities *are* entirely composed of individual actions, is there some way of describing and aggregating the latter, not before realized, that will hold the key to the statement of both realities simultaneously and without personification, tautology, or hypostatized agency? This is the difficult question by which sociologists and social psychologists inevitably *would have been faced* had they given up their use of fictions; and it is a question which, in the writer's judgment, they were not prepared to answer. It was not merely that they did not have the right words for their concepts; *the concepts themselves were lacking.*

And this issue still remains as unfinished business. In spite of advances in many areas of social psychology and the social sciences, we are still faced, if we view the situation candidly, with the realization that our theories of social causality, and of the relation of action at the "societal" level to what we recognize as the acts of individuals, are far from adequate either in denotation or explanatory significance. Again, the writer has no quarrel with those who do not think a methodological housecleaning in these respects is necessary, those who believe that it is possible to achieve useful results through individuals in groups without facing such apparently unanswerable questions. He would only state his opinion that unless we are to be content with good works alone, unless we are willing to accept the bankruptcy of the social sciences as empirical disciplines that are also denotational, we must try to discover some more satisfactory paradigm for "the group and the individual." Some way must be found to describe in general terms that layout of conditions surrounding and involving individuals which we have called "the

group," and to formulate, in the precise yet *universal* manner of science, what actually goes on in the situation we call "collective" action. In this broader sense the problem of the individual and the group is really the "master problem" of social psychology.

The present article and one to follow in a later issue are intended as a contribution to the solution of this problem. In this article an attempt will be made to trace some of the major developments that have occurred with respect to it in contemporary systems of social psychology. Every system, of course, has had to make some kind of terms with it, if only by implication. The reader's indulgence is asked for the recital of theories that may be already familiar, a procedure rendered unavoidable by the need of showing the specific ways in which their authors have dealt with the problem.[5] To these synopses of the theories there will be added in most cases a critical commentary by the present writer, prepared mainly with its following orientation. In two previous publications the writer (1954, 1955) has offered preliminary conceptualizations of the "patterned" or "articulated" aspect of phenomena, a model which he has hypothesized as being general and therefore as underlying integrated behavior both in the lone individual and in collective aggregates. He now believes that the formulations of the group-individual relationship that are to be found in the schools of modern social psychology will, if analyzed, reveal in latent form some of the outlines of this same structural pattern; or, if they are lacking, then by restating of the theory in such a manner as to take them into account its validity and usefulness can be enhanced. It would follow that if, in the working through of these systems, a further endeavor is made to reveal such "structural" strands and to reinterpret or extend the ideas which they involve, additional light might be thrown upon the prob-

[5] For additional statements of the group-individual problem and its modern setting see Doob (1952) and the very thoughtful chapter on "An Introduction to Group Theory" in Asch (1952b). (See also Allport, 1942, 1961.) The latter reference contains further suggestions on the logic of the problem of collective reality. We shall not here attempt any statement of the extensive *earlier* literature.

lem in hand. Through his critique of the theories and certain other added sections the writer has endeavored to do just this.

PHILOSOPHICAL APPROACHES—COGNITIVE VIEWPOINTS—ATTEMPT AT A GESTALT SYNTHESIS

The impetus toward group reification at the time the writer began his work, though not productive of formal models, had already acquired a philosophical underpinning. There was developing a background of superorganic theory in cultural anthropology, as well as a doctrine of "emergent evolution" in biology. "Supersummation" and "wholistic properties" were added by gestalt psychology. All these ideas, if not already at the social level, could be readily extrapolated to it. As time went on, the phenomenological tendencies of the configurational psychologists had to be reckoned with. Though the writer had collected the "social introspections" of his subjects in his experiments on "group influence," there were those who felt, as Asch did, that the comparative neglect of the way the individual was *perceiving* the particular situation he was in had stood in the way of a full investigation of the group phenomenon. The "distortion effects" elicited in group experiments by Asch (1952a) could be cited as evidence of the "pressure" of the judgments of the group upon the cognitions of the individual. In such phenomena the manner in which the subject is perceiving the reactions of those about him is all-important.

The gestalt position, in conformity with Koffka (1935) and as stated more recently by Asch (1952b), can be summarized as follows: *The concepts both of the individual and the group are necessary for a full explanation of social and individual behavior, and from a psychological standpoint the two go hand in hand. Groups and institutions have their existence as indispensable constructs in the mental life of individuals.* The doctrine that there is a "whole property" that is not to be found in the parts was said to apply no less to collective than to individual aggregates. A group process "is neither a sum of individual activities nor a fact added to the activities of individuals" (Asch, 1952b, p. 252). There was a similarity here with the emergence doc-

trine of the relationship between the levels. Macroscopically described phenomena express a reality no less genuine than, but totally different from, the reality of the same ensemble microscopically viewed.[6]

Though the philosophical and gestalt approaches were broadly conceived, their focus proved too indefinite for our problem. As for the cultural and biological holistic theories, it was hard to know just what a "superorganic" entity *is*, or what it is that "emerges' as the reality at a higher level. Since it seemed to be conceded that consciousness, purposes, and values exist only in individuals, we are at a loss to understand what kind of transphenonomenological existence or "macroscopic whole-character" the group whole may have to the cognitive experiences of its members (the parts). Even though we can agree that the whole is more than the sum of the parts, no one has been able to state in terms that are both denotational and general just what this "more than" or "different from" may be. We cannot expect this situation, however, to trouble a phenomenological theorist too greatly, since for him the property of denotability is not a uniquely significant criterion of reality.

EARLY GROUP INFLUENCE EXPERIMENTS— FRAME OF REFERENCE, SOCIAL NORM, AND REFERENCE GROUP

By 1924 the writer had published the results of the experiment assigned to him by Münsterberg. It should be stated that in these investigations, in the "together" sessions, the subjects did not communicate. They sat around a table in groups of from three to five, working independently, each individual having his own set of materials for the task in hand. From this work the following gen-

---

[6] Asch (1952b, pp. 265–267) makes some pertinent comments on the fact that many group (that is, interpersonal) happenings that are significant in the lives of individuals are happenings between *other* persons and lie outside the immediate knowledge or possibility of voluntary control by the individuals concerned. He also comments, by a "negatively" inferred method, on the control over individuals in a social situation as evidenced by the interfunctioning of social attitudes (pp. 577–579). These passages seem related to the present writer's theory of collective relations which will be developed later.

eralizations were forthcoming. Though these findings are here expressed as interpretations from data rather than as the data themselves, it should be borne in mind that each of them was based upon actual quantitative experiments.

Working in the presence of others, even though there is no direct contact nor communication, establishes certain fundamental attitudes. We are confused and distracted whenever we feel our reaction to be at variance with or inferior to the average behavior of those about us. In the association process we tend to inhibit egocentric trends and personal complexes. In our thinking we assume a conversational attitude, becoming more expansive and less precise. And finally, we avoid extremes in passing judgment, tending, often unconsciously, toward conformity with what we think to be the opinion of those about us.[7]

It should be stated that there was already some experimental background in the literature on group influence at the time of the writer's experiments; and in part his findings were confirmations of those of earlier investigators.

One can scarcely examine this record without a conviction that some kind of theory or generalization about "collective influence" is called for. For the present purpose attention is directed to the final sentence. The reference here is to experiments in which the subjects (graduate students in psychology) judged the degree of pleasantness of odors in a series, and the heaviness of a series of weights, in both the "social" and "solitary" situation. The results showed that in both these tasks they made *fewer* extreme judgments, that is, judgments toward either end of the scale, in the "together" condition than they did when working alone. This phenomenon of *group convergence* was considered by the writer at that time to be the indirect result of the adoption by the individual, when in the group, of an attitude to conform. That is, it was an evidence of a set, whether conscious or otherwise, to *avoid* the *non*conformity to the (unknown) judgments of others that would be more likely to result from judging the odor or the weight to lie at either extreme of the scale than it would to result from judging it as nearer to the middle.

Some years later Sherif (1935), working

[7] Allport, F. H., *Social psychology*, p. 285. Reprinted by permission of the publishers, Houghton Mifflin and Company.

under different assumptions, reported a similar finding concerning judgments (together and alone) of the extent of the apparent movement of a stationary point of light in a dark room (autokinetic effect). Here, however, the judgments of the subjects were spoken aloud. Again there was found in the collective situation a marked convergence of judgments toward the central tendency of the subjects' estimates. The convergence effect, moreover, was seen to persist when the subjects were subsequently tested alone. These findings have been interpreted by Sherif and Sherif (1956) as due to "an extension into the social field" of a psychological principle that operates in perception and elsewhere. This is the principle that what is experienced by the individual in a situation is influenced by "anchorages" in some "frame of reference" afforded by that situation. Here the frame of reference for anchoring the subjects' judgments (they were called in this case "perceptions") consisted of the array of judgments given by the other individuals. Sherif's contribution to the problem of group and individual can thus be given in approximately the following terms. *A "frame of reference" is afforded by the situation of a reacting or interacting group in which the individual participates as a member; and this frame of reference provides an "anchorage" for the individual's perceptions (or other activities). Such an anchorage can be assumed to be a kind of collective standard or "norm" that arises among the individuals as a result of their interaction.* Since one would probably wish to exclude the hypothesis of mental telepathy, it seems to be implied in Sherif's logic that the reactions of the others must be overt and must be *perceived* in order for the collective standard or norm to arise. If they were not perceived, as in the writer's investigation, the effect, as we have seen, might be experimentally the same, but we would probably not interpret it as due to anchorage to a norm.

Be that as it may, from these and similar observations Sherif evolved his impressive theory of "social norms," applying the frame of reference principle not only to perceptions but to beliefs, to attitudes, and even to overt behaviors. As a corollary, one that relates the theory usefully to the phenomenon of levels, it was conceived that a social norm, established originally by interaction at the overt, societal, level, becomes through continual use "interiorized" as a personal value or ideal of the individual himself.

In view of the fact that this effect was actually demonstrable only in the verbalized estimates of the (autokinetic) motion and not as an actual conscious perception, and more particularly since the present writer had previously obtained the same sort of result without any of the subjects knowing the judgments of the others, the hypothesis of the establishment in the group of a social norm, and especially of the anchoring of the perceptions of individuals to that norm, would seem overelaborate. That there was here an effect produced specifically by coacting with others was clear. But for the purpose of theorizing about the social realities involved, one could wish for a somewhat more parsimonious interpretation.

As an a fortiori principle, however, the theory of social norms has been very useful. By its very divergence from the writer's procedure, and by calling the influence in question a "norm" or "standard" instead of merely a "social influence," it did focus attention upon whatever in the situation *is* overt and capable of being conformed to, and upon the possibility that the character of the particular interactive situation (including especially the type of group involved) might affect the result. There might, in other words, be different kinds of norms for different groups; and, since the individual could participate in a number of groups, different norms for conformity might exist with relation to different phases of his activity as related to those different groups.

Once it was recognized that the individual might belong to a number of norm imposing groups, that is, that he might share group norms with others in many different contexts, a further important distinction arose. One could distinguish *different degrees of importance* to the individual of the collectivities to whose norms he was being "anchored." In particular, one could distinguish between the groups of which the individual was *merely* a member, and those with which, whether he was actually a member or not, he strove to

identify himself (that is, in which he wished to be *considered* as a member). Status classifications aspired to by the individual, to take only one instance, were added to "natural interest" groups as examples of this sort of affiliation. In order to distinguish groups of this special identification type, they have been called the *reference groups* of the individual concerned. *Reference groups, then, are those which provide the greatest satisfactions to the individual. They are the main anchorage for his values and beliefs, and their norms are reflected to a large extent in his attitudes, his standards, and even in his general behavior.* The concept of reference group affiliation has afforded a rationale for much provocative research.[8]

Although the social norm and frame of reference theory has proved attractive and has had some success in predicting behavior in collective situations, there are important matters bearing upon explanation which it leaves unsettled. For example, there is no generalized principle, beyond obvious teleological assumptions, stating what the norm represents in the nature of a strategic value to the collectivity. We are also not told the reason why the individuals conform so faithfully to it. Are group established anchors for perception any more effective than any other kinds of perceptual frames of reference? If so, why? Does the norm point only to something inside the individual, or is it a standard which he holds "on behalf" of a group; or is it implied that there is a distinct group reality in which the norm inheres? If the latter, what is the nature of that reality? Or again, does an individual perceive according to the norm because he actually believes there *is* a group which is imposing the norm on him, or is he implicitly agreeing, with others, to adopt the fiction that a group norm exists, and doing so for the conscious or unconscious purpose of

---

[8] We owe the concept of reference groups, as well as the term, to Hyman (1942). For a useful distinction regarding the use of reference groups, see also Kelley (1952). Newcomb (1950) has extended the idea by proposing that there are "negative" reference groups. These are the groups with which the individual wishes *not* to be identified ("negative" involvement), and whose norms and attitudes he therefore rejects or opposes.

using such a notion to control his fellow group members (as well as himself)?

The theory is concerned primarily with the fact of membership in or identification with a group, and with the "obligation" that is imposed (as if by the group) upon the members to perceive or act in certain ways. It is presumed, of course, that the individuals receive certain satisfactions through their membership, participation, and norm obedience. If the individual deviates from the norms and persists in doing so, he may find the rewards becoming increasingly uncertain and may eventually lose his membership in the group. In these respects the theory gives us a clue to the members' motivation for conformity to the norm. Our complaint, however, is that it fails to follow up the implications of the clue. Ought we not to consider more carefully how the so-called norms arise? Why, for example, did the original or "charter" members of a particular group come to espouse just these norms in the first place (as the group was being formed or thereafter) with the result that these particular standards and not others became the ones to be continually maintained and imposed upon all newcomers to this group. We are not so naive as to believe in a "group being" that gives them, or a "group mind" consensus that legislates them. There evidently must be some motivations on the part of *individuals,* motives not yet sufficiently explained as to their nature or their integrated action, that lead to norm creation as well as norm obedience. Let us return to the original experiments and see if we can formulate some hypotheses.

WHAT DID THE EARLY GROUP INFLUENCE
  EXPERIMENTS SHOW? INDICATIONS OF A
  PRIMITIVE LAW OF STRUCTURING—RE-
  INTERPRETATION OF SOCIAL NORMS

One of the reasons why the earlier experiments seemed so challenging was that there was no good a priori reason to expect the results obtained. The groups represented psychological laboratory sessions, a part of the regularly scheduled academic work of the leader and the subjects concerned. As thus constituted, it is hard to believe that these situations imposed any obligation regarding ways of perceiving or judging. The norm of

behavior expected on the part of the subjects in psychological work is usually just "to react naturally." Since there seems no other way of explaining these results on a group basis we are led to infer that, if such a basis did exist, it must have been because another (psychological) group had somehow arisen, interlaid as it were within the experimental groupings, just by virtue of the subjects being together and acting in one another's presence. There were, of course, the further facts that the subjects knew one another and that they were all doing the same kind of task. Such a hypothetical, situationally conditioned, group we shall suppose is the one within which the norm arose.

Now here we have a choice of at least two possible interpretations. Considering Sherif's (1935) experiment, we might first, as he seems to have done, conceive that the group was in some way established as a kind of causally prior condition. And then as the members announced their judgments, the norm emerged as a kind of estimated average (arrived at perhaps unconsciously) by each member, on the basis of the series of judgments he had heard expressed. Thus as the experiment proceeded, this subjective norm began to function psychologically as an anchor for the subjects' remaining judgments. The group (considered as here effective merely as a consensus of judgments) is the independent variable; and the direction of influence or control goes from it to the several members. And we infer that the influence is perceptual or cognitive: one's perceptions or judgments are actually modified by the evidence of what the others are experiencing.

This interpretation seems at least consistent an an example of alleged group determinism. Its chief drawback is that it lacks motivational dynamics. Either there is a "group entity" of some sort that acts to modify the individuals' reactions (an explanation one would probably reject), or the individuals do it themselves. If we choose the latter alternative, we are not told why they do it. Sherif (1935), of course, has said that "the group" has provided through the judgments of its members a frame of reference, and also, through its central tendency, an anchor. But frames of reference and anchors are not automatic. They have

12   FLOYD H. ALLPORT

to be of the individual's choosing in part at least; and we are not *told* why the individuals chose the group frame rather than some other. They might have chosen entirely, for example, their own earlier run of judgments (adaptation level), or those of some other single individual, or perhaps none at all. Furthermore, a direct effect of a *social* influence upon a perception of magnitude (if it is considered that the subject's report *does* describe an actual percept and not merely what he *says* he perceived) would be, as in all such cases, difficult to substantiate. There could be group effects upon judgments or spoken reactions without assuming the imposition of a norm of *perceiving.*

The second alternative, which in the writer's opinion involves fewer assumptions, is to consider that the norm (that is, the average of the judgments), instead of being a "one-way agency" of the group acting upon the individual, is circularly involved in the process of the formation of the group itself. The "group" depends on this norm no less than the norm upon the "group." In this case the (psychological) group, even if it is informal, sporadic, and perhaps fortuitous, is regarded as something whose formation and "very existence," depends upon the fact that it has a significant meaning to the individuals. Figuratively stated, it arises as a kind of theater of operations for the satisfaction of the individuals' needs, an implementation of their behavioral contacts, and a medium of their self-expression. It affords an opportunity that is generally (even if unconsciously) welcomed. It is against this background that the meaning of obedience to a "group norm" should be understood. The norm arises as a standard to be adhered to in that situation for a particular reason. This reason is that the relationship between the conduct which the norm prescribes and the cooperative activities of individuals which make the "group" possible is close and facilitating. The norm behavior is so positively related to the group and to its rewarding operations that it comes to be individually and spontaneously regarded by all as the effective (and *mandatory*) means by which the (valued) group condition can, and should, be maintained. A norm is thus not something that is "imposed upon" (or

even afforded to) the individuals by the group; it is one of the conditions of the existence of the group itself.

Let us canvass this situation in a little more detail, using as cases simple instances from daily life and the small co-working groupings of these earlier experiments. Unless there are special circumstances that determine otherwise, human beings when they are thrown together for any length of time develop sets or attitudes toward one another that reflect the perceptual realization of one another's presence and coactivity. Such sets may be scarcely conscious. They may give rise to words, signs, gestures of recognition, or similar "acknowledgments" of the other person; or they may remain purely covert. The subtle signs of the awareness of such interrelations are the most elementary forms of "rewards of participation" in such informal, scarcely conscious, types of groupings. They come to be expected, and in a sense, valued. At least one could say that their complete absence (that is, complete indifference of others to us) would probably be disturbing.

The satisfactions of an A in this situation come (back) to him in his perceptual recognition of the signs ("provisients") given off by B (or by a number of Bs), as A's "cycle" of behavior in its course toward "closure" becomes "tangent" to B's behavior in the environment. But we immediately note that the situation is mutual and reciprocal. B's rewards, under the usual boundary conditions of small groups, also come to him by way of some recognition given him through a stimulus afforded by A (or by a number of A's). When this happens, A and B are "bound together." That is, so long as this situation lasts they are more likely to stay in one another's presence or range of stimulation than to separate. If only *one* of them were to need or seek this sign of recognition or bonhomie from the other, the situation would be "linear," merely a case of A seeking and obtaining contact from B, but not B from A. There would thus be in the situation itself no guarantee of the likelihood or the recurrence of such contacts. The arrangement would therefore be momentary and undependable. But when each of them needs or seeks the other, be it ever so slightly or unconsciously, there arises a predictively operating condition that we can call a *"collective structure."* We are justified in calling it that since its parts will not act, dependably and repetitively through time, alone. Through their *inter*dependence the "ensemble" maintains that enduringly integrated character that we associate with the term structure.

It should be realized that it is really not the individuals as whole organisms, but *these particular give-and-take behaviors* of seeking and recognition, that can be most clearly said to constitute the group (that is, the "grouping"). And what is especially important for our purpose is the fact that this structure (A to B *and* B to A) *is self-closing or cyclical in character.* The give-and-take of two reciprocating individuals, in the manner above described, *is* a cycle in which the behavior of each receives closure from, and is bound through reciprocation to, the behavior of the other within a collective structure made up of the two.

In such episodes there is sometimes a *special* facilitating effect that arises because the individuals are not fully aware of the whole process. Probably neither person realizes in any deep or personal way the full extent of the other's involvement (desire for the rewards of the structure); hence the "binding" effect of the situation may exist (and exist in full force) without either being conscious of it. As each person is set to gain or retain the rewards from the other and also to pay the price of obtaining them by extending his own cordiality *to* the other, yet as each does not realize that the other also is motivated in exactly this same way, a state of special readiness which might be called "pluralistic ingratiation" becomes established. Such a condition can scarcely fail to be conducive to group formation or "group cohesiveness." Indeed we could almost say that the patterning of behaviors incident to, or resulting from, this binding effect *is* the group in question.[9]

[9] When we view human behavior, at either the individual or the collective level, in terms of its (self-closing) structure, important facts are seen which are not evident in the "linear-agent" view characteristic of molar stimulus response theory. In fact the whole problem of the ongoings and events of motivation, perception, and learning tends to take

Such, we may assume, was the state of affairs implicit in the co-working groups employed by Sherif (1935) and the present writer. One could expect that there was here in progress this subtle, perhaps unconscious, building up of self-closing structures among the individuals. Our earlier discussion of the results in this direction was limited to the quantitative convergence or conformity shown in perceptions or judgments made in the *together* situation. These results have been confirmed by other investigators. But in addition, other types of effects of co-working have been noted. Let us examine these to see if they also give evidence of the "structuration" effect before going on with our explanation of how norms arise.

The writer's researches (1920, 1924a, 1924b) included the performance of subjects working together, but individually, in small groups (as compared with the results of solitary work) in a number of activities. In one set of experiments the subjects did problems in multiplication, in another they looked at a reversible perspective figure and noted the number of fluctuations. Still other sets included the writing of words in free chain association, the responses being later classified by the experimenter as personal (that is, egocentric) or otherwise. The effect upon verbal reasoning was studied by having the subjects under the two conditions write brief essays on topics suggested by philosophical quotations.

Though some individual differences were shown in the results, the effects in general were as follows. In all situations in which speed and quantity of work (that is, amount of energy put forth) was taken as a variable more work was done in the group situation than while working alone. More problems were multiplied in the group, more reversals of perspective in the figure were noted, and more words were written in the association lists. This phenomenon was called by the writer "social facilitation." It was in part a confirmation of the work of earlier investigators. *Quality* of work, which could not always be graded objectively, did not seem to improve—perhaps the reverse. Errors made in multi-

on a different "format" and may be seen to exhibit a different set of laws.

14   FLOYD H. ALLPORT

plication problems, possibly through lapse of
attention, were evidently more disturbing to
the subject (as suggested by their bunching)
than when alone; or else the distractions
leading to the errors were of longer duration
when others were present. In any case the
presence of others seemed, to a considerable
extent, and in one way or another, either
challenging or preoccupying. Two other effects
of much interest were noted. In the essays
there seemed to be a more expansive conversational quality, with less profundity of
thought, when they were written in the presence of others who were also writing on the
same themes. (This effect, however, should
be checked by other investigators because of
small numbers of cases and the possible bias
of the experimenter's judgment.) And there
was in the group condition of the association
experiments a definite tendency to associate
(or at least to write down) fewer words that
were in the context of a "personal" or subjective train of thinking.

Though sets toward others in the vicinity
are subtle and difficult to formulate, it is
believed that the above summary expresses
the same general pattern of behavior that
was seen in the norm and "conformity of
judgment" experiments. Again there is suggested an effort to "belong with" or to "come
to terms with" those around us. And again,
the fact which is particularly interesting is
that the situation did not really call for any
such effort. There were no "terms with others"
that were required by any overt circumstances.
However *psychologically* imperative such tendencies may have been, there was nothing whatever to suggest to the subjects that they
were *logically* called for. In these experiments
the subjects did not even communicate. No
comparisons whatever of the subjects' activities or productions were to be made at that
time or later; and the subjects were well
aware of that fact.

In spite of all these precautions an apparent
drive to be "at one" with the others, or in
some way acceptable or equal to the others,
is an inference from the findings that is hard
to escape. The increase in pace of mental
activities on the part of most of the subjects
in the co-working situation suggested a concern (perhaps one could almost call it an

anxiety or a fear) that they might "fall behind" or "fail to measure up to (their own
or others') expectations." Some of the introspective reports were to the effect that "others
are writing and I must write too." This increase of energy could be interpreted in various ways; but it does seem, in any case, to
betoken an effort to adjust one's performance
or "articulate" one's actions to the presence
or actions of others, or to what one imagines
the quantitative level of their activity to be.
Even though one might prefer to attribute the
socially facilitating effect to unconscious
rivalry, level of aspiration, or ego feeling,
the inference is still plausible that there is
an attempt to adjust in one's own way to
others; and that this effort actually requires
the existence of some sort of group pattern.
A dependable collective situation or ensemble
is *necessary* for the expression of such trends
of personality; otherwise these characteristics
would have neither the milieu nor the standard of judgment needed for their exhibition
and appraisal. In the conversational expan-
siveness of style and the reduction of personal
associations in one's thought stream, the same
tendency toward "interstructuring" with
others appeared. Here again it seemed as
though the subject were reacting for the
benefit of present and watchful eyes, even
though he knew that, though they were
present, they were not watching; and in such
a fashion as to create the impression (even
though those so impressed would never be
giving any evidence of it) that he is "out-
going," "convivial," and "fitting-in."

Possibly one could sum all this up as an
intuitive effort for "security" among one's
fellows, a striving so habitual and deep that
it is represented in one's unconscious inner
meanings even when the overt situation does
not realistically call for it. From a more objective standpoint, the writer would prefer to
call it simply a deep-seated tendency so to
act as to establish some sort of a give-and-
take, *structural*, relation with one's fellows—
to be "not left adrift" but included as a part
of a present collectivity; or to help create, if
necessary, such a structural relationship so
that one *can* be a part of it. Let the motives,
interpreted consciously and teleologically, be
what they will, let them be manifest or latent

—they all "feed into," or "eventuate in," the fact or existence of some sort of *collective structure* that is being formed, and formed with all the greater inevitability, perhaps, because its genesis is largely unconscious. Nothing could be gained by adding a new (structurizing) "instinct" to the long and largely discredited list of instincts of the past. But where there seems to be such an inevitable result as this, may we not assume, as in all learned adjustments, that wherever the possibility of a ubiquitous and general means of fulfillment is present, probability alone (as in trial and error) might lead to its being employed. Collective structuring, in other words, could be considered as the result of the heightened probability of satisfactions through integrated or articulated behaviors, a probability that is afforded by the presence and potential interactions of others.

We can now return to the task of explaining how norms arise, and to the search for the basis of our explanation in these simple coworking or coexperiencing assemblies. In terms of the experiments, why did the mean of the estimates of the individuals' perceptions in Sherif's experiments come to be an anchor, so that the judgments converged toward it, giving a narrower spread of reactions in the group than when the subjects worked alone? And why was a similar convergence of judgments in the group situation found in the writer's experiments on judgments of odor pleasantness and weight, even when the subjects did not communicate?

For the purpose of weighing the plausibility of the interpretations of so-called group effects that we have given in this section, the reader is now asked to put himself, imaginatively, in the place of the subjects in these experiments, and to test our assumption of "collective structuration" and its possible relation to these convergence phenomena. Suppose that the reader is judging with others the extent of apparent movement of the spot of light. He believes it to have been a very extensive or extreme movement; but the others, reporting before him, have all given estimates centering about a considerably smaller figure. If now he were to give his original "extreme" estimate, unmodified, would he not feel somewhat ill at ease? Might

he not, perhaps, even refrain from giving this estimate and substitute a smaller one? And if so, why?

Let us first take the perceptual social norm theory at face value. Here we explain the convergence tendency by saying that the social stimulation actually changed the subjects' *conscious experience* of the light's movement. There was a direct social effect upon the process of perceiving and the percept as such. We might interpret this effect, perhaps, as similar to what happens in cases of extreme suggestibility where the experience borders upon hallucination. But this is a no man's land of psychology, too vague as to what is happening to afford good explanations. Besides, the really important question would still remain—why was the reader suggestible with respect to stimulation *from the group?* As an alternative explanation, the reader might say that though he "perceived" the movement as he did, in view of the strongly dissenting view of all the others, he might honestly think that he must be mistaken about its actual movement; and so he might tend to report a lesser movement to "correct his error." This reaction would be uncooperative so far as the investigation was concerned; for it would be a clear violation of the experimenter's instruction to report the movement of the light as it actually *looked.*

To take still another alternative, and usually a favored one, the reader might say that the reason why he would feel uncomfortable in giving the deviating judgment would be because it would make him appear conspicuous, different from the others, or "nonconforming," or that it might either reveal the fact, or give some ground for the others to believe (truly or falsely), that he was a less competent, perhaps even a less intelligent, judge than the others. These reasons may be sound so far as they go, but are they complete? Why does one avoid being conspicuous in a group? Shall we attribute it to some sort of "instinct"? And what is behind this desire always to conform? Is this also an instinct, or does one do it because he feels that others expect it? But if this is so, why *should* they expect it? What does it do that is in some way baneful to their interrelationships or modus vivendi if they do *not* all act alike?

16   Floyd H. Allport

Besides one is not required to conform in everything he does in a group at all times. What then "selects" the behaviors on which conformity will be expected, and how is the pressure to conform imposed?

The explanation that the subject by changing his estimate is avoiding the implication of being less competent than the others, has, like the other explanations, an element of plausibility. But still, if he changes his estimate to save face, he really does not deceive *himself*. He can scarcely regard himself as a more competent perceiver than if he stuck to his original estimate, though he might conceivably convince himself that he really did not see it in the way he thought he had originally. But suppose he did suffer, under the "social influence," this sort of self-deception, or self-uncertainty. Would this not show a fairly strong tendency of susceptibility to what others are experiencing and the judgments they are making? And should this factor therefore not be fully as basic in our explanation of his behavior as his desire for vindication or "consonance" in his self-concept? And if the subject changed his estimate merely because he just wanted to *appear* competent, then we must at once recognize, as a required prima-facie addition to the "ego" motive, the important role of the *others*, that is, of the collective pattern of which the subject's activity is a part and in which his "appearing" is done.

In every case, therefore, we come back to the realization that the answers given above do not tell the whole story. Until we have found additional answers or some broader basis or hypothesis we must conclude that the convergence phenomenon is not yet fully explained.

Is there any alternative we have not tried? Yes, there is one. It lies in the direction we have earlier staked out and have hinted at in the analysis of ego motives just given, namely, that of the coming into existence of a psychologically grounded "collective structuring" of the individuals. Let the reader now begin again in a "negative" way by asking himself what the full consequences would be if he did *not* "converge" in his judgments toward the mean of the group. If instead of giving a similar response, he gave a *widely deviating*

reaction, what would be the effect upon others and upon their relationships with him. If one grants the premise that there is developing in the situation a relationship of give-and-take and a sense of "camaraderie" or "belonging," subtle and scarcely conscious, but nonetheless real, one might find in this very fact a natural explanation for the avoidance of the deviant response. Would the reason why the reader might feel ill at ease in giving a deviant reaction not be because such a reaction would run counter to these subtle attitudes or feelings of bonhomie that were established or were beginning to develop? Would it not be like spurning those with whom ties of fellowship were beginning to develop? Is it not at least a mild form of rejection to let it be known, even as a part of some routine occupation, that "I do not agree with you"?

Such a sense of the others we might well suppose to have been present even in the group situations used by the writer, in which the subjects did not communicate. To make an extreme judgment of an odor or a weight is to *run greater chances* of spurning or disregarding the judgments of one's associates, in effect, than if one makes a more moderate estimate. Psychologically the subjects were probably sensitive to one another's presence fairly continually, as the summary of the experiments and the introspections would indicate. Our own "probability" estimate of the appraisals, attitudes, expectations, and values of our fellows is with us no less truly than overt indications of these states on their part, and probably more continuously. One could easily imagine what would happen to the developing "we" feeling, or sense of solidarity, in a group situation if everyone sought to *diverge* from his fellows as much as possible in his judgments. And with the loss of these psychological components (cognitions or meanings) of being "bound" or united, that is, of being in readiness for reciprocally giving and receiving the rewards of cordial affiliation in the situation, the potentiality for what we have called the collective structure would be no more. One may well suppose that it would be on its way to extinction even if the diverging judgments were unexpressed but the individuals were cognizant of their probable divergence.

Is this not, then, the answer to the problem of the norm? Is the norm not merely some behavioral stipulation or practice which if adhered to will be conducive to the formation, or continued existence and operation, of a structure in which the individuals have some degree of *"involvement,"* that is, which they value and wish to preserve, a practice any marked deviation from which would tend to preclude or disrupt such a structure?

This conception also elucidates the matter of conformity, for which we found it difficult to assign a basic motive. Conformity, from this view, would be an *effect* and not a *cause*. Because individuals are similarly constituted, and those acts or omissions which would tend to foster or to disrupt their (valued) collective structure will be the same for all, the practices which they *individually* follow will be uniform throughout the collectivity. Their behavior with respect to the so-called norm, in other words, will be similar; and the belief may arise that this similarity is pursued and fostered as an end in itself. The individuals are said "to conform." Such conformity, however, in the primary condition, is merely the clustering of a statistical distribution under the influence of a common variable, and not a psychological fact or motive.

Traditional thinking to the contrary notwithstanding, the writer would maintain that *there is in human beings no such thing as a general and basic tendency, or drive, to conform. Nor is any systematic control or pressure toward conformity exerted by leaders, or by individuals upon one another, except as such uniformity of behavior is the result of pressure toward some other objective.* Whenever there is a pluralistic situation in which in order for an individual (or class of individuals) to perform some act (or have some experience) that he "desires" to perform (or for which he is "set") it is necessary that *another* person (or persons) perform certain acts (either similar or different and complementary to his own), we have what can be called a fact of collective structure. The structure is either collectively actualized or "potential," according to whether the desires are being carried out through the enabling action of the other person, or remain merely covert as sets or meanings in the individuals concerned. Though this situation, in which a large number of persons are seen to be doing the same thing, or doing one or the other of two complementary types of things, has been called "conformity," such a term is misleading in that it wrongly implies some basic compulsion on the part of the individuals to do what other individuals are doing. It is as inaccurate, for example, to describe the action of two motorists in avoiding a collision as basically due to "conformity in obeying the rule of the road" as it would be to speak of the performance of the sex act as a matter of "conformity."

An individual really does not "perform a sex act." He performs certain behaviors. The sex act really represents (or contains) a fact of *structure*. The notion of human performance, since that means always performance of *individuals*, does not properly encompass it. It represents a juncture (or "event-region") of a collective structure that is composed of certain behaviors of two individuals. It is a reciprocating (that is, self-closing) articulating of the specific acts of two individuals, a structuring at the individual order, into one inclusive *collective* structure. A "marriage" consists of a mutually tangent *set* of such inclusive structures (of many sorts as to the "meanings" involved) articulated through event-contacts into a more complex (or "global") structuring of the behaviors of the two individuals (*à deux* collective structure). To call a marriage, or a family of husband and wife, a (dyadic) group is a loose way of speaking which gives the erroneous impression that the elements of the aggregate are total individuals (whole biological organisms and personalities) rather than the structured behaviors specifically involved. Such usage therefore conceals the true structural nature of the aggregate.

And so with every instance of a plurum in which a situation cannot be adequately described without tracing the interlocking or self-closing "juncturing" of the behaviors of individuals. This is the nature of *collective reality*. This is *structure* at the collective order. While dealing with this subject the writer would also express his conviction that the above is a *general principle of nature,* that it appears at *all* levels, organismic, molecular, atomic, etc., as well as at the societal order. Thing, particle, organism, individual, and group—these are all agent-like terms which, like the "corporate fiction" of jurisprudence, are used as conveniences in our thinking. Wholenesses, or totalities, must be sought not in "things" or "agents," for matter, as commonly conceived, does not provide a workable paradigm of wholeness. Nor do they lie in the notion of open-ended, linear, and "molarly" conceived acts of such agents. They lie, instead, in (completed or self-closed) structures of ongoings and events. Actually, we live in and through *structuring* at all levels; and it behooves us to try to understand its general forms and laws.

Conformity may of course be "worked up" into a secondary motive or principle of action; but its roots would probably reside as before in the desire to maintain a collective structure. A group leader may encourage the idea of a "group entity" or "agency" that is believed to be "imposing" such a norm upon the individuals and thus *demanding* conformity or obedience. By our hypothesis the fictitious character of the "conformity-demanding" referent of such thinking is evident. Psychologically, the fact that there *is such a way of thinking* is, of course, all too real. Individuals are *aided* in controlling others (and themselves), whether for good or for ill, through the belief that the standards they practice are the "rules" or "norms" actually laid down by a "superindividual" institution or a "society." The belief in such a "norm giver," or "obedience-enforcer," as an actual being, is usually disclaimed when the individual is pressed to make a logical analysis. But it is worthy of note that there is a certain reluctance to do so; and almost never do we find an attempt being made to think out or explore the full realities that must be substituted if one is to understand what actually happens in the situation we call obedience to social or juristic norms.

In explaining the origin of norms as the discovery and confirmation of practices that preserve and facilitate the structure we have automatically thrown some light on why certain practices or dimensions of behavior are

"chosen" as norms and not others, that is, on the question of why norms are specific to the group and the situation at hand. To return once more to the earlier group experiments, we have suggested that wide deviation of judgments in regard to what the subjects were experiencing probably would have led to the loss of a feeling of camaraderie and to the breakdown of the potentiality for the structure. If this is so then the opposite trend, a clinging fairly close to the central tendency of judgment, would help to forestall this undesired outcome. Hence judging fairly closely to the level of the group average, actual or probable, as the experiment progressed, became the norm. On this basis one might predict what behaviors would be likely, in any group situation, to *become* norms. The introspections in the writer's experiments reported, in connection with the facilitation effect, a certain feeling of obligation to keep working (keep writing) because the others were doing so. Again, such behavior facilitates the "structural" sense. If one had laid down his pencil and sat back, it would probably have been disturbing, no less to the individual himself than to the others.[10]

The multiplication task showed a possible tendency to become confused at what might have been the awareness that one is making mistakes that probably the others were not making. The collective structuring here leads to negative rather than positive self-feeling. It seems to imply an incipient, and perhaps unconscious, self-imposed standard of "accuracy" as a condition for "belonging with the others." Or again, if in the writing of the essays or the associative trains of words the subject had lapsed into subjective reflections or soliloquy, he would probably have felt ill

---

[10] This observation introduces a new element which of course was present in all these group situations and was omitted in the discussion only to simplify our argument. There was an obligation of the subjects also (and perhaps primarily) to the experimenter to carry out his instructions. The experimenter also (that is, his behaviors and attitudes) must be considered as a part of the total collective structure —or rather, as representing a *special* structure with each subject which existed at times independently of the structure with the subject's co-workers (when the subjects worked alone), and at times in tangency with the latter structure (in the *together* sessions).

at ease, as though he were "out of context." It would be as if the others, if they *could* know what he was thinking, would regard him as reclusive or withdrawn, and hence as "not participating in the structure." We thus see that the subjects, individually, were tacitly enacting what would probably have been overtly and explicitly stated as norms had circumstances warranted.

Here we have the structural version of the interiorization-exteriorization phenomenon so often recognized in systems of social psychology. One rather sharp realization, however, that comes in this connection is that the direction is here altered. There is an exteriorization *to* the collectivity, in our theory, from the "expansion" or environmental "actualization" of the structures of "meaning" within the individual's (interiorized) structure, rather than an effect in the reverse direction as social determinists have assumed. Structuring in other words must proceed from "lower" orders into "higher" orders of compounding. All this might well interest the social scientist as having a bearing on the question of social origins. Mores, customs, and other social norms, are as a rule unwritten, yet they are followed. They are sometimes considered by sociologists to go back to "time immemorial," and to be "vestiges" persisting by social inertia or lag. If our present view is correct, however, this is far from true. Instead, they should be thought to arise spontaneously; and their origin is not ancient but, in everything but a few formal details, continually present and immediate. Causation, in the structural view, is not historical nor linear, but continuous, time independent, and reciprocally cyclical. One looks for it neither in society *nor* in the individual, as traditionally seen as separate levels or agencies, but in the compounded patterns of structuring which are the essential reality underlying both.

Though we have traced the arising of norms as from interiorization to exteriorization, it should be noted that we are not coming back to individuals in the old telic-agent, or entity, sense. The same difficulty about referents for a "plurality of parts" that we have encountered in trying to find a referent for the group might face us in the last analysis with

respect to individuals. The conception we have arrived at is neither that of group nor of individuals in the older sense, but of the articulations or structurings of individuals' behaviors. These involve neither the total biological organism nor the (total) "personality" of the individual, but are patterns of "specialized segments" of behavior—cyclical acts and cyclical act sequences of such an explicit sort that through their "events of juncture" with the "act cycles" of other individuals they constitute the reciprocating, self-closing, patterns that we call the "individual" and the "social" orders. In all this, it will be noted that although we have discarded the group concept, at least in the older unanalyzed sense, we have by no means ignored the fact that there is a *collective* reality. This is represented by the fact that individuals' behaviors are not merely structured in and for themselves, but that they are also, in many instances, *inter*structured with one another to compose the more inclusive structures that we call collectivities. The collectivities also may in some cases be interstructured among themselves, composing assemblies of a still "higher" social order.

So much for the group experimental bases from which the reference frame and social norm theory were developed, and for our structural reconstruing of the evidence from that source. It remains now only to extend our methods to the larger organized, or institutional, situation within which also, the social norm theory has been elaborated. Many instances could be cited in which "conformity to a standard" takes on a more intelligible meaning when we see norm performance as a kind of behavioral structure or substructure that is, as it were, tangent to a certain collective structure, and necessary for the continuation of that structural pattern among the individuals concerned. Just as there are certain nonspecialized, convivial, "closures" gained in the smaller groups, (and indeed the group is predicated on just that fact) so in the operation of *any* enduring collectivity, such as an organization or institution, there are certain more specialized "rewards," the activities producing which bind the individuals together. And just as in the case of the small coacting group there arose certain implementing or facilitating behaviors, deviation from which

20   FLOYD H. ALLPORT

would have threatened this "cohesive" state
of affairs, so in every enduring collectivity
there are certain standards (or norms), arising
through experience, obedience to which is
conducive to the self-closing sequence of
events that constitute that structure's operation, and violation of which tends to be destructive of that same cycle of events. And
so, just as a statistical effect of "convergence"
toward the mean of estimates appeared in
the co-working situations, so uniformities of
behavior in a more elaborate, edict obeying,
or functional role sense appear in all the
larger institutional or societal aggregations,
the modal act in each case being uniquely
adapted to, and protective of, the structure
concerned.[11] Though deviation from the norm
folkway, custom, or rule of law is frowned on
and punished, the reason for this (like the
reason for the sense of being ill at ease in
deviations in experimental groups) lies not
in the desire for conformity as such, but in

---

[11] A documenting of this statement and this paragraph as a whole in behavior in various social institutions can be found in the experimental program
of the writer (Allport, 1934b, 1939; Allport &
Solomon, 1939) and his students that led to the
formulation of the "J-curve hypothesis of conforming
behavior." Due partly to certain inadequacies in its
presentation there were misunderstandings of the
earlier statement of this theory on the part of social
psychologists, especially as to the meaning of the
"telic continuum" on which the observed behaviors
were distributed. The matter can now be clarified
by conceiving the J-curve of clustering (not "conforming") behaviors as fitted into place at the
appropriate "event-regions" of space and time that
are the site of the junctures in the collective structure concerned. An example would be the J-distribu-
tion of "degree of stopping" that occurs in a traffic
intersection at the space-time region of a *stop
sign*, where the juncturing is such as to permit the
action of each motorist, in both of the two "direc-
tional" classes, to complete its cycle, without disruption, from the events of primary "need" (reason for
making the trip) back to "closure" (that is, reduction of that "need" or "reason") consequent to the
trip's completion. The norms we call traffic laws are
simply experience-based, codified stipulations which,
when practiced, enable these cyclical structures to
complete themselves, and when deviated from tend
to destroy (negate) these structures. The presence
of J-curve distributions has also recently been demonstrated on large populations by Woo (1948) and
the writer, in the practice of seven American male
customs (norms) as related to the specific collective
structures which they facilitate and protect.

its effect of diminishing the structure's operation, plus the damage or ultimate annihilation that might result to the structure itself
should such deviations go unchallenged.

It is not difficult to envisage such hazards
in any of our familiar collective structures.
Disobedience with respect to a norm of table
manners, for example, not merely mars a
social occasion and subjects the deviater to
reproof or perhaps to ostracism; it would, if
persistently or widely practiced, spell the
demise of the particular class distinction
known as the "elite," or "polite society." With
this would come the end of the usual give-
and-take relations among those who now make
up its personnel, the end of protocols and
practices that are predicated upon distinctions
of this sort. Failure of a man to earn a living
for his family, and marital infidelity, are discouraged not only for the immediate interests
of the parties involved, but because these
breaches of norms might, not only in this
particular case but generally, disrupt the
structures of "matrimony" and the "family."
To violate the norm of "freedom of the press"
by instituting censorship would challenge not
only the personality trends for "independence"
in Americans, but the large and elaborate
structures that constitute the news disseminat-
ing business. For church officials to cease
stressing the norm that labels birth control a
sin would not only go against the *personal*
convictions of many church adherents; it
might also weaken the significance to parish-
ioners of those important substructures of
ecclesiastic-parishioner behavior known as the
sacraments. Not to stand when the "Star
Spangled Banner" is played would bring reproof not merely because it shows a lack of
patriotism on the part of the deviant, but
because such behavior, if sufficiently multiplied, would result in uncertainty and distrust
with respect to our personal security, since it
would be a threat to the national structure
of which our life-sustaining activities are an
inalienable part. This list of norms and their
bases is stated, it is true, partly in terms of
all-or-none types of prescribed acts as well as
in terms of the threshold degrees or quantities
of action required. Perhaps, however, for that
very reason they give the logic of our structural explanation a wider basis.

A further principle that is both interesting and important is implied in the preceding examples. There are usually two classes of rewards (or "provisients") of structures, or perhaps two substructural processes in close relation, that are safeguarded by norm obedience. The first is what might be called the regular or *in-course* rewards. These are the continuing outcomes of individuals' participations. They can be immediate; for example, there are the ego satisfactions derived as one mingles as a member in polite society, the newsman's profits in news gathering and publishing enterprises, the benefits and satisfactions, in marriage, of living with a mate, and the feelings of spiritual uplift experienced in religious worship. Or they can be delayed as in the case of the wages paid to the worker. The second class of rewards in structural participation are of two types. They are the indications that the structure *will be likely to continue its operation* (that is, tokens are given by the individuals to one another symbolizing their intent and readiness to continue playing their parts); and the indications given to an individual that *he is accepted* in the structure and that he will probably be able in the future to *hold his place* in it. These rewards, are, of course, more in the nature of meanings rather than of material goods. But it is usually important that the over-all provisients, occurring in, or resulting from, the structure's operations, from time to time include such tokens of confidence in the structure. We might call these tokens, or the acts connected with them, *structural assurances*. They include formal signs, special phrases, shibboleths, and the like, that belong to certain circles and must be used upon certain occasions. They include also emblems of authority and membership validations, certifications in businesses and professions, symbols of national or governmental agencies, and tokens of the permanence and sanctity of religious institutions or personnel. Marriages and families with a feeling of unity and security among the members are not unlikely to be those in which anniversaries, birthdays, and similar occasions are remembered by suitable words or tokens. All these provisients are like the oil in the oil gauge that tells us the engine is working properly and will not be expected to break down.

The writer believes it to be one of the major supports of his hypothesis that so much is made of these "structural assurance" provisients in collective aggregates and organizations. If the negative of this were true, the hypothesis would certainly seem doubtful. For such assurances, having always a future reference, underlie the *time independence* (endurance) of these structurings, without which there would be no truly stable human relations. Though their "dynamic" is secondary, that is, it comes mainly and in the long run from the regular *in-course* rewards of the structure, they are necessary for the continuance of those rewards. It should be noted also that they are *specific to them*. To try, for example, to interchange the structural assurance acts or tokens of polite society with those peculiar to government, church, or marriage, or to try to interchange any of the latter with one another, would be a prima-facie absurdity. This way of putting it, however, brings out the structural or potentially structural character of collective facts.

Some assurance value of course attaches to the regular in-course provisients of the structure; but there are usually also special structural assurance provisients that are required. In certain cases there are whole *substructures* of reciprocal and formal token giving and receiving acts that are "tangent," as it were, to the main in-course cycle of the total structure or to other "assurance cycles." There are also corresponding "assurance needs," (primary upsets or disequilibria in individuals) that are attendant upon this process and must be occasionally or periodically satisfied through the "closure" of the formal substructure concerned. Especially important for our present purpose is the fact that such assurance providing substructures often become the focus of norms that are adhered to rigidly, often fanatically. Having the visibility of "oil gauges" they become the stipulations for efforts to create, preserve, and extend the structural bases concerned. So-called obedience to a norm, whether it be a norm of in-course participation or of structural assurance, is as truly, and even more basically, a *cause* or *support* of group existence and group action than it is an effect. We come nearer to understanding it when we consider it as continuing structural phenomenon (or structurizing process) rather than a manifestation of a "social influence" on perception or behavior, or an aspect of group determinism in the traditional and unanalyzed sense of the term.

The normative, perceptual, and cognitive systems of social psychology have done much, both experimentally and theoretically, to bring these important matters to attention and to show that collectivities, however they may be described, have a real existence and should be studied. A logical analysis of certain fictions, however, and a more intimate observational approach to what actually happens between or among individuals, are needed to bring us closer to a solution of the master problem. When these aids are enlisted one is able to reconstrue the facts so well adduced by the phenomenologically and normatively oriented theories into a more objective and explicit conceptual model. In this model not merely percepts, subjective anchors, and values, but the actual patterning of intra-individual events, producing collectivities in a more overt and physicalistic sense can be brought to bear.

We turn now to other theories. In the one next to be discussed the answer to the master problem is given through a revivified version of the more traditional notion of the group, in which a collectivity is conceived not merely as a norm giver, but as a truly dynamic and behavior determining agency.

Field Theory and Group Dynamics— Structural Reinterpretations

Although frame of reference theory leaned somewhat toward social determinism as the mean of individuals' perceptions, it did not elaborate the group concept by ascribing to it special dynamic processes or laws. It was but a step to this postulate however, and its development was spurred by the practical usefulness of such a view. If the investigator fixes his attention upon collective episodes wholly within a group frame of reference (without being too hesitant about using collective fictions), he may be able to formulate a science of group action or group perform-

ance, that is, a system having quantitative functional relations between variables stated entirely at the collective level. Such a program has actually been carried out in the movement known as *group dynamics*.

Any experimental program in social psychology will be likely to be based upon some background theory about individuals and groups. Serving this purpose for group dynamics, at least at the start, was the psychological field theory originated by Kurt Lewin (1936, 1947). The group reality was conveniently represented in this theory in the form of a topological field (life-space) with its boundaries, subregions, goals with their positive or negative valences, and vectors of "psychological forces" acting upon individuals. The life-spaces of the individuals overlapped and, taken together, represented the life-space of the group. The answer which this theory has given to the "master problem" is stated in phenomenological rather than physicalistic terms, as follows: *The individual is a point within the life-space (field) of the group. This field is under tension due to (unbalanced) social forces acting in it; and the individual is pulled this way and that by the resultant of whatever forces are operative, as the field seeks to come to equilibrium.* The forces were conceived as related to tensions *within the individual*. There was also said to be a "locomotion" of the *individual (or group) through intervening regions toward a goal* (or away from it if the goal was negative). The distinction between the individual and group in respect to life space, motivation, and locomotion was often blurred. It was not clear whether the individual goals were also the group goal, that is, as the combined similar objectives of so many individuals, or whether the "group as a whole" was conceived as having a separate goal of its own, resulting from the integration of the individuals' different goal directed behaviors. In the latter case, the problem of understanding, in terms of a single field model, the *interrelationships* of the individuals' goal directed activities, or of representing in a single diagram both the individual and group levels of action, was even more baffling. In spite of these handicaps the model has had great vogue and has led to many useful interpretations and many experiments.[12]

Started by Lewin (1947, 1951) and systematized and documented by Cartwright and Zander (1953), group dynamics has been a discipline mainly of relatively small groups. This limitation was necessary from both an experimental and a theoretical standpoint, since the group situations had to be capable of being controlled. Hence the relation of individuals to one another in "institutions," or in the "great society," had to be correspondingly slighted.

The topological field theory was operationalized for experimental purposes by a further analogy. One can "interpret" the theory of forces in a group field by measuring the social outcomes that are said to be due to these forces. Since the outcomes are assumed to be proportional to the strength of the forces, such measures will serve to quantify the forces involved. *The social forces within the group represent pressures that are due to "field conditions" of group organization or process, inherent or imposed. The pooled statistics of the behaviors of the individual members (acting under such field conditions) are taken as measures of the "locomotion of the group" that is produced by these pressures.* For such a program, the name group dynamics seems fairly appropriate. The field conditions exerting the "pressures," and thus representing the *independent* variables, are exemplified by such group influences as "solidarity" or "cohesion," "group goals," place of residence, competition or cooperation, type of leadership, "social atmospheres," "social climates," and the "importance of an issue" to the group. Among the *dependent* variables ("group locomotions") one might mention attitudes, productions (quantity and quality), amount of communication, discussion directed toward changing the opinions of dissident members, conflicts, acceptance or rejection of individuals as members, and the adoption of common standards. A number of such hypotheses has been formulated and tested by Festinger and his colleagues (1950). Within this general framework much has been learned

[12] For an instructive diagrammatic employment of the model as related to group dynamics, see French (1941).

about the effects of these independent "group variables" upon these "group outcomes" or "locomotions." Both the program and the theoretical model of group dynamics, however, are broader than the above formulation would imply. Cartwright and Zander (1953) have republished and summarized examples of various ideologies and methods. For the general subject of "behavior in groups" one can consult Hare, Borgatta, and Bales (1955) and Thibaut and Kelley (1960).

In group dynamics as in other theories of social psychology we become acutely aware of the problem of the levels (group and individual) and of the dilemmas that come from being compelled to take some sort of stand regarding them. As pointed out earlier, if one talks about the group but does so in terms that apply also to individuals (as one naturally must in dealing with the dependent *experimental* variables), one must expect to run into tautologies. Here the using of the concept of a group in connection with the description adds no new content or meaning. The same is often true when one speaks of group conditions, as when an investigator speaks of groups under frustration or tension. In other instances the invoking of individual terminology may lead to group metaphors which, when actually applied to the acts or interests of all the individuals, are not truly designative. On the other hand, there are cases occurring in group dynamics, as elsewhere, in which, if one *does* concede that the description (that is, the variable to be measured) *is* something that a *group might properly be said to do,* or a property that a group *could have,* there is then at hand no denotable evidence of any group that is doing this act or having this property. This is the case when one speaks of social norms, of group pressures, or of cohesiveness, as a property of a group. What is here *predicated* of the "agent" seems appropriate; but the agent itself, as an actual doer of the act, or a denotable possessor of the property, is missing. We see no group that is "pressing" on the individuals, or is "sticking together."

When the group dynamicist speaks of the "attraction of the group for the individual" does he not mean just the attraction of the individuals for one another? If individuals are all drawn toward one another, are they not *ipso facto* drawn to the group? Or, on the other hand, does the group dynamicist mean the attractiveness to the individuals of some complex of interrelationships, or of the interactions of each of them with each of the others, by virtue of which they are all classified as members of the group? Does he define "attraction" to mean, *inter alia*, the possession of some common interest or common bond? If such are his meanings, and if this complex of interactions, or the common interest, is not kept at the focus of attention and perhaps specified when the term attraction is used, then an ambiguity is likely to be fostered. If it *is* to be specified, we shall then probably have to recite a whole nexus of meanings (embracing various individuals) so complex as to make the notion of attraction to the group too inexplicit to serve as an experimental variable.

But we need at this point to clarify our position. The exponent of the theory may claim that for his purpose it makes no difference just what form our definitions take so long as we are consistent. All that he is trying to do, he will say, is to take some set of operations which *can be called* "measuring the attractiveness of the group" and relate them experimentally to other measurable variables. If he can do this, then he can say that he has achieved a useful purpose in making predictions possible; and he has, moreover, been able to do so without going into the minutiae of exactly what the term "attractiveness" means. One could cite as a parallel case the situation in S-R learning theory in which terms are invented whose full significance is not understood (reinforcement, drive, habit strength, etc.), but which facilitate operations of measuring and relating variables, operations which themselves are never vague or in doubt as to their meanings.

With this the writer has no serious quarrel. He is only saying that there are other objectives also for which concepts need to be defined. Though it is not essential to the prediction and control of outcomes of collective action that we subject such terms as group pressures, group goals, group attraction, and group cohesiveness to semantic scrutiny, it *is* necessary that we do so if we are to solve

the problem to which we are here committed. The exponents of group dynamics have devised their operations and their experiments at the individual level. This has been necessary because groups have for us no denotation independent of that of individuals. But they have then proceeded to talk about these matters at the group level. The question we are asking is this: What is the value of such a way of talking when we consider it not for the purpose of predicting group variables or outcomes significant for group management, but for the purpose of understanding what is happening as these changes in variables appear?

Let us examine the alleged parallel from learning theory. In the first place it must be noted that the cases are not strictly comparable. In learning theory, as pointed out in the opening section of this article, there was a much better denotational base (the rat) for postulating some nondenotable variable (such as habit strength) than existed in the group formulations for the group related variables; and this basis made it possible to attain better control and precision in experimenting. But even if this were not true, the citing of what is done in research in learning does still not justify the neglect of the more careful analysis of concepts that is required for basic formulations. In the case of learning theory though it is true that the operations and data which can be rationalized by such terms as "reinforcement" or "habit strength" lead, in part because they *are* so rationalized, to useful laws concerning the quantity of learning achieved under different conditions, can anyone seriously say that these concepts, both of them metaphorical, or even the quantitative laws into which they help to order the data, are adequate descriptions of the occurrences taking place *in an organism* as the organism "learns"? If learning is to be *completely* understood, these molar concepts of learning in which the process is seen "from the outside" must ultimately be related in some way to neuronic assemblies, synaptic and humoral transmission, and the relation of "information" to molecular processes. Even the most thoroughgoing molar psychologist would probably not be such an "isolationist" as to deny this statement. Is it not so, also, when we try to extrapolate our "individual" observations to description at the "group" level? If the antireduction experimentalist cannot deny at least the *relevance* of structurings at the organic level (that is, within the individual) to the level of description in which he is interested, can the group dynamicist, who must use the lower level elements (individuals) *to work with* or he will have nothing, escape in his account of group processes (group attractiveness, pressures, locomotion, and the like) the responsibility for describing what these individuals are doing as all this group activity takes place? Until the individual and the social levels have been tied together through some clear and systematic theory, a task that has not been accomplished in group dynamics, we must expect our social science to be *ad hoc* rather than distinterested and rigorous.

Even from their own pragmatic position there seems to be some need of caution lest predictions go awry. We may ask, first, what group sampling methods have been used for ascertaining the "laws of groups." Though there have been various degrees of permanence and stability in the group situations employed, such data and indices are usually obtained from the population of a small aggregates, under fairly specific conditions, sometimes involving a definite place basis or a set of particular circumstances.

Then too, the problem of "partial inclusion" becomes important. A familiar method in group dynamics experiments is to assemble and treat the data in group-wise fashion. Means of individuals, percentages, numbers of cases in certain categories, and the like, have been computed as indices of measurement of the group variable. The fact is not experimentally provided for that the individuals from whose behavior the "group laws" have to be derived belong also to other groups. The same individual can belong to many. What the individual does in one group, or merely his relation to that group, may have an important bearing upon what he does in another group; and the total "group membership manifold" of one individual who is a member of a particular group may be widely different from the manifolds of the other members. Personality characteristics of individuals

may also be related both to their choices of groups and to some degree to their behavior in those groups. How tenuous, shifting, and contingent group entities turn out to be!

If one wishes to say that although these things are true there is still in all groups a *residue of sameness* (other variables being held constant) just because they *are* groups (and since we are seeking laws of "the group" *as such*, we are interested *only* in these samenesses) or if one says that he wishes to consider a group, by definition, as a thing only of the moment, a "gathering"—then it is true that we do not need to worry about the other group involvements or the personality characteristics of the individuals who compose it. But in so limiting our problem we would have to be reconciled to overlooking not only group differences, uniquenesses, and inconsistencies, but a great deal of the significance of "group affiliation" in the lives of human beings. A "pure" collective level, with laws all to itself, might be a pretty arid thing. Laws of group dynamics that work perfectly at such levels might turn out to be more or less limited by the investigators' selection and methodology.

What we are dealing with as the group reality, both in simple co-working situations and in aggregations with high affiliative involvement, is, as has been previously noted, more like "segments" of individuals' behavior patterns that have become in one degree or another organized with similar segments of the behaviors of others, than it is like an aggregate of whole individuals. The individual himself is a sort of matrix in which these patterns of collectively organized segments meet and affect one another. Instead of saying that a group incorporates (or is composed of) many individuals, we would do almost better to say that an individual incorporates many groups. One group has salience for him (that is, he is present in it or acting in terms of it) at one time, and another has salience at another time. When not salient for the individual, a group to which he belongs could be said to be represented in his own organism as sets, latent meanings, or stored memories.

Though the problem of partial inclusion has been recognized by workers in group dynamics (Cartwright & Zander, 1953, p. 146; Festinger, 1950), they do not seem to have found a solution for it in terms of their own system. Then too, other types of questions that have arisen, and have been noted by these investigators themselves, betray a similar lack of clarity in the line which separates the ontology of individuals from that of groups. Who, for example, exerts the pressure upon individual members for conformity? Since this is perhaps seldom the work of a sole specific agent or group monitor, we must seek an additional explanation. Do the individual members coerce *one another* (and themselves)? If so, by what process do they do it? Or again, how can one explain the tenacity of group standards? Under what circumstances do they change? Or, when we say that certain questions for discussion are important for the *group,* what do we mean? Does this mean anything more than "important for the individuals"? If so, how do we spell it out? By what process does an individual goal become a group goal? What sense does it make to speak of a group goal becoming an individual goal? Was not the group goal always a goal of individuals? In such questions we see the logical difficulties attending almost any form of societal determinism.

It is suggested that these dilemmas arise from trying to treat an hypostatized entity (group) that cannot be uniquely denoted as though it *could* be denoted. Can we not resolve the difficulty by a different approach? The writer would again offer for this purpose the interpretation of a collectivity as a reciprocating structuring of the segments of individuals' behaviors. But we shall here first elaborate that conception a little more in quasigeometric terms. The collective or group level of structure is made up of, and only of, these acts of individuals. Such behaviors of individuals separately are in turn structures at a lower (individual) order. The model is thus self-closing, or cyclical, throughout and at all levels. It starts with an "upset," or events in a "primary event region" (disequilibrium, "need," etc.), in an individual, and returns through the sequence of actions of all concerned, including the individual himself, back to the original "region of upset" in that individual. This return of acts to the primary event region, which is called

"closure," changes the earlier state of affairs back toward equilibrium. It should be noted that if the collectivity is constant and enduring (as groups more or less are), each individual in it will probably be seen to be a possible "closure person." The model holds not only for two individuals but for any number. To mention the full geometric possibilities in the latter case would take us too far afield. But the structure, in any case, can readily be shown to be cyclical and self-closing and, as such, can be illustrated in aggregates of any size or degree of elaboration.

It will be remembered that the building of the informal or the co-working group (structure) was pictured as the beginnings of the operation of a self-closing sequence of acts and rewards of "bonhomie," involving an individual's segments of behavior "reciprocating" with those of others. Such self-closing sequences were said to be subtly valued or desired by the individuals. We pointed out that that which often *looks like* "group determinism," "direction," or "group pressure," may not really be such, but may be better understood as the things which the individuals are doing to establish or preserve just this cyclism of interactions and their rewards. What looks like "group controls" are really structurizing behaviors of individuals. We are dealing with a process of *collective structurization* of individuals' behaviors that *eventuates* in establishing or preserving the "group" (that is, the structure), rather than with a process of the determination of individual behavior *by* a group. The term group "influence," or the idea of the influence of the group *upon* the individual, is therefore a misnomer or a misconception. The laws we are concerned with, by this hypothesis, are laws of "structurogenesis" in the collective human sphere, *not* laws of "social agency" or the "dynamics of groups."

The writer concedes that this interpretation seems to apply more directly to such phases as structure *formation* and *assurance rewards* than to regular in-course operations of an "established" structure. The principle, however, will still hold in a broad sense, and this interpretation will help us to translate the working program of group dynamics into a somewhat more rational form.

Let us now take the questions quoted earlier as presenting dilemmas for this program. The question of who exerts the pressure to conform has already been answered, both here and in the discussion of norms, by pointing out that there *is* no such pressure. What looks like it is really only a narrowed statistical distribution that results from the fact that acting in a certain way in a certain situation is necessary on the part of all the (similarly constituted) individuals in order for a structure that was establishing itself among their segments of behaviors to be formed and survive. And when we speak of a discussion question that is "important for the group," we could, in this view, mean a question that closely bears upon this structuration process. We could mean the bearing of the acts of individuals, as specific events, on the collective structure per se, including both its operational (or in-course) provisients and its structural assurances. Considerations which we might call the "geometry of the structure" could here be important. In order to translate into structural concepts the notion of a group goal we would abandon the linear teleological implication of goal and substitute the cyclically accruing "provisient output" (material or nonmaterial) of the structure concerned. Where the individual goal is said to be identical with the group goal this phenomenon can be explained by the hypothesis that there is structure of meaning (meaning cycle) in the individual's organism that is, more or less, a conceptual replication of the *collective* structure concerned, a structure of which his own behaviors are a part. This is the event-structural interpretation of "exteriorization and interiorization." We must remember also that "partial inclusion," which is explained by the fact that the structure is one of "segmentalized" reactions and not anatomical persons, permits the individual many such group goal replications (identifications), and also permits that some of his organismic structures (as for example personality trends) are not in *any* collective structurization. The individual, we have said, is in part a "matrix," a relating (or tangency) in his own structural system of the many collective structures in which his (segments of) behavior play a part. Partial inclusion, it will be noted, is capable

of fairly clear formulation in terms of the structural hypothesis.

Finally, for group standards or prescriptions, a generalizing of our interpretation of norms will provide the needed clarification. We can think more broadly of the norm as typifying any structure of behavior that is tangent to a main collective structure. As we have seen, such tangent structures often have the probability of being either facilitating or inhibiting to the collective structure under consideration. The behaviors involved in such tangent structures as are facilitating represent the "positive" prescriptions, that is, the things which, one, as a participant in the structure, will be motivated to do, or the "quantities" or "degrees" in which one must act; while the behaviors inhibiting tangent structures become the "negative" prescriptions, the things one must not do. This further development of the topic opens up the employment of a basic concept that we can call *relevance* (really "interstructurance," in more rigorous terms); and through this notion we can relate not merely norm (structures) to the main collective structure, but any structure whatsoever to any other structure upon which it may impinge. Such interrelationships are of course, fundamental to motivation for (or in) a particular structure. The "intensity" of our behavior in a given structure is in part dependent upon these reinforcing or inhibiting effects received from positively or negatively related structures. The interstructurance relationship can be readily mathematized as a *relevance* (or *interstructurance*) *ratio*. It can have either a +, a −, or a 0 value. And as the reader will recognize, it is also a matter of degree. Certain tangent structures are *more* relevant (positively *or* negatively) to a main structure than certain other tangent structures; and the size of these relative ratios can be estimated upon a scale or otherwise empirically measured. Attempts to formulate and use such indices experimentally have met with success in the investigations of the writer and his students.

Group standards, therefore, can be conceived as tangent structures of stipulative, communicative, acts (or potential tangent structures represented in individuals' meanings) which have high positive relevance to

28   Floyd H. Allport

(interstructurance with) the main operational structuring of the collectivity concerned. They can also be conceived as "substructures" of this main structure. Circumstances, deliberate or fortuitous, may change the degrees, or perhaps even the sign, of their relevance to that structure. When that occurs the group standard will change.

As previously demonstrated, the structural cartography makes the behaviors of individuals integral (and integrated) parts of the group model. They must, in principle, be *shown*, and in their precise articulation with each other mapped out, or else no group (collective structure) can be either depicted or conceived. This consideration plays an important part in the translation into structural thinking of the experimental logic of group dynamics. Because of the conceptual vagueness and unsteadiness of the group as a working notion we have earlier expressed the wish for some other procedure than group indices as a method for the accumulation and treatment of the data. Such a basis is now afforded by the behaviors of *individuals*.

For an example let us turn to a question that has been central for group dynamics, namely, the definition of "group cohesiveness" as an independent variable, and the question as to how it can be measured. This task has been performed through a number of group indices, such as mean numbers of friendly comments or of friendships among the members, degree of the sharing of norms, and mean avoidance of absenteeism. For none of these methods do we seem to have any sure means of its validation as a measure of just this elusive variable.

To obtain a translation of the concept into structure theory terms let us go back to the early group experiments and seek its basis in connection with those findings. According to the interpretation we have given, the individuals, tacitly, perhaps unconsciously, desire the collective situation (structure) to come into existence or to endure. They receive provisients and closure from it; they have in it a definite interest and involvement. The one important quantitative variable we have not thus far exploited to any extent in our theory is the variable which is suggested by the question: *"how great* is that interest or involvement?"* And of course we must mean

"how great is it for the individual" (that is, for each participant)? This variable, as an index, expresses the concept we have called the *potency of involvement* of the individual in the structure concerned, or, in more general terms, his *index of structurance*. Its value will no doubt depend upon the number of provisients and the general amount of "closure" the individual receives through the structure's operation. It might also represent the amount of energy that goes into the individual's participating acts. For estimating it the writer has had success with a method of "equivalents" which he has called the "negative causation" method, which will presently be described. It is this structural index, then, the "structural quantics" or energy, or the "potency of involvement," that the writer offers as a basis for determining the equivalent in structural terms of group cohesiveness.

It is conceded that such an index may be more difficult to operationalize with certainty than the group-wise method of counting overt friendly contacts, tabulating instances of absenteeism, and the like. The following procedure used in the experiments of the writer and his students is offered merely as a suggestion. The logic of the concept of potency of involvement and the possibility of its role as a structural variable does not depend upon the employment of this particular method. In this procedure one asks the subject (on suitable questionnaire forms) to imagine that the group concerned (that is, one of the structures in which he is involved) is threatened with dissolution, or that he is in danger of losing his place in it. He is then asked what proportion of his spare time (or energy) he would be willing to give under these circumstances to "keep it going" or to "maintain his membership" in it. In individual terms, "cohesiveness of the group" is thus translated into "potency of involvement of the individual" in the structure. From those who hear of this method for the first time the almost inevitable reaction is that it is too introspective or subjective to be reliable. We shall not undertake to defend this point. The question here is merely whether, in the absence of an opportunity for more overt indications, this less than perfect method is better than no attempt to measure potency of involvement at all. In defense of the procedure we would note that the subject is not being asked to rate or appraise himself in any way; there is no apparent reason for any differential bias or evasive answering; and there is, in general, no one who could be expected to know better than the subject himself how important the group (that is, the structure) in question is to him. Still more to the point is the fact that, almost without exception, clear-cut positive results have been obtained upon hypotheses dealing with a considerable range of behaviors in which potency of involvement, measured in the way above indicated, was used as the basis of the independent variable.

If one grants that a measure of potency of involvement that is dependable can be made available, would not such a measure, when combined for all the members of a given group, represent in terms of individual meanings just what the group dynamicist is seeking as the referent of his group term "cohesiveness?" Such a "potency of involvement" of an individual in a group (structure) is probably not a simple thing. We would always regard our index (subject's answer to our question) as embodying also the effect of whatever increments of motivation (positive or negative) are accruing to the set to preserve the structure in question by reason of the subject's involvement in *other* (tangent) structures. For we remember that the individual is, in these respects, like a matrix of relationships of many groupings. We should also consider the individual's index of potency of involvement in a certain collective structure as embodying the effect of motivational increments, again positive *or* negative, that are received from his characteristics (inner "meaning" structures) of personality. There would thus be assumed to be attained in the organism a kind of algebraic summing of the effects from all these other sources, as well as from the structure immediately under investigation, to produce the individual's "net investment" in, or tendency to maintain, the collective structure concerned. Would not such a measure, when the individuals' indices are averaged (or totaled), give a clear operationalizing of the Festinger concept of group cohesiveness? What index could *better* represent "the resultant of all the forces acting upon all the individuals to leave, or to remain in," the group concerned?

With potency of involvement and relevance (that is, structurance and interstructurance) clearly defined and measured as variables, and applied to structural magnitudes and relations in all the different levels of structuring in an individual's (inner and outer) manifold, we now have before us the entire motivational basis of the individual as seen from the structural standpoint. We have in hand, in other words, the equipment for predicting the amount (or energies) in which almost any act structure typical of the individual's behavior may be expected to be performed. This means that we should be able to predict the amount of any dependent variable activity performed singly or jointly with others, such as the amount of discussion, "distortion" effects, acceptance or rejection of a proposal, attitudes, morale, conflicts, effort for consonance, energy put into any single or joint project, or any of the other dependent variables used in group dynamics or elsewhere. By weighting the amount of the subject's potency of involvement in all the structures of the subject's manifold having appreciable relevance to the behavior (structure) to be predicted, by the relevance ratios (+ or −) of those structures to the behavior (structure) to be predicted, and then summing all these increments algebraically, the independent variable for making such a prediction can be obtained. The sum or mean of such predictions for all the individuals in a group should provide one with the group index for the activity to be predicted, as dependent upon the combination of collective structures in the entire individual manifolds of the population making up the group from which the data were obtained.

This procedure would afford a prediction that *does* take into account all the other involvements of the individuals who happen to be in that group. The immediate group (structure) concerned, however, since it would be more "salient," might afford a greater increment of weight to the behavior to be predicted than other groups. Increments coming from relevance to *particular* groups (structures) can be separately studied as desired. If one wishes to find the strength of the *total* gamut of motivation, the increments from relevant personality trends (structures that are *in* the subject) are to be included.

30   Floyd H. Allport

One particular advantage of this translation
of group dynamics objectives into structural
methods is that the method is not limited
to small groups but can be used upon populations in larger collective aggregations, or institutions, of any size or scope.

The details and symbols of the "structural
quantics" equation explained verbally above
have been published elsewhere by the writer
(1954, 1955). To the reader is left the task
of envisaging its application to the prediction
of individuals' participations in significant
action programs or attitude commitments, between which actions and commitments and
the collectivities in which they are involved
there is appreciable interstructurance. A
résumé of experimental work already done in
this field will be published as soon as practicable. Judging from the positive results already
attained, there seems reason to hope that this
approach, through the aid of the event-structure principle, may be able to generalize and
unite in parsimonious fashion not only hypotheses of group dynamics but the findings
of many other classical experiments in social
psychology.

REFERENCES

Allport, F. H. The influence of the group upon
association and thought. *J. exp. Psychol.*, 1920,
3, 159–182.

Allport, F. H. The group fallacy in relation to
social science. *J. abnorm. soc. Psychol.*, 1924, 19,
60–73. (a)

Allport, F. H. *Social psychology*. Boston: Houghton
Mifflin, 1924. (b)

Allport, F. H. "Group" and "institution" as
concepts in a natural science of social phenomena.
Publ. Amer. Sociol. Soc., 1927, 22, 83–100. (a)

Allport, F. H. The psychological nature of political
structure. *Amer. pol. sci. Rev.*, 1927, 21, 611–
618. (b)

Allport, F. H. *Institutional behavior*. Chapel Hill:
Univer. North Carolina Press, 1933.

Allport, F. H. Individuals and their human environment. *Proc. Ass. Res. nerv. ment. Dis.*, 1934, 14,
234–252. (a)

Allport, F. H. The J-curve hypothesis of conforming behavior. *J. soc. Psychol.*, 1934, 5, 141–183. (b)

Allport, F. H. Toward a science of public opinion.
Publ. opin. Quart., 1937, 1, 7–23.

Allport, F. H. Rule and custom as individual variations of behavior distributed upon a continuum of
conformity. *Amer. J. Sociol.*, 1939, 44, 897–921.

Allport, F. H. Polls and the science of public
opinion. *Publ. opin. Quart.*, 1940, 4, 249–257.

Allport, F. H. Methods in the study of collective
action phenomena. *J. soc. Psychol.*, 1942, 15, 165–
185.

Allport, F. H. The structuring of events: Outline
of a general theory with applications to psychology.
Psychol. Rev., 1954, 61, 281–303.

Allport, F. H. *Theories of perception and the concept of structure*. New York: Wiley, 1955.

Allport, F. H. The contemporary appraisal of an
old problem. *Contemp. Psychol.*, 1961, 6, 195–196.

Allport, F. H., & Hartman, D. A. The measurement and motivation of atypical opinion in a
certain group. *Amer. pol. sci. Rev.*, 1924, 19,
735–760.

Allport, F. H., & Hartman, D. A. The prediction of
cultural change. In S. A. Rice (Ed.), *Methods in
social science*. Chicago: Univer. Chicago Press,
1931. Pp. 307–350.

Allport, F. H., & Solomon, R. S. Lengths of conversations: A conformity situation analyzed by the
telic contiuum and J-curve hypothesis. *J. abnorm.
soc. Psychol.*, 1939, 34, 419–464.

Asch, S. E. Effects of group pressures upon the
modification and distortion of judgments. In
G. E. Swanson, T. M. Newcomb, & E. L. Hartley
(Eds.), *Readings in social psychology*. (2nd ed.)
New York: Holt, 1952. Pp. 2–11. (a)

Asch, S. E. *Social psychology*. New York: Prentice-
Hall, 1952. (b)

Cartwright, D., & Zander, A. (Eds.) *Group dynamics*. Evanston: Row, Peterson, 1953.

Doob, L. W. *Social psychology; An analysis of human
behavior*. New York: Holt, 1952.

Festinger, L. Informal social communication.
Psychol. Rev., 1950, 57, 271–292.

French, J. R. P., Jr. The disruption and cohesion of
groups. *J. abnorm. soc. Psychol.*, 1941, 36, 361–377.

Hare, P., Borgatta, E. F., & Bales, R. F. (Eds.)
Small groups. New York: Knopf, 1955.

Hyman, H. H. The psychology of status. *Arch.
Psychol., N. Y.*, 1942, No. 269.

Kelley, H. H. Two functions of reference groups.
In G. E. Swanson, T. M. Newcomb, & E. L.
Hartley (Eds.), *Readings in social psychology*.
New York: Holt, 1952. Pp. 410–414.

Koffka, K. *Principles of gestalt psychology*. New
York: Harcourt, 1935.

Lewin, K. *Principles of topological psychology*. New
York: McGraw-Hill, 1936.

Lewin, K. Frontiers in group dynamics. *Hum.
Relat.*, 1947, 1, 143–153.

Lewin, K. Field theory in social science. (Ed. by D.
Cartwright) New York: Harper, 1951.

Newcomb, T. M. *Social psychology*. New York:
Dryden, 1950.

Sherif, M. A study of some social factors in perception. *Arch. Psychol., N. Y.*, 1935, No. 187.

Sherif, M., & Sherif, Carolyn W. An outline of
social psychology. New York: Harper, 1956.

Thibaut, J. W., & Kelley, H. H. *The social psychology of groups*. New York: Wiley, 1960.

Woo C.-L. Conformity in custom behavior. Unpublished doctoral dissertation, Syracuse University,
1948.

(Received February 5, 1961)

[5]

Educational Organizations as Loosely Coupled Systems

Karl E. Weick

In contrast to the prevailing image that elements in organizations are coupled through dense, tight linkages, it is proposed that elements are often tied together frequently and loosely. Using educational organizations as a case in point, it is argued that the concept of loose coupling incorporates a surprising number of disparate observations about organizations, suggests novel functions, creates stubborn problems for methodologists, and generates intriguing questions for scholars. Sample studies of loose coupling are suggested and research priorities are posed to foster cumulative work with this concept.[1]

Imagine that you're either the referee, coach, player or spectator at an unconventional soccer match: the field for the game is round; there are several goals scattered haphazardly around the circular field; people can enter and leave the game whenever they want to; they can throw balls in whenever they want; they can say "that's my goal" whenever they want to, as many times as they want to, and for as many goals as they want to; the entire game takes place on a sloped field; and the game is played as if it makes sense (March, personal communication).

If you now substitute in that example principals for referees, teachers for coaches, students for players, parents for spectators and schooling for soccer, you have an equally unconventional depiction of school organizations. The beauty of this depiction is that it captures a different set of realities within educational organizations than are caught when these same organizations are viewed through the tenets of bureaucratic theory.

Consider the contrast in images. For some time people who manage organizations and people who study this managing have asked, "How does an organization go about doing what it does and with what consequences for its people, processes, products, and persistence?" And for some time they've heard the same answers. In paraphrase the answers say essentially that an organization does what it does because of plans, intentional selection of means that get the organization to agree upon goals, and all of this is accomplished by such rationalized procedures as cost-benefit analyses, division of labor, specified areas of discretion, authority invested in the office, job descriptions, and a consistent evaluation and reward system. The only problem with that portrait is that it is rare in nature. People in organizations, including educational organizations, find themselves hard pressed either to find actual instances of those rational practices or to find rationalized practices whose outcomes have been as beneficent as predicted, or to feel that those rational occasions explain much of what goes on within the organization. Parts of some organizations are heavily rationalized but many parts also prove intractable to analysis through rational assumptions.

It is this substantial unexplained remainder that is the focus of this paper. Several people in education have expressed dissatisfaction with the prevailing ideas about organizations supplied by organizational theorists. Fortunately, they have

1
This paper is the result of a conference held at La Jolla, California, February 2–4, 1975 with support from the National Institute of Education (NIE). Participants in the conference were, in addition to the author, W.W. Charters, Center for Educational Policy and Management, University of Oregon; Craig Lundberg, School of Business, Oregon State University; John Meyer, Dept. of Sociology, Stanford University; Miles Meyers, Dept. of English, Oakland (Calif.) High School; Karlene Roberts, School of Business, University of California, Berkeley; Gerald Salancik, Dept. of Business Administration, University of Illinois; and Robert Wentz, Superintendent of Schools, Pomona (Calif.) Unified School District. James G. March, School of Education, Stanford University, a member of the National Council on Educational Research, and members of the NIE staff were present as observers. This conference was one of several on organizational processes in education which will lead to a report that will be available from the National Institute of Education, Washington, D.C. 20208. The opinions expressed in this paper do not necessarily reflect the position or policy of the National Institute of Education or the Department of Health, Education, and Welfare.

also made some provocative suggestions about newer, more unconventional ideas about organizations that should be given serious thought. A good example of this is the following observation by John M. Stephens (1967: 9–11):

[There is a] remarkable constancy of educational results in the face of widely differing deliberate approaches. Every so often we adopt new approaches or new methodologies and place our reliance on new panaceas. At the very least we seem to chorus new slogans. Yet the academic growth within the classroom continues at about the same rate, stubbornly refusing to cooperate with the bright new dicta emanating from the conference room . . . [These observations suggest that] we would be making a great mistake in regarding the management of schools as similar to the process of constructing a building or operating a factory. In these latter processes deliberate decisions play a crucial part, and the enterprise advances or stands still in proportion to the amount of deliberate effort exerted. If we must use a metaphor or model in seeking to understand the process of schooling, we should look to agriculture rather than to the factory. In agriculture we do not start from scratch, and we do not direct our efforts to inert and passive materials. We start, on the contrary, with a complex and ancient process, and we organize our efforts around what seeds, plants, and insects are likely to do anyway . . . . The crop, once planted, may undergo some development even while the farmer sleeps or loafs. No matter what he does, *some* aspects of the outcome will remain constant. When teachers and pupils foregather, some education may proceed even while the Superintendent disports himself in Atlantic City.

It is crucial to highlight what is important in the examples of soccer and schooling viewed as agriculture. To view these examples negatively and dismiss them by observing that "the referee should tighten up those rules," "superintendents don't do that," "schools are more sensible than that," or "these are terribly sloppy organizations" is to miss the point. The point is although researchers don't know what these kinds of structures are like but researchers do know they exist and that each of the negative judgments expressed above makes sense only if the observer assumes that organizations are constructed and managed according to rational assumptions and therefore are scrutable only when rational analyses are applied to them. This paper attempts to expand and enrich the set of ideas available to people when they try to make sense out of their organizational life. From this standpoint, it is unproductive to observe that fluid participation in schools and soccer is absurd. But it can be more interesting and productive to ask, how can it be that even though the activities in both situations are only modestly connected, the situations are still recognizable and nameable? The goals, player movements, and trajectory of the ball are still recognizable and can be labeled "soccer." And despite variations in class size, format, locations, and architecture, the results are still recognized and can be labeled "schools." How can such loose assemblages retain sufficient similarity and permanence across time that they can be recognized, labeled, and dealt with? The prevailing ideas in organization theory do not shed much light on how such "soft" structures develop, persist, and impose crude orderliness among their elements.

The basic premise here is that concepts such as loose coupling serve as sensitizing devices. They sensitize the observer to notice and question things that had previously been taken for granted. It is the intent of the program described here to develop a language for use in analyzing complex organizations, a language that may highlight features that have previously gone unnoticed. The guiding principle is a reversal of the common assertion, "I'll believe it when I see it' and

Loosely Coupled Systems

presumes an epistemology that asserts, "I'll see it when I
believe it." Organizations as loosely coupled systems may not
have been seen before because nobody believed in them or
could afford to believe in them. It is conceivable that preoccupation with rationalized, tidy, efficient, coordinated structures has blinded many practitioners as well as researchers to
some of the attractive and unexpected properties of less
rationalized and less tightly related clusters of events. This
paper intends to eliminate such blindspots.

THE CONCEPT OF COUPLING

The phrase "loose coupling" has appeared in the literature
(Glassman, 1973; March and Olsen, 1975) and it is important
to highlight the connotation that is captured by this phrase
and by no other. It might seem that the word coupling is
synonymous with words like connection, link, or interdependence, yet each of these latter terms misses a crucial nuance.

By loose coupling, the author intends to convey the image
that coupled events are responsive, *but* that each event also
preserves its own identity and some evidence of its physical
or logical separateness. Thus, in the case of an educational
organization, it may be the case that the counselor's office is
loosely coupled to the principal's office. The image is that the
principal and the counselor are somehow attached, but that
each retains some identity and separateness and that their
attachment may be circumscribed, infrequent, weak in its
mutual affects, unimportant, and/or slow to respond. Each of
those connotations would be conveyed if the qualifier loosely
were attached to the word coupled. Loose coupling also
carries connotations of impermanence, dissolvability, and
tacitness all of which are potentially crucial properties of the
"glue" that holds organizations together.

Glassman (1973) categorizes the degree of coupling between
two systems on the basis of the activity of the variables
which the two systems share. To the extent that two systems either have few variables in common or share weak
variables, they are independent of each other. Applied to the
educational situation, if the principal-vice-principal-
superintendent is regarded as one system and the teacher-
classroom-pupil-parent-curriculum as another system, then by
Glassman's argument if we did not find many variables in the
teacher's world to be shared in the world of a principal and/or
if the variables held in common were unimportant relative to
the other variables, then the principal can be regarded as
being loosely coupled with the teacher.

A final advantage of coupling imagery is that it suggests the
idea of building blocks that can be grafted onto an organization or severed with relatively little disturbance to either the
blocks or the organization. Simon (1969) has argued for the
attractiveness of this feature in that most complex systems
can be decomposed into stable subassemblies and that these
are the crucial elements in any organization or system. Thus,
the coupling imagery gives researchers access to one of the
more powerful ways of talking about complexity now available.

But if the concept of loose coupling highlights novel images
heretofore unseen in organizational theory, what is it about
these images that is worth seeing?

COUPLED ELEMENTS

There is no shortage of potential coupling elements, but neither is the population infinite.

At the outset the two most commonly discussed coupling mechanisms are the technical core of the organization and the authority of office. The relevance of those two mechanisms for the issue of identifying elements is that in the case of technical couplings, each element is some kind of technology, task, subtask, role, territory and person, and the couplings are task-induced. In the case of authority as the coupling mechanism, the elements include positions, offices, responsibilities, opportunities, rewards, and sanctions and it is the couplings among these elements that presumably hold the organization together. A compelling argument can be made that *neither* of these coupling mechanisms is prominent in educational organizations found in the United States. This leaves one with the question what *does* hold an educational organization together?

A short list of potential elements in educational organizations will provide background for subsequent propositions. March and Olsen (1975) utilize the elements of intention and action. There is a developing position in psychology which argues that intentions are a poor guide for action, intentions often follow rather than precede action, and that intentions and action are loosely coupled. Unfortunately, organizations continue to think that planning is a good thing, they spend much time on planning, and actions are assessed in terms of their fit with plans. Given a potential loose coupling between the intentions and actions of organizational members, it should come as no surprise that administrators are baffled and angered when things never happen the way they were supposed to.

Additional elements may consist of events like yesterday and tomorrow (what happened yesterday may be tightly or loosely coupled with what happens tomorrow) or hierarchial positions, like, top and bottom, line and staff, or administrators and teachers. An interesting set of elements that lends itself to the loose coupling imagery is means and ends. Frequently, several different means lead to the same outcome. When this happens, it can be argued that any one means is loosely coupled to the end in the sense that there are alternative pathways to achieve that same end. Other elements that might be found in loosely coupled educational systems are teachers-materials, voters-schoolboard, administrators-classroom, process-outcome, teacher-teacher, parent-teacher, and teacher-pupil.

While all of these elements are obvious, it is not a trivial matter to specify which elements are coupled. As the concept of coupling is crucial because of its ability to highlight the identity and separateness of elements that are momentarily attached, that conceptual asset puts pressure on the investigator to specify clearly the identity, separateness, and boundaries of the elements coupled. While there is some danger of reification when that kind of pressure is exerted, there is the even greater danger of portraying organizations in inappropriate terms which suggest an excess of unity, integration, coordination, and consensus. If one is nonspecific about

Loosely Coupled Systems

boundaries in defining elements then it is easy—and careless—to assemble these ill-defined elements and talk about integrated organizations. It is not a trivial issue explaining how elements persevere over time. Weick, for example, has argued (1974: 363–364) that elements may appear or disappear and may merge or become separated in response to need-deprivations within the individual, group, and/or organization. This means that specification of elements is not a one-shot activity. Given the context of most organizations, elements both appear and disappear over time. For this reason a theory of how elements become loosely or tightly coupled may also have to take account of the fact that the nature and intensity of the coupling may itself serve to create or dissolve elements.

The question of what is available for coupling and decoupling within an organization is an eminently practical question for anyone wishing to have some leverage on a system.

STRENGTH OF COUPLING

Obviously there is no shortage of meanings for the phrase loose coupling. Researchers need to be clear in their own thinking about whether the phenomenon they are studying is described by two words or three. A researcher can study "loose coupling" in educational organizations or "loosely coupled systems." The shorter phrase, "loose coupling," simply connotes things, "anythings," that may be tied together either weakly or infrequently or slowly or with minimal interdependence. Whether those things that are loosely coupled exist in a system is of minor importance. Most discussions in this paper concern loosely coupled systems rather than loose coupling since it wishes to clarify the concepts involved in the perseverance of sets of elements across time.

The idea of loose coupling is evoked when people have a variety of situations in mind. For example, when people describe loosely coupled systems they are often referring to (1) slack times—times when there is an excessive amount of resources relative to demands; (2) occasions when any one of several means will produce the same end; (3) richly connected networks in which influence is slow to spread and/or is weak while spreading; (4) a relative lack of coordination, slow coordination or coordination that is dampened as it moves through a system; (5) a relative absence of regulations; (6) planned unresponsiveness; (7) actual causal independence; (8) poor observational capabilities on the part of a viewer; (9) infrequent inspection of activities within the system; (10) decentralization; (11) delegation of discretion; (12) the absence of linkages that should be present based on some theory—for example, in educational organizations the expected feedback linkage from outcome back to inputs is often nonexistent; (13) the observation that an organization's structure is not coterminus with its activity; (14) those occasions when no matter what you do things always come out the same—for instance, despite all kinds of changes in curriculum, materials, groupings, and so forth the outcomes in an educational situation remain the same; and (15) curricula or courses in educational organizations for which there are few prerequistes—the longer the string of prerequisties, the tighter the coupling.

POTENTIAL FUNCTIONS AND DYSFUNCTIONS OF LOOSE COUPLING

It is important to note that the concept of loose coupling need not be used normatively. People who are steeped in the conventional literature of organizations may regard loose coupling as a sin or something to be apologized for. This paper takes a neutral, if not mildly affectionate, stance toward the concept. Apart from whatever affect one might feel toward the idea of loose coupling, it does appear a priori that certain functions can be served by having a system in which the elements are loosely coupled. Below are listed seven potential functions that could be associated with loose coupling plus additional reasons why each advantage might also be a liability. The dialectic generated by each of these oppositions begins to suggest dependent variables that should be sensitive to variations in the tightness of coupling.

The basic argument of Glassman (1973) is that loose coupling allows some portions of an organization to persist. Loose coupling lowers the probability that the organization will have to—or be able to—respond to each little change in the environment that occurs. The mechanism of voting, for example, allows elected officials to remain in office for a full term even though their constituency at any moment may disapprove of particular actions. Some identity and separateness of the element "elected official" is preserved relative to a second element, "constituency," by the fact of loosely coupled accountability which is measured in two, four, or six year terms. While loose coupling may foster perseverance, it is not selective in what is perpetuated. Thus archaic traditions as well as innovative improvisations may be perpetuated.

A second advantage of loose coupling is that it may provide a sensitive sensing mechanism. This possibility is suggested by Fritz Heider's perceptual theory of things and medium. Heider (1959) argues that perception is most accurate when a medium senses a thing and the medium contains many independent elements that can be externally constrained. When elements in a medium become either fewer in number and/or more internally constrained and/or more interdependent, their ability to represent some remote thing is decreased. Thus sand is a better medium to display wind currents than are rocks, the reason being that sand has more elements, more independence among the elements, and the elements are subject to a greater amount of external constraint than is the case for rocks. Using Heider's formulation metaphorically, it could be argued that loosely coupled systems preserve many independent sensing elements and therefore "know" their environments better than is true for more tightly coupled systems which have fewer externally constrained, independent elements. Balanced against this improvement in sensing is the possibility that the system would become increasingly vulnerable to producing faddish responses and interpretations. If the environment is known better, then this could induce more frequent changes in activities done in response to this "superior intelligence."

A third function is that a loosely coupled system may be a good system for localized adaptation. If all of the elements in a large system are loosely coupled to one another, then any

Loosely Coupled Systems

one element can adjust to and modify a local unique contingency without affecting the whole system. These local adaptations can be swift, relatively economical, and substantial. By definition, the antithesis of localized adaptation is standardization and to the extent that standardization can be shown to be desirable, a loosely coupled system might exhibit fewer of these presumed benefits. For example, the localized adaptation characteristic of loosely coupled systems may result in a lessening of educational democracy.

Fourth, in loosely coupled systems where the identity, uniqueness, and separateness of elements is preserved, the system potentially can retain a greater number of mutations and novel solutions than would be the case with a tightly coupled system. A loosely coupled system could preserve more "cultural insurance" to be drawn upon in times of radical change than in the case for more tightly coupled systems. Loosely coupled systems may be elegant solutions to the problem that adaptation can preclude adaptability. When a specific system fits into an ecological niche and does so with great success, this adaptation can be costly. It can be costly because resouces which are useless in a current environment might deteriorate or disappear even though they could be crucial in a modified environment. It is conceivable that loosely coupled systems preserve more diversity in responding than do tightly coupled systems, and therefore can adapt to a considerably wider range of changes in the environment than would be true for tightly coupled systems. To appreciate the possible problems associated with this abundance of mutations, reconsider the dynamic outlined in the preceding discussion of localized adaptation. If a local set of elements can adapt to local idiosyncracies without involving the whole system, then this same loose coupling could also forestall the spread of advantageous mutations that exist somewhere in the system. While the system may contain novel solutions for new problems of adaptation, the very structure that allows these mutations to flourish may prevent their diffusion.

Fifth, if there is a breakdown in one portion of a loosely coupled system then this breakdown is sealed off and does not affect other portions of the organization. Previously we had noted that loosely coupled systems are an exquisite mechanism to adapt swiftly to local novelties and unique problems. Now we are carrying the analysis one step further, and arguing that when any element misfires or decays or deteriorates, the spread of this deterioration is checked in a loosely coupled system. While this point is reminiscent of earlier functions, the emphasis here is on the localization of trouble rather than the localization of adaptation. But even this potential benefit may be problematic. A loosely coupled system can isolate its trouble spots and prevent the trouble from spreading, but it should be difficult for the loosely coupled system to repair the defective element. If weak influences pass from the defective portions to the functioning portions, then the influence back from these functioning portions will also be weak and probably too little, too late.

Sixth, since some of the most important elements in educational organizations are teachers, classrooms, principals, and so forth, it may be consequential that in a loosely coupled system there is more room available for self-determination by the actors. If it is argued that a sense of efficacy is crucial for human beings, then a sense of efficacy might be greater in a loosely coupled system with autonomous units than it would be in a tightly coupled system where discretion is limited. A futher comment can be made about self-determination to provide an example of the kind of imagery that is invoked by the concept of loose coupling.

It is possible that much of the teacher's sense of—and actual—control comes from the fact that diverse interested parties expect the teacher to link their intentions with teaching actions. Such linking of diverse intentions with actual work probably involves considerable negotiation. A parent complains about a teacher's action and the teacher merely points out to the parent how the actions are really correspondent with the parent's desires for the education of his or her children. Since most actions have ambiguous consequences, it should always be possible to justify the action as fitting the intentions of those who complain. Salancik (1975) goes even farther and suggests the intriguing possibility that when the consequences of an action are ambiguous, the stated *intentions* of the action serve as surrogates for the consequences. Since it is not known whether reading a certain book is good or bad for a child, the fact that it is intended to be good for the child itself becomes justification for having the child read it. The potential trade-off implicit in this function of loose coupling is fascinating. There is an increase in autonomy in the sense that resistance is heightened, but this heightened resistance occurs at the price of shortening the chain of consequences that will flow from each autonomous actor's efforts. Each teacher will have to negotiate separately with the same complaining parent.

Seventh, a loosely coupled system should be relatively inexpensive to run because it takes time and money to coordinate people. As much of what happens and should happen inside educational organizations seems to be defined and validated outside the organization, schools are in the business of building and maintaining categories, a business that requires coordination only on a few specific issues—for instance, assignment of teachers. This reduction in the necessity for coordination results in fewer conflicts, fewer inconsistencies among activities, fewer discrepancies between categories and activity. Thus, loosely coupled systems seem to hold the costs of coordination to a minimum. Despite this being an inexpensive system, loose coupling is also a nonrational system of fund allocation and therefore, unspecifiable, unmodifiable, and incapable of being used as means of change.

When these several sets of functions and dysfunctions are examined, they begin to throw several research issues into relief. For example, oppositions proposed in each of the preceding seven points suggest the importance of contextual theories. A predicted outcome or its opposite should emerge depending on how and in what the loosely coupled system is embedded. The preceding oppositions also suggest a fairly self-contained research program. Suppose a researcher starts with the first point made, as loose coupling increases the system should contain a greater number of anachronistic practices. Loosely coupled systems should be conspicuous for their cultural lags. Initially, one would like to know whether

Loosely Coupled Systems

that is plausible or not. But then one would want to examine in more fine-grained detail whether those anachronistic practices that are retained hinder the system or impose structure and absorb uncertainty thereby producing certain economies in responding. Similar embellishment and elaboration is possible for each function with the result that rich networks of propositions become visible. What is especially attractive about these networks is that there is little precedent for them in the organizational literature. Despite this, these propositions contain a great deal of face validity when they are used as filters to look at educational organizations. When compared, for example, with the bureaucratic template mentioned in the introduction, the template associated with loosely coupled systems seems to take the observer into more interesting territory and prods him or her to ask more interesting questions.

METHODOLOGY AND LOOSE COUPLING

An initial warning to researchers: the empirical observation of unpredictability is insufficient evidence for concluding that the elements in a system are loosely coupled. Buried in that caveat are a host of methodological intricacies. While there is ample reason to believe that loosely coupled systems can be seen and examined, it is also possible that the appearance of loose coupling will be nothing more than a testimonial to bad methodology. In psychology, for example, it has been argued that the chronic failure to predict behavior from attitudes is due to measurement error and not to the unrelatedness of these two events. Attitudes are said to be loosely coupled with behavior but it may be that this conclusion is an artifact produced because attitudes assessed by time-independent and context-independent measures are being used to predict behaviors that are time and context dependent. If both attitudes and behaviors were assessed with equivalent measures, then tight coupling might be the rule.

Any research agenda must be concerned with fleshing out the imagery of loose coupling—a task requiring a considerable amount of conceptual work to solve a few specific and rather tricky methodological problems before one can investigate loose compling.

By definition, if one goes into an organization and watches which parts affect which other parts, he or she will see the tightly coupled parts and the parts that vary the most. Those parts which vary slightly, infrequently, and aperiodically will be less visible. Notice, for example, that interaction data—who speaks to whom about what—are unlikely to reveal loose couplings. These are the most visible and obvious couplings and by the arguments developed in this paper perhaps some of the least crucial to understand what is going on in the organization.

An implied theme in this paper is that people tend to over-rationalize their activities and to attribute greater meaning, predictability, and coupling among them than in fact they have. If members tend to overrationalize their activity then their descriptions will not suggest which portions of that activity are loosely and tightly coupled. One might, in fact, even use the presence of apparent overrationalization as a potential clue that myth making, uncertainty, and loose coupling have been spotted.

J.G. March has argued that loose coupling can be spotted and examined only if one uses methodology that highlights and preserves rich detail about context. The necessity for a contextual methodology seems to arise, interestingly enough, from inside organization theory. The implied model involves cognitive limits on rationality and man as a single channel information processor. The basic methodological point is that if one wishes to observe loose coupling he has to see both what is and is not being done. The general idea is that time spent on one activity is time spent away from a second activity. A contextually sensitive methodology would record both the fact that some people are in one place generating events and the fact that these same people are thereby absent from some other place. The rule of thumb would be that a tight coupling in one part of the system can occur only if there is loose coupling in another part of the system. The problem that finite attention creates for a researcher is that if some outcome is observed for the organization, then it will not be obvious whether the outcome is due to activity in the tightly coupled sector or to inactivity in the loosely coupled sector. That is a provocative problem of interpretation. But the researcher should be forewarned that there are probably a finite number of tight couplings that can occur at any moment, that tight couplings in one place imply loose couplings elsewhere, and that it may be the *pattern* of couplings that produces the observed outcomes. Untangling such intricate issues may well require that new tools be developed for contextual understanding and that investigators be willing to substitute nonteleological thinking for teleological thinking (Steinbeck, 1941: chapt. 14).

Another contextually sensitive method is the use of comparative studies. It is the presumption of this methodology that taken-for-granted understandings—one possible "invisible" source of coupling in an otherwise loosely coupled system—are embedded in and contribute to a context. Thus, to see the effects of variations in these understandings one compares contexts that differ in conspicuous and meaningful ways.

Another methodological trap may await the person who tries to study loose coupling. Suppose one provides evidence that a particular goal is loosely coupled to a particular action. He or she says in effect, the person wanted to do this but in fact actually did that, thus, the action and the intention are loosely coupled. Now the problem for the researcher is that he or she may simply have focused on the wrong goal. There may be other goals which fit that particular action better. Perhaps if the researcher were aware of them, then the action and intention would appear to be tightly coupled. Any kind of intention-action, plan-behavior, or means-end depiction of loose coupling may be vulnerable to this sort of problem and an exhaustive listing of goals rather than parsimony should be the rule.

Two other methodological points should be noted. First, there are no good descriptions of the kinds of couplings that can occur among the several elements in educational organizations. Thus, a major initial research question is simply, what

Loosely Coupled Systems

does a map of the couplings and elements within an educational organization look like? Second, there appear to be some fairly rich probes that might be used to uncover the nature of coupling within educational organizations. Conceivably, crucial couplings within schools involve the handling of disciplinary issues and social control, the question of how a teacher gets a book for the classroom, and the question of what kinds of innovations need to get clearance by whom. These relatively innocuous questions may be powerful means to learn which portions of a system are tightly and loosely coupled. Obviously these probes would be sampled if there was a full description of possible elements that can be coupled and possible kinds and strengths of couplings. These specific probes suggest, however, in addition that what holds an educational organization together may be a small number of tight couplings in out-of-the-way places.

ILLUSTRATIVE QUESTIONS FOR A RESEARCH AGENDA

Patterns of Loose and Tight Coupling: Certification versus Inspection

Suppose one assumes that education is an intrinsically uninspected and unevaluated activity. If education is intrinsically uninspected and unevaluated then how can one establish that it is occurring? One answer is to define clearly who can and who cannot do it and to whom. In an educational organization this is the activity of certification. It is around the issues of certification and of specifying who the pupils are that tight coupling would be predicted to occur when technology and outcome are unclear.

If one argues that "certification" is the question "who does the work" and "inspection" is the question "how well is the work done," then there can be either loose or tight control over either certification or inspection. Notice that setting the problem up this way suggests the importance of discovering the distribution of tight and loosely coupled systems within any organization. Up to now the phrase loosely coupled systems has been used to capture the fact that events in an organization seem to be temporally related rather than logically related (Cohen and March, 1974). Now that view is being enriched by arguing that any organization must deal with issues of certification (who does the work) and inspection (how well is the work done). It is further being suggested that in the case of educational organizations there is loose control on the work—the work is intrinsically uninspected and unevaluated or if it is evaluated it is done so infrequently and in a perfunctory manner—but that under these conditions it becomes crucial for the organization to have tight control over who does the work and on whom. This immediately suggests the importance of comparative research in which the other three combinations are examined, the question being, how do these alternative forms grow, adapt, manage their rhetoric and handle their clientele. Thus it would be important to find organizations in which the controls over certification and inspection are both loose, organizations where there is loose control over certification but tight control over inspection, and organizations in which there is tight control both over inspection and over certification. Such comparative research might be conducted among different kinds of educational organiza-

tions within a single country (military, private, religious schooling in the United States), between educational and noneduca-
tional organizations within the same country (for example,
schools versus hospitals versus military versus business organizations) or between countries looking at solutions to the
problem of education given different degrees of centralization. As suggested earlier, it.may not be the existence or
nonexistence of loose coupling that is a crucial determinant of
organizational functioning over time but rather the patterning
of loose and tight couplings. Comparative studies should
answer the question of distribution.

If, as noted earlier, members within an organization (and
researchers) will see and talk clearly about only those regions
that are tightly coupled, then this suggests that members of
educational organizations should be most explicit and certain
when they are discussing issues related to certification for
definition and regulation of teachers, pupils, topics, space,
and resources. These are presumed to be the crucial issues
that are tightly controlled. Increasing vagueness of description
should occur when issues of substantive instruction—
inspection—are discussed. Thus, those people who primarily
manage the instructional business will be most vague in describing what they do, those people who primarily manage
the certification rituals will be most explicit. This pattern is
predicted *not* on the basis of the activities themselves—
certification is easier to describe than inspection—but rather
on the basis of the expectation that tightly coupled subsystems are more crucial to the survival of the system and
therefore have received more linguistic work in the past and
more agreement than is true for loosely coupled elements.

Core Technology and Organizational Form

A common tactic to understand complex organizations is to
explore the possibility that the nature of the task being performed determines the shape of the organizational structure.
This straightforward tactic raises some interesting puzzles
about educational organizations. There are suggestions in the
literature that education is a diffuse task, the technology is
uncertain.

This first question suggests two alternatives: if the task is
diffuse then would not any organizational form whatsoever be
equally appropriate *or* should this directly compel a diffuse
form of organizational structure? These two alternatives are
not identical. The first suggests that if the task is diffuse then
any one of a variety of quite specific organizational forms
could be imposed on the organization and no differences
would be observed. The thrust of the second argument is that
there is one and only one organizational form that would fit
well when there is a diffuse task, namely, a diffuse organizational form (for instance, an organized anarchy).

The second question asks if the task in an educational organization is diffuse then why do all educational organizations look
the way they do, and why do they all look the same? If there
is no clear task around which the shape of the organization
can be formed then why is it that most educational organizations do have a form and why is it that most of these forms
look indentical? One possibile answer is that the tasks of
educational organizations does not constrain the form of the

Loosely Coupled Systems

organization but rather this constraint is imposed by the ritual of certification and/or the agreements that are made in and by the environment. If any of these nontask possibilities are genuine alternative explanations, then the general literature on organizations has been insensitive to them.

One is therefore forced to ask the question, is it the case within educational organizations that the technology is unclear? So far it has been argued that loose coupling in educational organizations is partly the result of uncertain technology. If uncertain technology does not generate loose coupling then researchers must look elsewhere for the origin of these bonds.

Making Sense in/of Loosely Coupled Worlds

What kinds of information do loosely coupled systems provide members around which they can organize meanings, that is, what can one use in order to make sense of such fleeting structures? (By definition loosely coupled events are modestly predictable at best.) There is a rather barren structure that can be observed, reported on, and retrospected in order to make any sense. Given the ambiguity of loosely coupled structures, this suggests that there may be increased pressure on members to construct or negotiate some kind of social reality they can live with. Therefore, under conditions of loose coupling one should see considerable effort devoted to constructing social reality, a great amount of face work and linguistic work, numerous myths (Mitroff and Kilmann, 1975) and in general one should find a considerable amount of effort being devoted to punctuating this loosely coupled world and connecting it in some way in which it can be made sensible. Loosely coupled worlds do not look as if they would provide an individual many resources for sense making—with such little assistance in this task, a predominant activity should involve constructing social realities. Tightly coupled portions of a system should not exhibit nearly this preoccupation with linguistic work and the social construction of reality.

Coupling as a Dependent Variable

As a general rule, any research agenda on loose coupling should devote equal attention to loose coupling as a dependent and independent variable. Most suggestions have treated loose coupling as an independent variable. Less attention has been directed toward loose coupling as a dependent variable with the one exception of the earlier argument that one can afford loose coupling in either certification or inspection but not in both and, therefore, if one can locate a tight coupling for one of these two activities then he can predict as a dependent variable loose coupling for the other one.

Some investigators, however, should view loose coupling consistently as a dependent variable. The prototypic question would be, given prior conditions such as competition for scarce resources, logic built into a task, team teaching, conflict, striving for professionalism, presence of a central ministry of education, tenure, and so forth, what kind of coupling (loose or tight) among what kinds of elements occurs? If an organization faces a scarcity of resources its pattern of couplings should differ from when it faces an expansion of resources (for instance, scarcity leads to stockpiling leads to decoupling). Part of the question here is, what kinds of changes in the environment are the variables of tight and loose coupling sensitive to? In response to what kinds of activities or what kinds of contexts is coupling seen to change and what kinds of environments or situations, when they change, seem to have no effect whatsoever on couplings within an organization? Answers to these questions, which are of vital importance in predicting the outcomes of any intervention, are most likely to occur if coupling is treated as a dependent variable and the question is, under what conditions will the couplings that emerge be tight or loose?

Assembling Loosely Connected Events

Suppose one assumes that there is nothing in the world except loosely coupled events. This assumption is close to Simon's stable subassemblies and empty world hypothesis and to the idea of cognitive limits on rationality. The imagery is that of numerous clusters of events that are tightly coupled within and loosely coupled between. These larger loosely coupled units would be what researchers usually call organizations. Notice that organizations formed this way are rather unusual kinds of organizations because they are neither tightly connected, nor explicitly bounded, but they are stable. The research question then becomes, how does it happen that loosely coupled events which remain loosely coupled are institutionally held together in one organization which retains few controls over central activities? Stated differently, how does it happen that someone can take a series of loosely coupled events, assemble them into an organization of loosely coupled systems, and the events remain both loosely coupled but the organization itself survives? It is common to observe that large organizations have loosely connected sectors. The questions are, what makes this possible, how does it happen? What the structure in school systems seems to consist of is categories (for example, teacher, pupil, reading) which are linked by understanding and legitimated exogenously (that is, by the world outside the organization). As John Meyer (1975) puts it, "the system works because everyone knows everyone else knows roughly what is to go on . . . . Educational organizations are holding companies containing shares of stock in uninspected activities and subunits which are largely given their meaning, reality, and value in the wider social market." Note the potential fragility of this fabric of legitimacy.

It remains to be seen under what conditions loosely coupled systems are fragile structures because they are shored up by consensual anticipations, retrospections, and understanding that can dissolve and under what conditions they are resilient structures because they contain mutations, localized adaptation, and fewer costs of coordination.

Separate Intending and Acting Components

Intention and action are often loosely coupled within a single individual. Salancik (1975) has suggested some conditions under which dispositions within a single individual may be loosely coupled. These include such suggestions as follows.

Loosely Coupled Systems

(1) If intentions are not clear and unambiguous, then the use of them to select actions which will fulfill the intentions will be imperfect. (2) If the consequences of action are not known, then the use of intention to select action will be imperfect. (3) If the means by which an intention is transformed into an action are not known or in conflict, then the coupling of action to intention will be imperfect. (4) If intentions are not known to a person at the time of selecting an action, then the relationships between action and intention will be imperfect. This may be more common than expected because this possibility is not allowed by so-called rational models of man. People often have to recall their intentions after they act or reconstruct these intentions, or invent them. (5) If there exists a set of multiple intentions which can determine a set of similar multiple actions, then the ability to detect a relationship between any one intention and any one action is likely to be imperfect. To illustrate, if there is an intention A which implies selecting actions X and Y, and there is also an intention B which implies selecting actions X and Y, then it is possible that under both presence and absence of intention A, action X will be selected. Given these circumstances, an observer will falsely conclude that this relationship is indeterminant.

The preceding list has the potential limitation for organizational inquiry in that it consists of events within a single person. This limitation is not serious *if* the ideas are used as metaphors or if each event is lodged in a different person. For example, one could lodge intention with one person and action with some other person. With this separation, then all of the above conditions may produce loose coupling between these actors but additional conditions also come into play given this geographical separation of intention from action. For example, the simple additional requirement that the intentions must be communicated to the second actor and in such a way that they control his actions, will increase the potential for error and loose coupling. Thus any discussion of separate locations for intention and action within an organization virtually requires that the investigator specify the additional conditions under which the intending component can control the acting component. Aside from the problems of communication and control when intention and action are separated there are at least two additional conditions that could produce loose coupling.

1. If there are several diverse intending components all of whom are dependent on the same actor for implementing action, then the relationship between any one intention and any one action will be imperfect. The teacher in the classroom may well be the prototype of this condition.

2. The process outlined in the preceding item can become even more complicated, and the linkages between intention and action even looser, if the single acting component has intentions of its own.

Intention and action are often split within organizations. This paper suggests that if one were to map the pattern of intention and action components within the organization these would coincide with loosely coupled systems identified by other means. Furthermore, the preceding propositions begin to suggest conditions under which the same components might be at one moment tightly coupled and at the next moment loosely coupled.

CONCLUSION: A STATEMENT OF PRIORITIES

More time should be spent examining the possibility that educational organizations are most usefully viewed as loosely coupled systems. The concept of organizations as loosely coupled systems can have a substantial effect on existing perspectives about organizations. To probe further into the plausibility of that assertion, it is suggested that the following research priorities constitute a reasonable approach to the examination of loosely coupled systems.

1. Develop Conceptual Tools Capable of Preserving Loosely Coupled Systems

It is clear that more conceptual work has to be done before other lines of inquiry on this topic are launched. Much of the blandness in organizational theory these days can be traced to investigators applying impoverished images to organizational settings. If researchers immediately start stalking the elusive loosely coupled system with imperfect language and concepts, they will perpetuate the blandness of organizational theory. To see the importance of and necessity for this conceptual activity the reader should reexamine the 15 different connotations of the phrase "loose coupling" that are uncovered in this paper. They provide 15 alternative explanations for any researcher who claims that some outcome is due to loose coupling.

2. Explicate What Elements Are Available in Educational Organizations for Coupling

This activity has high priority because it is essential to know the practical domain within which the coupling phenomena occur. Since there is the further complication that elements may appear or disappear as a function of context and time, this type of inventory is essential at an early stage of inquiry. An indirect benefit of making this a high priority activity is that it will stem the counterproductive suspicion that "the number of elements in educational organizations is infinite." The reasonable reply to that comment is that if one is precise in defining and drawing boundaries around elements, then the number of elements will be less than imagined. Furthermore, the researcher can reduce the number of relevant elements if he has some theoretical ideas in mind. These theoretical ideas should be one of the outcomes of initial activity devoted to language and concept development (Priority 1).

3. Develop Contextual Methodology

Given favorable outcomes from the preceding two steps, researchers should then be eager to look at complex issues such as patterns of tight and loose coupling keeping in mind that loose coupling creates major problems for the researcher because he is trained and equipped to decipher predictable, tightly coupled worlds. To "see" loosely coupled worlds unconventional methodologies need to be developed and conventional methodologies that are underexploited need to be given more attention. Among the existing tools that should be refined to study loose coupling are comparative studies and longitudinal studies. Among the new tools that should be "invented" because of their potential relevance to loosely

Loosely Coupled Systems

coupled systems are nonteleological thinking (Steinbeck, 1941), concurrence methodology (Bateson, 1972: 180–201), and Hegelian, Kantian, and Singerian inquiring systems (Mitroff, 1974). While these latter methodologies are unconconventional within social science, so too is it unconventional to urge that we treat unpredictability (loose coupling) as our topic of interest rather than a nuisance.

4. Promote the Collection of Thorough, Concrete Descriptions of the Coupling Patterns in Actual Educational Organizations

No descriptive studies have been available to show what couplings in what patterns and with what strengths existed in current educational organizations. This oversight should be remedied as soon as possible.

Adequate descriptions should be of great interest to the practitioner who wants to know how his influence attempts will spread and with what intensity. Adequate description should also show practitioners how their organizations may be more sensible and adaptive than they suspect. Thorough descriptions of coupling should show checks and balances, localized controls, stabilizing mechanisms, and subtle feedback loops that keep the organization stable and that would promote its decay if they were tampered with.

The benefits for the researcher of full descriptions are that they would suggest which locations and which questions about loose coupling are most likely to explain sizeable portions of the variance in organizational outcomes. For example, on the basis of good descriptive work, it might be found that both tightly and loosely coupled systems "know" their environments with equal accuracy in which case, the earlier line of theorizing about "thing and medium" would be given a lower priority.

5. Specify the Nature of Core Technology in Educational Organizations

A suprisingly large number of the ideas presented in this paper assume that the typical coupling mechanisms of authority of office and logic of the task do not operate in educational organizations. Inquiry into loosely coupled systems was triggered partly by efforts to discover what *does* accomplish the coupling in school systems. Before the investigation of loose coupling goes too far, it should be established that authority and task are not prominent coupling mechanisms in schools. The assertions that they are not prominent seem to issue from a combination of informal observation, implausibility, wishful thinking, looking at the wrong things, and rather vague definitions of core technology and reward structures within education. If these two coupling mechanisms were defined clearly, studied carefully, and found to be weak and/or nonexistent in schools, *then* there would be a powerful justification for proceeding vigorously to study loosely coupled systems. Given the absence of work that definitively discounts these coupling mechanisms in education and given the fact that these two mechanisms have accounted for much of the observed couplings in other kinds of organizations, it seems crucial to look for them in educational organizations in the interest of parsimony.

It should be emphasized that if it *is* found that substantial coupling within educational organizations is due to authority of office and logic of the task, this does not negate the agenda that is sketched out in this paper. Instead, such discoveries would (1) make it even more crucial to look for patterns of coupling to explain outcomes, (2) focus attention on tight and loose couplings within task and authority induced couplings, (3) alert researchers to keep close watch for any coupling mechanisms other than these two, and (4) would direct comparative research toward settings in which these two coupling mechanisms vary in strength and form.

6. Probe Empirically the Ratio of Functions to Dysfunctions Associated with Loose Coupling

Although the word "function" has had a checkered history, it is used here without apology—and without the surplus meanings and ideology that have become attached to it. Earlier several potential benefits of loose coupling were described and these descriptions were balanced by additional suggestions of potential liabilities. If one adopts an evolutionary epistemology, then over time one expects that entities develop a more exquisite fit with their ecological niches. Given that assumption, one then argues that if loosely coupled systems exist and if they have existed for sometime, then they bestow some net advantage to their inhabitants and/or their constituencies. It is not obvious, however, what these advantages are. A set of studies showing how schools benefit and suffer given their structure as loosely coupled systems should do much to improve the quality of thinking devoted to organizational analysis.

7. Discover How Inhabitants Make Sense Out of Loosely Coupled Worlds

Scientists are going to have some big problems when their topic of inquiry becomes low probability couplings, but just as scientists have special problems comprehending loosely coupled worlds so too must the inhabitants of these worlds. It would seem that quite early in a research program on loose coupling, examination of this question should be started since it has direct relevance to those practitioners who must thread their way through such "invisible" worlds and must concern their sense-making and stories in such a way that they don't bump into each other while doing so.

Karl E. Weick is a professor of psychology and organizational behavior at Cornell University.

Loosely Coupled Systems

REFERENCES

Bateson, Mary Catherine
1972 Our Own Metaphor. New York: Knopf.

Cohen, Michael D., and James G. March
1974 Leadership and Ambiguity. New York: McGraw-Hill.

Glassman, R. B.
1973 "Persistence and loose coupling in living systems." Behavioral Science, 18: 83–98.

Heider, Fritz
1959 "Thing and medium." Psychological Issues, 1 (3): 1–34.

March, J. G., and J. P. Olsen
1975 Choice Situations in Loosely Coupled Worlds. Unpublished manuscript, Stanford University.

Meyer, John W.
1975 Notes on the Structure of Educational Organizations. Unpublished manuscript, Stanford University.

Mitroff, Ian I.
1974 The Subjective Side of Science. New York: Elsevier.

Mitroff, Ian I., and Ralph H. Kilmann
1975 On Organizational Stories: An Approach to the Design and Analysis of Organizations Through Myths and Stories. Unpublished manuscript, University of Pittsburgh.

Salancik, Gerald R.
1975 Notes on Loose Coupling: Linking Intentions to Actions.

Unpublished manuscript, University of Illinois, Urbana-Champaign.

Simon, H. A.
1969 "The architecture of complexity." Proceedings of the American Philosophical Society, 106: 467–482.

Steinbeck, John
1941 The Log from the Sea of Cortez. New York: Viking.

Stephens, John M.
1967 The Process of Schooling. New York: Holt, Rinehart, and Winston.

Weick, Karl E.
1974 "Middle range theories of social systems." Behavioral Science, 19: 357–367.

[6]

The autopoiesis of social systems

Niklas Luhmann

Meaning and life as different modes of autopoietic organization

The term 'autopoiesis' has been invented to define life. Its origin is clearly biological. Its extension to other fields has been discussed, but rather unsuccessfully and on the wrong premises. The problem may well be that we use a questionable approach to the issue, 'tangling' our 'hierarchies' of investigation.

At first sight it seems safe to say that psychic systems, and even social systems, are also living systems. Would there be consciousness or social life without (biological) life? And then, if life is defined as autopoiesis, how could one refuse to describe psychic systems and social systems as autopoietic systems? In this way we can retain the close relation between autopoiesis and life and apply this concept to psychic systems and to social systems as well. We are almost forced to do it by our conceptual approach (Maturana, 1980; Hejl, 1982; Bunge, 1979). However, we immediately get into trouble in defining precisely what the 'components' of psychic and social systems are whose reproduction by the same components of the same systems recursively defines the autopoietic unity of the system. And what does 'closure' mean in the case of psychic and social systems if our theoretical approach requires the inclusion of cells, neurophysiological systems, immune systems, etc. of living bodies into the encompassing (?) psychological or sociological realities?

Moreover, because it is tied to life as a mode of self-reproduction of autopoietic systems, the theory of autopoiesis does not really attain the level of general systems theory which includes brains and machines, psychic systems and social systems, societies and short-term interactions. From this point of view, living systems are a special type of systems. However, if we abstract from life and define autopoiesis as a general form of system-building using self-referential closure, we would have to admit that there are non-living autopoietic systems, different modes of autopoietic reproduction, and general principles of autopoietic organization which materialize as life, but also in other modes of circularity and self-reproduction. In other words, if we find non-living autopoietic systems in our world, then and only then will we need a truly general theory of autopoiesis which carefully avoids references which hold true only for living systems. But which attributes of autopoiesis will remain valid on this highest level, and which will have to be dropped on behalf of their connection with life?

Social systems' autopoiesis 173

The text that follows uses this kind of multi-level approach. It distinguishes a general theory of self-referential autopoietic systems and a more concrete level at which we may distinguish living systems (cells, brains, organisms, etc.), psychic systems and social systems (societies, organizations, interactions) as different kinds of autopoietic systems (see Figure 1).

FIGURE 1
Types of self-referential autopoietic systems

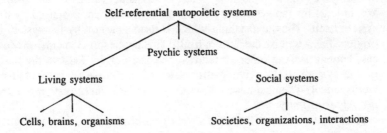

This scheme does not describe an internal systems differentiation. It is a scheme not for the operations of systems, but for their observation. It differentiates different types of systems or different modes of realization of autopoiesis.

This kind of approach is usable only if we are prepared to accept its anti-Aristotelian premise that social systems, and even psychic systems, are not living systems. The concept of autopoietic closure itself requires this theoretical decision, and leads to a sharp distinction between *meaning* and *life* as different kinds of autopoietic organization; and meaning–using systems again have to be distinguished according to whether they use *consciousness* or *communication* as modes of meaning-based reproduction. On the one hand, then, a psychological and a sociological theory have to be developed which meet these requirements; on the other hand, the concept of autopoiesis has to be abstracted from biological connotations. Both tasks are clearly interdependent. The general theory of autopoietic systems forms the foundation of the theories of psychic and social systems; the general theory itself, however, is meaningful only if this implementation succeeds, because otherwise we would be unable to determine which kind of attributes are truly general.

174 Sociocybernetic paradoxes

Communications as the basic elements of social systems

To use *ipsissima verba*, autopoietic systems 'are systems that are defined as unities, as networks of productions of components, that recursively, through their interactions, generate and realize the network that produces them and constitute, in the space in which they exist, the boundaries of the network as components that participate in the realization of the network' (Maturana, 1981: 21). Autopoietic systems, then, are not only self-organizing systems. Not only do they produce and eventually change their own *structures* but their self-reference applies to the production of other *components* as well. This is the decisive conceptual innovation. It adds a turbocharger to the already powerful engine of self-referential machines. Even *elements*, that is last components (in-dividuals), which are, at least for the system itself, undecomposable, are produced by the system itself. Thus, everything which is used as a unit by the system is produced as a unit by the system itself. This applies to elements, processes, boundaries and other structures, and last but not least to the unity of the system itself. Autopoietic systems, of course, exist within an environment. They cannot exist on their own. *But there is no input and no output of unity.*

Autopoietic systems, then, are sovereign with respect to the constitution of identities and differences. They do not create a material world of their own. They presuppose other levels of reality. Human life, for example, presupposes the small scope of temperature in which water exists as a liquid. But whatever they use as identities and as differences is of their own making. In other words, they cannot import identities and differences from the outer world; these are forms about which they have to decide themselves.

Social systems use communication as their particular mode of autopoietic reproduction. Their elements are communications which are recursively produced and reproduced by a network of communications and which cannot exist outside of such a network. Communications are not 'living' units, they are not 'conscious' units, they are not 'actions'. Their unity requires a synthesis of three selections: namely, information, utterance[1] and understanding (including misunderstanding).[2] This synthesis is produced by the network of communication, not by some kind of inherent power of consciousness, or by the inherent quality of the information. Also – and this goes against all kinds of 'structuralism' – communication is not produced by language. Structuralists have never been able to show how a structure can produce an event. At this point, the theory of autopoiesis offers a decisive advance. It is the network of events which reproduces itself, and structures are required for the reproduction of events by events.

The synthesis of information, utterance and understanding cannot be preprogrammed by language. It has to be recreated from situation to situation by referring to previous communications and to possibilities of further communications which are to be restricted by the actual event. This operation requires self-reference. It can in no way use the environment. Information, utterances and understandings are aspects which for the system cannot exist independently of the system; they are co-created within the process of communication. Even 'information' is not something which the system takes in from the environment. Pieces of information don't exist 'out there', waiting to be picked up by the system. As selections they are produced by the system itself in comparison with something else (e.g., in comparison with something which could have happened).

The communicative synthesis of information, utterance and understanding is possible only as an elementary unit of an ongoing *social* system. As the operating unit it is undecomposable, doing its autopoietic work only as an element of the system. However, further *units* of the same system can distinguish between information and utterance and can use this distinction to separate hetero-referentiality and self-referentiality. They can, being themselves undecomposable for the moment, refer primarily to the content of previous communications, asking for further information about the information; or they can question the 'how' and the 'why' of the communication, focusing on its utterance. In the first case, they will pursue hetero-referentiality, in the second case self-referentiality. Using a terminology proposed by Gotthard Günther (1979), we can say that the process of communication is not simply auto-referential in the sense that it is what it is. It is forced by its own structure to separate and to recombine hetero-referentiality and self-referentiality. Referring to itself, the process has to distinguish information and utterance and to indicate which side of the distinction is supposed to serve as the base for further communication. Therefore, self-reference is nothing but reference to this distinction between hetero-reference and self-reference. And, whereas auto-referentiality could be seen as a one-value thing (it is what it is), and could be described by a logic with two values only, namely, true and false, the case of social systems is one of much greater complexity because its self-reference (1) is based on an ongoing auto-referential (autopoietic) process, which refers to itself (2) as processing the distinction between itself and (3) its topics. If such a system did not have an environment, it would have to invent it as the horizon of its hetero-referentiality.

The elementary, undecomposable units of the system are communications of minimal size. This minimal size, again, cannot be determined independent of the system.[3] It is constituted by further communication or by the prospect of further communication. An elementary unit has the minimal meaning which is necessary for reference by further communication – for instance, the minimal meaning which still can be

176   Sociocybernetic paradoxes

negated. Further communication can very well separate pieces of
information, utterances and understandings and discuss them separately,
but this still would presuppose their synthesis in previous communication.
The system does not limit itself by using constraints for the constitution
of its elementary units. If need be, it can communicate about everything
and can decompose aspects of previous communication to satisfy actual
desires. As an operating system, however, it will not always do this to
the extreme.

Communication includes understanding as a necessary part of the
unity of its operation. It does not include the acceptance of its content.
It is not the function of communication to produce a consensus as
the favoured state of mind. Communication always results in an open
situation of either acceptance or rejection. It reproduces situations with
a specified and enforced choice. Such situations are not possible without communication; they do not occur as natural happenings. Only
communication itself is able to reach a point which bifurcates further
possibilities. The bifurcation itself is a reduction of complexity and, by
this very fact, an enforcement of selection. Automatically, the selection
of further communication is either an acceptance or rejection of previous
communication or a visible avoidance or adjournment of the issue.
Whatever its content and whatever its intention, communication reacts
within the framework of enforced choice. To take one course is not to
take the other. This highly artificial condition structures the self-reference
of the system; it makes it unavoidable to take other communications of
the same system into account, and every communication renews the same
condition within a varied context. If the system were set up to produce
consensus it soon would come to an end. It would never produce and
reproduce a society. In fact, however, it is designed to reproduce itself
by submitting itself to self-reproduced selectivity. Only this arrangement
makes social evolution possible, if evolution is seen as a kind of structural
selection superinduced on selectivity.

**Societies and interactions as different types
of social systems**
Social systems, then, are recursively closed systems with respect to
communication. However, there are two different meanings of 'closure'
which make it possible to distinguish between *societies* and *interactions*
as different types of social systems. Societies are encompassing systems
in the sense that they include all events which, for them, have the quality
of communication. They cannot communicate with their environment
because this would mean including their understanding partner in the
system, understanding being an essential aspect of the communication
itself.[4] By communication they extend and limit the societal system,
deciding about whether and what to communicate, and what to avoid.

Interactions, on the other hand, form their boundaries by the presence of people who are well aware that communication goes on around them without having contact with their own actual interaction. Interactions must take into account environmental communication, and have to acknowledge the fact that persons who are present and participate in the interaction have other roles and other obligations within systems which cannot be controlled here and now.

But interactions also are closed systems, in the sense that their own communication can be motivated and understood only in the context of the system. For example, if somebody approaches the interactional space and begins to participate, he has to be introduced and the topics of conversation eventually have to be adapted to the new situation. Interactions, moreover, cannot import communication ready-made from their environment. They communicate or they do not communicate, according to whether they decide to reproduce or not to reproduce their own elements. They continue or discontinue their autopoiesis like living systems which continue as living systems or die. There are no third possibilities, neither for life nor for communication. All selections have to be adapted to the maintenance of autopoietic reproduction. Something has to be said, or, at least, good and peaceful (or bad and aggressive) intentions have to be shown if others are present.[5] Everything else remains a matter of structured choice within the system. Some of its structures, then, become specialized in assuring that communication goes on even if nothing of informative quality remains and even if the communication becomes controversial and unpleasant (Malinowski, 1960).

The relation between action and communication

Confronted with the question of elementary units, most sociologists would come up with the answer: action. Sometimes 'roles' or even human individuals are preferred, but since the time of Max Weber and Talcott Parsons, action theory seems to offer the most advanced conceptualization.[6] Communication is introduced as a kind of action – for example, as 'kommunikatives Handeln' in the sense of Jürgen Habermas (1981). Usually this conceptualization is taken for granted, and classical sociological theory finds itself resumed under the title of 'Theory of Action' (Münch, 1982). Controversies are fought over headings such as action versus system, or individualistic versus holistic approaches to social reality. There is no serious conceptual discussion which treats the relation of actions and communications, and the important question of whether action or communication should be considered as the basic and undecomposable unit of social systems has not been taken up.

For a theory of autopoietic systems, only communication is a serious candidate for the position of the elementary unit of the basic self-referential process of social systems. Only communication is necessarily

178   Sociocybernetic paradoxes

and inherently social. Action is not. Moreover, social action already implies communication; it implies at least the communication of the meaning of the action or the intent of the actor, and it also implies the communication of the definition of the situation, of the expectation of being understood and accepted, and so on. Above all, communication is not a kind of action because it always contains a far richer meaning than the utterance or transmittance of messages alone. As we have seen, the perfection of communication implies understanding, and understanding is not part of the activity of the communicator and cannot be attributed to him. Therefore, the theory of autopoietic social systems requires a conceptual revolution within sociology: the replacement of action theory by communication theory as the characterization of the elementary operative level of the system.

The relation of action and communication has to be reversed. Social systems are not composed of actions of a special kind; they are not communicative actions, but require the attribution of actions to effectuate their own autopoiesis. Neither psychological motivation, nor reasoning or capacity of argumentation, constitutes action, but simply the attribution as such, that is, the linking of selection and responsibility for the narrowing of choice. [7] Only by attributing the responsibility for selecting the communication can the process of further communication be directed. One has to know who said what to be able to decide about further contributions to the process. Only by using this kind of simplifying localization of decision points can the process return to itself and communicate about communication.

Reflexive communication is not only an occasional event, but also a continuing possibility being co-reproduced by the autopoiesis itself. Every communication has to anticipate this kind of recursive elaboration, questioning, denial or correction, and has to preadapt to these future possibilities. Only in working out this kind of presumptive fitness can it become part of the autopoietic process. This, however, requires the allocation and distribution of responsibilities. And this function is fulfilled by accounting for action. The process therefore produces a second version of itself as a chain of actions. Contrary to the nature of communication itself, which includes the selectivity of information and the selectivity of understanding, and thereby constitutes its elements by overlapping and partial interpenetration, this action chain consists of clear-cut elements which exclude each other. Contrary to the underlying reality of communication, the chain of communicative actions can be seen and treated as asymmetric.

In this sense the constitution and attribution of actions serve as a *simplifying self-observation* of the communicative system. The system processes information but it takes responsibility only for the action part of this process, not for the information. It is congruent with the world, universally competent, including all exclusions, and at the same time it is a system within the world, able to distinguish and observe and control itself. It is a self-referential system and, thereby, a totalizing system. It cannot avoid operating within a 'world' of its own. Societies constitute worlds. Observing themselves, that is, communicating about themselves, societies cannot avoid using distinctions which differentiate the observing system from something else. Their communication observes itself within its world and describes the limitation of its own competence. Communication never becomes self-transcending.[8] It never can use operations outside its own boundaries. The boundaries themselves, however, are components of the system and cannot be taken as given by a pre-constituted world.

All this sounds paradoxical, and rightly so. Social systems as seen by an observer are paradoxical systems.[9] They include self-referential operations, not only as a condition of the possibility of their autopoiesis but also because of their self-observation. The distinction of communication and action and, as a result, the distinction of world and system are operative requirements. The general theory of autopoietic systems postulates a clear distinction between autopoiesis and observation. This condition is fulfilled in the case of social systems as well. Without using this distinction, the system could not accomplish the self-simplification necessary for self-observation. Autopoiesis and observation, communication and attribution of action are not the same and can never fuse. Nevertheless, self-observation in this specific sense of describing itself as a chain of clear-cut and responsible actions is a prerequisite of autopoiesis as such. Without this technique of using a simplified model of itself, the system could not communicate about communication and could not select its basic elements in view of their capacity to adapt themselves to the requirements of autopoiesis. This particular constellation may not be universally valid for all autopoietic systems. In view of the special case of social systems, however, the general theory has to formulate the distinction of autopoiesis and observation in a way which does not exclude cases in which self-observation is a necessary requirement of autopoiesis as such.

Observing such systems under the special constraints of logical analysis, we have to describe them as paradoxical systems or as 'tangled hierarchies'. It is not the task of an external observation to de-paradoxize the system and describe it in a way which is suitable for multi-level logical analysis.[10] The system de-paradoxizes itself. This requires 'undecidable' decisions. In the case of social systems these are decisions about the attribution of action. If desired, these decisions themselves can be attributed as actions, which again could be attributed as action, and so on in infinite regress. Logically, actions are always unfounded and decisions are decisions precisely because they contain an unavoidable

180   Sociocybernetic paradoxes

moment of arbitrariness and unpredictability. But this does not lead into lethal consequences. The system learns its own habits of acting and deciding, [11] accumulating experiences with itself and consolidating, on the basis of previous actions, expectations concerning future actions (structures). The autopoiesis does not stop in face of logical contradictions: it jumps, provided that possibilities of further communication are close enough at hand.

Maintenance of social systems by self-referential production of elements

The formal definition of autopoiesis gives no indication of the span of time during which components exist. Autopoiesis presupposes a recurring need for renewal. On the biological level, however, we tend to think about the process of replacement of molecules within cells or the replacement of cells within organisms, postponing for some time the final, inevitable decay. The limited duration of life seems to be a way of paying the cost of evolutionary improbability. All complex order seems to be wrested from decay.

This holds true for social systems as well, but with a characteristic difference. Conscious systems and social systems have to produce their own decay. They produce their basic elements, that is, thoughts and communications, not as short-term states but as events which vanish as soon as they appear. Events, too, occupy a minimal span of time, a specious present, but their duration is a matter of definition and has to be regulated by the autopoietic system itself: events cannot be accumulated. A conscious system does not consist of a collection of all its past and present thoughts, nor does a social system stockpile all its communications. After a very short time the mass of elements would be intolerably large and its complexity would be so great that the system would be unable to select a pattern of coordination and would produce chaos. The solution is to renounce all stability at the operative level of elements and to use events only. Thereby, the continuing dissolution of the system becomes a necessary cause of its autopoietic reproduction. The system becomes dynamic in a very basic sense. It becomes inherently restless. The instability of its elements is a condition of its duration.

All structures of social systems have to be based on this fundamental fact of vanishing events, disappearing gestures or words that are dying away. [12] Memory, and then writing, have their function in preserving not the events, but their structure-generating power. [13] The events themselves cannot be saved, but their loss is the condition of their regeneration. Thus, time and irreversibility are built into the system not only at the structural level, but also at the level of its elements. Its elements are operations, and there is no reasonable way to distinguish between 'points' and 'operations'. Disintegration and reintegration, disordering and ordering require each other, and reproduction comes about only by a recurring integration of disintegration and reintegration.

The theoretical shift from self-referential structural integration to self-referential constitution of elements has important consequences for systems maintenance. Maintenance is not simply a question of replication, of cultural transmission, of reproducing the *same patterns* under similar circumstances, such as using forks and knives while eating and only while eating; [14] its primary process is the production of *next elements* in the actual situation, *and these have to be different from the previous ones* to be recognizable as events. This does not exclude the relevance of pre-servable patterns; indeed, it even requires them for a sufficiently quick recognition of next possibilities. However, the system maintains itself not by storing patterns but by producing elements; not by transmitting 'memes' (units of cultural transmission analogous to 'genes') [15], but by recursively using events for producing events. Its stability is based on instability. This built-in requirement of discontinuity and newness amounts to a *necessity to handle and process information*, whatever the environment or the state of the system offers as occasions. Information is an internal change of state, a self-produced aspect of communicative events and not something which exists in the environment of the system and has to be exploited for adaptive or similar purposes. [16]

If autopoiesis bases itself on events, a description of the system needs not just one, but two dichotomies: the dichotomy of system and environment, and the dichotomy of event and situation. [17] Both dichotomies are 'world' formulas: system-plus-environment is one way, and event-plus-situation is another way, to describe the world. If the system (or its observer) uses the event/situation dichotomy, it can see the difference between system and environment as the structure of the situation, the situation containing not only the system, but also its environment from the point of view of an event. Processing information by producing events-in-situations, the system can orient itself to the difference of internal and external relevances. As the horizon (Husserl) of events, the situation refers to the system, to the environment and to its difference – but it does all this selectively, using the limited possibilities to produce the next event as a guideline. [18] Thus, the double dichotomy describes the way in which the system performs the 're-entry' of the difference between system and environment into the system. On the other hand, the difference between system and environment structures the limitation of choice which is needed to enable the system to proceed from one event-in-situation to another event-in-situation.

Systems based on events need a more complex pattern of time. For them, time cannot be given as an irreversibility alone. Events are happenings which make a difference between a 'before' and a 'thereafter'. They can be identified and observed, anticipated and remembered only

182 *Sociocybernetic paradoxes*

as such a difference. Their identity is their difference. Their presence is
a co-presence of the before and the thereafter. They have, therefore, to
present time within time and to reconstruct temporality in terms of a
shifting presence which has its quality as presence only owing to the
double horizons of past and future which accompany the presence on its
way into the future. [19] On this basis conscious time-binding can develop. [20]
The duality of horizons doubles as soon as we think of a future present
or a past present, both of which have their own future and their own
past. The temporal structure of time repeats itself within itself, and only
this reflexivity makes it possible to renounce a stable and enduring
presence (Luhmann, 1982a). By a slow process of evolution, the semantics
of time has adapted to these conditions. For a long time it used a religious
reservation – *aeternitas, aevum,* or the co-presence of God with all times
– to avoid the complete historization of time. Only modern society
recognizes itself – and consequently all previous societies – as constituting
its own temporality (Luhmann, 1980). The structural differentiation of
society as an autonomous autopoietic system requires the co-evolution of
corresponding temporal structures with modern historicism as the well-
known result.

The contribution of the general theory
of autopoietic systems
These short remarks by no means exhaust the range of suggestions that
the theory of social systems can contribute to the abstraction and refinement of the general theory of autopoietic systems (for a more extensive
treatment, see Luhmann, 1984). We can now return to the question,
What is new about it, given a long tradition of thinking about *creatio
continua,* continuance, duration, maintenance and so forth[21] (Ebeling,
1976)? Since the end of the sixteenth century, the idea of self-maintenance
has been used to displace teleological reasoning, and to reintroduce teleology
with the argument that the maintenance of the system is the goal of the
system or the function of its structures and operations. It is no surprise,
therefore, that the question of what is added by the theory of autopoiesis
to this well-known and rather futile traditional conceptualization has been
appended to this discussion. [22] An easy answer would be to mention
the sharp distinction between self-reference on the level of structures
(self-organization) and self-reference on the level of basic operations, or
elements. Moreover, we could point to the epistemological consequences
of distinguishing autopoiesis and observation, observing systems being
themselves autopoietic systems. We have only to look at the consequences
of an 'event-structure' approach for sociological theory to be aware
of new problems and new attempts at solution, compared with the
Malinowski/Radcliffe Brown/Parsons level of previous controversies.
There is, however, a further aspect which should be made explicit.

The theory of autopoietic systems formulates a situation of binary choice. A system either continues its autopoiesis or it does not. There are no in-between states, no third states. A woman may be pregnant or not: she cannot be a little pregnant. This is true, of course, for 'systems maintenance' as well. Superficial observers will find the same tautology. The theory of autopoietic systems, however, has been invented for a situation in which the theory of open systems has become generally accepted. Given this historical context, the concept of autopoietic closure has to be understood as the recursively closed organization of an open system. It does not return to the old notion of 'closed [versus open] systems' (Varela, 1979). The problem, then, is to see how autopoietic closure is possible in open systems. The new insight postulates closure as a condition of openness, and in this sense the theory formulates limiting conditions for the possibility of components of the system. Components in general and basic elements in particular can be reproduced only if they have the capacity to link closure and openness. For biological systems this does not require an 'awareness' of, or knowledge about, the environment. For meaning-based *conscious* or social systems the autopoietic mode of meaning gives the possibility of 're-entry',[23] that is, of presenting the difference between system and environment within the system. This re-entered distinction structures the elementary operations of these systems. In social, that is, communicative, systems, the elementary operation of communication comes about by an 'understanding' distinction between 'information' and 'utterance'. Information can refer to the environment of the system. Utterance, which is attributed to an agent as action, is responsible for the autopoietic regeneration of the system itself. In this way information and utterance are forced to cooperate, forced into unity. The emergent level of communication presupposes this synthesis. Without the basic distinction between information and utterance as different kinds of selection, the understanding would be not an aspect of communication, but a simple perception.

Thus, a sufficiently differentiated analysis of communication can show how the recurrent articulation of closure and openness comes about. It is a constitutive necessity of an emergent level of communication. Without a synthesis of three selections – information, utterance and understanding – there would be no communication but simply perception. By this synthesis, the system is forced into looking for possibilities of mediating closure and openness. In other words, communication is an evolutionary potential for building up systems which are able to maintain closure under the condition of openness and openness under the condition of closure. These systems face the continuing necessity to select meanings which satisfy these constraints. The result is our society.

In addition, the concept of autopoietic closure makes it possible to

184   Sociocybernetic paradoxes

understand the function of enforced binary choices. The system can
continue its autopoiesis or it can stop it. It can continue to live, to
produce conscious states or to communicate, or it can choose the only
alternative: to come to an end.[24] There are no third states. This is a
powerful technical simplification. On the other hand, the system lacks
any self-transcending power. It cannot enact operations from the outer
world. A social system can only communicate. A living system can only
live. Its autopoiesis as seen by an observer may have a causal impact on
its environment. But autopoiesis is production in the strict sense of a
process which needs further causes, not produced by itself, to attain
its effect. *The binary structure of autopoiesis seems to compensate for
this lack of totality.* It substitutes this kind of 'internal totality'. To be
or not to be, to continue the autopoiesis or not, serves as an internal
representation of the totality of possibilities. Everything which can happen
is reduced for the system to one of these two states. The system emerges
by inventing this choice, which does not exist without it. The negative
value is a value not of the world but of the system. But it helps to
simplify the totality of all conditions to one decisive question of how to
produce the next system state, the next element, the next communication
under the constraints of a given situation. Even unaware of the outer
world, the living system 'knows' that it is still alive and chooses its
operations in using life for reproducing life. A communicative system
too can continue to communicate on the base of the ongoing communication. This requires no reliable knowledge about outside conditions but
simply the distinction between system and environment as seen from the
point of view of the system. The unity of the autopoietic system is the
recursive processing of this difference of continuing or not which
reproduces the difference as a condition of its own continuity. Every
step has its own selectivity in choosing autopoiesis instead of stopping
it. This is not a question of preference, nor a question of goal attainment.
Rather, it has to be conceived as a 'code' of existence, if code is taken
as an artificial duplication of possibilities with the consequence that every
element can be presented as a selection.

This may become more clear if we consider the case of social systems.
Autopoiesis in this case means 'to continue to communicate'. This
becomes problematic in face of two different thresholds of discourage-
ment. The first tends to stop the process because the communication *has
not been understood*. The second tends to stop the process because *the
communication has been rejected*. These thresholds are related to each
other because understanding increases the chances of rejection.[25] It is
possible to refrain from communication in face of these difficulties, and
this is a rather common solution for interaction systems, particularly
under modern conditions of highly arbitrary interactions. Society however,
the system of all communications, cannot simply capitulate in the face

of these problems; it cannot stop all communications at once and decide to avoid any renewal. [26] The autopoiesis of society has invented powerful mechanisms to guarantee its continuity in the face of a lack of understanding or even open rejection. It continues by changing the interactional context or by reflexive communication. The process of communication returns to itself and communicates its own difficulties. It uses a kind of (rather superficial) self-control to become aware of serious misunderstandings, and it has the ability to communicate the rejection and restructure itself around this 'no'. In other words, the process is not obliged to follow the rules of logic. It can contradict itself. The system which uses this technique does not finish its autopoiesis and does not come to an end; it reorganizes itself as *conflict* to save its autopoiesis. When faced with serious problems of understanding and apparent misunderstandings, social systems very often tend to avoid the burden of argumentation and reasoned discourse to reach consensus – very much to the dismay of Habermas. Rather, they tend to favour the rejection of proposals and to embark on a course of conflict.

However this may be, the communication of contradiction, controversy and conflict seems to function as a kind of *immune system* of the social system (Luhmann, 1984). It saves autopoiesis by opening new modes of communication outside normal constraints. The law records experiences and rules for behaving under these abnormal conditions and, by some kind of epigenesis, develops norms for everyday behaviour which help to anticipate the conflict and to preadapt to its probable outcome (Luhmann, 1983a). In highly developed society we even find a functionally differentiated legal system which reproduces its own autopoietic unity. It controls the immune system of the larger societal system by a highly specialized synthesis of normative (not-learning) closure and cognitive (learning) openness (Luhmann, 1983b). At the same time, it increases the possibilities of conflict, makes more complex the immune system and limits its consequences. It cannot, of course, exclude conflicts outside the law, which may save the autopoieses of communication at even higher costs. [27]

The epistemological consequences of autopoietic closure
A final point of importance remains: the epistemological consequences of autopoietic closure. This problem also has to be discussed with respect to the present situation of scientific evolution in which the theory of autopoietic systems seems to offer advantages.

For many decades, scientific research has no longer operated under the guidance of an undoubted orthodoxy – be it a theory of cognition or a theory of science in particular. The universally accepted expedient is 'pragmatism'; the results are the only criteria of truth and progressive knowledge. This is clearly a self-referential, circular argument, based on a denial of circularity in theory and on its acceptance in practice. The avoidance of circularity becomes an increasingly desperate stance – a paradox which seems to indicate that the condemned solution, the paradox itself, is on the verge of becoming accepted theory.

One way to cope with this ambiguous situation is to test whether methodologies have the capacity to survive the coming scientific revolution. Functional analysis is one of them. It can be applied to all problems, including the problem of paradox, circularity, undecidability, logical incompleteness, etc. Stating such conditions as a problem of functional analysis invites one to look for feasible solutions, for strategies of de-paradoxization, of hierarchization (in the sense of the theory of types), of unfolding, of asymmetrization and so on. Functional analysis, in other words, reformulates the constitutive paradox as a 'solved problem' (which is and is not a problem) and then proceeds to compare problem solutions. [28]

In addition to this kind of preadaptation in scientific evolution to an expected change of the paradigm of the theory of cognition itself, the theory of autopoietic systems constructs the decisive argument. It is a theory of self-referential systems, to be applied to 'observing systems' as well – 'observing systems' in the double sense that Heinz von Foerster (1981) used when he chose the phrase as the title of a collection of his essays. The theory distinguishes autopoiesis and observation, but it accepts the fact that observing systems themselves are autopoietic (at least, living) systems. Observation comes about only as an operation of autopoietic systems, be it life, consciousness or communication. If an autopoietic system observes autopoietic systems, it finds itself constrained by the conditions of autopoietic self-reproduction (again, respectively, life, consciousness and communication, e.g., language), and it includes itself in the fields of its objects, because as an autopoietic system observing autopoietic systems, it cannot avoid gaining information about itself.

In this way, the theory of autopoietic systems integrates two separate developments of recent epistemological discussion. It uses a 'natural' or even 'material' epistemology, clearly distinct from all transcendental aspirations (Quine, 1969) – transcendentalism being in fact a title for the analysis of the autopoietic operations of conscious systems. In addition, it takes into account the special epistemological problems of universal or 'global' theories, referring to a class of objects to which they themselves belong. [29] Universal theories, logic being one of them, have the important advantage of seeing *and comparing* themselves with other objects of the same type. In the case of logic, this would require a many-valued structure and the corresponding abstraction. Classical logic did not eliminate self-reference, but it did not have enough space for its reflection. 'The very fact that the traditional logic, in its capacity of a place-value structure, contains *only* itself as a subsystem points to the specific and restricted role which reflection plays in the Aristotelian formalism. In order to become a useful theory of reflection a logic *has to encompass other sub-systems besides itself,'* (Günther, 1976: 310; emphasis added). Only under this condition does functional analysis become useful as a technique of self-exploration of universal theories.

The usual objection can be formulated, following Nigel Howard, as the 'existential axiom': knowing the theory of one's own behaviour releases one from its constraints (Howard, 1971: pp. xx, 2ff. and *passim*). For an empirical theory of cognition, this is an empirical question. The freedom, gained by self-reflection, can be used only if its constraints are sufficiently close at hand. Otherwise the autopoietic system simply will not know what to do next. It may know, for example, that it operates under the spell of an 'Oedipus complex' or a 'Marxist' obsession, but it does not know what else it can do.

A 'new epistemology' will have to pay attention to at least two fundamental distinctions: the distinction between autopoiesis and observation on the one hand, and the distinction between external observation and internal observation (self-observation) on the other. To combine these two distinctions is one of the unsolved tasks of systems theory.

Autopoiesis is the recursive production of the elements by the elements of the system. Observation, being itself an autopoietic operation, applies a distinction and indicates which side is used as a basis of further operations (including the operation of 'crossing' and indicating the other side). Self-observation is a special case of observation because it excludes other observers. Only the system can self-observe itself; others are by definition external observers. Therefore self-observation does not and cannot use criteria. It cannot choose between different perspectives.[30] It observes what it observes, and[31] can only change its focus and the distinction it applies. It is always sure about itself. External observers, on the other hand, are always a plurality. They have to presuppose other observers. They can observe other observers and other observations. They can compare their observations with others. They can be seduced into a reflexive observing of observations, and they need criteria when different observations yield different results.[32]

Classical epistemology looks for a set of conditions under which external observations yield identical results. It does not include self-observation (the 'subjective' or 'transcendental' approach, meaning only that these conditions can be found by introspection). This excludes, however, societies as observed and as observing systems. For within societies all observations of the society are self-observations. Societies cannot deny the fact that the observation itself is an element of the system which is observed. It is possible to differentiate subsystems within the societal system, giving them the special function of 'observing society'. This still implies self-observation, because the subsystem can only operate within the society. It can look at its social environment, at

188   Sociocybernetic paradoxes

political, economic, legal and religious affairs, but this observation itself (1) is part of the autopoiesis of the societal system and (2) becomes self-observation as soon as it tries to observe and control its epistemology. Somehow, a 'Third Position' (Bråten, 1984 and Chapter 12 below) would be required, one which contains the possibility of shifting between external observation and self-observation and of defining rules which tackle the paradox of being at the same time inside and outside of the system. It is within this context that universal theories become relevant. They are designed for external observation but are generalized in a way that includes the observing system as well. The rules and methodologies of universal theories may become the nucleus from which the development of a truly social epistemology can start. At least, they provide a field of experience in which we are logically forced to oscillate between external observation and self-observation.

We may leave as an unresolved question whether this kind of argument can generate not only sociological[33] but also biological (Maturana, 1978) and psychological (Campbell, 1970, 1974, 1975) epistemologies. This depends, last but not least, upon the possibility of applying the concept of self-observation not only to social systems and conscious systems, but also to living systems. In any case, advances in substantial theory may have side-effects on the theories which are supposed to control the research. Until the eighteenth century these problems were assigned to religion – the social system specialized for tackling paradoxes.[34] We have retained this possibility, but the normalization of paradoxes in modern art and modern science seems to indicate our desire eventually to get along without religion (Dupuy, 1982: 162ff). Apparently, our society offers the choice of trusting religion or working off our own paradoxes without becoming aware that this is religion.

Notes

1. In German I could use the untranslatable term, 'Mitteilung'.

2. The source of this threefold distinction (which also has been used by Austin and Searle) is Karl Bühler (1934). However, we modify the reference of this distinction. It refers not to 'functions', and not to types of 'acts', but to selections.

3. This argument, of course, does not limit the analytical powers of an observer, who, however, has to take into account the limitations of the system.

4. For problems of religion, and particularly for problems of 'communication with God' (revelation, prayer, etc.), see Niklas Luhmann (1985).

5. This again is not a motive for action but a self-produced fact of the social system. If nobody is motivated to say anything or to show his intentions, everybody would assume such communications and they would be produced without regard to such a highly improbable psychological environment.

6. See the discussion of 'The Unit of Action Systems' in Parsons (1937: 43 ff), which had a lasting impact on the whole theoretical framework of the later Parsons.

7. To elaborate on this point, of course, we would have to distinguish between 'behaviour'

and 'action'. A corresponding concept of 'motive' as a symbolic device facilitating the attribution of action has been used by Max Weber. See also Mills (1940), Burke (1945/1950) and Blum and McHugh (1971).

8. See the distinction between perceiving oneself and transcending oneself made by Hofstadter (1979).

9. The term 'paradox' refers to a logical collapse of a multi-level hierarchy, not to a simple contradiction. See Wilden (1972: 390 ff), Hofstadter (1979), Barel (1979).

10. I do not comment on the possibility of a logical analysis of self-referential systems which bypasses the Gödel limitations and avoids hierarchization.

11. 'Learning' understood as aspect of autopoiesis, that is, as a change of structure within a closed system (and not as adaptation to a changing environment): see Maturana (1983: 60–71).

12. It is rare that social scientists have a sense for the radicality and the importance of this insight; but see Allport (1940, 1954).

13. This explains that the invention of writing speeds up the evolution of complex societal systems, making it possible to preserve highly diversified structural information. This is, by now, a well explored phenomenon which still lacks a sufficient foundation in theory. See Yates (1966), Ong (1967), Havelock (1982).

14. This is the famous 'latent pattern maintenance' of Parsons – 'latent' because the system cannot actualize all its patterns all the time but has to maintain them as largely unused possibilities.

15. Dawkins's term; see Dawkins (1976).

16. See also (for systems) von Foerster (1981) especially p. 263: 'The environment contains no information: the environment is as it is.'

17. Using this theoretical framework, it is not permitted to speak of 'environment of events, of actions, etc.', or to speak of 'situations of a system'.

18. See Markowitz (1979) for further elaborations using the method of phenomenological psychology.

19. One of the best analyses of this complicated temporal structure remains Husserl (1928). For social systems see Bergmann (1981).

20. See Korzybski (1949). From an evolutionary point of view, see Stebbins (1982): 363 ff.

21 See Ebeling (1976), and of course the extensive 'functionalist' discussion about 'systems maintenance'.

22. See Jantsch (1981), who prefers the theory of thermodynamic disequilibrium and dissipative structures.

23. In the sense of Spencer Brown (1971). Gotthard Günther makes the same point in stating 'that these systems of self-reflection with centers of their own could not behave as they do unless they are capable of "drawing a line" between themselves and their environment'. And this leads Günther 'to the surprising conclusion that *parts of the universe have a higher reflective power than the whole of it*' (Günther, 1976: 319).

24. 'End' in this theory, therefore, is not 'telos' in the sense of the perfect state, but just the contrary: the zero-state, which has to be avoided by reproducing imperfect and improbable states. In a very fundamental way the theory has an anti-Aristotelian drift.

25. From an evolutionary point of view – see Luhmann (1981).

26. That the physical destruction of the possibility of communication has become possible, and that this destruction can be intended and produced by communication, is another question. In the same sense, life cannot choose to put an end to itself, but conscious systems can decide to kill their own bodies.

27. Recent tendencies to recommend and to domesticate symbolic illegalities as a kind of communication adapted to too high an integration of society and positive law seems to

190   Sociocybernetic paradoxes

postulate a second kind of immune system on the basis of a revived natural law, of careful choice of topics and highly conscientious practice; see Guggenberger (1983).

28. In a way, the problem remains a problem by 'oversolving' it, that is, by inventing several solutions which are of unequal value and differ in their appropriateness according to varying circumstances. This gives us, by a functional analysis of functional analysis, an example of how de-paradoxization can proceed. The happy pragmatist, on the other hand, would be content with stating that a problem becomes a problem only by seeing a solution; see Laudan (1977).

29. See Hooker (1975: 152–79). Many examples: the theory of sublimation may itself be a sublimation. Physical research uses physical processes. The theory of the Self has to take into account that the theorist himself is a Self (a healthy Self, a divided Self). For this last example see Holland (1977).

30. See, for the special case of conscious autopoietic systems (i.e. not for social systems!), Shoemaker (1963, 1968).

31. It can, of course, *distinguish* between self-observation and external observation, and it can observe external observation focusing on itself.

32. Not, of course, when different observations choose different objects; and the classical epistemology does not give useful criteria for the case in which different observations use different distinctions.

33. For a case study, using this mode of controlled self-reference, see Cole and Zuckermann (1975).

34. See the impasse as formulated by Bishop Huet: 'Mais lors que l'Entendement en vue de cette Idée forme un jugement de l'objet extérieur, d'où cette Idée est partie, il ne peut pas savoir très certainement et très clairement si ce jugement convient avec l'objet extérieur; et c'est dans cette convenance que consiste la Vérité, comme je l'ai dit. De sorte qu'encore qu'il connoisse la Vérité, il ne sçait pas qu'il connoît, et il ne peut être assuré de l'avoir connue' (Huet, 1723: 180).

References

Allport, Floyd H. (1940) 'An Event-System Theory of Collective Action: With Illustrations from Economic and Political Phenomena and the Production of War', *Journal of Social Psychology*, 11: 417–45.

Allport, Floyd H. (1954) 'The Structuring of Events: Outline of a General Theory with Applications to Psychology', *Psychological Review*, 61: 281–303.

Barel, Yves (1979) *Le Paradoxe et le Système: Essai sur le Fantastique Social*. Grenoble: Presses Universitaires.

Bergmann, Werner (1981) *Die Zeitstrukturen sozialer Systeme: Eine systemtheoretische Analyse*. Berlin: Duncker and Humblot.

Blum, Alan F. and Peter McHugh (1971) 'The Social Ascription of Motives', *American Sociological Review*, 36: 98–109.

Bråten, Stein (1984) 'The Third Position – Beyond Artificial and Autopoietic Reduction', *Kybernetes*, 13: 157–63.

Bühler, Karl (1934) *Sprachtheorie: Die Darstellungsfunktion der Sprache*. Jena: Fischer.

Bunge, Mario (1979) 'A Systems Concept of Society: Beyond Individualism and Holism', *Theory and Decision*, 10: 13–30.

Burke, Kenneth (1945) *A Grammar of Motives*. Reprinted together with *A Rhetoric of Motives* (1950). Cleveland, Ohio: World Publishing Company.

Campbell, Donald T. (1970) 'Natural Selection as an Epistemological Model', pp. 51–85 in Raoul Naroll and Ronald Cohen (eds), *A Handbook of Method in Cultural Anthropology*. Garden City, NY: Natural History Press.

Social systems' autopoiesis 191

Campbell, Donald T. (1974) 'Evolutionary Epistemology', pp. 413–65 in Paul A. Schilpp (ed.), *The Philosophy of Karl Popper*. La Salle, Ill.: Open Court Publications.

Campbell, Donald T. (1975) 'On the Conflicts between Biological and Social Evolution and between Psychological and Moral Tradition', *American Psychologist*, 30: 1103–26.

Cole, Jonathan R. and Harriet Zuckerman (1975) 'The Emergence of a Scientific Specialty: The Self-exemplifying Case of the Sociology of Science', pp. 139–74 in Lewis A. Coser (ed.), *The Idea of Social Structure: Papers in Honor of Robert K. Merton*. New York: Harcourt Brace Jovanovich.

Dawkins, R. (1976) *The Selfish Gene*. New York: Oxford University Press.

Dupuy, Jean-Pierre (1982) *Ordres et désordres: Enquête sur un nouveau paradigme*. Paris: Seuil.

Ebeling, Hans (ed.) (1976) *Subjektivität und Selbsterhaltung: Beiträge zur Diagnose der Moderne*. Frankfurt: Suhrkamp.

Guggenberger, Bernd (1983) 'An den Grenzen der Verfassung', *Frankfurter Allgemeine Zeitung*, no. 281, 3 December.

Günther, Gotthard (1976) 'Cybernetic Ontology and Transjunctional Operations', pp. 249–328 (esp. 319) in Gotthard Günther (ed.), *Beiträge zur Grundlegung einer operationsfähigen Dialektik*, Vol. 1. Hamburg: Meiner.

Günther, Gotthard (1979) 'Natural Numbers in Trans-classic Systems', pp. 241–64 in Gotthard Günther (ed.), *Beiträge zur Grundlegung einer operationsfähigen Dialektik*, Vol. 2. Hamburg: Meiner.

Habermas, Jürgen (1981) *Theorie des kommunikativen Handelns*. Frankfurt: Suhrkamp.

Havelock, Eric A. (1982) *The Literate Revolution in Greece and its Cultural Consequences*. Princeton: Princeton University Press.

Hejl, Peter M. (1982) *Sozialwissenschaft als Theorie selbstreferentieller Systeme*. Frankfurt: Campus.

Hofstadter, Douglas R. (1979) *Gödel, Escher, Bach: An Eternal Golden Braid*. Hassocks, Sussex: Harvester Press.

Holland, Ray (1977) *Self and Social Context*. New York: St Martin's Press.

Hooker, C. A. (1975) 'On Global Theories', *Philosophy of Science*, 42: 152–79.

Howard, Nigel (1971) *Paradoxes of Rationality: Theory of Metagames and Political Behaviour*. Cambridge, Mass.: MIT Press.

Huet, Pierre Daniël (1723) *Traité Philosophique de la Faiblesse de l'Esprit Humain*. Amsterdam: Du Sauzet.

Husserl, Edmund (1928) 'Vorlesungen zur Phänomenologie des inneren Zeitbewußtseins', *Jahrbuch für Philosophie und phänomenologische Forschung*, 9: 367–496.

Jantsch, Erich (1981) 'Autopoiesis: A Central Aspect of Dissipative Self-organization', pp. 65–88 in Milan Zeleny (ed.), *Autopoiesis: A Theory of Living Organization*. New York: North Holland.

Korzybski, Alfred (1949) *Science and Sanity: An Introduction to Non-Aristotelian Systems and General Semantics*, (3rd reprint ed.). Lakeville, Conn.: Institute of General Semantics.

Laudan, Larry (1977) *Progress and its Problems: Toward a Theory of Scientific Growth*. London: Routledge & Kegan Paul.

Luhmann, Niklas (1980) 'Temporalisierung von Komplexität: Zur Semantik neuzeitlicher Zeitbegriffe', pp. 235–300 in Niklas Luhmann, *Gesellschaftsstruktur und Semantik*, Vol. I. Frankfurt: Suhrkamp.

Luhmann, Niklas (1981) 'The Improbability of Communication', *International Social Science Journal*, 23(1): 122–32.

Luhmann, Niklas (1982a) 'The Future Cannot Begin: Temporal Structures in Modern Society', pp. 271–88 in Niklas Luhmann, *The Differentiation of Society*. New York: Columbia University Press.

192   Sociocybernetic paradoxes

Luhmann, Niklas (1982b) 'World-Time and System History: Interrelations between Temporal Horizons and Social Structures', pp. 289–323 in *The Differentiation of Society*. New York: Columbia University Press.

Luhmann, Niklas (1983a) *Rechtssoziologie* (2nd ed.). Opladen: Westdeutscher Verlag.

Luhmann, Niklas (1983b) 'Die Einheit des Rechtssystems', *Rechtstheorie*, 14: 129–54.

Luhmann, Niklas (1984) *Soziale Systeme: Grundriß einer allgemeinen Theorie*. Frankfurt: Suhrkamp.

Luhmann, Niklas (1985) 'Society, Meaning, Religion – Based on Self-Reference', *Sociological Analysis*, 46: 5–20.

Malinowski, Bronislaw (1960) 'The Problem of Meaning in Primitive Language', pp. 296–336 in C. K. Ogden and J. A. Richards (eds), *The Meaning of Meaning: A Study of the Influence of Language upon Thought and the Science of Symbolism* (10th ed.). London: Routledge & Kegan Paul.

Markowitz, Jürgen (1979) *Die Soziale Situation*. Frankfurt: Suhrkamp.

Maturana, Humberto R. (1978) 'Cognition', pp. 29–49 in Peter M. Hejl et al. (eds), *Wahrnehmung und Kommunikation*. Frankfurt: Lang.

Maturana, Humberto R. (1980) 'Man and Society', pp. 11–31 in Frank Benseler, Peter M. Hejl and Wolfram Köck (eds), *Autopoiesis, Communication and Society: The Theory of Autopoietic System in the Social Sciences*. Frankfurt: Campus.

Maturana, Humberto R. (1981) 'Autopoiesis', pp. 21–30 in Milan Zeleny (ed.), *Autopoiesis: A Theory of Living Organization*. New York: North Holland.

Maturana, Humberto R. (1983) *Reflexionen: Lernen oder ontogenetischer Drift. Delfin* II: 60–72.

Mills, C. Wright (1940) 'Situated Actions and Vocabularies of Motive', *American Sociological Review*, 5: 904–13.

Münch, Richard (1982) *Theorie des Handelns: Zur Rekonstruktion der Beiträge von Talcott Parsons, Emile Durkheim und Max Weber*. Frankfurt: Suhrkamp.

Ong, Walter J. (1967) *The Presence of the Word: Some Prolegomena for Cultural and Religious History*. New Haven, Conn.: Yale University Press.

Parsons, Talcott (1937) *The Structure of Social Action*. New York: McGraw-Hill.

Quine, Willard van O. (1969) 'Epistemology Naturalized', pp. 69–90 in Willard van O. Quine (ed), *Ontological Relativity and Other Essays*. New York.

Shoemaker, Sidney (1963) *Self-Knowledge and Self-Identity*. Ithaca, NY: Cornell University Press.

Shoemaker, Sidney (1968) 'Self-Reference and Self-Awareness', *Journal of Philosophy*, 65: 555–67.

Spencer Brown, George (1971) *Laws of Form* (2nd ed.). London: Allen & Unwin.

Stebbins, G. Ledyard (1982) *Darwin to DNA, Molecules to Humanity*. San Francisco: Freeman.

Varela, Francisco J. (1979) *Principles of Biological Autonomy*. New York: North Holland.

von Foerster, Heinz (1981) *Observing Systems*. Seaside, Cal.: Intersystems Publications.

Wilden, Anthony (1972) *System and Structure: Essays in Communication and Exchange*. London: Tavistock Press.

Yates, Frances A. (1966) *The Art of Memory*. London: Routledge & Kegan Paul.

Part III
Decision Making

One consequence of a *rapprochement* to cybernetics via systems theory was a cognitive slant in organization theory, expressed by its focus on decision making. Inspired by the seminal work of Herbert Simon, the organization theoreticians took strong interest in the actual practice of decision making in organizations, and soon reported surprising results. Michael Cohen, James March, and Johan Olsen (Chapter 7), like Weick studying educational organizations, constructed a 'garbage-can' model of decision making, a far cry from its rational predecessors. Admitting that the model might represent the extreme practice of decision making under ambiguity, these scholars continued to introduce political elements into the process nevertheless (Chapter 8). Their apprentice, Nils Brunsson (Chapter 9), arrived at the conclusion that, contrary to common knowledge, decisions, far from leading to action, actually prevent it from happening. Later trends concentrating on symbolic and cultural activities have enriched and changed the understanding of decision-making processes, revealing their complexity.

[7]

*Michael D. Cohen, James G. March, and
Johan P. Olsen*

A Garbage Can Model of Organizational Choice

*Organized anarchies are organizations characterized by problematic preferences,
unclear technology, and fluid participation. Recent studies of universities, a familiar form of organized anarchy, suggest that such organizations can be viewed for
some purposes as collections of choices looking for problems, issues and feelings
looking for decision situations in which they might be aired, solutions looking for
issues to which they might be an answer, and decision makers looking for work.
These ideas are translated into an explicit computer simulation model of a garbage can decision process. The general implications of such a model are described
in terms of five major measures on the process. Possible applications of the model
to more narrow predictions are illustrated by an examination of the model's predictions with respect to the effect of adversity on university decision making.*

Consider organized anarchies. These are organizations—or decision situations—characterized by three general properties.[1] The first is problematic preferences. In the organization it is difficult to impute a set of preferences to the decision situation that satisfies the standard consistency requirements for a theory of choice. The organization operates on the basis of a variety of inconsistent and ill-defined preferences. It can be described better as a loose collection of ideas than as a coherent structure; it discovers preferences through action more than it acts on the basis of preferences.

The second property is unclear technology. Although the organization manages to survive and even produce, its own processes are not understood by its members. It operates on the basis of simple trial-and-error procedures, the residue of learning from the accidents of past experience, and pragmatic inventions of necessity. The third property is fluid participation. Participants vary in the amount of time and effort they devote to different domains; involvement varies from one time to another. As a result, the boundaries of the organization are uncertain and changing; the audiences and decision makers for any particular kind of choice change capriciously.

These properties of organized anarchy have been identified often in studies of organizations. They are characteristic of any organization in part—part of the time. They are particularly conspicuous in public, educational, and illegitimate organizations. A theory of organized anarchy will describe a portion of almost any organization's activities, but will not describe all of them.

To build on current behavioral theories of organizations in order to accomodate the concept of organized anarchy, two major phenomena critical to an understanding of anarchy must be investigated. The first is the manner in which organizations make choices without consistent, shared goals. Situations of decision making under goal ambiguity are common in complex organizations. Often problems are resolved without recourse to explicit bargaining or to an explicit price system market—two common processes for decision making in the absence of consensus. The second phenomenon is the way members

[1] We are indebted to Nancy Block, Hilary Cohen, and James Glenn for computational, editorial, and intellectual help; to the Institute of Sociology, University of Bergen, and the Institute of Organization and Industrial Sociology, Copenhagen School of Economics, for institutional hospitality and useful discussions of organizational behavior; and to the Ford Foundation for the financial support that made our collaboration feasible. We also wish to acknowledge the helpful comments and suggestions of Søren Christensen, James S. Coleman, Harald Enderud, Kåre Rommetveit, and William H. Starbuck.

1

2   ADMINISTRATIVE SCIENCE QUARTERLY

of an organization are activated. This entails the question of how occasional members become active and how attention is directed toward, or away from, a decision. It is important to understand the attention patterns within an organization, since not everyone is attending to everything all of the time.

Additional concepts are also needed in a normative theory of organizations dealing with organized anarchies. First, a normative theory of intelligent decision making under ambiguous circumstances (namely, in situations in which goals are unclear or unknown) should be developed. Can we provide some meaning for intelligence which does not depend on relating current action to known goals? Second, a normative theory of attention is needed. Participants within an organization are constrained by the amount of time they can devote to the various things demanding attention. Since variations in behavior in organized anarchies are due largely to questions of who is attending to what, decisions concerning the allocation of attention are prime ones. Third, organized anarchies require a revised theory of management. Significant parts of contemporary theories of management introduce mechanisms for control and coordination which assume the existence of well-defined goals and a well-defined technology, as well as substantial participant involvement in the affairs of the organization. Where goals and technology are hazy and participation is fluid, many of the axioms and standard procedures of management collapse.

This article is directed to a behavioral theory of organized anarchy. On the basis of several recent studies, some elaborations and modifications of existing theories of choice are proposed. A model for describing decision making within organized anarchies is developed, and the impact of some aspects of organizational structure on the process of choice within such a model is examined.

THE BASIC IDEAS

Decision opportunities are fundamentally ambiguous stimuli. This theme runs through several recent studies of organizational choice.[2] Although organizations can often be

viewed conveniently as vehicles for solving well-defined problems or structures within which conflict is resolved through bargaining, they also provide sets of procedures through which participants arrive at an interpretation of what they are doing and what they have done while in the process of doing it. From this point of view, an organization is a collection of choices looking for problems, issues and feelings looking for decision situations in which they might be aired, solutions looking for issues to which they might be the answer, and decision makers looking for work.

Such a view of organizational choice focuses attention on the way the meaning of a choice changes over time. It calls attention to the strategic effects of timing, through the introduction of choices and problems, the time pattern of available energy, and the impact of organizational structure.

To understand processes within organizations, one can view a choice opportunity as a garbage can into which various kinds of problems and solutions are dumped by participants as they are generated. The mix of garbage in a single can depends on the mix of cans available, on the labels attached to the alternative cans, on what garbage is currently being produced, and on the speed with which garbage is collected and removed from the scene.

Such a theory of organizational decision making must concern itself with a relatively complicated interplay among the generation of problems in an organization, the deployment of personnel, the production of solutions, and the opportunities for choice. Although it may be convenient to imagine that choice opportunities lead first to the generation of decision alternatives, then to an examination of their consequences, then to an evaluation of those consequences in terms of objectives, and finally to a decision, this type of model is often a poor description of what actually happens. In the garbage can model, on the other hand, a decision is an outcome

---

[2] We have based the model heavily on seven recent studies of universities: Christensen (1971), Cohen and March (1972), Enderud (1971), Mood (1971), Olsen (1970, 1971), and Rommetveit (1971). The ideas, however, have a broader parentage. In particular, they obviously owe a debt to Allison (1969), Coleman (1957), Cyert and March (1963), Lindblom (1965), Long (1958), March and Simon (1958), Schilling (1968), Thompson (1967), and Vickers (1965).

or interpretation of several relatively independent streams within an organization.

Attention is limited here to interrelations among four such streams.

Problems. Problems are the concern of people inside and outside the organization. They might arise over issues of lifestyle; family; frustrations of work; careers; group relations within the organization; distribution of status, jobs, and money; ideology; or current crises of mankind as interpreted by the mass media or the nextdoor neighbor. All of these require attention.

Solutions. A solution is somebody's product. A computer is not just a solution to a problem in payroll management, discovered when needed. It is an answer actively looking for a question. The creation of need is not a curiosity of the market in consumer products; it is a general phenomenon of processes of choice. Despite the dictum that you cannot find the answer until you have formulated the question well, you often do not know what the question is in organizational problem solving until you know the answer.

Participants. Participants come and go. Since every entrance is an exit somewhere else, the distribution of "entrances" depends on the attributes of the choice being left as much as it does on the attributes of the new choice. Substantial variation in participation stems from other demands on the participants' time (rather than from features of the decision under study).

Choice opportunities. These are occasions when an organization is expected to produce behavior that can be called a decision. Opportunities arise regularly and any organization has ways of declaring an occasion for choice. Contracts must be signed; people hired, promoted, or fired; money spent; and responsibilities allocated.

Although not completely independent of each other, each of the streams can be viewed as independent and exogenous to the system. Attention will be concentrated here on examining the consequences of different rates and patterns of flows in each of the streams and different procedures for relating them.

THE GARBAGE CAN

A simple simulation model can be specified in terms of the four streams and a set of garbage processing assumptions.

Four basic variables are considered; each is a function of time.

A stream of choices. Some fixed number, m, of choices is assumed. Each choice is characterized by (a) an entry time, the calendar time at which that choice is activated for decision, and (b) a decision structure, a list of participants eligible to participate in making that choice.

A stream of problems. Some number, w, of problems is assumed. Each problem is characterized by (a) an entry time, the calendar time at which the problem becomes visible, (b) an energy requirement, the energy required to resolve a choice to which the problem is attached (if the solution stream is as high as possible), and (c) an access structure, a list of choices to which the problem has access.

A rate of flow of solutions. The verbal theory assumes a stream of solutions and a matching of specific solutions with specific problems and choices. A simpler set of assumptions is made and focus is on the rate at which solutions are flowing into the system. It is assumed that either because of variations in the stream of solutions or because of variations in the efficiency of search procedures within the organization, different energies are required to solve the same problem at different times. It is further assumed that these variations are consistent for different problems. Thus, a solution coefficient, ranging between 0 and 1, which operates on the potential decision energies to determine the problem solving output (effective energy) actually realized during any given time period is specified.

A stream of energy from participants. It is assumed that there is some number, v, of participants. Each participant is characterized by a time series of energy available for organizational decision making. Thus, in each time period, each participant can provide some specified amount of potential energy to the organization.

Two varieties of organizational segmentation are reflected in the model. The first is the mapping of choices onto decision makers, the decision structure. The decision structure of the organization is described by D, a v-by-m array in which d_{ij} is 1 if the ith participant is eligible to participate in the making of the jth choice. Otherwise, d_{ij} is 0. The second is the mapping of problems onto choices, the access structure. The access structure of the organization is described by A, a w-by-m array in which a_{ij} is 1 if the jth choice is accessible to the ith problem. Otherwise, a_{ij} is 0.

In order to connect these variables, three key behavioral assumptions are specified. The first is an assumption about the additivity of energy requirements, the second specifies the way in which energy is allocated to choices, and the third describes the way in which problems are attached to choices.

Energy additivity assumption. In order to be made, each choice requires as much effective energy as the sum of all requirements of the several problems attached to it. The effective energy devoted to a choice is the sum of the energies of decision makers attached to that choice, deflated, in each time period, by the solution coefficient. As soon as the total effective energy that has been expended on a choice equals or exceeds the requirements at a particular point in time, a decision is made.

Energy allocation assumption. The energy of each participant is allocated to no more than one choice during each time period. Each participant allocates his energy among the choices for which he is eligible to the one closest to decision, that is the one with the smallest energy deficit at the end of the previous time period in terms of the energies contributed by other participants.

Problem allocation assumption. Each problem is attached to no more than one choice each time period, choosing from among those accessible by calculating the apparent energy deficits (in terms of the energy requirements of other problems) at the end of the previous time period and selecting the choice closest to decision. Except to the extent that priorities enter in the organizational structure, there is no priority ranking of problems.

These assumptions capture key features of the processes observed. They might be modified in a number of ways without doing violence to the empirical observations on which they are based. The consequences of these modifications, however, are not pursued here. Rather, attention is focused on the implications of the simple version described. The

interaction of organizational structure and a garbage can form of choice will be examined.

ORGANIZATIONAL STRUCTURE

Elements of organizational structure influence outcomes of a garbage can decision process (a) by affecting the time pattern of the arrival of problems choices, solutions, or decision makers, (b) by determining the allocation of energy by potential participants in the decision, and (c) by establishing linkages among the various streams.

The organizational factors to be considered are some that have real-world interpretations and implications and are applicable to the theory of organized anarchy. They are familiar features of organizations, resulting from a mixture of deliberate managerial planning, individual and collective learning, and imitation. Organizational structure changes as a response to such factors as market demand for personnel and the heterogeneity of values, which are external to the model presented here. Attention will be limited to the comparative statics of the model, rather than to the dynamics produced by organizational learning.

To exercise the model, the following are specified: (a) a set of fixed parameters which do not change from one variation to another, (b) the entry times for choices, (c) the entry times for problems, (d) the net energy load on the organization, (e) the access structure of the organization, (f) the decision structure of the organization, and (g) the energy distribution among decision makers in the organization.

Some relatively pure structural variations will be identified in each and examples of how variations in such structures might be related systematically to key exogenous variables will be given. It will then be shown how such factors of organizational structure affect important characteristics of the decisions in a garbage can decision process.

Fixed Parameters

Within the variations reported, the following are fixed: (a) number of time periods—twenty, (b) number of choice opportunities—ten, (c) number of decision makers—ten, (d) number of problems—twenty, and (e) the solution coefficients for the 20 time periods—0.6 for each period.[3]

Entry Times

Two different randomly generated sequences of entry times for choices are considered. It is assumed that one choice enters per time period over the first ten time periods in one of the following orders: (a) 10, 7, 9, 5, 2, 3, 4, 1, 6, 8, or (b) 6, 5, 2, 10, 8, 9, 7, 4, 1, 3.

Similarly, two different randomly generated sequences of entry times for problems are considered. It is assumed that two problems enter per time period over the first ten time periods in one of the following orders: (a) 8, 20, 14, 16, 6, 7, 15, 17, 2, 13, 11, 19, 4, 9, 3, 12, 1, 10, 5, 18, or (b) 4, 14, 11, 20, 3, 5, 2, 12, 1, 6, 8, 19, 7, 15, 16, 17, 10, 18, 9, 13.

Net Energy Load

The total energy available to the organization in each time period is 5.5 units. Thus, the total energy available over twenty time periods is $20 \times 5.5 = 110$. This is reduced by the solution coefficients to 66. These figures hold across all other variations of the model. The net energy load on the organization is defined as the difference between the total energy required to solve all problems and the total effective energy available to the organization over all time periods. When this is negative, there is, in principle, enough energy available. Since the total effective energy available is fixed at 66, the net load is varied by varying the total energy requirements for problems. It is assumed that each problem has the same energy requirement under a given load. Three different energy load situations are considered.

Net energy load 0: light load. Under this condition the energy required to make a choice is 1.1 times the number of problems attached to that choice. That is, the energy required for each problem is 1.1. Thus, the minimum total effective energy required to

[3] The model has also been exercised under conditions of a set of solution coefficients that varies over the time periods. Specifically, the following series has been used: 1, 0.9, 0.7, 0.3, 0.1, 0.1, 0.3, 0.7, 0.9, 1, 0.6, 0.6, 0.6, 0.6, 0.6, 0.6, 0.6, 0.6, 0.6, 0.6. This simulation, using only one combination of choice and problem entry times, gives results consistent with all of the conclusions reported in the present article.

resolve all problems is 22, and the net energy load is $22 - 66 = -44$.

Net energy load 1: moderate load. Under this condition, the energy required for each problem is 2.2. Thus, the energy required to make a choice is 2.2 times the number of problems attached to that choice, and the minimum effective energy required to resolve all problems is 44. The net energy load is $44 - 66 = -22$.

Net energy load 2: heavy load. Under this condition, each problem requires energy of 3.3. The energy required to make a choice is 3.3 times the number of problems attached to that choice. The minimum effective energy required to resolve all problems is 66, and the net energy load is $66 - 66 = 0$.

Although it is possible from the total energy point of view for all problems to be resolved in any load condition, the difficulty of accomplishing that result where the net energy load is zero—a heavy load—is obviously substantial.

Access Structure

Three pure types of organizational arrangements are considered in the access structure (the relation between problems and choices).

Access structure 0: unsegmented access. This structure is represented by an access array in which any active problem has access to any active choice.

$$A_0 = \begin{matrix}
1111111111\\1111111111\\1111111111\\1111111111\\1111111111\\1111111111\\1111111111\\1111111111\\1111111111\\1111111111\\1111111111\\1111111111\\1111111111\\1111111111\\1111111111\\1111111111\\1111111111\\1111111111\\1111111111\\1111111111
\end{matrix}$$

Access structure 1: hierarchical access. In this structure both choices and problems are

6   ADMINISTRATIVE SCIENCE QUARTERLY

arranged in a hierarchy such that important problems—those with relatively low numbers—have access to many choices, and important choices—those with relatively low numbers—are accessible only to important problems. The structure is represented by the following access array:

$$
A_1 = \begin{array}{l}
1111111111 \\
1111111111 \\
0111111111 \\
0111111111 \\
0011111111 \\
0011111111 \\
0001111111 \\
0001111111 \\
0000111111 \\
0000111111 \\
0000011111 \\
0000011111 \\
0000001111 \\
0000001111 \\
0000000111 \\
0000000111 \\
0000000011 \\
0000000011 \\
0000000001 \\
0000000001
\end{array}
$$

Access structure 2: specialized access. In this structure each problem has access to only one choice and each choice is accessible to only two problems, that is, choices specialize in the kinds of problems that can be associated to them. The structure is represented by the following access array:

$$
A_2 = \begin{array}{l}
1000000000 \\
1000000000 \\
0100000000 \\
0100000000 \\
0010000000 \\
0010000000 \\
0001000000 \\
0001000000 \\
0000100000 \\
0000100000 \\
0000010000 \\
0000010000 \\
0000001000 \\
0000001000 \\
0000000100 \\
0000000100 \\
0000000010 \\
0000000010 \\
0000000001 \\
0000000001
\end{array}
$$

Actual organizations will exhibit a more complex mix of access rules. Any such combination could be represented by an appropriate access array. The three pure structures considered here represent three classic alternative approaches to the problem of organizing the legitimate access of problems to decision situations.

Decision Structure

Three similar pure types are considered in the decision structure (the relation between decision makers and choices).

Decision structure 0: unsegmented decisions. In this structure any decision maker can participate in any active choice opportunity. Thus, the structure is represented by the following array:

$$
D_0 = \begin{array}{l}
1111111111 \\
1111111111 \\
1111111111 \\
1111111111 \\
1111111111 \\
1111111111 \\
1111111111 \\
1111111111 \\
1111111111 \\
1111111111
\end{array}
$$

Decision structure 1: hierarchical decisions. In this structure both decision makers and choices are arranged in a hierarchy such that important choices—low numbered choices—must be made by important decision makers—low numbered decision makers—and important decision makers can participate in many choices. The structure is represented by the following array:

$$
D_1 = \begin{array}{l}
1111111111 \\
0111111111 \\
0011111111 \\
0001111111 \\
0000111111 \\
0000011111 \\
0000001111 \\
0000000111 \\
0000000011 \\
0000000001
\end{array}
$$

Decision structure 2: specialized decisions. In this structure each decision maker is associated with a single choice and each choice has a single decision maker. Decision makers specialize in the choices to which they attend. Thus, we have the following array:

$$D_2 = \begin{matrix} 1000000000 \\ 0100000000 \\ 0010000000 \\ 0001000000 \\ 0000100000 \\ 0000010000 \\ 0000001000 \\ 0000000100 \\ 0000000010 \\ 0000000001 \end{matrix}$$

As in the case of the access structure, actual decision structures will require a more complicated array. Most organizations have a mix of rules for defining the legitimacy of participation in decisions. The three pure cases are, however, familiar models of such rules and can be used to understand some consequences of decision structure for decision processes.

Energy Distribution

The distribution of energy among decision makers reflects possible variations in the amount of time spent on organizational problems by different decision makers. The solution coefficients and variations in the energy requirement for problems affect the overall relation between energy available and energy required. Three different variations in the distribution of energy are considered.

Energy distribution 0: important people— less energy. In this distribution important people, that is people defined as important in a hierarchial decision structure, have less energy. This might reflect variations in the combination of outside demands and motivation to participate within the organization. The specific energy distribution is indicated as follows:

Decision maker	Energy	
1	0.1	
2	0.2	
3	0.3	
4	0.4	
5	0.5	$= E_0$
6	0.6	
7	0.7	
8	0.8	
9	0.9	
10	1.0	

The total energy available to the organization each time period (before deflation by the solution coefficients) is 5.5.

Energy distribution 1: equal energy. In this distribution there is no internal differentiation among decision makers with respect to energy. Each decision maker has the same energy (0.55) each time period. Thus, there is the following distribution:

Decision maker	Energy	
1	0.55	
2	0.55	
3	0.55	
4	0.55	
5	0.55	$= E_1$
6	0.55	
7	0.55	
8	0.55	
9	0.55	
10	0.55	

The total energy available to the organization each time period (before deflation by the solution coefficients) is 5.5.

Energy distribution 2: important people— more energy. In this distribution energy is distributed unequally but in a direction opposite to that in E_0. Here the people defined as important by the hierarchical decision structure have more energy. The distribution is indicated by the following:

Decision maker	Energy	
1	1.0	
2	0.9	
3	0.8	
4	0.7	
5	0.6	$= E_2$
6	0.5	
7	0.4	
8	0.3	
9	0.2	
10	0.1	

As in the previous organizations, the total energy available to the organization each time period (before deflation by the solution coefficients) is 5.5.

Where the organization has a hierarchical decision structure, the distinction between important and unimportant decision makers is clear. Where the decision structure is unsegmented or specialized, the variations in energy distribution are defined in terms of the same numbered decision makers (lower numbers are more important than higher numbers) to reflect possible status differences which are not necessarily captured by the decision structure.

Simulation Design

The simulation design is simple. A Fortran version of the garbage can model is given in the appendix, along with documentation and an explanation. The $3^4 = 81$ types of organizational situations obtained by taking the possible combinations of the values of the four dimensions of an organization (access structure, decision structure, energy distribution, and net energy load) are studied here under the four combinations of choice and problem entry times. The result is 324 simulation situations.

SUMMARY STATISTICS

The garbage can model operates under each of the possible organizational structures to assign problems and decision makers to choices, to determine the energy required and effective energy applied to choices, to make such choices and resolve such problems as the assignments and energies indicate are feasible. It does this for each of the twenty time periods in a twenty-period simulation of organizational decision making.

For each of the 324 situations, some set of simple summary statistics on the process is required. These are limited to five.

Decision Style

Within the kind of organization postulated, decisions are made in three different ways.

By resolution. Some choices resolve problems after some period of working on them. The length of time may vary, depending on the number of problems. This is the familiar case that is implicit in most discussions of choice within organizations.

By oversight. If a choice is activated when problems are attached to other choices and if there is energy available to make the new choice quickly, it will be made without any attention to existing problems and with a minimum of time and energy.

By flight. In some cases choices are associated with problems (unsuccessfully) for some time until a choice more attractive to the problems comes along. The problems leave the choice, and thus it is now possible to make the decision. The decision resolves

no problems; they having now attached themselves to a new choice.

Some choices involve both flight and resolution—some problems leave, the remainder are solved. These have been defined as resolution, thus slightly exaggerating the importance of that style. As a result of that convention, the three styles are mutually exclusive and exhaustive with respect to any one choice. The same organization, however, may use any one of them in different choices. Thus, the decision style of any particular variation of the model can be described by specifying the proportion of completed choices which are made in each of these three ways.

Problem Activity

Any measure of the degree to which problems are active within the organization should reflect the degree of conflict within the organization or the degree of articulation of problems. Three closely related statistics of problem activity are considered. The first is the total number of problems not solved at the end of the twenty time periods; the second is the total number of times that any problem shifts from one choice to another, while the third is the total number of time periods that a problem is active and attached to some choice, summed over all problems. These measures are strongly correlated with each other. The third is used as the measure of problem activity primarily because it has a relatively large variance; essentially the same results would have been obtained with either of the other two measures.

Problem Latency

A problem may be active, but not attached to any choice. The situation is one in which a problem is recognized and accepted by some part of the organization, but is not considered germane to any available choice. Presumably, an organization with relatively high problem latency will exhibit somewhat different symptoms from one with low latency. Problem latency has been measured by the total number of periods a problem is active, but not attached to a choice, summed over all problems.

Cohen et al: A GARBAGE CAN MODEL   9

Decision Maker Activity

To measure the degree of decision maker activity in the system, some measure which reflects decision maker energy expenditure, movement, and persistence is required. Four are considered: (a) the total number of time periods a decision maker is attached to a choice, summed over all decision makers, (b) the total number of times that any decision maker shifts from one choice to another, (c) the total amount of effective energy available and used, and (d) the total effective energy used on choices in excess of that required to make them at the time they are made. These four measures are highly intercorrelated. The second was used primarily because of its relatively large variance; any of the others would have served as well.

Decision Difficulty

Because of the way in which decisions can be made in the system, decision difficulty is not the same as the level of problem activity. Two alternative measures are considered: the total number of choices not made by the end of the twenty time periods and the total number of periods that a choice is active, summed over all choices. These are highly correlated. The second is used, primarily because of its higher variance; the conclusions would be unchanged if the first were used.

IMPLICATIONS OF THE MODEL

An analysis of the individual histories of the simulations shows eight major properties of garbage can decision processes.

First, resolution of problems as a style for making decisions is not the most common style, except under conditions where flight is severely restricted (for instance, specialized access) or a few conditions under light load. Decision making by flight and oversight is

a major feature of the process in general. In each of the simulation trials there were twenty problems and ten choices. Although the mean number of choices not made was 1.0, the mean number of problems not solved was 12.3. The results are detailed in Table 1. The behavioral and normative implications of a decision process which appears to make choices in large part by flight or by oversight must be examined. A possible explanation of the behavior of organizations that seem to make decisions without apparently making progress in resolving the problems that appear to be related to the decisions may be emerging.

Second, the process is quite thoroughly and quite generally sensitive to variations in load. As Table 2 shows, an increase in the net energy load on the system generally increases problem activity, decision maker activity, decision difficulty, and the uses of flight and oversight. Problems are less likely to be solved, decision makers are likely to shift from one problem to another more frequently, choices are likely to take longer to make and are less likely to resolve problems. Although it is possible to specify an organization that is relatively stable with changes in load, it is not possible to have an organization that is stable in behavior and also has other desirable attributes. As load changes, an organization that has an unsegmented access structure with a specialized decision structure stays quite stable. It exhibits relatively low decision difficulty and decision maker activity, very low problem latency, and maximum problem activity. It makes virtually all decisions placed before it, uses little energy from decision makers, and solves virtually no problems.

Third, a typical feature of the model is the tendency of decision makers and prob-

TABLE 1. PROPORTION OF CHOICES THAT RESOLVE PROBLEMS UNDER FOUR CONDITIONS OF CHOICE AND PROBLEM ENTRY TIMES, BY LOAD AND ACCESS STRUCTURE

		Access structure			
		All	Unsegmented	Hierarchical	Specialized
Load	Light	0.55	0.38	0.61	0.65
	Moderate	0.30	0.04	0.27	0.60
	Heavy	0.36	0.35	0.23	0.50
	All	0.40	0.26	0.37	0.58

Organization Theory I

TABLE 2.   EFFECTS OF VARIATIONS IN LOAD UNDER FOUR CONDITIONS
OF CHOICE AND PROBLEM ENTRY TIMES

		Mean problem activity	Mean decision maker activity	Mean decision difficulty	Proportion of choices by flight or oversight
Load	Light	114.9	60.9	19.5	.45
	Moderate	204.3	63.8	32.9	.70
	Heavy	211.1	76.6	46.1	.64

lems to track each other through choices. Subject to structural restrictions on the tracking, decision makers work on active problems in connection with active choices; both decision makers and problems tend to move together from choice to choice. Thus, one would expect decision makers who have a feeling that they are always working on the same problems in somewhat different contexts, mostly without results. Problems, in a similar fashion, meet the same people wherever they go with the same result.

Fourth, there are some important interconnections among three key aspects of the efficiency of the decision processes specified. The first is problem activity, the amount of time unresolved problems are actively attached to choice situations. Problem activity is a rough measure of the potential for decision conflict in the organization. The second aspect is problem latency, the amount of time problems spend activated but not linked to choices. The third aspect is decision time, the persistence of choices. Presumably, a good organizational structure would keep both problem activity and problem latency low through rapid problem solution in its choices. In the garbage can process such a result was never observed. Segmentation of the access structure tends to reduce the number of unresolved problems active in the organization but at the cost of increasing the latency period of problems and, in most cases the time devoted to reaching decisions. On the other hand, segmentation of the decision structure tends to result in decreasing problem latency, but at the cost of increasing problem activity and decision time.

Fifth, the process is frequently sharply interactive. Although some phenomena associated with the garbage can are regular and flow through nearly all of the cases, for ex-

ample, the effect of overall load, other phenomena are much more dependent on the particular combination of structures involved. Although high segmentation of access structure generally produces slow decision time, for instance, a specialized access structure, in combination with an unsegmented decision structure, produces quick decisions.

Sixth, important problems are more likely to be solved than unimportant ones. Problems which appear early are more likely to be resolved than later ones. Considering only those cases involving access hierarchy where importance is defined for problems, the relation between problem importance and order of arrival is shown in Table 3. The system, in

TABLE 3.   PROPORTION OF PROBLEMS RESOLVED UNDER FOUR CONDITIONS OF CHOICE AND PROBLEM ENTRY TIMES, BY IMPORTANCE OF PROBLEM AND ORDER OF ARRIVAL OF PROBLEM (FOR HIERARCHICAL ACCESS)

		Time of arrival of problem	
		Early, first 10	Late, last 10
Importance of problem	High, first 10	0.46	0.44
	Low, last 10	0.48	0.25

effect, produces a queue of problems in terms of their importance, to the disadvantage of late-arriving, relatively unimportant problems, and particularly so when load is heavy. This queue is the result of the operation of the model. It was not imposed as a direct assumption.

Seventh, important choices are less likely to resolve problems than unimportant choices. Important choices are made by over-sight and flight. Unimportant choices are made by resolution. These differences are observed under both of the choice entry sequences but are sharpest where important choices enter relatively early. Table 4 shows

TABLE 4. PROPORTION OF CHOICES THAT ARE MADE BY FLIGHT OR OVERSIGHT UNDER FOUR CONDITIONS OF CHOICE AND PROBLEM ENTRY TIMES, BY TIME OF ARRIVAL AND IMPORTANCE OF CHOICE (FOR HIERARCHICAL ACCESS OR DECISION STRUCTURE)

		Time of arrival of choice	
		Early, first 5	Late, last 5
Importance of choice	High, first 5	0.86	0.65
	Low, last 5	0.54	0.60

the results. This property of important choices in a garbage can decision process can be naturally and directly related to the phenomenon in complex organizations of important choices which often appear to just happen.

Eighth, although a large proportion of the choices are made, the choice failures that do occur are concentrated among the most important and least important choices. Choices of intermediate importance are virtually always made. The proportion of choice failures, under conditions of hierarchical access or decision structures is as follows:

Three most important choices   0.14
Four middle choices   0.05
Three least important choices   0.12

In a broad sense, these features of the process provide some clues to how organizations survive when they do not know what they are doing. Much of the process violates standard notions of how decisions ought to be made. But most of those notions are built on assumptions which cannot be met under the conditions specified. When objectives and technologies are unclear, organizations are charged to discover some alternative decision procedures which permit them to proceed without doing extraordinary violence to the domains of participants or to their model of

what an organization should be. It is a hard charge, to which the process described is a partial response.

At the same time, the details of the outcomes clearly depend on features of the organizational structure. The same garbage can operation results in different behavioral symptoms under different levels of load on the system or different designs of the structure of the organization. Such differences raise the possibility of predicting variations in decision behavior in different organizations. One possible example of such use remains to be considered.

GARBAGE CANS AND UNIVERSITIES

One class of organization which faces decision situations involving unclear goals, unclear technology, and fluid participants is the modern college or university. If the implications of the model are applicable anywhere, they are applicable to a university. Although there is great variation among colleges and universities, both between countries and within any country, the model has general relevance to decision making in higher education.

General Implications

University decision making frequently does not resolve problems. Choices are often made by flight or oversight. University decision processes are sensitive to increases in load. Active decision makers and problems track one another through a series of choices without appreciable progress in solving problems. Important choices are not likely to solve problems.

Decisions whose interpretations continually change during the process of resolution appear both in the model and in actual observations of universities. Problems, choices, and decision makers arrange and rearrange themselves. In the course of these arrangements the meaning of a choice can change several times, if this meaning is understood as the mix of problems discussed in the context of that choice.

Problems are often solved, but rarely by the choice to which they are first attached. A choice that might, under some circumstances, be made with little effort becomes an arena for many problems. The choice becomes almost impossible to make, until the problems drift off to another arena. The matching of problems, choices, and decision makers is partly controlled by attributes of content, relevance, and competence; but it is also quite sensitive to attributes of timing, the particular combinations of current garbage cans, and the overall load on the system.

Universities and Adversity

In establishing connections between the hypothetical attributes of organizational structure in the model and some features of contemporary universities, the more detailed implications of the model can be used to explore features of university decision making. In particular, the model can examine the events associated with one kind of adversity within organizations, the reduction of organizational slack.

Slack is the difference between the resources of the organization and the combination of demands made on it. Thus, it is sensitive to two major factors: (a) money and other resources provided to the organization by the external environment, and (b) the internal consistency of the demands made on the organization by participants. It is commonly believed that organizational slack has been reduced substantially within American colleges and universities over the past few years. The consequences of slack reduction in a garbage can decision process can be shown by establishing possible relations between changes in organizational slack and the key structural variables within the model.

Net energy load. The net energy load is the difference between the energy required within an organization and the effective energy available. It is affected by anything that alters either the amount of energy available to the organization or the amount required to find or generate problem solutions. The energy available to the organization is partly a function of the overall strength of exit opportunities for decision makers. For example, when there is a shortage of faculty, administrators, or students in the market for participants, the net energy load on a university is heavier than it would be when there is no shortage. The energy required to find solutions depends on the flow of possible problem solutions. For example, when the environment of the organization is relatively rich,

solutions are easier to find and the net energy is reduced. Finally, the comparative attractiveness and permeability of the organization to problems affects the energy demands on it. The more attractive, the more demands. The more permeable, the more demands. Universities with slack and with relatively easy access, compared to other alternative arenas for problem carriers, will attract a relatively large number of problems.

Access structure. The access structure in an organization would be expected to be affected by deliberate efforts to derive the advantages of delegation and specialization. Those efforts, in turn, depend on some general characteristics of the organizational situation, task, and personnel. For example, the access structure would be expected to be systematically related to two features of the organization: (a) the degree of technical and value heterogeneity, and (b) the amount of organizational slack. Slack, by providing resource buffers between parts of the organization, is essentially a substitute for technical and value homogeneity. As heterogeneity increases, holding slack constant, the access structure shifts from an unsegmented to a specialized to a hierarchical structure. Similarly, as slack decreases, holding heterogeneity constant, the access structure shifts from an unsegmented to a specialized to a hierarchical structure. The combined picture is shown in Figure 1.

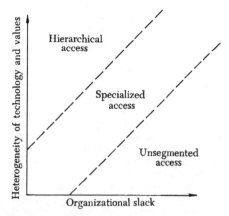

FIGURE 1. HYPOTHESIZED RELATIONSHIP BETWEEN SLACK, HETEROGENEITY, AND THE ACCESS STRUCTURE OF AN ORGANIZATION

Cohen et al: A GARBAGE CAN MODEL 13

Decision structure. Like the access structure, the decision structure is partly a planned system for the organization and partly a result of learning and negotiation within the organization. It could be expected to be systematically related to the technology, to attributes of participants and problems, and to the external conditions under which the organization operates. For example, there are joint effects of two factors: (a) relative administrative power within the system, the extent to which the formal administrators are conceded substantial authority, and (b) the average degree of perceived interrelation among problems. It is assumed that high administrative power or high interrelation of problems will lead to hierarchical decision structure, that moderate power and low interrelation of problems leads to specialized decision structures, and that relatively low administrative power, combined with moderate problem interrelation, leads to unsegmented decision structures. The hypothetical relations are shown in Figure 2.

there is an active external demand for attention affects the extent to which decision makers will have energy available for use within the organization. The stronger the relative outside demand on important people in the organization, the less time they will spend within the organization relative to others. Note that the energy distribution refers only to the relation between the energy available from important people and less important people. Thus, the energy distribution variable is a function of the relative strength of the outside demand for different people, as shown in Figure 3.

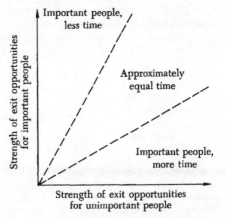

FIGURE 3. HYPOTHESIZED RELATIONSHIP BETWEEN EXIT OPPORTUNITIES AND THE DISTRIBUTION OF ENERGY WITHIN AN ORGANIZATION

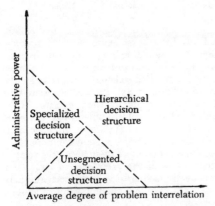

FIGURE 2. HYPOTHESIZED RELATIONSHIP BETWEEN ADMINISTRATIVE POWER, INTERRELATION OF PROBLEMS, AND THE DECISION STRUCTURE OF AN ORGANIZATION

Energy distribution. Some of the key factors affecting the energy distribution within an organization are associated with the alternative opportunities decision makers have for investing their time. The extent to which

Within a university setting it is not hard to imagine circumstances in which exit opportunities are different for different decision makers. Tenure, for example, strengthens the exit opportunities for older faculty members. Money strengthens the exit opportunities for students and faculty members, though more for the former than the latter. A rapidly changing technology tends to strengthen the exit opportunities for young faculty members.

Against this background four types of colleges and universities are considered: (a) large, rich universities, (b) large, poor universities, (c) small, rich colleges, and (d) small, poor colleges.

Important variations in the organizational variables among these schools can be expected. Much of that variation is likely to be within-class variation. Assumptions about these variables, however, can be used to generate some assumptions about the predominant attributes of the four classes, under conditions of prosperity.

Under such conditions a relatively rich school would be expected to have a light energy load, a relatively poor school a moderate energy load. With respect to access structure, decision structure, and the internal distribution of energy, the appropriate position of each of the four types of schools is marked with a circular symbol on Figures 4, 5, and 6. The result is the pattern of variations indicated below:

and unimportant people. The expected results of these shifts are shown by the positions of the square symbols in Figure 6.

At the same time, adversity affects both access structure and decision structure. Adversity can be expected to bring a reduction in slack and an increase in the average interrelation among problems. The resulting hypothesized shifts in access and decision structures are shown in Figures 4 and 5.

Table 5 shows the effects of adversity on the four types of schools according to the previous assumptions and the garbage can model. By examining the first stage of adversity, some possible reasons for discontent among presidents of large, rich schools can be seen. In relation to other schools they are not seriously disadvantaged. The large, rich

	Load	Access structure	Decision structure	Energy distribution
Large, rich	Light 0	Specialized 2	Unsegmented 0	Less 0
Large, poor	Moderate 1	Hierarchical 1	Hierarchical 1	More 2
Small, rich	Light 0	Unsegmented 0	Unsegmented 0	More 2
Small, poor	Moderate 1	Specialized 2	Specialized 2	Equal 1

With this specification, the garbage can model can be used to predict the differences expected among the several types of school. The results are found in Table 5. They suggest that under conditions of prosperity, overt conflict (problem activity) will be substantially higher in poor schools than in rich ones, and decision time will be substantially longer. Large, rich schools will be characterized by a high degree of problem latency. Most decisions will resolve some problems.

What happens to this group of schools under conditions of adversity—when slack is reduced? According to earlier arguments, slack could be expected to affect each of the organizational variables. It first increases net energy load, as resources become shorter and thus problems require a larger share of available energy to solve, but this effect is later compensated by the reduction in market demand for personnel and in the relative attractiveness of the school as an arena for problems. The market effects also reduce the differences in market demand for important

schools have a moderate level of problem activity, a moderate level of decision by resolution. In relation to their earlier state, however, large, rich schools are certainly deprived. Problem activity and decision time have increased greatly; the proportion of decisions which resolve problems has decreased from 68 percent to 21 percent; administrators are less able to move around from one decision to another. In all these terms, the relative deprivation of the presidents of large, rich schools is much greater, in the early stages of adversity, than that of administrators in other schools.

The large, poor schools are in the worst absolute position under adversity. They have a high level of problem activity, a substantial decision time, a low level of decision maker mobility, and a low proportion of decisions being made by resolution. But along most of these dimensions, the change has been less for them.

The small rich schools experience a large increase in problem activity, an increase in

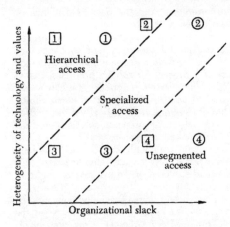

① Large, poor school, good times
② Large, rich school, good times
③ Small, poor school, good times
④ Small, rich school, good times

1 Large, poor school, bad times
2 Large, rich school, bad times
3 Small, poor school, bad times
4 Small, rich school, bad times

FIGURE 4. HYPOTHESIZED LOCATION OF DIF-
FERENT SCHOOLS IN TERMS OF SLACK AND HET-
EROGENEITY

decision time, and a decrease in the proportion of decisions by resolution as adversity
begins. The small, poor schools seem to move
in a direction counter to the trends in the
other three groups. Decision style is little affected by the onset of slack reduction, problem activity, and decision time decline, and
decision-maker mobility increases. Presidents
of such organizations might feel a sense of
success in their efforts to tighten up the organization in response to resource contraction.

The application of the model to this particular situation among American colleges
and universities clearly depends upon a large
number of assumptions. Other assumptions
would lead to other interpretations of the impact of adversity within a garbage can decision process. Nevertheless, the derivations

from the model have some face validity as a
description of some aspects of recent life in
American higher education.

The model also makes some predictions of
future developments. As adversity continues,
the model predicts that all schools, and particularly rich schools, will experience improvement in their position. Among large,
rich schools decision by resolution triples,
problem activity is cut by almost three-
fourths, and decision time is cut more than
one-half. If the model has validity, a series of
articles in the magazines of the next decade
detailing how President X assumed the presidency of large, rich university Y and guided
it to "peace" and "progress" (short decision
time, decisions without problems, low problem activity) can be expected.

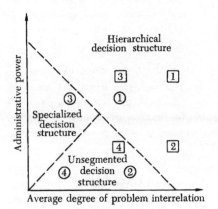

Average degree of problem interrelation

① Large, poor school, good times
② Large, rich school, good times
③ Small, poor school, good times
④ Small, rich school, good times

1 Large, poor school, bad times
2 Large, rich school, bad times
3 Small, poor school, bad times
4 Small, rich school, bad times

FIGURE 5. HYPOTHESIZED LOCATION OF DIF-
FERENT SCHOOLS IN TERMS OF ADMINISTRATIVE
POWER AND PERCEIVED INTERRELATION OF
PROBLEMS

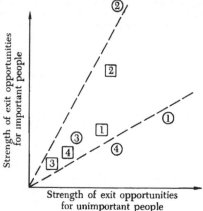

Strength of exit opportunities
for unimportant people

① Large, poor school, good times
② Large, rich school, good times
③ Small, poor school, good times
④ Small, rich school, good times

1 Large, poor school, bad times
2 Large, rich school, bad times
3 Small, poor school, bad times
4 Small, rich school, bad times

FIGURE 6. HYPOTHESIZED LOCATION OF DIF-
FERENT SCHOOLS IN TERMS OF EXIT OPPORTUNI-
TIES

CONCLUSION

A set of observations made in the study
of some university organizations has been
translated into a model of decision making in
organized anarchies, that is, in situations
which do not meet the conditions for more
classical models of decision making in some
or all of three important ways: preferences
are problematic, technology is unclear, or
participation is fluid. The garbage can process is one in which problems, solutions, and
participants move from one choice opportunity to another in such a way that the nature
of the choice, the time it takes, and the problems it solves all depend on a relatively complicated intermeshing of elements. These include the mix of choices available at any one
time, the mix of problems that have access to
the organization, the mix of solutions looking

for problems, and the outside demands on
the decision makers.

A major feature of the garbage can process
is the partial uncoupling of problems and
choices. Although decision making is thought
of as a process for solving problems, that is
often not what happens. Problems are
worked upon in the context of some choice,
but choices are made only when the shifting
combinations of problems, solutions, and decision makers happen to make action possible. Quite commonly this is after problems
have left a given choice arena or before they
have discovered it (decisions by flight or
oversight).

Four factors were specified which could be
expected to have substantial effects on the
operation of the garbage can process: the organization's net energy load and energy distribution, its decision structure, and problem
access structure. Though the specifications
are quite simple their interaction is extremely
complex, so that investigation of the probable
behavior of a system fully characterized by
the garbage can process and previous specifications requires computer simulation. No
real system can be fully characterized in this
way. Nonetheless, the simulated organization
exhibits behaviors which can be observed
some of the time in almost all organizations
and frequently in some, such as universities.
The garbage can model is a first step toward
seeing the systematic interrelatedness of organizational phenomena which are familiar,
even common, but which have previously
been regarded as isolated and pathological.
Measured against a conventional normative
model of rational choice, the garbage can
process does appear pathological, but such
standards are not really appropriate. The
process occurs precisely when the preconditions of more normal rational models are not
met.

It is clear that the garbage can process
does not resolve problems well. But it does
enable choices to be made and problems resolved, even when the organization is
plagued with goal ambiguity and conflict,
with poorly understood problems that
wander in and out of the system, with a variable environment, and with decision makers
who may have other things on their minds.

There is a large class of significant situa-

TABLE 5. EFFECT OF ADVERSITY ON FOUR TYPES OF COLLEGES AND
UNIVERSITIES OPERATING WITHIN A GARBAGE CAN DECISION PROCESS

Type of school/ type of situation	Organi- zational type	Deci- sion style propor- tion resolu- tion	Problem activity	Problem latency	Deci- sion maker activity	Deci- sion time
			Outcome			
Large, rich universities						
Good times	0200	0.68	0	154	100	0
Bad times, early	1110	0.21	210	23	58	34
Bad times, late	0111	0.65	57	60	66	14
Large, poor universities						
Good times	1112	0.38	210	25	66	31
Bad times, early	2112	0.24	248	32	55	38
Bad times, late	1111	0.31	200	30	58	28
Small, rich colleges						
Good times	0002	1.0	0	0	100	0
Bad times, early	1002	0	310	0	90	20
Bad times, late	0001	1.0	0	0	100	0
Small, poor colleges						
Good times	1221	0.54	158	127	15	83
Bad times, early	2211	0.61	101	148	73	52
Bad times, late	1211	0.62	78	151	76	39

tions in which the preconditions of the garbage can process cannot be eliminated. In some, such as pure research, or the family, they should not be eliminated. The great advantage of trying to see garbage can phenomena together as a process is the possibility that that process can be understood, that organizational design and decision making can take account of its existence and that, to some extent, it can be managed.

APPENDIX

Version five of the Fortran program for the garbage can model reads in entry times for choices, solution coefficients, entry times for problems, and two control variables, NA and IO. NA controls various combinations of freedom of movement for decision makers and problems. All results are based on runs in which NA is 1. Comment cards included in the program describe other possibilities. The latter variable, IO, controls output. At the value 1, only summary statistics are printed. At the value 2, full histories of the decision process are printed for each organizational variant.

The following are ten summary statistics:

1. (KT) Problem persistence, the total number of time periods a problem is activated and attached to a choice, summed over all problems.

2. (KU) Problem latency, the total number of time periods a problem is activated, but not attached to a choice, summed over all problems.

3. (KV) Problem velocity, the total number of times any problem shifts from one choice to another.

4. (KW) Problem failures, the total number of problems not solved at the end of the twenty time periods.

5. (KX) Decision maker velocity, the total number of times any decision maker shifts from one choice to another.

6. (KS) Decision maker inactivity, the total number of time periods a decision maker is not attached to a choice, summed over all decision makers.

7. (KY) Choice persistence, the total number of time periods a choice is activated, summed over all choices.

18   ADMINISTRATIVE SCIENCE QUARTERLY

8. (KZ) Choice failures, the total number of choices not made by the end of the twenty time periods.

9. (XR) Energy reserve, the total amount of effective energy available to the system but not used because decision makers are not attached to any choice.

10. (XS) Energy wastage, the total effective energy used on choices in excess of that required to make them at the time they are made.

In its current form the program generates both the problem access structure and the decision structure internally. In order to examine the performance of the model under other structures, modification of the code or its elimination in favor of Read statements to take the structures from cards will be necessary.

Under IO = 2, total output will be about ninety pages. Running time is about two minutes under a Watfor compiler.

Cohen et al: A GARBAGE CAN MODEL   19

APPENDIX TABLE: FORTRAN PROGRAM FOR GARBAGE CAN MODEL, VERSION FIVE

```
C      THE GARBAGE CAN MODEL. VERSION 5
C      ***
C      IO IS 1 FOR SUMMARY STATISTICS ONLY
C      IO IS 2 FOR SUMMARY STATISTICS PLUS HISTORIES
C      ***
C      NA IS 1 WHEN PROBS AND DMKRS BOTH MOVE
C      NA IS 2 WHEN DMKRS ONLY MOVE
C      NA IS 3 WHEN PROBS ONLY MOVE
C      NA IS 4 WHEN NEITHER PROBS NOR DMKRS MOVE
C      ***
C      IL IS A FACTOR DETERMINING PROB ENERGY REQ
C      ***
C      VARIABLES
C         ***
C         NUMBERS
C            COUNTERS   UPPER LIMITS      NAME
C            ***
C               I          NCH           CHOICES
C               J          NPR           PROBLEM
C               K          NDM           DECMKRS
C               LT         NTP           TIME
C         ***
C         ARRAYS
C            CODE         DIMEN          NAME
C            ***
C            ICH          NCH            CHOICE ENTRY TIME
C            ICS          NCH            CHOICE STATUS
C            JET          NPR            PROB. ENTRY TIME
C            JF           NPR            PROB. ATT. CHOICE
C            JFF          NPR            WORKING COPY JF
C            JPS          NPR            PROB. STATUS
C            KDC          NDM            DMKR. ATT. CHOICE
C            KDCW         NDM            WORKING COPY KDC
C            XEF          MCH            ENERGY EXPENDED
C            XERC         NCH            CHOICE EN. REQT.
C            XERP         NPR            PROB. EN. REQT.
C            XSC          NTP            SOLUTION COEFFICIENT
C         ***
C         2-DIMENSIONAL ARRAYS
C            ***
C            CODE         DIMEN          NAME
C            ***
C            IKA          NCH,NDM        DECISION STRUCTURE
C            JIA          NPR,NCH        ACCESS STRUCTURE
C            XEA          NDM,NTP        ENERGY MATRIX
C         ***
C         ***
C         ***
C      ***
C      SUMMARY STATISTICS FOR EACH VARIANT
C            COL 1: KZ: TOTAL DECISIONS NOT MADE
C            COL 2: KY: TOTAL NUMBER ACTIVE CHOICE PERIODS
C            COL 3: KX: TOTAL NUMBER CHANGES BY DECISION MAKERS
C            COL 4: KW: TOTAL PROBLEMS NOT SOLVED
C            COL 5: KV: TOTAL NUMBER CHANGES BY PROBLEMS
C            COL 6: KU: TOTAL NUMBER LATENT PROBLEM PERIODS
C            COL 7: KT: TOTAL NUMBER ATTACHED PROBLEM PERIODS
C            COL 8: KS: TOTAL NUMBER PERIODS DMKRS RESTING
C            COL 9: XR: TOTAL AMOUNT OF UNUSED ENERGY
```

```
C                COL 10:XS: TOTAL AMOUNT OF WASTED ENERGY
C      ***
C      INPUT BLOCK. READ-IN AND INITIALIZATIONS.
       DIMENSION ICH(20),JF(20),XERC(20),XEE(20),XSC(20),JFF(20),XERP(20
      *),JET(20),JPS(20),ICS(20),KDC(20),KDCW(20),JIA(20,20),IKA(20,20),
      CXEA(20,20),KABC(20,20),KBBC(20,20),KCBC(20,20)
1001   FORMAT(5(I3,1X))
1002   FORMAT(10(I3,1X))
1003   FORMAT(25(I1,1X))
1004   FORMAT(10F4.2)
       NTP=20
       NCH=10
       NPR=20
       NDM=10
   8   READ(5,1002)(ICH(I),I=1,NCH)
       READ(5,1004)(XSC(LT),LT=1,NTP)
       READ(5,1002)(JET(J),J=1,NPR)
       READ(5,1003) NA,IO
       WRITE(6,1050) NA
1050   FORMAT('1       DEC.MAKER MOVEMENT CONDITION (NA) IS  ',I1/)
       DO 998 IL=1,3
       IB=IL-1
       DO 997 JAB=1,3
       JA=JAB-1
       DO 996 JDB=1,3
       JD=JDB-1
       DO 995 JEB=1,3
       JE=JEB-1
       XR=0.0
       XS=0.0
       KS=0
       DO 10 I=1,NCH
       XERC(I)=1.1
       XEE(I)=0.0
  10   ICS(I)=0
       DO 20 K=1,NDM
       KDC(K)=0
  20   KDCW(K)=KDC(K)
       DO 40 J=1,NPR
       XERP(J)=IL*1.1
       JF(J)=0
       JFF(J)=0
  40   JPS(J)=0
C      SETTING UP THE DECISION MAKERS ACCESS TO CHOICES.
       DO 520 I=1,NCH
       DO 510 J=1,NDM
       IKA(I,J)=1
       IF(JD.EQ.1) GO TO 502
       IF(JD.EQ.2) GO TO 504
       GO TO 510
 502   IF(I.GE.J) GO TO 510
       IKA(I,J)=0
       GO TO 510
 504   IF(J.EQ.I) GO TO 510
       IKA(I,J)=0
 510   CONTINUE
 520   CONTINUE
C      SETTING UP THE PROBLEMS ACCESS TO CHOICES.
       DO 560 I=1,NPR
       DO 550 J=1,NCH
```

```
            JIA(I,J)=0
            IF(JA.EQ.1) GO TO 532
            IF(JA.EQ.2) GO TO 534
            JIA(I,J)=1
            GO TO 550
      532   IF ((I-J).GT.(I/2)) GO TO 550
            JIA(I,J)=1
            GO TO 550
      534   IF(I.NE.(2*J))  GO TO 550
            JIA(I,J)=1
            JIA(I-1,J)=1
      550   CONTINUE
      560   CONTINUE
            DO 590 I=1,NDM
            DO 580 J=1,NTP
            XEA(I,J)=0.55
            IF(JF.EQ.1)GO TO 580
            XXA=I
            IF(JE.EQ.0)GO TO 570
            XEA(I,J)=(11.0-XXA)/10.0
            GO TO 580
      570   XEA(I,J)=XXA/10.0
      580   CONTINUE
      590   CONTINUE
      C     *** FINISH READ    INITIALIZATION
            DO 994 LT=1,NTP
     1006   FORMAT(2X,6HCHOICE,2X,I3,2X,6HACTIVE )
      C     CHOICE ACTIVATION
            DO 101   I=1,NCH
            IF(ICH(I).NE.LT)GO TO 101
            ICS(I)=1
      101   CONTINUE
      C     PROB. ACTIVATION
            DO 110 J=1,NPR
            IF(JET(J).NE.LT)GO TO 110
            JPS(J)=1
      110   CONTINUE
      C     FIND MOST ATTRACTIVE CHOICE FOR PROBLEM J
            DO 120 J=1,NPR
            IF (JPS(J).NE.1) GO TO 120
            IF(NA.EQ.2)GO TO 125
            IF(NA.EQ.4)GO TO 125
            GO TO 126
      125   IF(JF(J).NE.0)GO TO 127
      126   S=1000000
            DO 121 I=1,NCH
            IF (ICS(I).NE.1) GO TO 121
            IF(JIA(J,I).EQ.0)GO TO 121
            IF(JF(J).EQ.0)GO TO 122
            IF(JF(J).EQ.1)GO TO 122
            IF((XERP(J)+XERC(I)-XEE(I)).GE.S)GO TO 121
            GO TO 123
      122   IF((XERC(I)-XEE(I)).GE.S)GO TO 121
            S=XERC(I)-XEE(I)
            GO TO 124
      123   S=XERP(J)+XERC(I)-XEE(I)
      124   JFF(J)=I
      121   CONTINUE
            GO TO 120
      127   JFF(J)=JF(J)
```

```
120     CONTINUE
        DO 130 J=1,NPR
131     JF(J)=JFF(J)
130     JFF(J)=0
        LTT=LT-1
        IF(LT.EQ.1)LTT=1
C       FIND MOST ATTRACTIVE CHOICE FOR DMKR K
        DO 140 K=1,NDM
        IF(NA.EQ.3)GO TO 145
        IF(NA.EQ.4) GO TO 145
        GO TO 146
 145    IF(KDC(K).NE.0)GO TO 147
 146    S=1000000
        DO 141 I=1,NCH
        IF (ICS(I).NE.1) GO TO 141
        IF(IKA(I,K).EQ.0)GO TO 141
        IF(KDC(K).EQ.0)GO TO 142
        IF(KDC(K).EQ.I)GO TO 142
 148    IF((XFRC(I)-XEE(I)-(XEA(K,LTT)*XSC(LTT))).GE.S)GO TO 141
        GO TO 143
 142    IF((XERC(I)-XEE(I)).GE.S)GO TO 141
        S=XERC(I)-XEE(I)
        GO TO 144
 143    S=XERC(I)-XEE(I)-XEA(K,LTT)*XSC(LTT)
 144    KDCW(K)=I
 141    CONTINUE
        GO TO 140
 147    KDCW(K)=KDC(K)
 140    CONTINUF
        DO 150 K=1,NDM
 151    KDC(K)=KDCW(K)
        IF(KDC(K).NE.0)GO TO 150
        XR=XR+(XEA(K,LT)*XSC(LT))
        KS=KS+1
 150    KDCW(K)=0
C       ESTABLISHING THE ENERGY REQUIRED TO MAKE EACH CHOICE.
        DO 199 I=1,NCH
        IF(ICS(I).EQ.0)GO TO 199
        XERC(I)=0.0
        DO 160 J=1,NPR
        IF (JPS(J).NE.1) GO TO 160
        IF(JF(J).NE.I)GO TO 160
        XERC(I)=XERC(I)+XERP(J)
 160    CONTINUE
        DO 170 K=1,NDM
        IF(IKA(I,K).EQ.0)GO TO 170
        IF(KDC(K).NE.I)GO TO 170
        XEE(I)=XEE(I)+XSC(LT)*XEA(K,LT)
 170    CONTINUE
 199    CONTINUE
C       MAKING DECISIONS
        DO 299 I=1,NCH
        IF (ICS(I).NE.1) GO TO 299
        IF(XERC(I).GT.XEE(I))GO TO 299
        XS=XS+XEE(I)-XERC(I)
        ICS(I)=2
        DO 250 J=1,NPR
        IF(JF(J).NE.I)GO TO 250
        JPS(J)=2
 250    CONTINUE
```

```
      IF(NA.EQ.3)GO TO 261
      IF(NA.EQ.4)GO TO 261
      GO TO 299
 261  DO 262 K=1,NDM
      IF(KDC(K).NE.1)GO TO 262
      KDCW(K)=1
 262  CONTINUE
 299  CONTINUE
      DO 200 I=1,NCH
 200  KABC(LT,I)=ICS(I)
      DO 210 K=1,NDM
      KBBC(LT,K)=KDC(K)
      IF(KDCW(K).EQ.0)GO TO 210
      KDC(K)=0
 210  KDCW(K)=0
      DO 220 J=1,NPR
      KCBC(LT,J)=JF(J)
      IF(JPS(J).EQ.0) GO TO 230
      IF(JPS(J).EQ.1) GO TO 220
      KCBC(LT,J)=1000
      GO TO 220
 230  KCBC(LT,J)=-1
 220  CONTINUE
 994  CONTINUE
C     FINISH TIME PERIOD LOOP. BEGIN ACCUMULATION OF 10 SUMMARY STATISTICS.
      KZ=0
      KY=0
      KX=0
      KW=0
      KV=0
      KU=0
      KT=0
      DO 310 I=1,NTP
      DO 320 J=1,NCH
      IF(KABC(I,J).NE.1)GO TO 320
      KY=KY+1
      IF(I.NE.NTP)GO TO 320
      KZ=KZ+1
 320  CONTINUE
 310  CONTINUE
      DO 330 I=2,NTP
      DO 340 J=1,NDM
      IF(KBBC(I,J).EQ.KBBC(I-1,J))GO TO 340
      KX=KX+1
 340  CONTINUE
 330  CONTINUE
      DO 350 I=1,NTP
      DO 360 J=1,NPR
      IF(KCBC(I,J).EQ.0)GO TO 351
      IF(KCBC(I,J).EQ.-1) GO TO 360
      IF(KCBC(I,J).EQ.1000) GO TO 352
      KT=KT+1
      GO TO 360
 351  KU=KU+1
      GO TO 360
 352  IF(I.NE.NTP)GO TO 360
      KW=KW+1
 360  CONTINUE
 350  CONTINUE
      KW=NPR-KW
```

```
      DO 370 I=2,NTP
      DO 380 J=1,NPR
      IF(KCBC(I,J).EQ.KCBC(I-1,J))GO TO 380
      KV=KV+1
380   CONTINUE
370   CONTINUE
C     BEGIN WRITEOUT OF MATERIALS FOR THIS ORGANIZATIONAL VARIANT.
1000  FORMAT(1H1)
1019  FORMAT(2X,'LOAD=',I1,' PR.ACC.=',I1,' DEC.STR.=',I1,' EN.DIST.=',
     BI1,2X,'STATS 1-10',3X,8I5,1X,2F6.2/)
      WRITE(6,1019)IB,JA,JD,JE,KZ,KY,KX,KW,KV,KU,KT,KS,XR,XS
      IF(IO.EQ.1) GO TO 995
2000  FORMAT(' CHOICE ACTIVATION HISTORY',34X,'DEC.MAKER ACTIVITY HISTOR
     BY'/' 20 TIME PERIODS,10 CHOICES',33X,'20 TIME PERIODS,10 DEC. MAKE
     CRS'/' 0=INACTIVE,1=ACTIVE,2=MADE',33X,'0=INACTIVE,X=WORHING ON CHO
     DICE X'//9X,'  1  2  3  4  5 6 7 8 9 10',30X,'1 2 3 4 5 6 7 8 9 10'/)
      WRITE(6,2000)
2001  FORMAT( 5X,I2,3X,10I2,25X,I2,3X,10I2)
      WRITE(6,2001)(LT,(KABC(LT,J),J=1,NCH),LT,( KBBC(LT,J),J=1,NDM),
     B LT=1,NTP  )
2002  FORMAT(/' PROBLEM HISTORY:ROWS=TIME,COLS=PROBS.. -1=NOT ENTERED..
     BO=UNATTACHED,X=ATT.TO CH.X,**=SOLVED'/10X,
     C'  1  2  3  4  5  6  7  8  9 10 11 12 13 14 15 16 17 18 19 20'/)
      WRITE(6,2002)
2003  FORMAT(20(5X,I2,3X,20(1X,I2)/))
      WRITE(6,2003)(LT,(KCBC(LT,J),J=1,NPR),LT=1,NTP)
      WRITE(6,1000)
995   CONTINUE
996   CONTINUE
997   CONTINUE
998   CONTINUE
      STOP
      END

*******   DATA AS FOLLOWS  (AFTER GUIDE CARDS)   ***********


0         1         2         3         4         5         6         7         8
12345678901234567890123456789012345678901234567890123456789012345678901234567890

008.005.006.007.004.009.002.010.003.001
1.000.900.700.300.100.100.300.700.901.00
0.600.600.600.600.600.600.600.600.600.60
009.005.008.007.010.003.003.001.007.009
006.008.005.002.004.002.004.010.006.001
1 2
```

Michael D. Cohen is an NSF-SSRC post-doctoral fellow at Stanford University; James G. March is David Jacks Professor of Higher Education, Political Science, and Sociology at Stanford University; and Johan P. Olsen is an assistant professor of Political Science at the University of Bergen.

BIBLIOGRAPHY

Allison, Graham T.
  1969 "Conceptual models and the Cuban missile crises." American Political Science Review, 63: 689–718.
Christensen, Søren
  1971 Institut og laboratorieorganisation på Danmarks tekniske Højskole. Copenhagen: Copenhagen School of Economics.
Cohen, Michael D., and James G. March
  1972 The American College President. New York: McGraw-Hill, Carnegie Commission on the Future of Higher Education.
Coleman, James S.
  1957 Community Conflict. Glencoe: Free Press.
Cyert, Richard M., and James G. March
  1963 Behavioral Theory of the Firm. Englewood Cliffs: Prentice-Hall.
Enderud, Harald
  1971 Rektoratet og den centrale administration på Danmarks tekniske Højskole. Copenhagen: Copenhagen School of Economics.
Lindblom, Charles E.
  1965 The Intelligence of Democracy. New York: Macmillan.
Long, Norton
  1958 "The local community as an ecology of games." American Journal of Sociology, 44: 251–261.
March, James G., and Herbert A. Simon
  1958 Organizations. New York: John Wiley.
Mood, Alexander (ed.)
  1971 More Scholars for the Dollar. New York: McGraw-Hill, Carnegie Commission on the Future of Higher Education.
Olsen, Johan P.
  1970 A Study of Choice in an Academic Organization. Bergen: University of Bergen.
  1971 The Reorganization of Authority in an Academic Organization. Bergen: University of Bergen.
Rommetveit, Kåre
  1971 Framveksten av det medisinske fakultet ved Universitetet i Tromsø. Bergen: University of Bergen.
Schilling, Warner R.
  1968 "The H-bomb decision: how to decide without actually choosing." In W. R. Nelson (ed.), The Politics of Science. London: Oxford University Press.
Thompson, James D.
  1967 Organizations in Action. New York: McGraw-Hill.
Vickers, Geoffrey
  1965 The Art of Judgment. New York: Basic Books.

[8]

Bounded rationality, ambiguity, and the engineering of choice

James G. March
Professor of Management
Stanford University

Rational choice involves two guesses, a guess about uncertain future conse-
quences and a guess about uncertain future preferences. Partly as a result of
behavioral studies of choice over a twenty-year period, modifications in the
way the theory deals with the first guess have become organized into
conceptions of bounded rationality. Recently, behavioral studies of choice have
examined the second guess, the way preferences are processed in choice be-
havior. These studies suggest possible modifications in standard assumptions
about tastes and their role in choice. This paper examines some of those
modifications, some possible approaches to working on them, and some
complications.

1. The engineering of choice and ordinary choice behavior

■ Recently I gave a lecture on elementary decision theory, an introduction
to rational theories of choice. After the lecture, a student asked whether it
was conceivable that the practical procedures for decisionmaking implicit in
theories of choice might make actual human decisions worse rather than better.
What is the empirical evidence, he asked, that human choice is improved by
knowledge of decision theory or by application of the various engineering forms
of rational choice? I answered, I think correctly, that the case for the usefulness
of decision engineering rested primarily not on the kind of direct empirical confirmation that he sought, but on two other things: on a set of theorems prov-
ing the superiority of particular procedures in particular situations if the situations are correctly specified and the procedures correctly applied, and on the
willingness of clients to purchase the services of experts with skills in decision
sciences.

The answer may not have been reasonable, but the question clearly was. It
articulated a classical challenge to the practice of rational choice, the possibility
that processes of rationality might combine with properties of human beings to

Presented at a conference on the new industrial organization at Carnegie-Mellon University,
October 14–15, 1977. The conference was organized to honor the contributions of Herbert A. Simon
to economics, and his contribution to this paper is obvious. In addition, I have profited from
comments by Richard M. Cyert, Jon Elster, Alexander L. George, Elisabeth Hansot, Nannerl O.
Keohane, Robert O. Keohane, Tjalling Koopmans, Mancur Olson, Louis R. Pondy, Roy Radner,
Giovanni Sartori, and Oliver E. Williamson. This research has been supported by a grant from
the Spencer Foundation.

produce decisions that are less sensible than the unsystematized actions of an intelligent person, or at least that the way in which we might use rational procedures intelligently is not self-evident. Camus (1951) argued, in effect, that man was not smart enough to be rational, a point made in a different way at about the same time by Herbert A. Simon (1957). Twenty years later, tales of horror have become contemporary clichés of studies of rational analysis in organizations (Wildavsky, 1971; Wildavsky and Pressman, 1974; Warwick, 1975).

I do not share the view of some of my colleagues that microeconomics, decision science, management science, operations analysis, and the other forms of rational decision engineering are mostly manufacturers of massive mischief when they are put into practice. It seems to me likely that these modern technologies of reason have, on balance, done more good than harm, and that students of organizations, politics, and history have been overly gleeful in their compilation of disasters. But I think there is good sense in asking how the practical implementation of theories of choice combines with the ways people behave when they make decisions, and whether our ideas about the engineering of choice might be improved by greater attention to our descriptions of choice behavior.

At first blush, pure models of rational choice seem obviously appropriate as guides to intelligent action, but more problematic for predicting behavior. In practice, the converse seems closer to the truth for much of economics. So long as we use individual choice models to predict the behavior of relatively large numbers of individuals or organizations, some potential problems are avoided by the familiar advantages of aggregation. Even a small signal stands out in a noisy message. On the other hand, if we choose to predict small numbers of individuals or organizations or give advice to a single individual or organization, the saving graces of aggregation are mostly lost. The engineering of choice depends on a relatively close articulation between choice as it is comprehended in the assumptions of the model and choice as it is made comprehensible to individual actors.

This relation is reflected in the historical development of the field. According to conventional dogma, there are two kinds of theories of human behavior: descriptive (or behavioral) theories that purport to describe actual behavior of individuals or social institutions, and prescriptive (or normative) theories that purport to prescribe optimal behavior. In many ways, the distinction leads to an intelligent and fruitful division of labor in social science, reflecting differences in techniques, objectives, and professional cultures. For a variety of historical and intellectual reasons, however, such a division has not characterized the development of the theory of choice. Whether one considers ideas about choice in economics, psychology, political science, sociology, or philosophy, behavioral and normative theories have developed as a dialectic rather than as separate domains. Most modern behavioral theories of choice take as their starting point some simple ideas about rational human behavior. As a result, new developments in normative theories of choice have quickly affected behavioral theories. Contemplate, for example, the impact of game theory, statistical decision theory, and information theory on behavioral theories of human problem-solving, political decisionmaking, bargaining, and organizational behavior (Rapoport, 1969; Vroom, 1964; Binkley, Bronaugh, and Marras, 1971; Tversky and Kahneman, 1974; Mayhew, 1974). It is equally obvious that prescriptive theories of choice have been affected by efforts to understand actual

Organization Theory I

choice behavior. Engineers of artificial intelligence have modified their perceptions of efficient problem solving procedures by studying the actual behavior of human problem solvers (Simon, 1969; Newell and Simon, 1972). Engineers of organizational decisionmaking have modified their models of rationality on the basis of studies of actual organizational behavior (Charnes and Cooper, 1963; Keen, 1977).

Modern students of human choice frequently assume, at least implicitly, that actual human choice behavior in some way or other is likely to make sense. It can be understood as being the behavior of an intelligent being or a group of intelligent beings. Much theoretical work searches for the intelligence in apparently anomalous human behavior. This process of discovering sense in human behavior is conservative with respect to the concept of rational man and to behavioral change. It preserves the axiom of rationality; and it preserves the idea that human behavior is intelligent, even when it is not obviously so. But it is not conservative with respect to prescriptive models of choice. For if there is sense in the choice behavior of individuals acting contrary to standard engineering procedures for rationality, then it seems reasonable to suspect that there may be something inadequate about our normative theory of choice or the procedures by which it is implemented.

Rational choice involves two kinds of guesses: guesses about future consequences of current actions and guesses about future preferences for those consequences (Savage, 1954; Thompson, 1967). We try to imagine what will happen in the future as a result of our actions and we try to imagine how we shall evaluate what will happen. Neither guess is necessarily easy. Anticipating future consequences of present decisions is often subject to substantial error. Anticipating future preferences is often confusing. Theories of rational choice are primarily theories of these two guesses and how we deal with their complications. Theories of choice under uncertainty emphasize the complications of guessing future consequences. Theories of choice under conflict or ambiguity emphasize the complications of guessing future preferences.

Students of decisionmaking under uncertainty have identified a number of ways in which a classical model of how alternatives are assessed in terms of their consequences is neither descriptive of behavior nor a good guide in choice situations. As a result of these efforts, some of our ideas about how the first guess is made and how it ought to be made have changed. Since the early writings of Herbert A. Simon (1957), for example, bounded rationality has come to be recognized widely, though not universally, both as an accurate portrayal of much choice behavior and as a normatively sensible adjustment to the costs and character of information gathering and processing by human beings (Radner, 1975a, 1975b; Radner and Rothschild, 1975; Connolly, 1977).

The second guess has been less considered. For the most part, theories of choice have assumed that future preferences are exogenous, stable, and known with adequate precision to make decisions unambiguous. The assumptions are obviously subject to question. In the case of collective decisionmaking, there is the problem of conflicting objectives representing the values of different participants (March, 1962; Olson, 1965; M. Taylor, 1975; Pfeffer, 1977). In addition, individual preferences often appear to be fuzzy and inconsistent, and preferences appear to change over time, at least in part as a consequence of actions taken. Recently, some students of choice have been examining the ways individuals and organizations confront the second guess under conditions of ambiguity (i.e., where goals are vague, problematic, inconsistent, or unstable) (Cohen and March, 1974; Weick, 1976; March and Olsen, 1976; Crozier and Friedberg, 1977). Those efforts are fragmentary, but they suggest that ignoring the ambiguities involved in guessing future preferences leads both to misinterpreting choice behavior and to misstating the normative problem facing a decisionmaker. The doubts are not novel; John Stuart Mill (1838) expressed many of them in his essay on Bentham. They are not devastating; the theory of choice is probably robust enough to cope with them. They are not esoteric; Hegel is relevant, but may not be absolutely essential.

2. Bounded rationality

■ There is a history. A little over twenty years ago, Simon published two papers that became a basis for two decades of development in the theory of choice (1955, 1956). The first of these examined the informational and computational limits on rationality by human beings. The paper suggested a focus on stepfunction utility functions and a process of information gathering that began with a desired outcome and worked back to a set of antecedent actions sufficient to produce it. The second paper explored the consequences of simple payoff functions and search rules in an uncertain environment. The two papers argued explicitly that descriptions of decisionmaking in terms of such ideas conformed more to actual human behavior than did descriptions built upon classical rationality, that available evidence designed to test such models against classical ones tended to support the alternative ideas.

Because subsequent developments were extensive, it is well to recall that the original argument was a narrow one. It started from the proposition that all intendedly rational behavior is behavior within constraints. Simon added the idea that the list of technical constraints on choice should include some properties of human beings as processors of information and as problem solvers. The limitations were limitations of computational capability, the organization and utilization of memory, and the like. He suggested that human beings develop decision procedures that are sensible, given the constraints, even though they might not be sensible if the constraints were removed. As a short-hand label for such procedures, he coined the term "satisficing."

Developments in the field over the past twenty years have expanded and distorted Simon's original formulation. But they have retained some considerable flavor of his original tone. He emphasized the theoretical difficulty posed by self-evident empirical truths. He obscured a distinction one might make between individual and organizational decisionmaking, proposing for the most part the same general ideas for both. He obscured a possible distinction between behavioral and normative theories of choice, preferring to view differences between perfect rationality and bounded rationality as explicable consequences of constraints. Few of the individual scholars who followed had precisely the same interests or commitments as Simon, but the field has generally maintained the same tone. Theoretical puzzlement with respect to the simplicity of decision behavior has been extended to puzzlement with respect to decision inconsistencies and instabilities, and the extent to which individuals and organizations do things without apparent reason (March and Olsen, 1976). Recent books on decisionmaking move freely from studies of organizations to studies of individuals (Janis and Mann, 1977). And recent books on normative decision-making accept many standard forms of organizational behavior as sensible (Keen, 1977).

Twenty years later, it is clear that we do not have a single, widely-accepted, precise behavioral theory of choice. But I think it can be argued that the empirical and theoretical efforts of the past twenty years have brought us closer to understanding decision processes. The understanding is organized in a set of conceptual vignettes rather than a single, coherent structure; and the connections among the vignettes are tenuous. In effect, the effort has identified major aspects of some key processes that appear to be reflected in decision-making; but the ecology of those processes is not well captured by any current theory. For much of this development, Simon bears substantial intellectual responsibility.

Simon's contributions have been honored by subsumption, extension, elabora-tion, and transformation. Some writers have felt it important to show that aspira-tion level goals and goal-directed search can be viewed as special cases of other ideas, most commonly classical notions about rational behavior (Riker and Ordeshook, 1973). Others have taken ideas about individual human be-havior and extended them to organizations (both business firms and public bureaucracies) and to other institutions, for example, universities (Bower, 1968; Allison, 1971; Steinbruner, 1974; Williamson, 1975). Simon's original precise commentary on specific difficulties in rational models has been ex-panded to a more general consideration of problems in the assumptions of rationality, particularly the problems of subjective understanding, perception, and conflict of interest (Cyert and March, 1963; Porat and Haas, 1969; Carter, 1971; R. N. Taylor, 1975; Slovic, Fischoff, and Lichtenstein, 1977). The original articles suggested small modifications in a theory of economic behavior, the substitution of bounded rationality for omniscient rationality. But the ideas ultimately have led to an examination of the extent to which theories of choice might subordinate the idea of rationality altogether to less intentional conceptions of the causal determinants of action (March and Olsen, 1976).

3. Alternative rationalities

■ The search for intelligence in decisionmaking is an effort to rationalize apparent anomalies in behavior. In a general way, that effort imputes either calculated or systemic rationality to observed choice behavior. Action is presumed to follow either from explicit calculation of its consequences in terms of objectives, or from rules of behavior that have evolved through processes that are sensible but which obscure from present knowledge full information on the rational justification for any specific rule.

Most efforts to rationalize observed behavior have attempted to place that behavior within a framework of calculated rationality. The usual argument is that a naive rational model is inadequate either because it focuses on the wrong unit of analysis, or because it uses an inaccurate characterization of the prefer-ences involved. As a result, we have developed ideas of limited rationality, contextual rationality, game rationality, and process rationality.

Ideas of *limited rationality* emphasize the extent to which individuals and groups simplify a decision problem because of the difficulties of anticipating or considering all alternatives and all information (March and Simon, 1958; Lindblom, 1959, 1965; Radner, 1975a, 1975b). They introduce, as reasonable responses, such things as step-function tastes, simple search rules, working backward, organizational slack, incrementalism and muddling through, uncertainty avoidance, and the host of elaborations of such ideas that are familiar to students of organizational choice and human problem solving.

Ideas of *contextual rationality* emphasize the extent to which choice behavior is embedded in a complex of other claims on the attention of actors and other structures of social and cognitive relations (Long, 1958; Schelling, 1971; Cohen, March, and Olsen, 1972; Wiener, 1976; Sproull, Weiner, and Wolf, 1978). They focus on the way in which choice behavior in a particular situation is affected by the opportunity costs of attending to that situation and by the apparent tendency for people, problems, solutions, and choices to be joined by the relatively arbitrary accidents of their simultaneity rather than by their *prima facie* relevance to each other.

Ideas of *game rationality* emphasize the extent to which organizations and other social institutions consist of individuals who act in relation to each other intelligently to pursue individual objectives by means of individual calculations of self-interest (Farquharson, 1969; Harsanyi and Selten, 1972; Brams, 1975). The decision outcomes of the collectivity in some sense amalgamate those calculations, but they do so without imputing a super-goal to the collectivity or invoking collective rationality. These theories find reason in the process of coalition formation, sequential attention to goals, information bias and interpersonal gaming, and the development of mutual incentives.

Ideas of *process rationality* emphasize the extent to which decisions find their sense in attributes of the decision process, rather than in attributes of decision outcomes (Edelman, 1964; Cohen and March, 1974; Kreiner, 1976; Christensen, 1976). They explore those significant human pleasures (and pains) found in the ways we act while making decisions, and in the symbolic content of the idea and procedures of choice. Explicit outcomes are viewed as secondary and decisionmaking becomes sensible through the intelligence of the way it is orchestrated.

All of these kinds of ideas are theories of intelligent individuals making calculations of the consequences of actions for objectives, and acting sensibly to achieve those objectives. Action is presumed to be consequential, to be connected consciously and meaningfully to knowledge about personal goals and future outcomes, to be controlled by personal intention.

Although models of calculated rationality continue to be a dominant style, students of choice have also shown considerable interest in a quite different kind of intelligence, systemic rather than calculated. Suppose we imagine that knowledge, in the form of precepts of behavior, evolves over time within a system and accumulates across time, people, and organizations without complete current consciousness of its history. Then sensible action is taken by actors without comprehension of its full justification. This characterizes models of adaptive rationality, selected rationality, and posterior rationality.

Ideas of *adaptive rationality* emphasize experiential learning by individuals or collectivities (Cyert and March, 1963; Day and Groves, 1975). Most adaptive models have the property that if the world and preferences are stable and the experience prolonged enough, behavior will approach the behavior that would be chosen rationally on the basis of perfect knowledge. Moreover, the postulated learning functions normally have properties that permit sensible adaptation to drifts in environmental or taste attributes. By storing information on past experiences in some simple behavioral predilections, adaptive rationality permits the efficient management of considerable experiential information; but it is in a form that is not explicitly retrievable—particularly across individuals or long periods of time. As a result, it is a form of intelligence that tends to separate current reasons from current actions.

Ideas of *selected rationality* emphasize the process of selection among individuals or organizations through survival or growth (Winter, 1964, 1971, 1975; Nelson and Winter, 1973). Rules of behavior achieve intelligence not by virtue of conscious calculation of their rationality by current role players but by virtue of the survival and growth of social institutions in which such rules are followed and such roles are performed. Selection theories focus on the extent to which choice is dominated by standard operating procedures and the social regulation of social roles.

Ideas of *posterior rationality* emphasize the discovery of intentions as an interpretation of action rather than as a prior position (Hirschman, 1967; Weick, 1969; March, 1973). Actions are seen as being exogenous and as producing experiences that are organized into an evaluation after the fact. The valuation is in terms of preferences generated by the action and its consequences, and choices are justified by virtue of their posterior consistency with goals that have themselves been developed through a critical interpretation of the choice. Posterior rationality models maintain the idea that action should be consistent with preferences, but they conceive action as being antecedent to goals.

These explorations into elements of systemic rationality have, of course, a strong base in economics and behavioral science (Wilson, 1975; Becker, 1976); but they pose special problems for decision engineering. On the one hand, systemic rationality is not intentional. That is, behavior is not understood as following from a calculation of consequences in terms of prior objectives. If such a calculation is asserted, it is assumed to be an interpretation of the behavior but not a good predictor of it. On the other hand, these models claim, often explicitly, that there is intelligence in the suspension of calculation. Alternatively, they suggest that whatever sense there is in calculated rationality is attested not by its formal properties but by its survival as a social rule of behavior, or as an experientially verified personal propensity.

In a general way, these explications of ordinary behavior as forms of rationality have considerably clarified and extended our understanding of choice. It is now routine to explore aspects of limited, contextual, game, process, adaptive, selected, and posterior rationality in the behavioral theory of choice. We use such ideas to discover and celebrate the intelligence of human behavior. At the same time, however, this discovery of intelligence in the ordinary behavior of individuals and social institutions is an implicit pressure for reconstruction of normative theories of choice, for much of the argument is not only that observed behavior is understandable as a human phenomenon, but that it is, in some important sense, intelligent. If behavior that apparently deviates from standard procedures of calculated rationality can be shown to be intelligent, then it can plausibly be argued that models of calculated rationality are deficient not only as descriptors of human behavior but also as guides to intelligent choice.

4. The treatment of tastes

■ Engineers of intelligent choice sensibly resist the imputation of intelligence to all human behavior. Traditionally, deviations of choice behavior from the style anticipated in classical models were treated normatively as errors, or correctable faults, as indeed many of them doubtless were. The objective was to transform subjective rationality into objective rationality by removing the needless informational, procedural, and judgmental constraints that limited the effectiveness of persons proceeding intelligently from false or incomplete informational premises (Ackoff and Sasieni, 1968). One of Simon's contributions to the theory of choice was his challenge of the self-evident proposition that choice behavior necessarily would be improved if it were made more like the normative model of rational choice. By asserting that certain limits on rationality stemmed from properties of the human organism, he emphasized the possibility that actual human choice behavior was more intelligent than it appeared.

Normative theories of choice have responded to the idea. Substantial parts of the economics of information and the economics of attention (or time) are tributes to the proposition that information gathering, information processing, and decisionmaking impose demands on the scarce resources of a finite capacity human organism (Stigler, 1961; Becker, 1965; McGuire and Radner, 1972; Marschak and Radner, 1972; Rothschild and Stiglitz, 1976). Aspiration levels, signals, incrementalism, and satisficing rules for decisionmaking have been described as sensible under fairly general circumstances (Hirschman and Lindblom, 1962; Spence, 1974; Radner, 1975a, 1975b; Radner and Rothschild, 1975).

These developments in the theory of rational choice acknowledge important aspects of the behavioral critique of classical procedures for guessing the future consequences of present action. Normative response to behavioral discussions of the second guess, the estimation of future preferences, has been similarly conservative but perceptible. That standard theories of choice and the engineering procedures associated with them have a conception of preferences that differs from observations of preferences has long been noted (Johnson, 1968). As in the case of the informational constraints on rational choice, the first reaction within decision engineering was to treat deviations from well-defined, consistent preference functions as correctable faults. If individuals had deficient (i.e., inconsistent, incomplete) preference functions, they were to be induced to generate proper ones, perhaps through revealed preference techniques and education. If groups or organizations exhibited conflict, they were to be induced to resolve that conflict through prior discussion, prior side payments (e.g., an employment contract), or prior bargaining. If individuals or organizations exhibited instability in preferences over time, they were to be induced to minimize that instability by recognizing a more general specification of the preferences so that apparent changes became explicable as reflecting a single, unchanging function under changing conditions or changing resources.

Since the specific values involved in decisionmaking are irrelevant to formal models of choice, both process rationality and contextual rationality are, from such a perspective, versions of simple calculated rationality. The criterion function is changed, but the theory treats the criterion function as any arbitrary set of well-ordered preferences. So long as the preferences associated with the process of choice or the preferences involved in the broader context are well defined and well behaved, there is no deep theoretical difficulty. But, in practice, such elements of human preference functions have not filtered significantly into the engineering of choice.

The record with respect to problems of goal conflict, multiple, lexicographic goals, and loosely coupled systems is similar. Students of bureaucracies have argued that a normative theory of choice within a modern bureaucratic structure must recognize explicitly the continuing conflict in preferences among various actors (Tullock, 1965; Downs, 1967; Allison and Halperin, 1972; Halperin, 1974). Within such systems "decisions" are probably better seen as strategic first-move interventions in a dynamic internal system than as choices in a classical sense. Decisions are not expected to be implemented, and actions that would be optimal if implemented are suboptimal as first moves. This links theories of choice to game-theoretic conceptions of politics, bargaining, and strategic actions in a productive way. Although in this way ideas about strategic choice in collectivities involving conflict of interest are well established in part of the choice literature (Elster, 1977a), they have had little impact on such obvious applied domains as bureaucratic decisionmaking or the design of organizational control systems. The engineering of choice has been more explicitly concerned with multiple criteria decision procedures for dealing with multiple, lexico-graphic, or political goals (Lee, 1972; Pattanaik, 1973). In some cases these efforts have considerably changed the spirit of decision analysis, moving it toward a role of exploring the implications of constraints and away from a conception of solution.

Behavioral inquiry into preferences has, however, gone beyond the problems of interpersonal conflict of interest in recent years and into the complications of ambiguity. The problems of ambiguity are partly problems of disagreement about goals among individuals, but they are more conspicuously problems of the relevance, priority, clarity, coherence, and stability of goals in both individual and organizational choice. Several recent treatments of organizational choice behavior record some major ways in which explicit goals seem neither particularly powerful predictors of outcomes nor particularly well represented as either stable, consistent preference orders or well-defined political constraints (Cohen and March, 1974; Weick, 1976; March and Olsen, 1976; Sproull, Weiner, and Wolf, 1978).

It is possible, of course, that such portrayals of behavior are perverse. They may be perverse because they systematically misrepresent the actual behavior of human beings or they may be perverse because the human beings they describe are, insofar as the description applies, stupid. But it is also possible that the description is accurate and the behavior is intelligent, that the ambiguous way human beings sometimes deal with tastes is, in fact, sensible. If such a thing can be imagined, then its corollary may also be imaginable: Perhaps we treat tastes inadequately in our engineering of choice. When we start to discover intelligence in decisionmaking where goals are unstable, ill-defined, or apparently irrelevant, we are led to asking some different kinds of questions about our normative conceptions of choice and walk close not only to some issues in economics but also to some classical and modern questions in literature and ethics, particularly the role of clear prior purpose in the ordering of human affairs.

Consider the following properties of tastes as they appear in standard prescriptive theories of choice:

Tastes are *absolute*. Normative theories of choice assume a formal posture of moral relativism. The theories insist on morality of action in terms of tastes; but they recognize neither discriminations among alternative tastes, nor the possibility that a person reasonably might view his own preferences and actions based on them as morally distressing.

Tastes are *relevant*. Normative theories of choice require that action be taken in terms of tastes, that decisions be consistent with preferences in the light of information about the probable consequences of alternatives for valued outcomes. Action is willful.

Tastes are *stable*. With few exceptions, normative theories of choice require that tastes be stable. Current action is taken in terms of current tastes. The implicit assumption is that tastes will be unchanged when the outcomes of current actions are realized.

Tastes are *consistent*. Normative theories of choice allow mutually inconsistent tastes only insofar as they can be made irrelevant by the absence of scarcity or reconcilable by the specification of trade-offs.

Tastes are *precise*. Normative theories of choice eliminate ambiguity about the extent to which a particular outcome will satisfy tastes, at least insofar as possible resolutions of that ambiguity might affect the choice.

Tastes are *exogenous*. Normative theories of choice presume that tastes, by whatever process they may be created, are not themselves affected by the choices they control.

Each of these features of tastes seems inconsistent with observations of choice behavior among individuals and social institutions. Not always, but often enough to be troublesome. Individuals commonly find it possible to express both a taste for something and a recognition that the taste is something that is repugnant to moral standards they accept. Choices are often made without respect to tastes. Human decisionmakers routinely ignore their own, fully conscious, preferences in making decisions. They follow rules, traditions, hunches, and the advice or actions of others. Tastes change over time in such a way that predicting future tastes is often difficult. Tastes are inconsistent. Individuals and organizations are aware of the extent to which some of their preferences conflict with other of their preferences; yet they do nothing to resolve those inconsistencies. Many preferences are stated in forms that lack precision. It is difficult to make them reliably operational in evaluating possible outcomes. While tastes are used to choose among actions, it is often also true that actions and experience with their consequences affect tastes. Tastes are determined partly endogenously.

Such differences between tastes as they are portrayed by our models and tastes as they appear in our experience produce ordinary behavioral phenomena that are not always well accommodated within the structure of our prescriptions.

We manage our preferences. We select actions now partly in terms of expectations about the effect of those actions upon future preferences. We do things now to modify our future tastes. Thus, we know that if we engage in some particularly tasty, but immoral, activity, we are likely to come to like it more. We know that if we develop competence in a particular skill, we shall often come to favor it. So we choose to pursue the competence, or not, engage in an activity, or not, depending on whether we wish to increase or decrease our taste for the competence or activity.

We construct our preferences. We choose preferences and actions jointly, in part, to discover—or construct—new preferences that are currently unknown. We deliberately specify our objectives in vague terms to develop an understanding of what we might like to become. We elaborate our tastes as interpretations of our behavior.

We treat our preferences strategically. We specify goals that are different from the outcomes we wish to achieve. We adopt preferences and rules of actions that if followed literally would lead us to outcomes we do not wish, because we believe that the final outcome will only partly reflect our initial intentions. In effect, we consider the choice of preferences as part of an infinite game with ourselves in which we attempt to deal with our propensities for acting badly by anticipating them and outsmarting ourselves. We use deadlines and make commitments.

We confound our preferences. Our deepest preferences tend often to be paired. We find the same outcome both attractive and repulsive, not in the sense that the two sentiments cancel each other and we remain indifferent, but precisely that we simultaneously want and do not want an outcome, experience it as both pleasure and pain, love and hate it (Catullus, 58 B.C., l.1).

We avoid our preferences. Our actions and our preferences are only partly linked. We are prepared to say that we want something, yet should not want it, or wish we did not want it. We are prepared to act in ways that are inconsistent with our preferences, and to maintain that inconsistency in the face of having it demonstrated. We do not believe that what we do must necessarily result from a desire to achieve preferred outcomes.

We expect change in our preferences. As we contemplate making choices that have consequences in the future, we know that our attitudes about possible outcomes will change in ways that are substantial but not entirely predictable. The subjective probability distribution over possible future preferences (like the subjective probability distribution over possible future consequences) increases its variance as the horizon is stretched. As a result, we have a tendency to want to take actions now that maintain future options for acting when future preferences are clearer.

We suppress our preferences. Consequential argument, the explicit linking of actions to desires, is a form of argument in which some people are better than others. Individuals who are less competent at consequential rationalization try to avoid it with others who are more competent, particularly others who may have a stake in persuading them to act in a particular way. We resist an explicit formulation of consistent desires to avoid manipulation of our choices by persons cleverer than we at that special form of argument called consistent rationality.

It is possible, on considering this set of contrasts between decisionmaking as we think it ought to occur and decisionmaking as we think it does occur to trivialize the issue into a "definitional problem." By suitably manipulating the concept of tastes, one can save classical theories of choice as "explanations" of behavior in a formal sense, but probably only at the cost of stretching a good idea into a doubtful ideology (Stigler and Becker, 1977). More importantly from the present point of view, such a redefinition pays the cost of destroying the practical relevance of normative prescriptions for choice. For prescriptions are useful only if we see a difference between observed procedures and desirable procedures.

Alternatively, one can record all of the deviations from normative specifications as stupidity, errors that should be corrected; and undertake to transform the style of existing humans into the styles anticipated by the theory. This has, for the most part, been the strategy of operations and management analysis for the past twenty years; and it has had its successes. But it has also had failures.

It is clear that the human behavior I have described may, in any individual case, be a symptom of ignorance, obtuseness, or deviousness. But the fact that such patterns of behavior are fairly common among individuals and institutions suggests that they might be sensible under some general kinds of conditions—that goal ambiguity, like limited rationality, is not necessarily a fault in human choice to be corrected but often a form of intelligence to be refined by the technology of choice rather than ignored by it.

Uncertainty about future consequences and human limitations in dealing with them are relatively easily seen as intrinsic in the decision situation and the nature of the human organism. It is much harder to see in what way ambiguous preferences are a necessary property of human behavior. It seems meaningful in ordinary terms to assert that human decisionmakers are driven to techniques of limited rationality by the exigencies of the situation in which they find themselves. But what drives them to ambiguous and changing goals? Part of the answer is directly analogous to the formulations of limited rationality. Limitations of memory organization and retrieval and of information capacity affect information processing about preferences just as they affect information processing about consequences (March and Simon, 1958; Cyert and March, 1963; Simon, 1973; March and Romelaer, 1976). Human beings have unstable, inconsistent, incompletely evoked, and imprecise goals at least in part because human abilities limit preference orderliness. If it were possible to be different at reasonable cost, we probably would want to be.

But viewing ambiguity as a necessary cost imposed by the information processing attributes of individuals fails to capture the extent to which similar styles in preferences would be sensible, even if the human organism were a more powerful computational system. We probably need to ask the more general question: Why might a person or institution intelligently choose to have ambiguous tastes? The answer, I believe, lies in several things, some related to ideas of bounded rationality, others more familiar to human understanding as it is portrayed in literature and philosophy than to our theories of choice.

First, human beings recognize in their behavior that there are limits to personal and institutional integration in tastes. They know that no matter how much they may be pressured both by their own prejudices for integration and by the demands of others, they will be left with contradictory and intermittent desires partially ordered but imperfectly reconciled. As a result, they engage in activities designed to manage preferences or game preferences. These activities make little sense from the point of view of a conception of human choice that assumes people know what they want and will want, or a conception that assumes wants are morally equivalent. But ordinary human actors sense that they might come to want something that they should not, or that they might make unwise or inappropriate choices under the influence of fleeting, but powerful, desires if they do not act now either to control the development of tastes or to buffer action from tastes (Elster, 1977b).

Second, human beings recognize implicitly the limitations of acting rationally on current guesses. By insisting that action, to be justified, must follow preferences and be consistent both with those preferences and with estimates of future states, we considerably exaggerate the relative power of a choice based consistently upon two guesses compared to a choice that is itself a guess. Human beings are both proponents for preferences and observers of the process by which their preferences are developed and acted upon. As observers of the process by which their beliefs have been formed and consulted, they recognize the good sense in perceptual and moral modesty (Williams, 1973; Elster, 1977c).

Third, human beings recognize the extent to which tastes are constructed, or developed, through a more or less constant confrontation between preferences and actions that are inconsistent with them, and among conflicting preferences. As a result, they appear to be comfortable with an extraordinary array of unreconciled sources of legitimate wants. They maintain a lack of coherence both within and among personal desires, social demands, and moral codes. Though they seek some consistency, they appear to see inconsistency as a normal, and necessary, aspect of the development and clarification of tastes (March, 1973).

Fourth, human beings are conscious of the importance of preferences as beliefs independent of their immediate action consequences. They appear to find it possible to say, in effect, that they believe something is more important to good action than they are able (or willing) to make it in a specific case. They act as though some aspects of their beliefs are important to life without necessarily being consistent with actions, and important to the long-run quality of choice behavior without controlling it completely in the short run. They accept a degree of personal and social wisdom in ordinary hypocrisy (Chomsky, 1968; March, 1973; Pondy and Olson, 1977).

Fifth, human beings know that some people are better at rational argument than others, and that those skills are not particularly well correlated with either morality or sympathy. As a result, they recognize the political nature of argumentation more clearly, and more personally, than the theory of choice does. They are unwilling to gamble that God made clever people uniquely virtuous. They protect themselves from cleverness by obscuring the nature of their preferences; they exploit cleverness by asking others to construct reasons for actions they wish to take (Shakespeare, 1623).

5. Tastes and the engineering of choice

■ These characteristics of preference processing by individual human beings and social institutions seem to me to make sense under rather general circumstances. As a result, it seems likely to me that our engineering of choice behavior does not make so much sense as we sometimes attribute to it. The view of human tastes and their proper role in action that we exhibit in our normative theory of choice is at least as limiting to the engineering applicability of that theory as the perfect knowledge assumptions were to the original formulations.

Since it has taken us over twenty years to introduce modest elements of bounded rationality and conflict of interest into prescriptions about decision-making, there is no particular reason to be sanguine about the speed with which our engineerings of choice will accept and refine the intelligence of ambiguity. But there is hope. The reconstruction involved is not extraordinary, and in some respects has already begun. For the doubts I have expressed about engineering models of choice to be translated into significant changes, they will have to be formulated a bit more precisely in terms that are comprehensible within such theories, even though they may not be consistent with the present form of the theories or the questions the theories currently address. I cannot accomplish such a task in any kind of complete way, but I think it is possible to identify a few conceptual problems that might plausibly be addressed by choice theorists and a few optimization problems that might plausibly be addressed by choice engineers.

The conceptual problems involve discovering interesting ways to reformulate some assumptions about tastes, particularly about the stability of tastes, their exogenous character, their priority, and their internal consistency.

Consider the problem of *intertemporal comparison* of preferences (Strotz, 1956; Koopmans, 1964; Bailey and Olson, 1977; Shefrin and Thaler, 1977). Suppose we assume that the preferences that will be held at every relevant future point in time are known. Suppose further that those preferences change over time but are, at any given time, consistent. If action is to be taken now in terms of its consequences over a period of time during which preferences change, we are faced with having to make intertemporal comparisons. As long as the changes are exogenous, we can avoid the problem if we choose to do so. If we can imagine an individual making a complete and transitive ordering over possible outcomes over time, then intertemporal comparisons are implicit in the preference orderings and cause no particular difficulty beyond the heroic character of the assumption about human capabilities. If, on the other hand, we think of the individual as having a distinct, complete, and consistent preference relation defined over the outcomes realized in a particular time period, and we imagine that those preferences change over time, then the problem of intertemporal comparisons is more difficult. The problem is technically indistinguishable from the problem of interpersonal comparison of utilities. When we compare the changing preferences of a single person over time to make tradeoffs across time, we are, in the identical position as when we attempt to make comparisons across different individuals at a point in time. The fact that the problems are identical has the advantage of immediately bringing to bear on the problems of intertemporal comparisons the apparatus developed to deal with interpersonal comparisons (Mueller, 1976). It has the disadvantage that that apparatus allows a much weaker conception of solution than is possible within a single, unchanging set of preferences. We are left with the weak theorems of social welfare economics, but perhaps with a clearer recognition that there is no easy and useful way to escape the problem of incomparable preference functions by limiting our attention to a single individual, as long as tastes change over time and we think of tastes as being defined at a point in time.

Consider the problem of *endogenous change* in preferences (Von Weiszäcker, 1971; Olson, 1976). Suppose we know that future tastes will change in a predictable way as a consequence of actions taken now and the consequences of those actions realized over time. Then we are in the position of choosing now the preferences we shall have later. If there is risk involved, we are choosing now a probability distribution over future preferences. If we can imagine some "super goal," the problem becomes tractable. We evaluate alternative preferences in terms of their costs and benefits for the "super goal." Such a strategy preserves the main spirit of normal choice theory but allows only a modest extension into endogenous change. This is the essential strategy adopted in some of the engineering examples below. In such cases desirable preferences cannot always be deduced from the "super goal," but alternative preferences can be evaluated. In somewhat the same spirit, we can imagine adaptive preferences as a possible decision procedure and examine whether rules for a sequence of adaptations in tastes can be specified that lead to choice outcomes better in some easily recognized sense than those obtained through explicit calculated rationality at the start of the process. One possible place is the search for cooperative solutions in games in which calculated rationality is likely to lead to outcomes desired by no one (Cyert and de Groot, 1973, 1975). Also in the same general spirit, we might accept the strict morality position and attempt to select a strategy for choice that will minimize change in values. Or we might try to select a strategy that maximizes value change. All of these are possible explorations, but they are not fully attentive to the normative management of adaptation in tastes. The problem exceeds our present concepts: How do we act sensibly now to manage the development of preferences in the future when we do not have now a criterion for evaluating future tastes that will not itself be affected by our actions? There may be some kind of fixed-point theorem answer to such a problem, but I suspect that a real conceptual confrontation with endogenous preferences will involve some reintroduction of moral philosophy into our understanding of choice (Friedman, 1967; Williams, 1973; Beck, 1975).

Consider the problem of *posterior preferences* (Schutz, 1967; Hirschman, 1967; Weick, 1969; Elster, 1976). The theory of choice is built on the idea of prior intentions. Suppose we relax the requirement of priority, allow preferences to rationalize action after the fact in our theories as well as our behavior. How do we act in such a way that we conclude, after the fact, that the action was intelligent, and also are led to an elaboration of our preferences that we find fruitful? Such a formulation seems closer to a correct representation of choice problems in politics, for example, than is conventional social welfare theory. We find meaning and merit in our actions after they are taken and the consequences are observed and interpreted. Deliberate efforts to manage posterior constructions of preferences are familiar to us. They include many elements of child rearing, psychotherapy, consciousness raising, and product advertising. The terms are somewhat different. We talk of development of character in child rearing, of insight in psychotherapy, of recognition of objective reality in political, ethnic, or sexual consciousness raising, and of elaboration of personal needs in advertising. But the technologies are more similar than their ideologies. These techniques for the construction (or excavation) of tastes include both encouraging a reinterpretation of experience and attempting to induce current behavior that will facilitate posterior elaboration of a new understanding of personal preferences. I have tried elsewhere to indicate some of the possibilities this suggests for intelligent foolishness and the role of ambiguity in sensible action (March, 1973, 1977). The problem is in many ways indistinguishable from the problem of poetry and the criticism of poetry (or art and art criticism). The poet attempts to write a poem that has meanings intrinsic in the poem but not necessarily explicit at the moment of composition (Ciardi, 1960). In this sense, at least, decisions, like poems, are open; and good decisions are those that enrich our preferences and their meanings. But to talk in such a manner is to talk the language of criticism and aesthetics, and it will probably be necessary for choice theory to engage that literature in some way (Eliot, 1933; Cavell, 1969; Steinberg, 1972; Rosenberg, 1975).

Finally, consider the problem of *inconsistency* in preferences (Elster, 1977c). From the point of view of ordinary human ideas about choice, as well as many philosophical and behavioral conceptions of choice, the most surprising thing about formal theories of choice is the tendency to treat such terms as

values, goals, preferences, tastes, wants, and the like as either equivalent or as
reducible to a single objective function with properties of completeness and
consistency. Suppose that instead of making such an assumption, we viewed
the decisionmaker as confronted simultaneously with several orderings of outcomes. We could give them names, calling one a moral code, another a social
role, another a personal taste, or whatever. From the present point of view
what would be critical would be that the several orderings were independent
and irreducible. That is, they could not be deduced from each other, and they
could not be combined into a single order. Then instead of taking the conventional step of imputing a preference order across these incomparables by some
kind of revealed preference procedure, we treat them as truly incomparable and
examine solutions to internal inconsistency that are more in the spirit of our
efforts to provide intelligent guidance to collectivities in which we accept the
incomparability of preferences across individuals. Then we could give better
advice to individuals who want to treat their own preferences strategically, and
perhaps move to a clearer recognition of the role of contradiction and paradox
in human choice (Farber, 1976; Elster, 1977c). The strategic problems are amen-
able to relatively straightforward modifications of our views of choice under
conflict of interest; the other problems probably require a deeper understanding of contradiction as it appears in philosophy and literature (Elster, 1977c).

Formulating the conceptual problems in these ways is deliberately conservative *vis-à-vis* the theory of choice. It assumes that thinking about human
behavior in terms of choice on the basis of some conception of intention is useful, and that the tradition of struggle between normative theories of choice and
behavioral theories of choice is a fruitful one. There are alternative paradigms
for understanding human behavior that are in many situations likely to be more
illuminating. But it is probably unwise to think that every paper should suggest
a dramatic paradigm shift, particularly when the alternative is seen only dimly.

Such strictures become even more important when we turn to the engineering
of choice. Choice theorists have often discussed complications in the usual abstract representation of tastes. But those concerns have had little impact on
ideas about the engineering of choice, perhaps because they pose the problems
at a level of philosophic complexity that is remote from decision engineering.
Thus, although I think the challenges that ambiguity makes to our models of
choice are rather fundamental, my engineering instincts are to sacrifice purity
to secure tractability. I suspect we should ask the engineers of choice not
initially to reconstruct a philosophy of tastes but to reexamine, within a familiar
framework, some presumptions of our craft, and to try to make the use of
ambiguity somewhat less of a mystery, somewhat more of a technology. Consider, for example, the following elementary problems in engineering.

The optimal ambition problem. The level of personal ambition is not a decision
variable in most theories of choice; but as a result of the work by Simon and
others on satisficing, there has been interest in optimal levels of aspiration.
These efforts consider an aspiration level as a trigger that either begins or ends the
search for new alternatives. The optimization problem is one of balancing the
expected costs of additional search with the expected improvements to be
realized from the effort (March and Simon, 1958).

But there is another, rather different, way of looking at the optimum ambition problem. Individuals and organizations form aspirations, goals, targets, or
ambitions for achievement. These ambitions are usually assumed to be con-

nected to outcomes in at least two ways: they affect search (either directly or through some variable like motivation) and thereby performance; they affect (jointly with performance) satisfaction (March and Simon, 1958). Suppose we wish to maximize some function of satisfaction over time by selecting among alternative ambitions over time, alternative initial ambitions, or alternatives defined by some other decision variable that affects ambition. Examples of the latter might be division of income between consumption and savings, tax policies, or choice among alternative payment schemes. In effect, we wish to select a preference function for achievement that will, after the various behavioral consequences of that selection are accounted for, make us feel that we have selected the best ambition. It is a problem much more familiar to the real world of personal and institutional choice than it is to the normative theory of choice, but it is something about which some things could be said.

The optimal clarity problem. Conventional notions about intelligent choice often begin with the presumption that good decisions require clear goals, and that improving the clarity of goals unambiguously improves the quality of decision-making. In fact, greater precision in the statement of objectives and the measurement of performance with respect to them is often a mixed blessing. There are arguments for moderating an unrestrained enthusiasm for precise performance measures: Where contradiction and confusion are essential elements of the values, precision misrepresents them. The more precise the measure of performance, the greater the motivation to find ways of scoring well on the measurement index without regard to the underlying goals. And precision in objectives does not allow creative interpretation of what the goal might mean (March, 1978). Thus, the introduction of precision into the evaluation of performance involves a tradeoff between the gains in outcomes attributable to closer articulation between action and performance on an index of performance and the losses in outcomes attributable to misrepresentation of goals, reduced motivation to development of goals, and concentration of effort on irrelevant ways of beating the index. Whether one is considering developing a performance evaluation scheme for managers, a testing procedure for students, or an understanding of personal preferences, there is a problem of determining the optimum clarity in goals.

The optimal sin problem. Standard notions of intelligent choice are theories of strict morality. That is, they presume that a person should do what he believes right and believe that what he does is right. Values and actions are to be consistent. Contrast that perspective with a view, somewhat more consistent with our behavior (as well as some theology), that there is such a thing as sin, that individuals and institutions sometimes do things even while recognizing that what they do is not what they wish they did, and that saints are a luxury to be encouraged only in small numbers. Or contrast a theory of strict morality with a view drawn from Nietzsche (1918) or Freud (1927) (see also Jones, 1926) of the complicated contradiction between conscience and self-interest. Although the issues involved are too subtle for brief treatment, a reasonably strong case can be made against strict morality and in favor of at least some sin, and therefore hypocrisy. One of the most effective ways of maintaining morality is through the remorse exhibited and felt at immoral action. Even if we are confident that our moral codes are correct, we may want to recognize human complexities. There will be occasions on which humans will be tempted by desires

Organization Theory I 197

604 / THE BELL JOURNAL OF ECONOMICS

that they recognize as evil. If we insist that they maintain consistency between ethics and actions, the ethics will often be more likely to change than the actions. Hypocrisy is a long-run investment in morality made at some cost (the chance that, in fact, action might otherwise adjust to morals). To encourage people always to take responsibility for their actions is to encourage them to deny that bad things are bad—to make evil acceptable. At the same time, sin is an experiment with an alternative morality. By recognizing sin, we make it easier for persons to experiment with the possibility of having different tastes. Moral systems need those experiments, and regularly grant licenses to experiment to drunks, lovers, students, or sinners. These gains from sin are purchased by its costs. Thus, the optimization problem.

The optimal rationality problem. Calculated rationality is a technique for making decisions. In standard versions of theories of choice it is the only legitimate form of intelligence. But it is obvious that it is, in fact, only one of several alternative forms of intelligence, each with claims to legitimacy. Learned behavior, with its claim to summarize an irretrievable but relevant personal history, or conventional behavior and rules, with their claims to capture the intelligence of survival over long histories of experience more relevant than that susceptible to immediate calculation, are clear alternative contenders. There are others: Revelation or intuition, by which we substitute one guess for two; or imitation, or expertise, by which we substitute the guess of someone else for our own. Among all of these, only calculated rationality really uses conscious preferences of a current actor as a major consideration in making decisions. It is easy to show that there exist situations in which any one of these alternative techniques will make better decisions than the independent calculation of rational behavior by ordinary individuals or institutions. The superiority of learned or conventional behavior depends, in general, on the amount of experience it summarizes and the similarity between the world in which the experience was accumulated and the current world. The superiority of imitation depends, in general, on the relative competence of actor and expert and the extent to which intelligent action is reproducible but not comprehendible. At the same time, each form of intelligence exposes an actor to the risks of corruption. Imitation risks a false confidence in the neutrality of the process of diffusion; calculated rationality risks a false confidence in the neutrality of rational argument; and so on. It is not hard to guess that the relative sizes of these risks vary from individual to individual, or institution to institution. What is harder to specify in any very precise way is the extent and occasions on which a sensible person would rely on calculated rationality rather than the alternatives.

6. A romantic vision

■ Prescriptive theories of choice are dedicated to perfecting the intelligence of human action by imagining that action stems from reason and by improving the technology of decision. Descriptive theories of choice are dedicated to perfecting the understanding of human action by imagining that action makes sense. Not all behavior makes sense; some of it is unreasonable. Not all decision technology is intelligent; some of it is foolish. Over the past twenty years, the contradiction between the search for sense in behavior and the search for improvement in behavior has focused on our interpretation of the way information about future consequences is gathered and processed. The effort built considerably on the idea of bounded rationality and a conception of human decision-making as limited by the cognitive capabilities of human beings. Over the next twenty years, I suspect the contradiction will be increasingly concerned with an interpretation of how beliefs about future preferences are generated and utilized. The earlier confrontation led theories of choice to a slightly clearer understanding of information processing and to some modest links with the technologies of computing, inference, and subjective probability. So perhaps the newer confrontation will lead theories of choice to a slightly clearer understanding of the complexities of preference processing and to some modest links with the technologies of ethics, criticism, and aesthetics. The history of theories of choice and their engineering applications suggests that we might appropriately be pessimistic about immediate, major progress. The intelligent engineering of tastes involves questions that encourage despair over their difficulty (Savage, 1954). But though hope for minor progress is a romantic vision, it may not be entirely inappropriate for a theory built on a romantic view of human destiny.

References

ACKOFF, R. L. AND SASIENI, M. W. *Fundamentals of Operations Research*. New York: Wiley, 1968.

ALLISON, G. T. *Essence of Decision: Explaining the Cuban Missile Crisis*. Boston: Little, Brown, 1969.

———— AND HALPERIN, M. H. "Bureaucratic Politics: Paradigm and Some Policy Implications" in R. Tanter and R. H. Ullman, eds., *Theory and Policy in International Relations*, Princeton: Princeton University Press, 1972.

BAILEY, M. J. AND OLSON, M. "Pure Time Preference, Revealed Marginal Utility, and Friedman-Savage Gambles." Unpublished manuscript, 1977.

BECK, L. W. *The Actor and the Spectator*. New Haven: Yale University Press, 1975.

BECKER, G. S. "A Theory of the Allocation of time." *Economic Journal*, Vol. 75 (1965), pp. 493–517.

————. "Altruism, Egoism, and Genetic Fitness: Economics and Sociobiology." *Journal of Economic Literature*, Vol. 14 (1976), pp. 817–826.

BINKLEY, R., BRONAUGH, R., AND MARRAS, A., EDS. *Agent, Action, and Reason*. Toronto: University of Toronto Press, 1971.

BOWER, J. L. "Descriptive Decision Theory from the 'Administrative Viewpoint' " in R. A. Bauer and K. J. Gergen, eds., *The Study of Policy Formation*, New York: Free Press, 1968.

BRAMS, S. J. *Game Theory and Politics*. New York: Free Press, 1975.

CAMUS, A. *L'Homme Révolte*. Paris: Gallimard, 1951. (Published in English as *The Rebel*.)

CARTER, E. E. "The Behavioral Theory of the Firm and Top-Level Corporate Decisions." *Administrative Science Quarterly*, Vol. 16 (1971), pp. 413–429.

CATULLUS, G. V. *Carmina*, 85. Rome: 58 B.C.

CAVELL, S. *Must We Mean What We Say?* New York: Scribner, 1969.

CHARNES, A. AND COOPER, W. W. "Deterministic Equivalents for Optimizing and Satisficing under Chance Constraints." *Operations Research*, Vol. 11 (1963), pp. 18–39.

CHRISTENSEN, S. "Decision Making and Socialization" in J. G. March and J. P. Olsen, eds., *Ambiguity and Choice in Organizations*, Bergen: Universitetsforlaget, 1976.

CHOMSKY, N. *Language and Mind*. New York: Harcourt, Brace, & World, 1968.

CIARDI, J. *How Does a Poem Mean?* Cambridge: Houghton Mifflin, 1960.

COHEN, M. D. AND MARCH, J. G. *Leadership and Ambiguity: The American College President*. New York: McGraw-Hill, 1974.

————, ————, AND OLSEN, J. P. "A Garbage Can Model of Organizational Choice." *Administrative Science Quarterly*, Vol. 17 (1972), pp. 1–25.

CONNOLLY, T. "Information Processing and Decision Making in Organizations" in B. M. Staw and G. R. Salancik, eds., *New Directions in Organizational Behavior*, Chicago: St. Clair, 1977.

CROZIER, M. AND FRIEDBERG, E. *L'Acteur et le Système*. Paris: Seuil, 1977.

CYERT, R. M. AND DE GROOT, M. H. "An Analysis of Cooperation and Learning in a Duopoly Context." *The American Economic Review*, Vol. 63, No. 1 (March 1973), pp. 24–37.

———— AND ————. "Adaptive Utility" in R. H. Day and T. Groves, eds., *Adaptive Economic Models*, New York: Academic Press, 1975.

606 / THE BELL JOURNAL OF ECONOMICS

—— AND MARCH, J. G. *A Behavioral Theory of the Firm.* Englewood Cliffs, N.J.: Prentice-Hall, 1963.
DAY, R. H. AND GROVES, T., EDS. *Adaptive Economic Models.* New York: Academic Press, 1975.
DOWNS, A. *Inside Bureaucracy.* Boston: Little, Brown, 1967.
EDELMAN, M. *The Symbolic Uses of Politics.* Champaign, Ill.: University of Illinois Press, 1960.
ELIOT, T. S. *The Use of Poetry and the Use of Criticism.* Cambridge: Harvard University Press, 1933.
ELSTER, J. "A Note on Hysteresis in the Social Sciences." *Synthese*, Vol. 33 (1976), pp. 371–391.
——. *Logic and Society.* London: Wiley, 1977a.
——. "Ulysses and the Sirens: A Theory of Imperfect Rationality." *Social Science Information*, Vol. 16, No. 5 (1977b), pp. 469–526.
——. "Some Unresolved Problems in the Theory of Rational Behavior." Unpublished manuscript, 1977c.
FARBER, L. *Lying, Despair, Jealousy, Envy, Sex, Suicide, Drugs, and the Good Life.* New York: Basic Books, 1976.
FARQUHARSON, R. *Theory of Voting.* New Haven: Yale University Press, 1969.
FREUD, S. *The Ego and the Id.* London: Hogarth, 1927.
FRIEDMAN, M. *To Deny Our Nothingness: Contemporary Images of Man.* New York: Delacorte, 1967.
HALPERIN, M. H. *Bureaucratic Politics and Foreign Policy.* Washington, D.C.: The Brookings Institution, 1974.
HARSANYI, J. C. AND SELTEN, R. "A Generalized Nash Solution for Two-Person Bargaining Games with Incomplete Information." *Management Science*, Vol. 18 (1972), pp. 80–106.
HEGEL, G. W. F. *G. W. F. Hegel's Werke.* Berlin: Duncker und Humblot, 1832.
HIRSCHMAN, A. O. *Development Projects Observed.* Washington, D.C.: The Brookings Institution, 1967.
—— AND LINDBLOM, C. E. "Economic Development, Research and Development, Policy Making: Some Converging Views." *Behavioral Science*, Vol. 7 (1962), pp. 211–222.
JANIS, I. L. AND MANN, L. *Decision Making.* New York: Free Press, 1977.
JOHNSON, E. *Studies in Multiobjective Decision Models.* Lund: Studentlitteratur, 1968.
JONES, E. "The Origin and Structure of the Superego." *International Journal of Psychoanalysis*, Vol. 7 (1926), pp. 303–311.
KEEN, P. G. W. "The Evolving Concept of Optimality." *TIMS Studies in the Management Sciences*, Vol. 6 (1977), pp. 31–57.
KOOPMANS, T. C. "On Flexibility of Future Preferences" in M. W. Shelly and G. L. Bryan, eds., *Human Judgments and Optimality*, New York: Wiley, 1964.
KREINER, K. "Ideology and Management in a Garbage Can Situation" in J. G. March and J. P. Olsen, eds., *Ambiguity and Choice in Organizations*, Bergen: Universitetsforlaget, 1976.
LEE, S. M. *Goal Programming for Decision Analysis.* Philadelphia: Auerbach, 1972.
LINDBLOM, C. E. "The Science of Muddling Through." *Public Administration Review*, Vol. 19 (1959), pp. 79–88.
——. *The Intelligence of Democracy.* New York: Macmillan, 1965.
LONG, N. E. "The Local Community as an Ecology of Games." *American Journal of Sociology*, Vol. 44 (1958), pp. 251–261.
MAO, T. T. *On Contradiction.* Published in English in 1952 by Foreign Language Press, Peking.
MARCH, J. G. "The Business Firm As a Political Coalition." *Journal of Politics*, Vol. 24 (1962), pp. 662–678.
——. "Model Bias in Social Action." *Review of Educational Research*, Vol. 42 (1973), pp. 413–429.
——. "Administrative Leadership in Education." Unpublished manuscript, 1977.
——. "American Public School Administration: A Short Analysis." *School Review*, Vol. 86 (1978), pp. 217–250.
—— AND OLSEN, J. P., EDS. *Ambiguity and Choice in Organizations.* Bergen: Universitetsforlaget, 1976.
—— AND ROMELAER, P. J. "Position and Presence in the Drift of Decisions" in J. G. March and J. P. Olsen, eds., *Ambiguity and Choice in Organizations*, Bergen: Universitetsforlaget, 1976.
—— AND SIMON, H. A. *Organizations.* New York: Wiley, 1958.
MARSCHAK, J. AND RADNER, R. *Economic Theory of Teams.* New Haven: Yale University Press, 1972.

MAYHEW, D. R. *Congress: The Electoral Connection.* New Haven: Yale University Press, 1974.

McGUIRE, C. B. AND RADNER, R., EDS. *Decision and Organization.* Amsterdam: North-Holland, 1972.

MILL, J. S. *Bentham.* (1838). Reprinted in *Mill on Bentham and Coleridge.* London: Chatoo and Windus, 1950.

MUELLER, D. C. "Public Choice: A Survey." *Journal of Economic Literature,* Vol. 14 (1976), pp. 395–433.

NELSON, R. R. AND WINTER, S. G. "Towards an Evolutionary Theory of Economic Capabilities." *The American Economic Review,* Vol. 63 (1973), pp. 440–449.

NEWELL, A. AND SIMON, H. A. *Human Problem Solving.* Englewood Cliffs, N.J.: Prentice-Hall, 1972.

NIETZSCHE, F. *The Geneology of Morals.* New York: Boni and Liveright, 1918.

OLSON, M. *The Logic of Collective Action.* New York: Schocken, 1965.

——. "Exchange, Integration, and Grants" in M. Pfaff, ed., *Essays in Honor of Kenneth Boulding,* Amsterdam: North-Holland, 1976.

PATTANAIK, P. K. "Group Choice with Lexicographic Individual Orderings." *Behavioral Science,* Vol. 18 (1973), pp. 118–123.

PFEFFER, J. "Power and Resource Allocation in Organizations in B. M. Staw and G. R. Salancik, eds., *New Directions in Organizational Behavior,* Chicago: St. Clair, 1977.

PONDY, L. R. AND OLSON, M. L. "Organization and Performance." Unpublished manuscript, 1977.

PORAT, A. M. AND HAAS, J. A. "Information Effects on Decision Making." *Behavioral Science,* Vol. 14 (1969), pp. 98–104.

RADNER, R. "A Behavioral Model of Cost Reduction." *The Bell Journal of Economics,* Vol. 6, No. 1 (Spring 1975a), pp. 196–215.

——. "Satisficing." *Journal of Mathematical Economics,* Vol. 2 (1975b), pp. 253–262.

—— AND ROTHSCHILD, M. "On the Allocation of Effort." *Journal of Economic Theory,* Vol. 10 (1975), pp. 358–376.

RAPOPORT, A. *Fights, Games, and Debates.* Ann Arbor: University of Michigan Press, 1960.

RIKER, W. AND ORDESHOOK, P. *An Introduction to Positive Political Theory.* Englewood Cliffs, N.J.: Prentice-Hall, 1974.

ROSENBERG, H. *Art on the Edge: Creators and Situations.* New York: Macmillan, 1975.

ROTHSCHILD, M. AND STIGLITZ, J. "Equilibrium in Competitive Insurance Markets: An Essay on the Economics of Imperfect Information." *Quarterly Journal of Economics,* Vol. 90 (1976), pp. 629–649.

SAVAGE, L. J. *Foundations of Statistics.* New York: Wiley, 1954.

SCHELLING, T. "On the Ecology of Micro-Motives." *Public Interest,* Vol. 25 (1971), pp. 59–98.

SCHUTZ, A. *The Phenomenology of the Social World.* Evanston, Ill.: Northwestern, 1967.

SHAKESPEARE, W. *Hamlet, Prince of Denmark.* Stratford-upon-Avon: 1623.

SHEFRIN, H. M. AND THALER, R. "An Economic Theory of Self-Control." Unpublished manuscript, 1977.

SIMON, H. A. "A Behavioral Model of Rational Choice." *Quarterly Journal of Economics,* Vol. 69 (1955), pp. 99–118.

——. "Rational Choice and the Structure of the Environment." *Psychological Review,* Vol. 63 (1956), pp. 129–138.

——. *Models of Man.* New York: Wiley, 1957.

——. *The Science of the Artificial.* Cambridge: MIT Press, 1969.

——. "The Structure of Ill-Structured Problems," *Artificial Intelligence,* Vol. 4 (1973), pp. 181–201.

SLOVIC, P., FISCHHOFF, B., AND LICHTENSTEIN, S. "Behavioral Decision Theory." *Annual Review of Psychology,* Vol. 28 (1977), pp. 1–39.

SPENCE, A. M. *Market Signalling.* Cambridge: Harvard University Press, 1974.

SPROULL, L. S., WEINER, S. S., AND WOLF, D. B. *Organizing an Anarchy.* Chicago: University of Chicago Press, 1978.

STEINBRUNER, J. D. *The Cybernetic Theory of Decision.* Princeton: Princeton University Press, 1974.

STEINBERG, L. *Other Criteria: Confrontations with Twentieth Century Art.* New York: Oxford University Press, 1972.

STIGLER, G. J. "The Economics of Information." *Journal of Political Economy,* Vol. 69 (1961), pp. 213–225.

608 / THE BELL JOURNAL OF ECONOMICS

────── AND BECKER, G. S. *"De Gustibus Non Est Disputandum."* *The American Economic Review*, Vol. 67 (March 1977), pp. 76–90.

STROTZ, R. H. "Myopia and Inconsistency in Dynamic Utility Maximization." *Review of Economic Studies*, Vol. 23 (1956).

TAYLOR, M. "The Theory of Collective Choice" in F. I. Greenstein and N. W. Polsby, eds., *Handbook of Political Science*, Vol. 3, Reading, Mass.: Addison-Wesley, 1975.

TAYLOR, R. N. "Psychological Determinants of Bounded Rationality: Implications for Decision-making Strategies." *Decision Sciences*, Vol. 6 (1975), pp. 409–429.

THOMPSON, J. *Organizations in Action.* New York: McGraw-Hill, 1967.

TULLOCK, G. *The Politics of Bureaucracy.* Washington, D.C.: Public Affairs, 1965.

TVERSKY, A. AND KAHNEMAN, D. "Judgment under Uncertainty: Heuristics and Biases." *Science*, Vol. 185 (1974), pp. 1124–1131.

VON WEISZÄCKER, C. C. "Notes on Endogenous Change of Taste." *Journal of Economic Theory*, Vol. 3 (1971), pp. 345–372.

VROOM, V. H. *Work and Motivation.* New York: Wiley, 1964.

WARWICK, D. P. *A Theory of Public Bureaucracy: Politics, Personality, and Organization in the State Department.* Cambridge: Harvard University Press, 1975.

WEICK, K. E. *The Social Psychology of Organizing.* Reading, Mass.: Addison-Wesley, 1969.

──────. "Educational Organizations as Loosely Coupled Systems." *Administrative Science Quarterly*, Vol. 21 (1976), pp. 1–18.

WEINER, S. S. "Participation, Deadlines, and Choice" in J. G. March and J. P. Olsen, eds., *Ambiguity and Choice in Organizations*, Bergen: Universitetsforlaget, 1976.

WILDAVSKY, A. *Revolt Against the Masses and Other Essays on Politics and Public Policy.* New York: Basic Books, 1971.

────── AND PRESSMAN, H. *Implementation.* Berkeley: University of California Press, 1973.

WILLIAMS, B. A. O. *Problems of the Self.* Cambridge: Cambridge University Press, 1973.

WILLIAMSON, O. E. *Markets and Hierarchies.* New York: Free Press, 1975.

WILSON, E. O. *Sociobiology.* Cambridge: Harvard University Press, 1975.

WINTER, S. G. "Economic 'Natural Selection' and the Theory of the Firm." *Yale Economic Essays*, Vol. 4 (1964), pp. 225–272.

──────. "Satisficing, Selection, and the Innovating Remnant." *Quarterly Journal of Economics*, Vol. 85 (1971), pp. 237–261.

──────. "Optimization and Evolution in the Theory of the Firm" in R. H. Day and T. Groves, eds., *Adaptive Economic Models*, New York: Academic Press, 1975.

[9]

Journal of Management Studies, **19**, 1, 1982

THE IRRATIONALITY OF ACTION AND ACTION RATIONALITY: DECISIONS, IDEOLOGIES AND ORGANIZATIONAL ACTIONS

NILS BRUNSSON

Stockholm School of Economics

ABSTRACT

Irrationality is a basic feature of organizational behaviour. Organizational decision making tends to be irrational, and organizational ideologies bias organizations' perceptions. Much effort has been spent on prescribing how organizations should achieve more rationality. However, rational decision making affords a bad basis for action. Some irrationalities are necessary requirements for organizational actions. Choices are facilitated by narrow and clear organizational ideologies, and actions are facilitated by irrational decision-making procedures which maximize motivation and commitment.

THE DECISION-MAKING PERSPECTIVE AND IRRATIONALITY

A characteristic of social science is the multitude perspectives used by different researchers. The significant differences between research fields lie less often in what is described than in how it is described. One important way of developing a social science is to apply new perspectives to a part of reality, thereby highlighting new features of the reality. Perspectives determine what data are seen, what theories are developed, and what kinds of results turn up.

One of the most influential perspectives has been the decision-making perspective which conceives of human behaviour as resulting from decisions made by individuals, group, or organizations. A decision is normally described as a conscious choice between at least two alternative actions. Researchers have studied the choosing among alternatives, the generating of alternatives, and the forming of criteria for choice (goals, objectives).

The attractiveness of the decision-making perspective has several explanations. One explanation is that diverse social theories can be stated in decision-making terms. This is true for parts of microeconomics and of political science. Another explanation is that the perspective lends itself to experimentation; psychological researchers can create experimental decision situations by giving people objectives and information, and then they

Address for reprints: Professor N. Brunsson, Stockholm School of Economics, Box 6501, s-11383 Stockholm, Sweden.

30 NILS BRUNSSON

study the resulting choices. In addition, social development has spawned situations where the decision-making perspective seems relevant from a common-sense point of view. The establishment and growth of large organizations have added hierarchy to society and, consequently, many actions are determined by forces outside the actors themselves (Chandler, 1977; Galbraith, 1967; Lindblom, 1977). This separates cognition from action and makes it natural to say some individuals decide and others carry out the decisions. The decision-making perspective seems almost imperative in democratic conventions. According to the existing law for industrial democracy in Sweden, for example, the employees' influence should be guaranteed by their participation in decisions. These imperatives may result from a spread of the decision-making perspective from researchers to practitioners.

Still, the decision-making perspective has derived from studies of individual behaviour rather than organizational. An individual has less difficulty going from decision to action than does an organization. This emphasis on individual behaviour might explain why the choosing of actions has received much more attention than the carrying out of actions. Organizational decision processes are described in essentially the same terms as individual decision processes, and research has often characterized organizations as being led by single powerful entrepreneurs (as in microeconomic theory) or by coalitions (as described by Cyert and March, 1963).

The decision-making perspective has been most elaborated in normative research which prescribes how decisions should be made. This kind of research sets the criteria for a 'rational' decision. Strong efforts have been devoted to prescribing how a best choice should be made, given a specific problem, specific alternatives and specific information. Typically, a problem is described as one where there is either too little information or too much. Little attention has been paid to other phases of decision-making processes or to implementing the decisions made.

Normative research has engendered an increasing consensus among researchers as to what kinds of decision making should be called rational. At the same time, empirical research has found ample evidence of decision-making processes that appear irrational by the normative standards (Cyert and March, 1963; Janis, 1972; Lindblom, 1959; March and Olsen, 1976; Nisbett and Ross, 1980; Tversky and Kahneman, 1974). What is more, the apparent irrationalities are not limited to insignificant decisions: people behave similarly when making major decisions on strategic issues. It can even be argued that the apparent irrationalities are largest in major decisions. Janis (1972) demonstrated how decisions with serious actual or potential effects—such as the decision by the Kennedy administration to start the invasion in the Bay of Pigs—were made without normative rationality. Disturbing information was suppressed, and false illusions of unanimity were built up among the decision makers, who took immense and unjustified risks.

There are three common ways of explaining the irrationality found in practice. One chauvinist explanation is that the people studied are not clever enough to behave rationally. For instance, difficulties of implementing models from operations research have been explained by managers' emotional reactions or by their cognitive styles (Huysmans, 1970; Tarkowsky, 1958). If decision makers only had the brain capacities and knowledge of scientists, they would behave as the rational decision models prescribe. Thus, decision makers ought to be selected better and trained better.

A second explanation derives from recent psychological research, which indicates that certain types of irrationality are inherent characteristics of human beings, and these characteristics are difficult to change by training (Goldberg, 1968; Kahneman and Tversky, 1973). Consequently, not even experts can be fully rational, and full rationality can only be reached by mathematical formulae or computer programs.

A third way of explaining apparently irrational behaviour is to point out practical restrictions. In realistic decision situations, values, alternatives and predictions interact; so decision makers have incomplete information, or they have more information than human beings can grasp. This view implies that normative research should design systems for gathering and processing data. Not many years ago, some people expected computer-based information systems to solve numerous management problems (Murdick and Ross, 1975). Also, recognizing that objectives may be difficult to compare with each other, normative research has produced cost-benefit analysis and multiple-criteria methods (Keeney and Raiffa, 1976; Prest and Turvey, 1965).

These traditional explanations are made within the decision-making perspective. They refer to diverse phenomena that disturb decision processes. Like the decision processes themselves, the disturbances are described as being cognitive; they arise from deficiencies in perceived information or deficiencies in decision makers' mental abilities.

These ways of explaining irrationality cannot be said to be inherently wrong, but there is much evidence that these explanations do not suffice. Computer-based information systems have not been used in the prescribed ways; recommendations given by operations-research models have not been followed; cost-benefit analyses have not been done or have been neglected even by competent and successful managers and politicians (Ackerman et al., 1974; Argyris, 1977; Churchman, 1964; Harvey, 1970).

If actual behaviour is to be understood, other explanations are needed. As long as actual behaviour is not fully understood, the recommendations of normative research may be irrelevant, confusing or even harmful.

The main purpose of this article is to argue that an action perspective will be more fruitful for understanding large areas of organizational behaviour. The action perspective explains behaviour within attempts to change and differences in abilities to achieve changes. Because organizational actions do not lend themselves to laboratory experiments, the article is based on studies of major organizational changes or stabilities in seven organizations. The organizations include industrial companies, governmental agencies and local governments. Processes of change were observed, and people's ways of describing both the changes and the general situations were measured.

The decision-making perspective fails to recognize that practitioners do more than make decisions. Making a decision is only a step towards action. A decision is not an end product. Practitioners get things done, act and induce others to act.

An action perspective makes it easier and important to observe that there exist both decisions without actions and actions without decisions. Some actions are not preceded by weighing of objectives, evaluating of alternatives or choosing; and decision processes and decisions do not always influence actions, particularly not when the actions precede the decisions. On the other hand, decision processes often comprise some of the processes associated with actions. Because managers and representatives in political bodies describe part of their work as decision making, decisions and decision making should remain important topics for study.

In fact, the very relationship between decision making and action helps explain why decisions deviate from normative rationality. Since decision processes aim at action, they should not be designed solely according to such decision-internal criteria as the norms of rationality; they should be adapted to external criteria of action. Rational decisions are not always good bases for appropriate and successful actions.

How can decisions lay foundations for actions? The next section attempts to answer this question.

DECISIONS AS INITIATORS OF ACTIONS

Making decisions is just one way among several of initiating actions in organizations. However, it is a familiar one. Actions are often preceded by group activities which the participants describe as decision-making steps. Certain issues are posed in forms that allow them to be handled by decision processes: several alternative actions are proposed, their probable effects are forecasted, and finally actions are chosen. Sometimes the decision makers even formulate goals or other explicit criteria by which the alternatives can be evaluated. The final results are called decisions.

For decisions to initiate actions, they must incorporate cognitive, motivational and committal aspects. One cognitive aspect of a decision is expectation: the decision expresses the expectation that certain actions will take place. A decision also demonstrates motivation to take action, and it expresses the decision makers' commitments to specific actions. By making a decision, decision makers accept responsibility both for getting the actions carried out and for the appropriateness of the actions.

ACTION AND ACTION RATIONALITY 33

To go from decision to action is particularly complicated and difficult when there are several decision makers and several actors and when decision makers and actors are different persons. These conditions are typical of organizations. Thus, organizations should provide motivational and social links from decisions to actions. Strong motivations, sometimes even enthusiasm, are needed to overcome big intellectual or physical obstacles. Cooperating actors should be able to rely on certain kinds of behaviours and attitudes from their collaborators, so they should construct mutual commitments: the actors should signal to one another that they endorse proposed actions, for example, by presenting arguments in favour of them or by expressing confidence in success. Actors should also elicit commitments from those who will evaluate their actions afterwards, because committed evaluators are more likely to judge actions as successful (Brunsson, 1976).

Thinking, motivation and commitment are aspects of all actions. However, the importance of each aspect might differ in various situations, depending on such variables as the actors' time horizons, the degrees of change that the actions involve, and the power relationships within the organization. Cognitive activities probably become more important where the actors expect more information to be beneficial. Motivations would be more important where actors lack information needed for predicting the consequences of acting, where the negative consequences could be great, or where great efforts are essential; motivations would be less important where the actions are highly complex and the actors must collaborate extensively (Zander, 1971). Commitments would be more important where many people are involved in actions, agreements from many people are necessary, efforts must be tightly coordinated, or results depend upon the actions or evaluations of collaborators who are accessible through communication. Since motivations and commitments represent internal pressures for action, they are particularly influential where external pressures are weak. This is true of wait-and-see situations where people think that it may be possible to take no action: the actors can reject one proposed action without having to accept another at the same time.

The stronger the expectation, motivation and commitment expressed in a decision, the more power that decision exerts as a basis for action. Insofar as the constituents of decisions are determined by decision processes, the likelihoods of actions can be influenced by designing the decision processes. However, effective decision processes break nearly all the rules for rational decision making: few alternatives should be analyzed, only positive consequences of the chosen actions should be considered, and objectives should not be formulated in advance.

The following subsections explain how irrationalities can build good bases for organizational actions.

NILS BRUNSSON

Searching for Alternatives

According to the rational model, all possible alternatives should be evaluated. This is impossible, so the injunction is often reformulated as evaluating
as many alternatives as possible.

In reality, it seems easier to find decision processes which consider few
alternatives (typically two) than ones which consider many alternatives. It
is even easy to find decision processes which consider only one alternative.
This parsimony makes sense from an action point of view, because considering
multiple alternatives evokes uncertainty, and uncertainty reduces motivation and commitment. If actors are uncertain whether a proposed action is
good, they are less willing to undertake it and to commit themselves to
making it succeed. For example, in order to facilitate product-development
projects, uncertainty should not be analyzed but avoided (Brunsson, 1980).
If people do not know which action will actually be carried out, they have
to build up motivations for several alternatives at the same time, and this
diffuses the motivations supporting any single alternative For the same
reasons, commitments may be dispersed or destroyed by the consideration
of several alternatives. Therefore, very early in decision processes, if possible
before the processes even start, decision makers should get rid of alternatives
that have weak to moderate chances of being chosen.

On the other hand, alternatives with no chance to being chosen do not
have these negative effects: they may even reinforce motivation and commitment. One strategy is to propose alternatives which are clearly unacceptable but which highlight by comparison the virtues of an acceptable
alternative. This defines the situation as not being of the wait-and-see type:
rejecting one alternative means accepting another. Another and more
important effect is that commitments become doublesided: commitments
arise not only through endorsements of acceptable alternatives but also
through criticisms of unacceptable alternatives. Thus, considering two
alternatives can lay a stronger foundation for action than considering only
one alternative if one of the two alternatives is clearly unacceptable.

One example is the decision process following the merger of Sweden's
three largest steel companies. The merger was supposed to make production
more efficient by concentrating each kind of production in one steelworks.
A six-month-long decision process considered several alternative ways of
redistributing production. Besides the alternative that was actually chosen,
however, only one alternative was investigated thoroughly. This was the
alternative to make no change at all. Because this alternative would have
made the merger meaningless, no one considered it a practical action.

Estimating Consequences

Decision makers who want to make rational decisions are supposed to consider
all relevant consequences that alternatives might have; positive and negative

consequences should get equal attention. But such a procedure evokes much uncertainty, for inconsistent information produces bewilderment and doubt, and stimulates conflicts among decision makers (Hoffman, 1968). Also, it is difficult to weigh positive and negative consequences together (Slovic, 1966).

One way of avoiding uncertainty is to search for consequences in only one direction—to seek support for the initial opinion about an alternative. People tend to anchor their judgements in the first cues they perceive (Slovic, 1972; Tversky and Kahneman, 1974). Searching for positive consequences of an acceptable alternative has high priority, while negative consequences are suppressed. The purpose is not only to avoid uncertainty: active search for arguments in favour of an alternative also helps to create enthusiasm and to increase commitments. If negative consequences do pop up, adding more positive consequences can at least help to maintain commitment and motivation.

For example, in a company with high propensity to undertake innovative product-development projects, personnel spent most of their discussions collecting arguments in favour of specific projects. This helped them to build up enthusiasm for projects—an enthusiasm that they deemed necessary to overcome difficulties (Brunsson, 1976).

Evaluating Alternatives

The rational model prescribes that alternatives and their consequences should be evaluated according to predetermined criteria, preferably in the form of objectives. Decision makers are told to start with objectives and then to find out what effects the alternatives would have on them. This is a dangerous strategy from the action point of view because there is a high risk that decision makers will formulate inconsistent objectives and will have difficulties assessing alternatives. Data are needed that are difficult or impossible to find, and different pieces of information may point in conflicting directions.

For producing action, a better strategy is to start from the consequences and to invent the objectives afterwards (Lindblom, 1959). Predicted consequences are judged to be good because they can be reformulated as desirable objectives. The relations between alternatives and objectives are not investigated in detail, only enough to demonstrate some positive links. The objectives are arguments, not criteria for choice; they are instruments for motivation and commitment, not for investigation. The argumentative role of objectives becomes evident in situations where objectives are abandoned after data indicate that they will not be promoted by preferred actions.

For instance, the calculations in the merged steel company actually demonstrated that the no-change alternative would be at least as profitable as the alternative that was chosen. The decision makers then shifted their criterion from profitability as defined in the calculations to criteria such as access to a harbour and the age of a steelworks—criteria which favoured the alternative to be chosen.

Choosing

Within the decision-making perspective, a decision is normally described as a choice which follows automatically from preceding analysis. But when decision making initiates action, a choice is not merely a statement of preference for one alternative but an expression of commitment to carrying out an action. A choice can be formulated in diverse ways which express different degrees of commitment and enthusiasm. Which people participate in choosing influences which people participate in acting.

A local government with an unstable majority postponed for eight years a decision about where to build new houses. Yet, at every time, there existed a majority favouring one location. Majority support was not thought to be a sufficient basis for the complicated and time-consuming planning work to follow (Brunsson, 1981; Jönsson, 1982).

Making Rational Use of Irrationality

The purpose of action calls for irrationality. Some irrationalities are consistent with the prescriptions of Lindblom (1959) who argued that thorough rational analyses are irrelevant for the incremental steps in American national policy. But irrationality is even more valuable for actions involving radical changes, because motivation and commitment are crucial.

Much of the decision irrationality observed in decision processes can be explained as action rationality. The hypothesis that such may be the case is worth considering at least in situations where motivation and commitment are highly beneficial. For example, this kind of explanation can be applied to some of the strategic decisions described by Janis (1972). Much of the irrationality Janis observed in the decision of the Kennedy administration to invade Cuba can be explained by the fact that such risky and normally illegitimate actions needed extreme motivation and commitment to be adopted. Strong motivations and commitments seem actually to have arisen, and they led to very strong efforts to complete the action in spite of great difficulties and uncertainties.

According to Janis, better alternatives would have been found if the decision process had been more rational, giving room for more criticism, alternative perspectives and doubts. Perhaps so. But deciding more rationally in order to avoid big failures is difficult advice to follow. If the decisions should initiate actions, the irrationality is functional and should not be replaced by more rational decision procedures. Rational analyses are more appropriate where motivation and commitment offer weak benefits. This is true for actions which are less significant, less complicated and short-term. Lundberg (1961) observed that investment calculations are made for small, marginal investments but not for large, strategic ones. If one believes that rational decision processes lead to better choices, this observation should be disquieting. Moreover, important actions tend to be carried out with strong motivations and commitments, which make it difficult to stop or change directions if the actions prove to be mistakes.

There is also the opposite risk—that decision rationality impedes difficult but necessary actions. For actions involving major organizational changes, the magnitudes of the issues and the uncertainties involved may frighten people into making analyses as carefully as possible At the same time, the uncertainty potentials and the involvements of many people heighten the risks that rational decision making will obstruct action

One extreme and pathological case of decision making giving no basis for action is decision orientation This occurs when people regard decision making as their only activities, not caring about the actions and not even presuming that there will be actions In full accordance with the decision-making perspective, these people look upon decisions as end points. In one political organization, for instance, the politicians facilitated their decision making substantially by concentrating on making decisions and ignoring subsequent actions. Since the decisions were not to be carried out, the politicians did not have to worry about negative effects, and they could easily reach agreements. On the other hand, the lack of actions threatened the survival of the organization.

To sum up, rational decision-making procedures fulfill the function of choice—they lead to the selection of action alternatives. But organizations face two problems: to choose the right thing to do and to get it done. There are two kinds of rationality, corresponding to these two problems: decision rationality and action rationality. The one is not better than the other, but they serve different purposes and imply different norms. The two kinds of rationality are difficult to pursue simultaneously because rational decision-making procedures are irrational from an action perspective; they should be avoided if actions are to be facilitated.

How can the problem of choice and the problem of action be solved concurrently? One way is to solve the problem of choice by means of ideologies instead of by decisions. Ideologies can fulfill the function of choice without impeding actions. This is the theme of the next section.

IDEOLOGIES THAT FACILITATE ACTIONS

Recent research has stressed other cognitive aspects of organizational life than decision making. Organizational members share interests which determine their participation in an organization. They also perceive similarly the organization, its environment, its history and its future. Some shared knowledge, perspectives and attitudes persist over time (Clark, 1972; Jönsson and Lundin, 1977; Starbuck, 1976; Starbuck et al., 1978). These cognitive phenomena, or parts of them, have been given names such as frames of reference, myths or strategies; here they are called organizational ideologies.

An ideology is a set of ideas. A person's ideas about one particular object or situation is here called a cognitive structure. Because people can be more or less closely related to their ideas, it is possible to distinguish three kinds of organizational ideologies. One kind is the members' individual cognitive structures. These can be called *subjective ideologies*. The members also have ideas of the cognitive structures of their colleagues. These ideas are *perceived ideologies;* what people think other people think. Finally, *objective ideologies* are ideas which are shared by all organizational members and which afford common bases for discussion and action. These different kinds of ideologies are at least partly inconsistent.

Ideologies describe both how things are and how they should be, and these two aspects are often strongly interdependent. Both the descriptive and the normative aspects answer questions about reality. One question is *how*? How do the members act in relation to each other or to people outside the organization? Another question is *what*? What has happened (history), or what will (expectations)? Ideologies define not only what is perceived as fact but also which facts appear important. Thirdly, ideologies can answer the question *why*? Causes may be attributed to an individual member, to the whole organization (self-attribution), or to the organization's environments (environmental attribution).

Organizational ideologies interrelate closely with decisions, since they make it easier for people to agree on what objectives to pursue, on what action alternatives hold promise, and on what outcomes are probable. Ideologies afford short-cuts in decision making by enabling decision makers to omit or abbreviate some steps and by filtering out some alternatives and consequences (March and Simon, 1958).

Ideologies also substitute for decisions. Many organizational actions do not follow decision processes; agreement and coordination arise without decision making, because the actors perceive situations similarly and share expectations and general values (Danielsson and Malmberg, 1979).

In the innovative company mentioned earlier, most ideas for product-development projects clearly matched the ideology. Such proposals could be accepted and projects started without explicit decisions. Instead of carrying out decision-making processes, management engaged in supporting the proposals by arousing commitments and strengthening the expectations that the projects would succeed.

Organizational ideologies tend to arise by themselves in any organization, but according to some authors, they can also be consciously moulded by an organization's members (Ansoff et al., 1976; Lorange and Vancil, 1977;

Starbuck et al., 1978). This suggests that ideologies can be formed with the direct purpose of avoiding rational decision making, thus reinforcing the potential for taking difficult actions. In fact, organizational ideologies might reconcile the tasks of thinking and of acting, because ideologies might identify appropriate actions and also contribute to their accomplishment.

If ideologies are to take the place of rational decision making, confrontations between proposed actions and ideologies should give clear results. It should be possible to classify a proposal as acceptable or unacceptable after little analysis and discussion. There should be high consistency among the cognitive structures of individual organizational members. There should not only be common ideologies to undergird discussions, but these objective ideologies should be very conclusive—so clear and so narrow that additional filters for ideas are unnecessary.

Conclusiveness could be accomplished by objective ideologies that include just a few, precise normative statements. However, a confrontation between very simple ideologies and a nonconforming action proposal might throw the ideologies into question rather than the proposal. Complex ideologies that make contingent statements about an organization and its environments can also be conclusive, and such ideologies are unlikely to be challenged by a single action proposal.

A comparison between two companies revealed that the one with narrow, clear and complex objective ideologies was able to accomplish great changes in its product mix, whereas the company with broad, ambiguous and simple ideologies had great difficulties getting new products into production (Brunsson, 1979). Ideologies which are clear, narrow, differentiated, complex and consistent can provide good bases for action because they solve a large part of the choice problem. Such ideologies can determine what actions are right, so analysis is minimized, and efforts can concentrate on reinforcing actions. Decision rationality can be used for forming ideologies, and action rationality can be used for forming actions. Thinking can be separated from acting.

Attribution is important too. If the outcomes of action are believed to depend on environmental events, an organization should construct forecasts of the type prescribed by rational models. If the outcomes seem to depend on what members do within an organization itself, the key task is to create motivations and commitments. Thus, environmental attribution fits decision rationality, whereas self-attribution facilitates action rationality.

IDEOLOGICAL SHIFTS THAT FOSTER RADICAL CHANGES

Actions that would radically change an organization's relations to its environments are typically difficult to carry out and need strong commitments and high motivations, so ideologies should endorse these actions precisely and enthusiastically. But such ideologies constrain the possibilities for change, because only changes that match the ideologies receive ideological support.

Changes within narrow ideologies do sometimes suffice. Often, however, organizations need quick and radical changes to accommodate rapid environmental changes, and precise ideologies would rule out changes which are radical enough to cope with these situations. Yet, broad and ambiguous ideologies would not afford strong bases for action. A company which regards itself a transportation company may be no more flexible than one which considers railways its domain. There seems to be a dilemma: radical changes require conflicting qualities of organizational ideologies.

There is a solution, however. Again, the trick is to separate thinking from acting. If change actions are preceded by ideological shifts, they can attract enough support to be accomplished. This implies that change actions should wait until new ideologies have been established.

If ideologies are to serve as bases for choice, they must resist pressures for change and change slowly. In fact, the slowness of ideological shifts can explain the long time-lags before organizations respond to important threats in their environments, even when the threats seem obvious to external observers (Starbuck et al., 1978).

The need for complex and precise ideologies that shift explains the 'myth cycles' reported by Jönsson and Lundin (1977). They found that organizations jump from one dominant ideology, or myth, to another. Belief in a dominant ideology is strong under normal conditions, and the dominant ideology is questioned only during crises. When members lose faith in a dominant ideology, they replace it by another. Such myth cycles imply a strong belief in one objective ideology and a consistency between subjective and objective ideologies which seem irrational from a decision-making point of view. On the other hand, the cycles contain much action rationality. A dominant ideology maximizes an organization's ability to act. Consensus and strong adherence to one ideology are not merely results of people's analytical and perceptual deficiencies; they are necessary conditions for organizational survival.

If radical changes have to be initiated by ideological shifts, it becomes a crucial issue how ideologies can be changed. External factors—such as crises or shifts in leadership—may be important, as may the properties of ideologies themselves. What properties make ideologies apt to shift when shifts are needed? Fortunately, the same properties that make ideologies good bases for action make them apt to change. Precision and complexity facilitate both.

Because descriptive statements in ideologies can be checked against reality, changes in reality provide incentives for ideological shifts. The more factors an ideology considers, the greater is the chance that some of them will change; and the more causal links among these factors, the more repercussions a change in one of them will have. If statements are clear, they can be proved false, and they have weak chances of surviving drastic changes in reality. The most stable ideologies are simple ones which are both vague and widely applicable—such as, our goal is profitability, or we shall operate in the transportation industry.

Paradoxically, the refining and elaborating of ideologies are steps toward abandoning them. However, a situation from which a change is initiated need not have much in common with the situation in which the change occurs. Existing ideologies are threatened when their implications contradict observations. If these threats cannot be met by making ideologies more ambiguous, inconsistencies arise within both subjective and objective ideologies. If subjective ideologies change more rapidly than the objective ideologies, inconsistencies arise between the subjective and the objective ideologies, so belief in objective ideologies decreases. Diverse subjective ideologies appear, and these may correspond to social structures different from the ones founded upon the old ideologies. The result is inconsistency between an organization's social and its ideological structures, inconsistency which gives less room for compromise and authority. Differences between what people think privately and the ideologies to which they can refer publicly in their discussions give rise to misunderstandings. When people misinterpret each others' statements, conflicts arise, escalate and remain difficult to resolve. Once the objective ideologies have been questioned, many people see chances to change the organization's environments, its internal functioning and their own positions. The differences increase between what is and what should be, with regard to what goals to pursue, how things should be done, and who should control events.

Ideological shifts afford very bad contexts for action. Ideological inconsistencies increase uncertainty and make it extremely difficult to marshall commitments for organizational actions. Conflicts interfere with coordination. Simultaneous attempts to change environments, the ways things are done, and who has control may easily exceed an organization's problem-solving abilities. Thus, an ideological shift has to be completed before acting begins. In fact, an ideological shift in one organization produced a complete inability to act, a social deadlock where everyone worked for change, but their individual actions actually impeded change, and where no one understood how to break out of this frustrating situation (Brunsson, 1981). A social deadlock is a steady state: it is full of activities, but these activities stabilize the situation, reinforcing the deadlock. A productive ideological shift must be a step in a process which leads to something new.

The difference between social deadlocks and productive ideological shifts has two implications. The first implication concerns observers of organizational changes: they might mistake confused situations for productive ideological states. Since confused situations precede the actions that create radical changes, observers might infer that confused situations produce changes, and that organizations should try to remain confused in order to have high propensities to change and high abilities to adapt to changing environments (Hedberg and Jönsson, 1978). This inference neglects the transitional character of confused situations, and it mistakes processes of change for initiators of change. The confused situation during an ideological shift may resemble neither its predecessor nor its successor. On the contrary, consistent, clear and complex ideologies are both good starting points for ideological shifts and desirable results of the shifts. Consensus rather than conflict breeds change.

The second implication is more practical: ideological shifts may become steady states. Social deadlocks are created and maintained by vicious circles in which ideological confusion leads to more confusion, and conflicts lead to still more conflicts. The confusion and conflict during an ideological shift bring an organization to the brink of social deadlock. How to prevent social deadlocks is an intriguing question for research.

CONCLUSIONS

This article discusses two aspects of organizations' thinking: decision making and ideologies. Observations of organizations demonstrate that both aspects tend to be irrational in the traditional meaning of the word. Many decisions are based on biased information about a biased set of two alternatives, sometimes only one, and the information is weighed improperly. Organizational ideologies focus members' perceptions on just a few aspects of reality, and members' confidence in their biased perceptions greatly exceeds what seems justified. Organizational processes systematically reduce, rather than exploit, the multitude perceptions that numerous people could have brought in.

These irrationalities appear both harmful and difficult to explain if the main purpose of an organization's thinking is to choose the right actions. However, the main problem for organizations is not choice but taking organized actions. Decision making and ideologies form bases for action and can be fully understood only by recognizing that function. Thinking must be adapted to the purpose of action; and, in that perspective, irrational decision making and narrow, prejudicial ideologies are necessary ingredients of viable organizations inhabiting complex and rough environments.

Organizations have two problems in relation to action—to find out what to do and to do it. When confronting difficult actions, organizations separate these problems. Organizations solve the problem of choice by forming ideologies, then the activities preceding specific actions focus on creating motivations and commitments.

Getting things done is particularly problematic in political organizations. These organizations institutionalize conflict: people are recruited on the basis that they adhere to disparate ideologies, and these ideological differences persist in spite of common membership in the same organizations. The ideological differences block radical actions because each proposed action is scrutinized from diverse viewpoints. Actions are supposed to be initiated by rational decision procedures that integrate the disparate viewpoints. Thus, proposed actions that involve major changes are rejected, and the organizations move in small steps (Brunsson and Jönsson, 1979). Generally, political organizations try to generate action by forming strong majorities. Where this is impossible, the problems aggravate.

Lindblom (1959) argued that irrationalities can be accepted in national policy making because policies develop incrementally. The conclusion here is instead that the high degree of rationality in political organizations produces incrementalism. It is rationality, not irrationality, that is tied to incrementalism.

Decisions and actions can also be separated organizationally. Civil servants can take actions, while the politicians discuss and debate. This heightens the chances of powerful actions but decreases the politicians' influence over what actions to take. Strong political influence seems to hinder radical changes even if there is a strong majority.

In Sweden, the control of industrial companies is shifting from managers to groups representing diverse interests, such as unions, local governments, and regional and national authorities. The industrial companies are becoming more and more like political organizations. Finding ways to combine influence by diverse groups with ability to act is a pressing challenge for organizational research.

REFERENCE

ACKERMAN, B. A., ROSS-ACKERMAN, S., SAWYER, J. W. and HENDERSON, D. W. (1974). *The Uncertain Research for Environmental Quality.* New York: Free Press.

ANSOFF, H. I., DECLERCK, R. P. and HAYES, R. L. (Eds.) (1976). *From Strategic Planning to Strategic Management.* New York: Wiley.

ARGYRIS, C. (1977). 'Organizational learning and management information systems'. *Accounting, Organizations and Society*, **2**, 113–23.

BRUNSSON, N. (1976). *Propensity to Change.* Göteborg, Sweden: B.A.S.

BRUNSSON, N. (1979). 'The fallacy of accepting everything as a strategy for change'. *Munich Social Science Review*, **2**, 29–39.

BRUNSSON, N. (1980). 'The functions of project evaluation'. *R & D Management*, **10**, 61–5.

BRUNSSON, N. (1981). *Politik och administration.* Stockholm: Liber.

BRUNSSON, N. and JÖNSSON, S. (1979). *Beslut och handling.* Falköping, Sweden: Liber.

CHANDLER, A. D. (1977). *The Visible Hand.* Cambridge, Mass.: Belknap.

CHURCHMAN, C. W. (1964). 'Managerial acceptance of scientific recommendations'. *California Management Review*, **7**, 31–8.

CLARK, B. R. (1972). 'The organizational saga in higher education'. *Administrative Science Quarterly*, **17**, 178–84.

CYERT, R. M. and MARCH, J. G. (1963). *A Behavioral Theory of the Firm.* Englewood Cliffs, N.J.: Prentice-Hall.

DANIELSSON, A. and MALMBERG, A. (1979). *Beslut fattas.* Stockholm: S.A.F.

GALBRAITH, J. K. (1967). *The New Industrial State.* Boston, Mass.: Houghton Mifflin.

44 NILS BRUNSSON

GOLDBERG, L. R. (1968). 'Simple models or simple processes? Some research on clinical judgments'. *American Psychologist*, **23**, 483–96.

HARVEY, A. (1970). 'Factors making for implementation success and failure'. *Management Science, Series B*, **16**, 312–20.

HEDBERG, B. L. T. and JÖNSSON, S. A. (1978). 'Designing semi-confusing information systems for organizations in changing environments'. *Accounting, Organizations and Society*, **3**, 47–64.

HOFFMAN, P. J. (1968). 'Cue-consistency and configurality in human judgement'. In Kleinmetz B. (Ed.), *Formal Representation of Human Judgement*. New York: Wiley.

HUYSMANS, J. H. (1970). 'The effectiveness of the cognitive style constraint in implementing operations research proposals'. *Management Science*, **17**, 99–103.

JANIS, I. L. (1972). *Victims of Groupthink*. Boston, Mass.: Houghton Mifflin.

JÖNSSON, S. A. (1982). 'Cognitive turning in municipal problem solving'. *Journal of Management Studies*, **19**, 63–73.

JÖNSSON, S. A. and LUNDIN, R. A. (1977). 'Myths and wishful thinking as management tools'. In Nystrom, P. C. and Starbuck, W. H. (Eds.), *Prescriptive Models of Organizations*. Amsterdam: North-Holland, 157–70.

KAHNEMAN, D. and TVERSKY, A. (1973). 'On the psychology of prediction'. *Psychological Review*, **80**, 237–51.

KEENEY, R. L. and RAIFFA, H. (1976). *Decisions with Multiple Objectives*. New York: Wiley.

LINDBLOM, C. E. (1959). 'The science of "muddling through" '. *Public Administration Review*, **19**, 79–88.

LINDBLOM, C. E. (1977). *Politics and Markets*. New York: Basic Books.

LORANGE, P. and VANCIL, R. F. (1977). *Strategic Planning Systems*. Englewood Cliffs, N.J.: Prentice-Hall.

LUNDBERG, E. (1961). *Produktivitet och räntabilitet*. Stockholm: S.N.S.

MARCH, J. G. and OLSEN, J. P. (Eds.) (1976). *Ambiguity and Choice in Organizations*. Bergen: Universitetsforlaget.

MARCH, J. G. and SIMON, H. A. (1958). *Organizations*. New York: Wiley.

MURDICK, R. G. and ROSS, J. E. (1975). *Information Systems for Modern Management*. Englewood Cliffs, N.J.: Prentice-Hall.

NISBETT, R. and ROSS, L. (1980). *Human Inference*. Englewood Cliffs, N.J.: Prentice-Hall.

PREST, A. R. and TURVEY, R. (1965). 'Cost-benefit analysis: a survey'. *Economic Journal*, **75**, 685–705.

SLOVIC, P. (1966). 'Cue consistency and cue utilization in judgement'. *American Journal of Psychology*, **79**, 427–34.

SLOVIC, P. (1972). *From Shakespeare to Simon*. Portland: Oregon Research Institute.

STARBUCK, W. H. (1976). 'Organizations and their environments'. In Dunnette, M. D. (Ed.), *Handbook of Industrial and Organizational Psychology*. Chicago: Rand McNally, 1069–123.

STARBUCK, W. H., GREVE, A. and HEDBERG, B. L. T. (1978). 'Responding to Crises'. *Journal of Business Administration*, **9**, 2, 111–37.

TARKOWSKY, Z. M. (1958). 'Symposium: problems in decision taking'. *Operational Research Quarterly*, **9**, 121–3.

TVERSKY, A. and KAHNEMAN, D. (1974). 'Judgement under uncertainty: heuristics and biases'. *Science*, **185**, 1124–31.

ZANDER, A. (1971). *Motives and Goals in Groups*. New York: Academic Press.

Part IV
Organizational Learning

One point of interest related to decision making was its potential to change over time: thus an interest in organizational, as different from individual, learning. Chris Argyris and Donald Schön's *Organizational Learning: A Theory of Action Perspective*[3] has become the central work on this issue, and is announced in Argyris's article (Chapter 10). But organizational learning also came to be portrayed with increasing complexity. Bo Hedberg (Chapter 11) pointed out that the unlearning could be as important as learning in organizations. Later Scott D.N. Cook and Dvora Yanow (Chapter 12) summarized earlier research on organizational learning and opened it up to new trends – cultural approaches and knowledge management – where the topic still remains.

Note

3. 1978, Reading, MA: Addison-Wesley.

[10]

Single-Loop and
Double-Loop Models in
Research on Decision
Making

Chris Argyris

Some current research and theory on organizational decision making from the political science literature is
examined, in which the potential role of learning and
feedback in the decision-making process is largely ignored. An espoused theory of action based on single-loop
learning is found to be the most general model of action.
A double-loop model is proposed as providing feedback
and more effective decision making.

RESEARCH AND THE STATUS QUO

Cohen and March (1974: 205) state explicitly: "First, we do
not believe that any major new cleverness that would conspicuously alter the prevailing limits in our ability to change
the course of history (in organizational theory and practice)
will be discovered." However, a few pages later (Cohen and
March, 1974: 215), in the fascinating section on "Technology
of Foolishness," they raise questions about certain "robust
faiths" that have become segments of contemporary Western civilization, such as the concept of choice, which assumes
pre-existence of purpose, the necessity of consistency, and
the primacy of rationality. Their questions seem to imply that
the course of history may be alterable, and it is not surprising
that this inconsistency appears in a section in which Cohen
and March attempt to apply their framework to develop practical advice to administration.

The problem has two aspects. The first is that Cohen and March
recommend a leadership strategy that has been called (by
March) mini-Machiavellian and derivable from the major properties of decision making in organized anarchies that Cohen and
March found as a result of their research. They recommended
that the leader should (1) be involved in the organization in order
to provide the energy needed to influence major decisions, (2)
become informed so that in an information poor system (characteristic of organized anarchies) he will then become valued, (3)
persist in promoting his views, since a decision defeated today
may be accepted tomorrow, (4) exchange status for substance,
(5) facilitate opposing factors to participate, and (6) overload the
system thereby making themselves more necessary.

This advice appears to be a framework for maintaining organizations as Cohen and March found them: mini-Machiavellian
and organized anarchies. The advice could also perpetuate the
expectations of subordinates, especially the ineffective and/or
less involved ones, that organizations and their leadership will
never change, and can lead to physical and psychological
exhaustion in leaders. Imagine being advised to work hard, to
be present at most meetings, to provide energy in a system
whose participants refuse to energize (and through their
bickering are capable of using up any energy input), and to
facilitate opposition because it is the best way to correct
excesses or polarizations of positions.

Finally, the advice appears to sanction deceit. The effectiveness of a mini-Machiavellian leadership is based on the assumption that the reasons for behavior or strategy are kept
secret. For example, Cohen and March (1974: 211) recommend that if the president of a university wants to untangle a

curriculum reform from an issue of social justice, he should create a garbage can attractive enough to seduce the social justice proponents away from the immediate action.

To those familiar with organizational activity, Cohen and March have elevated leadership strategy to what some would consider dysfunctions in organizations.

Cohen and March might object to calling the strategy dysfunctional, since they described organizations as they were and since they provided a section on the technology of foolishness which raised some basic questions about orthodoxy in decision making. The term, foolishness, indicates that Cohen and March were aware how radical their questions would appear to many theorists on decision making. What Cohen and March reported was a rational theory of leadership, consistent with their model, which, in turn, was consistent with the organizations they studied.

In examining other literature, to learn what can be done about this problem, one finds mostly conjectures and almost no empirical research. The primary objective stated in almost all of the studies is to attempt a rigorous description of the problem. This position is predictable because the underlying assumption of much research in social science is to conduct rigorous research about conditions, systems, relationships, and so forth as they are (Argyris, 1968, 1971, 1973, 1974, 1975; Hackman and Morris, 1975). Such an assumption is considered in that useful insights for correcting problems can be derived from the accurate description of a problem.

A paradoxical assumption is that change is possible even though the factors causing the problems are taken as given. For example, Cohen and March (1974) view intergroup coalition rivalries, avoidance of uncertainty, interpersonal threat, and mistrust as factors inhibiting decision-making effectiveness; but they were viewed as factors to be understood, not altered. This does not mean that suggestions are not made in the literature to increase decision-making effectiveness. For example, a collegial style of decision making might be recommended, but no insight provided on this could be attained without first reducing conflict, mistrust, and so on.

ALTERNATIVE VIEWS

An earlier model called "synoptic" described a decision maker going through a set of processes where he or she (1) identified and systematically ordered objectives and values, (2) comprehensively surveyed all possible means of achieving those values, (3) exhaustively examined the sequences, and (4) made a choice that maximized or reached some acceptable level of achievement. Lindblom (1959, 1965: 137–138, 1968) described this model, but with other researchers argued that this view was not adapted to man's limited intellectual capacities, to the inadequacy of information, to the high cost of analysis, to learning from failures, or to the close relationship between fact and value in policy making. Consequently they proposed a third model described as an incremental approach to decision making (Pressman and Wildavsky, 1973; Moynihan, 1972). Researchers proposing this model consider analysis to be drastically limited and the definition of a good policy arbitrary, and it is probably not possible

Single-Loop and Double-Loop

to select rigorous criteria for effectiveness. The closest one could come to understanding effectiveness would be to define key questions, which, if answered, would make it possible to evaluate effectiveness. Effective action is more a succession of comparisons between actions and feedback from the environment, which provide information for the next action or decision. Since decisions are made on necessarily incomplete information, once executed, feedback is required to evaluate their effectiveness.

It is not the purpose here to argue for any of these approaches, but rather to explore the importance that learning processes play in problem solving and decision making. The effectiveness of this approach depends upon being able to subdivide problems and upon the actions being repeatable enough so that decision makers can learn from their actions and adapt their decision making and behavior accordingly; also upon the availability of valid information from the environment within realistic time constraints to make corrections possible.

Underlying Role of Learning in Decision Making

Learning is here defined as the detection and correction of errors, and error as any feature of knowledge or of knowing that makes action ineffective. Error is a mismatch: a condition of learning, and matching a second condition of learning. The detection and correction of error produces learning and the lack of either or both inhibits learning.

It is difficult to conceive of how decision-making processes that include such activities as search, design, and choice could operate effectively without valid information. It is here assumed that the more complex and ill-structured a problem, the higher the probability of ambiguity and so the higher the probability of errors; that is, the lower the probability that actions will match plans effectively. Furthermore, problems become increasingly complex and ill-structured, the need for learning increases, but so does the difficulty in carrying out effective learning.

An assumption in the three models of decision-making processes just described is that complex decisions can be subdivided and the subordinate problems solved in some sort of functional sequence. Such an approach would be especially appropriate for decisions that once made are not intended to be altered. This makes crucial the learning processes before the decision. For example, Allison (1971), George (1973), and Neustadt (1970) provide illustrations of decisions where the learning could have occurred before the decisions were made, though in many cases, it did not.

Factors That Inhibit Learning

At least two important sets of variables can be altered to increase the effectiveness of learning, no matter at what point the learning is to occur. One is the degree to which interpersonal, group, intergroup, and bureaucratic factors produce valid information for the decision makers to use to monitor the effectiveness of their decisions. The other is the receptivity to corrective feedback of the decision-making unit—that is, individual, group, or organization.

Allison (1971) presented evidence that organizational and
bureaucratic political factors significantly influenced the
amount and quality of the learning during decision making.
Examples of organizational factors are partial resolutions of
interdepartmental and interpersonal conflicts, ineffective and
incomplete search, avoidance of uncertainty, political exchanges, and annexation of other units. Examples of bureaucratic and political factors among individuals are competitive
games; bargaining, parochial priorities, personal goals, interests, stakes, and stands; use of power; misperception,
and miscommunication.

Halperin (1974: 235–279) suggested that there were "ma-
neuvers" to affect the information given and received; for
example, (1) reporting only those factors that support one's
view, (2) biasing reports to senior participants to promote
one's own view, (3) not reporting facts that indicate danger,
and (4) avoiding senior officers who might report facts that
one wished to suppress.

Hoopes (1969) described the distortion and manipulation of
information by subordinates and the lack of open debate.
Wildavsky (1964) and Wildavsky and Pressman (1974) focused especially on the competitiveness and bureaucratic
win-lose politics among bureaus and departments. Thomson
(1968) and Halberstam (1969) provided vivid examples of how
personal ideologies, cognitive rigidities, and concepts of loyalty inhibited the generation and communication of valid information to upper levels. Geyelin (1966) and Halberstam
(1969) provided evidence that key officials repeatedly and
privately attributed motives to others, which then influenced
the information that the officials gave or expected to receive.
Schlesinger (1973) and Sorenson (1963) stated that secrecy
had been a governing principle of presidential decision making
nationally, and that conflict was the "one quality which
characterizes most issues likely to be brought to the President." Moynihan (1972) suggested that bureaucratic political
strife and competitiveness led to "competitive depreciation."
Wildavsky (1964) provided informative descriptions of the
political warfare, one-upmanship, and power maneuverings
that occurred during budgetary processes. Donavan (1970:
32, 33) described how the decision related to the Bay of Pigs
moved to execution without President Kennedy being able
either to control or to reverse it, and how President Johnson
was misled into signing community-action legislation that
provided for citizen participation, a concept which he did not
like. Gawthrop (1971) described administrative politics as
games in which the basic rules were to maximize winning
and self-interest. Schlesinger (1973) described the compelling
need, especially of the President, for "passports to reality"
since the world that immediately surrounds superiors is so
often unreal. Neustadt's (1960, 1970) work presaged many of
the observations above and suggested that key top figures
seem to forget the constraints others have placed upon them
by their national governance processes as well as by deeply
held norms developed over years of national political activity.

Moreover, the literature suggests that the factors that inhibit
valid feedback tend to become increasingly more operative as
the decisions become more important and as they become

Single-Loop and Double-Loop

more threatening to participants in the decision-making processes; that is, valid information appears to be more easily generated for less important and less threatening decisions. This is a basic organizational problem for it is found not only in governmental organizations, but also in business organizations, schools, religious groups, trade unions, hospitals, and so on (Argyris, 1964, 1970, 1972).

One might say that participants in organizations are encouraged to learn to perform as long as the learning does not question the fundamental design, goals, and activities of their organizations. This learning may be called single-loop learning. In double-loop learning, a participant would be able to ask questions about changing fundamental aspects of the organization (Allison, Neustadt, Halperin, and others).

Furthermore, most groups and organizations studied in their usual settings permit only single-loop learning. Recent research on individual adult learning suggests that human beings are also acculturated to be primarily single-loop learners in dealing with other human beings and with substantive, controversial issues (Argyris and Schon, 1974). This high degree of consonance between learning acculturation and the kind of limitations placed on learning within groups and organizations results in processes that limit exploration and information and so help provide stability but also inhibit learning in fundamental organizational issues.

To intervene in these circular processes, one needs a model that helps to explain what aspects of current behavior of decision makers and policy makers inhibit double-loop learning, a model that would increase the effectiveness of decision making and policy making, and finally one that would make it possible to use the explanatory model to achieve effectiveness.

THEORIES OF ACTION

Argyris and Schon (1974) stated that all human action was based on theories of action. One can differentiate between espoused theories of action and theories-in-use. Espoused theories of action are those that people report as a basis for actions. Theories-in-use are the theories of action inferred from how people actually behave (taken from video or audio tapes, or other instruments that focus on collecting relatively directly observable behavior). Most individuals studied seem to be able to detect the discrepancies between their espoused theories and theories-in-use of others, but were not able to detect similar discrepancies in themselves. People observe the discrepancies manifested by others but they are programmed with theories-in-use that say, "If you observe others behaving incongruently with what they espouse, in the name of effectiveness, concern, diplomacy, do not tell them."

Single-Loop Model

A model of the theory-in-use was found to account for much of the behavior relevant to this study (Argyris and Schon, 1974). It was hypothesized that human behavior, in any situation, represents the most satisfactory solution people can find consistent with their governing values or variables, such as achieving a purpose as others define it, winning, suppressing negative feelings, and emphasizing rationality.

It was also hypothesized that human beings learned to associate behavioral strategies with their governing values or variables. The primary strategies are to control the relevant environment and tasks unilaterally and to protect themselves and their group unilaterally. The underlying behavioral strategy is control over others, although people vary widely in how they control others. Giving the meaning of a concept to others and defining its validity for them is one of the most powerful ways to control others.

Control as a behavioral strategy influences the leader, others, and the environment in that it tends to produce defensiveness and closedness, because unilateral control does not tend to produce valid feedback. Moreover, controlling behavior unilaterally may be seen by others as defensiveness. Groups composed of individuals using such strategies will tend to create defensive group dynamics, reduce the production of valid information, and reduce free choice. Consequently it was hypothesized that a particular kind and quality of learning would take place. There would be relatively little public testing of ideas, especially important or threatening ones. As a result, leaders would tend to receive little genuine feedback and others would tend not to violate their governing values and so disturb the accepted fundamental framework. Many of the hypotheses or hunches that the leaders generate would then tend to become limited and accepted with little opposition. Moreover, whatever a leader learned would tend to be within the confines of what was acceptable.

Under these conditions, problem solving about technical or interpersonal issues would be rather ineffective. Effective problem solving occurs to the extent individuals are aware of the major variables relevant to their problem and solve the problem in such a way that it remains solved (at least until the external variables change); and, moreover, that they accomplish these without reducing the current level of problem-solving effectiveness (Argyris, 1970). Under these conditions, top administrators tend to become frustrated with the ineffectiveness of the decision-making process and react by striving to increase control, by increasing secrecy about their own strategies, and by demanding loyalty of subordinates that borders on complete agreement with their views.

Besides the acculturation of individuals to these interpersonal group and intergroup dynamics, the consequences just described would be compounded by pyramidal structures, management information systems, including budgets (Argyris, 1964, 1965). In other words, the activities documented in the literature cited above exist at the individual, interpersonal, group, intergroup, organizational, and intraorganizational level in such a way that they mutually reinforce each other to create a stable, indeed, an ultra stable slate (Schon, 1972).

Double-Loop Model

A model incorporating double-loop-learning can avoid the consequences of a model based on single-loop learning (Argyris and Schon, 1974). The governing variables or values of Model II are not the opposite of Model I. The governing variables are valid information, free and informed choice, and internal commitment. The behavior required to satisfice these

Single-Loop and Double-Loop

values also is not the opposite of Model I. For example, Model I emphasizes that the individuals are expected to be articulate about their purposes, goals, and so forth, and simultaneously control the others and the environment in order to ensure achievement of their goals. However, in the double-loop model, the unilateral control that usually accompanies advocacy is rejected because the typical purpose of advocacy is to win; and so, articulateness and advocacy are coupled with an invitation to confront one another's views and to alter them, in order to produce the position that is based on the most complete valid information possible and to which participants can become internally committed. This means that the leader must be skilled in eliciting double-loop learning. Every significant action in the double-loop model is evaluated in terms of the degree it helps the participants generate valid and useful information, including relevant feelings, and solve the problem so that it remains solved without reducing the level of problem-solving effectiveness.

The behavioral strategies of this model involve sharing power with anyone who has competence, and with anyone who is relevant in deciding or implementing the action, in the definition of the task, or the control over the environment. Face saving is resisted because it is seen as a defensive nonlearning activity, and any face-saving action that must be taken is planned jointly with the people involved, with the exception of individuals vulnerable to such candid and joint solutions.

Under these conditions individuals would not tend to compete to make decisions for others or to outdo others for self-gratification. They would try to find the most competent people for the decision to be made, and would try to build viable decision-making networks in which the major function of the group would be to maximize the contributions of each member so that when a synthesis was developed, the widest possible exploration of views would have taken place.

Finally, if new concepts were formulated, the meaning given to them by the formulator and the inference processes used to develop them would be open to scrutiny by those who were expected to use them. Evaluations and attributions would be the result of directly observable data after the concepts were used. Also, the formulator would feel responsible to present the evaluations and attributions so as to encourage open and constructive confrontations.

If the governing values and behavioral strategies just outlined are used, then the degree of defensiveness in individuals, within, between, and among groups, would tend to decrease and free choice would tend to increase, as would feelings of commitment. The end result should be increased effectiveness in decision making or policy making in the monitoring of the decisions and policies and in the probabilities that errors and failures would be communicated openly and that actors would learn from the feedback.

TRANSITIONAL MODEL

It is not easy to conceptualize models of transition from a single-loop to a double-loop model that do not violate the requirements of the latter. Moreover, if one is able to design such processes, the probability of being able to test them empirically is low. Few subjects are interested in genuinely new options, especially if learning them may be difficult and if having learned them there is little support from subordinates' peers, and superiors, as well as from organizational policies and practices to use the new skills.

Learning to become aware of one's present theory-in-use and then altering it is a very difficult process, because it requires that individuals question the theories of action that have formed the framework for their actions. Learning about double-loop learning through lectures, reading, and case discussions will lead to learning at the espoused level rather than at the level of theory-in-use.

For example, the single-loop model teaches individuals to be high on articulate advocacy and simultaneously high on unilateral control over others in order to win. Governmental and private executives can be taught to be articulate advocates in such a way that control is shared in order to increase time for study, and the executives might even come to value the new behavior highly, yet they are unable to behave according to the new requirements, or to experience the appropriate feelings. In the single-loop model inquiry may be seen as weakness; in the double-loop model, it is seen as strength.

Another difficulty is that in organizations, human beings are acculturated to accept a role in a pervasive atmosphere of deception. For example, A would not tell B that he or she was about to act destructively toward B; C would not tell D that he or she was distorting information to D; and E would not tell F that he or she was flattering F. Yet all six know that they and others act in such ways, and that the accepted behavior is to act as if no one knows that such activities go on.

Second, if theories-in-use are the basis of behavior, then they represent a source of confidence that one has in functioning effectively in one's world. To change one's theory-in-use would be risky. There are few group, organizational, or societal supports for significantly different behaviors. New behavior, for example, a focus on real-time inquiry and shared power and trust, could actually cause difficulties for a person because it would be considered deviant behavior. New behavior could also harm the individual because others might use the new power and the trust against him or her.

Third, changing to a double-loop model involves exploration of certain basic values and feelings. For example, if an individual decides to explore reducing his unilateral control over others, he will soon confront himself with the question, why does he control others? Typically, he may respond by saying that if he did not control others, he could not get things done. "People respect what I inspect." All this is confirmable in a Model I world.

In exploring new behaviors some top officials have checked their hypotheses about their lack of confidence with their subordinates. To their dismay they have learned that their subordinates felt the officials' mistrust, and that they kept this knowledge hidden just as the officials were keeping their attributions of mistrust of the subordinates hidden. Also the subordinates could give officials valid reasons for behaving in

Single-Loop and Double-Loop

ways that required the officials' control. In short, the officials learned that much of their sense of a need for unilateral control was a self-fulfilling prophecy (Argyris 1976a).

Such experiences help one to understand why people accustomed to single-loop learning find it difficult to change. For example, many "alternative schools" were started because certain teachers and students were against the Model I schools. A major strategy of alternative schools included going from a highly structured to a very loose school; from unilateral control by teachers to complete equality with students; from teachers evaluating students to students evaluating teachers. These strategies did not work for two reasons. One cannot have effective school organizations without structure with complete equality, and without evaluations of performance of students. Moreover, when one examines carefully the actual behavior of the teachers and the students, it went from the opposite of Model I to an oscillating Model I (Argyris 1974). The same analysis appears to be relevant to the experiments for community participation projects. Many floundered between the competitive win-lose tactics of militant minorities to the opposite role of withdrawal of power and structure related to such learning experiences as T-groups or sensitivity training. A large portion of T-group practice (not theory) is based on a model that is the opposite to the single-loop model; that is, one characterized by withdrawal and passivity. Such a model is not apt to produce more effective decision making; it may actually produce an increase in participant narcissism and, therefore, increased problems when the participant strives to behave with others who have not been in his or her T-groups (Argyris, 1972).

Such data raise questions about two commonly held assumptions by researchers in this field. The first assumption is that changes can be produced directly from descriptive research. Bauer (1974),for example, suggested that there is a continuous relationship from understanding a given situation, to designing a new one and then realizing it. Research tends to suggest that change based on the double-loop model would require a shift in the behavior of individuals and in group, intergroup, and organizational processes.

The second assumption is that changes to make the environment approximate the requirements of the double-loop model would lead to behavior and values appropriate to the model. This assumption is not predicted by the theory, which states that no changes will occur toward a double-loop model unless the individuals change their current theories-in-use. This also means that changes in organizational structure, management information systems, and organizational norms will not lead directly to changes in behavior of the people within the new system.

MULTIPLE ADVOCACY MODEL

George (1972) showed that it is possible for researchers to develop normative prescriptive models that are systematic and empirically testable. He (1972: 758) hypothesized that a system of multiple advocacy worked best and was likely to produce better decisions when three conditions were satisfied:

(1) no major maldistribution of power, weight, influence, competence, information, or analytical resources; (2) bargaining and persuasive skills among members, participation of chief executives to monitor and regulate the workings of multiple advocacy; and (3) time for adequate debate and exchange of ideas.

On the basis of espoused theories and theories-in-use, however, if for example, power, weight, and influence are functions of a role, then maldistribution of such variables would be alterable by order of the chief executive. However, the theories-in-use of individual members also influence their power, weight, and influence in groups. In studies (Argyris, 1969) of nearly 300 policy-making and decision-making sessions in the government and private sectors, such theory-in-use variables made significant differences in the effectiveness of individual members and in the quality of the decisions. However, the variables were rarely, if ever, discussed openly because such discussions violated the governing values of suppressing threatening issues and the negative feelings against the norms against interpersonal risk taking. Questions can also be raised about bargaining and persuasive skills. In a single-loop model, such skills are closely correlated with unilateral control and manipulation of information, secrecy, and so on, which inhibit the kind of discussion required in multiple advocacy if it is to be effective.

Analysis of tapes (Argyris, 1969) of policy-making and decision-making meetings suggests that groups rarely have enough time for adequate debate partially because the win-lose dynamics coupled with single-loop learning and the emphasis on control of others make discussions competitive. Consequently, if the theories-in-use of groups inhibit effective discussion, how effective can the chief executive be in monitoring such factors? George (1972: 761) stated that the multiple advocacy required that the chief executive define his or her own role as that of a magistrate who evaluates, judges, and chooses among the various policies proposed by advocates. Some research (Argyris, 1956, 1968, 1974; Blake and Mouton, 1968) would indicate that this would tend to magnify the win-lose dynamics and/or create a greater sense of hidden conformity.

George suggested that with the introduction of the magistrate role, the advocates will no longer compete against each other but they will compete for the magistrate's attention. Our research would raise some doubts because some of the key variables that influence the magistrate's attention are related to the effectiveness with which the members compete with each other. George may wish that the individuals carrying out the custodian role focus on reducing the competitiveness that is destructive. But there is nothing in George's model to suggest that presently such behavior would be seen, by the participants, as deviant and odd. Also, if our research to date is valid, there are few top administrators who hold such skills.

George also suggests that collegial decision making coupled with the three conditions mentioned would increase the effectiveness of decision making. The path to increased effectiveness may be more difficult. Several decades ago execu-

Single-Loop and Double-Loop

tives in government and private industry associated with the production of complex electronic equipment developed what they called product planning groups, task forces, and matrix organizations. The idea was congruent with the one espoused by George. If one could bring together competent people, with adequate resources and time, and with relatively equal weight of power and influence, more effective decisions should be made. A study of nine such teams in matrix organizations showed that as time progressed the participants, through their behavior (theory-in-use),altered these groups to look more like little pyramidal organizations with little genuine collegial style (Argyris, 1967).

Finally, George identified nine possible malfunctions of policy making that could not be ignored, no matter what model of decision making was used. These included: (1) the chief executive and his other advisors agree too readily on the kind of problem and on a response to it; (2) disagreements do not cover the full range of relevant hypotheses and options; (3) there is no advocate for an unpopular policy action, and so on. These malfunctions were confirmed by other research (Janis, 1972).

George's case for multiple advocacy, with which this writer agrees, points up some important gaps that can begin to be reduced by examining literature and by pursuing further empirical research. The gaps become evident when the distinction is made between espoused theory and theory-in-use. The latter type of data is necessary for the empirical test of any model as well as for knowledge that will be helpful in practice, but these data are still lacking.

DISCUSSION AND SUMMARY

It is acknowledged that the research on the two models is only beginning, although from the data available so far, one can conclude that many espouse the double-loop model or some combination of both models. The data on theory-in-use indicate that most behavior may be categorized as approximately the single-loop model.

One difficulty with these results is that they may be based on research in which the categories are poorly defined. A more differentiated conceptual scheme might produce different results. The results of studies so far range from high interobserver reliability to studies where the subjects scored their own behavior and judged it to approximate the single-loop model, even though they had originally claimed it to be double-looped (Argyris, 1976c). Finally, predictions on the basis of the present conceptual scheme were confirmed (Argyris and Schon, 1974).

Double-loop learning can occur under the conditions of the single-loop model under extreme crisis or revolution. Unfortunately, there are no directly observable data, such as tape recordings, that could lead to inferences if the changes in behavior were those of the double-loop model. Under such extreme conditions, members can be brutally candid, discount the negative impact upon them from such behavior on the grounds that the stakes are very high and the members' motives are sincere; that is, they are not capable of more effective behavior, yet the need for honesty is greater than the need to avoid hurt feelings (Janis). An excellent example of this state in the deliberations of the Marshall Plan is where Kennan felt so punished that he left the meeting to cry and regain his composure (Janis, 1972).

This mode of behavior depends upon having members who can tolerate competitiveness in the group, but this may exclude individuals who may have substantive contributions to make, but cannot tolerate severe competition. Groups composed of highly competitive people also tend to create norms that make other groups "outsiders" and "competitors" if not enemies (Janis, 1972). Moreover, participants from other groups coming into these groups in order to give reports, tend to feel intimidated and then presentations tend to be less effective, which may be viewed by the competitive group as evidence of their superiority. In short, the presentation may be pessimistic and there may be more individuals, groups, and organizations falling into the double-loop model, implied by our admittedly incomplete research; but further empirical research is needed to make the case convincing. Such research would have to obtain directly observable data (for instance, transcripts) and not remain at the espoused level (questionnaires and reports). Another way of interpreting the findings is that they illustrate the scope and depth of the problem and help to explain why much research in social science tends to support the status quo.

Chris Argyris is James Bryant Conant Professor of Education and Organization Behavior, Graduate School of Education, Harvard University.

REFERENCES

Alderfer, Clayton P., and L. Dave Brown
Learning from Changing. Beverly Hills, Calif.: Sage Publications, in press.

Allison, Graham T.
1971 Essence of Decision: Explaining the Cuban Missile Crisis. Boston, Mass.: Little Brown.

Argyris, Chris
1965 Organization and Innovation. Homewood, Ill.: Irwin-Dorsey.
1966 Some Causes of Organizational Ineffectiveness within the Dept. of State, Center for International Systems Research, Occasional Paper, No. 2.
1967 "Today's problems with tomorrow's organizations." Journal of Management Studies, 4: 31–55.
1969 "The incompleteness of social psychology theory." American Psychologist, 24: 893–908.
1970 Intervention Theory and Method. Reading, Mass.: Addison-Wesley.
1971 Management and Organizational Development. New York: McGraw Hill.

1972 "Do personal growth laboratories represent an alternative culture?" Journal of Applied Behavioral Science, 8: 7–28.
1973 On Organizations of the Future. Albert Schweitzer Lecture given at Syracuse University on May 11, 1972. Published as Sage Professional Paper in Administration and Policy Studies #03-006.
1973 The CEO's Behavior: Key to Organizational Development, Harvard Business Review, March-April, Vol. 51, No. 2: 55–64.
1973 "Some limits of rational man organizational theory." Public Administration Review, 33: 253–267.
1974 "Alternative schools: a behavioral analysis." Teachers College Record, 75: 429–452.
1975 "Some dangers in applying results from experimental social psychology." American Psychologist, 30: 469–485.
1976a Increasing Leadership Effectiveness. New York: Interscience, John Wiley.

1976b "Problems and new directions for industrial psychology." In Marvin Dunnette, ed., Handbook of Industrial and Organizational Psychology. Chicago: Rand-McNally.
1976c "Theories of action that inhibit individual learning." American Psychologist, in press.

Bauer, Raymond A.
1974 The Convergence of What Is and What Should Be. Division of Research, Harvard Business School HBS-7.

Blake, Robert R., and Jane Mouton
1968 Corporate Excellence through Good Organizational Development, Houston, Texas: Gulf Publishing Co.

Cohen, Michael D., and James G. March
1974 Leadership and Ambiguity, The American College President. New York: McGraw Hill Book Co.

Cyert, Richard M., and James G. March
1963 A Behavioral Theory of the Firm. Englewood Cliffs, N.J., Prentice-Hall.

Single-Loop and Double-Loop

Donovan, John C.
1970 The Policy Makers. Indianapolis, In.: Pegasus-Western Publishers.

Gawthrop, Louis
1971 Administrative Politics and Social Change. New York: St. Martin's Press.

George, Alexander
1973 "The case for multiple advocacy in making foreign policy." American Political Science Review, LXVI: 751–785.

Geyelin, Philip
1966 Lyndon B. Johnson and the World. New York: Frederick A. Praeger.

Golembiewski, R. T.
1972 Renewing Organizations. Itasca, Ill.: F. E. Peacock.

Hackman, J. Richard, and C. G. Morris
1975 "Group tasks, group interaction process, and group performance effectiveness—a review and proposed integration." In L. Berkowitz (ed.), Advances in Experimental Social Psychology, Vol. 8, N.Y. Academic Press.

Halberstam, David
1974 The Best and the Brightest. New York: Random House.

Halperin, Morton H.
1974 Bureaucratic Politics and Foreign Policy. Washington, D.C.: The Brookings Institution.

Janis, Irving L.
1972 Victims of Groupthink. Boston: Houghton Mifflin.

Katz, Daniel, and Robert L. Kahn
1966 The Social Psychology of Organizations. New York: John Wiley.

Lawrence, Paul R., and Jay W. Lorsch
1967 Organization and Environment Managing Differentiation and Integration. Boston: Division of Research, Harvard University, Graduate School of Business Administration.

Likert, Rensis
1961 The Human Organization. New York: McGraw Hill.

Lindblom, Charles E.
1959 "The science of 'muddling through.'" Public Administration Review, XIX: 79–88.
1965 The Intelligence of Democracy: Decision Making through Mutual Adjustment. New York: The Free Press.
1968 The Policy Making Process. Englewood Cliffs, N.J.: Prentice-Hall.

Marrow, A. J., D. G. Bowers, and S. E. Seashore
1967 Management by Participation. New York: Harper and Row.

Moynihan, Daniel P.
1972 Coping. New York: Random House.

Neustadt, Richard E.
1960 Presidential Power: The Politics of Leadership. New York: Wiley.
1970 Alliance Politics. New York: Columbia University Press.

Porter, Lyman W., E. E. Lawler, and J. R. Hackman
1975 Behavior in Organizations. New York: McGraw Hill.

Pressman, Jeffrey L., and Aaron Wildavsky
1973 Implementation. Berkeley, Calif.: University of California Press.

Schein, Edgar
1965 Organizational Psychology. Englewood Cliffs, N.J., Prentice-Hall.

Schlesinger, Arthur M. Jr.
1973 The Imperial Presidency. Boston: Houghton Mifflin.

Schon, Donald
1971 Beyond the Stable State. New York: Random House.

Simon, Herbert A.
1970 The Sciences of the Artificial. Cambridge, Mass.: M.I.T.

Sofer, Cyril
1961 The Organization from Within. London: Tavistock Publications.

Steinbruner, John D.
1974 The Cybernetic Theory of Decision. Princeton, N.J.: Princeton University Press.

Thomson, James C., Jr.
1968 "How could Vietnam happen?" The Atlantic, pp. 47–53.

Wildavsky, Aaron
1964 The Politics of the Budgetary Process. Boston: Little Brown.

[11]

BO HEDBERG

How organizations learn and unlearn

This chapter discusses how organizations continue to learn as they travel through different environments. Effective learning makes organizations more able to cope with problems. Learning takes place when organizations interact with their environments: organizations increase their understanding of reality by observing the results of their acts. Often the acts are experimental ones. In other instances, organizations learn by imitating other organizations' behavior, or by accepting others' experiences and maps of the environment.

The term organizational learning raises the issue about whether organizations as entities can do anything in their own right. Is it meaningful to think of organizations as having objectives, learning abilities, and memories, or do organizations only learn and remember through their current members? The literature on organizational learning mostly avoids these questions. Although the concept of organizational learning is widely used, the empirical observations are almost always taken from studies of how individuals and animals learn in laboratories.

March and Olsen (1976) described the learning cycle as a stimulus-response system in which individuals' actions lead to organizational actions which evoke environmental responses. The latter are, in turn, reported back to the organizations, where they affect individuals' cognitions and preferences and so influence future actions. Figure 1 portrays this model.

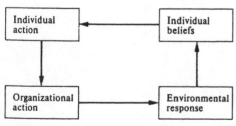

Figure 1 The cycle of organizational learning

The model spells out the interactions between individuals and organizations in organizational learning: it is individuals who act and who learn from acting; organizations are the stages where acting takes place. Experiences from acting are stored in individuals' minds, and these experiences modify organizations' future behaviors. The acting generally accumulates into trial-and-error sequences that incorporate experiments by both organizations and their environments.

Other descriptions of the learning cycle have been less explicit about individuals' roles in organizational learning; these descriptions give the impression that organizations are the entities that act and learn. Cyert and March (1963:99), for example, pictured the learning cycle as follows. An organization may be in various, alternative states. There exist a number of states of the system. At any time, an organization prefers some of these states to others. External sources of disturbance shock an organization: these shocks cannot be controlled. There exist decision variables inside an organization which are manipulated according to decision rules. Each combination of external shocks and decision variables changes the state of an organization. Thus, the next state is determined by the previous state, external shocks, and decision. Any decision rule that has led to a preferred state becomes more likely to be used in the future than it was in the past.

The experimental relationships between organizations and their environments differ from scientific experiments in at least three important ways. Firstly, organizations' environments change frequently, so different experimental situations replace each other over time. Knowledge grows, and simultaneously it becomes obsolete as reality changes. Understanding involves both learning new knowledge and discarding obsolete and misleading knowledge. The discarding activity—unlearning—is as important a part of understanding as is adding new knowledge. In fact, it seems as if slow unlearning is a crucial weakness of many organizations.

Secondly, in contrast to many scientists who, as experimenters, consider the environment as given and attempt to explore reality without influencing it, organizations as experimenters blend adaptive adjustment with manipulative enactment. They select and enact their environments, and they learn for both defensive and offensive purposes (Nystrom *et al*., 1976; Starbuck, 1976; Weick, 1969). It is misleading to equate learning with adaptation. Organizational learning includes both the processes by which organizations adjust themselves defensively to reality and the processes by which knowledge is used offensively to improve the fits between organizations and their environments.

Thirdly, although the paradigm of scientific experimenting assumes that stimuli precede responses and that knowledge and beliefs follow from observations of the results of actions—as in Figure 1—, organizational learning may well occur also in situations where beliefs and realities are little, if at all, connected. Cognitive limitations often distort organizations' interpretations of experiments, and ambiguity may be so great that learning cycles are blocked off and incomplete (March and Olsen, 1976).

This chapter begins by discussing the concept of learning and how organizational and individual learning relate to each other. A stimulus-response paradigm is then employed to describe how organizations select their stimuli, enact their environments, and assemble their responses, and how action programs and theories of action develop as organizations continue to act. The SR model, with its complete learning cycles, is then challenged in a discussion on incomplete learning cycles. Conditions for learning are discussed with respect to inner and outer learning environments. The description ends by discussing how learning is triggered and how unlearning occurs. These aspects are often closely related so that one initiates the other. A concluding, prescriptive section identifies research needs and develops four design strategies that organizational designers could follow in order to facilitate organizations' learning and unlearning.

How researchers understand learning

The concept of learning has many interpretations. It is frequently a summary label for all kinds of processes that map aspects of environments into systems that learn. Habit forming and conditioning are simple forms of one-way learning in which the restricted aim is to establish repertoires of responses or attitudes in the learners (Mowrer, 1960; Thorpe, 1956). According to this view, the systems that learn need not understand the reality behind the stimuli to which they respond. Learning is merely the retention of response patterns for subsequent use, and behavior requires no understanding of causal relationships (Campbell, 1965). But learning can involve more active processes. Learners can perform experiments in order to explore their surroundings. They can engage in undirected or spontaneous searches which bring about trial-and-error learning or evoke latent learning. They can also undertake to explore and exploit their environments, through systematic searches.

Active forms of learning lead to insight (Thorpe, 1956). Attempts to act expose the conditions for acting; causal relationships in the environment, or in the interface between learner and environment, are gradually untangled. Learning, in this sense, is discovery. Learners

discover themselves and their environments; these discoveries lead to comprehending of reasons beyond events, and ultimately to mental maps of relevant aspects of the environment (Lembo, 1972; Morine and Morine, 1973). Learning also takes place when learners integrate new constructs into existing cognitive structures and, in the process, reconcile incongruent experiences and beliefs (Laszlo, 1972). Learning, in this sense, arises from positive feedback between learners and their environments.

Learning that cumulates, maintains, and restructures knowledge

Learning can be cumulative (Samstag, 1973). Learners can build up dominance over their habitats if their environments are stable and manageable. Learning in stable environments is like mental bricklaying, in that pieces of knowledge add to each other. But environments are seldom stable. Most learners have to work actively in order to maintain the understanding which they acquired earlier. The few organization theories which depict learning focus on these ongoing adjustments—the repair work (Bonini, 1963; Cyert and March, 1963; March and Simon, 1958).

Understanding environments that change requires tearing down obsolete mental maps and starting anew. Organizations which encounter environmental discontinuities that threaten their survival (Hedberg, 1974) or which discover new environmental niches (Starbuck and Dutton, 1973) may have to unlearn old behaviors and learn new ones.

Piaget (1968) described learning as a continuous genesis, a process of creation and recreation, where gestalts and logical structures are added or deleted from memory over time. Ongoing empirical observations change, expand, differentiate, and intensify a learner's stored experience. Few, if any, organization theories even try to describe these cyclic developments. Cyert and March (1963) noted that modification and restructuring of knowledge must be incorporated in theories of organizations' long-term behavior, but few significant attempts in that direction have been reported.

Learning that enslaves and learning that liberates

Charging that assumptions about simple-minded, conditioning learning characterize most contemporary approaches to teaching, Illich (1971) concluded that a de-schooling society might do less harm than do most current educational systems. Likewise, Freire (1970a) characterized traditional teaching as a banking approach to learning. Teachers, he said, deposit knowledge in supposedly empty students. The surrounding world remains unknown and unchangeable to the learners because they get no chance to explore and name their reality, and they lack opportunities for discovering or experimenting. Learners can thus never master their environments, but are gradually conditioned to perform imposed behaviors. Such teaching, said Freire, is both domesticating and oppressive, and it pacifies those who learn. The learners become the captives of a culture of silence. Learners who only learn to respond and who imitate others' behaviors have little power over their environments. Living in a culture of silence, they cannot change the language or the rules through which behaviors are imposed.

Learning that helps learners to grow and develop has very different power implications from the enslaving forms criticized by Illich and Freire. Learners become experimenters who take initiatives to explore their habitats. Such learning can only take place in the language of the learners and on their terms. The learners themselves must act, reflect, and name their findings. In directing their explorations and naming their observations, they begin to understand their environments and become more able to manipulate and change their situations (Freire, 1970b).

Learning that changes environments

Another aspect of learning involves processes through which learners create their environments. Katona (1940) emphasized that the purpose of learning is to improve performance and to master the environment. Reality is constructed anew each time a learner acquires a new concept or structure (Piaget, 1968). Learning should not be imitative, but should emphasize generative processes through which learners create environments which they can master (Chomsky, 1966).

The aim of Freire's (1970b) pedagogy of conscientization was to enable Latin America's masses to change their reality, not only to understand it. He proposed processes through which people not only as recipients, but as knowing subjects, would develop awareness of the sociocultural reality shaping their lives and through which people would be increasingly able to transform that reality. Such learning is revolutionary; it challenges the existing structures.

Freire's approach highlights the interactive nature of learning processes. Understanding helps people to manipulate their environments, but learning cannot precede manipulative acts, for acting is the means to acquire knowledge (Freire, 1973).

Learning as the result of both adaptive and manipulative behavior

Learning thus encompasses the processes whereby learners iteratively map their environments and use

their maps to alter their environments. Figure 2 shows this adaptive-manipulative cycle.

The cycle implies that learning requires both change and stability in the relationships between learners and their environments. Too much turbulence can prohibit learners from mapping their environments. Experimenting becomes meaningless when the experimental situations change too frequently. If too much time elapses between observations of the environment and their translation into actions, experience-based actions will be obsolete. Yet too much stability is also dysfunctional to learning. There is little inducement to learn if established and successful behaviors almost never grow obsolete. Situations with much stability produce little information and few opportunities for learning. These are important balances because environmental stability is a design variable which can be altered by those who are responsible for the viability and efficiency of organizations.

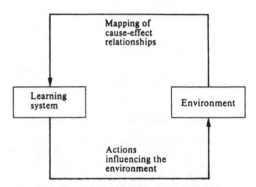

Figure 2 Learning as an adaptive-manipulative relationship between a system and its environment

Learning in open, cognitive systems takes the form of positive feedback which changes the systems or their knowledge, whereas learning in closed, natural systems is the function of negative feedback which aims at maintaining the genotype unchanged (Laszlo, 1972). If a system cannot reorganize itself, it has to use its behavior repertoire to resist and counteract outside threats. To the extent that organizations' decision makers try to treat subsystems as closed, organizational learning is likely to aim at self-stabilization (J. R. Galbraith, 1973; Thompson, 1967). But organizations themselves are open systems that can reorganize themselves, move into new niches, or create more benevolent habitats (Metcalfe et al., 1975; Pondy and Mitroff, 1979).

How individuals' and organizations' learning relate

Do organizations learn? Many organization theorists feel uncomfortable about treating organizations as living systems. Organizations, they say, are merely constructs. Organizations cannot do anything. They have no properties aside from those which channel through people (Hunt, 1968). Organizations cannot have goals; only people and coalitions of people can (Cyert and March, 1963). Organizations, as such, do not learn; members of organizations learn. Yet, most organization theorists keep using concepts such as organizational behavior, organizational slack, and organizational learning, because there are many situations where it is meaningful to interpret organizations as cohesive entities that act purposely and that learn from their actions.

The literature on organizational learning borrows heavily from research on individuals' cognition and learning. One example is the search theory in the behavioral theory of the firm (Cyert and March, 1963), which much resembles Feigenbaum's (1970) assumptions about how individuals search their memories—as depicted in his Elementary Perceiver and Memorizer computer program. In fact, no theory of organizational learning is based primarily on observations of organizations' behavior. Instead, experiments with individual humans, mice, and pigeons provide the bases upon which theories of organizational learning are mostly built.

Individuals' learning is doubtless important in organizational learning. Organizations have no other brains and senses than those of their members. Besides, as Laszlo (1972) demonstrated in detail, there are many similarities between human brains and organizations in their roles as information-processing systems. Insights into how human brains process and store information can suggest important processes in organizations' learning.

Although organizational learning occurs through individuals, it would be a mistake to conclude that organizational learning is nothing but the cumulative result of their members' learning. Organizations do not have brains, but they have cognitive systems and memories. As individuals develop their personalities, personal habits, and beliefs over time, organizations develop world views and ideologies. Members come and go, and leadership changes, but organizations' memories preserve certain behaviors, mental maps, norms, and values over time. For example, standard operating procedures constitute behavior repertoires which are available to many members and which are frequently inherited between office holders (Cyert and March, 1963; Simon, 1957). Customs and symbols are bearers of organizations' traditions and norms, and they help to perpetuate

organizations' social patterns (Blau, 1969; Cohen, 1974). Myths and organizational sagas function as organizational long-term memories from which strategies are derived and in terms of which consistency arguments are voiced (Clark, 1972; Hedberg and Jönsson, 1977; Jönsson and Lundin, 1977; MacIver, 1947; Mitroff and Kilmann, 1976). Also, social systems such as managerial cultures (Dalton, 1959; Harbison and Myers, 1959) and professional groups (Hedberg and Mumford, 1975; Rhenman, 1973) uphold norms and values which affect organizations' behavior and learning (Stymne, 1970). All these phenomena influence individuals' learning within organizations and then transmit the organizational heritage to new generations of members. As leaders and myths shift, sediments of behaviors and beliefs are added to this organizational memory (Danielsson, 1975).

Organizations do quite frequently know less than their members. Problems in communication, such as filtering, distortion, and insufficient channel capacity, make it normal for the whole to be less than the sum of the parts (Argyris and Schön, 1978). This appears to be particularly prevalent when organizations face crises, or when rapid changes in an environment overload communication networks (Hedberg, 1974; Starbuck and Hedberg, 1977).

Organizations do not drift passively with their members' learning: organizations influence their members' learning, and they retain the sediments of past learning after the original learners have left. Organizations can be thought of as stages where repertoires of plays are performed by individual actors. The actors act, but they are directed. They are assigned roles, they are given scripts, and they become socialized into a theatre's norms, beliefs, and behaviors. Although the repertoires of plays shift, especially with the arrivals of new leaders, directors, or schools, there are rich traditions of plays and standards that remain as time passes.

Knowledge of how organizations influence their members' learning and how they store and transmit the products of learning is important to anyone who manages, designs, or studies organizations. Yet their bases in studies of how individuals learn in laboratory settings imply that existing theories have restricted validity. Most learning experiments have been performed in simple environments with one-dimensional goal structures, few and controlled stimuli, high degrees of environmental stability, specified selections of choices, linear reward functions, immediate and accurate feedbacks, and vacuous social contexts (Lieberman, 1972). Real organizations pursue multiple goals and operate in complex environments with heterogeneous stimuli and unstable characteristics. Real organizations have to invent action alternatives, their reward systems are dysfunctional or nonexistent, their feedbacks are lagged and incomplete, and their social contexts consist of layers of formal and informal networks. The interplay between individual, group, and organizational levels has been poorly described in the literature, and research into the interactions between learning individuals and learning organizations is badly needed.

How organizations assemble responses

Almost all theories of organizational learning assume that learning rests on cognitive processes, and most of the theories build on the stimulus-response (SR) paradigm. Organizational learning does involve the detection and correction of errors, and it involves repeated testing, construction, and reconstruction of knowledge (Argyris and Schön, 1978). But in addition to trial-and-error learning, organizations occasionally learn by imitating others' behaviors or by accepting behavior repertoires from others. These latter forms of learning do not necessarily imply SR mechanisms. Neither do they assume that stimuli always precede responses.

SR learning models describe how organizations gather experience and knowledge as they respond to stimuli from encountered situations. Responses that match stimuli well become increasingly likely to be evoked by the same—or similar—stimuli in the future, and searches for proper responses are gradually replaced by programmed SR chains (Cyert and March, 1963; March and Simon, 1958). To identify stimuli properly and to select adequate responses, organizations map their environments and infer what causal relationships operate in their environments. These maps constitute theories of action which organizations elaborate and refine as new situations are encountered.

Responses can be single acts that match single stimuli one-to-one, but responses can also be assemblies incorporating many subroutines. Feigenbaum's (1970) Elementary Perceiver and Memorizer, which is a theory of how humans store experiences for later stimulus-triggered recall, illustrates how responses may be put together. This theory asserts that human cognitive systems store tokens of information at terminal nodes in a list-structured long-term memory; the tokens are words in a vocabulary from which the cognitive systems can build responses. An arriving stimulus is identified by a discrimination network that tests the properties of the stimulus in a sequence of conditional comparisons. When a stimulus has been identified, the discrimination network provides an address indicating the area of the long-term memory which contains an appropriate response. The discrimination network is restructured dynamically so that frequently appearing stimuli are identified more promptly, and frequently occurring responses are placed into the discrimination network

itself so that the reference addresses to long-term memories are replaced by the stored responses. Associative links among responses allow the formation of standard operating procedures.

Newell and Simon (1972) have laid forth the hitherto most extensive theory about cognition in human problem solving and learning. Their models resemble Feigenbaum's, although they are much more detailed. They concluded that human cognitive systems store tokens of information and action subroutines in long-term memory, and that these chunks of information are recalled and concatenated into response assemblies when humans respond to stimuli.

The notion that a single stimulus can evoke a sophisticated response (March and Simon, 1958) is consistent with the complexity theory proposed by Schroder *et al.* (1967). These researchers claimed that earlier studies of human information processing had used experimental environments that were too simple, and so these earlier studies had overlooked variables such as how learners organize information in their memories and how they combine information into responses. Schroder *et al.* found that individuals and groups responded quite differently to identical stimuli in complex settings. The researchers surmised that individuals and groups differ in integrative complexity: integrative complexity takes account of the rules through which people see facets of a problem and also the connections between these alternative perspectives. People who make naive responses evidently organize their memories into few-dimensional, hierarchical structures and they possess few discrimination rules for identifying stimuli. People making sophisticated responses seem to possess multi-dimensional stimulus-discrimination networks. They perceive several perspectives of a problem, and they select preferred interpretations and responses out of many alternatives. However, specific people may range from low to high integrative complexity for different problem situations. Individuals can, for example, have highly complex cognitive structures for their professional fields and show low integrative complexity in areas where they are lay persons. Decision makers' cognitive styles also have important implications for how they perceive situations and how they respond to discovered problems (Doktor, 1969; Keen, 1973; McKenney and Keen, 1974). Learners who encounter certain stimuli frequently or who receive important rewards for mastering situations, enrich their knowledge and move towards higher levels of integrative complexity and so improve their maps of the environments and improve their responses to stimuli.

Theories of action (Argyris and Schön, 1978) or myths and sagas (Clark, 1972; Hedberg and Jönsson, 1977; Jönsson and Lundin, 1977) are for organizations what cognitive structures are for individuals. They filter and interpret signals from the environment and tie stimuli to responses. They are metalevel systems that supervise the identification of stimuli and the assembling of responses.

That learners are multilevel systems is an important idea. Learning that occurs on the primary level and that serves merely to adjust parameters in a fixed structure to varying demands differs profoundly from learning that occurs on metalevels and that redefines the rules for low-level learning. Low-level learning is what Argyris (1976) called single-loop learning; it is generally the only thing described in theories of organizational learning (Cyert and March, 1963). Metalevel learning is what Argyris (1976) called double-loop learning and what Bateson (1972) called deutero-learning; it changes norms, values, and world views. Theories of metalevel learning are few—which suggests that few instances of it have been observed. Low-level learning produces successive replacements or refinements of responses, but metalevel learning can open up totally new ways to assemble responses and to connect stimuli to responses (Kelly, 1955).

How organizations select and organize stimuli

Organizations select the stimuli to which they respond because they typically face much more information than they can sensibly process. Limitations in humans' short-term memories prevent many stimuli from being perceived (Bjork, 1970; Miller, 1956; Newell and Simon, 1972; Norman, 1969, 1970; Simon, 1969; Sperling, 1967; Waugh and Norman, 1965). Both organizations and individuals use attention-directing mechanisms to cope with these limitations: they develop standard operating procedures to guide search and problem identification (Cyert and March, 1963); they refrain from searching for opportunities and they concentrate on overt problems (Thompson, 1967); and they filter incoming signals using rules that reflect members' cognitive styles and preferences (Doktor, 1969; Keen, 1973) and rules that are designed to hold down uncertainty and complexity (Cyert and March, 1963).

Organizations aggregate the selected stimuli into compound stimuli that supposedly map their environments. But there is no one-to-one correspondence between events in the real world and organizations' mapping of these events. Interactions between events and people may give rise to many interpretations of reality, so organizations face multiple realities (Schutz, 1967).

Sociologists have referred to such a perceptual filter as a definition of the situation (McHugh, 1968) and March and Simon (1958) used the same concept to describe the rules that organizations use to interpret stimuli. A defi-

nition of a situation is a set of rules that interprets stimuli in a way that is meaningful to an observer. Definitions of situations transform events scattered in chronological time into events cohesive in social time, and they glue events separated in physical space into units in social space (Mead, 1932). Hegel's (1959) term Weltanschauung—world view—recognizes that individuals, groups, and societies reorganize the world inside themselves. A Weltanschauung is a definition of the situation: it influences what problems are perceived, how these problems are interpreted, and what learning ultimately results.

Perceptual filters make observations meaningful, but these filters also bias beliefs and actions. Myrdal (1958) argued that researchers' and disciplines' world views bias the production of knowledge in social sciences, and Radnitsky (1970) and Törnebohm (1973) widened this discussion to scientific inquiry in general. These and many other authors have concluded that scientists' values direct their searches and mold their findings. Churchman (1971: 149–179) showed how Weltanschauungen similarly affect the designs of management models and information systems and determine organizations' mappings of their environments. Stimson and Thompson (1975) illustrated how different world views about racial integration led to vastly different operations-research models for achieving integration.

That organizations select stimuli is consistent with Weick's (1969) observation that organizations can enact their environments, and also with Starbuck's (1976) claim that organizations make choices among alternative environments. In a sense, the environment is inside an organization. The real world provides the raw material of stimuli to react to, but the only meaningful environment is the one that is born when stimuli are processed through perceptual filters.

Little has been written about how organizations develop their perceptual filters and define situations. Again, the possibly relevant theories describe how individuals use discrimination networks to identify stimuli (Feigenbaum, 1970; Newell and Simon, 1972) and how stimuli are integrated into constructs in human brains (Bieri, 1955; Kelly, 1955; Schroder et al., 1967; Scott, 1974; Zajonc, 1960).

A few attempts have been made to describe organizations' world views. Clark (1972) found that some liberal-arts colleges had cherished sagas which influenced their interpretations of the past and present as well as their choices of actions. Hedberg and Jönsson (1977) labelled as myths the theories that organizations use to interpret their situations and to formulate strategies. Jönsson and Lundin (1977) showed how competing myths struggle for dominance when organizations pass through crises; the particular mechanisms of myth changes were described by Hedberg and Jönsson (1977) and by Jönsson *et al*. (1974). A more general analysis was provided by Kuhn (1962), who showed how the development of scientific knowledge can be understood as a process of replacing paradigms.

Most attempts to describe how organizations' definitions of the situations change assume that evolutionary processes are at work, and that the deterioration of one world view—or myth—contributes to the development of replacements (Jönsson and Lundin, 1977; Kuhn, 1962). However, sudden restructuring is also possible. Kelly (1955) found that individuals' constructs shift abruptly rather than evolve, and Watzlawick *et al*. (1974) described how psychotherapists can employ reframing to stimulate radical modifications in clients' behaviors. Organizations may adopt new world views rather suddenly when their leaders change (Clark, 1972; Hedberg, 1974; Starbuck and Hedberg, 1977).

How organizations learn, assuming that learning cycles are complete

Together the mechanisms that select and interpret stimuli and the mechanisms that enable organizations to store and assemble responses imply a two-level SR model. This model assumes that learning results when organizations interact with their environments: each action adds information and strengthens or weakens linkages between stimuli and responses. In the most common interactions, discovered stimuli evoke response assemblies.

When environments change, there are typically time delays between the environmental changes and changes in the organizations' responses. Minor changes can normally be handled through adjustments in existing action programs, or through switching back and forth within repertoires of behaviors. This is the kind of short-term learning that Cyert and March (1963) described in their behavioral theory of the firm: adjusting search rules and attention rules, changing goals and expectations, and modifying parameters in decision rules. In other instances, organizations negotiate their environments, buffer their inputs and outputs, or manipulate their settings so that impacts from the environment are blunted or forestalled. Thompson (1967) described the vast repertoire of procedures with which organizations hedge themselves from environments.

More substantial changes in organization-environment relationships require that old responses be deleted and sometimes replaced. This unlearning is often difficult, and it takes time. Environmental changes create uncertainty, so organizations are tempted to rely on previously successful behaviors (Hedberg, 1975b). Observed changes are belittled at first, or they are looked upon as stories which someone made up or which

resulted from misperceptions. Ghost myths (Jönsson *et al*., 1974) may have to struggle with the authorized myths for a long time before the organizations realize that the ghost is real and that reorientations are necessary.

Profound changes in the relationships between organizations and their environments may involve total restructurings of the rules by which responses are assembled, and total restructurings are often strongly resisted. Organizations' environmental maps tend to be rigid (Weick, 1969), because socially constructed reality and logical congruence in human brains stabilize established perceptions and beliefs and ward off ambiguous cues until there is enough counter evidence to justify radical reorganizations (Festinger, 1957; Kelly, 1955). However, metalevel shifts do occur, and both people and organizations sometimes unlearn and restructure their mental maps. Watzlawick *et al*. (1974) called one class of metalevel shifts reframings, implying that they are mainly matters of learners' changing their definitions of situations. Other metalevel shifts restructure the responses or the linkages which connect stimuli and responses. New causal models, or new response assemblies, result from the latter shifts.

Argyris and Schön (1978) proposed that a whole learning system is bound together by a theory of action. Radically new situations require that theories of action be replaced, but organizations have difficulties doing this. From his research and consulting, Beer (1972) concluded that organizations' metalogic—the rules for assembling responses and the rules which define situations—typically are inaccessible even to managers and other policy makers, so that these people lack the ability to implement new behavior modes in their organizations. Because people mostly lack languages in which to express and change metarules, organizational changes are constrained to shifts inside behavioral modes. New world views or new theories of action are required in order to restructure organizations (Argyris and Schön, 1978; Freire, 1970b).

The SR model—Figure 3—follows the basic logic of Campbell's (1959) suggested mechanism for variation, selection, and retention. The real world provides the stimuli and is the source of variation. One metalevel of an organization selects stimuli to perceive and interprets them. Another metalevel assembles responses that appear to match the perceived stimuli. Stimuli are perceived and responses are assembled on the basis of theories of action.

The rules that assemble responses develop gradually through series of partial replacements, but changes in the mechanisms that handle stimuli are typically discrete. Three modal situations—adjustment, turnover, and turnaround—can be identified, as shown in Table 1. Adjustment learning is applicable when a world view

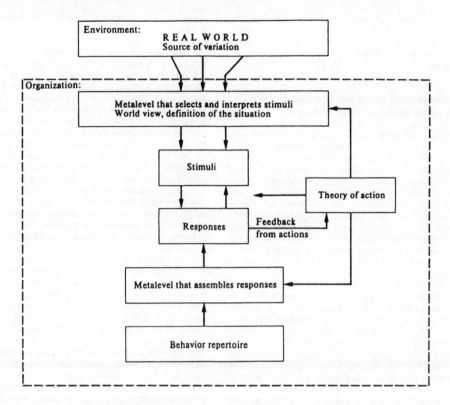

Figure 3 An SR model of how an organization interacts with its environment

remains the same and temporary changes can be handled inside the behavior repertoire. Turnover learning involves modifications of the interpretative system and development of new combinations of responses. Turnaround learning involves restructuring of one or both of the metasystems that handle stimuli and responses.

Reality is only the provider of potential inputs to a learner. Reality offers ranges of alternative environments from which an organization selects and enacts one from time to time. The environment perceived by a learner has been filtered and invented through the stimulus-processing mechanisms. This notion opens interesting opportunities for changing organizational behavior: not only can an organization reorient itself by inventing new responses, it can also ask new questions. An organization can discover new environments when real environments cannot be enacted. Unlearning and reframing can enable an organization to move between environments.

Table 1 Three modes of organizational learning

Learning mode	Change in organization-environment relationship	Organizational responses	Ease and rate of response
Adjustment learning	Fluctuations, minor changes that are reversible.	Adjustments of parameters or rules. Selection from response repertoires. Negotiate or manipulate the environment.	Relatively easy and fast, often routinized.
Turnover learning	Significant, partial changes that are irreversible.	Unlearning and replacement by new behaviors.	Difficult and time-consuming.
Turnaround learning	Substantial changes that are irreversible.	Changing theory of action or part thereof.	Impossible or very difficult, but rapid when change occurs.

This section dealt with complete learning cycles, but learning occurs also under conditions of ambiguity and in situations where causes are not easily tied to effects. The next section describes incomplete learning cycles.

How organizations learn, assuming that learning cycles are incomplete

Figure 1 pictured a learning cycle with uninterrupted links between actions and responses, between responses and beliefs, and between beliefs and new actions. But learning cycles are often interrupted or disturbed. Organizations have difficulties in tracing which actions caused environmental responses. Individuals in organizations sometimes form their beliefs on misinterpretations of cause-effect relationships or even through influences from outside sources. This gives room for theories of action—myths—with low or no validity to the concerned organizations. Schools of thought substitute for actors' own first-hand experience. Myths are created on spotty evidences.

March and Olsen (1976) identified four kinds of incompleteness in organizations' learning cycles. Firstly, role-constrained learning occurs where the couplings between individuals' beliefs and individuals' actions are blocked. Constraining role definitions and standard operating procedures prevent individuals in organizations from changing their behaviors in response to new knowledge. Role-constrained learning contributes significantly to organizational inertia in that it delays the transformation of knowledge into actions.

Secondly, audience learning occurs where the couplings between individuals' actions and organizations' actions are weak. The reasons may be that organizational politics counteract and neutralize individuals' initiatives, that organizations' capacities to resist change exceed individuals' capacities to instigate change, or that individuals misunderstand how their organizations function.

Thirdly, superstitious learning happens where individuals' actions affect organizational actions but where the couplings between organizational actions and environmental responses are ambiguous. Individuals form their beliefs and modify their actions appropriately on the basis of apparent environmental responses, but the latter responses are erroneously interpreted as resulting from preceding organizational actions. The reason may be that complex interactions between organizations and their environments exceed people's cognitive capacities for mapping, so that faulty inferences are drawn. Superstitious learning thus, in effect, separates one subsystem that produces actions from another subsystem that forms beliefs. Organizational learning proceeds, but the coupling between actions and knowledge is weak.

Finally, there are incomplete learning cycles where the couplings between environmental responses and individuals' beliefs are problematic. March and Olsen (1976) named this fourth variety learning under ambiguity. This label is somewhat unfortunate in that ambiguity plays an important role also in audience learning and superstitious learning where unclear relationships inside organizations or between organizations and their environments weaken or sever the links of the learning cycle. The point about this fourth form of incompleteness is that there exists no single, objective explanation of an outcome or of its causes. Different individuals may interpret situations and processes differently because of excessive problem complexity, selective perception, different cognitive styles, and mental maps. A leader or a dominant coalition then selects one of these interpretations and provides legitimacy by referring to a world view that lends meaning and structure to the situation.

Discussions of human rationality (Lindblom, 1959; Simon, 1957) and observations of organizational decisions (Cohen *et al.*, 1972; Cyert *et al.*, 1956; Dufty and Taylor, 1962; March and Olsen, 1976) have made it clear that complete learning cycles and unbroken SR chains describe rare phenomena. Yet, there are very few studies of how organizations learn through incomplete learning cycles and of the consequences of loose couplings between organizations' action-generating systems and their knowledge production. Role-constrained learning is not very interesting to study from this perspective. Its major impact is to delay necessary adaptions of individuals' or organizations' behaviors. Superstitious learning, audience learning, and learning under ambiguity are all pathologies under which organizations form theories of action with questionable validity (Argyris and Schön, 1978). The SR learning model assumes that organizations develop theories of action which may well be simplified but which basically are valid descriptions of the reality, of causalities, and of the instrumentality of actions. Incomplete learning cycles lead to theories of action that have low validity in their descriptions of the reality or in their understanding of causalities, or in both, yet these imperfect theories of action can enable organizations to act and to learn.

Many authors have recognized the role of theories of action in organizations' learning. Argyris and Schön (1978) discussed how both valid and invalid theories of action guide organizational learning. Clark (1972) described how colleges store experiences and performance standards in sagas that develop over time and that often shift with the advent of new leaders. Kuhn's (1962) discussion of paradigm shifts in sciences is

12 *Handbook of Organizational Design*

another recognition of the incompleteness of learning cycles.

Several organization theorists have used the concept of myths to denote organizations' theories of action. The term myth emphasizes the multiple origins that theories of action may have. Some are born out of observations from reality, others are sheer fantasies, but most myths have some connections with reality. Myths are told and carried by groups of believers, often from generation to generation. Myths and rites belong together. The former shape the latter and the latter develop and consolidate the former. Hedberg and Jönsson (1977) proposed that myths change cyclically. Figure 4 shows the feedback paths which produce these cycles. A ruling myth is a theory that generates strategies and actions. Strategies are hypotheses, and actions test these hypotheses, verifying or falsifying the theory.

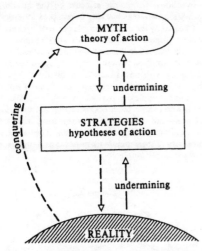

Figure 4 The interplay between myth, strategies, and reality

Strategies are reformulated when actions fail to produce desired results. A ruling myth is challenged when it no longer can produce convincing strategies; it is also challenged by the arrival of competing myths.

Myths change through various mechanisms. They can be undermined as their strategies and actions fail to produce desired results. Since all myths are, at best, partial mappings of reality, there will sooner or later appear events that raise doubts about the validity of the myths. Also, myths are mappings of past realities. They grow obsolete as time goes on. Undermining works through the failures of a ruling myth itself. New myth candidates thrive as doubt in a ruling myth spreads.

Ruling myths can also be conquered by new myths that arrive from outside an organization. New leaders frequently bring in new myths (Clark, 1972; Hedberg, 1974; Jönsson and Lundin, 1977). Schools of thought and consultants spread myths in managerial cultures. Conquering does not necessarily require that ruling myths are undermined. A strong outsider myth can remove a well functioning ruling myth, but it is often the case that conquering speeds up replacement in organizations where ruling myths begin to be undermined.

Myths change through different mechanisms. When learning cycles are complete and organizations have instrumental theories of action, changes in the environment in an organization, or between the two, are normally the triggers that initiate myth replacement. Old theories of action are then undermined by the results that their actions produce.

Direct empirical falsification does not work when learning cycles are incomplete. There are, however, means to discard and replace myths. Undermining can relax constraints in role-constrained learning so that individuals' beliefs can affect individuals' and organizations' actions. Feedback can also challenge ruling myths in cases where organizations expect outcomes which do not occur and in cases where organizations misinterpret outcomes which actually should have confirmed the strategies and the myths. Incomplete learning cycles also change myths through conquering. Because ruling myths are based on distorted observations, they may well be challenged by competing myths which present other world views or interpret past outcomes differently. New leaders (Clark, 1972; Starbuck and Hedberg, 1977), reframing (Watzlawick *et al.*, 1974), and new political coalitions (Jönsson and Lundin, 1977) are instances which may overturn organizations' old myths.

How environments affect learning

Viewing learning as the result of an experimental relationship between learners and their environments implies that ideal learning conditions fall somewhere between the extremes of environmental stability and turbulence. If an experimental situation remains unchanged for long periods of time, there are no variations to explore and the marginal return from experimenting declines. If, on the other hand, environments shift too rapidly, learning deteriorates as well. Rapid environmental change may stimulate metalearning in which the people in organizations learn to identify patterns of environmental behavior, but organizations in turbulent environments mostly find it very difficult to cope and survive (Emery and Trist, 1965).

How rapidly do environments shift? And what will organizations' environments look like in the future?

Bennis (1966) predicted that future changes will be so rapid that demands for adaptation will cause the deterioration of rigid organizational structures—such as bureaucracies—and severely overload managerial systems. Katz and Kahn (1966) foresaw that organizations will have to pay increasing attention to assessing forces that are emerging in their environments. But Emery and Trist (1965) claimed that organizations' environments are changing at increasing rates towards increasing complexity, and both they and Terreberry (1968) concluded that turbulent environments are becoming more common. Thus, foresight and good predictions may be rare commodities. Environmental complexity and unwise uses of modern information technologies have led to an information-rich society that threatens to overload both organizations' and individuals' information-processing capacities (Simon, 1971).

Complex, fast-moving industrial societies appear to afford bad conditions for learning. But many organizations have learned to cope with uncertainty and information overload. They structure themselves so as to reduce the demands for information processing and to facilitate learning in complex and changing environments (J. R. Galbraith, 1973; Simon, 1971; Weinshall and Twiss, 1973). They select and enact their environments, influencing the amounts of information and the rates of change to which they are exposed (Starbuck, 1976; Weick, 1969). Organizations also reduce their information loads by limiting their time perspectives and by attending to stimuli sequentially (Cyert and March, 1963). They employ buffers and regulations to smooth out environmental demands over time (Thompson, 1967), and they exploit information technologies to upgrade their abilities to cope with information-rich environments (Simon, 1971).

Outer environments and learning

Emery and Trist (1965) classified environments as (a) placid-randomized, (b) placid-clustered, (c) disturbed-reactive, and (d) turbulent. Placid-randomized environments have randomly scattered and unconnected elements: there are no patterns of behavior and no provisions for learning. Each element attempts to optimize its local situation. Turbulent environments are the opposite extreme: their elements are highly interconnected, and they change rapidly. Turbulent environments demand more control capacity than organizations normally possess, so organizations in turbulent environments float with their surroundings, almost unable to learn and to control their development. Between the extremes of total unconnectedness and total interconnectedness are settings for organizational learning. Both clustered and reactive environments offer rich opportunities for experimental learning. Elements gather together in groups in placid-clustered environments; understanding the behavior of one element of a cluster facilitates the understanding of other elements' behavior. Elements compete with each other in disturbed-reactive environments, and organizations can explore their environments by analyzing the reactions that their actions evoke.

Schroder *et al.* (1967) showed that, over time, individuals' cognitive maps develop from simplicity and low integration to high integrative complexity, but that the maps begin to lose complexity when environmental complexity becomes too great. The ∩-shaped curve that relates integrative complexity to environmental complexity is shown in Figure 5. This curve suggests that optimal environments for learning make maximal use of—but do not overload—individuals' information-handling capacity. But what is optimal depends on many things. Streufert (1973) has shown that learning in simple situations is primarily affected by the quantity of information, whereas learning in complex situations is also affected by the nature and relevance of information. Streufert argued that individuals who receive much feedback indicating failures—noxity feedback—must split their attention between solving unsolved problems and coping with new situations. Individuals who face complex situations are then easily overloaded and their integrative complexity peaks at a low level. But individuals who receive feedback indicating success—eucity feedback—can concentrate on integrating their knowledge and on solving new problems. The integrative complexity of their mental maps peaks at a high level of environmental complexity.

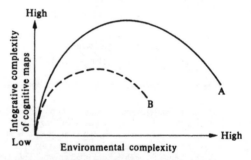

Figure 5 How integrative complexity relates to environmental complexity: A = when individuals receive a high portion of eucity feedback; B = when individuals receive a high portion of noxity feedback

Duncan (1972) classified organizations' environments along two dimensions. The simplicity-complexity dimension describes the number of decision factors and components in the environment, and the static-dynamic dimension denotes the rate of change in environmental elements and the consequent frequency with which decision models ought to be adjusted. The resulting measure of perceived environmental complexity estimates the number of stimuli an organization faces. The extreme ends of each dimension are difficult environments for learning. Environments that are highly complex, or that change very rapidly, overload organizations' information-processing capacity and limit the level of integrative complexity in individuals' mental maps. Very simple environments and environments that change very slowly are eventually explored and permit organizations to use many standard operating procedures. Such environments offer few challenges to learners.

Environmental benevolence or hostility is another property that affects organizational learning. Because organizations in benevolent environments often have weaker incentives to improve their performances, they may be subject to strategic stagnation (Child, 1974; Miller and Mintzberg, 1974). Only rare organizations in benevolent environments use their slack resources for experiments and undirected searches. Organizations in hostile environments face new problems and are often forced to develop new niches, but their possibilities to learn are often restricted by scarce resources and limited strategic opportunities (Olofsson *et al.*, 1973). Benevolence may breed somnolence, hostility may lead to paralysis, and neither condition promotes learning (Hedberg *et al.*, 1976). The degree of interconnectedness (Emery and Trist, 1965), the rate of change (Duncan, 1972; Emery and Trist, 1965), and environmental complexity (Schroder *et al.*, 1967) are all physical properties of the outer environment. The benevolence or hostility of an environment (Nystrom *et al.*, 1976) is a subjective matter and relates to the fit between the amount and kind of information processing that the environment forces an organization to do in order to survive and the same organization's ability to meet these challenges. Streufert's (1973) findings about eucity and noxity feedbacks point at the dynamics that develop between organizations and environments. If an environment demands too much of an organization—hostility—or if an organization has little luck with its initial actions, a backlog of unsolved problems adds on to the information-processing demands. Learners' ability to learn is thus not only a function of the nature of an environment but also of their coping capacity, and of the dynamics that develop during the learning process.

Schroder *et al.* (1967) found that individuals vary greatly with respect to their level of integrative complexity for different problem areas. Frequent problem exposures tend to stimulate mental maps with high integrative complexity, and individuals with such developed maps have high ability to cope with difficult environments. These findings suggest assuming similar relationships at the organizational level: that organizations' capacity to learn in different environments, and to deal with negative and positive performance feedback, varies greatly depending upon their previous problem exposure, the nature of the mental maps they possess, and the amount of information-processing capacity that they can mobilize to attack problems.

Inner environments and learning

Outer environments put some conditions on learning. Other conditions come from the inner environments that exist inside organizations. Organizations can, to some extent, control their outer environments. These environments are partly enacted or selected (Starbuck, 1976; Weick, 1969) and successful organizations find and develop niches through which they can control, for example, the rate of change to which they are exposed. But many organizations have not realized these possibilities, or they have not developed the necessary abilities to create niches. They float along passively and attribute their problems to hostile environments (Hedberg and Jönsson, 1977). Other organizations find themselves in environments that they cannot control. They have to rely on regulating their inner environments in order to facilitate or impede learning (Lieberman, 1972). Inner environments for learning can be managed in many ways. For example, organizations determine what information to acquire and how accurate, timely, and exhaustive that information shall be (Carroll, 1967; Glimell, 1975). Information systems filter information differently and affect the conditions for learning. Organizations also determine the amount of discretion their members have and they stimulate their members' willingness and ability to explore alternative environments (Lieberman, 1972; Thompson, 1967; Thompson, 1965). Decentralization and participative management can reduce demands on information channels, can diminish individuals' cognitive work loads, can improve the quality of upward communications, and can stimulate innovation and learning (Hedberg, 1975a; Wilson, 1966). Time targets, regulations, and rules constrain members' freedom and substitute for supervisory controls. By providing resources, organizations facilitate the invention and implementation of new strategies, but affluence may undermine the incentives to improve procedures, to delete ineffective behaviors, and to invent better methods (Bonini, 1963; Cyert and March, 1963). There are balances to strike if learning is to remain vital (Hedberg *et al.*, 1976).

Numerous laboratory experiments have investigated the impacts of rewards and punishments on learning. Immediate rewards reinforce behaviors and facilitate learning, whereas punishments tend to suppress behaviors and to cause inaction. Organizations can use their rewards and punishments to induce their members to search for new problems and solutions (Wilson, 1966). They can also inadvertently paralyze their members by punishing them, either by emphasizing the costs of failure or by offering inappropriate rewards. Somewhat unclear roles, tasks, and rewards and ambiguous problem definitions can stimulate innovative search in organizations (Burns and Stalker, 1961), but high levels of ambiguity with respect to tasks and rewards and insecurity with respect to jobs disrupt organizational learning (Thompson, 1965).

Slevin (1971, 1973) found that innovative behavior is confined within well defined boundaries. The innovative boundaries depend upon cost-to-reward ratios, and individuals' willingness to explore new alternatives can be predicted if the innovative boundaries are known. Slevin's experiments suggest that organizations can design their innovative boundaries by setting costs of search, costs of failure, and rewards for activity and discovery so as to encourage search, risk taking, and learning. The study raises the issue as to whether innovative boundaries can be tied to individualized or even impersonal reward systems so that organizations can regulate the number of members in the innovation space.

Lieberman (1972) studied how rewards and feedbacks about performance interact to create learning environments for the decision makers in a management game. The decision makers operated either a salary-based reward system or a profit-sharing reward system; they received lagged, aggregate feedbacks about their performances, but some of them could buy feedback improvements—more accurate, more up-to-date information. Lieberman found that the decision makers in salary-based reward systems spent more resources evaluating their activities than did those in profit-sharing systems, but increased evaluation did not raise profits. Purchases of improved feedbacks correlated with reduced profits because the costs of improved feedbacks were not recovered through improved decision making. Also, the decision makers who did not have opportunities to purchase feedback improvements showed greater adaptability to changing external conditions than did those who had such opportunities. Changes from one learning environment to another activated searches, regardless of the environments involved. Decision makers who moved into environments where they could buy improved feedbacks increased their information purchases under both reward systems.

Lieberman's findings resemble those of Hedberg (1970), who found that changes from intermittent, hard-copy reports to interactive computer terminals substantially affected teams' information searches in another management game. Teams which acquired information through computer terminals more than doubled their information gathering on the average, but the additional information did not improve teams' performances. Likewise, Glimell (1975) found weak impacts on learning when marketing managers changed from a traditional information system to an interactive, computerized information system in a chemical firm. However, other attempts to improve information have been more successful. Gerrity (1970) and Morton (1971) designed interactive information systems for marketing and for investment-trust management: they reported that decisions and learning improved after the currency, accuracy, and scope of information were improved.

The costs of search—both the actual costs of acquiring information and the subjective perceptions of efforts that are needed in order to know more—are important aspects of inner environments. Search increases when decision makers have inexpensive and easy access to information (Hedberg, 1970; Morton, 1971). But organizational learning depends on whether there is capacity to digest additional information. Studies of computer-aided decision making emphasize that the numbers of stimuli in an environment should match decision makers' capacities for information handling. If additional information overloads decision makers, or if it cannot be used to recover its costs, less information-rich environments are better learning environments, or at least more cost-effective (Ackoff, 1967; Simon, 1971). The costs of acquiring information should be set so that decision makers are both encouraged to gather relevant information and reminded of the declining returns from extensive search.

Decision makers' propensities to search and organizations' level of curiosity also depend upon organizational structure. Structural diversity can stimulate innovation and attempts to change organizations (Wilson, 1966). Overlapping work roles, ambiguous goals and responsibilities, and informal communication channels can stimulate learning (Burns and Stalker, 1961; Grinyer and Norburn, 1975). Hedberg et al. (1976) described a set of balances whereby uncertainty, inconsistency, doubt, conflict, and scarcity are used to counterbalance organizations' stabilizing forces, and Hedberg and Jönsson (1977) applied these ideas in designing information systems which use confusion to trigger searches and change.

Thus, there are many ways in which organizations can influence their own learning. They can select and enact their outer environments, and they can redesign their inner environments. Organizations learn when they interact with their environments, but their environments are largely artifacts of the organizations' mental maps. Figure 6 summarizes the determinants of organizations' outer and inner environments.

16   *Handbook of Organizational Design*

Outer environments: Inner environments: Organization:

enacting and choosing

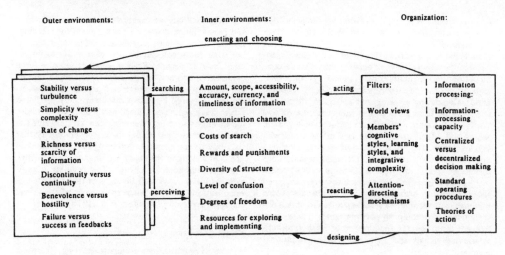

Figure 6 Factors that influence organizations' learning

How learning is triggered

Organizations cannot afford to scan their environments, continuously searching for conditions that require actions. They search intermittently, they rely on attention-directing standard operating procedures, and they question these procedures only when problems begin to mount. Although affluence sometimes initiates searches for opportunities (Lewin and Wolf, 1975), it is usually the case that scarcity, conflict, and substandard performances lead to actions, whereas wealth, harmony, and goal accomplishment breed complacency and reinforce current behaviors. Learning is typically triggered by problems.

Problems as triggers

March and Simon (1958) designated dissatisfaction as the major trigger of organizational problem solving. Organizations begin to search when problems are discovered or when gaps between performance and expectations become large enough (Downs, 1976). Organizations scan only the parts of their environments where competitors and other outside forces threaten their survival (Terreberry, 1968). Doubts about viability lead to reexaminations and reevaluations of strategies in theatened segments of environments (Starbuck, 1976).

Cyert and March (1963) coined the concept of organizational slack to provide a buffer mechanism which absorbed the results of postulated imperfections in organizations' problem solving. They defined slack as the difference between an organization's necessary and available reward resources. Organizational slack accumulated in successful organizations and provided fat to live from in times of crisis. Slack reductions were postulated to trigger organizational problem solving.

Bonini (1963) operationalized the idea of slack-triggered learning in his index-of-felt-pressure, which was used to initiate reassessments and problem solving in a simulation model of a hypothetical firm. Bonini's index measure is a function of performance relative to expectations for key decision centers in the model firm. When the pressure stays within an acceptable range, previous strategies are continued. If performance exceeds or equals expectations for a period of time, expectations are adjusted upwards.

Organizations do not react to all problems. Many stimuli disappear in perceptual filters. Other stimuli are buried in aggregates. Because standard operating procedures must tolerate some fluctuations in the variables which they monitor, minor problems are often ignored. Deviations from normal must be large before adjustments or reorganizations occur (Bonini, 1963).

The concept of organizational slack has been criticized by subsequent researchers. It leaves many unanswered questions about why organizations initiate search, for example. The concept of organizational slack has helped to explain organizations' behavior retrospectively, but this concept has failed to predict reorientations prospectively (Lewin and Wolf, 1975). Slack mechanisms appear to function during periods of growth, but fail to work during times of decline. Organizations' members raise their expectations after successful performances, but they do not as readily reduce their expectations when performance declines (Bonini, 1963). Comparing growing and stagnating firms in a sample of 60 firms from fifteen industries, Lewin and Wolf (1972) found no significant reductions in general selling and administrative expenses in the firms with sagging profits. They concluded that long-term declines in performance are not sufficient to make organizations reconsider their strategies. Williamson (1964) found many cases where diminishing slack resources triggered reorientations by organizations, but he also discovered that managers manipulate slack resources to obtain discretion and to accomplish personal goals. These interferences disturbed the functioning of slack resources as warning signals and as triggers of organizational learning.

Opportunities as triggers

But if problems were the only triggers of learning, problem-ridden organizations would be the best innovators. Noting the lack of empirical support for this hypothesis (Mansfield, 1961) and also observing that affluence sometimes fosters experimentation and discovery, Cyert and March (1963) proposed that both excess amounts of organizational slack and sharp reductions of slack trigger search and learning.

How accumulations of organizational slack trigger learning has been studied very little. Thompson (1967) observed that organizations need to explore opportunities in order to develop new domains, but he concluded that problemistic search almost always dominates opportunistic surveillance in organizations. Wealthy and successful organizations can of course afford to explore their environments and to experiment with innovative actions, but few appear to do so. Instead, success reinforces current behaviors and makes organizations less inclined to try new strategies. Never change a winning team!

Organizations which have gone from growth to stagnation illustrate the dangers of excessive slack resources (Hedberg, 1974; Starbuck and Hedberg, 1977). Many organizations become too content with their past and grow insensitive to changes in their environments. They drift into backwaters, and discover suddenly that their markets are gone and that their procedures have become obsolete (Olofsson *et al.*, 1973). Affluence breeds strategic stagnation, but the stagnation does not surface until affluence turns into scarcity (Miller, 1977; Miller and Mintzberg, 1974).

Neither scarcity and severe problems nor affluence and benevolence provide a good climate for learning. Low levels of organizational slack may trigger search, but slack resources may be needed in order to implement new strategies. Problems and crises can force organizations to act, but problem-ridden organizations can often not afford to take risks. If organizational learning was triggered by excess resources or by predicted future slack reductions, there would be resources both for inventing and implementing new actions. But the dilemma of organizational-slack mechanisms is that they buy tolerances and routinizing for organizational problem solving at the expense of organizational curiosity and readiness for change. The resulting organizational inertia may well be so large that it threatens organizations' survival when environmental conditions change irreversibly (Hedberg *et al.*, 1976).

People as triggers

Actions by organizations' members also trigger learning. Hirschman (1970) claimed that members in organizations have two basic ways to react to the way their system is managed; they can voice their opinion and engage in organizational governance, or they can leave the organization and engage in new memberships. As long as the members' loyalty suffices, they stay and use their voice. When the voice option is exhausted, or if the loyalty is too low, members exit. The most competent and opinionated members are often the first to leave when the voice option is blocked. Left without vivid opposition, an organization deteriorates rapidly and loses its ability to invent and implement new strategies. Triggers of learning can also consist of conditions that merely question the present without giving future directions. A moment of hesitation is necessary in order to allow an organization to change from the execution of action programs to genuine problem solving (March and Simon, 1958). Leadership crises may provide such moments of healthy confusion. Pettigrew (1974) found periods of self-doubt and hesitation typically preceded the entrance into new development phases in developing computer departments. Hedberg (1973, 1975b), Jönsson (1973), and Wilson (1966) found that major reorientations in stagnating, expanding, and innovating organizations, respectively, frequently emerged from financial crises in combination with leadership crises. Although the crises as such did not provide new learning or new directions, they contributed to rapid unlearning and facilitated the implementation of new strategies.

Wolf (1971) found that changes in management often correlated with substantial strategic reorientations and reallocations of slack resources. Even though it intuitively makes sense that a new management can unfreeze organizational strategies, the causality can also go in the other direction. Sarason (1972) observed that the departure of key decision makers often precedes strategic reorientations. The firing of top executives and the subsequent rearrangement of an organization are both parts of the same organizational adjustment. The new leader is not the initiator of change, but rather a solution to change actions. Unlearning and triggering of learning can thus be intimately related and sometimes overlapping phenomena. Triggers cause unlearning, and unlearning can trigger new learning. For example, the removal of knowledge often signals change and initiates new learning. New leaders can be seen as triggers of change, but their arrival has usually been preceded by the dismissal or departure of old leaders. Removing people is an important way in which organizations get rid of their past and unlearn. With the departing individuals' procedures and experiences disappear parts of an organization's memory.

How unlearning occurs

Unlearning is a process through which learners discard knowledge. Unlearning makes way for new responses and mental maps. How capable then are organizations to unlearn old behaviors and world views and to relearn when they face new situations? Several authors have expressed pessimistic views on this matter. For instance, Beer (1972) concluded that managers and policy makers in organizations typically lack the tools and the language for getting free of their contexts and implementing changes. Instead, large organizations frequently allocate their resources to manipulate and change their environments rather than to change their own behaviors (J. K. Galbraith, 1973). And designers of decision models and information systems discover over and over again that organizations are highly resistant to change (Glimell, 1975; Huysmans, 1970).

Success reinforces organizations' theories of action (Argyris and Schön, 1978; Starbuck and Hedberg, 1977) and makes unlearning difficult. There are times when organizations should treat their memories as enemies (March and Olsen, 1976). Unlearning poses particular problems to organizations that travel from stable, benevolent environments into unstable, hostile ones (Hedberg *et al.*, 1976).

How one conceptualizes organizational development is also a matter of attitude, however. What appears as adaptive development from a macro perspective may be viewed as a series of deaths and rebirths on micro levels (Starbuck, 1976). If organizations are identified by the names they carry and the buildings they occupy, one must conclude that organizations indeed learn, unlearn, and relearn over time; but if organizations are identified by their myths and their leaders, the death-rebirth

analogue describes most situations better. Organizations that have replaced their people, abandoned their founders' ideas, and invented new goals have both unlearned and relearned, but are they the same organizations?

Organizations learn and unlearn via their members. Unlearning in the human mind is a cumbersome and energy-consuming process. Suppose that a person has learned to expect that event B will follow event A. Then the situation changes so that event C follows event A. The person's expectations about event B have to be unlearned and expectations have to be established concerning event C. Postman and Stark (1965) and Postman and Underwood (1973) provided two partly different theories of unlearning in cases such as this. The earlier theory asserts that responses are deleted and replaced by new ones which are coupled to the old stimuli: event C actually takes the place of event B in long-term memory. Unlearning and relearning are thus seen as abrupt phenomena which go together; at some point, the expectation of event C replaces the expectation of event B. The later theory claims that unlearning is separate from relearning and that both phenomena proceed gradually: the expectation of event B is unlearned gradually, and the expectation of event C is established gradually. The new association A–C, at some point, begins to suppress the old association A–B which is moved to a less accessible area of the memory. The latter theory is consistent with the notion that humans' associative memories are updated through dynamic reallocations which are based on the frequencies of observed relationships (Feigenbaum, 1970). Newell and Simon's (1972) model of human memory also suggests that unlearning is a gradual process where new responses become easily available at the expense of old ones. Postman and Underwood (1973) concluded that the most crucial activities of unlearning arise in the perceptions of stimuli, and not in assembling responses or associating stimuli with new responses. Watzlawick *et al.* (1974) drew similar conclusions from their experiences with psychotherapy: reframing perceptions is a powerful way to change behaviors. People who are able to perceive reality in different terms can redefine their problems, unlearn old behaviors, and replace them with new responses almost instantaneously.

In the SR framework of Figure 3, unlearning has three modes of operation. The first one goes through the disconfirmation—or disassembly—of mechanisms for selecting and identifying stimuli, so that a perceiver no longer knows what is perceived. People or organizations unlearn their world views. The second mode of unlearning involves the disconfirmation of connections between stimuli and responses, so that a person or an organization no longer knows what responses to make to identified stimuli. The third mode involves the disconfirmation of connections between responses—the disconfirmation of response assemblies—so that a person or an organization no longer knows how to assemble responses to new situations. Unlearning thus threatens a learner's theory of action, or part thereof. In the case of incomplete learning cycles in organizations, it is either the myth or the strategy that is abandoned—Figure 4. Organizations that face the double problem of learning both new questions and new responses cannot unlearn overnight. Their unlearning takes time and resources, and in the meantime they are quite disoriented or paralyzed. Such organizations may appear naive and incompetent to outside observers who watch them issuing inconsistent problem statements and implementing various strategies for recovery (Hedberg, 1974). They may lose their environments' trust and support during this disoriented phase and never manage to overcome the transition (Nystrom *et al.*, 1976).

Knowledge that has resulted from complete learning cycles in organizations can normally be unlearned through complete cycles too. The same SR mechanisms which established and reinforced a mental map, a behavior program, or a single SR coupling, can remove this piece of knowledge as it is disconfirmed by further acting. However, unlearning cycles can be blocked so that incomplete cycles develop. Organizations which have been poisoned by their own success are often unable to unlearn obsolete knowledge in spite of strong disconfirmations (Nystrom *et al.*, 1976). And myths which arrived from the outside, carried by a leader or a school of thought, are often removed by new myths arriving in the same fashion (Hedberg and Jönsson, 1977). Unlearning can thus occur either through complete unlearning cycles—where acting according to SR chains produces inconsistent results which challenge and remove old knowledge—or through incomplete unlearning cycles—where imitation, the sharing of external disorientations, or the departures of leaders play important roles.

Learning through incomplete learning cycles can be partly or totally unconnected to what is happening in the real world, and so can unlearning. If it makes sense to talk about role-constrained organizational learning, superstitious learning, audience learning, and learning under ambiguity (March and Olsen, 1976), there is also unlearning that is role-constrained or superstitious, unlearning that happens in individuals but that fails to spread to audiences in organizations, and unlearning under ambiguity. Organizations' myths or strategies—Figure 4—can remain, although individuals realize that their organizations must unlearn. Also, organizations can unlearn and discover that their members have not. Incomplete unlearning cycles are problematic in that they frequently add to dysfunctional organizational inertia. But they can also have the opposite effect by enabl-

ing external forces swiftly to blank out organizational memories.

Very little is known about how organizational unlearning differs from that of individuals. To the extent that unlearning cycles are complete, one must assume that similar disconfirming SR mechanisms are at work. A threshold level of counter evidence to a previously assumed coupling blanks out the mapping in organizational memory. But, unlike what happens in individuals, disconfirmations can be voiced by individual pressure groups, and leaders can leave as pressures mount—which deletes the attacked parts of organizational memory as these leaders depart. When unlearning cycles are incomplete, shifts of leaders and internal struggles between organizational groups are even more important to determining what is, and what is not, in an organization's memory.

Organizational unlearning is typically problem-triggered. Funds shortages, falling revenues, actual losses, diminishing popular support, or public criticism from evaluators are some examples. These triggers cause hesitancy and build up distrust in procedures and leaders. A turbulent period then frequently follows. Inconsistent messages are issued by the leaders, and organizational members and outside evaluators begin to search for new leadership and alternative strategies and myths. Ultimately the world view and the standard operating procedures break down. The organization has unlearned its yesterday (Hedberg *et al.*, 1976) and finds itself either paralyzed or busily relearning.

When new myths—with or without new leaders—are the basic triggers of unlearning, organizations can relearn and reorient almost instantaneously. A new theory of action replaces the old one. When this is not the case, organizations must first establish new world views, new action programs, or new amendments to their response repertoires before they can begin to recover. Not all organizations manage to do so. A certain amount of excess resources are needed in order to invent and implement new orientations but, although diminishing slack often triggers organizational search (Cyert and March, 1963), the slack that remains at the time of unlearning is often insufficient for survival. Other organizations get so disoriented during their unlearning that they never manage to pull their act together. Their goals erode, their members develop apathy, and their leaders leave nothing but a strategic vacuum as they exit.

Myth cycles that nicely tie into each other and that provide organizations with new and useful theories of action just before obsolete theories are discarded appear to be the ideal thing to strive for. Balances between organizations' abilities to learn and to unlearn appear necessary for long-term survival. Unlearning abilities are needed in order to make room for more adequate interpretative frameworks and responses in organizational memory. Learning abilities are needed to generate new knowledge and to adjust and update existing knowledge.

How to facilitate organizational learning

Improving organizations should be the ultimate purpose of exploring how organizations learn and unlearn. But the current knowledge about organizational learning is weak, partial, and often generalized from individual learning. The prescriptions below must now absorb considerable uncertainty and they can only be formulated in a rather sketchy way. Further research is therefore badly needed.

Learning about organizational learning

There are two areas in particular where current knowledge is weak or nonexistent. The first area has to do with the relationships between individual and organizational learning and unlearning. In what respects is the collective information processing in organizations different from individuals' information processing? How important are organizational sagas (Clark, 1972), myths (Jönsson and Lundin, 1977; Mitroff and Kilmann, 1976), and habits (Simon, 1957) as memories which give organizations consistent properties regardless of their temporary memberships? How do hierarchies, status systems, and perceptual filters affect organizations' abilities to learn and unlearn? Understanding of organizational learning will have to derive either from a separately developed body of theories about how organizations learn as organizations, or from better assessments of how individual learning is modified when it occurs in organizations.

The second area concerns studies and models of how organizations shift their theories of action—or myths—as they develop. Little is known about how organizations' cognitive structures are challenged, modified, abolished, and restored as time passes and as inner and outer environments change (Michael, 1963). A theory of long-term behavior in organizations must contain a theory of how organizations learn, unlearn, and relearn. Very little has happened since Cyert and March (1963) made this observation. If organizations—as Beer (1972) suggested—lack the ability to change their metarules and modes of behaviors, then it is understandable why organizational researchers have obtained little insight into how organizations unlearn and relearn. But if, on the other hand, organizations are rigid and fail to unlearn and relearn in time because managers, organizational designers, and scientists envisage stability as desirable and normal and conse-

quently focus their interest on organizations' stabilizing processes and structural properties, then destabilizers and processes that reorient organizations will never be researched or developed. It is possible that the past two or three decades of steadily growing, benevolent industrial environments never really put organizations' reorienting abilities to a test. But it is equally possible that the two or three decades ahead will do so. Organization theory must therefore develop knowledge about how organizations evolve and revolve over time, and mechanisms for organizational unlearning and relearning must be important parts of these theories.

Awaiting this development, some clusters of prescriptive topics deserve particular attention: (a) making organizations more experimental, (b) regulating organizations' sensitivity to change signals, (c) redesigning organizations' inner and outer environments, and (d) balancing organizations' stabilizers and destabilizers.

Promoting experimentation

Learning results from the adaptive and manipulative interactions between an organization and its environments: experimental actions are important because organizations rarely master their environments so that they can develop lasting optimal responses. But organizations are not very experimental, as a rule. Inexhaustible flows of information easily use up organizations' information-processing capacities, so they program themselves to avoid uncertainty. They question their actions only sporadically, typically after problems have mounted. One result is that many organizations lock themselves into strategies and development patterns. Exploring the past and the present dominates over prospecting alternative futures. Long-term survival calls for surveillance of opportunities, whereas short-term coping concentrates upon problemistic search. Most organizations have much of the latter and little of the former (Thompson, 1967). Yet, if organizations are to survive in hostile and changing environments, they must change strategies and pursue new development patterns. Organizational designs should encourage experimenting so that organizations attain long-term viability.

Starbuck (1974) argued that organizational decision makers generally face the task of optimizing unknown criteria. Optima are not easily found, and even if they can be located, they vanish over time. Criteria for evaluating solutions are seldom explicit or compatible, if they are spelled out at all. Organizations would probably act more realistically if they planned their decisions as sequences of experiments, and kept on experimenting even after their experimenting has led to acceptable solutions (Hedberg et al., 1977). Box and Draper (1969) outlined a methodology for such experimental searches for moving optima: they proposed evolutionary operation as a reasonable alternative to traditional, optimum-seeking decision methods. Campbell's (1969) argument that political reforms should be treated as experiments is based upon a similar attitude toward the difficulty of finding optimal solutions to complex problems.

Experimental attitudes can be stimulated in several ways. Improved consciousness of how rare optimal solutions are and how swiftly good responses become obsolete can illuminate the inevitability of endless sequences of learning and unlearning in response to changing conditions. Individuals with low needs for uncertainty avoidance, high tolerances for ambiguity, and lusts to experiment should be recruited as decision makers (Hedberg *et al.*, 1977). Personnel selection could help identify such people.

Reward systems can be designed to favor organizational curiosity and to discourage complacency: lowered costs of failure and support for risk taking can substantially increase search and experimenting (Hedberg, 1974; Normann, 1975; Thompson, 1967).

Organizational revisions can be institutionalized through discontinuities such as time-constrained management contracts, job-exchange schemes, sunset procedures for activities, zero-base budgeting, and built-in obsolescence in planning models and computerized information systems (Hedberg and Jönsson, 1978; March and Simon, 1958). Training techniques such as role reversal, brainstorming, role playing, and simulation can be used to free organizations' members from preconceptions and to encourage experimentation and reframing (McCall, 1977).

Regulating awareness

The SR model—Figure 3—provides several indications for how organizational learning can be enhanced. One major problem in SR learning in relatively stable environments is that self-stabilizing forces easily pick up so much momentum that they freeze the stimulus-response repertoires. If the variety of stimuli is small, and if similar stimuli recur frequently, standard operating procedures take control of the acting. It becomes increasingly difficult to change the metasystems which identify stimuli and assemble responses. Organizations which want to stay prepared for future reorientations should therefore attempt to regulate their awareness by exposing themselves to external variation.

Outside sources of variation are crucial to self-organizing (Buckley, 1967; Campbell, 1969; Weick, 1969), because exposure to a wide variety of stimuli keeps learning systems alert. This alertness can most easily be maintained by removing some perceptual filters. Information systems should spend less effort trying to reduce uncertainties and ambiguities in the informa-

tion presented to decision makers (Hedberg and Jönsson, 1978). If the outside world does not make sense, the image of the world presented through reports and performance statistics should not give false senses of security. Reducing the filters on organizations' perceptual systems and communication channels is a basic strategy for making organizations aware of how their environments develop.

Instead of striving for clarity and harmony, perceptual filters should let decision makers see important properties of the real world. Crises, conflicts, dialectics, self-doubt, and hesitancy can facilitate unlearning and reframing (Assael, 1969; Jönsson, 1973; Nystrom *et al.*, 1976; Pettigrew, 1974; White, 1969).

The variety of stimuli can also be improved by short-circuiting information channels within organizations, and between organizations and their environments, so that established perceptual filters are bypassed and cross-divisional and other lateral communication links are created. Participative decision-making is one forum for such encounters. Systems that collect and disseminate information from clients', customers', and patients' perspectives can also contribute (Hedberg *et al.*, 1977).

Organizations can also institutionalize repeated searches among their programs. Recognizing the tendencies for organizational behaviors to become rigid and obsolete, March and Simon (1958) suggested that organizations that want to stay adaptive and to avoid being cut off from changing environments should use programs to challenge their programs. Repeatedly revising programs can serve to let new stimuli into organizations; it weakens the defense against relevant threats.

These prescriptions assume that organizations need to promote their awareness—that is, to discover more— in order to become better learners. But regulating awareness can also mean directing awareness or even discouraging awareness. Organizations in very information-rich environments may need additional filters to avoid stimuli overload. They may benefit from lowering their conflict levels and from reducing the variety of stimulus to which they expose themselves. Most of these prescriptions should apply also to this reverse aim of reducing organizations' awareness. Decision groups can be made more homogeneous in terms of members' cognitive styles, experiences, and professions. Ruling myths can be emphasized. Costs of search can be upgraded, and informal communications can be discouraged. The shift from environment attribution to ego attribution when organizations unite around new myths also serves to reduce awareness (Hedberg and Jönsson, 1977).

Semi-confusing information systems in self-designing organizations (Hedberg and Jönsson, 1978) should vary their filtering depending upon environmental contingencies so that organizations' awareness matches their ability to cope with incoming information. In times of excessive stability and monotony, filtering should be reduced. Conflict levels should be raised, and heterogeneity should be encouraged. But in times when organizations have just embarked on new, brave strategies, perceptual filters and mechanisms which reduce variety and unite organizational processes should be used. In the first case, it is a matter of challenging a possibly over-mature ruling myth. In the latter case, a new myth must be sheltered.

Redesigning environments

Inner and outer environments provide other design variables for improved organizational learning. Organizations cannot do much about the properties of their outer environments—although they can choose their own environments from among the available alternatives—, but those who design and manage organizations can do a lot to improve inner environments.

Lieberman's (1972) experiments suggest a number of environmental conditions that facilitate learning. Rewards and punishments can encourage risk taking and stimulate experimenting. The costs of failure can be shared and recognized as necessary investments in future domains. Resources for experimentation can be secured if searches are triggered early enough, while there are slack resources available for inventing and implementing new solutions (Hedberg et al., 1976). Personal security can be granted so that the insecurities arising from problems can be better borne. Information systems can free organizational decision makers from information overloads. Perceptual filters can be made more or less instrumental to search and discovery (Glimell, 1975). Finally, individuals with different cognitive styles, different tolerances for ambiguity, and different emotional flexibility produce very different mappings of the same reality. Because the willingness to learn and unlearn varies with the relationship between perceived problem complexity and estimated problem-solving capacity, selection of personnel who are able to structure problems effectively and who are less inclined to overestimate difficulties can heighten organizations' abilities to build up and tear down knowledge.

Achieving dynamic balances

Nystrom et al. (1976) spelled out how blends of interacting processes can keep organizations in dynamic equilibrium. Wildavsky (1972) proposed that self-evaluating organizations might employ dual-management groups in order to secure dialectics, competing world views, and action alternatives. Maybe organizations of the future ought to be governed by two-party systems, where one group manages while another group tries to formulate a

convincing alternative strategy: if the opposition group at election time convinces an organization's members that their alternative strategies are better than those of the ruling group, the two management groups would trade positions. White (1969) proposed similar ideas for strengthening decision dialectics by recognizing more than one frame of reference and more than one way to assemble responses; he believed that such dialectical organizations would be less prone to be captured in their own old behaviors.

Anchoring their proposal in the notion of slack-triggered search and in designs composed of counteracting and interacting processes, Hedberg et al. (1976: 41) delineated six principles for a balanced and viable organization. They proposed that a learning organization should rely on minimal amounts of consensus, contentment, affluence, faith, consistency, and rationality. That is, for each of these organizational assets, there should be a counterbalancing one. Dissatisfaction is needed to trigger action so that long-term contentment results. Shortages are useful to prevent organizations from dying from wealth. Distrust in forecasts makes forecasts useful. There should be balances and counterbalances, processes and counteracting processes. Self-designing organizations should have minimal amounts—that is, just a little bit more than not enough—of the properties that characterize good and orderly organizations. This would provide for enough frequent triggering, reasonably easy unlearning, sufficiently low trust in previous successes, and enough slack resources to implement new strategies. The desired balances—organizational seesaws—were caricatured with six aphorisms:

Cooperation requires minimal consensus.
Satisfaction rests upon minimal contentment.
Wealth arises from minimal affluence.
Goals merit minimal faith.
Improvement depends on minimal consistency.
Wisdom demands minimal rationality.

The previous prescriptive topics have dealt with how such balances can be achieved. Promoting experimentation gives means to keep down consistency, challenge optimal solutions, and question forecasts and goals. Regulating awareness is a way to cope with excessive consensus, contentment, and faith. Redesigning environments allows organizations to do away with consistency, to abandon plans and goals, and to unlearn their world views and established response assemblies. Dynamic balances of this sort should keep organizations on the move.

Post scriptum: how self-sufficiency becomes insufficiency

The author's interest in how organizations learn and

unlearn started when he studied how once successful organizations gradually got captured in their own self-sufficiency and stagnated into final crises with which they could not cope. He pictured this life cycle—the development from organizational tents to organizational palaces—in the following story:

Once upon a time there was a tribe that lived in the grassland. They hunted deer, drank from the brook, and set up their tents when the evening embraced them with darkness. One morning, after a gorgeous night in a pleasant campsite, some tribesmen went hunting at daybreak. They came back with deer for another day or two. Let us stay, they suggested. This is a good site to be at. So the tribe stayed one more day, and one more, and one more . . .

Soon the hunters learned to breed their cattle, farm the land, and dam the water. As they grew wealthier and more secure, they turned their tents into houses and then into palaces. And they fenced themselves against their enemies.

The latter were known as Uncertainty, Conflict, and Ambiguity. There were enemies. Oh, yes! But the fence was sufficient. And the tribesmen bettered the defense after each attack.

Pilgrims came by and told tales about better campsites and different deer. But the tribesmen paid little attention. The last hunter was dead. One summer there was less water in the brook than there used to be. No one noticed the change at first, but as the brook continued to dry out, the water manager notified the tribe council. The council fired the manager, and decided that there was water in the brook. The vote was eight to one. The tribe added to the fence, which had become so dense that one could no longer see the surrounding grassland.

A few days later, the cattle were dead, suffering from the heat and the lack of water. Looking over the fence, the tribesmen discovered that the grassland had turned into desert. They decided to move, but it was too late. Palaces have no tentpegs.

There is too much waste of human resources, capital, knowledge, and enthusiasm in letting organizations develop with learning abilities only. Such organizations build walls around them, and grow defensive. They become insensitive to signals from the environment, and they accumulate so many resources that they cannot afford to move when times are changing. That is why abilities for learning, unlearning, and relearning must be equally developed. To learn, unlearn, and relearn is the organizational walk: development comes to an end when one of these legs is missing.

References

Ackoff, Russell L. (1967). "Management misinformation systems." Management Science, 14: B147–B156.

Argyris, Chris (1976). "Leadership, learning, and changing the status quo." Organizational Dynamics, 4 (Winter): 29–43.

Argyris, Chris, and Schön, Donald A. (1978). Organizational Learning. Reading, Mass: Addison-Wesley.

Assael, Henry (1969). "Constructive role of interorganizational conflict." Administrative Science Quarterly, 14: 573–582.

Bateson, Gregory (1972). Steps to an Ecology of Mind. New York: Ballantine.

Beer, Stafford (1972). Brain of the Firm. New York: Herder and Herder.

Bennis, Warren G. (1966). Changing Organizations. New York: McGraw-Hill.

Bieri, James (1955). "Cognitive complexity-simplicity and predictive behavior." Journal of Abnormal and Social Psychology, 51: 263–268.

Bjork, Robert A. (1970). "Repetition and rehearsal mechanisms in models for short-term memory." In Donald A. Norman (ed.), Models of Human Memory: 307–330. New York: Academic Press.

Blau, Peter M. (1969). "Objectives of sociology." In Robert Bierstedt (ed.), A Design for Sociology: 43–71. Philadelphia: American Academy of Political and Social Science.

Bonini, Charles P. (1963). Simulation of Information and Decision Systems in the Firm. Englewood Cliffs, N.J.: Prentice-Hall.

Box, George E. P., and Draper, Norman R. (1969). Evolutionary Operation. New York: Wiley.

Buckley, Walter Frederick (1967). Sociology and Modern Systems Theory. Englewood Cliffs, N.J.: Prentice-Hall.

Burns, Tom, and Stalker, Gerald M. (1961). The Management of Innovation. London: Tavistock.

Campbell, Donald T. (1959). "Methodological suggestions from a comparative psychology of knowledge processes." Inquiry, 2: 152–182.

—— (1965). "Variation and selective retention in socio-cultural evolution." In Herbert R. Barringer, George I. Blanksten, and Raymond W. Mack (eds.), Social Change in Developing Areas: 19–49. Cambridge, Mass.: Schenkman.

—— (1969). "Reforms as experiments." American Psychologist, 24: 409–429.

Carroll, Donald C. (1967). "Implications of on-line, real-time systems for managerial decision making." In Walter L. Johnson (ed.), The Management of Aerospace Programs: 345–370. Tarzana, Cal.: American Astronautical Society.

Child, John (1974). Organization, Management and Adaptiveness. Working paper, University of Aston.

Chomsky, Noam (1966). Cartesian Linguistics. New York: Harper & Row.

Churchman, C. West (1971). The Design of Inquiring Systems. New York: Basic Books.

Clark, Burton R. (1972). "The organizational saga in higher education." Administrative Science Quarterly, 17: 178–184.

Cohen, Abner (1974). Two-dimensional Man. Berkeley: University of California Press.

24 *Handbook of Organizational Design*

Cohen, Michael D., March, James G., and Olsen, Johan P. (1972). "A garbage can model of organizational choice." Administrative Science Quarterly, 17: 1–25.

Cyert, Richard M., and March, James G. (1963). A Behavioral Theory of the Firm. Englewood Cliffs, N.J.: Prentice-Hall.

Cyert, Richard M., Simon, Herbert A., and Trow, Donald B. (1956). "Observation of a business decision." Journal of Business, 29: 237–248.

Dalton, Melville (1959). Men Who Manage. New York: Wiley.

Danielsson, Albert (1975). Företagsekonomi. Lund: Studentlitteratur.

Doktor, Robert H. (1969). The Development and Mapping of Certain Cognitive Styles of Problem Solving. Doctoral dissertation, Stanford University.

Downs, Anthony (1967). Inside Bureaucracy. Boston: Little, Brown.

Dufty, Norman Francis, and Taylor, P. M. (1962). "The implementation of a decision." Administrative Science Quarterly, 7: 110–119.

Duncan, Robert B. (1972). "Characteristics of organizational environments and perceived environmental uncertainty." Administrative Science Quarterly, 17: 313–327.

Emery, Fred E., and Trist, Eric L. (1965). "The causal texture of organizational environments." Human Relations, 18: 21–32.

Feigenbaum, Edward A. (1970). "Information processing and memory." In Donald A. Norman (ed.), Models of Human Memory: 451–468. New York: Academic Press.

Festinger, Leon (1957). A Theory of Cognitive Dissonance. Stanford, Cal.: Stanford University Press.

Freire, Paulo (1970a). "The adult literacy process as cultural action for freedom." Harvard Educational Review, 40: 205–225.

—— (1970b). "Cultural action and conscientization." Harvard Educational Review, 40: 452–477.

—— (1973). Education for Critical Consciousness. New York: Seabury Press.

Galbraith, Jay R. (1973). Designing Complex Organizations. Reading, Mass.: Addison-Wesley.

Galbraith, John Kenneth (1973). Economics and the Public Purpose. New York: Houghton Mifflin.

Gerrity, Thomas P. (1970). The Design of Man-Machine Decision Systems. Doctoral dissertation, Massachusetts Institute of Technology.

Glimell, Hans R. (1975). Designing Interactive Systems for Organizational Change. Gothenburg: Business Administration Studies.

Grinyer, Peter H., and Norburn, David (1975). "Planning for existing markets: perceptions of executives and financial performance." Journal of the Royal Statistical Society, Series A, 138 (1): 70–97.

Harbison, Frederick Harris, and Myers, Charles A. (1959). Management in the Industrial World. New York: McGraw-Hill.

Hedberg, Bo L. T. (1970). On Man-Computer Interaction in Organizational Decision-making. Gothenburg: Business Administration Studies.

—— (1973). Organizational Stagnation and Choice of Strategy. Working paper, International Institute of Management, Berlin.

—— (1974). Reframing as a Way to Cope with Organizational Stagnation. Working paper, International Institute of Management, Berlin.

—— (1975a). "Computer systems to support industrial democracy." In Enid Mumford and Harold Sackman (eds.), Human Choice and Computers: 211–230. Amsterdam: North-Holland.

—— (1975b). "Growth stagnation as a managerial discontinuity." In Proceedings of the INSEAD Seminar on Management under Discontinuity: 34–59. Brussels: European Institute for Advanced Studies in Management.

Hedberg, Bo L. T., and Jönsson, Sten A. (1977). "Strategy formulation as a discontinuous process." International Studies of Management and Organization, 7: 89–109.

—— (1978). "Designing semi-confusing information systems for organizations in changing environments." Accounting, Organizations and Society, 3: 47–64.

Hedberg, Bo L. T., and Mumford, Enid (1975). "The design of computer systems: man's vision of man as an integral part of the systems design process." In Enid Mumford and Harold Sackman (eds.), Human Choice and Computers: 31–59. Amsterdam: North-Holland.

Hedberg, Bo L. T., Nystrom, Paul C., and Starbuck, William H. (1976). "Camping on seesaws: prescriptions for a self-designing organization." Administrative Science Quarterly, 21: 41–65.

—— (1977). "Designing organizations to match tomorrow." In Paul C. Nystrom and William H. Starbuck (eds.), Prescriptive Models of Organizations: 171–181. Amsterdam: North-Holland.

Hegel, Georg Wilhelm Friedrich (1959). Enzyklopädie der philosophischen Wissenschaften im Grundrisse. Hamburg: F. Meiner.

Hirschman, Albert O. (1970). Exit, Voice and Loyalty. Cambridge, Mass.: Harvard University Press.

Hunt, Raymond G. (1968). "Review of E. J. Miller and K. A. Rice's Systems of Organization." Administrative Science Quarterly, 13: 360–362.

Huysmans, Jan H. B. M. (1970). The Implementation of Operations Research. New York: Wiley.

Illich, Iván D. (1971). De-schooling Society. New York: Harper & Row.

Jönsson, Sten A. (1973). Decentralisering och utveckling. Gothenburg: Business Administration Studies.

Jönsson, Sten A., and Lundin, Rolf A. (1977). "Myths and wishful thinking as management tools." In Paul C. Nystrom and William H. Starbuck (eds.), Prescriptive Models of Organizations: 157–170. Amsterdam: North-Holland.

Jönsson, Sten A., Lundin, Rolf A., and Sjöberg, Lennart (1974). Frustrations in Decision Processes. Working paper, University of Gothenburg.

Katona, George (1940). Organizing and Memorizing. New York: Columbia University Press.

Katz, Daniel, and Kahn, Robert L. (1966). The Social Psychology of Organizations. New York: Wiley.

Keen, Peter George Wills (1973). The Implications of Cognitive Style for Individual Decision Making. Doctoral dissertation, Harvard University.

Kelly, George Alexander (1955). The Psychology of Personal Constructs (two vols.). New York: Norton.

Kuhn, Thomas S. (1962). The Structure of Scientific Revolutions. Chicago: University of Chicago Press.

Laszlo, Ervin (1972). Introduction to Systems Philosophy. New York: Gordon and Breach.

Lembo, John M. (1972). When Learning Happens. New York: Schocken.

Lewin, Arie Y., and Wolf, Carl W. (1972). Organizational Slack III. Working paper, New York University.

—— (1975). "The theory of organizational slack: a critical review." In Eliezer Shlifer (ed.), Proceedings—XX International Meeting, The Institute of Management Sciences, Vol. 2: 648–654. Jerusalem: Jerusalem Academic Press.

Lieberman, Arnold J. (1972). Organizational Learning Environments: Effects and Perceptions of Learning Constraints. Doctoral dissertation, Stanford University.

Lindblom, Charles E. (1959). "The science of muddling through." Public Administration Review, 19: 79–88.

McCall, Morgan W., Jr. (1977). "Making sense with nonsense: helping frames of reference clash." In Paul C. Nystrom and William H. Starbuck (eds.), Prescriptive Models of Organizations: 111–123. Amsterdam: North-Holland.

McHugh, Peter (1968). Defining the Situation. Indianapolis: Bobbs-Merrill.

MacIver, Robert Morrison (1947). The Web of Government. New York: Macmillan.

McKenney, James L., and Keen, Peter G. W. (1974). "How managers' minds work." Harvard Business Review, 52 (3): 79–90.

Mansfield, Edwin (1961). "Technical change and the rate of imitation." Econometrica, 29: 741–766.

March, James G., and Olsen, Johan P. (1976). Ambiguity and Choice in Organizations. Bergen: Universitetsforlaget.

March, James G., and Simon, Herbert A. (1958). Organizations. New York: Wiley.

Mead, George Herbert (1932). The Philosophy of the Present. Chicago: Open Court.

Metcalfe, J. Leslie, McQuillan, William F. O., and Hutchinson, Peter (1975). Organizations are Open Systems. Working paper, London Graduate School of Business Studies.

Michael, Donald N. (1973). On Learning to Plan and Planning to Learn. San Francisco: Jossey-Bass.

Miller, Danny (1977). A Study of Strategy Making at Volkswagenwerk AG. Working paper, McGill University.

Miller, Danny, and Mintzberg, Henry L. (1974). Strategy Formulation in Context. Working paper, McGill University.

Miller, George A. (1956). "The magical number seven, plus or minus two: some limits on our capacity for processing information." Psychological Review, 63: 81–97.

Mitroff, Ian I., and Kilmann, Ralph H. (1976). "On organization stories: an approach to the design and analysis of organizations through myths and stories." In Ralph H. Kilmann, Louis R. Pondy, and Dennis P. Slevin (eds.), The Management of Organization Design, Vol. I: 189–207. New York: Elsevier North-Holland.

Morine, Harold, and Morine, Greta (1973). Discovery. Englewood Cliffs, N.J.: Prentice-Hall.

Morton, Michael S. Scott (1971). Management Decision Systems. Boston: Harvard University, Graduate School of Business Administration.

Mowrer, Orval Hobart (1960). Learning Theory and the Symbolic Processes. New York: Wiley.

Myrdal, Gunnar (1958). Value in Social Theory. New York: Harper.

Newell, Allen, and Simon, Herbert A. (1972). Human Problem Solving. Englewood Cliffs, N.J.: Prentice-Hall.

Norman, Donald A. (1969). Memory and Attention. New York: Wiley.

—— (1970). Models of Human Memory. New York: Academic Press.

Normann, Richard (1975). Skapande företagsledning. Stockholm: Aldus.

Nystrom, Paul C., Hedberg, Bo L. T., and Starbuck, William H. (1976). "Interacting processes as organization designs." In Ralph H. Kilmann, Louis R. Pondy, and Dennis P. Slevin (eds.), The Management of Organization Design, Vol. I: 209–230. New York: Elsevier North-Holland.

Olofsson, Christer, Schlasberg, Johan, and Svalander, Per-Axel (1973). "Sjukvårdens nyfattigdom." Läkartidningen, 70: 2312–2314.

Pettigrew, Andrew M. (1974). Internal Politics and the

Emergence and Decline of Departmental Groups. Working paper, London Graduate School of Business Studies.

Piaget, Jean (1968). Le Structuralisme. Paris: Presses Universitaires de France.

Pondy, Louis R., and Mitroff, Ian I. (1979). "Beyond open system models of organizations." In Barry M. Staw (ed.), Research in Organizational Behavior, Vol. 1: 3–39. Greenwich, Conn.: JAI Press.

Postman, Leo, and Stark, Karen (1965). "The role of response set in tests of unlearning." Journal of Verbal Learning and Verbal Behavior, 4: 315–322.

Postman, Leo, and Underwood, Benton J. (1973). "Critical issues in interference theory." Memory and Cognition, 1: 19–40.

Radnitsky, Gerard (1970). Contemporary Schools of Metascience (2nd ed.). New York: Humanities Press.

Rhenman, Eric (1973). Organization Theory for Long-range Planning. London: Wiley.

Samstag, Karl (1973). "Das Entwicklungsstufenmodell in der PIAGET-Diskussion. Ein Interpretationsversuch." In Walter Breunig (ed.), Das Zeitproblem im Lernprozess: 9–33. München: Ehrenwirth.

Sarason, Seymour B. (1972). The Creation of Settings and the Future Societies. San Francisco: Jossey-Bass.

Schroder, Harold M., Driver, Michael J., and Streufert, Siegfried (1967). Human Information Processing. New York: Holt, Rinehart and Winston.

Schutz, Alfred (1967). "On multiple realities." In Alfred Schutz, Collected Papers, Vol. 1. The Problem of Social Reality: 207–259. The Hague: Martinus Nijhoff.

Scott, William A. (1974). "Varieties of cognitive integration." Journal of Personality and Social Psychology, 30: 563–578.

Simon, Herbert A. (1957). Administrative Behavior (2nd ed.). New York: Macmillan.

—— (1969). The Sciences of the Artificial. Cambridge, Mass.: MIT Press.

—— (1971). "Designing organizations for an information-rich world." In Martin Greenberger (ed.), Computers, Communications, and the Public Interest: 37–52. Baltimore: Johns Hopkins Press.

Slevin, Dennis P. (1971). "The innovation boundary: a specific model and some empirical results." Administrative Science Quarterly, 16: 515–531.

—— (1973). "The innovation boundary: a replication with increased costs." Administrative Science Quarterly, 18: 71–75.

Sperling, George (1967). "Successive approximations to a model for short term memory." Acta Psychologica, 27: 285–292.

Starbuck, William H. (1974). "Systems optimization with unknown criteria." In Proceedings of the 1974 International Conference on Systems, Man, and Cybernetics: 67–76. New York: Institute of Electrical and Electronics Engineers.

—— (1976). "Organizations and their environments." In Marvin D. Dunnette (ed.), Handbook of Industrial and Organizational Psychology: 1069–1123. Chicago: Rand McNally.

Starbuck, William H., and Dutton, John M. (1973). "Designing adaptive organizations." Journal of Business Policy, 3: 21–28.

Starbuck, William H., and Hedberg, Bo L. T. (1977). "Saving an organization from a stagnating environment." In Hans B. Thorelli (ed.), Strategy + Structure = Performance: 249–258. Bloomington: Indiana University Press.

Stimson, David H., and Thompson, Ronald P. (1975). "The importance of 'Weltanschauung' in operations research: the case of the school busing problem." Management Science, 21: 1123–1132.

Streufert, Susan C. (1973). "Effects of information relevance on decision making in complex environments." Memory and Cognition, 1: 224–228.

Stymne, Bengt (1970). Values and Processes. Lund: Studentlitteratur.

Terreberry, Shirley (1968). "The evolution of organizational environments." Administrative Science Quarterly, 12: 590–613.

Thompson, James D. (1967). Organizations in Action. New York: McGraw-Hill.

Thompson, Victor A. (1965). "Bureaucracy and innovation." Administrative Science Quarterly, 10: 1–20.

Thorpe, William Herman (1956). Learning and Instinct in Animals. Cambridge, Mass.: Harvard University Press.

Törnebohm, Håkan (1973). "United studies." In Ervin Laszlo (ed.), The World System: 141–160. New York: Brazillier.

Watzlawick, Paul, Weakland, John H., and Fisch, Richard (1974). Change. New York: Norton.

Waugh, Nancy C., and Norman, Donald A. (1965). "Primary memory." Psychological Review, 72: 89–104.

Weick, Karl E. (1969). The Social Psychology of Organizing. Reading, Mass.: Addison-Wesley.

Weinshall, Theodore D., and Twiss, Brian C. (1973). Organizational Problems in European Manufacture. London: Longman.

White, Orion F., Jr. (1969). "The dialectical organization—an alternative to bureaucracy." Public Administration Review, 29: 32–42.

Wildavsky, Aaron B. (1972). "The self-evaluating organization." Public Administration Review, 32: 509–520.

Williamson, Oliver E. (1964). The Economics of Discretionary Behavior. Englewood Cliffs, N.J.: Prentice-Hall.

Wilson, James Q. (1966). "Innovation in organization: notes toward a theory." In James D. Thompson (ed.), Approaches to Organizational Design: 193–218. Pittsburgh: University of Pittsburgh Press.

Wolf, Carl W. (1971). An Investigation into the Theory of Organizational Slack. Doctoral dissertation, New York University.

Zajonc, Robert B. (1960). "The process of cognitive tuning in communication." Journal of Abnormal and Social Psychology, 61: 159–167.

[12]

Culture and
Organizational Learning

SCOTT D. N. COOK

San Jose State University

DVORA YANOW

California State University, Hayward

Traditionally, theories of organizational learning have taken one of two approaches that share a common characterization of learning but differ in focus. One approach focuses on learning by individuals in organizational contexts; the other, on individual learning as a model for organizational action. Both base their understanding of organizational learning on the cognitive activity of individual learning. However, there is something organizations do that may be called organizational learning, that is neither individuals learning in organizations nor organizations employing processes akin to learning by individuals. This form of organizational learning can be seen in the case of three small workshops that make "the finest flutes in the world." This essay proposes a perspective on organizational learning, drawing on the concept of organizational culture, that can be useful in understanding the case. This perspective provides a fruitful basis for exploring the above distinctions in both theory and practice.

Two questions underlie the phrase "organizational learning": Can organizations learn? What is the nature of learning when it is done by organizations? How these questions have been addressed in the organizational learning literature, directly and indirectly, reveals a particular orientation toward the topic. Our analysis of this orientation and discussion of another view are the subjects of this essay.

In writing on organizational learning, most authors (e.g., Argyris & Schön, 1978; Bolman, 1976; Duncan & Weiss, 1979; Etheredge & Short, 1983; Gahmberg, 1980; Hedberg, 1981; Herriott, Levinthal, & March, 1985; Lant & Mezias, 1990; Levitt & March, 1988; March & Olsen, 1976; Miles & Randolph, 1981; Shrivastava, 1983; Sims & Gioia, 1986; Sitkin, 1992; Weick, 1991; Weiss, 1980) have examined how individuals learn in organizational contexts or have explored ways that

AUTHORS' NOTE: The authors thank Mats Alvesson, Lee Bolman, Gideon Kunda, Craig Lundberg, Ed Schein, Deborah Stone, Sharon Traweek, Barry A. Turner, Karl Weick, and the anonymous reviewers of this essay for their careful readings of the text and for their many helpful suggestions. An earlier version was presented at the Second Annual Symposium of the Public Administration Theory Network, Los Angeles, April 1990.

JOURNAL OF MANAGEMENT INQUIRY, Vol. 2 No. 4, December 1993 373-390
© 1993 Sage Publications, Inc.

374   JOURNAL OF MANAGEMENT INQUIRY / December 1993

theories of individual learning can be applied to organizations or both. In the first instance, the typical argument is that organizational learning is a particular sort of learning done in organizations by key individuals whose learning is tied to subsequent organizational change. The second approach holds that organizations can learn because they possess capacities that are identical or equivalent to the capacities that individuals possess that enable them to learn— that is, with respect to learning, this approach treats organizations *as if* they were individuals. Despite their differences, both approaches tend to address the questions just mentioned from a common perspective: They typically base their account of the nature of *organizational* learning, explicitly or implicitly, on an understanding of what it means for an *individual* to learn. This grounding in learning by individuals suggests a link between discussions of organizational learning and theories of cognition. For this reason, we call this orientation the "cognitive perspective" on organizational learning.

Although the cognitive perspective has been and continues to be a wellspring of insight and utility, we have found it less useful in efforts to understand a phenomenon that we believe is central to the subject of organizational learning: specifically, where learning is understood to be done by the organization as a whole, not by individuals in it, and where the organization is not understood as if it were an individual (that is, as if it were in some way ontologically a cognitive entity). We hold that learning can indeed be done by organizations; that this phenomenon is neither conceptually nor empirically the same as either learning by individuals or individuals learning within organizations; and that to understand organizational learning as learning by organizations, theorists and practitioners need to see organizations not primarily as cognitive entities but as cultural ones.

Our intention here is to outline a "cultural perspective" on organizational learning (in keeping with recent attention to organizational culture; e.g., Frost, Moore, Louis, Lunderberg, & Martin, 1985, 1991; Schein, 1985). We see this perspective as a complement to, not a substitute for, the cognitive perspective. From the cultural perspective, we argue, the question, "Can organizations learn?" is not an epistemological one about cognitive capacities, but an empirical one about organizational actions—to which the answer is, yes. Further, we hope to show that the second question, "What is the nature of learning as done by organizations?" can be addressed from the cultural perspective

in a way that avoids some specific conceptual difficulties found in the cognitive perspective, while also suggesting some new avenues for exploration.

The theoretical argument presented here has grown out of our analysis of three small companies manufacturing flutes. In the sections that follow, we describe what we see as some of the conceptual difficulties inherent in the cognitive view, discuss the meanings of the concept of organizational learning, and outline a cultural perspective on organizational learning, which we illustrate through the case example of the flute companies.

THE COGNITIVE PERSPECTIVE

Most of the literature on organizational learning has addressed the topic from a perspective that entails various concepts traditionally associated with cognition. Many authors, for example, have used the notion of learning from mistakes, a concept central to cognition, to address organizational learning both at the level of the organizational aggregate and at the level of key actors within an organizational setting. In this vein, Etheredge and Short (1983) see governmental learning as a reflection of increased intelligence and behavioral effectiveness: If government behaves more effectively, then we may say that it has learned, often from its own mistakes. Lant and Mezias (1990) hold that "an organizational learning model suggests that the impetus for organizational change is triggered by performance below aspiration level" (p. 149). Some theories of cognition are modeled on principles of systems theory; reflecting this, some authors have understood organizational learning to be tied to the detection and correction of errors linked to a change in course or improved performance. For Bolman (1976) and Argyris and Schön (1978), organizational learning is error detection and correction geared to improving the effectiveness of individual behavior in organizations. Similarly, Sitkin (1991) refers to "the action/failure/feedback/correction cycle" in making the provocative argument that organizations may learn more effectively through "strategic failure" than through a singularly success-oriented strategy of failure avoidance.

However, there are problems inherent in transferring to organizations concepts whose origin is cognition by individuals. These problems, which come both from the nature of cognition and from its application to organizations, are rarely acknowledged or explored. For example, the sorts of activities that we conventionally and unproblematically associate with cognition in individuals (acquiring knowledge of history, mastering skills useful in fixing machines, solving geometric problems, gaining facility at programming or sailing or singing, etc.) are neither conventionally nor unproblematically associated with organizations. Further, it is not readily apparent how the sort of organizational activities commonly described in discussions of organizational learning (e.g., the rearrangement of departmental structure, the adoption of new technologies or strategies, etc.) are in fact activities than can meaningfully be called learning, particularly learning on the part of the organization itself.[1]

A fundamental problem derives from the fact that it is impossible to *see* cognition taking place in the actions of organizations. This has led to the common assertion in the literature that organizational learning has taken place when actions by organizationally key individuals that are understood to entail learning are followed by observable changes in the organization's pattern of activities. In this vein, Miles and Randolph (1981), drawing on Simon's work, define organizational learning as individuals' insights reflected "in the structural elements and outcomes of the organization itself" (p. 50).

Having accepted generally the inference that organizational learning entails observable organizational change linked to individual cognition, the cognitive perspective splits into two major approaches. One approach has focused on individual learning in an organizational context. The other has used individual learning as a model for understanding certain types of collective organizational activity. Most authors have followed one approach or the other; a few have explored both.

The first approach treats organizational learning explicitly as learning by individuals within an organizational context. For example, March and Olsen (1976) focus on the experiential learning of individuals within organizations. Argyris and Schön (1978) examine the actions of members of organizations, whom they see as agents for the organization. Etheredge and Short (1983) treat governmental learning, in large part, as learning by individual politicians, officials, advisors, analysts, bureaucrats, and other decision makers within government agencies. Weiss (1980) similarly presents societal learning as the accretion over time of government officials' knowledge, which is transferred into the policy-making process. Simon (1991) aligns

himself with this approach quite definitively in stating, "All learning takes place inside individual human heads; an organization learns in only two ways: a) by the learning of its members, or b) by ingesting new members who have knowledge the organization didn't previously have" (p. 125).

Some authors state that they take organizational learning to be different in some sense from individual learning. Fiol and Lyles (1985), in a review of the literature, found this stance to be one of the points of consensus among theorists. Nonetheless, the accounts and illustrations offered by these authors typically describe episodes of individual learning that occur within organizational contexts. For example, Bolman (1976) treats organizational learning as "learning experiences for key decision makers." For Shrivastava (1983), organizational learning "occurs through the medium of individual members" and involves the development of better interpersonal skills. In a broader sense, for Sims and Gioia (1986), "organizational social cognition" within the "thinking organization" essentially concerns understanding "our own cognitive processes" and "how other people think" (p. x). Organizational learning as approached in such cases, although conceived of as different from individual learning, is nevertheless described as a form of learning by individuals; it is not treated as learning by organizations.[2]

The second approach develops theories of organizational action largely by applying to organizations concepts that are commonly found in models of individual learning. Hedberg (1981) and Gahmberg (1980), for example, extend stimulus-response models of individual learning to explain organizational selection of stimuli and choice of responses. For Weick (1991), the traditional "defining property of learning is the combination of same stimulus and different response," but the fact that this "is rare in organizations" leads him to consider how organizations might employ stimulus-response learning in "nontraditional ways" (p. 117). In a fashion that suggests the themes of adaptation and conditioned response from behaviorist psychology, Cyert and March (1963) see organizational learning as entailed in organizational adaptation that "uses individual members of the organization as instruments" in a way that constitutes "adaptation at the aggregate level of the organization" (p. 123). For them, organizational learning is understood to occur when an organization, in response to "an external source of disturbance or shock," selects "decision rules" that lead the organization "to a preferred state" (p. 99). Lant and Mezias (1991) add the notion of learning to the language of systemic adaptation in describing "an ecology of strategic learning" and arguing that "organizational change is governed by an experiential learning process" within which entrepreneurship is seen as a "search activity" that can bring about "change to the core dimensions of organizational activity" (p. 148). Duncan and Weiss (1979), meanwhile, present a cognitive model of the production of organizational knowledge: Individual decision makers possess specialized knowledge about the organization, which is shared through paradigmatic frameworks that generate a set of beliefs that provide a way of seeing the organizational world.[3] Similarly, in applying the notion of memory to organizations, Levitt and March (1988) argue that "organizational learning depends on features of individual memories . . . but our present concern is with organizational aspects of memory" (p. 326).

It is clear that individuals do indeed learn within the context of organizations, that this context influences the character of that learning and, in turn, that such learning can have operational consequences for the activities of the organization. Also, there is nothing inherently invalid in applying models of individual learning to organizations. A great deal of important work has come out of these efforts. It is not clear, however, either conceptually or empirically, that such instances of learning constitute learning by organizations. And because it is not obvious, a priori, that organizations are cognitive entities, in drawing on individual cognition as a way of understanding organizational phenomena, we must take care not to lose sense of the "as if" quality of the metaphor, forgetting that organizations and individuals are not the same sorts of entities. The nature of the difference, as we will argue later, bears on how each can be understood to learn.

In both approaches, the application to organizations of a model of learning based on cognition by individuals entails, in our view, at least three substantive problems. First, it raises a set of complex arguments concerning the ontological status of organizations as cognitive entities—specifically, arguments about how organizations exist and how the nature of their existence entails an ability to learn that is identical or akin to the human cognitive abilities associated with learning. In other words, because the cognitive perspective adopts its understanding of learning from theories about individuals, it follows that to discuss cognitive organizational learning, one

must first show how, in their capacity to learn, organizations are like individuals.

Further, because theories of cognition already carry with them an understanding of learning, many who have adopted the cognitive perspective on organizational learning have seen *organizations*, although not always *learning*, as the term calling for explanation. In this vein, Argyris and Schön (1978) begin their discussion of organizational learning with the section, "What is an organization that it may learn?" Others (e.g., Duncan & Weiss, 1979; Gahmberg, 1980) similarly begin with definitions and discussions of the concept of organization that, in part, constitute arguments concerning the ontological status of organizations with respect to learning. Morgan (1986) looks at how organizations can be understood to be brains (metaphorically at least) and how this might help us design organizations "so that they can learn and self-organize in the manner of a fully functioning brain" (p. 105). Sandelands and Stablein (1987), meanwhile, consider the existence of the "organizational mind" as a way of understanding an organization's ability to engage in "ideational processes" or a "commerce of ideas" (pp. 138-139). The idea of attributing an ontological status to organizations as cognitive entities, which has been fundamental to the views of the cognitive perspective, has often proven to be conceptually as problematic as it is provocative: What has been taken as self-evident in the case of individuals has proved a lightning rod for debate when applied to organizations. Although this debate has produced many challenging and useful insights, it remains fundamentally unresolved.

Second, the study of individual learning is itself complex, in flux, and bounded by its own theoretical constraints. Adopting the perspective (or the metaphor) of cognition for the study of organizational learning has yielded many insights; yet these insights are limited by what we understand about learning from the field of individual cognition. Although much work is being done that advances our understanding of individual cognition, the absence of an established, commonly accepted model of individual learning leaves its useful application to organizations inherently problematic. Linking our understanding of organizational learning to cognitive theory, at the very least, obligates us to account in organizational terms for developments in that theory or to explain why this is not necessary.

Apart from the problems posed by debates concerning organizational ontology and the nature of theories of individual learning, the cognitive perspective presents a third difficulty: its proposition (often implicit) that learning for organizations is the same as learning for individuals. This is a difficulty for several reasons. In a fundamental sense, it does not follow from anything essential about organizations or about learning that learning must be the same for individuals and organizations. Nor is it clear how two things that are in so many ways so obviously different as individuals and organizations could nonetheless carry out identical or even equivalent activities. Further, even if it were shown that organizations and individuals are ontologically equivalent in the possession of cognitive capacities required for learning, it would not necessarily follow that they would both learn in the same fashion or, as Weick (1991) notes, that the results of their learning would be the same. Indeed, even among individuals, we can observe significantly different "learning styles."[4] This issue has been left largely unaddressed by theorists of organizational learning.

There is a further problematic point that is found in many parts of the literature that derives, we believe, in large measure from its systems origins. Although the idea is not inherent in the concept of cognition itself, organizational learning has typically been linked to organizational change and, particularly, to increased effectiveness. Many authors share the view (or assumption) that "learning will improve future performance" (Fiol & Lyles, 1985). Conversely, the absence of observable change has commonly been taken to mean that learning did not take place or, in fact, that learning was "impeded" (Jenkins-Smith, St. Clair, & James, 1988).

Although change is often associated with individual learning, it seems clear that some forms of learning entail little or no change that is meaningfully discernible, particularly in observable behavior. For example, maintaining the mastery of a technique may involve perceptual or kinesthetic learning that need not involve behavioral change or any observable change in ability—as when a dancer, accommodating an injury, learns new ways to perform the identical movements that were performed before the injury. Likewise, we can learn new knowledge that is not linked at all to behavioral change. One may, for example, learn a phone number and never use it or bring it to mind again. Nor does learning always produce increased effectiveness or improved performance, as the learning of faulty skills or self-destructive habits makes all too clear.

We infer from what has been written in the organizational learning literature a normative concern with learning as change and/or improvement, which typically ignores other notions of learning. The focus on overt behavioral change inherent in the experiments of cognitive psychology may in part account for this tendency to equate learning with change. We will argue, however, that change does not always accompany learning by organizations, and moreover, equating learning with change may leave out much of interest.[5] Here, we turn to an exploration of learning by organizations.

KNOWING AND LEARNING BY ORGANIZATIONS

Organizations act. The Boston Celtics play basketball. The Concertgebouw Orchestra performs Mahler symphonies. These are activities done by groups; they are not and cannot be done by single individuals. A single basketball player cannot play a game of basketball by herself; only the several players, together as a team, are able to carry out the team's strategies, moves, and style of play. A violinist alone cannot perform Mahler's Third Symphony; the execution of the phrasing, dynamics, and tempi of the piece requires the collective actions of the orchestra as a group.

Further, the ability to play basketball games or perform symphonies, we argue, is only meaningfully attributed to a group, not to individual players. It is not meaningful to say that the ability to play Mahler symphonies is possessed by an individual musician, because no individual person can perform symphonies. An individual musician possesses the ability to carry out merely a portion of what only an orchestra can do. Moreover, musicians can act on that ability only in the context of the orchestra: They may each play their parts alone (to practice, say), but to perform the symphony they must participate in an activity of the orchetra.

Although it has become more common to attribute abilities to groups, there has been an equally common reluctance to attribute to them any form of knowledge or knowing associated with those abilities: Traditionally, it has been accepted, usually unquestioningly, that matters of knowing are exclusively matters about what or how individuals know. This reluctance is consistent with the cognitive perspective's origins in theories of individual cognition. From this perspective, therefore, it would typically be argued that it is

378   JOURNAL OF MANAGEMENT INQUIRY / December 1993

the knowledge of all the individuals in an orchestra taken together that constitutes the know-how behind the ability to perform symphonies—and thus it is not know-how possessed by a group. This argument has two shortcomings. First, it implies that the performance of a symphony is meaningfully reducible to the playing of 100 different parts by individuals. This is an implication that belies the experiential reports of musicians and their audiences, and it can never be meaningfully tested because the performance of symphonies is always a group activity. Second, it is conceptually unsound to attribute to individuals know-how that no individual can demonstrate. Just as the ability to perform symphonies is meaningfully attributed only to a group, so is possession of the know-how necessary to do so. Removed from the traditional assumptions of the cognitive perspective, the same reasoning that supports the concept of group abilities would also suggest the concept of group know-how.

In this sense, the statement, "The Celtics know how to play basketball" is meaningful as a statement about organizational knowing. Other "ensembles" that are more commonly thought of as organizations, such as IBM or Saab or the U.S. Environmental Protection Agency, similarly know how to do what they do. The know-how entailed in producing a computer, a Saab 9000, or a set of standards for air quality resides in the organization as a whole, not in individual members of the organization.[6] These are propositions about organizational knowing.

Learning is related to knowing; in one sense, it is the act of acquiring knowledge. Thus the knowledge demonstrated by the Concertgebouw when it plays a symphony or by Saab when it produces a car can be understood as having been learned. The individuals in the organization were not born with the ability to perform their parts of these activities, nor has the organization always possessed these abilities. What can be said of the abilities can be said of the know-how associated with them: It has to be acquired; it has to be learned. The statement, "The Celtics know how to play basketball" suggests something about organizational learning as well as organizational knowing. Organizational learning, then, describes a category of activity that can only be done by a group. It cannot be done by an individual.

In this respect, organizational learning, as we use the term, refers to the capacity of an organization to learn how to do what it does, where what it learns is possessed not by individual members of the organiza-

tion but by the aggregate itself. That is, when a group acquires the know-how associated with its ability to carry out its collective activities, that constitutes organizational learning.[7]

From the perspective of this understanding, the foregoing examples of organizational activities are descriptions of things that organizations as collectives actually do that can be meaningfully understood as learning. The answer to our initial question is, yes, organizations do indeed learn. We acknowledge that the term *learning* is borrowed from the realm of individual behavior: When individuals demonstrate a new ability, it is meaningful to assert that they have acquired the know-how associated with that ability. However, we believe that the similarity between individual and organizational learning ends there. We do not infer that because there is an apparent likeness in activity, the underlying processes are necessarily alike. In particular, we argue that what organizations do when they learn is necessarily different from what individuals do when they learn. Specifically, we believe that organizational learning is not essentially a cognitive activity, because, at the very least, organizations lack the typical wherewithal for undertaking cognition: They do not possess what people possess and use in knowing and learning—that is, actual bodies, perceptive organs, brains, and so forth. To understand organizational learning, we must look for attributes that organizations can be meaningfully understood to possess and use, that can be seen to give rise to the sorts of activities outlined in the organizational learning examples above. This is a central concern of the arguments that follow.[8]

At this juncture, three additional points can be raised. First, in our view, organizational learning, like individual learning, does not necessarily imply change, particularly observable change. An organization can, for example, learn something in order *not* to change. Second, organizational learning need not, as the systems notion of feedback would suggest, be a response to an environmental stimulus (such as error detection). The impetus for learning can also come from within the organization itself. Third, in a significant measure, organizational knowledge or know-how is unique to each organization. That is, two organizations performing the same task do not necessarily perform it identically. Even two very similar organizations know how to do somewhat different things. The Celtics do not play basketball in the same way as do the 76ers. The Concertgebouw and the New York Philharmonic perform the same Mahler Symphony differently. IBM and Apple have different management styles, although both manufacture computers. Organizational knowing and learning are always in some part intimately bound to a particular organization.

In the case analysis that follows, we examine in greater detail how understanding organizational learning in terms of organizational culture helps address the issues we have identified so far. Organizational culture has been defined and treated in many ways (see, for example, Frost et al., 1985, 1991; Ouchi & Wilkins, 1985; Schein, 1985; Smircich, 1983). For our purposes at hand, we define culture in application to organizations as a set of values, beliefs, and feelings, together with the artifacts of their expression and transmission (such as myths, symbols, metaphors, rituals), that are created, inherited, shared, and transmitted within one group of people and that, in part, distinguish that group from others. This definition is in keeping with an interpretive approach to human action and social reality (see, for example, Berger & Luckmann, 1966; Mead, 1934; Taylor, 1979).[9]

Such an approach to organizational learning builds on the following. Human action includes the ability to act in groups. Over time and in the course of joint action or practice, a group of people creates a set of intersubjective meanings that are expressed in and through their artifacts (objects, language, and acts). Such artifacts include the symbols, metaphors, ceremonies, myths, and so forth with which organizations and groups transmit their values, beliefs, and feelings to new and existing members, as well as in part to strangers. As new members join the group, each acquires a sense of these meanings through the everyday practices in which the organization's artifacts are engaged. Through such "artifactual interactions," shared meanings are continually maintained or modified; these are acts that create, sustain, or modify the organization's culture.[10]

The concept of culture, because it takes human groups as its subject, allows us to begin with the empirical observation that a group of people can and does act collectively—and can do so in ways that suggest learning. The concept of organizational learning, then, is not encountered as a theoretical hypothesis (Can organizations learn?) to be tested and proved. Rather, the concept is addressed through empirical observations that call to be understood. The ontological problem of the existence of an organization as a cognitive entity is, thus, not encountered. The focus of the cultural theorist concerned with organizational learning shifts to the second question, "What

is the nature of learning when it is done by organizations?" and the task is to develop concepts with which to describe how a group of individuals acting collectively, as an organization, does those things that might meaningfully and usefully be understood as learning.

THE FINEST FLUTES IN THE WORLD: ORGANIZING CRAFTSMANSHIP

Most of the finest flutes produced in this century have been made in a style reminiscent of old world craftsmanship by three small workshops in and around Boston, Massachusetts: the Wm. S. Haynes Company; Verne Q. Powell Flutes, Inc.; and Brannen Brothers—Flutemakers, Inc. Haynes, the oldest of the three, was founded in 1900. In 1927, Verne Q. Powell, who was shop foreman for Haynes, left the company to make flutes on his own. Two of Powell's mastercraftsmen, Bickford and Robert Brannen, founded Brannen Brothers in 1977.[11]

Instruments made by these three companies have been regarded by flutists internationally as the "best flutes in the world." The idea of excellence has been central to the identities of all three companies. Until the early 1980s, when changing economics and a growing challenge by large-scale, highly tooled Japanese flute manufacturers affected demand, it was common for the Boston companies to have a 5-year backlog of orders.

The companies themselves are rather small, each having begun with 1 or 2 people and expanding slowly to typically about 25. Apart from a secretary or a bookkeeper, all people in the companies work on the instruments. In each workshop, the owners and/or managers (3 to 4 people in each) may have offices and administrative work to do, but each also spends time, in some cases the bulk of it, at a workbench.

The companies are also similar in terms of physical layout. There are areas where work is done with die machines or casting equipment and other areas for cleaning and polishing or storage. But the central area of activity at each shop consists of rows of workbenches stocked mostly with hand tools where flutemakers sit side by side doing the delicate mechanical and aesthetic work that makes the instruments what they are.

The flutemakers themselves are in many ways a varied lot. The range of ages has been wide, yet most of the flutemakers have been in their 20s or 30s. Until recently, they were almost exclusively men; now, at

380   JOURNAL OF MANAGEMENT INQUIRY / December 1993

Brannen Brothers, for example, about 40% are women. Some flutemakers are musicians; very few have ever been flutists. A growing number have been to college. Many have hobbies or previous professions that complement the detail and finesse of their work with the flutes (silversmithing, fine woodworking, a "fanatical interest" in high-end stereo equipment, or specialty car engines). Many—for reasons unknown—are astigmatic.

In all three shops, flutes have been made following similar procedures and organization of production. The tube that becomes the body of the flute is made outside the shop to each company's precise specifications. Screws and steel rods for the key mechanism and strips of silver for various parts are also brought in. The parts are collected, carefully inspected, and given an initial polishing. Next, the body is formed. Tone holes are put into the tube, and the structure that holds the key mechanism is soldered on. The key mechanism is assembled and precisely fit to the body. Then, pads are put into the keys and the mechanism adjusted by hand to remarkably fine tolerances. Meanwhile, the head joint and embouchure hole are put together and delicately hand finished. Finally, the flute is polished, packed up, and shipped to its new owner.

At Powell (which we will use here as the primary example), it would take about 2 weeks to make an instrument from start to finish. At all times there would be several flutes at each step of manufacture. Typically, each flute would be worked on by several flutemakers in succession. Each individual craftsman, typically skilled in only a few aspects of the process, would work on his part of a flute (or a small batch) until that work was finished, whereupon the flute (or batch) would be handed on to the next craftsman. The second flutemaker would base her work on the former's. And so on down the line. If at any point a flutemaker felt that earlier work was not right, that person would return the piece to the appropriate prior flutemaker to be reworked to their mutual satisfaction.

In describing why a piece might need to be reworked, a flutemaker would typically make only cryptic remarks, such as, "It doesn't feel right" or "This bit doesn't look quite right." The first flutemaker would then rework the piece until both were in agreement that it had "the right feel" or "the right look." In working on a portion of the key mechanism, say, one flutemaker might tell the previous one that a key "doesn't feel right; it's cranky." This would lead the other to check the key over until he got a sense of how the feel was off. Ultimately he would trace the problem down, for example, to a need for adjusting the way the

key fit into the mechanism or, perhaps, to a need to reset the tension on the spring that operates the key. The language in such interchanges is inexact in no small part because many of the actual physical dimensions and tolerances of the flutes have never been made explicit; and many that have been are not commonly referred to in explicit terms by the flutemakers in daily practice. Yet the extremely precise standards of the instruments, on which the flute's ultimate style and quality depend, have been maintained through just these sorts of individual and mutual judgments of hand and eye.

This process has resulted in two very important things. First, it has made sure that at any one step of manufacture not only had work been done properly with respect to the work each flutemaker needed to accomplish, but it was also done properly from the perspective of the next flutemaker who needed to base her work on that of the former. The second result has been that when a flute reached the final inspection at the end of manufacture, almost without exception, it required no further work. The hand-to-hand checking of the flutes has amounted to a very successful, informal quality control system.

Apprentices have typically been trained by sitting at a workbench to do one of the steps of manufacture as would any other flutemaker. As an apprentice finished each piece of work, he would show it to a master-craftsman who would judge it, just as she would judge the work of any other flutemaker: If it did not feel right or look right, it would be handed back to the apprentice to be reworked until it did. Eventually, the apprentice would become a judge of his own work (this would be a mark of the end of his apprenticeship). Similarly, he would become able to judge work by other flutemakers on flutes coming to him for work and be able to recognize when they needed to be taken back because the look or feel was "not right." In this way, at one and the same time, an apprentice would both acquire a set of skills in flutemaking and become a member of the informal quality control system that has unfalteringly maintained the style and quality of these instruments.

No two Powell flutes are exactly alike. Each has its own strengths and quirks, its own personality. Yet a knowledgeable fluteplayer would never fail to recognize a Powell by the way it feels and plays, nor would she confuse a Powell with a Haynes or a Brannen Brothers. Each Powell flute, although unique, shares an unambiguous family resemblance with all other Powells. This family resemblance is the essence of Powell style and quality. And although each Powell has its own personality and aspects of the flute's physical design have been changed from time to time, the Powell style has been maintained. In this sense, a Powell flute made 50 years ago plays and feels the same as one made recently.

This principle is equally true of Haynes and Brannen Brothers flutes. Each company has developed a distinctly recognizable product, transcending individual variations among flutes and design changes over time. Further, this constancy of style and quality has been maintained through the years, even though each instrument has typically been the product of several flutemakers and the workshops have passed through several generations of flutemakers.

ORGANIZATIONAL
LEARNING IN THE FLUTE WORKSHOP

Like playing basketball or a symphony, the knowledge needed to make these flutes of the finest quality resides not in any one individual, but in the organization as a whole. The organization was not "born" with that knowledge; it had to learn it.

We may say that each of the Boston companies, as an organization, knows how to make flutes. Indeed, the know-how required to make one of their instruments from start to finish rarely has been known by a single flutemaker; typically, producing a flute has been a group effort.

Each organization has learned how to produce a flute. The knowledge has been learned collectively, not individually. It is true that each flutemaker knows how to perform his or her individual tasks; but the know-how required to make the flute as a whole resides with the organization, not with the individual flutemaker because only the workshop as a whole can make the flute. This is demonstrated in the fact that when flutemakers have left one of the workshops, the know-how needed to make the flute has not been lost to the organization, as evidenced in the sameness of play and feel of instruments produced by that workshop over the years. The workshop has continued to make flutes of the same quality and style as before because it—the organization, not the individual—possesses the know-how and the ability to make its own particular style of instrument. Typically, neither the flutes nor the way they are made have changed when flutemakers have left one of the workshops.

Moreover, the organizational know-how entailed in flutemaking at each workshop is, in a significant measure, different from that at the others. Although all three know how to make flutes and all follow similar production operations, each makes its own particular flute, one with a unique, unambiguously recognizable style. Thus part of what each workshop knows is unique to it.

Further, such organizational know-how is not meaningfully transferable from one shop to the next; it is deeply embedded in the practices of each workshop. A Haynes flutemaker, for example, could not walk into the Powell workshop, sit down at a bench, and begin making Powell flutes. Over the years, several flutemakers have, in fact, moved from one company to another, and in every instance they have had to be partially retrained, even to do the same jobs they were doing at the other company. They have had to learn a new "feel," a different way of "handling the pieces." Overall, this know-how has been learned not by being given explicit measurements and tolerances, but tacitly, in the hand-to-hand judgments of feel and eye, by working on flutes and having that work judged by the other flutemakers. These judgments are typically expressed in terms of the right look or right feel that are unique to that workshop.

What such a flutemaker knows can be learned only within the context of a specific workshop and only by joining in the collective activity of the workshop as a whole, making its particular instrument. The knowledge of how a finished mechanism, say, should feel can be used only in that workshop. Although each individual possesses the know-how needed to do her portion of the work on the flute, she cannot use that knowledge to produce an entire flute on her own, nor could she produce quality work in the style of a particular workshop except in that particular organizational context.

In this lies an example of organizational learning that does not require overt change on the part of the organization. As a new member, for example, is socialized or acculturated into the organization, learning by the organization takes place: The organization learns how to maintain the style and quality of its flutes through the particular skills, character, and quirks of a new individual. The organization engages in a dynamic process of maintaining the norms and practices that assure the constancy of its product. This is learning in a sense quite different from change-oriented learning: It is the active reaffirmation or maintenance

382   JOURNAL OF MANAGEMENT INQUIRY / December 1993

of the know-how that the organization already possesses. We argue that such organizational learning is better explained from a cultural perspective that assumes the group and group attributes as its unit of analysis than from an individually oriented cognitive perspective. We will expand on this reasoning shortly, after considering an example of explicit change at Powell.

POWELL AND THE COOPER SCALE

Along with more routine changes in personnel, one exceptional episode at Powell reflects how an innovation in product design was also a means of maintaining the organization's identity.

In 1974, Powell became aware of a new scale (the particular arrangement and size of a flute's tone holes that determines the way the flute plays "in tune"). Albert Cooper, an independent English flutemaker, had begun making flutes with a scale he had developed himself. Although he produced only a few flutes a year, several flutists had come to favor his scale over any other. Word of the Cooper scale soon came to Powell's attention, and Powell got in touch with Mr. Cooper. Powell's assessment of the Cooper scale led them to consider the possibility of making a Cooper-scale Powell flute.

For Powell, this possibility was not only a matter of the design of the instrument; it also meant that the workshop would have to accommodate something "new and foreign" within what it knew of itself and of flutemaking. What made this possibility challenging for Powell was that the design of the existing flute—already "the best damned flute in the world," as Powell's president at the time put it—was an integral part of the workshop's identity. Its scale had been developed by Mr. Powell himself and was felt to be an intimate part of the Powell flute. The flutemakers were concerned that in changing the scale, they could be changing the style of the Powell flute, and that would be, in their words, "totally unthinkable."

Their concern seems to have been that adopting a different scale would amount to changing the identity of the company. Yet they had been impressed with the Cooper scale, as had a growing number of flutists. The dilemma was summed up when one flutemaker asked, "If the Powell flute is the best there is, and we want to keep it that way, does that mean we need to change when something new and maybe better comes along?"

The debate continued for some weeks. A prototype Powell flute with a Cooper scale was made. Questions were raised and concerns discussed: Is a Powell flute with a Cooper scale still a Powell flute? Can we make a new scale and still be the same company? Can we change and not let go of quality?

The physical changes in design that the adoption of the Cooper scale would entail were actually quite small. In fact, to the eye, the flute with the new scale and those with the old were very hard to tell apart. Nor would the change be any great threat or challenge to the day-to-day aspects of craftsmanship: Virtually every bit of work could be done without noticing which scale a particular flute was built to. Even with respect to tooling, the change would be a minor matter. For example, once dies were made for the new scale, they could be used in place of the old dies, and work could proceed as usual.

Finally, Powell adopted the Cooper scale. By unanimous vote, the company decided to offer its customers the Powell flute with the new scale. But only as a special option: They would continue to make the Powell flute with the original scale, "and we will do so," Powell's president said, "until we die."

Within a few months, Powell, having brought the Cooper scale to the broad attention of the flute world, saw over 90% of its incoming orders opt for the new scale, and most of the orders on the waiting list were changed by customers to the new option. This soon became the normal pattern, with only a few flutists maintaining their preference for the original Powell scale. The workshop viewed Powell flutes with either scale to be consistent with Powell's standards of quality and style and felt that the Powell flute was "still the best there is."

ORGANIZATIONAL
LEARNING AND THE COOPER SCALE

The Cooper scale episode reflects learning by Powell that in some ways entailed observable change and in others did not. Powell became aware of and assessed the new scale and ultimately made new tooling and offered a new product. All of these are observable changes in a meaningful sense. But Powell also learned in other ways that were equally significant but that did not entail overt change, nor was it a matter of change solely through the vehicle of organizationally key individuals. The workshop succeeded in making an innovation that came to constitute an important shift in the history of flutemaking; yet it did so while leaving unchanged the essential style of the Powell flute and the unique culture of the Powell workshop, in particular, its tacit mode of manufacturing know-how.

The flutes that were made with the Cooper scale were accepted by the flutemakers and by fluteplayers as "Powell flutes." No one ever claimed that the style of the Powell flute had been altered by the change. As one flutemaker observed, "We have only made the best, better."

This particular case of technological change did not involve any essential changes in daily work activities. The only explicit changes were some new tooling that produced the nearly imperceptible changes in the physical dimensions of the instrument necessary for the new scale.

In an important sense, the impetus for change was internal, not external: It did not arise out of a need to improve effectiveness or efficiency or to meet any perceived external challenge to market share or to correct an error. At root, Powell adopted a new technology to maintain and reaffirm its own self-image as makers of "the best"—that is, to sustain what the group felt, believed, and valued.

The decision to produce Powell flutes with both scales was not the resolution of a company conflict: There were no warring camps within the organization over which scale was better, nor was there a feeling that the original scale was in error. Offering both scales was Powell's way of accommodating something new while sustaining the organization's image of itself.

The central issue was the question of organizational identity: Could the organization make a flute with a Cooper scale and still be the Powell organization? For Powell flutemakers specifically, this question focused on their product: Could the organization absorb a new scale into its existing image or sense of "the Powell style"? Would the instrument still be "a Powell"? As organizational members put it, "Can we make a Powell flute with the Cooper scale without it ceasing to be the Powell flute?"

In a very real way, this set of questions can be interpreted to mean, Can we change without changing? Can we make a very deliberate design change and manage it organizationally (strategize about it, implement it, incorporate it into company policy, develop new tooling, etc.) without changing the Powell product and organization into different entities?

This suggests a relationship between change and learning that is different from the customary focus of the cognitive approach. In learning how to make the Cooper scale, Powell mostly learned how to build a flute that was subtly but significantly different without changing the style or identity of their product. Powell's primary concern was as much preservative as it was innovative: learning how to do and make something different without becoming a new and different company; learning how to produce a new scale without changing the essence of the Powell flute.

This concern is reflected both in the making of the instrument and in the deliberations about choosing to go with the Cooper scale. Evaluating the possibility of making a Cooper scale at Powell was both an explicit and implicit exercise. A prototype instrument was made, so some things were necessarily explicit: measurements had to be taken, dies had to be cut, and so forth. Yet this was not done to test the Cooper scale: Mr. Cooper had already made flutes with the Cooper scale, which Powell had seen and tested earlier. Making the prototype enabled Powell, almost ceremonially, to go through the motions of making a Cooper-scale Powell flute and in doing so, to assure itself that the flutes and the company's style would be preserved through the Cooper innovation. Powell was not so much learning a new technology as learning—collectively, as an organization—how to maintain its identity in the face of a new undertaking.

Essentially, the exercise of making the prototype and the discussions about being "the Powell style" were actions aimed at preserving the organization's particular identity. The learning accomplished by Powell involved no reorganization, restructuring of tasks, or recasting criteria for effectiveness; it entailed neither explicit reflections on the practice of flutemaking nor the redrawing of organizational maps.

REFLECTIONS ON CULTURAL LEARNING

Several aspects of the cultural perspective on organizational learning can be noted at this point. First, intuitively it is a much shorter conceptual leap to see organizations as cultural entities than it is to see them as cognitive ones. Organizations, being human groups, are more readily understood as being like tribes than they are as being like individuals or brains. Second, because organizational learning here is understood to involve shared meanings associated with and carried out through cultural artifacts, it is understood as an activity *of* the organization, that is, an activity at the level of the group, not at the level of the individual.

384   JOURNAL OF MANAGEMENT INQUIRY / December 1993

Accordingly, it is seen as conceptually and empirically distinct from learning by individuals in the organization. Third, it is also, then, unnecessary to argue that organizations learn in a way that is fundamentally the same as or similar to individual learning. The cultural perspective makes it possible to explore the meaning of organizational learning by beginning with empirical observations of group action rather than relying on conceptual arguments about likenesses between theories of individual cognition and theories of organizations. Fourth, it allows us to view organizational learning as both an innovative and a preservative activity, thus incorporating into the discussion of organizational learning the rather considerable amount of effort that organizations, like all human groups, put into maintaining the patterns of activity that are unique to each organization.

The cultural perspective and the cognitive perspective both include the study of the activities of individuals. The difference is one of focus: The cognitive perspective takes individual action as its primary point of reference; the cultural perspective focuses on a group of individuals moving within a "net of expectations" ranging from the organization's "explicit constitution to the most subtle mutual understandings between its members" (Vickers, 1976, p. 6). Within the cultural perspective, organizational knowledge is not held by an individual, nor do we see it as the aggregated knowledge of many individuals. What is known is known and made operational only by several individuals acting "in congregate."

The case analysis presented here exemplifies organizational learning as a collective activity rather than an individual one and, quite importantly, as an activity of preservation as well as one of innovation. From this analysis we derive a definition of organizational learning as *the acquiring, sustaining, or changing of intersubjective meanings through the artifactual vehicles of their expression and transmission and the collective actions of the group.*

These meanings, whether they are acquired by new members or created by existing ones, come about and are maintained through interactions among members of the organization. They need not be face-to-face verbal interactions: meaning-making and meaning-sustaining interactions take place just as importantly through the medium of the artifacts of the organization's culture—its symbolic objects, symbolic language, and symbolic acts. Such "artifactual interaction" happens not only in exceptional circumstances of disruption or change but also routinely as part of

"normal" day-to-day work (whether that be production, management, marketing, etc.). Such was the case at Powell.

This means that much of organizational learning, in our view, is tacit, occasioned through experiences of the artifacts of the organization's culture that are part of its daily work. No one says during the course of a typical working day, for example, "Powell values its identity as producer of the flutes with a particular feel to the mechanism." Rather, that part of Powell's culture is incorporated into the artifacts of daily life in the organization. It is reflected, for example, in the company's stories and myths, in the daily judgments of feel and eye, and in the ceremony of making a prototype Powell with a Cooper scale. Through such largely tacit practice and interpretation of artifactual interaction, the members of each workshop sustain their shared "web of meanings" and the group's expectations concerning the quality of workmanship and the style of its product. This sense of artifactual interaction follows Polanyi's formulation (Polanyi & Prosch, 1975) for tacit knowledge: something learned while focusing on something else.[12] Similarly, we argue, organizations learn tacitly, while focusing on "normal" work.

This incorporation of tacit expression and communication is a further point of distinction from the cognitive perspective, which typically requires that those things essential to organizational learning be made explicit, so that they can be communicated. What is to be learned must be "capable *of being stated* [italics added] in terms that are in principle understandable to other members of the organization" (Duncan & Weiss, 1979, p. 86). By contrast, the cultural perspective we propose here argues that what the organization learns may be, and often is, tacitly known, communicated, and understood. In the flute case, not only do the daily hand-to-hand judgments constitute tacit expressions of organizational know-how, but learning and knowing how to recognize the right feel are also transmitted tacitly—for example, in the mastercraftsman's judgments of an apprentice's work. Indeed, in large measure, it was such tacit knowledge that guided the decision making around the adoption of the Cooper scale.

A central concern of organizational learning from this cultural perspective is how an organization constitutes and reconstitutes itself. We have described organizational learning as the acquiring, sustaining, and changing, through collective actions, of the meanings embedded in the organization's cultural artifacts.

Following this, organizational activities, from ordinary daily tasks to major innovations, can be seen to entail the ongoing reconstitution of what is essential to the organization's identity and its ability to do what it does.

One way in which organizations reconstitute themselves is through the acquisition of new members. As new members are successfully integrated into an organization, their actions increasingly exhibit aspects of the group's or organization's culture. Accordingly, the meanings embedded in a new member's actions become compatible with—indeed, become part of—the "web of meaning" embedded in the actions of the group. This is what happens, for example, when an apprentice at one of the workshops begins to use that workshop's metaphors successfully in interactions with other flutemakers or when he becomes able to work within the informal quality control system by judging his own work and that of others as having the right feel, without checking with a mastercraftsman. When a new member's actions "fit in" to group activity, the organization's concerns are thereby confirmed and sustained; that is to say, the organization has reconstituted itself. Organizations also reconstitute themselves through the ordinary day-to-day activities of veteran members. Such activities and their underlying web of meaning mutually confirm and sustain each other.

The flute workshops have engaged in a form of organizational learning that amounts to organizational reconstitution over time as they have passed through successive generations of flutemakers. The personnel have undergone a complete turnover (in some cases more than once), whereas the form of workmanship and the style and quality of the products have remained constant. A provocative parallel can be found in Weick's (1979) example of the Duke Ellington Orchestra continuing long after the Duke had been replaced by his son. Weick reasons that this has been possible because the concept of that orchestra has been continually recreated by the perceptions of its audiences. We suggest that another likely factor is that the orchestra has sustained its identity through long-term organizational learning. Specifically, the ongoing maintenance of the patterns of collective action among the players, intimately bound up with performance itself, has enabled the organization to survive over the years and through a change in personnel (indeed, its leadership!) because the orchestra continued to learn what it needed to do—how it needed to play—to be the Duke Ellington Orchestra.[13]

The focus here is less on what goes on inside the heads of individuals and more on what goes on in the practices of the group (including how those practices are manifested, in part, in individual action). To paraphrase Douglas (1986), rather than seeing the organization as the individual writ large, we would do well to see the individual as the group writ small, each individual carrying those parts of the collective knowledge that make possible individual action with respect to organizational concerns.[14]

Further, organizational reconstitution can be seen as an important feature of organizational change. As the Cooper innovation at Powell suggests, preservation of organizational identity can be a central concern in organizational innovation. Typically, the aim of innovation is for the organization to take on a new situation, not a new identity. Accordingly, a significant part of the effort put into mastering what is new is often concerned with keeping stable what is old. Asking, as the Powell flutemakers did, "Can we undergo this innovation and still remain who we are?" suggests that a major concern of such innovations is the reconstitution of what makes up the identity of the organization, of what it does and how it does it.

In a somewhat similar fashion, Duncan and Weiss (1979), in considering a social basis for organizational learning, focus on shared cognitive frameworks particular to specific organizations. However, echoing the systems view, they maintain that organizational learning involving such frameworks takes place through the detection of a "performance gap" and its closing by the acquisition of organizational knowledge. In contrast, the cultural perspective we have proposed would not limit organizational learning to the closing of performance gaps (although we would certainly wish to include them). The maintenance of patterns of organizational activity (i.e., the reconstitution of the organization) is ongoing, is not dependent on error detection and corrective change, and does not necessarily entail responses to external stimuli. In our view, the dynamic, ongoing preservation of organizational identity is as compelling as an exclusive focus on learning new things and unlearning outlived ones.[15]

CULTURE AND ORGANIZATIONAL LEARNING: CONCLUSION

We began this article by focusing on two questions: Can organizations learn? What is the nature of learning when it is done by organization? It is our view that

386   JOURNAL OF MANAGEMENT INQUIRY / December 1993

in addressing these questions, most authors have adopted a cognitive perspective. They have taken as their common point of reference learning by individuals and have seen organizational learning either as learning by individuals in organizational contexts or as activities of organizations that are akin to learning by individuals. We have argued that the first position tends to blur the useful distinction between learning *in* organizations and learning *by* organizations. The second, we have maintained, raises the conceptually problematic notion that organizations learn the same way people do, which itself entails an unresolved debate about the ontological status of organizations as cognitive entities (an assertion that the cognitive perspective nonetheless seems to require in order to claim that organizations learn). We have noted that, in ways rarely addressed, the cognitive perspective and its insights are dependent on or conceptually linked to theories of individual cognition that are themselves controversial, complex, multiple, and changing. Finally, we have argued that the cognitive perspective's tendency to associate learning with behavioral change derives perhaps as much from its own conceptual predilections as from the realities of organizational life.

By comparison, from a cultural perspective, we have argued (a) that one aspect of the human capacity to act is the ability to act in groups; (b) that a group of people with a history of joint action or practice is meaningfully understood as a culture; (c) that a culture is constituted, at least in part, from the intersubjective meanings that its members express in their common practice through objects, language, and acts; (d) that such meaning-bearing objects, language, and acts are cultural artifacts through which an organization's collective knowledge or know-how is transmitted, expressed, and put to use; and (e) that organizations are constantly involved in activities of modifying or maintaining those meanings and their embodiments—that is, of changing or preserving their cultural identity. Finally, it has been our position that such activities constitute organizational learning. That is, when organizations are seen as cultures, they are seen to learn through activities involving cultural artifacts, and that learning, in turn, is understood to entail organizations' acquiring, changing, or preserving their abilities to do what they know how to do.

This is not to suggest that an organization has only one culture—there is always the possibility that an organization will have multiple cultures, no one of which is dominant, or that there will be a dominant culture and one or more subcultures—nor does it indicate that organizational cultures are created only by managers or founders (see Davis, 1985; Louis, 1985; Yanow, 1992, for discussions and examples of multiple cultures, including those not managerially created). Indeed, the flute case illustrates the role of members in sustaining an organization's culture, even when the original ones are long gone. Although we do not wish to minimize the potential for conflict within or across cultural groups, such is not present in this case. What cultural organizational learning might look like in the face of conflict is a subject for future research. What we have described here is the process of learning by a group that does share cultural meanings. In the flute case, the whole organization constituted such a group; in another context, this might not be so.

The cultural perspective we have proposed rests on a particular understanding of culture that is itself part of a debate in the field. Those who understand culture as an organization's artifacts alone may not find in this essay the sorts of stories, rituals, metaphors, and so forth that add up to culture for them.[16]

But because we see culture as the values, beliefs, and feelings of the organization's members along with their artifacts, we do find culture in the case. Powell identified itself, for example, as a maker of "the finest flutes in the world"; this belief, and the value the organization placed on it, ultimately meant for them that they had to learn how to accommodate the Cooper scale within their practice. And they had to learn this in the face of a paradox. They already made what they held to be the finest flute, and it had a Powell scale. This belief was unchallenged. They had to learn how to think of the Powell flute with the Cooper scale as *also* "the finest flute"—in the face of what might appear as a logical and historical impossibility that there could be two different finest Powell flutes at once. This required them to learn to change not just their beliefs—what Gagliardi (1991, p. 13) calls the "logos" or cognitive part of culture—but also their values and feelings—the "ethos" (the moral experience) and the "pathos" (the sensuous experience) of culture. To see culture in the Powell case, one has to have a theory of culture that includes values, beliefs, and feelings along with their artifactual embodiments. Although calling on the study of organizational learning to include organizational culture as well as cognition, we are also joining those who would like to see the field of organizational culture make its work more inclusive of the noncognitive aspects of human action.

In addition to the above, we find a cultural understanding of organizational learning to be a fruitful approach that suggests further areas of exploration. We would like to speculate on some of these.

Organizations commonly acquire new members. As we noted above, such occasions present an opportunity for an organization to learn, where that learning can be understood to constitute the maintenance or preservation of the know-how associated with an organization's activities and abilities. There is a need for a fuller understanding of how the group and the individual come to hold the shared intersubjective meanings that constitute organizational cultures, as well as of processes by which both "agree to disagree." This cultural perspective suggests that organizational socialization is not simply a question of "How do you socialize Smith into IBM?" (because that constitutes learning by Smith, the individual, not IBM, the organization) but rather the fuller question, "How does IBM renourish itself with new members, yet ensure its continuity?" Socialization typically suggests movement in a single direction: IBM socializes Smith, where Smith is relatively passive, a receptive vessel. From the cultural perspective, for Smith to become a member of IBM (or of a unit within IBM), she must form an understanding of the meaning of those elements of IBM's culture that enable her to carry out her role effectively within it (a point where individual cognition may properly and profitably enter the discussion). IBM, meanwhile, must learn how to make Smith's actions compatible with the actions (and underlying meanings) of other members of its culture and to do so in a way that fosters its own continuity, flourishing, and survival. Cultural organizational learning would focus on the *mutual* creation of compatible and shared meanings.

Would one find the same tacit, artifactual interaction in a larger, more highly differentiated organization? We agree with Ed Schein (personal communication, June 1988) that the theoretical premises remain the same, regardless of differences in size and structure. We suggest, however, that cultural learning as we have described it may be more easily seen when size is small and structure is simple. Such would be the case with subunits of large organizations.

Similarly, our presentation of culture as an organization-wide phenonmenon may be an artifact of Powell's relatively small size. We do not mean to suggest that organizations have only single cultures. It does seem to us, however, that cultural learning across subcultures within a single organization, even in the presence of differences, disagreements, perhaps hostility, will take place—if at all—through the tacit

processes of artifactual interaction we have discussed. The question indeed is whether learning will take place under such circumstances, whether it will be preservative or not, and if so, of what. How and whether it happens is likely to be context specific; that it might be preservative learning is a possibility to entertain in any context. As the field of organizational culture itself develops theories of power, our understanding of cultural learning will benefit.

Finally, from the emphasis on error detection and correction inherited from the systems view, it has been a logical step for the cognitive perspective to develop the normative position that organizations *ought* to have the ability to detect and correct errors. This, in turn, has supported the claim that when organizations detect and correct errors, they have "learned." In this fashion, the cognitive perspective has evolved a substantially problem-oriented and problem-solving understanding of organizational learning: If learning is about correcting errors, then learning is about things that have gone wrong.

But, as Vickers (personal communication, January 1981) has pointed out, an orientation toward what goes wrong does not necessarily yield the sum total of what is interesting or vital about organizational life. What goes right can also be of interest, and is so, we would argue, for the very reason that it accounts for much of what organizations do. We hold that a cultural theory of organizational learning enables one to focus as much on the right as on the wrong and as much on continuity and preservation as on change. We believe this to be a fruitful area for further exploration.

Vickers (1976) intended his focus on the cultural nature of institutional change "to challenge some widely held beliefs about the role and dominance of cognition" (p. 7). We do not assume for ourselves the whole of this challenge, but we would be pleased if our observations were to further the current explorations of the role that culture plays in our lives, particularly that growing portion that is spent in maintaining and changing our institutions.

NOTES

1. This discussion of organizational learning as individual learning has a parallel in organizational behavior that has at times been a source of confusion—specifically, whether "organizational behavior" refers to the behavior of individuals within organizations or to the collective behaviors of organizations themselves. The use of the individual as a model for the group, and vice versa, has a long history.

It may be found in philosophy and social science in discussions that trace their lineage, in one sense, to Mead (1934) or, in another sense, to Hobbes (1651/1958). Indeed, it can be found as far back as Plato (Hamilton & Cairns, 1961) when, for example, Socrates suggests that just as large letters can be easier to read than small ones, we should not look first to discover justice in the individual but rather in the state, where the "letters exist . . . larger," and only after finding it there should we look for it in individuals, recognizing then "the likeness of the greater in the form of the less."

2. Duncan and Weiss (1979) develop a similar critique in their finding that individual learning within an organizational setting, as presented by March and Olsen (1976) and Argyris and Schön (1978), has limitations for producing understanding of "systematic organization action."

3. In other respects, however, their work is an exception to the following discussion.

4. For that matter, even within research on individual cognition there is a great deal of attention given to variations in how learning occurs across individuals and within one individual over time (see, for example, Gardner, 1983).

5. It seems to us that the concept of organizational learning began to attract attention in the mid-1970s, in part in response to theories of organizational change from the previous decade that called for radical changes in the social, political, and corporate worlds. The concept of organizational *learning* provided a noncontroversial, conservative, yet dynamic, alternative for addressing the issue of change because, traditionally, learning is not seen as a controversial or radical activity. It also provided a tool for intervention. Its psychological origins made it a manageable tool, in that it targeted problems in single individuals, who could be helped to learn, in contrast with radical change theories rooted in analyses of the sociopolitical structure that demanded change in "the system."

We also note that a learning approach to organizational change addresses implicitly one of the problems that arose in early T-group change efforts. Practitioners using T-groups came to note that although T-groups produced learning and change in individuals, those changes were often challenged when these individuals returned from the training to the organization, and, as a consequence, what those individuals learned was sometimes lost. Seeing organizational change as the result of learning by key individuals within an organization conceptually avoids the problem of translating individual learning into organizational learning.

6. Although inventions and innovations are often the products of single individuals, part of the process of building an organization is a matter of embedding the know-how required for the ongoing production and adaptation of these products into the organization itself. Karl Weick has called to our attention a series of social psychological experiments that modeled cultural transmission within a group, similar to our discussion here, as subjects are replaced over successive generations of the experiment. The research found that the small group's simple strategy survived changes in membership. This research is reported in Weick and Gilfillan (1971).

7. Bateson (1958) was perhaps the first to analyze the problem of learning by a group, in his 1936 study of how the Iatmul culture learned to accommodate change. In his epilogue to the later edition of the book, he elaborated on the concept of "schismogenesis" to describe this process. Much influenced by his interim studies in psychology, Bateson introduced the concept of "deutero-learning"—"learning to learn"—as the way in which groups and individuals manage a changing environment.

8. We are, of course, limited by the English language to describing organizational actions using verbs appropriate to individual action, thereby appearing ourselves to anthropomorphize organizations. This conceptualization of organizational activity is further promoted by the use of a singular verb for group action—for example, the organization *knows*—mandated by accepted rules of English usage. On the other hand, such usage bolsters our conceptualization of the organization as an entity that can take action that is other than the sum of its parts.

9. There is no single definition or theory of culture in either the interdisciplinary field of organizational culture studies or in its disciplinary "homes" of anthropology or sociology. Ouchi and Wilkins (1985) noted this quite thoroughly in their review of the several literatures whose theories and debates underlie and inform work in organizationally oriented culture studies. We place ourselves in the school that considers both meanings and their artifactual expressions to be necessary components of culture. When we refer to a cultural perspective in this essay, we have in mind one informed by such an interpretive theoretical position. We cannot in this article explore the ways in which cultural learning might look different according to one's theoretical position regarding the nature of culture, but we wish to acknowledge that this might be the case and might be a useful area for further research.

10. Properly speaking, symbols, rituals, myths, and so forth are *not* the artifacts of an organization's culture; annual reports, statements of corporate philosophy, award celebrations, daily talk about the specifics of work, and so forth are the artifacts. The former terms are analytic vocabulary that characterize and categorize the actual artifacts. As tools of research, these terms draw attention to certain features of organizational life; in fact, they incorporate the rules and conventions by which such categories are formed. This point is germane to a central methodological issue in the study of organizational cultures: Because the analytic categories are essentially constructs of the observer, care must be taken not to confuse them with organizational experience itself.

11. This case is based on extensive observation and interviewing over a period of several years, including numerous visits to all three workshops, detailed interviews with all key personnel, and "shop floor" interviews with flutemakers and apprentices at all levels. The case as presented here draws, as well, on Cook (1982). Our theoretical interest in culture as an approach to organizational learning initially grew out of our considerations of the flute case. Since then, we have moved back and forth between theory building and exploration of the case in developing the view presented here. In this sense, both our experience and the form of this essay reflect a recursive interpretive, or hermeneutic, circle.

12. One of Polanyi's examples is of bicycle riding, where balance is learned tacitly while focusing on pedaling or

steering or some other target of attention. On a related subject, Brown and Duguid (1991) have explored ways that practitioners communicate and learn skills tacitly in daily practice.

13. We have had this point further confirmed in a personal conversation with a member of the Juilliard String Quartet. Over more than two decades the quartet has replaced all but one of its original members. One of the newest members reports that his experience of learning to play in the style of the Juilliard and his contributions to the evolution of that style were never a subject of explicit conversation but were carried out through the playing of the music itself in rehearsal and performance.

14. For Douglas (1986), such concerns in a societal context include classification systems, institutional memory and forgetfulness, and group identity. She addresses the issue of attributing emotions, behaviors, or thought to institutions, and argues that thinking itself forms the social bond among individuals and binds them in a corporate entity. In a similar sense, Bougon, Weick, and Binkhorst (1977) held that "what ties an organization together is what ties thought together" (p. 626). What we are suggesting is an approach that adds to thinking what Vickers (1973) called "appreciating," that would include values and feelings along with artifacts and practices as the organizational glue.

15. It is possible that we have been disposed to find ongoing conservation, preservation, and reconstitution at work in seeing learning as an aspect of culture. As anthropologists Marcus and Fischer (1986) noted about work in their field, "The drive remains strong . . . to show repeatedly how the tradition and the deep structures of cultures shine through despite change" (p. 181). One of the criticisms levied at phenomenological analyses of human reality is that they are concerned with societal stability and order to the exclusion of change. We hope we have sufficiently illustrated our concern with change as a part of human action. The exception that we take with the cognitive approach to organizational learning is its nearly exclusive concern with change.

16. Related to this, we differ with those who see culture as one of several elements of an organization. Levitt and March (1988), for example, in arguing that organizations learn "by encoding inferences from history into routines that guide behavior," use the term *routines* to include "forms, rules, procedures, conventions, strategies and technologies" along with "beliefs, frameworks, paradigms, codes, cultures and knowledge" (p. 320). Because we understand culture not as something that an organization possesses, but as something constitutive of it, we would not see culture as one of several avenues for carrying out routines, but rather would see routines, as well as many of the other items on their list, as elements or artifacts of an organizational culture.

REFERENCES

Argyris, C., & Schön, D. A. (1978). *Organizational learning.* Reading, MA: Addison-Wesley.

Bateson, G. (1958). *Naven* (2nd ed.). Stanford, CA: Stanford University Press.

Berger, P. L., & Luckmann, T. (1966). *The social construction of reality.* New York: Doubleday.

Bolman, L. (1976). Organizational learning. In C. Argyris (Ed.), *Increasing leadership effectiveness.* New York: Wiley.

Bougon, M., Weick, K., & Binkhorst, D. (1977). Cognition in organizations: An analysis of the Utrecht Jazz Orchestra. *Administrative Science Quarterly, 22,* 606-639.

Brown, J. S., & Duguid, P. (1991). Organizational learning and communities-of-practice: Toward a unified view of working, learning, and innovation. *Organizational Science, 2,* 40-57.

Cook, S.D.N. (1982). *Part of what judgment is.* Doctoral dissertation, Massachusetts Institute of Technology.

Cyert, R. M., & March, J. G. (1963). *A behavioral theory of the firm.* Englewood Cliffs, NJ: Prentice-Hall.

Davis, T.R.V. (1985). Managing culture at the bottom. In R. H. Kilmann, M. J. Saxton, R. Serpa, & Associates (Eds.), *Gaining control of the corporate culture.* San Francisco: Jossey-Bass.

Douglas, M. (1986). *How institutions think.* Syracuse, NY: Syracuse University Press.

Duncan, R., & Weiss, A. (1979). Organizational learning. *Research in Organizational Behavior, 1,* 75-123.

Etheredge, L. S., & Short, J. (1983). Thinking about government learning. *Journal of Management Studies, 20,* 41-58.

Fiol, C. M., & Lyles, M. A. (1985). Organizational learning. *Academy of Management Review, 10,* 803-813.

Frost, P. J., Moore, L. F., Louis, M. R., Lundberg, C. C., & Martin, J. (1985). *Organizational culture.* Beverly Hills, CA: Sage.

Frost, P. J., Moore, L. F., Louis, M. R., Lundberg, C. C., & Martin, J. (1991). *Reframing organizational cultures.* Newbury Park, CA: Sage.

Gagliardi, P. (1991). Artifacts as pathways and remains of organization life. In P. Gagliardi (Ed.), *Symbols and artifacts.* New York: Aldine de Gruyter.

Gahmberg, H. (1980). *Contact patterns and learning in organizations: With a network analysis in two industrial organizations.* Helsinki, Finland: Helsinki School of Economics.

Gardner, H. (1983). *Frames of mind.* New York: Basic Books.

Hamilton, E. & Cairns, H. (Eds.). (1961). *The collected dialogues of Plato.* Princeton, NJ: Princeton University Press.

Hedberg, B. (1981). How orgnizations learn and unlearn. In P. C. Nystrom & W. H. Starbuck (Eds.), *Handbook of organizational design.* London: Oxford University Press.

Herriott, S. R., Levinthal, D. A., & March, J. G. (1985). Learning from experience in organizations. *American Economic Review, 75,* 298-302.

Hobbes, T. (1958). *Leviathan.* New York: Bobbs-Merrill. (Original work published in 1651)

Jenkins-Smith, H. C., & St. Clair, G. with the assistance of James, R. (1988, March). *Analysis of change in elite policy beliefs within subsystems.* Paper presented at the annual meeting of the Western Political Science Association, San Francisco.

Lant, T. K., & Mezias, S. J. (1990). Managing discontinuous change: A simulation study of organizational learning and entrepreneurship. *Strategic Management Journal, 11,* 147-179.

390   JOURNAL OF MANAGEMENT INQUIRY / December 1993

Levitt, B., & March, J. G. (1988). Organizational learning. *Annual Review of Sociology, 14,* 319-340.

Louis, M. R. (1985). Sourcing workplace cultures. In R. H. Kilmann, M.J. Saxton, R. Serpa, & Associates (Eds.), *Gaining control of the corporate culture.* San Francisco: Jossey-Bass.

March, J. G., & Olsen, J. P. (1976). Organizational learning and the ambiguity of the past. In *Ambiguity and choice in orgnizations.* Oslo, Norway: Universitetsforlaget.

Marcus, G. & Fischer, M.M.J. (1986). *Anthropology as cultural critique.* Chicago: University of Chicago Press.

Mead, G. H. (1934). *Mind, self and society.* Chicago: University of Chicago.

Miles, R. H., & Randolph, W. A. (1981). Influence of organizational learning styles on early development. In J. R. Kimberly & R. H. Miles (Eds.), *The organizational life cycle.* San Francisco: Jossey-Bass.

Morgan, G. (1986). *Images of organization.* Beverly Hills, CA: Sage.

Ouchi, W. G., & Wilkins, A. L. (1985). Organizational culture. *Annual Review of Sociology, 11,* 457-483.

Polanyi, M., & Prosch, H. (1975). *Meaning.* Chicago: University of Chicago Press.

Sandelands, L. E., & Stablein, R. E. (1987). The concept of organization mind. *Research in the Sociology of Organizations, 5,* 135-161.

Schein, E. H. (1985). *Organizational culture and leadership.* San Francisco: Jossey-Bass.

Shrivastava, P. (1983). A typology of organizational learning systems. *Journal of Management Studies, 20*(1), 7-28.

Simon, H. A. (1991). Bounded rationality and organizational learning. *Organization Science, 2,* 125-134.

Sims, H. P., Jr., Gioia, D. A., & Associates. (1986). *The thinking organization: Dynamics of organizational social cognition.* San Francisco: Jossey-Bass.

Sitkin, S. B. (1992). Learning through failure: The strategy of small losses. *Research in Organizational Behavior, 14,* 231-266.

Smircich, L. (1983). Concepts of culture and organizational analysis. *Administrative Science Quarterly, 28*(3), 339-358.

Taylor, C. (1979). Interpretation and the sciences of man. In P. Rabinow & W. M. Sullivan (Eds.), *Interpretive social science: A reader.* Berkeley: University of California Press.

Vickers, G. (1973). *Making institutions work.* London: Associated Business Programmes.

Vickers, G. (1976, November). *Institutional learning as controlled cultural change.* Paper presented at the Division for Study in Research and Education, Massachusetts Institute of Technology.

Weick, K. E. (1979). Cognitive processes in organizations. *Research in Organizational Behavior, 1,* 41-74.

Weick, K. E. (1991). The nontraditional quality of organizational learning. *Organizational Science, 2*(1), 41-73.

Weick, K. E., & Gilfillan, D. P. (1971). Fact of arbitrary traditions in a lab microculture. *Journal of Personality and Social Psychology, 17,* 179-191.

Weiss, C. (1980, December). *Policy evaluation as societal learning.* Paper presented at the Pinhas Sapir Conference on Development, Tel Aviv, Israel.

Yanow, D. (1992). Supermarkets and culture clash: The epistemological role of metaphors in administrative practice. *American Review of Public Adminstration, 22*(2), 89-109.

Part V
Leadership

Another classical theme, leadership, was inherited from social psychology and transformed according to the needs of organization theory. A review article by Gary Yukl (Chapter 13) has served as a passage point, summarizing older research and pointing towards new venues. But soon enough, the cultural and symbolist wave reached this issue as well. Jeffrey Pfeffer's article (Chapter 14) on the symbolic role of leaders continues to inspire today's research for the new turn it took towards dramatic performances and representation. But it was Linda Smircich and Gareth Morgan's (Chapter 15) inspired use of *gestalt* psychology that powerfully re-framed leadership as management of meaning, a notion that was further developed by Karl Weick in his concept of sensemaking (see Volume II, Part III).

[13]

ORGANIZATIONAL BEHAVIOR AND HUMAN PERFORMANCE **6**, 414–440 (1971)

Toward a Behavioral Theory of Leadership[1]

Gary Yukl

*Department of Psychology, The University of Akron,
Akron, Ohio 44304*

A great deal of the apparent inconsistency in the leadership literature may be due to semantic confusion about leader behavior and to the absence of a conceptual framework which includes intermediate and situational variables. A system of three distinct leader behavior dimensions is proposed to reduce this confusion. Two of the dimensions are similar to the familiar variables, Consideration and Initiating Structure. The third dimension, Decision-Centralization, refers to the extent to which a leader allows his subordinates to participate in decision-making. A discrepancy model is developed to explain the relation between leader behavior and subordinate satisfaction with the leader. A multiple linkage model is developed to explain how the leader behavior variables interact with situational variables to determine group productivity. A review of the leadership literature revealed that the results of previous research are generally consistent with the proposed models. The compatibility of the linkage model with Fiedler's Contingency Model is discussed, and suggestions for future research are offered.

Despite over two decades of extensive leadership research, the relation of leader behavior to subordinate productivity and satisfaction with the leader is still not very clear. The apparent absence of consistent relationships in the research literature (Sales, 1966; Korman, 1966; Lowin, 1968) may be due in part to several related problems. First, there is a great deal of semantic confusion regarding the conceptual and operational definition of leadership behavior. Over the years there has been a proliferation of leader behavior terms, and the same term is often defined differently from one study to the next. Secondly, a great deal of empirical data has been collected, but a theoretical framework which adequately explains causal relationships and identifies limiting conditions has not yet emerged. Finally, the research has often failed to include intermediate and situational variables which are necessary in order to understand how a leader's actions can affect his subordinates' productivity.

The purpose of this article is to begin the development of a theory which explains how leader behavior, situational variables, and inter-

---

[1] The author is grateful to Ken Wexley and Alexis Anikeeff for their helpful comments.

mediate variables interact to determine subordinate productivity and satisfaction with the leader. In the first section of the article, a system of three distinct and generally applicable leader behavior dimensions will be proposed. In the next two sections, these leadership dimensions will be used to develop a discrepancy model of subordinate satisfaction and a multiple linkage model of leader effectiveness. Finally, the extent to which the research literature supports these behavioral models will be evaluated.

CLASSIFICATION OF LEADER BEHAVIOR

Consideration and Initiating Structure

Some early investigators began with a list of very specific leadership activities (e.g., "inspection," "write reports," "hear complaints") and attempted to determine how performance of these activities or the amount of time allocated to them related to leader success. Since the number of specific leader activities that are possible is nearly endless, several Ohio State University psychologists attempted to find a few general behavior dimensions which would apply to all types of leaders. Factor analyses of leadership behavior questionnaires were carried out, and two orthogonal factors were found (Hemphill & Coons, 1957; Halpin & Winer, 1957). These factors were called Consideration and Initiating Structure. Consideration refers to the degree to which a leader acts in a warm and supportive manner and shows concern and respect for his subordinates. Initiating Structure refers to the degree to which a leader defines and structures his own role and those of his subordinates toward goal attainment.

The principal method for measuring these variables has been the use of either the Leader Behavior Description Questionnaire (Hemphill & Coons, 1957) or the Supervisory Behavior Description questionnaire (Fleishman, 1957a). These questionnaires are administered to a leader's subordinates. A related questionnaire, called the Leadership Opinion Questionnaire (Fleishman, 1957b), is administered to the leader himself. This questionnaire is considered to be a measure of leader attitudes rather than leader behavior. Occasionally other observers, such as peers or superiors, are the source of leader behavior descriptions, and in some studies Consideration and Initiating Structure are experimentally manipulated by having leaders play predetermined roles.

Decision-Centralization

A somewhat different approach to the classification of leaders was initiated by Lewin's (1944) theoretical typology of democratic, autocratic, and laissez-faire leaders. Studies following in this tradition have usually focused on the relative degree of leader and subordinate influence over the group's decisions. The various decision-making procedures used by a leader, such as delegation, joint decision-making, consultation, and autocratic decision-making, can be ordered along a continuum ranging from high subordinate influence to complete leader influence. Although a leader will usually allow more subordinate participation and influence for some decisions than for others, the average degree of participation can be computed for any specified set of typical decisions. Heller and Yukl (1969) have used the term "Decision-Centralization" to refer to this average. A high Decision-Centralization score means a low amount of subordinate participation. Naturally, a leader is capable of voluntarily sharing decision-making with his subordinates only to the extent that he has authority to make decisions.

Most methods that have been used to measure participation can also be regarded as a measure of Decision-Centralization. Participation and Decision-Centralization have been measured by subordinate ratings of their perceived autonomy or influence in decision-making, by subordinate responses to a questionnaire concerning the leader's decision behavior, and by leader responses to a decision behavior questionnaire. In some studies the leader's actual decision-making behavior has been experimentally manipulated. The term Decision-Centralization was introduced for two reasons. First, this term emphasizes the behavior of the leader rather than the behavior of the subordinates. Second, the definition of Decision-Centralization explicitly encompasses a greater variety of leader decision procedures than does the typical definition of participation (Heller & Yukl, 1969).[2]

Reconciling the Two Approaches to Leader Behavior Classification

Is Decision-Centralization equivalent to Consideration and Initiating Structure, or is it a distinct leadership dimension? The degree to which the three dimensions are independent depends upon the precise definitions given them. Since the definitions vary from study to study, it is not surprising that there is some disagreement regarding the relation between these dimensions. For example, Lowin (1968) has suggested that Initiating Structure is conceptually similar to autocratic supervision, Sales (1966) has suggested that "employee orientation" (which includes high Consideration) is usually associated with democratic leadership, and Newport (1962) has suggested that Consideration and Initiating Struc-

---

[2] Despite my preference for the term Decision-Centralization, the more familiar term participation will usually be used when discussing the direction of correlations in order to avoid confusion.

ture are similar, respectively, to democratic and autocratic leadership. On the other hand, Gomberg (1966), McMurry (1958), Schoenfeld (1959), and Stanton (1962) have claimed that high Consideration and autocratic leadership are not incompatible, or in other words, that Consideration and Decision-Centralization are separate dimensions.

There are several sound theoretical arguments for treating Decision-Centralization as a separate dimension of leader behavior. Let us look first at the relation between Consideration and Decision-Centralization. The Consideration scale in the Ohio State questionnaires includes several items pertaining to the decision-making participation of subordinates, and Consideration is sometimes defined as including the sharing of decision-making with subordinates. However, one can argue that this sharing is only considerate of subordinates when they clearly desire participation, and the desire for participation can vary substantially from person to person and from situation to situation. Inclusion of participation items in a Consideration scale results in scores which are not comparable across persons unless first adjusted for differences in participation preferences. It is more practical to define Consideration as simply the degree to which a leader's behavior expresses a positive attitude rather than an indifferent or negative attitude toward subordinates. When defined in this manner, Consideration can be regarded as conceptually distinct from Decision-Centralization. In general, a high Consideration leader is friendly, supportive, and considerate; a low Consideration leader is hostile, punitive, and inconsiderate. A leader who acts indifferent and aloof is between these extremes but is closer to the low end of the continuum. The specific behaviors used in scaling Consideration should be generally applicable to all types of leadership situations.

What about the relation between Decision-Centralization and Initiating Structure? Although Initiating Structure is defined broadly as task-oriented behavior, it appears to include at least three types of task behavior: (1) Behavior indicating the leader's concern about productivity (e.g., goal-oriented comments to subordinates, and use of various rewards and punishments to encourage productivity), (2) behavior insuring that necessary task decisions are made, and (3) behavior insuring that these decisions and directives from higher levels in the organization are carried out (e.g., training and supervision). Note that this definition does not specify who will actually make the decisions. The task orientation of the leader does not appear to be very closely related to the amount of influence he will allow subordinates in the making of task or maintenance decisions. Even very autocratic leaders can differ considerably with respect to their task orientation and concern about group performance. Therefore, it seems reasonable to treat Initiating Structure and Decision-Centralization as separate dimensions of leader behavior.

The empirical evidence on the relation of Decision-Centralization to Consideration and Initiating Structure is scanty, and the research which will be cited should be regarded as suggestive rather than conclusive. Most of these studies use the Consideration scale of the Leader Behavior Description Questionnaire, which includes some participation items. Naturally these items increase the likelihood of finding a significant correlation between Consideration and Decision-Centralization.

In a study of 67 second-line supervisors in three companies, this author found a low but significant correlation ($r = -.24$; $p < .05$) between Consideration and Decision-Centralization. Decision-Centralization was measured by means of leader responses on the decision procedure questionnaire (Form C) described in Heller and Yukl (1968). There was no significant correlation between Decision-Centralization and Initiating Structure.

Other evidence is provided by analyses of a more recent version of the Leader Behavior Description Questionnaire, which has ten new subscales in addition to the original scales for Consideration and Initiating Structure. One of the new scales, called "Tolerance of Member Freedom," can be regarded as a measure of participation or Decision-Centralization. Stogdill, Goode, and Day (1962, 1963, 1964) administered this questionnaire to "subordinates" of corporation presidents, labor union presidents, community leaders, and ministers. The correlations between Consideration and Tolerance of Member Freedom for the four samples, respectively, were .41, .42, .40, and .49. For a sample of office supervisors rated by female subordinates on this questionnaire, the correlation was .50 (Beer, 1966).[3] Decision-Centralization and Initiating Structure were not significantly correlated in any of the five samples just described.

Argyle, Gardner, and Cioffi (1957) analyzed the relation among leadership dimensions as measured by questionnaires administered to managers in England. Democratic (vs authoritarian) leadership correlated .41 with nonpunitive (vs punitive) leadership. Democratic leadership was not significantly correlated with pressure for production, a component of Initiating Structure.

If we remember to reverse the sign of the correlation when necessary in order to correct for the fact that high participation equals low Decision-Centralization, then it is obvious that the results of these studies are remarkably consistent. Decision-Centralization and Initiating Struc-

---

[3] Significance levels for the correlations were not given, but judging from the sample sizes, they should all be significant at the .05 level or better.

ture appear to be independent dimensions. Decision-Centralization and Consideration should probably be regarded as oblique rather than orthogonal dimensions. That is, there will tend to be a low to moderate negative correlation between them, but some leaders will have high scores on both dimensions ("benevolent autocrat") and some leaders will have low scores on both dimensions ("malevolent democrat").

A DISCREPANCY MODEL OF SUBORDINATE SATISFACTION WITH THE LEADER

In this section, a discrepancy model of satisfaction will be used to explain the relation of the three leadership dimensions to subordinate satisfaction with the leader. Discrepancy or subtraction models of job satisfaction have been proposed by a number of psychologists (Morse, 1953; Schaffer, 1953; Rosen & Rosen, 1955; Ross & Zander, 1957; Porter, 1962; Katzell, 1964; Locke, 1969). In a discrepancy model, satisfaction is a function of the difference between a person's preferences and his actual experience. The less the discrepancy between preferences and experience, the greater the satisfaction. This hypothesis has received some support in the studies cited above, but the evidence is by no means conclusive. In some versions of the discrepancy model there is a second hypothesis which states that the amount of dissatisfaction with a given discrepancy also depends upon the importance of the needs affecting the preference level. If importance varies from person to person, the discrepancy scores cannot be compared unless first adjusted for importance. Whether such a correction is necessary, and if so, how it should be made appears to be a matter of growing controversy.

Although the discrepancy model appears to be applicable to the analysis of subordinates' satisfaction with their leader, only a few studies have used it for this purpose. In two of these studies (Foa, 1957; Greer, 1961), leadership variables other than Consideration, Initiating Structure, and Decision-Centralization were used. No studies were found which included subordinate preferences for Consideration and Initiating Structure as a moderating variable. The results from studies which have included subordinate preferences for participation in decision-making tend to be consistent with the discrepancy model.

According to the proposed discrepancy model, the shape of the curve relating leader behavior to subordinate satisfaction will vary somewhat depending upon a subordinate's preference level. A preference level will be defined tentatively as a range of leader behavior acceptable to subordinates rather than as a single point on a behavior continuum. Figure 1 shows the theoretical curves for a low, medium, and high preference level. The curves represent the relation for a single subordinate. When

GARY YUKL

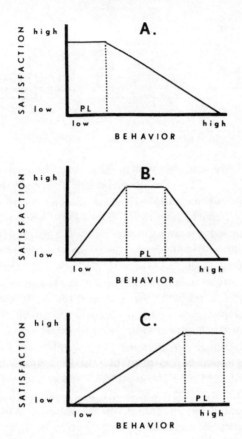

FIG. 1. The relation between leader behavior and subordinate satisfaction for a low, medium, and high preference level (PL).

the preference levels of group members are relatively homogeneous, the relation between leader behavior and average group satisfaction with their leader will yield a curve similar to that for an individual. However, the more variable the preferences are in a group, the less likely it is that any significant relation will be found between leader behavior and average group satisfaction.

Subordinate preference levels are determined both by subordinate personality and by situational variables (see Fig. 2). Preferences can be expected to vary more for Initiating Structure and Decision-Centralization than for Consideration. Except for a few masochists, is is probably safe to assume that subordinates will desire a high degree of considerate behavior by their leaders. As a result, the function relating Consideration and subordinate satisfaction should resemble curve C in Fig. 1.

Preference levels for Decision-Centralization, i.e., the subordinate's

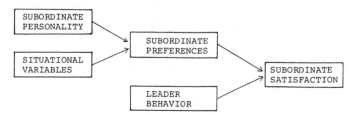

FIG. 2. A discrepancy model of subordinate satisfaction with the leader.

desire for participation in decision-making, may be partially determined by two personality traits: Authoritarianism (Vroom, 1959) and "need for independence" (Trow, 1957; Ross & Zander, 1957; Vroom, 1959; Beer, 1966, p. 51; French, Kay, & Meyer, 1966). Although none of these investigators assessed the relation between a personality measure and expressed behavior preferences, they did find that personality had the expected moderating effect upon the relation between Decision-Centralization and subordinate satisfaction. However, it should be noted that Tosi (1970) was not able to replicate the results of the study by Vroom (1959). The measurement of subordinate preferences in future replications may aid in clearing up the contradiction between these two studies.

The major situational determinant of the preference level for participation in making a decision is probably the importance of that decision for the subordinate (Maier, 1965, p. 165). When a decision is very important to subordinates, they are likely to prefer as much influence as possible (e.g., joint decision-making or delegation). When decisions do not involve matters of importance, consultation or even autocratic decision-making is more likely to be preferred. Of course, the more that subordinates trust their leader to make a decision favorable to them, the less need they will feel to participate in order to protect their interests. Also, when the subordinates are committed to group goal attainment or survival and the task or environment favors centralized decision-making (e.g., a crisis), then they are likely to expect the leader to make most of the decisions (Mulder & Stemerding, 1963).

Preference levels for Initiating Structure are partially determined by the subordinates' commitment to group goals and their perception of the amount of structuring that is necessary to help the group attain these goals. Subordinates who are indifferent about or hostile toward the goal of maximum productivity are likely to prefer a leader who is not very task oriented in his behavior.

Summary of the Discrepancy Model

The major features of the proposed discrepancy model can be summarized in terms of the following hypotheses:

Hyp 1: Subordinate satisfaction with the leader is a function of the discrepancy between actual leader behavior and the behavior preferences of subordinates.

Hyp 2: Subordinate preferences are determined by the combined effect of subordinate personality and situational variables.

Hyp 3: Subordinates usually prefer a high degree of leader Consideration, and this preference level results in a positive relation between Consideration and subordinate satisfaction.

The discrepancy model in its present form is only a static model representing one-way causality at one point in time. No attempt has been made to include additional complexities such as the effects of leader behavior on subordinate preferences. For example, a leader who gradually allows greater subordinate participation may find that the subordinates' preference for decision-making increases over time. Nor does the model explicitly deal with such other determinants of subordinate satisfaction with the leader as his intelligence or the feedback effects from successful or unsuccessful group performance. Finally, the influence of various components of the model on leader behavior has also been ignored. For example, subordinate preferences represent one of several sources of role expectations for the leader, and these role expectations interact with other situational variables and leader personality to determine his behavior.

A MULTIPLE LINKAGE MODEL OF LEADER EFFECTIVENESS

When a leader is dependent upon his subordinates to do the work, subordinate performance is unlikely to improve unless the leader can increase one or more of the following three intermediate variables: (1) Subordinate task motivation (i.e., effort devoted to their tasks), (2) subordinate task skills, and (3) Task-Role Organization (i.e., the technical quality of task decisions).[4] Consideration, Initiating Structure, Decision-Centralization, and various situational variables interact in their effects on these intermediate variables. The intermediate variables interact in turn to determine group performance (see Fig. 3).

Consideration, Initiating Structure, and Subordinate Motivation

Consideration and Initiating Structure interact in their effect upon subordinate task motivation. Subordinate task motivation will be highest when the leader is high on both Consideration and Initiating Structure.

---

[4] The leader can also improve productivity by obtaining necessary information, resources, and cooperation from other organization members and outside agencies, but this involves leader behavior outside the context of the work group.

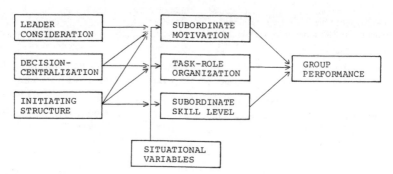

Fɪɢ. 3. A multiple linkage model of leader effectiveness.

The ordering of the other combinations is less certain, because the interaction appears to be highly complex and irregular. If leaders were subgrouped according to their Initiating Structure scores, for high structuring leaders there would probably be a positive relation between Consideration and subordinate task motivation. For low structuring leaders, there is some reason to suspect that the relation between Consideration and subordinate motivation is described by an inverted U-shaped curve. In other words, subordinate task motivation can be adversely affected when the low structuring leader is either very supportive and friendly or very hostile and punitive.

There are at least two hypotheses for explaining the interaction between Consideration and Initiating Structure, and it is not yet clear if either or both are correct. From instrumentality theory (Vroom, 1964, p. 220; Galbraith & Cummings, 1967), comes the hypothesis that a leader can improve subordinate performance by being highly considerate to subordinates who make an effort to perform well, while withholding Consideration from subordinates who show little task motivation. In effect, considerate behavior is a reward which is contingent upon the display of certain task-motivated behavior by subordinates.

The "identification" hypothesis proposes that subordinate motivation is a response to previous leader Consideration rather than an attempt to obtain future Consideration. As Consideration increases, subordinate attitudes toward the leader become more favorable and his influence over the subordinates increases correspondingly. In effect, the considerate leader has greater "referent power" (French & Raven, 1959). However, in order for subordinate loyalty to be translated into task motivation, it is necessary for the leader to communicate a concern for productivity. If the leader is highly considerate but does not stress productivity, the subordinates are likely to feel that they can safely neglect their tasks.

424   GARY YUKL

If a leader actually becomes hostile and punitive, it is likely that subordinate task motivation will be adversely affected, regardless of the level of Initiating Structure. Punitive leadership can lead to counter-aggression by subordinates in the form of slowdowns and subtle sabotage (Day & Hamblin, 1964).

Decision-Centralization and Subordinate Motivation

Although there is some direct evidence that subordinate participation can result in increased task motivation (Baumgartel, 1956), the nature and relative importance of the psychological processes accounting for the relation and the prerequisite conditions for their occurrence are not yet clear. A number of explanations for the effect of participation on subordinate motivation have been proposed during the last two decades.

Probably the most important of the proposed processes is the possibility that subordinates become "ego-involved" with a decision which they have helped to make. When subordinates identify with a decision, they become motivated to help make the decision successful, if only to maintain a favorable self-concept. However, there may be several limiting conditions for this causal sequence (Strauss, 1964; Vroom, 1964; Lowin, 1968). It is possible that there is some minimal amount of individual influence, actual or perceived, which is necessary before identification will occur. As a group gets larger, the influence of each member over a decision will necessarily decline; thus the size of the group may be one limiting factor. Also, it is not clear whether a person who supports a proposal that is rejected will become committed to the proposal finally selected by the group. Another prerequisite may be the subordinate's perception that the decision process is a test of his decision ability and those skills of his which are used in implementing the decision. In the case where subordinates participate in making decisions unrelated to their tasks, there is no reason to assume that any increased commitment to these decisions will generalize to task decisions. Finally, if responsibility for making decisions is thrust upon subordinates who do not want it or who see it as the legitimate role of the leader, then these subordinates may fail to identify with the decisions (French, Israel, & As, 1960).

Another explanation of the relation between Decision-Centralization and task motivation is that participation facilitates reduction of subordinate resistance to change (Coch & French, 1948). One way this could occur is through direct persuasion. Since the leader is usually not aware of all the subordinates' fears and doubts regarding a proposed change, consultation provides him with an opportunity to uncover these fears and to persuade subordinates that the change will be beneficial rather

BEHAVIORAL THEORY OF LEADERSHIP   425

than harmful. When a leader's proposal involves features which clearly are detrimental to subordinates, mere persuasion is not likely to win their support. However, consultation or joint decision-making provides the opportunity for bargaining and agreement on a compromise proposal which the subordinates can support (Strauss, 1964).

When the leader allows his subordinates to make a group decision, the interaction dynamics of the group are yet another possible source of increased task motivation. If the work group is cohesive, its members are subject to direct social pressure to conform to group norms (Schachter, Willerman, Festinger, & Hyman, 1961; Berkowitz, 1954; Seashore, 1954). In addition, the work group may function as a "reference group" for its members (Newcomb, 1965, p. 109). Subordinates who have positive attitudes toward their work group will tend to support group norms, including group decisions made in a legitimate manner. This tendency for member attitudes and behavior to be consistent with reference group norms will occur even in the absence of direct social pressure.

Of course, increased commitment to carry out decisions is not conceptually equivalent to increased task motivation. Subordinates can make task decisions which in effect restrict output or resist change. Subordinate attitudes toward the leader and the organization constitute an important situational variable which moderates the effect of participation upon task motivation. If relations between the leader and the subordinates are very poor, or the subordinates are in opposition to the goal of maximum group performance, then participation in decisions involving production goals, standards, quotas, etc., is not likely to result in increased subordinate task motivation (Strauss, 1964). Since Consideration is an important determinant of subordinate attitudes toward the leader, participation is more likely to be effective if combined with high Consideration than if combined with low Consideration.

Leader Behavior and Subordinate Task Skill

The second way in which leaders can increase group performance is to increase the ability of subordinates to perform their individual tasks. A number of studies (reviewed in Vroom, 1964, p. 197) support Maier's (1965) hypothesis that performance is a function of a person's Motivation $\times$ Ability. According to this hypothesis, even highly motivated subordinates will not perform well if they lack the necessary knowledge or skills to carry out their assignments. Therefore, one way for a leader to improve group performance is to correct deficiencies in subordinate task skills and knowledge by means of on-the-job instruction and improved downward communication of task-relevant information. Instruction and communication of this nature are, by definition, elements of Initiating Structure. A more complex analysis of the relation between Initiating Structure and subordinate task skill was beyond the scope of this article.

The Nature of Task-Role Organization

Task-Role Organization refers to how efficiently the skill resources of subordinates are utilized to perform the group's formal tasks. Adequacy of Task-Role Organization depends upon how well job assignment decisions and work method decisions are made. The making of job assignment decisions is usually referred to in industrial psychology as "placement" or "classification." When the jobs of each subordinate are identical and subordinates work independently of each other, it doesn't matter what subordinates are assigned to what jobs. However, when jobs are highly specialized, each job has different skill requirements, and skill differences among subordinates are substantial, then job assignments are an important type of task decision. If work assignments are not made carefully, the skills of some workers will not be fully utilized, while other workers will be placed in jobs which they cannot perform adequately. Furthermore, if the jobs are interdependent, bottlenecks will occur at various points in the flow of work.

Work method decisions are important whenever a task can be performed in many different ways, and some ways are better than others. Work methods and procedures can be designed with the available skills of a particular work group in mind, but it is common practice in industrial engineering to ignore individual differences and develop methods which maximize the efficiency of the typical worker. Decisions about work procedures are not always the responsibility of the leader. In some organizations, work methods are designed by staff specialists or are rigidly prescribed by company or union regulations.

Task-Role Organization was included in the multiple linkage model to account for any variability in group productivity which is not attributable to subordinate motivation, subordinate ability, or to extraneous events such as an improvement in the flow of material inputs, a breakdown in equipment, etc. The identification of Task-Role Organization as a separate variable is analogous to Maier's (1965) distinction between the quality of a decision and group acceptance of the decision. Although Task-Role Organization is an important conceptual component of the multiple linkage model, measurement of this variable is likely to prove troublesome. Any measure of Task-Role Organization will be highly specific to a given set of tasks and subordinates. Within a specific situation, one could attempt to scale the adequacy of job assignment decisions by evaluating the match between job requirements and subor-

dinate skills for all possible combinations of job assignments. Adequacy
of work method decisions could be evaluated in several ways. In some
situations, the accumulated knowledge of industrial engineering specialists may permit the subjective ranking of various possible work procedures according to their relative efficiency. When objective measures of
group performance (e.g., quantity or quality of output, labor time, errors)
are available to use as a criterion of efficiency, then alternative work
methods may be experimentally compared. However, it may be difficult
to hold task motivation constant, even within a single work group, because job design can affect the intrinsic motivation of workers as well
as their efficiency.

Initiating Structure, Decision-Centralization, and
  Task-Role Organization

Both Initiating Structure and Decision-Centralization appear to be
related to Task-Role Organization. By definition, a leader who is high in
Initiating Structure will attempt to improve the efficiency of his group.
However, simply engaging in structuring behavior does not guarantee
that Task-Role Organization will improve. The leader's success depends
upon his organizing skills, technical knowledge, and the extent to which
he taps the knowledge of his subordinates by allowing them some degree
of participation in making task decisions. The relation between Decision-
Centralization and Task-Role Organization is moderated by the relative
amount of leader and subordinate organizing skills and task knowledge.
When the leader is very capable in this respect but the subordinates
lack the appropriate talents, then there will be a negative relation between participation and Task-Role Organization. When the subordinates
have more relevant knowledge and organizing talent than the leader, we
would expect a positive relation between participation and Task-Role
Organization. We have already seen that Decision-Centralization can
affect the task motivation of subordinates as well as the quality of task
decisions. This means that in the situation where there is a negative
relation between participation and Task-Role Organization, there may
also be a positive relation between participation and subordinate motivation. When such a trade-off dilemma occurs, some intermediate degree of Decision-Centralization will probably be optimal with respect
to group performance.

In some situations, the quality of task decisions involves a time dimension. That is, the effectiveness of decisions depends in part upon
how quickly they are made (Strauss, 1964; Lowin, 1968). Autocratic
decision-making is faster than other decision procedures because little
communication with subordinates is necessary. Therefore, participation

GARY YUKL

is likely to be negatively related to group performance when rapid
decision-making is required. The magnitude of this negative relation will
be greatest when the leader already has the necessary knowledge and
ability to make good decisions, the subordinates are motivated by the
urgency of the situation, and the task group is very large.

Summary of the Multiple Linkage Model

The major features of the multiple linkage model of leadership effectiveness can be summarized by means of the following hypotheses:

Hyp 1: Group productivity is a function of the interaction among
subordinate task motivation, subordinate task skills, and Task-Role
Organization for the group.

Hyp 2: Initiating Structure and Consideration interact in the determination of subordinate task motivation. Task motivation is highest when
the leader is high on both behavior variables.

Hyp 3: Decision-Centralization is negatively correlated with subordinate task motivation (i.e., high participation causes high motivation)
when subordinate relations with the leader are favorable, the decisions
are relevant to subordinate tasks, and subordinates perceive their participation to be a test of valued abilities.

Hyp 4: Initiating Structure interacts with Decision-Centralization in
the determination of Task-Role Organization. The relationship is moderated by the level and distribution of task knowledge and planning
ability in the group.

Hyp 5: Initiating Structure is positively related to the level of subordinate task skill.

REVIEW OF RELATED RESEARCH

Most studies of the relation between leader behavior and subordinate
satisfaction with the leader have not measured subordinate preferences
or the personality and situational variables which determine these
preferences. Most studies of the relation between leader behavior and
group productivity have not included measures of the intermediate and
situational variables in the proposed linkage model. The approach typical
of most leadership research has been to look for a linear relation between
leader behavior and one of the criterion variables. Nevertheless, previous
research does provide some direct and some indirect evidence for evaluating the proposed models.

In the following sections of this article, relevant leadership research
will be reviewed. The review will include studies dealing with variables
which are reasonably similar to those in the proposed discrepancy and
linkage models. However, it should be emphasized that in many of these

studies, the operational measurement of a variable only approximates the conceptual definition presented in this article. Studies using scales which can be regarded as a measure of leader attitudes (e.g., LPC scale, F scale, Leadership Opinion Questionnaire) rather than leader behavior were not included. Also excluded were studies of general vs close supervision. This leadership dimension, as usually defined, confounds Decision-Centralization with Initiating Structure. Finally, the review does not include studies of emergent leaders in informal groups, studies using children, studies involving an entire organization rather than individual work groups or departments, and studies in which leader behavior is obviously confounded with organizational variables such as the incentive system.

Consideration and Satisfaction

In seven studies of the relation between Consideration and subordinate satisfaction with their leader, Consideration was measured by means of subordinate responses on leader behavior description questionnaires. In five of these studies (Halpin, 1957; Halpin & Winer, 1957; Nealey & Blood, 1968; Yukl, 1969a; Anderson, 1966) there was a strong positive relation between Consideration and subordinate satisfaction. In the remaining two studies (Fleishman & Harris, 1962; Skinner, 1969) there was a significant curvilinear relation between Consideration and two objective measures which reflect subordinate satisfaction, namely turnover and grievances. The curve describing the relation corresponded roughly to curve C in Fig. 1. If subordinate preferences were homogeneous, this curve would represent supporting evidence for the concept of a zone of indifference within which leader behavior does not affect subordinate satisfaction. Below this indifference zone, the relation between Consideration and satisfaction was positive.

In research reported in Likert (1961, p. 17), aspects of Consideration such as "supervisor takes an interest in me and understands my problems" and "supervisor thinks of employees as human beings rather than as persons to get the work done," were related to favorable attitudes on job-related matters. In two laboratory experiments (Day & Hamblin, 1964; Misumi & Shirakashi, 1966) punitive leader behavior (i.e., low Consideration) was associated with low subordinate satisfaction. In another laboratory experiment, Lowin (1969) found a significant positive relation between subordinates' satisfaction and their ratings of leader Consideration, but the difference in satisfaction between high and low Consideration conditions, although in the right direction, was not significant.

Only two studies were found in which a positive relation between Consideration and subordinate satisfaction with the leader did not occur. In a study by Argyle, Gardner, and Cioffi (1958), leader self-reports of punitive behavior did not correlate significantly with subordinate turnover and absences. Pelz (1952) found an interaction between the degree to which a leader acts as a representative of his subordinates when dealing with higher management (one form of Consideration) and the leader's upward influence in the organization. For leaders with little upward influence, subordinates were less satisfied when the leader "went to bat" for them than when he did not go to bat. Presumably the leader representation raised expectations which he could not fulfill, thereby frustrating subordinates. In terms of the discrepancy model, the subordinates' preferences for leader representation are probably lower when it repeatedly causes frustration. Whether the negative effects of unsuccessful representation can completely cancel out the positive effects of other considerate behavior by the leader is not clear. It does not seem likely.

In summary, the research literature indicates that in most situations, considerate leaders will have more satisfied subordinates. Although none of the investigators included subordinate preferences in their analysis, the results are consistent with the discrepancy model if we can make the relatively safe assumption that most subordinates prefer considerate leaders.

Initiating Structure and Satisfaction

A consistent linear relation between Initiating Structure and subordinate satisfaction was not found, even within sets of studies using comparable measures. Unfortunately, none of the studies reviewed included subordinate preferences. Baumgartel (1956), Halpin and Winer (1957), Argyle *et al.* (1958), Misumi and Shirakashi (1966), Lowin (1969), Anderson (1966), and Likert (1961, pp. 16–18) failed to find a significant relation. Halpin (1957) and Yukl (1969a) found positive correlations. Vroom and Mann (1960) found a significant negative correlation between pressure for production and job satisfaction for delivery truck drivers but not for loaders. Nealey and Blood (1968) found a negative correlation between Initiating Structure and subordinate satisfaction for second-level supervisors and a positive correlation for first-level supervisors.

Only three studies were found which examined the possibility of a curvilinear relation between Initiating Structure and subordinate satisfaction. Likert (1955) found that the relation between pressure for productivity and subordinate satisfaction took the form of an inverted U-shaped curve which is similar to curve B in Fig. 1. Fleishman and

Harris (1962) and Skinner (1969) found a curvilinear relation between Initiating Structure and both turnover and grievances. Although subordinate preferences were not measured, the relationships in these studies were roughly comparable to curve A in Fig. 1.

Fleishman and Harris also tested for an interaction between Initiating Structure and Consideration. The results of their analysis suggest that Consideration has a greater effect upon subordinate satisfaction than does Initiating Structure. High Consideration leaders could increase Initiating Structure with little accompanying increase in turnover or grievances. Fleishman and Harris provide two possible explanations for this interaction. One explanation is that considerate leaders are more likely to deal with any dissatisfaction caused by high structuring behavior before the dissatisfaction results in official grievances or withdrawal (i.e., turnover). Another explanation is that Consideration affects the way subordinates perceive structuring behavior. In terms of the discrepancy model, subordinates of highly considerate leaders are more likely to have a higher preference level for Initiating Structure because they do not perceive leader structuring as threatening and restrictive.

Decision-Centralization and Satisfaction

Six studies were found which examined the correlation between subordinate satisfaction and participation as perceived either by the leaders or by the subordinates (Baumgartel, 1956; Argyle *et al.*, 1958; Vroom, 1959; Bachman, Smith, & Slesinger, 1966; Yukl, 1969a; Tosi, 1970). In each of these studies, evidence was found to support a positive relation between participation and subordinate satisfaction, although within some of the studies, a significant relation was not obtained for every subsample or for every alternative measure of the variables. A significant positive relation was also found in each of five studies in which participation was experimentally manipulated (Coch & French, 1948; Shaw, 1955, Morse & Reimer, 1956; Solem, 1958; Maier & Hoffman, 1962). The results of these studies are generally consistent with the discrepancy model if one can assume that the subordinates preferred a substantial degree of participation.

In those cases where a significant relation between participation and subordinate satisfaction was not found, there was usually some reason to expect that the subordinates preferred a moderate or low amount of participation. In the study by Vroom (1959), a positive correlation occurred for subordinates with a high need for independence but not for subordinates with a low need for independence. Bass (1965, pp. 169–170) and French *et al.* (1960) found that subordinate participation did not result in more favorable attitudes toward a leader unless the subordinates per-

ceived the decision-making as a legitimate part of their role. Further
evidence for the moderating effect of subordinate preferences can be found
in a study by Baumgartel (1956) and in two unpublished studies (Jacobson, 1951; Tannenbaum, 1954) which were reported in Likert (1961, pp.
92–93). In the Tennenbaum study, some subordinates reacted adversely
to a sudden substantial increase in participation. Finally, Morse (1953,
p. 64) found that, regardless of whether workers made some decisions
or none, they reported more intrinsic job satisfaction when the amount
of decision-making equalled the amount desired than when they were
not allowed to make as many decisions as they desired. Although intrinsic
job satisfaction is conceptually distinct from satisfaction with the leader,
these two variables are probably highly correlated when the leader determines how much responsibility a subordinate has for making task
decisions.

Consideration, Initiating Structure, and Productivity

Considering the complexity of the interaction between Consideration
and Initiating Structure, it is not surprising that research on the relation
between Consideration and productivity does not yield consistent results.
In the large majority of studies there was either a significant positive
relation (Katz, Maccoby, Gurin, & Floor, 1951; Argyle *et al.*, 1958;
Besco & Lawshe, 1959; Schachter *et al.*, 1961; Kay, Meyer, & French,
1965) or there was no significant linear relation (Bass, 1957; Halpin,
1957; Rambo, 1958; Day & Hamblin, 1964; Anderson, 1966; Nealey &
Blood, 1968; Rowland & Scott, 1968). Lowin (1969) found a positive
relation for objectively manipulated Consideration in an experiment but
not for subordinate ratings of Consideration. A significant negative relation was found by Halpin and Winer (1957) for aircraft commanders and
by Fleishman, Harris, and Burtt (1955, p. 80) for foremen of production
departments but not for nonproduction departments. In both of these
studies, productivity was measured by superior ratings, and the highest
ratings went to leaders low on Consideration but high on Initiating
Structure. It is possible that the ratings were influenced more by the
raters' task-oriented stereotype of the ideal leader than by actual group
performance.

Turning to research on the relation between Initiating Structure and
productivity, we again find mixed results. In a number of studies a
significant positive relation was reported (Fleishman *et al.*, 1955; Likert,
1955; Halpin & Winer, 1957; Maier & Maier, 1957; Besco & Lawshe,
1959; Anderson, 1966; Nealey & Blood, 1968). For some subsamples in
three of these studies, and for leaders studied by Argyle *et al.* (1958),
Bass (1957), Halpin (1957), Rambo (1958), and Lowin (1969), a signifi-

cant relation was not found. In no case was a significant negative relation reported.

It is unfortunate that so few investigators measured intermediate variables or tested for an interaction between Consideration and Initiating Structure. However, the few studies which are directly relevant to the proposed linkage model do provide supporting evidence. In a laboratory experiment in Japan, Misumi and Shirakashi (1966) found that leaders who were both task oriented and considerate in their behavior had the most productive groups. Halpin (1957) found that aircraft commanders were rated highest in effectiveness when they were above the mean on both Consideration and Initiating Structure. Hemphill (1957) obtained the same results for the relation between the behavior of department chairmen in a Liberal Arts College and faculty ratings of how well the department was administered. Fleishman and Simmons (1970) translated the Supervisory Behavior Description into Hebrew and administered this questionnaire to the superiors of Israeli foremen. Proficiency ratings for the foremen were also obtained from their superiors. Once again, the foremen with the best ratings tended to be high on both Consideration and Initiating Structure. Patchen (1962) found that personal production norms (i.e., task motivation) of workers were highest when the leader encouraged proficiency as well as "going to bat" for them. These production norms were related in turn to actual group production. Finally, although he didn't measure Consideration, Baumgartel (1956) found a significant positive relation between subordinate motivation and the concern of research laboratory directors for goal attainment (i.e., Initiating Structure).

Decision-Centralization and Productivity

Seventeen studies were found which examined the relation between Decision-Centralization and group productivity. A significant positive relation between participation and productivity was found by Bachman *et al.* (1966), Coch and French (1948), Fleishman (1965), French (1950), French, Kay, and Meyer (1966), Lawrence and Smith (1955), Likert (1961, p. 20), Mann and Dent (1954), McCurdy and Eber (1953), Meltzer (1956), and Vroom (1959). Argyle *et al.* (1958) found a positive relation only for departments without piece rates, suggesting that the organizational incentive system, a situational variable, interacts with Decision-Centralization in determining the subordinates' task motivation. Tosi (1970), French *et al.* (1960), and McCurdy and Lambert (1952) failed to find a significant relation between participation and productivity. In two other studies (Shaw, 1955; Morse & Reimer, 1956) a significant negative relation was found. Several of these studies demon-

434   GARY YUKL

strate that various situational variables can moderate the effects of leader decision behavior on group performance. Nevertheless, the high percentage of studies reporting a positive relation is an indication that some degree of participation leads to an increase in group performance in most situations. However, this generalization is *not* equivalent to concluding "the more participation there is, the greater will be group productivity." For a particular group, there is probably some optimal pattern of decision-making which will consist of various amounts of delegation, joint decision-making, consultation, and autocratic decision-making (Heller & Yukl, 1969). The optimal pattern is likely to involve some intermediate amount of subordinate influence, rather than the greatest possible amount.

DISCUSSION

The Multiple Linkage Model and Fiedler's Contingency Model

A considerable number of leadership studies have been conducted by Fred Fiedler and his associates at the University of Illinois (Fiedler, 1967). Fiedler has developed a theory of leadership effectiveness to explain the results of this research. According to Fiedler's theory, group performance is a function of the interaction between the leader's "esteem for his least preferred co-worker" (LPC) and three situational variables: task structure, leader–member relations, and the position power of the leader. Leaders with low LPC scores have the most productive groups when the leadership situation, in terms of the three situational variables, is either very favorable or very unfavorable. Leaders with high LPC scores are more effective when the situation is intermediate in favorableness. Although Fiedler provides a behavioral explanation for these hypothesized relations, most of his studies did not measure leader behavior. The few studies which have attempted to identify the behavioral correlates of LPC scores have not yielded consistent results (Sample & Wilson, 1965; Fiedler, 1967, p. 53; Nealey & Blood, 1968; Yukl, 1970; Gruenfeld, Rance, & Weissenberg, 1969; Reilly, 1969). Thus, it is not possible at this time to determine whether Fiedler's model is compatible with the proposed linkage model. Both theories are generally supported by their own separate bodies of empirical research. Reconciliation of the two approaches will probably require additional research which includes variables from both theories.

Direction for Future Research

The theoretical framework and the literature review presented earlier point out some empirical gaps which badly need filling. The central feature of the linkage model is the set of intermediate variables. A leader can do little to improve group productivity unless he can alter one or more of these variables. Yet the mediating role of these variables, their relation to each other, and their interaction in the determination of productivity have seldom been investigated in leadership studies. Future research should be more comprehensive in scope. Leader behavior variables, intermediate variables, situational variables, subordinate preferences, criterion variables (i.e., satisfaction and productivity), and relevant leader traits should all be included. Situational variables other than those discussed in this article also need to be investigated. Likely candidates are the organizational limiting conditions for participation suggested by Lowin (1968) and Strauss (1964), the structural variables found to be associated with leader decision behavior by Heller and Yukl (1969), the situational variables in Fiedler's model, the situational variables cluster-analyzed by Yukl (1969b), and Woodward's (1965) system for classifying production technology. Finally, the way in which the three behavior dimensions interact in determining the intermediate variables should be investigated. If possible, the leader behavior variables should be experimentally manipulated in order to avoid the measurement problems associated with leader behavior descriptions by subordinates.

The analysis of leader effectiveness has utilized leader behavior variables which maintain a basic continuity with traditional conceptualization and research. However, in speculating about future research, it is appropriate to evaluate the continued usefulness of these broadly defined behavior dimensions. It is obvious that Consideration and Initiating Structure are composed of relatively diverse elements, while Decision-Centralization is an average based on many different types of decisions. In order to improve the predictive power of the model, it may be necessary to identify which components of the behavior variables are the most important determinants of each intermediate variable.

The discrepancy model and the multiple linkage model provide only the skeleton of a static leadership theory which purposely ignores the additional complexities of feedback loops and circular causality. Much additional research and revision will be necessary to transform the skeleton into a full-fledged dynamic model which permits accurate predictions about leader effectiveness in formal task groups.

REFERENCES

ANDERSON, L. R. Leader behavior, member attitudes, and task performance of intercultural discussion groups. *Journal of Social Psychology*, 1966, **69**, 305–319.

ARGYLE, M., GARDNER, G., & CIOFFI, F. The measurement of supervisory methods. *Human Relations,* 1957, **10**, 295–313.

ARGYLE, M., GARDNER, G., & CIOFFI, F. Supervisory methods related to productivity, absenteeism, and labor turnover. *Human Relations*, 1958, **11**, 23–40.

BACHMAN, J. G., SMITH, C. G., & SLESINGER, J. A. Control, performance, and satisfaction: An analysis of structural and individual effects. *Journal of Personality and Social Psychology*, 1966, **4**, 127–136.

BASS, B. M. Leadership opinions and related characteristics of salesmen and sales managers. In R. M. Stogdill and A. E. Coons (Eds.), *Leader behavior: Its description and measurement*. Columbus: Bureau of Business Research, Ohio State University, 1957.

BASS, B. M. *Organizational psychology*. Boston: Allyn & Bacon, 1965.

BAUMGARTEL, H. Leadership, motivations, and attitudes in research laboratories. *Journal of Social Issues*, 1956, **12**, (2), 24–31.

BEER, M. *Leadership, employee needs, and motivation*. Columbus: Bureau of Business Research, Ohio State University, Monograph No. 129, 1966.

BERKOWITZ, L. Group Standards, cohesiveness, and productivity. *Human Relations*, 1954, **7**, 509–519.

BESCO, R. O., & LAWSHE, C. H. Foreman leadership as perceived by supervisor and subordinate. *Personnel Psychology*, 1959, **12**, 573–582.

COCH, L., & FRENCH, J. R. P. Overcoming resistance to change. *Human Relations*, 1948, **1**, 512–532.

DAY, R. C., & HAMBLIN, R. L. Some effects of close and punitive styles of supervision. *American Journal of Sociology*, 1964, **16**, 499–510.

FIEDLER, F. E. *A theory of leadership effectiveness*. New York: McGraw-Hill, 1967.

FLEISHMAN, E. A. A leader behavior description for industry. In R. M. Stogdill and A. E. Coons (Eds.), *Leader behavior: Its description and measurement*. Columbus: Bureau of Business Research, Ohio State University, 1957 (a).

FLEISHMAN, E. A. The Leadership Opinion Questionnaire. In R. M. Stogdill and A. E. Coons (Eds.), *Leader behavior: Its description and measurement*. Columbus: Bureau of Business Research, Ohio State University, 1957 (b).

FLEISHMAN, E. A. Attitude versus skill factors in work group productivity. *Personnel Psychology*, 1965, **18**, 253–266.

FLEISHMAN, E. A., & SIMMONS, J. Relationship between leadership patterns and effectiveness ratings among Israeli foremen. *Personnel Psychology*, 1970, **23**, 169–172.

FLEISHMAN, E. A., & HARRIS, E. F. Patterns of leadership behavior related to employee grievances and turnover. *Personnel Psychology*, 1962, **15**, 43–56.

FLEISHMAN, E. A., HARRIS, E. F., & BURTT, H. E. *Leadership and supervision in industry*. Columbus: Bureau of Educational Research, Ohio State University, Research monograph No. 33, 1955.

FOA, U. G. Relation of worker's expectations to satisfaction with his supervisor. *Personnel Psychology*, 1957, **10**, 161–168.

FRENCH, J. R. P. Field experiments: Changing group productivity. In J. G. Miller (Ed.), *Experiments in social process: A symposium on social psychology*. New York: McGraw-Hill, 1950.

FRENCH, J. R. P., ISRAEL, J., & AS, D. An experiment on participation in a Norwegian factory. *Human Relations*, 1960, **13**, 3–19.

FRENCH, J. R. P., KAY, E., & MEYER, H. Participation and the appraisal system. *Human Relations*, 1966, **19**, 3–20.

FRENCH, J. R. P., & RAVEN, B. The bases of social power. In D. Cartwright (Ed.), *Studies in social power*. Ann Arbor: Institute for Social Research, University of Michigan, 1959.

GALBRAITH, J., & CUMMINGS, L. L. An empirical investigation of the motivational determinants of task performance: Interactive effects between instrumentality-valence and motivation-ability. *Organizational Behavior and Human Perform-ance*, 1967, **2**, 237–257.

GOMBERG, W. The trouble with democratic management. *Transaction*, 1966, **3**, (5), 30–35.

GREER, F. L. Leader indulgence and group performance. *Psychological Monographs*, 1961, **75** (12, Whole No. 516).

GRUENFELD, L. W., RANCE, D. E., & WEISSENBERG, P. The behavior of task-oriented (low LPC) and socially-oriented (high LPC) leaders under several conditions of social support. *Journal of Social Psychology*, 1969, **79**, 99–107.

HALPIN, A. W. The leader behavior and effectiveness of aircraft commanders. In R. M. Stogdill and A. E. Coons (Eds.), *Leader behavior: Its description and measurement*. Columbus: Bureau of Business Research, Ohio State University, 1957.

HALPIN, A. W., & WINER, B. J. A factorial study of the leader behavior descriptions. In R. M. Stogdill and A. E. Coons (Eds.), *Leader behavior: Its description and measurement*. Columbus: Bureau of Business Research, Ohio State University, 1957.

HELLER, F., & YUKL, G. Participation, managerial decision-making, and situational variables. *Organizational Behavior and Human Performance*, 1969, **4**, 227–241.

HEMPHILL, J. K. Leader behavior associated with the administrative reputations of college departments. In R. M. Stogdill and A. E. Coons (Eds.), *Leader behavior: Its description and measurement*. Columbus: Bureau of Business Research, Ohio State University, 1957.

HEMPHILL, J. K., & COONS, A. E. Development of the leader behavior description questionnaire. In R. M. Stogdill and A. E. Coons (Eds.), *Leader behavior: Its description and measurement*. Columbus: Bureau of Business Research, Ohio State University, 1957.

JACOBSON, J. M. Analysis of interpersonal relations in a formal organization. Unpublished doctoral dissertation, University of Michigan, 1953.

KATZ, D., MACCOBY, N., GURIN, G., & FLOOR, L. *Productivity, supervision, and morale among railroad workers*. Ann Arbor: Survey Research Center, University of Michigan, 1951.

KATZELL, R. A. Personal values, job satisfaction, and job behavior. In H. Borrow (Ed.), *Man in a World of Work*. Boston: Houghton-Mifflin, 1964.

KAY, E., MEYER, H. H., & FRENCH, J. R. P. Effects of threat in a performance appraisal interview. *Journal of Applied Psychology*, 1965, **49**, 311–317.

KORMAN, A. K. Consideration, initiating structure, and organizational criteria—A review. *Personal Psychology*, 1966, **19**, 349–362.

LAWRENCE, L. C., & SMITH, P. C. Group decision and employee participation. *Journal of Applied Psychology*, 1955, **39**, 334–337.

LEWIN, K. The dynamics of group action. *Educational Leadership*, 1944, **1**, 195–200.

LIKERT, R. Developing patterns in management. *Strengthening management for the new technology*. New York: American Management Association, 1955.

LIKERT, R. *New patterns of management*. New York: McGraw-Hill, 1961.

LOCKE, E. A. What is job satisfaction? *Organizational Behavior and Human Performance*, 1969, **4**, 309–336.

LOWIN, A. Participative decision-making: A model, literature critique, and prescriptions for research. *Organizational Behavior and Human Performance*, 1968, **3**, 68–106.

LOWIN, A., HRAPCHAK, W. J., & KAVANAGH, M. J. Consideration and Initiating

Structure: An experimental investigation of leadership traits. *Administrative Science Quarterly*, 1969, **14**, 238–253.

MAIER, N. R. F. *Psychology in industry*. Third ed. Boston: Houghton-Mifflin Co., 1965.

MAIER, N. R. F., & HOFFMAN, L. R. Group decision in England and the United States. *Personnel Psychology*, 1962, **15**, 75–87.

MAIER, N. R. F., & MAIER, R. A. An experimental test of the effects of "developmental" vs. "free" discussions on the quality of group decisions. *Journal of Applied Psychology*, 1957, **41**, 320–323.

MANN, F. C., & DENT, J. The supervisor: Member of two organizational families. *Harvard Business Review*, 1954, **32**, (6), 103–112.

McCURDY, H. G., & EBER, H. W. Democratic vs. authoritarian: A further investigation of group problem-solving. *Journal of Personality*, 1953, **22**, 258–269.

McCURDY, H. G., & LAMBERT, W. E. The efficiency of small groups in the solution of problems requiring genuine cooperation. *Journal of Personality*, 1952, **20**, 478–494.

McMURRAY, R. N. The case for benevolent autocracy. *Harvard Business Review*, 1958, **36**, (1), 82–90.

MELTZER, L. Scientific productivity in organizational settings. *Journal of Social Issues*, 1956, **12**, (2), 32–40.

MISUMI, J., & SHIRAKASHI, S. An experimental study of the effects of supervisory behavior on productivity and morale in a hierarchical organization. *Human Relations*, 1966 **19**, 297–307.

MORSE, N. *Satisfaction in the white-collar job*. Ann Arbor: Institute for Social Research, University of Michigan, 1953.

MORSE, N. C., & REIMER, E. The experimental change of a major organizational variable. *Journal of Abnormal and Social Psychology*, 1956, **52**, 120–129.

MULDER, M., & STEMERDING, A. Threat, attraction to group and strong leadership: A laboratory experiment in a natural setting. *Human Relations*, 1963, **16**, 317–334.

NEALEY, S. M., & BLOOD, M. R. Leadership performance of nursing supervisors at two organizational levels. *Journal of Applied Psychology*, 1968, **52**, 414–422.

NEWCOMB, T. H., TURNER, R. H., & CONVERSE, P. E. *Social psychology*. New York: Holt, Rinehart, & Winston, 1965.

NEWPORT, G. A study of attitudes and leadership behavior. *Personnel Administration*, 1962, **25** (5), 42–46.

PATCHEN, M. Supervisory methods and group performance norms. *Administrative Science Quarterly*, 1962, **7**, 275–294.

PELZ, D. C. Influence: A key to effective leadership in the first-line supervisor. *Personnel*, 1952, **29**, 209–217.

PORTER, L. W. Job attitudes in management: I. Perceived deficiencies in need fulfillment as a function of job level. *Journal of Applied Psychology*, 1962, **46**, 375–384.

RAMBO, W. W. The construction and analysis of a leadership behavior rating form. *Journal of Applied Psychology*, 1958, **42**, 409–415.

REILLY, A. J. The effects of different leadership styles on group performance: A field experiment. Paper presented at the American Psychological Association Convention, Washington, D. C., Sept. 1, 1969.

ROSEN, R. A. H., & ROSEN, R. A. A. Suggested modification in job satisfaction surveys. *Personnel Psychology*, 1955, **8**, 303–314.

Ross, I. C., & Zander, A. Need satisfactions and employee turnover. *Personnel Psychology*, 1957, **10**, 327–338.

Rowland, K. M., & Scott, W. E. Psychological attributes of effective leadership in a formal organization. *Personnel Psychology*, 1968, **21**, 365–378.

Sales, S. M. Supervisory style and productivity: Review and theory. *Personnel Psychology*, 1966, **19**, 275–286.

Sample, J. A., & Wilson, T. R. Leader behavior, group productivity, and rating of least preferred coworker. *Journal of Personality and Social Psychology*, 1965, **1**, 266–270.

Schachter, S., Willerman, B., Festinger, L., & Hyman, R. Emotional disruption and industrial productivity. *Journal of Applied Psychology*, 1961, **45**, 201–213.

Schaffer, R. H. Job satisfaction as related to need satisfaction in work. *Psychological Monograph*, 1953, **67**, (14, Whole No. 364).

Schoenfeld, E. Authoritarian management: A reviving concept. *Personnel*, 1959, **36**, 21–24.

Seashore, S. *Group cohesiveness in the industrial work group*. Ann Arbor: Institute for Social Research, University of Michigan, 1954.

Shaw, M. E. A comparison of two types of leadership in various communication nets. *Journal of Abnormal and Social Psychology*, 1955, **50**, 127–134.

Skinner, E. W. Relationships between leadership behavior patterns and organizational-situational variables. *Personnel Psychology*, 1969, **22**, 489–494.

Solem, A. R. An evaluation of two attitudinal approaches to delegation. *Journal of Applied Psychology*, 1958, **42**, 36–39.

Stanton, E. S. Which approach to management—democratic, authoritarian, or . . .? *Personnel Administration*, 1962, **25** (2), 44–47.

Stogdill, R. M., Goode, O. S., & Day, D. R. New leader behavior description subscales. *Journal of Psychology*, 1962, **54**, 259–269.

Stogdill, R. M., Goode, O. S., & Day, D. R. The leader behavior of corporation presidents. *Personnel Psychology*, 1963, **16**, 127–132.

Stogdill, R. M., Goode, O. S., & Day, D. R. The leader behavior of presidents of labor unions. *Personnel Psychology*, 1964, **17**, 49–57.

Strauss, G. Some notes on power equalization. In H. J. Leavitt (Ed.), *The social science of organizations: Four perspectives*. Englewood Cliffs, New Jersey: Prentice-Hall, 1964.

Tosi, H. A re-examination of personality as a determinant of the effects of participation. *Personnel Psychology*, 1970, **23**, 91–99.

Tannenbaum, A. S. The relationship between personality and group structure. Unpublished doctoral dissertation. Syracuse University, 1954.

Trow, D. B. Autonomy and job satisfaction in task-oriented groups. *Journal of Abnormal and Social Psychology*, 1957, **54**, 204–209.

Vroom, V. H. Some personality determinants of the effects of participation. *Journal of Abnormal and Social Psychology*, 1959, **59**, 322–327.

Vroom, V. H. Work and Motivation. New York: John Wiley and Sons, 1964.

Vroom, V. H., & Mann, F. C. Leader authoritarianism and employee attitudes. *Personnel Psychology*, 1960, **13**, 125–140.

Woodward, J. *Industrial organization:* Theory and practice. London: Oxford University Press, 1965.

Yukl, G. A. Conceptions and consequences of leader behavior. Paper presented at

440 GARY YUKL

the annual convention of the California State Psychological Association, Newport Beach, January, 1969 (a).

YUKL, G. A. A situation description questionnaire for leaders. *Educational and Psychological Measurement*, 1969, **29**, 515–518 (b).

YUKL, G. A. Leader LPC scores: Attitude dimensions and behavioral correlates. *Journal of Social Psychology*, 1970, **80**, 207–212.

RECEIVED: April 29, 1970

[14]

The Ambiguity of Leadership [1]

JEFFREY PFEFFER
University of California, Berkeley

Problems with the concept of leadership are addressed: (a) the ambiguity of its definition and measurement, (b) the issue of whether leadership affects organizational performance, and (c) the process of selecting leaders, which frequently emphasizes organizationally-irrelevant criteria. Leadership is a process of attributing causation to individual social actors. Study of leaders as symbols and of the process of attributing leadership might be productive.

Leadership has for some time been a major topic in social and organizational psychology. Underlying much of this research has been the assumption that leadership is causally related to organizational performance. Through an analysis of leadership styles, behaviors, or characteristics (depending on the theoretical perspective chosen), the argument has been made that more effective leaders can be selected or trained or, alternatively, the situation can be configured to provide for enhanced leader and organizational effectiveness.

Three problems with emphasis on leadership as a concept can be posed: (a) ambiguity in definition and measurement of the concept itself; (b) the question of whether leadership has discernible effects on organizational outcomes; and (c) the selection process in succession to leadership positions, which frequently uses organizationally irrelevant criteria and which has implications for normative theories of leadership. The argument here is that leadership is of interest primarily as a phenomenological construct. Leaders serve as symbols for representing personal causation of social events. How and why are such attributions of personal effects made? Instead of focusing on leadership and its effects, how do people make

Jeffrey Pfeffer (Ph.D. — Stanford University) is Associate Professor in the School of Business Administration and Associate Research Sociologist in the Institute of Industrial Relations at the University of California, Berkeley.

Received 12/17/75, Accepted 2/27/76; Revised 4/20/76.

[1] An earlier version of this paper was presented at the conference, Leadership: Where Else Can We Go?, Center for Creative Leadership, Greensboro, North Carolina, June 30 - July 1, 1975.

inferences about and react to phenomena labelled as leadership (5)?

The Ambiguity of the Concept

While there have been many studies of leadership, the dimensions and definition of the concept remain unclear. To treat leadership as a separate concept, it must be distinguished from other social influence phenomena. Hollander and Julian (24) and Bavelas (2) did not draw distinctions between leadership and other processes of social influence. A major point of the Hollander and Julian review was that leadership research might develop more rapidly if more general theories of social influence were incorporated. Calder (5) also argued that there is no unique content to the construct of leadership that is not subsumed under other, more general models of behavior.

Kochan, Schmidt, and DeCotiis (33) attempted to distinguish leadership from related concepts of authority and social power. In leadership, influence rights are voluntarily conferred. Power does not require goal compatability — merely dependence — but leadership implies some congruence between the objectives of the leader and the led. These distinctions depend on the ability to distinguish voluntary from involuntary compliance and to assess goal compatibility. Goal statements may be retrospective inferences from action (46, 53) and problems of distinguishing voluntary from involuntary compliance also exist (32). Apparently there are few meaningful distinctions between leadership and other concepts of social influence. Thus, an understanding of the phenomena subsumed under the rubric of leadership may not require the construct of leadership (5).

While there is some agreement that leadership is related to social influence, more disagreement concerns the basic dimensions of leader behavior. Some have argued that there are two tasks to be accomplished in groups — maintenance of the group and performance of some task or activity — and thus leader behavior might

be described along these two dimensions (1, 6, 8, 25). The dimensions emerging from the Ohio State leadership studies — consideration and initiating structure — may be seen as similar to the two components of group maintenance and task accomplishment (18).

Other dimensions of leadership behavior have also been proposed (4). Day and Hamblin (10) analyzed leadership in terms of the closeness and punitiveness of the supervision. Several authors have conceptualized leadership behavior in terms of the authority and discretion subordinates are permitted (23, 36, 51). Fiedler (14) analyzed leadership in terms of the least-preferred-co-worker scale (LPC), but the meaning and behavioral attributes of this dimension of leadership behavior remain controversial.

The proliferation of dimensions is partly a function of research strategies frequently employed. Factor analysis on a large number of items describing behavior has frequently been used. This procedure tends to produce as many factors as the analyst decides to find, and permits the development of a large number of possible factor structures. The resultant factors must be named and further imprecision is introduced. Deciding on a summative concept to represent a factor is inevitably a partly subjective process.

Literature assessing the effects of leadership tends to be equivocal. Sales (45) summarized leadership literature employing the authoritarian-democratic typology and concluded that effects on performance were small and inconsistent. Reviewing the literature on consideration and initiating structure dimensions, Korman (34) reported relatively small and inconsistent results, and Kerr and Schriesheim (30) reported more consistent effects of the two dimensions. Better results apparently emerge when moderating factors are taken into account, including subordinate personalities (50), and situational characteristics (23, 51). Kerr, et al. (31) list many moderating effects grouped under the headings of subordinate considerations, supervisor considerations, and task considerations. Even if each set of considerations consisted of only one factor (which it does not), an attempt to account for the effects of leader behavior would necessitate considering four-way interactions. While social reality is complex and contingent, it seems desirable to attempt to find more parsimonious explanations for the phenomena under study.

The Effects of Leaders

Hall asked a basic question about leadership: is there any evidence on the magnitude of the effects of leadership (17, p. 248)? Surprisingly, he could find little evidence. Given the resources that have been spent studying, selecting, and training leaders, one might expect that the question of whether or not leaders matter would have been addressed earlier (12).

There are at least three reasons why it might be argued that the observed effects of leaders on organizational outcomes would be small. First, those obtaining leadership positions are selected, and perhaps only certain, limited styles of behavior may be chosen. Second, once in the leadership position, the discretion and behavior of the leader are constrained. And third, leaders can typically affect only a few of the variables that may impact organizational performance.

Homogeneity of Leaders

Persons are selected to leadership positions. As a consequence of this selection process, the range of behaviors or characteristics exhibited by leaders is reduced, making it more problematic to empirically discover an effect of leadership. There are many types of constraints on the selection process. The attraction literature suggests that there is a tendency for persons to like those they perceive as similar (3). In critical decisions such as the selections of persons for leadership positions, compatible styles of behavior probably will be chosen.

Selection of persons is also constrained by the internal system of influence in the organization. As Zald (56) noted, succession is a critical decision, affected by political influence and by environmental contingencies faced by the or-

ganization. As Thompson (49) noted, leaders may be selected for their capacity to deal with various organizational contingencies. In a study of characteristics of hospital administrators, Pfeffer and Salancik (42) found a relationship between the hospital's context and the characteristics and tenure of the administrators. To the extent that the contingencies and power distribution within the organization remain stable, the abilities and behaviors of those selected into leadership positions will also remain stable.

Finally, the selection of persons to leadership positions is affected by a self-selection process. Organizations and roles have images, providing information about their character. Persons are likely to select themselves into organizations and roles based upon their preferences for the dimensions of the organizational and role characteristics as perceived through these images. The self-selection of persons would tend to work along with organizational selection to limit the range of abilities and behaviors in a given organizational role.

Such selection processes would tend to increase homogeneity more within a single organization than across organizations. Yet many studies of leadership effect at the work group level have compared groups within a single organization. If there comes to be a widely shared, socially constructed definition of leadership behaviors or characteristics which guides the selection process, then leadership activity may come to be defined similarly in various organizations, leading to the selection of only those who match the constructed image of a leader.

Constraints on Leader Behavior

Analyses of leadership have frequently presumed that leadership style or leader behavior was an independent variable that could be selected or trained at will to conform to what research would find to be optimal. Even theorists who took a more contingent view of appropriate leadership behavior generally assumed that with proper training, appropriate behavior could be produced (51). Fiedler (13), noting how hard it was to change behavior, suggested changing the situational characteristics rather than the person, but this was an unusual suggestion in the context of prevailing literature which suggested that leadership style was something to be strategically selected according to the variables of the particular leadership theory.

But the leader is embedded in a social system, which constrains behavior. The leader has a role set (27), in which members have expectations for appropriate behavior and persons make efforts to modify the leader's behavior. Pressures to conform to the expectations of peers, subordinates, and superiors are all relevant in determining actual behavior.

Leaders, even in high-level positions, have unilateral control over fewer resources and fewer policies than might be expected. Investment decisions may require approval of others, while hiring and promotion decisions may be accomplished by committees. Leader behavior is constrained by both the demands of others in the role set and by organizationally prescribed limitations on the sphere of activity and influence.

External Factors

Many factors that may affect organizational performance are outside a leader's control, even if he or she were to have complete discretion over major areas of organizational decisions. For example, consider the executive in a construction firm. Costs are largely determined by operation of commodities and labor markets; and demand is largely affected by interest rates, availability of mortgage money, and economic conditions which are affected by governmental policies over which the executive has little control. School superintendents have little control over birth rates and community economic development, both of which profoundly affect school system budgets. While the leader may react to contingencies as they arise, or may be a better or worse forecaster, in accounting for variation in organizational outcomes, he or she may account for relatively little compared to external factors.

Second, the leader's success or failure may

be partly due to circumstances unique to the organization but still outside his or her control. Leader positions in organizations vary in terms of the strength and position of the organization. The choice of a new executive does not fundamentally alter a market and financial position that has developed over years and affects the leader's ability to make strategic changes and the likelihood that the organization will do well or poorly. Organizations have relatively enduring strengths and weaknesses. The choice of a particular leader for a particular position has limited impact on these capabilities.

Empirical Evidence

Two studies have assessed the effects of leadership changes in major positions in organizations. Lieberson and O'Connor (35) examined 167 business firms in 13 industries over a 20 year period, allocating variance in sales, profits, and profit margins to one of four sources: year (general economic conditions), industry, company effects, and effects of changes in the top executive position. They concluded that compared to other factors, administration had a limited effect on organizational outcomes.

Using a similar analytical procedure, Salancik and Pfeffer (44) examined the effects of mayors on city budgets for 30 U.S. cities. Data on expenditures by budget category were collected for 1951-1968. Variance in amount and proportion of expenditures was apportioned to the year, the city, or the mayor. The mayoral effect was relatively small, with the city accounting for most of the variance, although the mayor effect was larger for expenditure categories that were not as directly connected to important interest groups. Salancik and Pfeffer argued that the effects of the mayor were limited both by absence of power to control many of the expenditures and tax sources, and by construction of policies in response to demands from interests in the environment.

If leadership is defined as a strictly interpersonal phenomenon, the relevance of these two studies for the issue of leadership effects becomes problematic. But such a conceptualization seems unduly restrictive, and is certainly inconsistent with Selznick's (47) conceptualization of leadership as strategic management and decision making. If one cannot observe differences when leaders change, then what does it matter who occupies the positions or how they behave?

Pfeffer and Salancik (41) investigated the extent to which behaviors selected by first-line supervisors were constrained by expectations of others in their role set. Variance in task and social behaviors could be accounted for by role-set expectations, with adherence to various demands made by role-set participants a function of similarity and relative power. Lowin and Craig (37) experimentally demonstrated that leader behavior was determined by the subordinate's own behavior. Both studies illustrate that leader behaviors are responses to the demands of the social context.

The effect of leadership may vary depending upon level in the organizational hierarchy, while the appropriate activities and behaviors may also vary with organizational level (26, 40). For the most part, empirical studies of leadership have dealt with first line supervisors or leaders with relatively low organizational status (17). If leadership has any impact, it should be more evident at higher organizational levels or where there is more discretion in decisions and activities.

The Process of Selecting Leaders

Along with the suggestion that leadership may not account for much variance in organizational outcomes, it can be argued that merit or ability may not account for much variation in hiring and advancement of organizational personnel. These two ideas are related. If competence is hard to judge, or if leadership competence does not greatly affect organizational outcomes, then other, person-dependent criteria may be sufficient. Effective leadership styles may not predict career success when other variables such as social background are controlled.

Belief in the importance of leadership is fre-

quently accompanied by belief that persons occupying leadership positions are selected and trained according to how well they can enhance the organization's performance. Belief in a leadership effect leads to development of a set of activities oriented toward enhancing leadership effectiveness. Simultaneously, persons managing their own careers are likely to place emphasis on activities and developing behaviors that will enhance their own leadership skills, assuming that such a strategy will facilitate advancement.

Research on the bases for hiring and promotion has been concentrated in examination of academic positions (e.g., 7, 19, 20). This is possibly the result of availability of relatively precise and unambiguous measures of performance, such as number of publications or citations. Evidence on criteria used in selecting and advancing personnel in industry is more indirect.

Studies have attempted to predict either the compensation or the attainment of general management positions of MBA students, using personality and other background information (21, 22, 54). There is some evidence that managerial success can be predicted by indicators of ability and motivation such as test scores and grades, but the amount of variance explained is typically quite small.

A second line of research has investigated characteristics and backgrounds of persons attaining leadership positions in major organizations in society. Domhoff (11), Mills (38), and Warner and Abbeglin (52) found a strong preponderance of persons with upper-class backgrounds occupying leadership positions. The implication of these findings is that studies of graduate success, including the success of MBA's, would explain more variance if the family background of the person were included.

A third line of inquiry uses a tracking model. The dynamic model developed is one in which access to elite universities is affected by social status (28) and, in turn, social status and attendance at elite universities affect later career outcomes (9, 43, 48, 55).

Unless one is willing to make the argument

that attendance at elite universities or coming from an upper class background is perfectly correlated with merit, the evidence suggests that succession to leadership positions is not strictly based on meritocratic criteria. Such a conclusion is consistent with the inability of studies attempting to predict the success of MBA graduates to account for much variance, even when a variety of personality and ability factors are used.

Beliefs about the bases for social mobility are important for social stability. As long as persons believe that positions are allocated on meritocratic grounds, they are more likely to be satisfied with the social order and with their position in it. This satisfaction derives from the belief that occupational position results from application of fair and reasonable criteria, and that the opportunity exists for mobility if the person improves skills and performance.

If succession to leadership positions is determined by person-based criteria such as social origins or social connections (16), then efforts to enhance managerial effectiveness with the expectation that this will lead to career success divert attention from the processes of stratification actually operating within organizations. Leadership literature has been implicitly aimed at two audiences. Organizations were told how to become more effective, and persons were told what behaviors to acquire in order to become effective, and hence, advance in their careers. The possibility that neither organizational outcomes nor career success are related to leadership behaviors leaves leadership research facing issues of relevance and importance.

The Attribution of Leadership

Kelley conceptualized the layman as:

an applied scientist, that is, as a person concerned about applying his knowledge of causal relationships in order to *exercise control* of his world (29, p. 2).

Reviewing a series of studies dealing with the attributional process, he concluded that persons were not only interested in understanding their world correctly, but also in controlling it.

The view here proposed is that attribution processes are to be understood not only as a means of providing the individual with a veridical view of his world, but as a means of encouraging and maintaining his effective exercise of control in that world (29, p. 22).

Controllable factors will have high salience as candidates for causal explanation, while a bias toward the more important causes may shift the attributional emphasis toward causes that are not controllable (29, p. 23). The study of attribution is a study of naive psychology — an examination of how persons make sense out of the events taking place around them.

If Kelley is correct that individuals will tend to develop attributions that give them a feeling of control, then emphasis on leadership may derive partially from a desire to believe in the effectiveness and importance of individual action, since individual action is more controllable than contextual variables. Lieberson and O'Connor (35) made essentially the same point in introducing their paper on the effects of top management changes on organizational performance. Given the desire for control and a feeling of personal effectiveness, organizational outcomes are more likely to be attributed to individual actions, regardless of their actual causes.

Leadership is attributed by observers. Social action has meaning only through a phenomenological process (46). The identification of certain organizational roles as leadership positions guides the construction of meaning in the direction of attributing effects to the actions of those positions. While Bavelas (2) argued that the functions of leadership, such as task accomplishment and group maintenance, are shared throughout the group, this fact provides no simple and potentially controllable focus for attributing causality. Rather, the identification of leadership positions provides a simpler and more readily changeable model of reality. When causality is lodged in one or a few persons rather than being a function of a complex set of interactions among all group members, changes can be made by replacing or influencing the occupant of the leadership position. Causes of organizational actions are readily identified in this simple causal structure.

Even if, empirically, leadership has little effect, and even if succession to leadership positions is not predicated on ability or performance, the belief in leadership effects and meritocratic succession provides a simple causal framework and a justification for the structure of the social collectivity. More importantly, the beliefs interpret social actions in terms that indicate potential for effective individual intervention or control. The personification of social causality serves too many uses to be easily overcome. Whether or not leader behavior actually influences performance or effectiveness, it is important because people believe it does.

One consequence of the attribution of causality to leaders and leadership is that leaders come to be symbols. Mintzberg (39), in his discussion of the roles of managers, wrote of the symbolic role, but more in terms of attendance at formal events and formally representing the organization. The symbolic role of leadership is more important than implied in such a description. The leader as a symbol provides a target for action when difficulties occur, serving as a scapegoat when things go wrong. Gamson and Scotch (15) noted that in baseball, the firing of the manager served a scapegoating purpose. One cannot fire the whole team, yet when performance is poor, something must be done. The firing of the manager conveys to the world and to the actors involved that success is the result of personal actions, and that steps can and will be taken to enhance organizational performance.

The attribution of causality to leadership may be reinforced by organizational actions, such as the inauguration process, the choice process, and providing the leader with symbols and ceremony. If leaders are chosen by using a random number table, persons are less likely to believe in their effects than if there is an elaborate search or selection process followed by an elaborate ceremony signifying the changing of control, and if the leader then has a variety of perquisites and symbols that distinguish him or

her from the rest of the organization. Construction of the importance of leadership in a given social context is the outcome of various social processes, which can be empirically examined.

Since belief in the leadership effect provides a feeling of personal control, one might argue that efforts to increase the attribution of causality to leaders would occur more when it is more necessary and more problematic to attribute causality to controllable factors. Such an argument would lead to the hypothesis that the more the *context* actually effects organizational outcomes, the more efforts will be made to ensure attribution to *leadership*. When leaders really do have effects, it is less necessary to engage in rituals indicating their effects. Such rituals are more likely when there is uncertainty and unpredictability associated with the organization's operations. This results both from the desire to feel control in uncertain situations and from the fact that in ambiguous contexts, it is easier to attribute consequences to leadership without facing possible disconfirmation.

The leader is, in part, an actor. Through statements and actions, the leader attempts to reinforce the operation of an attribution process which tends to vest causality in that position in the social structure. Successful leaders, as perceived by members of the social system, are those who can separate themselves from organizational failures and associate themselves with organizational successes. Since the meaning of action is socially constructed, this involves manipulation of symbols to reinforce the desired process of attribution. For instance, if a manager knows that business in his or her division is about to improve because of the economic cycle, the leader may, nevertheless, write recommendations and undertake actions and changes that are highly visible and that will tend to identify his or her behavior closely with the division. A manager who perceives impending failure will attempt to associate the division and its policies and decisions with others, particularly persons in higher organizational positions, and to disassociate himself or herself from the division's performance, occasionally even transferring or moving to another organization.

Conclusion

The theme of this article has been that analysis of leadership and leadership processes must be contingent on the intent of the researcher. If the interest is in understanding the causality of social phenomena as reliably and accurately as possible, then the concept of leadership may be a poor place to begin. The issue of the effects of leadership is open to question. But examination of situational variables that accompany more or less leadership effect is a worthwhile task.

The more phenomenological analysis of leadership directs attention to the process by which social causality is attributed, and focuses on the distinction between causality as perceived by group members and causality as assessed by an outside observer. Leadership is associated with a set of myths reinforcing a social construction of meaning which legitimates leadership role occupants, provides belief in potential mobility for those not in leadership roles, and attributes social causality to leadership roles, thereby providing a belief in the effectiveness of individual control. In analyzing leadership, this mythology and the process by which such mythology is created and supported should be separated from analysis of leadership as a social influence process, operating within constraints.

REFERENCES

1. Bales, R.F. *Interaction Process Analysis: A Method for the Study of Small Groups* (Reading, Mass.: Addison-Wesley, 1950).
2. Bavelas, Alex. "Leadership: Man and Function," *Administrative Science Quarterly*, Vol. 4 (1960), 491-498.
3. Berscheid, Ellen, and Elaine Walster. *Interpersonal Attraction* (Reading, Mass.: Addison-Wesley, 1969).
4. Bowers, David G., and Stanley E. Seashore. "Predicting Organizational Effectiveness with a Four-Factor Theory of Leadership," *Administrative Science Quarterly*, Vol. 11 (1966), 238-263.
5. Calder, Bobby J. "An Attribution Theory of Leadership," in B. Staw and G. Salancik (Eds.), *New Directions in Organizational Behavior* (Chicago: St. Clair Press, 1976), in press.
6. Cartwright, Dorwin C., and Alvin Zander. *Group Dynamics: Research and Theory*, 3rd ed. (Evanston, Ill.: Row, Peterson, 1960).
7. Cole, Jonathan R., and Stephen Cole. *Social Stratification in Science* (Chicago: University of Chicago Press, 1973).
8. Collins, Barry E., and Harold Guetzkow. *A Social Psychology of Group Processes for Decision-Making* (New York: Wiley, 1964).
9. Collins, Randall. "Functional and Conflict Theories of Stratification," *American Sociological Review*, Vol. 36 (1971), 1002-1019.
10. Day, R. C., and R. L. Hamblin. "Some Effects of Close and Punitive Styles of Supervision," *American Journal of Sociology*, Vol. 69 (1964), 499-510.
11. Domhoff, G. William. *Who Rules America?* (Englewood Cliffs, N.J.: Prentice-Hall, 1967).

12. Dubin, Robert. "Supervision and Productivity: Empirical Findings and Theoretical Considerations," in R. Dubin, G. C. Homans, F. C. Mann, and D. C. Miller (Eds.), *Leadership and Productivity* (San Francisco: Chandler Publishing Co., 1965), pp. 1-50.
13. Fiedler, Fred E. "Engineering the Job to Fit the Manager," *Harvard Business Review*, Vol. 43 (1965), 115-122.
14. Fiedler, Fred E. *A Theory of Leadership Effectiveness* (New York: McGraw-Hill, 1967).
15. Gamson, William A., and Norman A. Scotch. "Scapegoating in Baseball," *American Journal of Sociology*, Vol. 70 (1964), 69-72.
16. Granovetter, Mark. *Getting a Job* (Cambridge, Mass.: Harvard University Press, 1974).
17. Hall, Richard H. *Organizations: Structure and Process* (Englewood Cliffs, N.J.: Prentice-Hall, 1972).
18. Halpin, A. W., and J. Winer. "A Factorial Study of the Leader Behavior Description Questionnaire," in R. M. Stogdill and A. E. Coons (Eds.), *Leader Behavior: Its Description and Measurement* (Columbus, Ohio: Bureau of Business Research, Ohio State University, 1957), pp. 39-51.
19. Hargens, L. L. "Patterns of Mobility of New Ph.D.'s Among American Academic Institutions," *Sociology of Education*, Vol. 42 (1969), 18-37.
20. Hargens, L. L., and W. O. Hagstrom. "Sponsored and Contest Mobility of American Academic Scientists," *Sociology of Education*, Vol. 40 (1967), 24-38.
21. Harrell, Thomas W. "High Earning MBA's," *Personnel Psychology*, Vol. 25 (1972), 523-530.

22. Harrell, Thomas W., and Margaret S. Harrell. "Predictors of Management Success." *Stanford University Graduate School of Business, Technical Report No. 3 to the Office of Naval Research.*

23. Heller, Frank, and Gary Yukl. "Participation, Managerial Decision-Making, and Situational Variables," *Organizational Behavior and Human Performance,* Vol. 4 (1969), 227-241.

24. Hollander, Edwin P., and James W. Julian. "Contemporary Trends in the Analysis of Leadership Processes," *Psychological Bulletin,* Vol. 71 (1969), 387-397.

25. House, Robert J. "A Path Goal Theory of Leader Effectiveness," *Administrative Science Quarterly,* Vol. 16 (1971), 321-338.

26. Hunt, J. G. "Leadership-Style Effects at Two Managerial Levels in a Simulated Organization," *Administrative Science Quarterly,* Vol. 16 (1971), 476-485.

27. Kahn, R. L., D. M. Wolfe, R. P. Quinn, and J. D. Snoek. *Organizational Stress: Studies in Role Conflict and Ambiguity* (New York: Wiley, 1964).

28. Karabel, J., and A. W. Astin. "Social Class, Academic Ability, and College 'Quality'," *Social Forces,* Vol. 53 (1975), 381-398.

29. Kelley, Harold H. *Attribution in Social Interaction* (Morristown, N.J.: General Learning Press, 1971).

30. Kerr, Steven, and Chester Schriesheim. "Consideration, Initiating Structure and Organizational Criteria—An Update of Korman's 1966 Review," *Personnel Psychology,* Vol. 27 (1974), 555-568.

31. Kerr, S., C. Schriesheim, C. J. Murphy, and R. M. Stogdill. "Toward A Contingency Theory of Leadership Based Upon the Consideration and Initiating Structure Literature," *Organizational Behavior and Human Performance,* Vol. 12 (1974), 62-82.

32. Kiesler, C., and S. Kiesler. *Conformity* (Reading, Mass.: Addison-Wesley, 1969).

33. Kochan, T. A., S. M. Schmidt, and T. A. DeCotiis. "Superior-Subordinate Relations: Leadership and Headship," *Human Relations,* Vol. 28 (1975), 279-294.

34. Korman, A. K. "Consideration, Initiating Structure, and Organizational Criteria—A Review," *Personnel Psychology,* Vol. 19 (1966), 349-362.

35. Lieberson, Stanley, and James F. O'Connor. "Leadership and Organizational Performance: A Study of Large Corporations," *American Sociological Review,* Vol. 37 (1972), 117-130.

36. Lippitt, Ronald. "An Experimental Study of the Effect of Democratic and Authoritarian Group Atmospheres," *University of Iowa Studies in Child Welfare,* Vol. 16 (1940), 43-195.

37. Lowin, A., and J. R. Craig. "The Influence of Level of Performance on Managerial Style: An Experimental Object-Lesson in the Ambiguity of Correlational Data," *Organizational Behavior and Human Performance,* Vol. 3 (1968), 440-458.

38. Mills, C. Wright. "The American Business Elite: A Collective Portrait," in C. W. Mills, *Power, Politics, and People* (New York: Oxford University Press, 1963), pp. 110-139.

39. Mintzberg, Henry. *The Nature of Managerial Work* (New York: Harper and Row, 1973).

40. Nealey, Stanley M., and Milton R. Blood. "Leadership Performance of Nursing Supervisors at Two Organizational Levels," *Journal of Applied Psychology,* Vol. 52 (1968), 414-442.

41. Pfeffer, Jeffrey, and Gerald R. Salancik. "Determinants of Supervisory Behavior: A Role Set Analysis," *Human Relations,* Vol. 28 (1975), 139-154.

42. Pfeffer, Jeffrey, and Gerald R. Salancik. "Organizational Context and the Characteristics and Tenure of Hospital Administrators," *Academy of Management Journal,* Vol. 20 (1977), in press.

43. Reed, R. H., and H. P. Miller. "Some Determinants of the Variation in Earnings for College Men," *Journal of Human Resources,* Vol. 5 (1970), 117-190.

44. Salancik, Gerald R., and Jeffrey Pfeffer. "Constraints on Administrator Discretion: The Limited Influence of Mayors on City Budgets," *Urban Affairs Quarterly,* in press.

45. Sales, Stephen M. "Supervisory Style and Productivity: Review and Theory," *Personnel Psychology,* Vol. 19 (1966), 275-286.

46. Schutz Alfred. *The Phenomenology of the Social World* (Evanston, Ill.: Northwestern University Press, 1967)

47. Selznick, P. *Leadership in Administration* (Evanston, Ill.: Row, Peterson, 1957).

48. Spaeth, J. L., and A. M. Greeley. *Recent Alumni and Higher Education* (New York: McGraw-Hill, 1970).

49. Thompson, James D. *Organizations in Action* (New York: McGraw-Hill, 1967).

50. Vroom, Victor H. "Some Personality Determinants of the Effects of Participation," *Journal of Abnormal and Social Psychology,* Vol. 59 (1959), 322-327.

51. Vroom, Victor H., and Phillip W. Yetton. *Leadership and Decision-Making* (Pittsburgh: University of Pittsburgh Press, 1973).

52. Warner, W. L., and J. C. Abbeglin. *Big Business Leaders in America* (New York: Harper and Brothers, 1955).

53. Weick, Karl E. *The Social Psychology of Organizing* (Reading, Mass.: Addison-Wesley, 1969).

54. Weinstein, Alan G., and V. Srinivasan. "Predicting Managerial Success of Master of Business Administration (MBA) Graduates," *Journal of Applied Psychology,* Vol. 59 (1974), 207-212.

55. Wolfle, Dael. *The Uses of Talent* (Princeton: Princeton University Press, 1971).

56. Zald, Mayer N. "Who Shall Rule? A Political Analysis of Succession in a Large Welfare Organization," *Pacific Sociological Review,* Vol. 8 (1965), 52-60.

[15]

Leadership:
The Management of Meaning

LINDA SMIRCICH
GARETH MORGAN

The concept of leadership permeates and structures the theory and practice of organizations and hence the way we shape and understand the nature of organized action, and its possibilities. In fact, the concept and practice of leadership, and variant forms of direction and control, are so powerfully ingrained into popular thought that the absence of leadership is often seen as an absence of organization. Many organizations are paralyzed by situations in which people appeal for direction, feeling immobolized and disorganized by the sense that they are not being led. Yet other organizations are plagued by the opposite situation characterized in organizational vernacular as one of "all chiefs, no Indians"— the situation where the majority aspire to lead and few to follow. Thus, successful acts of organization are often

seen to rest in the synchrony between the initiation of action and the appeal for direction; between the actions of leaders and the receptivity and responsiveness of followers.

In this paper we focus on understanding the phenomenon of leadership, not merely to improve the practice of leadership, but as a means for understanding the phenomenon of organization. For, in leading, managers enact a particular form of social reality with far- reaching, but often poorly understood and appreciated, consequences. We engage in our analysis to reveal how concepts and ideas that dominate management theory and ideology shape managerial practice and the reality of organization. Our approach is to analyze leadership as a

The Journal of Applied Behavioral Science,
Volume 18, Number 3, Pages 257-273
Copyright © 1982 by JAI Press Inc.
All rights of reproduction in any form reserved.
ISSN: 0021-8863

Linda Smircich is an associate professor of organizational behavior in the School of Business Administration, University of Massachusetts, Amherst, Massachusetts 01003. Gareth Morgan is an associate professor of organizational behavior in the Faculty of Administrative Studies of York University, Toronto, Ontario, Canada.

258   THE JOURNAL OF APPLIED BEHAVIORAL SCIENCE Vol. 18/No. 3/1982

distinctive kind of social practice, present a case study of leadership in an organizational context, and analyze its consequences for understanding the basic nature of modern corporate life.

THE PHENOMENON OF LEADERSHIP

Leadership is realized in the process whereby one or more individuals succeeds in attempting to frame and define the reality of others. Indeed, leadership situations may be conceived as those in which there exists an *obligation* or a perceived *right* on the part of certain individuals to define the reality of others.

This process is most evident in unstructured group situations where leadership emerges in a natural and spontaneous manner. After periods of interaction, unstructured leaderless groups typically evolve common modes of interpretation and shared understandings of experience that allow them to develop into a social organization (Bennis & Shepard, 1965). Individuals in groups that evolve this way attribute leadership to those members who structure experience in meaningful ways. Certain individuals, as a result of personal inclination or the emergent expectations of others, find themselves adopting or being obliged to take a leadership role by virtue of the part they play in the definition of the situation. They emerge as leaders because of their role in framing experience in a way that provides a viable basis for action, e.g., by mobilizing meaning, articulating and defining what has previously remained implicit or unsaid, by inventing images and meanings that provide a focus for new attention, and by consolidating, confronting, or changing prevailing wisdom (Peters, 1978; Pondy, 1976).

Through these diverse means, individual actions can frame and change situations, and in so doing enact a system of shared meaning that provides a basis for organized action. The leader exists as a formal leader only when he or she achieves a situation in which an obligation, expectation, or right to frame experience is presumed, or offered and accepted by others.

Leadership, like other social phenomena, is socially constructed through interaction (Berger & Luckmann, 1966), emerging as a result of the constructions and actions of both leaders and led. It involves a complicity or process of negotiation through which certain individuals, implicitly or explicitly, surrender their power to define the nature of their experience to others. Indeed, leadership depends on the existence of individuals willing, as a result of inclination or pressure, to surrender, at least in part, the powers to shape and define their own reality. If a group situation embodies competing definitions of reality, strongly held, no clear pattern of leadership evolves. Often, such situations are characterized by struggles among those who aspire to define the situation. Such groups remain loosely coupled networks of interaction, with members often feeling that they are "disorganized" because they do not share a common way of making sense of their experience.

Leadership lies in large part in generating a point of reference, against which a feeling of organization and direction can emerge. While in certain circumstances the leader's image of reality may be hegemonic, as in the case of charismatic or totalitarian leaders who mesmerize their followers, this is by no means always the case. For the phenomenon of leadership in being interactive is by nature dialectical. It is shaped through the interaction of at least two points of reference, i.e., of leaders and of led.

This dialectic is often the source of powerful internal tensions within leadership situations. These manifest themselves in the conflicting definitions of those who aspire to define reality and in the fact that while the leader of a group may forge a unified pattern of meaning, that very same pattern often provides a point of reference for the negation of leadership (Sennett, 1980). While individuals may look to a leader to frame and concretize their reality, they may also react against, reject, or change the reality thus defined. While leadership often emerges as a result of expectations projected on the emergent leader by the led, the surrender of power involved provides the basis for negation of the situation thus created. Much of the tension in leadership situations stems from this source. Although leaders draw their power from their ability to define the reality of others, their inability to control completely provides seeds of disorganization in the organization of meaning they provide.

The emergence of leadership in unstructured situations thus points toward at least four important aspects of leadership as a phenomenon. First, leadership is essentially a social process defined through interaction. Second, leadership involves a process of defining reality in ways that are sensible to the led. Third, leadership involves a dependency relationship in which individuals surrender their powers to interpret and define reality to others.[1] Fourth, the emergence of formal leadership roles represents an additional stage of institutionalization, in which rights and obligations to define the nature of experience and activity are recognized and formalized.

LEADERSHIP IN FORMALIZED SETTINGS

The main distinguishing feature of formal organization is that the way in which experience is to be structured and defined is built into a stock of taken for granted meanings, or "typifications" in use (Schutz, 1967) that underlie the everyday definition and reality of the organization. In particular, a formal organization is premised upon shared meanings that define roles and authority relationships that institutionalize a pattern of leadership. In essence, formal organization truncates the leadership process observed in natural settings, concretizing its characteristics as a mode of social organization into sets of predetermined roles, relationships, and practices, providing a blueprint of how the experience of organizational members is to be structured.

Roles, for example, institutionalize the interactions and definitions that shape the reality of organizational life. Rules, conventions, and work practices present ready-made typifications through which experience is to be made sensible. Authority relationships legitimize the pattern of dependency relations that characterize the process of leadership, specifying who is to define organizational reality, and in what circumstances. Authority relationships institutionalize a hierarchical pattern of interaction in which certain individuals are expected to define the experience of others—to lead, and others to have their experience defined—to follow. So powerful is this process of institutionalized leadership and the expectation that someone has the right and obligation to define reality, that leaders are held to account if they do not lead "effectively." Those expecting to be led, for example, often rational-

260   THE JOURNAL OF APPLIED BEHAVIORAL SCIENCE Vol. 18/No. 3/1982

ize their own inaction or ineffectiveness by scapegoating through statements such as "she is a poor manager" or "he is messing things up." On the other hand, occupancy of an authority role presents the leader in every situation with an existential dilemma—how to define and structure the element of organizational reality encountered at a given time. Formal organizations are often heavily populated by those who feel obliged to define the reality and experience of others in a way that is consistent with their idea of "being a good leader." To fail in this obligation is to fail in one's organizational role.

In these ways, patterns of formal organization institutionalize aspects of the leadership process within the context of a unified structure that specifies patterns of desired interaction, sense making, and dependency. As in the case of leadership as an emergent process, formal structures of organized action also contain a dialectical tension between the pattern of action and meaning that the structure seeks to establish, and the tendency of individuals to reinterpret, or even react against, the structure thus defined. While submitting to the dominant pattern of meaning, individuals frequently strive to develop patterns of their own, a phenomenon well documented in studies of the so-called "informal organization" (Roethlisberger & Dickson, 1939).

It is this inherent tension that calls for the development of a mediating form of leadership, bridging the gulf between the requirements of institutionalized structure and the natural inclinations of its human agents. It is this form of leadership that we most often recognize as leadership in informal organizations—the interpersonal process linking structure and the human beings who inhabit this struc-

ture. The person that is most easily recognized as an organizational leader is one who rises above and beyond the specification of formal structure to provide members of the organization with a sense that they are organized, even amidst an everyday feeling that at a detailed level everything runs the danger of falling apart.

Similarly, successful corporate leaders who give direction to the organization in a strategic sense frequently do so by providing an image or pattern of thinking in a way that has meaning for those directly involved (Quinn, 1980). This is reflected in part in Selznick's (1957) conception of leadership as involving the embodiment of organizational values and purpose. Strategic leadership, in effect, involves providing a conception and direction for organizational process that goes above and beyond what is embedded in the fabric of organization as a structure, i.e., a reified and somewhat static pattern of meaning.

Formal organization thus embodies at least two distinctive, yet complementary aspects of the phenomenon of leadership: (1) the structure of organization institutionalizes the leadership process into a network of roles, often in an overconcretized and dehumanizing form; (2) mediating or interpersonal leadership—what is most evident as leadership in action, operationalizes the principles of leadership as an emergent process within the context of the former. This is usually as a means of transcending the limitations of the former for containing the dialectical tension that it embodies, and as a means of giving the whole coherence and direction over time. These two aspects of leadership have been well recognized in leadership research (Katz & Kahn, 1966) and are frequently interpreted and studied in terms of a relationship between "initiating structure" and "consideration" (e.g., Stogdill, 1974).

The phenomenon of leadership in formal organizations has been conceptualized and studied in many ways. Leadership research has sought for an understanding of leadership in terms of the personal traits of leaders (Mann, 1959), in terms of situations in which they lead (Fiedler, 1967), in terms of what they do (Mintzberg, 1973) or some combination thereof. Such approaches to the study of leadership tap into important attributes of what leadership may involve in day to day practice, particularly in terms of action requirements, and identify those practices most likely to work in different situations. Other approaches have viewed leadership as a process of exchange and influence (Barnard, 1938; Jacobs, 1971), and attempts have been made to understand the nature of the interactions and transactions necessary for effective leadership to occur (Bougon, Note 1). In the remainder of this paper, we wish to supplement these views with an approach to studying leadership that focuses on the way detailed interactive situations acquire meaningful form.

LEADERSHIP AS THE MANAGEMENT OF MEANING

A focus on the way meaning in organized settings is created, sustained, and changed provides a powerful means of understanding the fundamental nature of leadership as a social process. In understanding the way leadership actions attempt to shape and interpret situations to guide organizational members into a common interpretation of reality, we are able to understand how leadership

works to create an important foundation for organized activity. This process can be most easily conceptualized in terms of a relationship between figure and ground. Leadership action involves a moving figure—a flow of actions and utterances (i.e., what leaders do) within the context of a moving ground—the actions, utterances, and general flow of experience that constitute the situation being managed. Leadership as a phenomenon is identifiable within its wider context as a form of action that seeks to shape its context.

Leadership works by influencing the relationship between figure and ground, and hence the meaning and definition of the context as a whole. The actions and utterances of leaders guide the attention of those involved in a situation in ways that are consciously or unconsciously designed to shape the meaning of the situation. The actions and utterances draw attention to particular aspects of the overall flow of experience, transforming what may be complex and ambiguous into something more discrete and vested with a specific pattern of meaning. This is what Schutz (1967) has referred to as a "bracketing" of experience, and Goffman (1974) as a "framing" of experience, and Bateson (1972) and Weick (1979) as the "punctuation of contexts." The actions and utterances of leaders frame and shape the context of action in such a way that the members of that context are able to use the meaning thus created as a point of reference for their own action and understanding of the situation.

This process can be represented schematically in terms of the model presented in Figure 1. When leaders act they punctuate contexts in ways that provide a focus for the creation of

262   THE JOURNAL OF APPLIED BEHAVIORAL SCIENCE Vol. 18/No. 3/1982

Figure 1. Leadership: A Figure-Ground Relationship Which
Creates Figure-Ground Relationships

Framing Experience ⟶	*Interpretation* ⟶	*Meaning and Action*
Leadership action creates a focus of attention within the ongoing stream of experience which characterizes the total situation.	The action assumes significance, i.e., is interpreted within its wider context. The leader has a specific figure-ground relation in mind in engaging in action; other members of the situation construct their own interpretation of this action.	Action is grounded in the interpretive process which links figure and ground.
Such action "brackets" and "frames" an element of experience for interpretation and meaningful action.		

meaning. Their action isolates an element of experience, which can be interpreted in terms of the context in which it is set. Indeed, its meaning is embedded in its relationship with its context. Consider, for example, the simple situation in which someone in a leadership role loses his or her temper over the failure of an employee to complete a job on time. For the leader this action embodies a meaning that links the event to context in a significant way, e.g., "This employee has been asking for a reprimand for a long time"; "This was an important job"; "This office is falling apart." For the employees in the office, the event may be interpreted in similar terms, or a range of different constructions placed upon the situation, e.g., "Don't worry about it, he always loses his temper from time to time"; "She's been under pressure lately because of problems at home."

The leader's action may generate a variety of interpretations that set the basis for meaningful action. It may serve to redefine the context into a situation where the meeting of deadlines assumes greater significance, or merely serves as a brief interruption in daily routine, soon forgotten. As discussed earlier, organized situations are often characterized by complex

patterns of meaning, based on rival interpretations of the situation. Different members may make sense of situations with the aid of different interpretive schemes, establishing "counter-realities," a source of tension in the group situation that may set the basis for change of an innovative or disintegrative kind. These counter-realities underwrite much of the political activities within organizations, typified by the leader's loyal lieutenants—the "yes men" accepting and reinforcing the leader's definition of the situation and the "rebels" or "out" groups forging and sustaining alternative views.

Effective leadership depends upon the extent to which the leader's definition of the situation, e.g., "People in this office are not working hard enough," serves as a basis for action by others. It is in this sense that effective leadership rests heavily on the framing of the experience of others, so that action can be guided by common conceptions as to what should occur. The key challenge for a leader is to manage meaning in such a way that individuals orient themselves to the achievement of desirable ends. In this endeavor the use of language, ritual, drama, stories, myths, and symbolic construction of all kinds may play an important role (Pfeffer, 1981; Pondy,

Frost, Morgan & Dandridge, 1982; Smircich, 1982). They constitute important tools in the management of meaning. Through words and images, symbolic actions and gestures, leaders can structure attention and evoke patterns of meaning that give them considerable control over the situation being managed. These tools can be used to forge particular kinds of figure-ground relations that serve to create appropriate modes of organized action. Leadership rests as much in these symbolic modes of action as in those instrumental modes of management, direction, and control that define the substance of the leader's formal organizational role.

A CASE STUDY IN THE MANAGEMENT OF MEANING

In order to illustrate the way leadership involves the management of meaning, we present here a case study drawn from an ethnographic study of the executive staff of an insurance company. The company was a division of a larger corporation (10,000 employees), was 11 years old, and employed 200 people. The case focuses on the way the president of the insurance company, Mr. Hall, sought to structure the experience of staff members by creating a particular figure-ground relationship—"Operation June 30th" (OJ30). OJ30 emerged as a prominent organizational event during the fieldwork and provided a focus for studying the process of leadership in action, in this instance, one of limited success.

Methodology

The research was conducted by one of the authors during the summer of 1979. An agreement was reached whereby the researcher was invited to spend six weeks in the insurance company as an observer of the executive staff. The purpose of the research was to learn about the ways of life within the 10-member top management group, to uncover the structures of meaning in use in the setting, and to synthesize an image of the group's reality.

The specific techniques used to gather data in the setting, consistent with the ethnographic tradition (Bogdan & Taylor, 1975; Schatzman & Strauss, 1973; Smircich, Note 2), were oriented toward understanding the realms of intersubjective meaning which gave that organization a semblance of unity and character to its membership.

In this study the researcher maintained the work hours of the organization. Early on she met individually with each of the staff members and explained the project as an attempt to learn about their organization. Each day's activity consisted of observing the management staff in a variety of situations: staff meetings, planning sessions, interactions with their subordinates, on coffee breaks, and in casual conversation. The guiding principle in this endeavor was to obtain a multi-sided view of the situation in order to build a holistic image of the group's understanding of itself. Toward the end of the stay in the company, tape recorded conversations/interviews were held with all staff members, including the president. The raw data from this study consist of daily field notes, documents, tapes of conversations, and the researcher's experience of the situation.

During the field work, the organization was in the midst of OJ30, and it was a prominent topic of discussion by the staff and in the researcher's con-

264   THE JOURNAL OF APPLIED BEHAVIORAL SCIENCE Vol. 18/No. 3/1982

versations with the staff. For the purposes of this paper, the data were culled for all references to the OJ30 program so that an account of the situation from multiple viewpoints could be presented.

Ideally, the research would have proceeded in a way that allowed the researcher to reflect back to the group the many-sided image of the meaning system in use that had emerged. As the case study shows, the president's unwillingness to proceed with this aspect of the research was representative of the way of life he strived to maintain in the organization and in that sense provides a form of validation for some of the data presented here.

The background to Operation June 30th

"Operation June 30th" was instigated by Mr. Hall, the president, in direct response to complaints by the district sales managers that the agents in the field were not getting adequate service from the home office. Insurance claims, applications, endorsements, and renewals were not being handled promptly. The agents were getting complaints from their custom-ers about long delays; consequently, they submitted second and third work requests that only served to make the volume of paperwork greater. The slowdown in processing of paperwork also meant that the agents' commission checks were slow in going out so that they did not receive their commissions in the month of sale.

After hearing the frustration of the Sales Department, Hall considered what might be done.[2] He conferred with the vice-president of administrative operations and the vice-president of claims and asked them if they thought it would be possible to have processing operations current by June 30th, the end of the fiscal year. President Hall then wrote an announcement (Figure 2), showed it to the vice-presidents for their comments and approval, and released it to the district sales managers.

With the initiation of OJ30, make-shift posters proclaiming "Operation June 30th Goals Week of June ____" were attached to file cabinets in the operations area. To bring the work-flow up to date, overtime work (evenings and Saturdays) was expected, and other departments were encouraged to help out wherever possible by

Figure 2. Operation June 30

WHAT:	A special program designed to bring all insurance processing activities up to date by June 30, 1979.
WHY:	The present work backlog is having an adverse impact on total insurance operations.
HOW:	1. All departments will make a concerted effort to eliminate all backlogs. The goal is to have work conditions current in all departments by June 30.
	2. All insurance home office employees who have the time will be expected to "volunteer" to assist other departments by performing certain assigned processing tasks until June 30. Procedures relative to this will be developed.
TIMING:	Operation June 30 will commence on Monday, May 14 and will terminate on Saturday, June 30.
PRIORITY:	This program has the highest priority. Nothing else in insurance is of more importance.
REPORTS:	Each staff member will report in writing weekly to Mr. Hall on the status of work conditions in his or her department.

loaning people during the week or by urging their people to come in on the weekends. Each week at the staff meeting a status report was made by the vice-president of operations on the number of files that had been processed through each of the operating units.

At Hall's staff meeting of July 2nd, the vice-president of operations declared OJ30 a "success." During that meeting an energetic discussion about how to express gratitude to the employees took place. The company ultimately provided a free lunch for the employees to thank them for their efforts, and a written statement of progress was prepared for the district sales managers. But privately some staff members expressed quite differing views about what had occurred. In fact some held the opinion that the whole affair was a failure because it did not address the real problems in the company.

OJ30 was a focus for the construction of different interpretations of reality. While the president and some of his staff constructed the situation in one way, other members forged their own view of the situation through the interplay of quite a different figure-ground relationship. It is instructive to examine the way the dynamics of the leadership process in this situation are reflected in the constructions of those involved.

Operation June 30: An attempt to manage meaning

How OJ30 structured meaning is reflected in the way it was created, named, and managed as a significant event within day to day work life. OJ30 was presented to staff members in a way that attempted to orient attention

away from the current situation to a desired future state. No attempt was made to analyze or interpret the significance of the backlog of work; the intent was just to eliminate it. This is reflected in the president's choice of language in the creation and naming of Operation June 30th. In the announcement the backlog was labelled "adverse," but not otherwise interpreted. The backlog is defined as the problem, and OJ30 was conceived as a military style operation to overcome it, implying a gathering of troops for an all-out assault. The name chosen by the president was not oriented to an explanation of the present conditions (e.g., "Operation Backlog" or "Operation Clean Sweep") but instead served to focus attention on a desired future state. Moreover, the inclusion of a date gave the program the status of a concrete event with an end point.

In this effort the president chose to emphasize certain temporal, perceptual ("special program," "highest priority") and interpersonal horizons ("concerted effort," "volunteer") to serve as context. By choosing a future time horizon, a perceptual space of tightness/closeness to respond to urgency, and an interpersonal horizon of smoothness and nonconflict, the president implied that the message of Operation June 30th was one of a forward focus. He placed no blame for current conditions and viewed the organization as a team, each member having an important role. When the vice-president of operations declared Operation June 30th a success, Hall saw the free lunch as an appropriate way to draw the event to a close.

This same pattern of emphasis was reflected in other examples of the president's talk, as in this instance of elaborating his management philosophy:

266   THE JOURNAL OF APPLIED BEHAVIORAL SCIENCE Vol. 18/No. 3/1982

We all need each other. You really don't go very far unless everybody's got their shoulder to the wheel.... You can't over-do this (teamwork) to the point where you threaten to suppress some spirited debate in an organization.... You could have people not speaking their minds just be-cause they feel they might undermine the teamwork philosophy, or the image you're trying to build. That would be wrong, because you've got to have some con-frontation between people as you go along, as long as it doesn't get personal. This is what I keep saying to the staff. You can't get personal about these things, because once you get personal and take on a person individually and affect your relationship, then you've injected a little poison into the outfit. But as long as you're sincere and you're talking about the issues instead of personalities, then debate should be encouraged if you're going to make the best decisions ... and the main thing is just to keep the per-sonalities out of it.

The president does not speak of his role in terms of charting the direction of the organization but instead focuses his efforts at establishing and main-taining internal harmony. His ap-proach toward OJ30 was quite con-sistent with this focus.

The staff members' reactions

Although the president sought to shape a reality of cooperation and urgency in the face of adverse condi-tions, it is apparent from the talk of executive staff that he did not succeed in generating these feelings among these staff members. Indeed, the reality for them was basically one of dis-harmony, disaffection, and noninvolve-ment. This is evidenced by remarks of the vice-president of operations, whose department was the main focus of Operation June 30th.

Tom (the president) talks about "sprinting to the finish," "we all have to put our shoulder to the wheel," but you know nobody responds.... To tell you the truth, I'm pretty fed up, I'm agitated by working every Saturday that I've been working, and to see very few other peo-ple who are helping or anything...."

The vice-president of operations maintained a chart to keep track of who had been helping during Opera-tion June 30th and expressed dissatis-faction with what it showed. "See, Di-rector of Personnel, all dashes by his name, he hasn't helped out.... We have no team around here."

The president's use of military im-agery was noted by the director of personnel but not seen as effective.

It's (OJ30) probably a good thing in a lot of ways because say somebody at-tacked our country, we got called into a world war.... I kind of thought that when this initially came out it would serve as a common cause, a unification of the different forces we have in the company. It started off in that direction, but it's eased up quite a bit.

There was no urgency about OJ30 for the staff members. "We'll be in the same boat on July 30th," said one executive and he explained why.

As long as ... the president or someone else that has some involvement with that department doesn't challenge them, every-one's going to think everything is fine. And it will be, until some agents or some insured ... begin to ask more questions as to why this isn't being done. I know for a fact that they aren't up-to-date. I could go over there and find errors.

But at the July 2nd staff meeting this same executive did not question the vice-president of operations' de-scription of OJ30 as a success, justify-ing his own behavior by saying his de-partment was not directly involved and that it was the president's responsibility to check and ask questions. But he believed the president incapable of doing so because he didn't know what to look for. In his own way, this executive also participated in burying the problems, but he saw that as the only option available to him.

The staff members' interpretations

The executive staff members rejected the meaning that the president sought to attach to the OJ30 program. They made sense of the project not in terms of some desired future state of task performance, but against the background of what they knew and felt about their organization.[3]

They were not a team, but instead a group in which conflict was repressed but close to the surface. Their group enacted a continued pattern of not dealing with problems effectively. The executive staff attributed this pattern to the preferences and style of the president. They considered him "too trusting" and "not wanting to hear if things are bad." Although he espoused that "you have to have some confrontation between people," he and the staff participated in avoiding confrontation.

To the executive staff, OJ30 was symbolic of the way of life in their organization. It represented one more instance of the president's continued reluctance to deal fully and directly with problems. He may have labelled OJ30 "highest priority" and attempted to mobilize their energies, but he got little more than business as usual. For the staff did not interpret it as an occasion in which to behave in tight and helpful coordination. They made sense of OJ30, not as an organizational imperative emphasizing interdependence, but as an organizational malaise encouraging an isolationist response.

The executive staff expressed feelings of powerlessness; they saw no way to do things differently. For them it was a choice of resigning or going along with the way it is. Neither alternative seemed attractive. They shared a common understanding of the expected mode of behavior, basically a passive posture and a shared perception of the president's preferences. Paradoxically, the president's attempt to manage the meaning of OJ30 ("everybody get their shoulder to the wheel") was actually sabotaged by his staff's adherence to what they saw as the "real" organizational value—the value which Hall, to them, embodied: If you do nothing, no harm will come to you.

The competing interpretations of reality

Figure 3 presents a summary of the competing interpretive schemes through which the president and his executive staff made sense of the OJ30 project. For the president, OJ30 sought to define the situation in a way that created a high priority, future-oriented program addressed to the question, "What do we do now?" His interpretation of the final "success" of the program was framed against the relative success of OJ30 in getting rid of the backlog of work. For the staff, OJ30 was framed against an understanding of why they were "in a mess" and had a very different significance. It was just another sign of the inadequate way the fragmented organization was being run. They saw it as the act of a manager who was afraid to confront the real issues, who insisted on seeing the organization as a team, whereas the reality was that of a poorly managed group characterized by narrow self-interest, and noncooperation at anything but a surface level. OJ30 for

Figure 3. Competing Interpretations of OJ30

Framing Experience	Interpretation	Meaning and Action
OJ30 frames significant elements of work experience (work backlog, customer and staff complaints) in a form that makes them amenable to action.	**The President's Interpretation** OJ30 provides an opportunity for the company to work together in the resolution of a problem. It will solve the problem and help develop a cooperative spirit. **The Staff Members' Interpretation** OJ30 represents another futile act which will do nothing to solve the organization's basic problems. It symbolizes the way we do things here.	**For the President** OJ30 does much to clear the backlog of work and can be judged a success. Meaning framed against an *idealized image* **For Staff Members** Will call for no more than minimal action; do not take too seriously for it can't do much to remedy the basic problem. Meaning framed against *past history*

them was symbolic of the status quo, and hence they were not effectively mobilized into action.

IMPLICATIONS FOR THE THEORY AND PRACTICE OF CONTEMPORARY ORGANIZATION

The OJ30 case illustrates a leadership action concerned with managing the meaning of a particular situation. As an action designed to catch up on a work-flow problem, OJ30 was partially successful, for it did generate extra work from many staff who felt obliged to do something in conformity with the president's wishes. As an action designed to define the meaning of a situation, it was for the most part a failure, for it was interpreted by the executive staff in a manner that ran counter to what the president desired. Indeed the president's most powerful impact on the pattern of meaning within the organization was of a negative kind— his inaction and avoidance of problems creating an atmosphere of drifting and inaction.

At the surface our analysis may lead to the conclusion that Hall was a weak and ineffective leader. But to quickly judge him so is to risk losing sight of the larger dynamics that are at work in this leadership situation. Although Hall's view of organizational reality is not shared by the executive staff, he exerted a major impact on the broader definition of the situation. His style and presence provided the most powerful point of reference for action. The executive staff in this case adopts a passive nonconfronting posture, living a somewhat uncomfortable organizational reality defined and symbolized by the president. Hall provides evidence of how even weak leadership, by its fundamental nature, involves the definitions of situations.

Leaders symbolize the organized situation in which they lead. Their actions and utterances project and shape imagery in the minds of the led, which is influential one way or another in shaping actions within the setting as a whole. This is not to deny the importance of the voluntary nature of the enactments and sense-making activities initiated by members of the situation being managed. Rather, it is to recognize and emphasize the special and important position accorded to the leader's view of the situation in the frame of reference of others. Leaders, by nature of their leadership role, are provided with a distinctive opportunity to influence the sense making of others. Our case study illustrates the importance of the leader recognizing the nature of his or her influence and managing the meaning of situations in a constructive way. At a minimum this involves that he or she (a) attempt to deal with the equivocality that permeates many interactive situations; (b) attend to the interpretive schemes of those involved, and (c) embody through use of appropriate language, rituals, and other forms of symbolic discourse, the meanings and values conducive to desired modes of organized action. A focus on leadership as the management of meaning encourages us to develop a theory for the practice of leadership in which these three generalizations are accorded a central role.

Our analysis also draws attention to the role of power as a defining feature of the leadership process. With the OJ30 case we see the way the power relations embedded in a leadership role oblige others to take particular note of the sense-making activities emanating from that role. We have

270   THE JOURNAL OF APPLIED BEHAVIORAL SCIENCE Vol. 18/No. 3/1982

characterized this in terms of a dependency relation between leaders and led, in which the leader's sense-making activities assume priority over the sense-making activities of others.

The existence of leadership depends on and fosters this dependency, for insofar as the leader is expected to define the situation, others are expected to surrender that right. As we have noted, leadership as a phenomenon depends upon the existence of people who are prepared to surrender their ability to define their reality to others. Situations of formal leadership institutionalize this pattern into a system of rights and obligations whereby the leader has the prerogative to define reality, and the led to accept that definition as a frame of reference for orienting their own activity.

Organized action in formal settings constitutes a process of enactment and sense making on the part of those involved, but one shaped in important ways by the power relations embedded in the situation as a whole. Leadership and the organizational forms to which it gives rise enact a reality that expresses a power relationship. An understanding of the power relationship embedded in all enactment processes is thus fundamental for understanding the nature of organization as an enacted social form, for enactments express power relationships.

Thus our analysis of the leadership process tells us much about the nature of organization as a hierarchical phenomenon. Most patterns of formal organization institutionalize the emergent characteristics of leadership into roles, rules, and relations that give tangible and enduring form to relationships between leaders and led. Our analysis of leadership as a social phenomenon based on interaction, sense

making, and dependency implies a view of much modern organization in which these factors are seen as defining features. To see leadership as the management of meaning is to see organizations as networks of managed meanings, resulting from those interactive processes through which people have sought to make sense of situations.

This view of leadership and organization provides a framework for reconsidering the way leadership has been treated in organizational research. By viewing leadership as a relationship between traits, roles, and behaviors and the situations in which they are found, or as a transactional process involving the exchange of rewards and influence, most leadership research has focused upon the dynamics and surface features of leadership as a tangible social process. The way leadership as a phenomenon involves the structuring and transformation of reality has with notable exceptions (e.g., Burns, 1978), been ignored, or at best approached tangentially. The focus on the exchange of influence and rewards has rarely penetrated to reveal the way these processes are embedded in, and reflect a deeper structure of power-based meaning and action. Leadership is not simply a process of acting or behaving, or a process of manipulating rewards. It is a process of power-based reality construction and needs to be understood in these terms.

The concept of leadership is a central building block of the conventional wisdom of organization and management. For the most part the idea that good organization embodies effective leadership practice passes unquestioned. Our analysis here leads us to question this wisdom and points toward the unintended consequences that leadership situations often generate.

The most important of these stem from the dependency relations that arise when individuals surrender their power and control over the definition of reality to others. Leaders may create situations in which individuals are crippled by purposelessness and inaction when left to guide efforts on their own account. Leadership may actually work against the development of self-responsibility, self-initiative, and self-control, in a manner that parallels Argyris's (1957) analysis of the way the characteristics of bureaucratic organization block potentialities for full human development. These blocks arise whenever leadership actions divert individuals from the process of defining and taking responsibility for their own action and experience.

Leadership situations may generate a condition of "trained inaction" in the led, a variant form of Veblen's (1904) "trained incapacity," observed by Merton (1968) as a dominant characteristic of the bureaucratic personality. This trained inaction is clearly illustrated in the 0J30 study where the executive staff experienced problems in their work situation as something beyond their control. The situation here emanates from the way a relatively weak leader defines the situation; but it is equally evident in situations of strong, dominating leadership illustrated in a graphic but extreme way in situations such as the tragedy in Jonestown, Guyana.

An awareness of the dependency relationships that characterize leadership situations sensitizes us to potentially undesirable consequences and also points toward ways in which leadership action can be directed for the avoidance of such states through the crea-

tion of patterns of meaning construction that facilitate constructive tension and innovation rather than passivity. In this regard our analysis points toward an important focus for both the practice of contemporary organization and for future research—on the processes through which the management of meaning in organized situations can develop in ways that enhance, rather than deny, the ability of individuals to take responsibility for the definition and control of their world.

It is important to investigate forms of organized action that depart from the traditional leadership model. We are persuaded to suggest that the study of nonleadership situations would focus attention on a phenomenon of some importance.

Patterns of organization that replace hierarchical leadership with patterns of more equalized interaction in which each has an obligation to define what is happening, and respond accordingly, changes the very basis of organization. Such arrangements increase the adaptive capacity of organization through what Emery and Trist (1972) have described as a redundancy of functions. These embody a model of human development in line with the ability of human beings to take responsibility for their actions. In situations characterized by hierarchical dependency, those in leadership roles are obliged to interpret and assimilate all that there is to observe and understand about a situation before initiating the action of others. In situations of more equalized power, this obligation and ability is more widely spread. Members of a situation are unable to look to authority relations to solve problems; adaptive capacities have to be developed at the level at which they are needed, increas-

272   THE JOURNAL OF APPLIED BEHAVIORAL SCIENCE Vol. 18/No. 3/1982

ing the learning and adaptive ability of the whole. Autonomous work groups and leaderless situations of all kinds present concrete opportunities for the study of emergent principles of organization that offer alternatives to the dependency relations that have permeated Western culture as an organizational norm.

The conventional wisdom that organization and leadership are by definition intertwined has structured the way we see and judge alternative modes of organized action. Approaching this subject from a perspective that treats organization as a phenomenon based on the management of meaning, we can begin to see and understand the importance of developing and encouraging alternative means through which organized action can be generated and sustained.

NOTES

1. A minor qualification is appropriate here in that certain charismatic leaders may inspire others to restructure their reality in creative ways. The dependency relation is evident, however, in that the individual takes the charismatic leader as a point of reference in this process.

2. The president of the insurance company had been involved in the day to day management of the company for 18 months. Previously, all nine executive staff members had reported to an executive vice-president so that the president could devote his attention to external relationships. When the executive vice-president died in January 1978, a decision was made not to replace him. Instead, all executive staff members reported directly to the president. The executive staff was a stable group; all had been employed in the company for no less than seven years.

3. The staff members were concerned about the equivocality surrounding the cause of the backlog. In a conversation with the researcher, the director of sales asked himself, "How did the company get into this position?" And replied, "It started two years ago with the decision to microfilm. It ate us up. I could have my head handed to me for this, the president backed

it." The sales director expressed the view that the past decision to install microfilming equipment and to microfilm all stored records as well as microfilm all incoming work had been the major factor in the operating department's falling so far behind in the processing of work. The other executives agreed with this interpretation.

REFERENCE NOTES

1. Bougon, M. *Schemata, leadership, and organizational behavior.* Doctoral dissertation, Cornell University, 1980.
2. Smircich, L. Studying organizations as cultures. In G. Morgan (Ed.), *Organizational research strategies: Links between theory and method.* Unpublished manuscript.

REFERENCES

Argyris, C. *Personality and organization.* New York: Harper, 1957.

Barnard, C. *The functions of the executive.* Cambridge, Mass.: Harvard University Press, 1938.

Bateson, G. *Steps to an ecology of mind.* New York: Ballantine Books, 1972.

Bennis, W. G., & Shepherd, H. A. A theory of group development. *Human Relations*, 1965, 9, 415–457.

Berger, P., & Luckmann, T. *The social construction of reality.* New York: Anchor Books, 1966.

Bogdan, R., & Taylor, S. J. *Introduction to qualitative methods.* New York: Wiley, 1975.

Burns, J. M. *Leadership.* New York: Harper & Row, 1978.

Emery, F. E., & Trist, E. L. *Towards a social ecology.* Harmondsworth: Penguin, 1973.

Fiedler, F. E. *A theory of leadership effectiveness.* New York: McGraw-Hill, 1967.

Goffman, E. *Frame analysis.* New York: Harper Colophon Books, 1974.

Jacobs, T. O. *Leadership and exchange in formal organizations.* Alexandria, Va.: Human Resources Organization, 1971.

Katz, D., & Kahn, R. L. *The social psychology of organizations.* New York: Wiley, 1966.

Mann, R. D. A review of the relationships between personality and performance in small groups. *Psychological Bulletin*, 1959, 56, 241–270.

Merton, R. K. *Social theory and social structure.* (enlarged ed.). New York: Free Press, 1968.

Mintzberg, H. *The nature of managerial work.* Englewood Cliffs, N.J.: Prentice-Hall, 1973.

Peters, T. J. Symbols, patterns and settings: An optimistic case for getting things done. *Organizational Dynamics*, 1978, 3–22.

Pfeffer, J. Management as symbolic action: The creation and maintenance of organizational paradigms. *Research in Organizational Behavior*, 1981, *3*, 1–52.

Pondy, L. R. Leadership is a language game. In M. McCall & M. Lombardo (Eds.), *Leadership: Where else can we go?* Durham, N.C.: Duke University Press, 1976.

Pondy, L. R., Frost, P., Morgan, G., & Dandridge, T. (Eds.). *Organizational symbolism*. Greenwich, Conn.: JAI Press, 1982.

Quinn, J. B. *Strategies for change*. New York: Irwin, 1980.

Roethlisberger, F. J., & Dickson, W. J. *Management and the worker*. Cambridge, Mass.: Harvard University Press, 1939.

Schatzman, L., & Strauss, A. *Fieldwork*. Englewood Cliffs, N.J.: Prentice-Hall, 1973.

Schutz, A. *Collected papers I: The problem of social reality*. (2nd ed.). The Hague: Martinus Nijhoff, 1967.

Selznick, P. *Leadership in administration*. New York: Harper & Row, 1957.

Sennett, R. *Authority*. New York: Knopf, 1980.

Smircich, L. Organizations as shared meanings. In Pondy, L. R., Frost, P., Morgan, G. & Dandridge, T. (Eds.). *Organizational symbolism*. Greenwich , Conn.: JAI Press, 1982.

Stogdill, R. M. *Handbook of leadership: A survey of theory and research*. New York: The Free Press, 1974.

Veblen, T. *The theory of business enterprise*. Clifton, N.J.: Augustus M. Kelly, 1975 (originally published 1904).

Weick, K. *The social psychology of organizing*. Reading, Mass.: Addison-Wesley, 1979.

Part VI
Power and Control

Leadership can be seen as one way of conceptualizing control in organizations; an alternative way would focus on systemic mechanisms rather than on persons and their interactions or would replace the socio-psychological approach with a sociological one, typically addressing power.

In 1961, Tom Burns and G.M. Stalker published *The Management of Innovation*,[4] a book that reviewed some 20 cases of postwar Scottish and English organizations, arriving at the conclusion that 'mechanistic' organizational structures were appropriate and effective in stable, simple environments, but that dynamic and complex environments call for flexible and self-adaptive 'organic' structures. By the 1960s, the idea launched by Burns and Stalker had developed into what was later called 'contingency theory'. Contingency theory, in all its variations, matched some attributes of internal organization with those of the environment. The British Aston Group, by now legendary, consequently elaborated on this model to create 'a strategic contingencies' theory of intraorganizational power', exemplified here by one of their many articles (Chapter 16).

On the other side of the Atlantic and the other side of the disciplinary divide, Olivier Williamson in economics developed his own organization theory, contrasting markets and hierarchies and comparing their relative transaction costs.[5] Although his work has influenced many scholars directly, the concepts that remained engraved in a collective memory of organization theory were those coined by William G. Ouchi (Chapter 17): markets, bureaucracies, and clans. The addition of clans softened the sharp dichotomy introduced by Williamson, and alluded to other notions increasingly popular in organization theory: loose couplings and culture.

Yet another angle was taken by critical theorists – first Marxists, and later Foucauldians.[6] Stewart Clegg and David Dunkerley's *Organization, Class and Control*[7] of 1980 remained for many years the leading representative of this trend, and is summarized here in Clegg's later article (Chapter 18).

Notes

4. Oxford: Oxford University Press.
5. Williamson, Olivier E. (1975), *Markets and Hierarchies: Analysis and Anti-trust Implications: A Study in Economics of Internal Organization*. New York: The Free Press.
6. Linda Smircich and Marta B. Calás have edited a reader entitled *Critical Perspectives on Organization and Management Theory* (1995), Aldershot: Dartmouth. For this reason, this perspective is signalled rather than exhaustively included in the present volume.
7. London: Routledge & Kegan Paul.

[16]

D. J. Hickson, C. R. Hinings, C. A. Lee, R. E. Schneck,
and J. M. Pennings

A Strategic Contingencies'
Theory of Intraorganizational Power

A strategic contingencies' theory of intraorganizational power is presented in which it is hypothesized that organizations, being systems of interdependent subunits, have a power distribution with its sources in the division of labor. The focus is shifted from the vertical-personalized concept of power in the literature to subunits as the units of analysis. The theory relates the power of a subunit to its coping with uncertainty, substitutability, and centrality, through the control of strategic contingencies for other dependent activities, the control resulting from a combination of these variables. Possible measures for these variables are suggested.

Typically, research designs have treated power as the independent variable. Power has been used in community studies to explain decisions on community programs, on resource allocation, and on voting behavior: in small groups it has been used to explain decision making; and it has been used in studies of work organizations to explain morale and alienation. But within work organizations, power itself has not been explained. This paper sets forth a theoretical explanation of power as the dependent variable with the aim of developing empirically testable hypotheses that will explain differential power among subunits in complex work organizations.[1]

The problems of studying power are well known from the cogent reviews by March (1955, 1966) and Wrong (1968). These problems led March (1966: 70) to ask if power was just a term used to mask our ignorance, and to conclude pessimistically that the power of the concept of power "depends on the kind of system we are confronting."

Part of March's (1966) pessimism can be attributed to the problems inherent in community studies. When the unit of analysis is the community, the governmental, political, economic, recreational, and other units which make up the community do not necessarily interact and may even be oriented outside the supposed boundaries of the community. However, the subunits of a work organization are mutually related in the interdependent activities of a single identifiable social system. The perspective of the present paper is due in particular to the encouraging studies of subunits by Lawrence and Lorsch (1967a, 1967b), and begins with their (1967a: 3) definition of an organization as "a system of interrelated behaviors of people who are performing a task that has been differentiated into several distinct subsystems."

Previous studies of power in work organizations have tended to focus on the individual and to neglect subunit or departmental power. This neglect led Perrow (1970: 84) to state: "Part of the problem, I suspect, stems from the persistent attempt to define power in terms of individuals and as a social-psychological phenomenon. . . . Even sociological studies tend to measure

[1] This research was carried out at the Organizational Behavior Research Unit, Faculty of Business Administration and Commerce, University of Alberta, with the support of Canada Council Grants numbers 67-0253 and 69-0714.

power by asking about an individual. . . . I am not at all clear about the matter, but I think the term takes on different meanings when the unit, or power-holder, is a *formal group* in an *open system* with *multiple goals,* and the system is assumed to reflect a political-domination model of organization, rather than only a cooperative model. . . . The fact that after a cursory search I can find only a single study that asks survey questions regarding the power of functional *groups* strikes me as odd. Have we conceptualized power in such a way as to exclude this well-known phenomenon?"

The concept of power used here follows Emerson (1962) and takes power as a property of the social relationship, not of the actor. Since the context of the relationship is a formal organization, this approach moves away from an overpersonalized conceptualization and operationalization of power toward structural sources. Such an approach has been taken only briefly by Dubin (1963) in his discussion of power, and incidentally by Lawrence and Lorsch (1967b) when reporting power data. Most research has focused on the vertical superior-subordinate relationship, as in a multitude of leadership studies. This approach is exemplified by the extensive work of Tannenbaum (1968) and his colleagues, in which the distribution of perceived power was displayed on control graphs. The focus was on the vertical differentiation of perceived power, that is the exercise of power by managers who by changing their behavior could vary the distribution and the total amount of perceived power.

By contrast, when organizations are conceived as interdepartmental systems, the division of labor becomes the ultimate source of intraorganizational power, and power is explained by variables that are elements of each subunit's task, its functioning, and its links with the activities of other subunits. Insofar as this approach differs from previous studies by treating power as the dependent variable, by taking subunits of work organizations as the subjects of analysis, and by attempting a multivariate explanation, it may avoid some of the previous pitfalls.

ELEMENTS OF A THEORY

Thompson (1967: 13) took from Cyert and March (1963) a viewpoint which he hailed as a newer tradition: "A newer tradition enables us to conceive of the organization as an open system, indeterminate and faced with uncertainty, but subject to criteria of rationality and hence needing certainty . . . we suggest that organizations cope with uncertainty by creating certain parts specifically to deal with it, specializing other parts in operating under conditions of certainty, or near certainty."

Thus organizations are conceived of as interdepartmental systems in which a major task element is coping with uncertainty. The task is divided and allotted to the subsystems, the division of labor creating an interdependency among them. Imbalance of this reciprocal interdependence (Thompson, 1967) among the parts gives rise to power relations. The essence of an organization is limitation of the autonomy of all its members or parts, since all are subject to power from the others; for subunits, unlike individuals, are not free to make a decision to participate, as March and Simon (1958) put it, nor to decide whether or not to come together in political relationships. They must. They exist to do so. Crozier (1964: 47) stressed in his discussion of power "the necessity for the members of the different groups to live together; the fact that each group's privileges depend to quite a large extent on the existence of other group's privileges." The groups use differential power to function within the system rather than to destroy it.

If dependency in a social relation is the reverse of power (Emerson, 1962), then the crucial unanswered question in organizations is: what factors function to vary dependency, and so to vary power? Emerson (1962: 32) proposed that "the dependence of actor A upon actor B is (*1*) directly proportional to A's motivational investment in goals mediated by B, and (*2*) inversely proportional to the availability of those goals to A outside of the A–B relation." In organizations, subunit B will have more power than other subunits to the extent that (*1*) B has the capacity to fulfill the requirements of the other subunits and (*2*) B monopolizes this ability. If a central problem facing modern organizations is uncertainty, then B's power in the organization will be partially determined by the extent to which B copes with uncertainties for other subunits, and by the extent to which B's coping activities are available elsewhere.

Thus, intraorganizational dependency can be associated with two contributing variables: (1) the degree to which a subunit copes with uncertainty for other subunits, and (2) the extent to which a subunit's coping activities are substitutable. But if coping with uncertainty, and substitutability, are to be in some way related to power, there is a necessary assumption of some degree of task interconnection among subunits. By definition, organization requires a minimum link. Therefore, a third variable, centrality, refers to the varying degree above such a minimum with which the activities of a subunit are linked with those of other subunits.

Before these three variables can be combined in a theory of power, it is necessary to examine their definition and possible operationalization, and to define power in this context.

Power

Hinings et al. (1967: 62) compared power to concepts such as bureaucracy or alienation or social class, which are difficult to understand because they tend to be treated as "large-scale unitary concepts." Their many meanings need disentangling. With the concept of power, this has not yet been accomplished (Cartwright, 1965), but two conceptualizations are commonly employed: (1) power as coercion, and (2) power as determination of behavior.

Power as coercive force was a comparatively early conceptualization among sociologists (Weber, 1947; Bierstedt, 1950). Later, Blau (1964) emphasized the imposition of will despite resistance.

However, coercion is only one among the several bases of power listed by French and Raven (1959) and applied across organizations by Etzioni (1961); that is, coercion is a means of power, but is not an adequate definition of power. If the direction of dependence in a relationship is determined by an imbalance of power bases, power itself has to be defined separately from these bases. Adopting Dahl's (1957) concept of power, as many others have done (March, 1955; Bennis et al., 1958; Emerson, 1962; Harsanyi, 1962; Van Doorn, 1962; Dahlstrom, 1966; Wrong, 1968; Tannenbaum, 1968; Luhmann, 1969), power is defined as the determination of the behavior of one social unit by another.

If power is the determination of A's behavior by B, irrespective of whether one, any, or all the types of bases are involved, then authority will here be regarded as that part of power which is legitimate or normatively expected by some selection of role definers. Authority may be either more or less than power. For subunits it might be represented by the formally specified range of activities they are officially required to undertake and, therefore, to decide upon.

Discrepancies between authority and power may reflect time lag. Perrow (1970) explored the discrepancy between respondent's perceptions of power and of what power should be. Perhaps views on a preferred power distribution precede changes in the exercise of power, which in turn precede changes in expectations of power, that is in its legitimate authority content. Perhaps today's authority hierarchy is partly a fossilized impression of yesterday's power ranking. However this may be, it is certainly desirable to include in any research not only data on perceived power and on preferred power, but also on positional power, or authority, and on participation, or exercised power (Clark [ed.], 1968).

Kaplan (1964) succinctly described three dimensions of power. The weight of power is defined in terms of the degree to which B affects the probability of A behaving in a certain way, that is, determination of behavior in the sense adopted here. The other dimensions are domain and scope. Domain is the number of A's, persons or collectivities, whose behavior is determined; scope is the range of behaviors of each A that are determined. For subunit power within an organization, domain might be the number of other subunits affected by the issues, scope the range of decision issues affected, and weight the degree to which a given subunit affects the decision process on the issues. In published research such distinctions are rarely made. Power consists of the sweeping undifferentiated perceptions of respondents when asked to rank individuals or classes of persons, such as supervisors, on influence. Yet at the same time the complexity of power in organizations is recognized. If it is taken for granted that, say, marketing has most to do with sales matters, that accounting has most to do with finance matters, supervisors with supervisory matters, and so on, then the validity of forcing respondents to generalize single opinions across an unstated range of possibilities is questionable.

To avoid these generalized opinions, data collected over a range of decision topics or issues are desirable. Such issues should in principle include all recognized problem areas in the organization, in each of which more than one subunit is involved. Examples might be marketing strategies, obtaining equipment, personnel training, and capital budgeting.

Some suggested subvariables and indicators of power and of the independent variables are summarized in Table 1. These are

TABLE 1.   VARIABLES AND OPERATIONALIZABLE SUBVARIABLES

Power (weight, domain, scope)
Positional power (authority)
Participation power
Perceived power
Preferred power
Uncertainty
Variability of organizational inputs
Feedback on subunit performance;
Speed
Specificity
Structuring of subunit activities
Coping with uncertainty, classified as:
By prevention (forestalling uncertainty)
By information (forecasting)
By absorption (action after the event)
Substitutability
Availability of alternatives
Replaceability of personnel
Centrality
Pervasiveness of workflows
Immediacy of workflows

intended to include both individual perceptions of power in the form of questionnaire responses and data of a somewhat less subjective kind on participation in decision processes and on formal position in the organization.

It is now possible to examine coping with uncertainty, substitutability and centrality.

Uncertainty and Coping with Uncertainty

Uncertainty may be defined as a lack of information about future events, so that alternatives and their outcomes are unpredictable. Organizations deal with environmentally derived uncertainties in the sources and composition of inputs, with uncertainties in the processing of throughputs, and again with environmental uncertainties in the disposal of outputs. They must have means to deal with these uncertainties for adequate task performance. Such ability is here called coping.

In his study of the French tobacco manufacturing industry, Crozier (1964: 164) suggested that power is related to "the kind of uncertainty upon which depends the life of the organization." March and Simon (1958) had earlier made the same point, and Perrow (1961) had discussed the shifting domination of different groups in organizations following the shifting uncertainties of resources and the routinization of skills. From studies of industrial firms, Perrow (1970) tentatively thought that power might be due to uncertainty absorption, as March and Simon (1958) call it. Lawrence and Lorsch (1967b) found that marketing had more influence than production in both container-manufacturing and food-processing firms, apparently because of its involvement in (uncertain) innovation and with customers.

Crozier (1964) proposed a strategic model of organizations as systems in which groups strive for power, but his discussion did not clarify how uncertainty could relate positively to power. Uncertainty itself does not give power: coping gives power. If organizations allocate to their various subunits task areas that vary in uncertainty, then those subunits that cope most effectively with the most uncertainty should have most power within the organization, since coping by a subunit reduces the impact of uncertainty on other activities in the organization, a shock absorber function. Coping may be by prevention, for example, a subunit prevents sales fluctuations by securing firm orders; or by information, for example, a subunit forecasts sales fluctuations; or by absorption, for example, a drop in sales is swiftly countered by novel selling methods (Table 1). By coping, the subunit provides pseudo certainty for the other subunits by controlling what are otherwise contingencies for other activities. This coping confers power through the dependencies created.

Thus organizations do not necessarily aim to avoid uncertainty nor to reduce its absolute level, as Cyert and March (1963) appear to have assumed, but to cope with it. If a subunit can cope, the level of uncertainty encountered can be increased by moving into fresh sectors of the environment, attempting fresh outputs, or utilizing fresh technologies.

Operationally, raw uncertainty and coping will be difficult to disentangle, though theoretically the distinctions are clear. For all units, uncertainty is in the raw situation which would exist without the activities of the other relevant subunits, for example, the uncertainty that would face production units if the sales subunit were not there to forecast and/or to obtain a smooth flow of orders. Uncertainty might be indicated by the variability of those inputs to the organization which are taken by the subunit. For instance, a production subunit may face variability in raw materials and engineering may face variability in equipment performance. Lawrence and Lorsch (1967a) attempted categorizations of this kind. In addition, they (1967a: 14) gave a lead with "the time span of definitive feedback from the environment." This time span might be treated as a secondary indicator of uncertainty, making the assumption that the less the feedback to a subunit on the results of what it is doing, and the less specific the feedback, the more likely the subunit is to be working in a vague, unknown, unpredictable task area. Both speed and specificity of feedback are suggested variables in Table 1.

Furthermore, the copious literature on bureaucratic or mechanistic structures versus more organic and less defined structures could be taken to imply that routinized or highly structured subunits, for example, as conceptualized and measured by Pugh *et al.* (1968), will have stable homogeneous activities and be less likely to face uncertainty. This assumption would require empirical testing before structuring of activities could be used as an indicator of uncertainty, but it is tentatively included in Table 1.

In principle, coping with uncertainty might be directly measured by the difference between the uncertainty of those inputs taken by a subunit and the certainty with which it performs its activities nonetheless. This would indicate the degree of shock absorption.

The relation of coping with uncertainty to power can be expressed by the following hypothesis:

Hypothesis 1. The more a subunit copes with uncertainty, the greater its power within the organization.

The hypothesis is in a form which ignores any effects of centrality and substitutability.

Substitutability

Concepts relating to the availability of alternatives pervade the literature on power. In economics theory the degree of competition is taken as a measure of the extent to which alternatives are available from other organizations, it being implied that the power of an organization over other organizations and customers is a function of the amount of competition present. The same point was the second part of Emerson's (1962) power-dependency scheme in social relations, and the second requirement or determinant in Blau's (1964) model of a power relationship.

Yet only Mechanic (1962) and Dubin (1957, 1963) have discussed such concepts as explanations of organizational power. Mechanic's (1962: 358) hypothesis 4 stated: "Other factors remaining constant, a person difficult to replace will have greater power than a person easily replaceable." Dubin (1957) stressed the very similar notion of

Hickson et al: STRATEGIC CONTINGENCIES' THEORY   221

exclusiveness, which as developed later (Dubin, 1963: 21), means that: "For any given level of functional importance in an organization, the power residing in a functionary is inversely proportional to the number of other functionaries in the organization capable of performing the function." Supporting this empirically, Lipset *et al.* (1956) suggested that oligarchy may occur in trade unions because of the official's monopoly of political and negotiating skills.

The concept being used is represented here by the term substitutability, which can, for subunits, be defined as the ability of the organization to obtain alternative performance for the activities of a subunit, and can be stated as a hypothesis for predicting the power of a subunit as follows:

Hypothesis 2. The lower the substitutability of the activities of a subunit, the greater its power within the organization.

Thus a purchasing department would have its power reduced if all of its activities could be done by hired materials agents, as would a personnel department if it were partially substituted by selection consultants or by line managers finding their staff themselves. Similarly, a department may hold on to power by retaining information the release of which would enable others to do what it does.

The obvious problem in operationalization is establishing that alternative means of performing activities exist, and if they do, whether they could feasibly be used. Even if agents or consultants exist locally, or if corporation headquarters could provide services, would it really be practicable for the organization to dispense with its own subunit? Much easier to obtain are data on replaceability of subunit personnel such as length of training required for new recruits and ease of hiring, which can be regarded as secondary indicators of the substitutability of a subunit, as indicated in Table 1.

Centrality

Given a view of organizations as systems of interdependent roles and activities, then the centrality of a subunit is the degree to which its activities are interlinked into the system. By definition, no subunit of an organization can score zero centrality. With-

out a minimum of centrality, coping with uncertainty and substitutability cannot affect power; above the minimum, additional increments of centrality further differentiate subunit power. It is the degree to which the subunit is an interdependent component, as Thompson (1967: 54) put it, distinguishing between pooled, sequential, and reciprocal interdependence patterns. Blau and Scott (1962) made an analogous distinction between parallel and interdependent specialization. Woodward (1965: 126) also introduced a concept of this kind into her discussion of the critical function in each of unit, large batch and mass, and process production: "there seemed to be one function that was central and critical in that it had the greatest effect on success and survival."

Within the overall concept of centrality, there are inconsistencies which indicate that more than one constitutive concept is being used. At the present stage of conceptualization their identification must be very tentative. First, there is the idea that the activities of a subunit are central if they are connected with many other activities in the organization. This workflow pervasiveness may be defined as the degree to which the workflows of a subunit connect with the workflows of other subunits. It describes the extent of task interactions between subunits, and for all subunits in an organization it would be operationalized as the flowchart of a complete systems analysis. For example, the integrative subsystems studied by Lawrence and Lorsch (1967a: 30), "whose members had the function of integrating the sales-research and the production-research subsystems" and which had structural and cultural characteristics intermediate between them, were presumably high on workflow pervasiveness because everything they did connected with the workflows of these several other subsystems. Research subsystems, however, may have been low on this variable if they fed work only to a single integrative, or production, subsystem.

Secondly, the activities of a subunit are central if they are essential in the sense that their cessation would quickly and substantially impede the primary workflow of the organization. This workflow immediacy is defined as the speed and severity with which the workflows of a subunit affect the final outputs of the organization. Zald (1962) and Clark (1956) used a similar idea when they explained differential power among institution staff and education faculty by the close relation of their activities to organization goals.

The pervasiveness and immediacy of the workflows of a subunit are not necessarily closely related, and may empirically show a low correlation. A finance department may well have pervasive connections with all other subunits through the budgeting system, but if its activities ceased it would be some time before the effects were felt in, say, the production output of a factory; a production department controlling a stage midway in the sequence of an automated process, however, could have high workflow immediacy though not high pervasiveness.

The two main centrality hypotheses can therefore be stated as follows:

Hypothesis 3a. The higher the pervasiveness of the workflows of a subunit, the greater its power within the organization.

Hypothesis 3b. The higher the immediacy of the workflows of a subunit, the greater its power within the organization.

CONTROL OF CONTINGENCIES

Hypotheses relating power to coping with uncertainty, substitutability, and the subvariables of centrality have been stated in a simple single-variable form. Yet it follows from the view of subunits as interdependent parts of organizational systems that the hypotheses in this form are misleading. While each hypothesis may be empirically upheld, it is also hypothesized that this cannot be so without some values of both the other main independent variables. For example, when a marketing department copes with a volatile market by forecasting and by switching sales staff around to ensure stable orders, it acquires power only because the forecast and the orders are linked to the workflow of production, which depends on them. But even then power would be limited by the availability of a successful local marketing agency which could be hired by the organization, and the fact that

salesmen were low skilled and easily replaceable.

To explain this interrelationship, the concept of control of contingencies is introduced. It represents organizational interdependence; subunits control contingencies for one another's activities and draw power from the dependencies thereby created. As a hypothesis:

Hypothesis 4. The more contingencies are controlled by a subunit, the greater its power within the organization.

A contingency is a requirement of the activities of one subunit which is affected by the activities of another subunit. What makes such a contingency strategic, in the sense that it is related to power, can be deduced from the preceding hypotheses. The independent variables are each necessary but not sufficient conditions for control of strategic contingencies, but together they determine the variation in interdependence between subunits. Thus contingencies controlled by a subunit as a consequence of its coping with uncertainty do not become strategic, that is, affect power, in the organization without some (unknown) values of substitutability and centrality. A strategic contingencies theory of power is therefore proposed and is illustrated by the diagram in Figure 1.

In terms of exchange theory, as developed by Blau (1964), subunits can be seen to be exchanging control of strategic contingencies one for the other under the normative regulation of an encompassing social system, and acquiring power in the system through the exchange. The research task is to elucidate what combinations of values of the independent variables summarized in hypotheses 1–3 allow hypothesis 4 to hold. Ultimately and ideally the aim would be to discover not merely the weightings of each in the total effect upon power, but how these variables should be operationally interrelated to obtain the best predictions. More of one and less of another may leave the resulting power unchanged. Suppose an engineering subunit has power because it quickly absorbs uncertainty by repairing breakdowns which interfere with the different workflows for each of several organization outputs. It is moderately central and non-

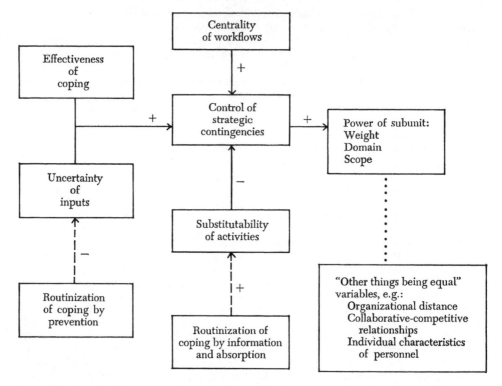

⟶ Direct relationship with power; ------- indirect relationship with power; ....
relationship with power other than by control of contingencies.

FIGURE 1. THE STRATEGIC CONTINGENCIES THEORY AND ROUTINIZATION

substitutable. A change in organization policy bringing in a new technology with a
single workflow leading to a single output
would raise engineering's centrality, since
a single breakdown would immediately stop
everything, but simultaneously the uncertainty might be reduced by a maintenance
program which all but eliminates the possibility of such an occurrence.

Though three main factors are hypothesized, which must change if power is to
change, it is not assumed that all subunits
will act in accord with the theory to increase
their power. This has to be demonstrated.
There is the obvious possibility of a cumulative reaction in which a subunit's power
is used to preserve or increase the uncertainty it can cope with, or its centrality, or
to prevent substitution, thereby increasing

its power, and so on. Nor is it argued that
power or authority are intentionally allocated in terms of the theory, although the
theory is open to such an inference.

Routinization

Most studies that refer to uncertainty contrast is with routinization, the prior prescription of recurrent task activities. Crozier
(1964) held that the power of the maintenance personnel in the tobacco plants was
due to all other tasks being routinized. A
relative decline in the power of general
medical personnel in hospitals during this
century is thought to be due to the routinization of some tasks, which previously presented uncertainties which could be coped
with only by a physician, and the transfer

of these tasks to relatively routinized sub-units, such as inoculation programs, mass X-ray facilities, and so on (Perrow, 1965; Gordon and Becker, 1964). Crozier (1964: 165) crystallized the presumed effects of routinization; "But the expert's success is constantly self-defeating. The rationalization process gives him power, but the end results of rationalization curtail his power. As soon as a field is well covered, as soon as the first intuitions and innovations can be translated into rules and programs, the expert's power disappears."

The strategic contingencies' theory as developed in Figure 1 clarifies this. It suggests that research has been hampered by a confusion of two kinds of routinization, both of which are negatively related to power but in different ways. Routinization may be (*a*) of coping by prevention, which prevents the occurrence of uncertainty; and (*b*) of coping by information or absorption which define how the uncertainty which does occur shall be coped with.

Preventive routinization reduces or removes the uncertainty itself, for example, planned maintenance, which maintenance in Crozier's (1964) tobacco factories would have resisted; inoculation or X-ray programs; and long-term supply contracts, so that the sales staff no longer have to contend with unstable demand. Such routinization removes the opportunity for power, and it is this which is self-defeating (Crozier, 1964: 165) if the expert takes his techniques to a point when they begin not only to cope but to routinely diminish the uncertainty coped with. Thus reducing the uncertainty is not the same as reducing the impact of uncertainty. According to the hypothesis, a sales department which transmits steady orders despite a volatile market has high power; a sales department which reduces the uncertainty itself by long-term tied contracts has low power.

Routinization of coping by information and absorption is embodied in job descriptions and task instructions prescribing how to obtain information and to respond to uncertainty. For maintenance personnel, it lays down how to repair the machine; for physicians, it lays down a standard procedure for examining patients and sequences of reme-

dies for each diagnosis. How does this affect power, since it does not eliminate the uncertainty itself, as preventive routinization does? What it does is increase substitutability. The means of coping become more visible and possible substitutes more obvious, even if those substitutes are unskilled personnel from another subunit who can follow a standard procedure but could not have acquired the previously unexpressed skills.

There is probably some link between the two kinds of routinization. Once preventive routinization is accomplished, other coping routinization more easily follows, as indeed it follows any reduction of uncertainty.

STUDIES OF SUBUNIT POWER

Testing of Hypotheses on Earlier Work

The utility of the strategic contingencies theory should be tested on published work, but it is difficult to do this adequately, since most studies stress only one possibility. For example, Crozier (1964) and Thompson (1967) stressed uncertainty, Dubin (1963) stressed exclusiveness of function, and Woodward (1965) spoke of the critical function.

The difficulty is also due to the lack of data. For example, among several studies in which inferences about environmental uncertainty are drawn, only Lawrence and Lorsch (1967b) presented data. They combine executive's questionnaire responses on departmental clarity of job requirements, time span of definitive feedback on departmental success in performance, and uncertainty of cause and effect in the department's functional area.

Lawrence and Lorsch (1967b: 127) found that in two food-processing organizations, research was most influential, then marketing, excluding the field selling unit, and then production. However, influence, or perceived power as it is called here, was rated on the single issue of product innovation and not across a range of issues as suggested earlier in this paper; validity therefore rests on the assumption of equal potential involvement of each function in this one issue. Would research still be most influential if the issues included equipment purchase, or capital budgeting, or personnel training? Even so, on influence over product innovation, an uncertainty hypothesis could be said to fit neatly, since the subunits were ordered on perceived uncertainty of subenvironment exactly as they were on influence.

But uncertainty alone would not explain power in the other firms studied. Although in six plastics firms, coordinating sections or integrating units were perceived as having more influence than functional subunits because "integration itself was the most problematic job" (Lawrence and Lorsch 1967b: 62), it was also a central job in terms of workflow pervasiveness.

Furthermore, in two container manufacturing organizations, although the market subenvironment was seen as the least uncertain, the sales subunit was perceived as the most influential (Lawrence and Lorsch 1967b: 111). An explanation must be sought in the contingencies that the sales subunit controls for production and for research. In this industry, outputs must fit varying customer requirements for containers. Scheduling for production departments and design problems for research departments are therefore completely subject to the contingencies of orders brought in by the sales department. Sales has not only the opportunity to cope with such uncertainty as may exist over customer requirements, it is highly central; for its activities connect it directly to both the other departments—workflow pervasiveness—and if it ceased work production of containers would stop—workflow immediacy. The effects of centrality are probably bolstered by nonsubstitutability, since the sales subunit develops a necessary particularized knowledge of customer requirements. Production and research are, therefore, comparatively powerless in face of the strategic contingencies controlled by the sales subunit.

In short, only a sensitive balancing of all three factors can explain the patterns of contingencies from which power strategically flows.

This is plain also in Crozier's (1964) insightful study of small French tobacco-manufacturing plants. Crozier (1964: 109) had the impression that the maintenance engineers were powerful because "machine stoppages are the only major happenings that cannot be predicted"; therefore the engineers had (Crozier, 1964: 154) "control over the last source of uncertainty remaining in a completely routinized organizational system." But this is not enough for power. Had it been possible to contract maintenance work to consulting engineers, for example, then programs of preventive maintenance might have been introduced, and preventive routinization would have removed much of the uncertainty. However, it is likely that union agreements ensured that the plant engineers were nonsubstitutable. In addition, in these small organizations without specialist control and service departments, the maintenance section's work linked it to all production subunits, that is, to almost every other subunit in the plant. So workflow pervasiveness was high, as was workflow immediacy, since cessation of maintenance activities would quickly have stopped tobacco outputs. The control of strategic contingencies which gave power to the engineers has to be explained on all counts and not by uncertainty alone.

Crozier's (1964) study is a warning against the facile inference that a power distribution fitting the strategic contingencies theory is necessarily efficient, or rational, or functional for an organization; for the power of the engineers to thwart the introduction of programmed maintenance was presumably neither efficient, rational, nor functional.

A challenge to the analysis made is presented by Goldner's (1970) description of a case where there was programmed maintenance and yet the maintenance section held power over production. Goldner (1970) attributed the power of the maintenance subunit to knowing how to install and operate such programs, to coping with breakdowns as in the Crozier (1964) cases, and to knowing how to cope with a critical problem of parts supplies. The strategic contingencies theory accords with his interpretation so long as knowing how to install a program takes effect as coping with uncertainty and not yet as preventive routinization which stops breakdowns. This is where an unknown time element enters to allow for changes in the variables specified and in any associated variables not yet defined. For a time, knowing the answer to an uncertainty does confer power, but the analyses of routinization derived from the theory, as shown in Figure 1, suggests that if this becomes successful preventive routinization, it takes a negative effect upon power. The net result for power in Goldner's (1970) case would then be from the interplay of the opposed effects of activities some of which are preventively routinized, thus decreasing power, and some of which continue to be nonroutine, thus increasing power.

On the other hand, Goldner's (1970) description of the powerful industrial relations subunit in the same plant clearly supports the strategic contingencies theory by showing that coping with uncertainty, centrality, and substitutability had the effect predicted here. The industrial relations subunit exploited uncertainty over the supply and cost of personnel, which arose from possible strikes and pay increases, by (Goldner, 1970: 104) "use of the union as an outside threat." It coped effectively by its nonroutinized knowledge of union officials and of contract interpretation; and its activities were centrally linked to those of other subunits by the necessity for uniform practice on wages and employment. Industrial relations staff developed nonsubstitutable interpersonal and bargaining skills.

There are no means of assessing whether the univariate stress on uncertainty in the handful of other relevant studies is justified. Perrow (1970) explained the greater perceived power of sales as against production, finance, and research, in most of 12 industrial firms, by the concept of uncertainty absorption (March and Simon, 1958). Sales was strategic with respect to the environment. Is the one case where it came second to production the only case where it was also substitutable? Or not central?

White (1961) and Landsberger (1961) both suggested that power shifts over periods of time to follow the locus of uncertainty. Both studied engineering factories. From the histories of three firms, Landsberger (1961) deduced that when money was scarce and uncertain, accounting was powerful; when raw materials were short, purchasing was powerful; and, conversely, when demand was insatiable sales were

weakened. In the Tennessee Valley Authority, a nonmanufacturing organization, Selznick (1949) attributed the eventual power of the agricultural relations department to its ability to cope with the uncertain environmental threat represented by the Farm Bureau.

Yet while these earlier studies emphasized uncertainty in one way or another, others called attention to substitutability and probably also to centrality. Again the implication is that contingencies are not strategically controlled without some combination of all three basic variables. For example, the engineers described by Strauss (1962, 1964) appeared to have more power than purchasing agents because the latter were substitutable, that is, the engineers can set specifications for what was to be bought even though the purchasing agents considered this their own responsibility. Thompson (1956: 300) attributed variations in perceived power within and between two U.S. Air Force wings to the changing "technical requirements of operations," which may have indicated changing centralities and substitutabilities.

In the absence of data, consideration of further different kinds of organization must remain pure speculation, for example, the power of surgical units in hospitals, the power of buyers in stores, the power of science faculties in universities.

Other Variables Affecting Power

In order that it can be testable, the strategic contingencies theory errs on the side of simplicity. Any theory must start with a finite number of variables and presume continual development by their alteration or deletion, or by the addition of new variables. As stated, the theory uses only those variables hypothesized to affect power by their contribution to the control of contingencies exercised by a subunit. Other possible explanations of power are not considered. This in itself is an assumption of the greater explanatory force of the theory. Blalock (1961: 8) put the problem clearly: "The dilemma of the scientist is to select models that are at the same time simple enough to permit him to think with the aid of the model but also sufficiently realistic that the simplifications required do not lead to predictions that are highly inaccurate."

In recognition of this, Figure 1 includes several "other things being equal" variables as they are called, that may affect power, but are assumed to do so in other ways than by control of contingencies. One such range of possible relevant variables is qualities of interdepartmental relationships, such as competitiveness versus collaborativeness (Dutton and Walton, 1966). Does the power exercised relate to the style of the relationship through which the power runs? Another possibility is pinpointed by Stymne (1968: 88): "A unit's influence has its roots partly in its strategical importance to the company and partly in nonfunctional circumstances such as tradition, or control over someone in top management through, for example, family relationship." The tradition is the status which may accrue to a particular function because chief executives have typically reached the top through it. Many case studies highlight the personal links of subunits with top personnel (Dalton, 1959; Gouldner, 1955). The notion might be entitled the organizational distance of the subunit, a variant of social distance.

Finally, but perhaps most important, individual differences must be accepted, that is, differences in the intelligence, skills, ages, sexes, or personality factors such as dominance, assertiveness, and risk-taking propensity, of personnel in the various subunits.

CONCLUSION

The concept of work organizations as interdepartmental systems leads to a strategic contingencies theory explaining differential subunit power by dependence on contingencies ensuing from varying combinations of coping with uncertainty, substitutability, and centrality. It should be stressed that the theory is not in any sense static. As the goals, outputs, technologies, and markets of organizations change so, for each subunit, the values of the independent variables change, and patterns of power change.

Many problems are unresolved. For example, does the theory implicitly assume perfect knowledge by each subunit of the contingencies inherent for it in the activities of the others? Does a workflow of informa-

tion affect power differently to a workflow of things? But with the encouragement of the improved analysis given of the few existing studies, data can be collected and analyzed, hopefully in ways which will afford a direct test.

David J. Hickson is Ralph Yablon professor of behavioural studies, organizational analysis research unit, University of Bradford Management Centre, England; Christopher R. Hinings is a senior lecturer in sociology, industrial administration research unit, University of Aston-in-Birmingham, England; Charles A. Lee and Rodney E. Schneck are professors in the faculty of business administration and commerce, University of Alberta, Canada; and Johannes M. Pennings is an instructor and doctoral student at the institute for social research, University of Michigan.

REFERENCES

Bennis, Warren G., N. Berkowitz, M. Affinito, and M. Malone
  1958 "Authority, power and the ability to influence." Human Relations, 11: 143–156.
Bierstedt, Robert
  1950 "An analysis of social power." American Sociological Review, 15: 730–736.
Blalock, Hubert M.
  1961 Causal Inferences in Nonexperimental Research. Chapel Hill: University of North Carolina Press.
Blau, Peter
  1964 Exchange and Power in Social Life. New York: Wiley.
Blau, Peter, and W. Richard Scott
  1962 Formal Organizations: A Comparative Approach. London: Routledge and Kegan Paul.
Cartwright, Darwin
  1965 "Influence, leadership, control." In James G. March (ed.), Handbook of Organizations: 1–47. Chicago: Rand McNally.
Clark, Burton R.
  1956 "Organizational adaptation and precarious values: a case study." American Sociological Review, 21: 327–336.
Clark, Terry N. (ed.)
  1968 Community Structure and Decision-Making: Comparative Analyses. San Francisco: Chandler.

Crozier, Michel
1964 The Bureaucratic Phenomenon. London: Tavistock.
Cyert, Richard M., and James G. March
1963 A Behavioral Theory of the Firm. Englewood Cliffs, N.J.: Prentice-Hall.
Dahl, Robert A.
1957 "The concept of power." Behavioral Science, 2: 201–215.
Dahlstrom, E.
1966 "Exchange, influence, and power." Acta Sociologica, 9: 237–284.
Dalton, Melville
1959 Men Who Manage. New York: Wiley.
Dubin, Robert
1957 "Power and union-management relations." Administrative Science Quarterly, 2: 60–81.
1963 "Power, function, and organization." Pacific Sociological Review, 6: 16–24.
Dutton, John M., and Richard E. Walton
1966 "Interdepartmental conflict and cooperation: two contrasting studies." Human Organization, 25: 207–220.
Emerson, R. E.
1962 "Power-dependence relations." American Sociological Review, 27: 31–41.
Etzioni, Amitai
1961 A Comparative Analysis of Complex Organizations. New York: Free Press.
French, John R. P., and Bertram Raven
1959 "The bases of social power." In D. Cartwright (ed.), Studies in Social Power: 150–167. Ann Arbor: University of Michigan.
Goldner, Fred H.
1970 "The division of labor: process and power." In Mayer N. Zald (ed.), Power in Organizations: 97–143. Nashville: Vanderbilt University Press.
Gordon, Gerald, and Selwyn Becker
1964 "Changes in medical practice bring shifts in the patterns of power." The Modern Hospital (February): 89–91, 154–156.
Gouldner, Alvin W.
1955 Wildcat Strike. London: Routledge.
Harsanyi, John C.
1962 "Measurement of social power, opportunity costs, and the theory of two-person bargaining games." Behavioral Science, 7: 67–80.
Hinings, Christopher R., Derek S. Pugh, David J. Hickson, and Christopher Turner
1967 "An approach to the study of bureaucracy." Sociology, 1: 61–72.
Kaplan, Abraham
1964 "Power in perspective." In Robert L.

Kahn and Elise Boulding (eds.), Power and Conflict in Organizations: 11–32. London: Tavistock.
Landsberger, Henry A.
1961 "The horizontal dimension in bureaucracy." Administrative Science Quarterly, 6: 299–332.
Lawrence, Paul R., and Jay W. Lorsch
1967a "Differentiation and integration in complex organizations." Administrative Science Quarterly, 12: 1–47.
1967b Organization and Environment. Cambridge: Division of Research, Graduate School of Business Administration, Harvard University.
Lipset, Seymour M., Martin A. Trow, and James A. Coleman
1956 Union Democracy. Glencoe, Ill.: Free Press.
Luhmann, Niklaus
1969 "Klassische theorie der macht." Zeitschrift fur Politik, 16: 149–170.
March, James G.
1955 "An introduction to the theory and measurement of influence." American Political Science Review, 49: 431–450.
1966 "The power of power." In David Easton (ed.), Varieties of Political Theory: 39–70. Englewood Cliffs. N.J.: Prentice-Hall.
March, James G., and Herbert A. Simon
1958 Organizations. New York: Wiley.
Mechanic, David
1962 "Sources of power of lower participants in complex organizations." Administrative Science Quarterly, 7: 349–364.
Perrow, Charles
1961 "The analysis of goals in complex organizations." American Sociological Review, 26: 854–866.
1965 "Hospitals: technology, structure, and goals." In James G. March (ed.), Handbook of Organizations: 910–971. Chicago: Rand McNally.
1970 "Departmental power and perspectives in industrial firms." In Mayer N. Zald (ed.), Power in Organizations: 59–89. Nashville: Vanderbilt University Press.
Pugh, Derek S., David J. Hickson, Christopher R. Hinings, and Christopher Turner
1968 "Dimensions of organization structure." Administrative Science Quarterly, 13: 65–105.
Selznick, Philip
1949 T.V.A. and the Grass Roots. Berkeley: University of California Press.

Strauss, George
    1962   "Tactics of lateral relationship: the
            purchasing   agent."   Administrative
            Science Quarterly, 7: 161–186.
    1964   "Work-flow frictions, interfunctional
            rivalry, and professionalism." Human
            Organization, 23: 137–150.
Stymne, Bengt
    1968   "Interdepartmental   communication
            and intraorganizational strain." Acta
            Sociologica, 11: 82–100.
Tannenbaum, Arnold S.
    1968   Control in Organizations. New York:
            McGraw-Hill.
Thompson, James D.
    1956   "Authority and power in 'identical'
            organizations." American Journal of
            Sociology, 62: 290–301.
    1967   Organizations in Action. New York:
            McGraw-Hill.
Van Doorn, Jaques A. A.
    1962   "Sociology and the problem of power."
            Sociologica Neerlandica, 1: 3–47.

Weber, Max
    1947   The Theory of Social and Economic
            Organization.   Glencoe,   Ill.:   Free
            Press.
White, Harrison
    1961   "Management conflict and sociometric
            structure." American Journal of So-
            ciology, 67: 185–199.
Woodward, Joan
    1965   Industrial Organization: Theory and
            Practice. London: Oxford University
            Press.
Wrong, Dennis H.
    1968   "Some problems in defining social
            power." American Journal of Sociol-
            ogy, 73, 673–681.
Zald, Mayer N.
    1962   "Organizational control structures in
            five correctional institutions." Ameri-
            can Journal of Sociology, 68: 335–
            345.

[17]

MANAGEMENT SCIENCE
Vol. 25, No. 9, September1979
Printed in U.S.A.

A CONCEPTUAL FRAMEWORK FOR THE DESIGN OF ORGANIZATIONAL CONTROL MECHANISMS*

WILLIAM G. OUCHI†

The problem of organization is the problem of obtaining cooperation among a collection of individuals or units who share only partially congruent objectives. When a team of individuals collectively produces a single output, there develops the problem of how to distribute the rewards emanating from that output in such a manner that each team member is equitably rewarded. If equitable rewards are not forthcoming, members will, in future cooperative ventures, adjust their efforts in such a manner that all will be somewhat worse off (cf. Simon [41], Marschak [26], Alchian and Demsetz [1]).

It is the objective of this paper to describe three fundamentally different mechanisms through which organizations can seek to cope with this problem of evaluation and control. The three will be referred to as markets, bureaucracies, and clans. In a fundamental sense, markets deal with the control problem through their ability to precisely measure and reward individual contributions; bureaucracies rely instead upon a mixture of close evaluation with a socialized acceptance of common objectives; and clans rely upon a relatively complete socialization process which effectively eliminates goal incongruence between individuals. This paper explores the organizational manifestations of these three approaches to the problem of control.

The paper begins with an example from a parts distribution division of a major company which serves to give some flesh to what might otherwise be overly-abstract arguments. Through the example, each of the three mechanisms is explicated briefly and discussed in terms of two prerequisite conditions, one social and the other informational. The more concrete organization design features of the three forms are considered, along with some consideration of the unique costs accompanying each form.

(ORGANIZATIONAL DESIGN; CONTROL; ORGANIZATIONAL GOALS)

1. Introduction

Organizational control has many meanings and has been interpreted in many ways. Tannenbaum [42], whose view has dominated organizational theory, interprets control as the sum of interpersonal influence relations in an organization. In a similar vein, Etzioni [13] finds it useful to treat control in organizations as equivalent to power. Other than the power-influence approach to control, organization theorists have also treated control as a problem in information flows (Galbraith [15], Ouchi and Maguire [30]), as a problem in creating and monitoring rules through a hierarchical authority system as specified by Weber [46] and interpreted by Perrow [33], Blau and Scott [7], and many organizational sociologists, and as a cybernetic process of testing, measuring, and providing feedback (Thompson [43], Reeves and Woodward [35]).

This paper considers a more simple-minded view of organizational control stated in the following two questions: What are the mechanisms through which an organization can be managed so that it moves towards its objectives? How can the design of these mechanisms be improved, and what are the limits of each basic design?

2. An Example: The Parts Supply Division

For the last two years, the author has worked with the parts distribution division of a major company. From the outset, I was struck with this problem: the purchasing department buys approximately 100,000 different items each year from about 3,000

*Accepted by Arie Y. Lewin; received January 11, 1979. This paper has been with the author 3 months for 2 revisions.
†University of California, Los Angeles.

0025-1909/79/2509/0833$01.25

different manufacturers, and it accomplishes this huge volume of work with only 22 employees, of whom 3 are managerial-level. On the other hand, the warehousing operation, which stores these items until they are ordered by a customer and then fills the customer orders, has about 1,400 employees, of whom about 150 are managers. Why is it that it takes relatively so few people to accomplish the very complex task of evaluating the quality and price of so many items, compared to the number of people required to store and then to distribute them?

Out in a warehouse, the "pickers" must pick out the proper items to fill an order from a customer, the "packers" must check the items to be sure that the order is as specified and then must pack them properly for shipping, and the foreman must see to it that the work is going along properly. What we are interested in is the control process which the foreman uses to get the work out. The foreman is engaged in an elaborate task: he gathers information concerning the flow of work by watching the actions of the workers, knowing from their behavior which workers are doing their jobs well or poorly; he confirms his observations by checking a record of output for each worker at the end of each day. As he observes the pickers and packers at work, the foreman also, from time to time, will stop to inquire of a worker why he or she is doing a job in a particular manner. He may also ask someone to stop what they are doing and to do a different job instead; in some cases, he will angrily confront a "trouble maker" and demand that they behave as he directs. In all of these actions, the supervisor is working within a well-defined set of rules which prescribe both his behavior and that of the pickers and packers; he does so within both the formal limits of authority which are given him by virtue of his rank and within the informal limits of authority granted to him by the workers as a result of their trust in and respect for him as an individual. These formal limits of authority and of power are not implicit, they are written down in black and white, and each employee, both picker and foreman, knows them by memory. The informal agreements, while equally effective, remain implicit.

In the purchasing department, each purchasing officer does his or her work by sending out a description of the item desired to three or four different manufacturers, asking each one to quote a price for it. After the prices are in, the purchaser adds in any information that he may have concerning the honesty and reliability of the supplier and the past performance that he has demonstrated, and then decides to order from one of them. The supervisor occasionally consults with each purchasing agent to see if they need help, and the supervisor strictly reminds each and every person that under no conditions are they ever to accept gifts of any sort from any supplier. Now what is the control mechanism here?

Analysis of the Example

Three mechanisms have been identified: a market mechanism, which primarily characterized the purchasing function; a bureaucratic mechanism, which primarily characterized the warehousing function; and an informal social mechanism, which was mentioned in passing. This example illustrates that the mechanisms themselves overlap in organizations; although it may be helpful to treat them as conceptually distinct from one another, they in fact occur in various combinations.

Market Mechanisms

The work of the purchasing agent is, largely, subject to market mechanisms. At least two important effects are evident. First, the work of each agent is greatly simplified because he is relieved of the necessity of determining, for each part purchased, whether the supplier's intended manufacturing and delivery process is the most efficient possible. Instead, he simply puts each part out for competitive bids and permits the competititve process to define a fair price. In the second place, the work of the manager who supervises these agents is also greatly simplified, because he needs only to check their decisions against the simple criterion of cost minimization rather than observing the steps through which they work and forming an assessment of their unique skills and effort (however, this is a bureaucratic mechanism). Clearly, a parts division which chose to ignore market information and relied instead upon its own internal evaluation of the particulars of each bid would be at a significant cost disadvantage due to the much greater administrative overhead that it would incur.

As a pure model, a market is a very efficient mechanism of control (cf. Arrow [4, pp. 1–29]). In a market, prices convey all of the information necessary for efficient decision-making. In a frictionless market, where prices exactly represent the value of a good or service, decision-makers need no other information. Arbitrary rules such as those found in the warehouse are unnecessary. In addition to information, prices provide a mechanism for solving the problem of goal incongruity. Given a frictionless price mechanism, the firm can simply reward each employee in direct proportion to his contribution, so that an employee who produces little is paid little, and all payments, being exactly in proportion to contribution, are fair.

Of course, in this perfect example of a frictionless market, there is little reason for a formal organization to exist at all (Coase [9]). The fact that purchasing takes place within the corporate framework in our example suggests that some major market defects must exist. At least some of the parts purchased are sufficiently unique that only one or two potential manufacturers exist, so that a more detailed evaluation of those contracts is necessary, and a more thorough bureaucratic surveillance of the purchasing agents in such cases is also called for (see Williamson, [48] for a more complete discussion). More importantly, the work of the purchasing agents themselves is controlled through a process of bureaucratic surveillance rather than through a price mechanism. That is, the director of purchasing does not simply determine a market price for purchasing agents and then occasionally audit performance. Rather, he agrees upon an employment contract with each purchasing agent at some price (cf. Simon [37, pp. 183–195]) and then resorts to hierarchical order-giving and performance evaluation to control them. It is important to distinguish between the market mechanism employed by purchasing agents and the bureaucratic mechanism to which they are subject. Thus, in reality, there is a mixture of market and bureaucratic mechanisms which provide control in the case of purchasing, although it is the market mechanisms which are most clearly evident in this example.

Bureaucratic Mechanisms

In marked contrast to purchasing, warehousing in our example is subject to a variety of explicit routines of monitoring and directing which conform quite closely to the bureaucratic model described by Weber [46]. The fundamental mechanism of control involves close personal surveillance and direction of subordinates by superiors. The information necessary for task completion is contained in rules; these may be rules concerning processes to be completed or rules which specify standards of output or quality. In any case, rules differ from prices in the important sense that they are partial rather than complete bundles of information. A price implies that a comparison has taken place; a comparison between alternative buyers or sellers of the value of the object in question. A rule, however, is essentially an arbitrary standard against which a comparison is yet to be made. In order to use a rule (e.g., a budget, or cost standard), a manager must observe some actual performance, assign some value to it, and then compare that assigned value to the rule in order to determine whether the actual performance was satisfactory or not. All of this consumes a good deal of administrative overhead. If the rule is expressed qualitatively rather than quantitatively, the cost of administration can be expected to be even higher.

Given these inadequacies of bureaucracy, one might reasonably ask why the warehouse does not emulate the purchasing office and rely instead upon a price mechanism. The answer to that question has been the subject of a good deal of recent work by institutional economists, but an organization theorist might focus on one or two dimensions of the problem. Let us approach the question by beginning with the scenario of a warehouse manager who indeed decides to manage through an internal price mechanism. His first task is to set a price for each task, a job that may be impossible since many of the tasks are at least in part unique and thus not subject to market comparisons. Supposing that he can establish reasonable prices for a number of tasks, he must then have a mode of determining when an assigned task has been completed. Unlike the purchasing manager, who can sample delivered products for the purposes of determining contractual satisfaction, the warehouse manager has no correspondingly inexpensive way to determine performance and will have to establish a set of performance standards. In order to see that these standards are applied, he will have to create a system of hierarchical superiors who will closely monitor the performance of individual workers. Furthermore, he will have to create an atmosphere in which the workers willingly permit this close surveillance, or else morale and productivity will suffer. In some cases, tasks will inherently require teamwork, and then superiors will have to apply judgment to attribute value added among the team members. In order to simplify these problems of surveillance, the manager will attempt to create sub-specialties within the warehouse to more readily permit comparison of performance between like workers. Finally, when one task becomes particularly critical, the manager will want to increase the price that he will pay for it in order to increase the supply of workers who are willing to perform it. If he is unable to exactly price the critical task, he will have either an oversupply or an undersupply of workers performing it, to the detriment of the warehouse. Given the difficulty of correctly pricing any task, he will instead invest hierarchical superiors with the right to direct the efforts of subordinates on an *ad hoc* basis; and again he will need to create an atmosphere in which such directives will be willingly followed.

Having done all of these things, our warehouse manager who set out to create an internal market will have exactly instituted a bureaucratic hierarchy instead. Both bureaucratic and market mechanisms are directed towards the same objectives. Which form is more efficient depends upon the particulars of the transactions in question. Indeed, at this point we have an answer to the original dilemma: how can the purchasing department carry out its tasks with so few people compared to the number in warehousing? Purchasing in this example participates in a market mechanism, which is a far more efficient mechanism of control in terms of the administrative overhead consumed. Prices are a far more efficient means of controlling transactions than are rules. However, the conditions necessary for frictionless prices can rarely be met, and in such conditions the bureaucratic form, despite its inadequacies, is preferred.

Clan Mechanisms

The example also mentioned briefly the informal social structure which, in addition to market and bureaucratic mechanisms, also contributes to control in the warehouse. In order to illustrate the operation of these clan mechanisms, let us return briefly to the example.

Consider the foreman in the warehouse. His task is to oversee the work of pickers and packers. How is the warehouse manager to evaluate the work of the foreman? To some extent, he can rely on bureaucratic mechanisms such as output schedules, budgets, and inventory rules, but these in turn require surveillance. Given that the task of the foreman is significantly more subtle than that of the picker, the manager's task of bureaucratically supervising the foreman becomes very complex. However, if the manager is capable of selecting for promotion to foreman only that subset of workers who display a high internal commitment to the firm's objectives, and if he can maintain in them a deep commitment to these objectives, then his need for explicit surveillance and evaluation is reduced. In short, once the manager knows that they are trying to achieve the "right" objectives, he can eliminate many costly forms of auditing and surveillance.

Consider a different example—the general hospital. In the case of many health care employees, even the most dedicated attempts at systematic performance auditing would be frustrated. Task performance is inherently ambiguous, and teamwork is common, so that precise evaluation of individual contribution is all but impossible. In such cases, we observe a highly formalized and lengthy period of socialization during which would-be doctors and nurses are subjected not only to skill training but also to value training or indoctrination. When they are certified, they are certified with respect not only to their technical skills but also with respect to their integrity or purity of values.

When these socialization processes characterize groups such as physicians or nurses who occupy different organizations but with similar values, we refer to them as professions. When the socialization process refers to all of the citizens of a political unit, we refer to it as a culture. When it refers to the properties of a unique organization, we may refer to it as a clan. The functions of socialization are similar in professions, cultures, and clans, but our present interest centers on the clan.

The discovery that an informal social system characterizes most work organizations was noted first in the Hawthorne Studies (Roethlisberger and Dickson [36]). The subtle and widespread impact of local values on behavior has been thoroughly documented (Selznick [38], Gouldner [16]) as well as theoretically treated (Blau [6], Blau and Scott [7, pp. 89–99]). In organizational studies, the socialization mechanisms have been found to be unique to a particular organization (Trist and Bamforth [44]), to an industry (Lipset, Trow, and Coleman [24], Kaufmann [19]), or they may characterize most of the firms in an economy, as in the case of Japan (Nakane [29], Dore [12], Rohlen [37]).

Until recently, however, organization theorists have regarded this informal social system as either an anomaly or an epiphenomenon, not as the subject of analysis central to the problem of organization. However, a clan may serve as the basis of control in some organizations, just as the market was the basic form in the purchasing function and bureaucracy the basic form in the warehouse.

3. The Social and Informational Prerequisites of Control

It is possible to arrange the three modes of control along each of two dimensions: the informational requirements necessary to operate each control type, and the social underpinnings necessary to operate each control type. These are summarized in Table 1.

Let us consider first the social requirements, and then we will consider the informational issues. What we mean by social requirements is that set of agreements between people which, as a bare minimum, is necessary for a form of control to be employed. Any real organization, of course, will have developed a highly elaborated set of understandings which goes far beyond this. At the moment, however, our task is to understand the bare minimum without which a control mechanism cannot function.

838 WILLIAM G. OUCHI

TABLE 1
Social and Informational Prerequisites of Control

Type of Control	Social Requirements	Informational Requirements
Market	Norm of Reciprocity	Prices
Bureaucracy	Norm of Reciprocity Legitimate Authority	Rules
Clan	Norm of Reciprocity Legitimate Authority Shared Values, Beliefs	Traditions

A market cannot exist without a norm of reciprocity, but it requires no social agreements beyond that. A norm of reciprocity assures that, should one party in a market transaction attempt to cheat another, that the cheater, if discovered, will be punished by all members of the social system, not only by the victim and his or her partners. The severity of the punishment will typically far exceed the crime, thus effectively deterring potential future opportunists (Gouldner [17]). The norm of reciprocity is critical in a market if we think, for a moment, about the costs of running a market mechanism as opposed to the costs of any mechanism of control. In a market mechanism, the costs of carrying out transactions between parties have mostly to do with assuring oneself that the other party is dealing honestly, since all information relevant to the substance of the decision is contained in prices and is therefore not problematic. If honesty cannot be taken for granted, however, then each party must take on the cripplingly high costs of surveillance, complete contracting, and enforcement in order not to be cheated (Williamson [48]). These costs can quickly become so high that they will cause a market to fail.

When a market fails as the mechanism of control, it is most often replaced by a bureaucratic form. A bureaucracy contains not only a norm of reciprocity, but also agreement on legitimate authority, ordinarily of the rational/legal form (see Blau and Scott [7, pp. 27–36] for a discussion). In a bureaucratic control system, the norm of reciprocity is reflected in the notion of "an honest day's work for an honest day's pay", and it particularly contains the idea that, in exchange for pay, an employee gives up autonomy in certain areas to his organizational superiors, thus permitting them to direct his work activities and to monitor his performance. These steps are possible only if organization members accept the idea that higher office holders have the legitimate right to command and to audit or monitor lower persons, within some range (also known as the "zone of indifference", see Barnard [5]). Given social support for a norm of reciprocity and for the idea of legitimate authority, a bureaucratic control mechanism can operate successfully.

A Clan requires not only a norm of reciprocity and the idea of legitimate authority (often of the "traditional" rather than the "rational/legal" form), but also social agreement on a broad range of values and beliefs. Because the clan lacks the explicit price mechanism of the market and the explicit rules of the bureaucracy, it relies for its control upon a deep level of common agreement between members on what constitutes proper behavior, and it requires a high level of commitment on the part of each individual to those socially prescribed behaviors. Clearly, a clan is more demanding than either a market or a bureaucracy in terms of the social agreements which are prerequisite to its successful operation.

The Informational Prerequisites of Control

While a Clan is the most demanding and the Market the least demanding with respect to social underpinnings, the opposite is true when it comes to information. It has been observed (see Galbraith [15], Lawrence and Lorsch [21]) that, within large corporations, each department tends to develop its own peculiar jargon; it does so because the jargon, being suited to the particular task needs of the department, provides it with a very efficient set of symbols with which to communicate complex ideas, thus conserving on the very limited information-carrying capacity of an organization. We can also think of the accounting system in an organization as the smallest set of symbols which conveys information that is relevant to all organizational subunits. An accounting system is a relatively explicit information system compared, say, to the traditions of the U.S. Senate (see Matthews [27]). Each of these mechanisms carries information about how to behave, but the accounting system, being explicit, is easily accessed by a newcomer while the traditions of the Senate, being implicit, can be discovered by a freshman senator only over a period of years. On the other hand, the explicit system is far less complete in its ability to convey information and it has often been noted (see, for example, Vancil [45]) that there is no accounting measurement which fully captures the underlying performance of a department or corporation, since many of the dimensions of performance defy measurement (see Ouchi and Maguire [30]). Typically, an explicit information system must be created and maintained intentionally and at some cost, while an implicit information system often "grows up" as a natural by-product of social interaction.

In a true market, prices are arrived at through a process of competitive bidding, and no administrative apparatus is necessary to produce this information. However, many economists have argued that the conditions necessary for such perfect prices are rarely if ever met in reality, with the result that inefficiencies are borne by the parties to the market. Although some would contend that markets are explicitly not organizations (Arrow [4]), we can consider as a limit case the profit—or investment—center in a business as an attempt to control an organization through a price mechanism. In some large organizations, it is possible, with great effort and a huge accounting staff, to create internal numbers which will serve the function of prices. That is, if division general managers and department heads attempt simply to maximize their profit by taking the best prices available within the firm, then the firm as a whole will benefit. These "transfer prices" should not be confused with output, cost, or performance standards which are common in all organizations: those measures are effectively bureaucratic rules. The critical difference is that an internal price does not need a hierarchy of authority to accompany it. If the price mechanism is at work, all that is needed in addition to prices is a norm of reciprocity, accompanied by self-interest.

Only rarely is it possible for an organization to arrive at perfect transfer prices, however, because technological interdependence and uncertainty tremendously complicate the problem for most organizations, to the point where arriving at prices is simply not feasible. Under that condition, the organization can create an explicit set of rules, both rules about behavior and rules about levels of production or output. Although an organization can never create an explicit set of rules that will cover every situation that could possibly confront any of its employees, it can cut the information problem down to size by writing a relatively small set of rules that will cover 90% of all events and depending upon hierarchical authority to settle the remaining 10% of events. Thus, we see again that acceptance of legitimate authority is critical to a bureaucracy, since it is that property which enables the organization to incompletely specify the duties of an employee, instead having the employee agree that, within bounds, a superior may specify his or her duties as the need arises (Williamson [48, pp. 57–81]). In this manner, the organization deals with the future one step at a time, rather than having to anticipate it completely in advance in a set of explicit rules.

In a Clan, the information is contained in the rituals, stories, and ceremonies which convey the values and beliefs of the organization (Clark [8]). An outsider cannot quickly gain access to information concerning the decision rules used in the organization, but the information system does not require an army of accountants, computer experts, and managers: it is just there. Ivan Light [22] has described the Chinese-American *Hui* and the Japanese-American *Tanomoshi*, revolving-credit lending societies which provide venture capital for starting new businesses. They carry out all of the functions of any Wall Street investment bank, but, within their ethnic group, they are able to make loans which would be far too risky for any bank because they enjoy considerable advantages in obtaining, interpreting, and evaluating information about potential borrowers or members. None of their practices are explicit—even the rate of interest paid by borrowers is left unspecified and implicit. Entry into a *Hui* or *Tanomoshi* is strictly limited by birthright, a practice which guarantees that each member is a part of a social and kinship network which will support the values and beliefs upon which the control mechanism is founded. Clearly, the Clan information system cannot cope with heterogeneity nor with turnover, disadvantages which make it all but infeasible as a central mechanism of control in modern organizations, but the Clan, like the market, can operate with great efficiency if the basic conditions necessary to its operation can be met.

If the price requirements of a Market cannot be met and if the social conditions of the Clan are impossible to achieve, then the Bureaucratic mechanism becomes the preferred method of control. In a sense, the Market is like the trout and the Clan like the salmon, each a beautiful, highly-specialized species which requires uncommon conditions for its survival. In comparison, the bureaucratic method of control is the catfish—clumsy, ugly, but able to live in the widest possible range of environments and, ultimately, the dominant species. The bureaucratic mode of control can withstand high rates of turnover, a high degree of heterogeneity, and it does not have very demanding informational needs.

In reality, of course, we will never observe a pure market, a pure bureaucracy, or a pure clan. Real organizations will each contain some features of each of the modes of control. The design problem thus becomes one of assessing the social and informational characteristics of each division, department, or task and determining which of the forms of control ought to be emphasized in each case. Present organization theory, however, concentrates on the bureaucratic form to the exclusion of all else. The work of March and Simon [25] deals with decision-making in bureaucratic organizations, Parsons [32] describes problems of vertical control in bureaucracies, Perrow [33] concentrates on rules as a control mechanism in bureaucracies, and Argyris [3], Likert [23], and Tannenbaum [42] prescribe techniques for reducing some of the undesirable by-products of what remains an essentially bureaucratic mode of control.

Let us next consider some of the cost implications of each form of control. We will approach this task by looking at each of the stages at which an organization can exercise discretion over people. By doing so, we may discover some additional design variables which can influence the form of organizational control.

4.   Designing Control Mechanisms: Costs and Benefits

Basically, there are two ways in which an organization can achieve effective people control: either it can go to the expense of searching for and selecting people who fit its needs exactly, or else it can take people who do not exactly fit its needs and go to the expense of putting in place a managerial system to instruct, monitor, and evaluate them.

Which of these approaches is best depends on the cost to the organization of each. On the one hand, there is a cost of search and of acquisition: some skills are rare in the labor force and the organization wanting to hire people with those skills will have to search widely and pay higher wages. Once hired, however, such people will be able to perform their tasks without instruction and, if they have also been selected for values (motivation), they will be inclined to work hard without close supervision, both of which will save the organization money. On the other hand, there is the cost of training the unskilled and the indifferent to learn the organization's skills and values, and there is the cost of developing and running a supervisory system to monitor, evaluate, and correct their behavior. Once in place, however, such a system can typically take in a heterogeneous assortment of people and effectively control them; in addition, its explicit training and monitoring routines enable it to withstand high rates of turnover. High turnover is costly if search and acquisition costs are high, but turnover is relatively harmless to the organization if it hires all comers.

It has also been observed, by sociologists (Etzioni [13]), social psychologists, (Kelman [20]), and economists, (Williamson [48]), that various forms of evaluation and control will result in differing individual levels of commitment to or alienation from the organization and its objectives. In general, a control mode which relies heavily on selecting the appropriate people can expect high commitment as a result of internalized values.

At the other extreme, a control mode which depends heavily upon monitoring, evaluating, and correcting in an explicit manner is likely to offend people's sense of autonomy and of self-control and, as a result, will probably result in an unenthusiastic, purely compliant response. In this state, people require even more close supervision, having been alienated from the organization as a result of its control mechanism. Indeed, as is always true of any form of measurement, it is not possible for an organization to measure or otherwise control its employees without somehow affecting them through the very process that it uses to measure them: there is no completely unobtrusive measurement in most organizations. In general, the more obvious and explicit the measurement, the more noxious it is to employees and thus, the greater the cost to the organization of employing such methods. However, other conditions may demand the use of these more explicit yet offensive techniques of control. We can summarize these in Table 2.

TABLE 2
Organizational Control: People Treatment

People Treatment	Form of Commitment*	Corresponding Control Type
Totally Unselective; take anyone, no further treatment	Internalization	Market
Selection/Screening		Clan
Training —Skill Training —Value Training	Identification	Bureaucracy
Monitoring —Monitor Behavior —Monitor Output	Compliance	

* Taken from Kelman [20].

At one extreme, an organization could be completely unselective about its members, taking anyone (although we assume that everyone is to some extent self-interested, hedonistic, or profit-maximizing). At the other extreme, an organization could be highly selective, choosing only those individuals who already have both the skills and the values which the organization needs; this practice is most common in the "professional bureaucracies" such as hospitals, public accounting firms, and universities. In an apparent paradox, these most and least selective kinds of organizations will both have high levels of commitment; that is, members will have internalized the underlying objectives of the organization. Of course, the paradox is resolved by noting that the completely unselective organization relies on commitment of each individual to self, since it employs a market mechanism of control in which what is desired is that each person simply maximize his or her personal well-being (profit). Since the organization's objective is thus identical to the individual's objective, we can say that internalization of objectives exists and thus no close supervision will be necessary, and enthusiasm for pursuing the organization's goals will be high (since they are also the individual's selfish goals).

Most organizations, however, cannot take on all comers (they do not have a price mechanism) and they can rely upon selection and screening only to a limited extent, that is, they can select partially for the skills and values desired but will not be able to find people who fit exactly their needs. In this case, the organization may rely on training, both in the form of formalized training programs and in the form of on-the-job or apprenticeship training, to impart the desired skills and values. Typically, training will result in the trainee identifying with either the trainer (who may also be a respected superior) or with the work group or department. In this case, the employee will possess the necessary skills and will pursue the organization's objective, but only because he or she identifies with and wants to emulate the respected person or group, not because the underlying objectives have been internalized to the point where the employee believes them to be good and desirable objectives in their own right.

The link between forms of commitment and types of control is quite direct. Internalized commitment is necessary for a market, since a market possesses no hierarchical monitoring or policing capabilities. Internalization is also necessary to a clan, which has weak monitoring abilities, that is, evaluation is subtle and slow under this form of control, and thus, without high commitment, the mechanism is capable of drifting quite far off course before being corrected. A clan can also be supported with identification, however, and over time, the identification may be converted into internalization of the values of the clan.

Identification is also compatible with bureaucratic control, although it exceeds the minimum commitment that is necessary in a bureaucracy. Compliance is the minimum level of commitment necessary for bureaucratic control, but it is beneath the threshold of commitment necessary for the clan and market forms. The social agreement to suspend judgment about orders from superiors and to simply follow orders (see Blau and Scott [7, pp. 29–30]) is fundamental to bureaucratic control.

The issue of commitment and control may also pose a moral question of some significance. If organizations achieve internalized control purely through selection, then, it would seem, both the individual and the organization are unambiguously satisfied. If internalization is achieved through training of employees into the values and beliefs of the organization, however, then it is possible that some individuals may be subject to economic coercion to modify their values. Indeed, this kind of forced socialization is common in certain of our institutions (what Etzioni refers to as "coercive" organizations) such as the U.S. Marine Corps and many mental hospitals. In some such cases, we accept the abrogation of individual rights as being secondary to a more pressing need. In the case of a company town or a middle-aged employee with few job options, however, we are less likely to approve of this kind of pressure. As long as organizations maintain an essentially democratic power structure, this danger remains remote. If the hierarchy of authority becomes relatively autocratic, however, the possibility of loss of individual freedom becomes real.

5. Loose Coupling and The Clan as a Form of Control

In the present literature on organizations, a new and somewhat revolutionary view of "organizational rationality" is developing which has direct implications for our view of designing control mechanisms. This new view, which is coming to be known as "loose coupling" (see Weick [47]), implies that bureaucratic forms of control are unsuitable for many contemporary organizations. Let us briefly consider the underlying "organizational rationality" which dominates the current view of control, and then we will consider the loose coupling perspective.

The essential element which underlies any bureaucratic or market form of control is the assumption that it is feasible to measure, with reasonable precision, the performance that is desired. In order to set a production standard which effectively controls, it is essential that the industrial engineers or accountants be able to measure the desired output with some precision. In order to effectively control through the use of rules, it is essential that the personnel department know which rules to specify in order to achieve the desired performance. Indeed, the ability to measure either output or behavior which is relevant to the desired performance is critical to the "rational" application of market and bureaucratic forms of control. Table 3 specifies the contingencies which determine whether or not measurement is possible.

TABLE 3

Conditions Determining the Measurement of Behavior and of Output

		Knowledge of The Transformation Process	
		Perfect	*Imperfect*
	High	Behavior or Output Measurement (Apollo Program)	Output Measurement (Women's Boutique)
Ability to Measure Outputs			
	Low	Behavior Measurement (Tin Can Plant)	Ritual and Ceremony, "Clan" Control (Research Laboratory)

In order to understand Table 3, let us agree, for the moment, that if we wanted to control an organization, we would have to monitor or measure something and that, essentially, the things which we can measure are limited to the behavior of employees or the results, the outputs of those behaviors. If we understand the technology (that is, the means-ends relationships involved in the basic production or service activities) perfectly, as is the case in a tin-can plant, then we can achieve effective control simply by having someone watch the behavior of the employees and the workings of the machines: if all behaviors and processes conform to our desired transformation steps, then we know with certainty that proper tin cans are coming out the other end, even without looking. By specifying the rules of behavior and of process, we could create an effective bureaucratic control mechanism in this case.

On the other hand, suppose that we are designing a control system for a high-fashion women's boutique. What it takes to be a successful buyer or merchandiser is beyond our understanding, so we could not possibly hope to create a set of rules which, if followed by our buyers, would assure success. We can measure with precision, however, the average markdowns which each buyer's leftover dresses must

844   WILLIAM G. OUCHI

take, the average inventory turnover for each buyer, and the sales volume and profit margin of each buyer, thus giving us the alternative of an output control mechanism. If our output control mechanism consists of this multiple set of objectives, then it is effectively a bureaucratic mechanism which will be managed by having a superior in the hierarchy who will monitor the various indicators for each buyer and, using the legitimate authority of office, will enforce not only close monitoring but also will order the necessary corrections in the buyer's decisions.

In the third case, we could be designing a control mechanism for the Apollo moon-shot program. We can completely specify each step of the transformation process which must occur in order for a manned capsule to get to the surface of the moon and back to earth, thus giving us the possibility of behavior control. However, we also have an unambiguous measure of output: either the capsule gets there and back, or it doesn't. Thus we have a choice of either behavior control or of output control. In such a case, the lower cost alternative will be preferred; clearly, since the cost of one failure is prohibitive, we will choose an elaborate behavior control mechanism, with literally hundreds of ground controllers monitoring every step of the process.

Finally, suppose that we are running a research laboratory at a multibillion dollar corporation. We have no ability to define the rules of behavior which, if followed, will lead to the desired scientific breakthroughs which will, in turn, lead to marketable new products for the company. We can measure the ultimate success of a scientific discovery, but it may take ten, twenty, or even fifty years for an apparently arcane discovery to be fully appreciated. Certainly, we would be wary of using a strong form of output control to encourage certain scientists in our lab while discouraging others. Effectively, we are unable to use either behavior or output measurement, thus leaving us with no "rational" form of control. What happens in such circumstances is that the organization relies heavily on ritualized, ceremonial forms of control. These include the recruitment of only a selected few individuals, each of whom has been through a schooling and professionalization process which has taught him or her to internalize the desired values and to revere the appropriate ceremonies. The most important of those ceremonies, such as "hazing" of new members in seminars, going to professional society meetings, and writing scientific articles for publication in learned journals, will continue to be encouraged within the laboratory.

Now, it is commonly supposed that such rituals, which characterize not only research laboratories but also hospitals, schools, government agencies and investment banks, constitute quaint but essentially useless and perhaps even harmful practice. But if it is not possible to measure either behavior or outputs and it is therefore not possible to "rationally" evaluate the work of the organization, what alternative is there but to carefully select workers so that you can be assured of having an able and committed set of people, and then engaging in rituals and ceremonies which serve the purpose of rewarding those who display the underlying attitudes and values which are likely to lead to organizational success, thus reminding everyone of what they are supposed to be trying to achieve, even if they can't tell whether or not they are achieving it?

Whereas output and behavior control (see also Ouchi and Maguire [30], Ouchi [31]) can be implemented through a market or a bureaucracy, ceremonial forms of control (see Meyer and Rowan [28]) can be implemented through a clan. Because ceremonial forms of control explicitly are unable to exercise monitoring and evaluation of anything but attitudes, values, and beliefs, and because attitudes, values, and beliefs are typically acquired more slowly than are manual or cognitive abilities, ceremonial forms of control require the stability of membership which characterizes the clan.

Loose Coupling

It has recently become fashionable among organization theorists to argue that relatively few real organizations possess the underlying "rationality" which is assumed in market and bureaucratic forms of control. Parsons [32], Williamson [48], and Ouchi [31] have argued that most hierarchies fail to transmit control with any accuracy from top to bottom. Simon has made a convincing case that most organizations do not have a single or an integrated set of goals or objectives [41] and that the subunits of organizations are, as a matter of necessity, only loosely joined to each other [40]. Evan [14], Pfeffer [34], and Aldrich [2] have argued that the structure of most organizations is determined more by their environment than by any purposive, technologically-motived managerial strategy. Hannan and Freeman [18] have argued even more strongly that organizational form is isomorphic with ecological conditions, thus implying that organizations can be designed only by nature, through a process of selection; and Cohen, March, and Olsen [10] have argued that organizational decision processes are far from our view of "rationality" and have chosen instead the metaphor of the "garbage can" to describe them.

If there is any truth in this very considerable attack on our notions of the orderliness and rationality with which organizations function, then we must guess that the forms of control which are dominant today may be inappropriate in future organizations.

Under conditions of ambiguity, of loose coupling, and of uncertainty, measurement with reliability and with precision is not possible. A control system based on such measurements is likely to systematically reward a narrow range of maladaptive behavior, leading ultimately to organizational decline. It may be that, under such conditions, the clan form of control, which operates by stressing values and objectives as much as behavior, is preferable. An organization which evaluates people on their values, their motivation, can tolerate wide differences in styles of performance; that is exactly what is desirable under conditions of ambiguity, when means-ends relationships are only poorly understood; it encourages experimentation and variety.

6. A Few Closing Observations

Organizations vary in the degree to which they are loosely or tightly coupled. Many organizations, particularly those in relatively stable manufacturing industries, fit the requirements for behavior control or for output control. Control mechanisms of the market or bureaucratic variety can be designed into such organizations. Organizations in the public sector, in service industries, and in fast-growing technologies may not fit these specifications and perhaps should have cultural or clan forms of control instead.

The student of organizational control should take care to understand that clans, which operate on ceremony and on ritual, have forms of control which by their nature are subtle and are ordinarily not visible to the inexperienced eye. Many is the eager young manager who has taken a quick look around, observed that no control mechanisms exist, and then begun a campaign to install a bureaucratic or market mechanism of some sort, only to trip over the elaborate ceremonial forms of control which are in place and working quite effectively.

This paper has presented the argument that the design of organizational control mechanisms must focus on the problems of achieving cooperation among individuals who hold partially divergent objectives. Basically, such a collection of people can be moved towards cooperative action through one of three devices: a market mechanism which precisely evaluates each person's contribution and permits each to pursue non-organizational goals, but at a personal loss of reward; a clan mechanism which attains cooperation by selecting and socializing individuals such that their individual objectives substantially overlap with the organization's objectives; and a bureaucratic mechanism which does a little of each: it partly evaluates performance as closely as possible, and it partly engenders feelings of commitment to the idea of legitimate authority in hierarchies.

There are two underlying issues which are of central importance in determining which form of control will be more efficient. First is the question of the clarity with which performance can be assessed. Second is the degree of goal incongruence. These two dimensions are intimately related in determining the forms of control that will emerge, but each of these dimensions is shaped by an independent set of forces.

The intimate relationship between the two dimensions is evidenced in the observation that high levels of goal incongruity can be tolerated only so long as performance can be evaluated with precision. Conversely, high ambiguity concerning performance can be tolerated only if goal incongruity is trivial. In everyday language, people must either be able to trust each other or to closely monitor each other if they are to engage in cooperative enterprises.

However, the possibility of goal compatibility is shaped by forces independent of those which determine the level of performance evaluation. It has long been argued by sociologists and organization theorists that geographical mobility, urbanization, and industrialization, which tend to occur together, all undermine the basic forms of goal compatibility on which communal trust is founded. While these arguments have been advanced to explain the increasing bureaucratization of whole societies, they apply equally to work organizations. Growth, turnover, and specialization all undermine the possibility of developing goal congruence in work organizations and thus imply the dominance of bureaucratic and market forms.

On the other hand, it has equally been argued by organization theorists that technological interdependence is inimical to clear performance assessment, and that such interdependence will increase over time among organizations generally. This argument forecloses the development of market and bureaucratic forms, which require clarity of assessment.

In the immediate sense, the problem of organization design is to discover that balance of socialization and measurement which most efficiently permits a particular organization to achieve cooperation among its members. In the longer run, the problem is to understand how, in a society that is increasingly pluralistic and thus goal-incongruent, in which interest groups become more distinct and in which a sense of community seems remote, the control of organizations can be achieved without recourse to an unthinking bureaucratization which is at odds with the increasing interdependence and ambiguity which characterize economic organizations.[1]

[1] I am indebted to Thomas R. Hofstedt, with whom I first taught a course on Organizational Control, to Thomas L. Whisler, who introduced me to this topic, and to John W. Meyer and Oliver E. Williamson, whose creative insights to the problem of control have opened up my mind. I am also indebted to Arie Lewin, Patrick Connor, Kathleen Eisenhardt, and Charles T. Horngren for their constructive criticisms.

References

1. ALCHIAN, ARMEN A. AND DEMSETZ, HAROLD, "Production, Information Costs, and Economic Organization," *Amer. Econom. Rev.*, Vol. 62 (1972), pp. 777–795.
2. ALDRICH, HOWARD, "An Organization-Environment Perspective on Cooperation and Conflict Between Organizations in the Manpower Training System," in Anant Negandhi, ed., *Conflict and Power in Complex Organizations*, Kent State Univ., Kent, Ohio, 1972.
3. ARGYRIS, CHRIS, *Integrating the Individual and the Organization*, Wiley, New York, 1964.

DESIGN OF ORGANIZATIONAL CONTROL MECHANISMS   847

4. ARROW, KENNETH J., *The Limits of Organization*, Norton, New York, 1974, pp. 1–29.
5. BARNARD, CHESTER I., *The Functions of the Executive*, Harvard Univ. Press, Cambridge, Mass., 1938.
6. BLAU, PETER M., *The Dynamics of Bureaucracy*, Univ. of Chicago Press, Chicago, Ill., 1955.
7. ——— AND SCOTT, W. RICHARD, *Formal Organizations*, Scott, Foresman, San Francisco, Calif., 1962.
8. CLARK, BURTON R., *The Distinctive College: Antioch, Reed, and Swarthmore*, Aldine, Chicago, Ill., 1970.
9. COASE, R. H., "The Nature of the Firm," *Economica*, New Series, Vol. 4 (1937), pp. 386–405.
10. COHEN, MICHAEL D., MARCH, JAMES G. AND OLSEN, JOHAN P., "A Garbage Can Model of Organizational Choice," *Admin. Sci. Quart.*, Vol. 17 (1972), March, pp. 1–25.
11. DAVIS, STANLEY M. AND LAWRENCE, PAUL R., *Matrix*, Addison-Wesley, Reading, Mass., 1977.
12. DORE, RONALD, *British Factory—Japanese Factory*, Univ. of California Press, Berkeley, Calif., 1973.
13. ETZIONI, AMITAI, "Organizational Control Structure," in J. G. March, ed., *Handbook of Organizations*, Rand McNally, Chicago, Ill., 1965, pp. 650–677.
14. EVAN, WILLIAM M., "The Organization-Set," in James D. Thompson, ed., *Approaches to Organizational Design*, Univ. of Pittsburgh Press, Pittsburg, Pa., 1966.
15. GALBRAITH, JAY, *Designing Complex Organizations*, Organization Development Series, Addison-Wesley, Reading, Mass., 1973.
16. GOULDNER, ALVIN W., *Patterns of Industrial Bureaucracy*, Free Press, New York, 1954.
17. ———, "The Norm of Reciprocity," *Amer. Sociological Rev.*, Vol. 25 (1961), pp. 161–179.
18. HANNAN, MICHAEL T. AND FREEMAN, JOHN H., "The Population Ecology of Organizations," *Amer. J. Sociology*, Vol. 82 (1977), pp. 929–964.
19. KAUFMAN, HERBERT, *The Forest Ranger: A Study in Administrative Behavior*, The Johns Hopkins Univ. Press, Baltimore, Md., 1967.
20. KELMAN, H. C., "Compliance, Identification, and Internalization: Three Processes of Attitude Change," *J. Conflict Resolution*, Vol. 2 (1958), pp. 51–60.
21. LAWRENCE, PAUL R. AND LORSCH, JAY W., *Organization and Environment: Managing Differentiation and Integration*, Harvard University, Graduate School of Business Administration, Boston, Mass., 1967.
22. LIGHT, IVAN H., *Ethnic Enterprise in America*, Univ. of California Press, Berkeley, Calif., 1972.
23. LIKERT, RENSIS, *The Human Organization: Its Management and Value*, McGraw-Hill, New York, 1967.
24. LIPSET, SEYMOUR M., TROW, MARTIN A. AND COLEMAN, JAMES S., *Union Democracy*, Free Press, Glencoe, Ill., 1956.
25. MARCH, JAMES G. AND SIMON, HERBERT A., *Organizations*, Wiley, New York, 1958.
26. MARSCHAK, THOMAS A., "Economic Theories of Organization," in J. G. March (ed.), *Handbook of Organizations*, Rand McNally, Chicago, Ill., 1965, pp. 423–450.
27. MATTHEWS, DONALD R., *U.S. Senators and Their World*, Univ. of North Carolina Press, Chapel Hill, N.C., 1960.
28. MEYER, JOHN W. AND ROWAN, BRIAN, "Institutionalized Organizations: Formal Structure as Myth and Ceremony," *Amer. J. Sociology*, Vol. 83, No. 2 (September 1977), pp. 340–363.
29. NAKANE, CHIE, *Japanese Society*, Penguin Books, Middlesex, 1973.
30. OUCHI, W. G., AND MAGUIRE, M. A., "Organizational Control; Two Functions," *Admin. Sci. Quart.*, Vol. 20 (December 1975), pp. 559–569.
31. ———, "The Transmission of Control Through Organizational Hierarchy," *Acad. Management J.*, Vol. 21, No. 2 (1978).
32. PARSON, TALCOTT, *Structure and Process in Modern Society*, Free Press, New York, 1960.
33. PERROW, CHARLES, *Complex Organizations: A Critical Essay*, Scott, Foresman, Glenview, Ill., 1972.
34. PFEFFER, JEFFREY, "Beyond Management and the Worker: The Institutional Function of Management," *Acad. Management Rev.*, Vol. 1 (1976), pp. 36–46.
35. REEVES, T. KYNASTON AND WOODWARD, JOAN, "The Study of Managerial Control," in J. Woodward, ed., *Industrial Organization: Behaviour and Control*, Oxford Univ. Press, London, 1970.
36. ROETHLISBERGER, FRITZ J. AND DICKSON, WILLIAM J., *Management and the Worker*, Harvard Univ. Press, Cambridge, Mass., 1939.
37. ROHLEN, THOMAS P., *For Harmony and Strength: Japanese White-Collar Organization in Anthropological Perspective*, Univ. of California Press, Berkeley, Calif., 1974.
38. SELZNICK, PHILIP, *TVA and the Grass Roots*, Univ. of California Press, Berkeley, Calif., 1949.
39. SIMON, H. A., "A Formal Theory of the Employment Relation," in H. A. Simon, *Models of Man*, Wiley, New York, 1957, pp. 183–195.
40. ———, "The Architecture of Complexity," *Proc. Amer. Philos. Soc.*, Vol. 106 (December 1962), pp. 467–482.
41. ———, "On the Concept of Organizational Goal," *Admin. Sci. Quart.*, Vol. 9, No. 1 (June 1964), pp. 1–22.
42. TANNENBAUM, ARNOLD, *Control in Organizations*, McGraw-Hill, New York, 1968.
43. THOMPSON, JAMES D., *Organizations In Action*, McGraw-Hill, New York, 1969.

44. TRIST, ERIC L. AND BAMFORTH, K. W., "Some Social and Psychological Consequences of the Longwall Method of Goal-Getting," *Human Relations*, Vol. 4 (February 1951), pp. 3–38.
45. VANCIL, RICHARD F., "What Kind of Management Control Do You Need?," in *Harvard Business Review—On Management*, Harper and Row, New York, 1975, pp. 464–481.
46. WEBER, MAX, *The Theory of Social and Economic Organization*, translated by A. M. Henderson and T. Parsons, Free Press, New York, 1947.
47. WEICK, KARL E., "Educational Organizations As Loosely Coupled Systems," *Admin. Sci. Quart.*, Vol. 21 (March 1976), pp. 1–19.
48. WILLIAMSON, OLIVER A., *Markets and Hierarchies: Analysis and Antitrust Implications*, Free Press, New York, 1975.

[18]

Organization and Control

Stewart Clegg

Organizations are complex structures-in-motion that are best conceptualized as historically constituted entities. The analytic focus of their constitution is the control of the labor process. This control is conceptualized in terms of different "rules" operative at different levels of the class structure in organizations. These rules are historically structured principles of organization. They may be related in a causal argument to the "long waves" of economic life. These arguments are not common in organization theory, and this paper draws upon an extensive literature from related research areas. The paper concludes by sketching some of the empirical research possibilities of this new perspective in organization analysis.•

INTRODUCTION

Control is not a new concept to students of organizations. As early as 1920, Carter Goodrich (1975) analyzed the struggle between management and workers over the "frontier of control." Management of this period, in attempting to win the frontier, employed the work of F.W. Taylor (1947). Subsequently, Taylor's work was elaborated into one of the mainstreams of organization theory. Different writers came to agree (i.e., Hickson, 1966) on the theoretical centrality of the degree of specificity of role prescription attached to various positions in the organization. This degree of specificity, which indicates the variability of autonomy, discretion, and freedom from direction, was implicitly a concept of control. More recently, the concept of control has reemerged in sharper perspective in a literature that has significant implications for organization theory, although it is not usually considered to be part of the theoretical mainstream.

This paper argues that this literature is relevant to organization theory. The literature stresses the control of the labor process by variables that have historical structure — that is, variables that change both temporally and spatially. In organization analysis it seems more appropriate to study the whole organization rather than to study individual role prescriptions. Studying the organization as a whole entails a far more elaborate concept than role prescription. Although organizations are composed of people, persons are not particularly important for analysis; it is their organization in a specific labor process that is important. This labor process includes not only the purposeful activity of work itself but also the instruments of labor and the objects that are worked upon. These may be as real as bricks and mortar, trowel and concrete, or as abstract as lofty thoughts of conceptual design. The lowliest laborer and the most ambitious architect are related by their involvement in a common labor process (Marx, 1976: 284).

•

This paper has benefited considerably from the comments of three anonymous *ASQ* reviewers. I have also had helpful comments from Chilla Bulbeck, Gibson Burrell, Mike Emmison, David Hickson, and Peter Williams. I am responsible for any errors or infelicities that remain despite all this good advice.

Control in organizations is achieved through what may be termed "rules." These rules are not necessarily formally defined by members of the organization, although they may be. They do not depend on the members' cognizance of them for their analytic utility. "Rules" is meant merely as a term by which one can formulate the structure underlying the apparent surface of organizational life, rather as rules of grammar are formulated in structural linguistics (Chomsky, 1968). Unlike in structural linguistics, the concept of rules to be developed here is historical: the organization is a historically produced object. Rules are the fundamental organizing principles underlying decisive breaks of or interventions into control of the labor process. Each rule represents a distinct and historically evolved principle of organization that is embedded in the actual functioning of the organization.

Not all organizations have the same type of control in different times and places; so a key sociological question must be: what are the conditions of existence of these types of control? That is, how are different types of organization possible?

How one answers this question defines both the type of organization theorist one is and the theoretical "organization" one constructs for analysis. Typical answers refer to determination of organizations by "environments" (Aldrich, 1979) or by voluntaristic constructions of individuals (Weick, 1969; Silverman, 1970).

In the theory advanced here, organization is the result of economic agents calculating, miscalculating, and constructing the historical accumulation of capital. Organization structures are thus not necessarily determined by any thing, nor are they freely constructed.

CONTROL

Previous Statements

The recent restatements of the importance of the concept of control have been scattered in the literature in areas related to organization theory, such as the labor process (Braverman, 1974; Stark, 1980), the political economy of U.S. capitalism (Aglietta, 1979), the role of the new technical petty bourgeoisie (Gorz, 1972; Poulantzas, 1974), and the class struggle in the United States (Edwards, 1979). There have been three recent restatements in organization theory (Clegg, 1979; Salaman, 1979; Clegg and Dunkerley, 1980). Almost all of these draw on Marx (1976) and Braverman (1974).

Marx termed the process whereby capital develops its control over labor a development from "formal" to "real" subordination. In the earliest stage of the capitalist mode of production, in which labor produces surplus value through traditional methods and skills, the capitalists' major problem is how to appropriate as much of labor's value as possible. In the absence of technologies that enhance the productivity of labor, the limits to the accumulation of surplus value are the *absolute* limits of the working day (hence the chapters of *Capital* that concerned the struggle over the length of the working day). Without new technologies, additional surplus value can be accumulated only by extending the working day or by intensifying its drudgery. In this early stage, when the methods of production still belong to the workers but the means have been appropriated, capital's control over the labor process is still "formal."

"Real subordination" comes with the development of specifically capitalist processes of production that erode and diminish labor's ownership and control of the methods of production. The development of real subordination enlarges the possibilities of surplus-value accumulation. The possibilities are no longer bounded absolutely by the length and intensity of the

Organization and Control

working day; they are enlarged enormously through the extraction of *relative* surplus value. In its modern form, this relative exploitation of labor is based on intensifying labor and increasing its productivity. These are achieved not only through technology, but also by the development both of a complex organization of specialized laborers and of an organizational apparatus to support the objective domination of the machine.

Control and Power

Our understanding of this organizational apparatus was significantly improved by Claus Offe (1976). Offe argued that Max Weber's (1968) model of bureaucracy depicts what Offe terms a task-continuous status organization, in which both functional and hierarchical differentiation coincide.[1] Historically, as a result of the increasing application of technique to technology, labor has become increasingly specialized. A consequence of this increasing specialization is the development of a "task-discontinuous status organization," which parallels the rational-legal hierarchy of office; both are examples of "functional differentiation." Offe noted that "hierarchical differentiation and functional differentiation both produce status systems [which] in the course of industrial development can become independent of one another" (Offe, 1976: 24).

In the task-continuous status organization, a relationship among different positions in the hierarchy exists "such that there is a wide area of technical rules to which equal obedience is required from all the occupants of the positions in the structure" (Offe, 1976: 25). A superordinate position dominates a subordinate position "in terms of greater mastery of the rules and greater ability, knowledge and experience in production" (Offe, 1976: 25). The rules that a subordinate must obey become, in their entirety, components of the role definition of a superordinate. Offe's example of this organizational structure is "the production organization of the small craft workshop, with its triple hierarchical division of master, journeyman and apprentice" (Offe, 1976: 25). In such a structure, power clearly is derived from ownership and control of the means of production, and, overlying this, from knowledge of the methods of production. Offe's example is not typical of the modern large-scale organization and presents no particular problems for analysis. In this example, power is derived from ownership and control of the key resources of production: means and method.

The separation that developed historically between the ownership and control of the means of production and the ownership and control of the methods of production can generate opposing and contradictory interests and strategies. Control of methods on an individualistic rather than a collective basis gives rise to the problem of "power," defined in organization theory as "illegitimate" and "informal" bases of control derived from knowledge of methods of production (skills) that are non-routinized, unsubstitutable, and central to the organization. (See Hickson et al., 1971; Hinings et al., 1974; Clegg, 1975, 1977, 1979. This literature is well known; the most cited example is Crozier's [1964] maintenance men.) When an organization acts to reassert control over the "informal," "illegitimate" bases, changes may be seen in the social relations within the organization's occupation structure.

[1]
One must assume an equal probability of open access to all levels of the bureaucracy on the basis of competitive examination. Of course, once one introduces the variables of class, racial, ethnic, and sexual structure of the population, the structure becomes more discontinuous.

Power is exercised through these individualistic bases. More importantly, however, power is exercised in class struggle, where trade unions and employers' associations have attempted to represent, respectively, the control of methods and the control of means of production on a collective basis. The practice of power in such a struggle results in practices of, for example, cooptation, incorporation, de-skilling and hyper-qualification, technological substitution, or buying out.

The structurally generated effects of the practice of power in class struggle may be more systematically identified. Carchedi's (1977) work on the economic identification of social classes enables us to construct a typology that encompasses much of the literature. This typology (Table) arranges the structurally generated situations in which power conflicts have a collective basis rather than an individualistic one. The typology is generated by cross-classification (see Baldamus, 1979).

Table

Schematic Representation of Class-Structured Power Conflicts in Organizations

	Working Class	New Middle Class	Ruling Class
Working Class	Demarcation disputes; closed shop exclusions; local, regional, and international division of labor.	Men in the middle engaged in disputes about bonus, productivity, speeds, for example.	Disputes about liquidation; bankruptcy; capital strikes and starvation; lock-outs; "rationalization" through productivity and restrictive practices deals.
New Middle Class		Line vs. staff conflicts; cosmopolitans vs. locals; bureaucrats vs. professionals.	Disputes about the cheapening of non-surplus value producing labor process, through automation; standardization, via, for example, Electronic Data Processing (EDP) and other microprocess-related technology.
Ruling Class			Disputes about takeovers, mergers, trustification.

Note: The criteria for identification are the relations of agents to the production of value and to its appropriation (see Figure).

This typology elucidates the structurally generated conflicts within organizations. These conflicts operate through the non-neutrality of job design, technology, and organization structure as ideological practices. These have real effects on the experience of control as a more or less legitimate structure of goals, means, and distribution of resources (Fox, 1974).

This typology lacks process and action. Conflicts and uses of power are organized around something that people find worth struggling to control: the labor process, the site of most of our mature lives, the source of our wages and profits.

If we wish to add process and action, we have to recall that the transition from formal to real subordination is not conceptualized as unproblematic. The transition is conditioned, if not determined, by the class struggle, the state of the labor markets (particularly vis-à-vis the reserve army of the unemployed), the tendency toward the rising organic composition of capital, and the capacity of the markets to absorb additional production and, thus, for the value to be realized.

Organization and Control

LIMITATIONS OF THE LABOR-PROCESS PERSPECTIVE

Braverman's (1974) analysis of the development of the labor process has been criticized both for neglecting the variables — particularly class struggle — that condition the transition from formal to real subordination, and for positing a one-dimensional and unidirectional thesis of "de-skilling" (e.g., Palmer, 1975; Friedman, 1977; Jacoby, 1976; Aronowitz, 1978; Coombs, 1978; Edwards, 1978; Stark, 1980). In particular, Braverman was criticized for his "romance" of labor (Cutler, 1978). Stark (1980: 89) recently suggested that Braverman's work, although a "powerful moral document," has major limitations inasmuch as it failed to focus "on relations of conflict and alliance between and within the historically determined organizations which are constitutive of class formation across the various levels of social structure." Because of this lack of focus, Braverman condensed, simplified and truncated what was in fact an uneven process of the development of Taylorism (Maier, 1970; Palmer, 1975; Littler, 1978; Stark, 1980). Braverman also understated the "perennial resistance to rationalization and the real limitations to any managerial strategy for complete control of the labor process" (Stark, 1980: 92–93) that workers were able to generate.

Although de-skilling has undoubtedly taken place, it has frequently occurred in the context of what Gramsci (1971) called "Fordism." Fordism involves assembly-line production, and it increases the workers' interdependence and thus their ability to disrupt production through "individual acts of sabotage, collective activity, or the more passive forms of simply not showing up for work" (Stark, 1980: 93). This interdependence gives workers a far more active role than Braverman allowed. Additionally, there is the need to reconsider Braverman's picture of the ruling class; he viewed the ruling class as having almost Lucaksian subjectivity that is represented as an unproblematic and unified "capital-logic" (Aronowitz, 1978). The Brighton Labor Process Group (1977) also noted the tendency toward de-skilling in the move from formal to real subordination but, unlike Braverman, located it within the organizational totality. According to this view, de-skilling is not as pervasive or unitary as Braverman suggested. Labor, materials, and instruments in production can always be combined in more than one way, and so capital attempts to control the combination. But of course, since control can never be total, not all roles can be exactly and absolutely prescribed. Independent skilled work, in particular, may remain a functional necessity, even when the organization is formally totally hierarchical. Not every aspect of the labor process will be de-skilled, nor can it be.

De-skilling is only a part of the overall process of change. Because some work roles are de-qualified, others are simultaneously "hyper-qualified". These are managerial, discretionary work elements. Minimization of trust in one sphere may well entail its maximization in another (Fox, 1974). These differentials are not only intraorganizational. They become interorganizational and regionally specific in the world-wide division of labor.

ORGANIZATION AS A STRUCTURE-IN-PROCESS: STATEMENTS

Recently, a number of writers have conceived of the organization of the labor process as a totality that is a *structure-in-process*. In this conception, structure evolves; the focus is on social dynamics rather than on social statics. This conception of organization clears the way for a delimitation of the types of control that are linked to stages in the development of capital accumulation, the motive force for which can be explained as the articulations of contradictions generated by each stage of development.

The idea that there are types of control that do not necessarily correspond to a unidirectional evolution of de-skilling was offered by Edwards (1978). He began in the now-familiar manner, criticizing Braverman while acknowledging his brilliance. Notably, Edwards' (1978: 110) major criticism was that "Braverman has left class conflict out of his analysis of the labor process" (a point developed skillfully by Aronowitz (1978) in the same issue of *The Insurgent Sociologist*). Edwards' analysis put class conflict back in the labor process by focusing on the development of discrete systems of control. According to Edwards (1978: 112), control of the labor process has three elements: (1) directing work tasks; (2) evaluating the work done; and (3) rewarding and disciplining workers.

Edwards (1978) identified three "historically important and essentially quite different ways of organizing these three elements." The first, "simple control," is direct, open, and interpersonal; it seems to correspond more or less to Simon's (1952) notion of direct, extensive, formal control (see Offe, 1976; Clegg, 1979: 118). In the second, "technical control," "the control mechanism is embedded in the physical technology of the firm." In the third, "bureaucratic control," "control becomes embedded in the social organization of the enterprise, in the contrived social relations of production at the point of production." The key feature of this social organization is the widespread acceptance and use of Weber's (1968) formally rational ideal type of legal-rational bureaucracy. The second and third are "structural" ways of organizing control.

In Edwards' argument, the transition from simple control to technical control developed from the employer's efforts to control conflict in the areas of production; the transition from simple control to bureaucratic control developed from similar efforts to control conflict in administration. Such simple differentiations are no longer possible because of "the incompleteness of technical control and the increasingly factory character of administrative work" (Edwards, 1978). Furthermore, not only the employers, but also the unions now staff and manage the contemporary forms of bureaucratic control (see Edwards, 1979).

A developmental logic is clear in Edwards' analysis. An example is his observation that developments within the firm reflected and interacted with a broader reorganization: the development of monopoly capitalism, itself a response to the driving force of capital accumulation. Indeed, he argued that "each form of control corresponds to a definite stage in the development of the "representative" or most important firms, and so the systems of control correspond to or characterize stages of capitalism" (Edwards, 1978: 112). The development of these systems of control has been uneven across different sectors of the economy.

Organization and Control

Edwards' (1978) analysis, while insightful, contained some lacunae. Its most significant lacuna was its lack of an adequate theorization of the organization *as a complex unity* of distinct types of control; it simply identified the three types in a developmental logic. Furthermore, although Edwards offered a distinction between the monopoly and competitive sectors of a modern economy, the distinction was hardly adequate as a realistic sectoring, largely because a consideration of the role of the state was absent.

The major advance in Aglietta's (1979) work was its attempt to integrate the type of concrete history that Edwards attempted with a more rigorous analysis of the laws of motion of the capitalist-accumulation process that underlie the changes in control. This led to the idea that the labor process is a complex unity that is a "structure-in-motion." Aglietta's (1979) key concepts were that changes in the regulation of structural forms are conditioned by crises. Davis (1978: 212) described crises as "creative ruptures" in the continuity of the reproduction of social relations which lead to their restructuring in new forms. Structural forms, such as organizations, are complex social relations that are historical products both of the class struggle and of changing cycles of capital accumulation. Recognizing this relationship, Davis proposed a periodic succession of intraorganizational regimes that were constructed to correspond with the averaged succession of Kondratieffian "long waves" (Davis, 1978: 259; see also Mandel, 1975; Barr, 1979). Major changes in the organization of the labor process thus take on a historically rational evolution. They emerge as responses by dominant economic agents (i.e., dominant coalitions) within organizations to changed conditions of accumulation. In order to try to construct more profitable conditions, economic agents effect reorganization. New underlying principles of organization are tried, widely adopted, and accepted as the rules for particular aspects of particular labor processes. The genesis and adoption of these rules are not random, but are conditioned by fundamental movements. These movements are long waves.

CONTROL AND STRUCTURE: A THEORY GENERATION

A specific, realistic theory of contested control and class struggle requires a more complex notion of what organization entails. First, it requires a representation of a spatial structuring of relations of production that is not simply physical but is especially social. Organizations are the sites of the social relations of production that define class structure. Different types of organizations are constructed at different levels of the class structure, and different levels of the organization are constructed at different levels of the class structure. Consequently, different types of control tend to evolve in specific relationships to different levels of the class structure, and this occurs both intra- and interorganizationally. Within the organization, different control rules evolve at different times and at different stages of functional complexity. Earlier rules may persist at specific levels in the organization, despite the later development of more complex rules. These rules may be represented as a superimposed series. As is in the nature of social reality, the articulation of relations among the different levels may produce not only unanticipated consequences but also contradictions. The layers of rules exist in a dynamic relationship with each other. The metaphor most apt for representing this layering is drawn from geology: sedimentation.

Layers of sediment (or strata) provide a record of historically evolved structure. Classes are the strata of society. They may be represented in an ideal and abstract form through a series of categorical distinctions. These are depicted in the Figure. The definitions of the working class, the middle class, and the ruling class hinge on the relationship to the value of the different categories of agents. Simple descriptions of the typical range of occupations are also provided. In the Figure, the class categories run horizontally across the page. The concrete history of organizational strategic calculations, management techniques, and practices provides the temporal coordinates of the vertical axis. These correspond to the rules that represent ways of formulating decisive breaks or interventions in principles of organization. In their moment of dominance, the rules may be related to the development of long waves in the world economy. The rules become dominant at particular moments because they represent strategies appropriate to the conjunctural possibilities of accumulation. The locus of their decision making may be either within or outside the focal organization. The locus is less important than are the effects registered in the structure of social relations of production. These effects constitute the organization's structure through introducing the different rules of control. In this way, the task-discontinuity develops.

The Figure is a matrix; the diagonal, stepped series represents the level of the class structure at which the rules operate in their greatest specificity. Although historical in conception, they persist and endure at different levels of the organization. Developments in strategic calculations, management techniques, and practices transform the evolving task-discontinuous organization. Different interventions are specific to different levels of the class structure as it is produced, re-produced, and transformed in organization structures. These interventions have their dominant moments, but they may persist and endure as residues of earlier practices. I conceive of these rules as selecting what is enacted for the organization, so I call them *sedimented selection rules.*

The role of the state as the overall agency of organizational life that makes, defines, and enforces rules is not neglected. In the most recent postwar era of the post-Keynesian "managed" economy, the state has become dominant, particularly in the monopoly sector and, of course, in the state-capitalist sector (see Clegg and Dunkerley, 1980: Chapter 13). The effects of the state have a feedback function at all levels of organizational practice; specific state interventions have specific effects at specific levels.

Finally, since we are dealing with a sedimented structure, we need to look at the interrelationships between levels. These are represented in the diagram by the hatched lines that depict the interrelations between rules. For instance, dual labor markets generate low-wage labor that can be utilized through job design, which de-skills more complex elements of the labor process; such de-skilling, particularly in full-employment conditions, can generate such organization problems as absenteeism

Organization and Control

and turnover. These are remedied through enriched job design, the principles of which are taught as part of the dominant ideology of organization theory in business schools. Students of these schools are drawn primarily from the ranks of the state-capitalist and monopoly-capitalist sectors, and they learn through studying cases drawn from the literature of organization problems. Students who survive the corporate race to executive positions then become the nexus between the state (as regulator and as market) and monopoly capital.

Figure: The sedimented structure of selection rules.

	Working Class	Middle Class	Ruling Class
Relations to value	producers, exploited, non-owners, laborers, wage earners	non-producers, exploiters, non-owners, non-laborers, revenue-receivers	non-producers, exploiters, owners, non-laborers, revenue-receivers
Simple description	Occupational range unskilled — skilled	Occupational range supervisory — managerial professional	Ownership and control of the organization as a whole private — public

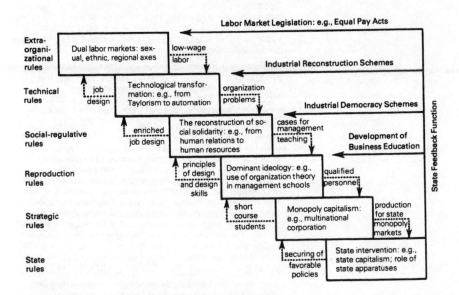

Note: The figure is a diagonal matrix. The stepped series represent the intersection of types of rules and levels of class structure in the organization. Hatched lines represent the articulation between levels while the solid lines represent the effect of the state.

Sedimented Selection Rules and Long Waves

A whole era may be characterized as having had relatively fast or slow accumulation. Accumulation depends on the rate of profit. A heightened rate of profit leads to relatively fast accumulation. The relationship between periods of fast and slow accumulation is one of succeeding cycles of "long waves of accelerated and decelerated accumulation determined by long waves in the rise and decline of the rate of profit" (Mandel, 1975: 129). The expansionary, accelerating phase of a long wave occurs when the rate of profit is triggered by factors that lower the organic composition of capital or raise the rate of surplus value. As these factors are exhausted, the rate of profit begins to fall because of unfavorable changes in either the organic composition of capital or the rate of surplus value. The long wave moves back into expansion when the rate of profit is once again lifted radically by a further combination of factors. New technologies, particularly energy technology, play a lead- ing role as triggers. However, as Rowthorn (1976: 64) stressed, the role of social technologies of control should not be ne- glected when considering these cycles. An example of social technologies is the general adoption of specific practices of organization. Certain speculative possibilities may be sketched for organization analysis.

We can distinguish the following long cycles of capitalist development that occurred in the past hundred years. The general depression that lasted from the early 1870s until the mid-1890s marked the downturn of a long wave; an upturn occurred from the mid-1890s to the first World War. The next downturn persisted through the 1920s to the beginning of the Second World War, which marked an accelerated renewal of accumulation that persisted until the late 1960s. Since then, we have clearly been in a downturn.

Each upturn in accumulation has seen the emergence of institutions that have intervened in, and thus framed, the organization of the labor process. The institutions have been major determinants of renewed accumulation, and they have been historically sedimented, as depicted in the Figure.

The upturn that began in the 1890s marked the emergence of attempts to apply formal abstract theories of organization to the labor process. One of these theories was F.W. Taylor's (1947) scientific management. The development of scientific man- agement depended upon a number of interrelated radical innovations in technology. In particular, it was possible because of the development of electricity as an energy source capable of powering new production technologies such as high-speed lathes. Such innovations were the technological foundations for the erosion of craft and personal skill. This erosion, a tactical move in the class struggle, was facilitated by Taylor's system, initially in the steel industry and later more generally. We can refer to interventions of this type as technical rules, since they stress the rule of technique over the will of the worker.

Because of the increasingly routinized, simplified, and de- skilled labor process (made possible by innovations such as Taylor's), during the First World War the capitalist labor process assimilated many raw recruits. Most notable among these were women,[2] young people, and aged peasants, who, through the real subordination of the labor process, were able to be rapidly

2
This was true at least in the U.K. In the U.S., where migration was of considerable im- portance in easing labor shortages (and in limiting working-class collective power) this was to be less significant.

Organization and Control

inducted into these new forms of labor. In the postwar period, this Taylorist simplification of the labor process was extended from the shop floor to the office, where female labor became increasingly a cheap and unskilled source of commercial work.

During the downturn of the inter-war period, the increase in de-skilling and routinizing white collar office work was a major device for increasing the efficiency of capital. This increase created a more homogenous labor process and a less skilled and less differentiated labor force that was recruited from increasingly differentiated labor markets. The major axes of differentiation, ethnicity and sex, were used to construct institutionalized skill and wage differences. We can refer to this form of labor market segmentation as an intervention constructed through the use of existing extraorganizational divisions. They may be termed *extraorganizational rules* (Clegg, 1979).

The individual enterprise or organization is not the overall economy. The economy of full employment during WW II and the long postwar boom posed particular problems for the organization and control of the labor process at the level of specific enterprises. Specifically, the war and postwar economies minimized the coercive domination of the reserve army of the unemployed, and so, as we might anticipate, the balance of domination became more hegemonic. In Mayo's (1975) studies, the breakdown of social solidarity and the subsequent articulation from human relations to human resources and work humanization during the long postwar boom may be identified as an intervention into the *social-regulative rules* of the organization, precisely because more coercive controls were unavailable due to the absence of the reserve army of the unemployed.

A major effect of full employment in the postwar period was the specialization of forms of labor control contingent upon the class structure of occupations. Friedman (1977) suggested that the two strategies which I have termed *technical rules* and *social-regulative rules* may have been applied to the labor process not only in different moments of the world's economic history (particularly since its rhythm has been modulated by two world wars), but also to different elements in the labor process. Technical rules tend to be applied to workers who are more peripheral to the labor process (less strategically contingent); social regulative rules tend to be applied to workers who are more central (more strategically contingent). This differential strategy arises as a way of handling inflexibilities that are generated by three contradictions within each intervention into the labor process.

First, Taylorist technical rules could not be applied universally. Not everyone could be de-skilled, nor could everyone be a high-wage laborer. In both spheres, differentials would have to be preserved for the strategy to work. Second, the affluent worker is not necessarily a happy worker. Third, the affluent worker is not necessarily a very satisfactory worker in situations demanding flexibility and some discretion. It is precisely the more strategically contingent workers that management will attempt to control through more subtle hegemonic domination, that is, through social-regulative rules.

This division of the work force can be carried further by *extraorganizational rules* (Clegg, 1979). The specialization of forms of labor control contingent upon the class structure of occupations can be extended through a sexual, racial, or ethnic division of labor that is extraorganizational in its dividing principle. Those skills that are not strategically contingent — generally those with low status, relatively low pay, and low job entrance requirements — can be further distinguished from the rest of the labor process, with the effect of minimizing the possibility of labor's developing a collective consciousness of itself *for* itself. In this way, the contradictory possibility that the concept participation might become a collective and liberating catchword would be minimized. Taylorizing unstrategic skills in the organization has promoted this distinction. Because of their low social status in the labor market, unstrategic skills tend to attract the most socially disadvantaged groups in the labor force. These are groups that are sexually and racially discriminated against: women and ethnic minorities, such as blacks or recent migrants. It has frequently been observed that management will often actively encourage this distinction by overqualifying managerial skills and other strategically contingent skills or by locating administration and research tasks only where white male, native-born workers can easily get to them. Friedman (1977) argued that there is substantial evidence ''from several countries concerning the more volatile unemployment levels for blacks, immigrants and women.'' One can cite Edwards, Reich, and Weisskopf (1972) and Castles and Kosack (1973) as evidence. These extraorganizational rules relate, then, to the structure of the secondary labor force.

Social-regulative rules tend to be aimed at workers in the "new middle class" (Carchedi, 1977) who perform contradictory supervisory functions as collective workers *and* as global capitalists. If this thesis is correct, we would expect to find that controls on the working class will tend to be either technical rules or extraorganizational rules. Extraorganizational rules function through the development of secondary labor markets, largely at the level of relatively unskilled workers. Technical rules tend to be developed in relation to technological transformations such as Taylorism or automation, processes that increase the amount of surplus that can be obtained from skilled workers. It is this phenomenon of intervention by technical rules that can generate the limited discretionary powers of decision making (e.g., Crozier's [1964] maintenance workers). These discretionary powers are historically sedimented in residual craft skills that escaped rationalization by scientific management.

Any organization based on mass production has to harness its labor power to its machine power for the maximum utilizable time because of the peculiarities of modern plant economy. The more that a modern plant is utilized by the organization below its rated capacity, the greater will be the cost of the plant's output. Hence, economy of production is achieved and the greatest surplus is potentially produced when maximal production is achieved. However, the market must be able to absorb the increased output. In a market economy, "no intrinsic correlation exists between increased output and the capacity of effective demand to absorb production" (Sohn-Rethel, 1976: 31). The consequence is that, although technical and social-regulative

Organization and Control

rules may maintain productivity, they are not sufficient by themselves. Sometimes they are not even necessary. This analysis of the need for such strategies applies best to developed market economy social formations, in which the national proletariat, on the average, forms part of an international labor aristocracy. In low-wage, less developed social formations — the periphery and semi-periphery of the world economy — hegemony will recede in importance. For this reason, a large number (Vernon's 1973 estimate was 187) of U.S., European, and Japanese international firms are established in the more peripheral regions. The enterprises have been located there precisely because of the reduced cost of the labor process, the possibility of multi-factor supply for core production (as in the U.S.), and transfer pricing. The firms, as Karpik (1977) and Adam (1975) argued, tend to be large technological enterprises. That part of their control of the labor process that is not assured by their relatively high pay scales and by the large reserve army of the unemployed can frequently be assured by the policies of the domestic state. This assurance is the existence of a compliant workforce that asserts little or no power.

We can now consider the organizations that operate primarily in the core states of the world economy — in particular, those organizations generated by the upturn of the cycle of accumulation in the postwar era. This developed on the basis of an important bunching of inventions in production and energy use during the inter-war period. These inventions were associated in particular with the automobile industry (the postwar boom is often called "the age of the internal combustion engine"). Associated with this age was the impact on mass consumption of the development of large electronics and plastics industries. The leading firms in these industries are primarily monopoly capitalist organizations. The developing domination of technological capitalism and other forms of monopoly capitalism in the postwar boom necessitated a further intervention in organizations that we can call *strategic rules*. Strategic rules are an intervention in both production and circulation of commodities. (In contrast, social regulative rules and technical rules are interventions only in the production of commodities. As such, they are a one-sided intervention that necessitates the further intervention of strategic rules.)

Intraorganizational interventions into production have to be buttressed and supported by strategic rules: interventions into the market in order to exert rational control (Sohn-Rethel, 1978: 32; see also Baran and Sweezy, 1966). The significance of organizations' capacity to plan becomes apparent when we consider that during 1970–1971, multinational organizations controlled 20 percent of industrial output in the capitalist world and 30 percent of world trade. At the same time, they possessed three times the gold and currency reserves of the United States (Mandel, 1975: 23). It has been forecast that, by the end of this century, between two and three hundred multinationals will control 75 percent of the private assets of the capitalist world (Wheelwright, 1974).

Two aspects of corporate dominance hinge on problems of control. The first aspect is the control by the corporate organizations of the new, massively expanded middle class strata of supervisors, managers, and professionals within these organizations. The second aspect is the control of the large corporate

organizations by the expanded strata of middle class professional workers within the state apparatuses. This aspect entails
a rejection of the classical liberal conception of state/market
relations in the face of corporate dominance.

The development of both state and private organizations gave
rise to strata of non-producers/exploiters/non-owners/
revenue-receivers who operate extensive controls over and in
the organization. These agents do not necessarily have the
decisive material interest of ownership (legal possession) of the
means of production that they control. Then how are the means
of production to be controlled? That is, in terms of the Figure,
what are the *reproduction rules* of late capitalism and where
are they located? It was argued elsewhere (Clegg and Dunkerley, 1980) that the business and management schools have
become the institutional sites for the reproduction of the
contemporary dominant ideology of late capitalism (see also
Marceau, Thomas, and Whitley, 1978). This dominant ideology
functions mainly to control the actions of the organizational
agents who enjoy the most discretion or the least specificity of
role prescription and who are not constrained simply by the
practices of routinely designed work. As both Marcuse (1964)
and Perrow (1972) argued, control is best achieved by employing agents that have rules and rationality built into them through
educational socialization.

Finally, as was argued in considerably more detail elsewhere
(Clegg, 1979; Clegg and Dunkerley, 1980), we have to consider
the role of the state in the interventions into the labor process.
The state cannot be conceived of as a polity parallel to and
outside of the economy. Its resources are one of the major
prizes to be fought over, bribed for, and won among corporate
executives. The state, through defining, making, and enforcing
rules, structures the space in which organizations operate.
Large organizations, being powerful, attempt to arrange this
structure to suit their own interests.

The state is a potential source of protection for capitalist
organizations operating on the market (see McCullough and
Shannon, 1977). Polanyi (1957) described two central features
of the market system. First, greater profit accrues to organizations that possess larger amounts of resources. There is
therefore continual pressure toward monopolization and
toward the creation of privileged access to resources. Second,
the market system is dynamic; it creates risks and uncertainties
for any specific organization, since new areas of demands and
new profit opportunities can be continually exploited. This
dynamism often undercuts existing organization profit centers.
Hence, in order to protect and to increase their advantages,
organizations continually attempt to control the contingencies
that are strategic for their profit-centered activity. Organization
agents therefore attempt to use the state to affect the market
in their interests (Wallerstein, 1974: 405) and to secure favorable state interventions in the socialization of costs, risks, and
losses. Additionally, the state becomes the major consumer of
much monopoly production, particularly of defense systems
and of electronic data-processing equipment. This state/capital
interdependence, particularly as mediated through taxes and
inflation, may well generate profound "fiscal crises" (O'Connor,
1974) and "legitimation crises" (Habermas, 1976).

Organization and Control

The state is also important as both a factor of cohesion and as a disarticulator of the totality, as depicted in the state's feedback functions in the Figure. These functions can have anticipated and unanticipated consequences. For example, the Crawford Report (Crawford et al., 1979), a federal government report on the manufacturing industry in Australia, argued that equal-pay legislation (extraorganizational level) has increased the rate of adoption of new technology (level of technical rules). This legislation has thus exacerbated industrial-relations conflicts and unemployment, both of which have profound effects at the state level. Exchange values involved in the labor process have increased because of equal-pay legislation, and so organizations have attempted to cheapen their labor process by substituting technologically advanced computerized intelligence systems.

Computerized intelligence systems may be similar to the bunched technological innovations that characterized the upturns of earlier long waves, but their effects are likely to be even more dramatic in their impact on the organization and control of the labor process. Earlier long waves, in their ascendant phase, created employment. However, the available but scanty evidence does not suggest that this is now the case (Hill, 1980). Microprocessors and allied technology have enormous potential for reducing production costs (by minimizing labor), but their effect on demand is potentially harsh. The de-laborization that is progressing in the advanced economies will not restore aggregate effective demand as long as income is distributed to individuals according to their economic activity. Restoring demand will require allocating income socially, on the basis of a massive redistribution of increasingly scarce employment opportunities. This redistribution would involve changing work hours, sharing jobs, and radically restructuring labor processes around principles different from those that underlie the "rules" discussed here. Decision making would have to shift from private intraorganizational criteria to public, societal criteria. Such a transformation will hardly be achieved through existing forms, either organizational or state.

CONCLUSION

The concept of control has been developed in this paper in an ideal typical analysis of organization. The concept already suggests new relationships and patterns in organizational phenomena. Considerable unifying potential attaches to the concept, particularly in as much as both macro- and micro-phenomena can be developed together within the same framework. What type of research might be generated from this exercise in conceptual clarification and development?

The contention of this paper is that organizations have been constructed on the basis of differential modes of control of their overall labor process and that different modes of control become specialized at different levels of the class structure in organizations. Intensive control characterizes lower-class participants, internal control characterizes middle-class participants, and extensive control characterizes ruling-class participants.

This exercise has been highly abstract. As such, it offers a simple sketch of complexities that might be encountered at the level of concrete organization that are open to empirical scrutiny. To bridge the gap between organization as theoretical abstraction and the organization as concrete particular, resistant to abstraction, an intermediate level of analysis is required. This intermediate analysis concerns the uneven development of organizations' labor processes through three dimensions: time (with long waves as hypothetical structuring frames for breaks); space (the internal class structure of organizations; the location of the specific organizations in particular regions of the world economy with their peculiar histories); and economy (the dominant sector, e.g., monopoly capital, within the particular branch, e.g., coal mining). Space and economy are the dependent variables; the independent variable is time, measured by the modalities of historically specific long waves. If one holds constant the branch within an industry in which a particular sector of capital dominates, do organizations drawn from the dominant sector display the same patterns of evolution within a given internal class structure and across different regions of the world economy? Contingency theory, which emphasizes internal determination by size or external determination by environment, would suggest a positive answer. Contingency theory stresses different aspects of organization than those elaborated here (see, for example, Lammers and Hickson, 1979, particularly "Conclusions").

The research effort would be of two kinds. The first, consisting of documentary analysis of archival materials drawn from and focusing on a sample of organizations within a particular branch of industry, would construct an ideal typical model of the major breaks in organizational control rules. Here the work of Dan Clawson (1980) must be regarded as a landmark, particularly in its emphasis on how the choices of organizational designers are conditioned by the imperatives of class struggle (ruling-class accumulation of value and working-class resistance to increased control).

The second kind of research would be ongoing. We are clearly entering an age of uncertainty in organization structure. Technological developments such as the possibly bunched innovations in computerized intelligence systems seem poised to produce very different organizations that will certainly have unforeseen political effects. Over the next decade, research could investigate the range of organization design options in particular industries by canvassing unions, management, and the state. The findings could be most usefully compared with the range of decisions actually implemented at the organization level.

The first phase would represent a revision of organization analysis, particularly inasmuch as it might confirm the "sedimentation" of control empirically discovered by Burawoy (1979). Organization theory would then have to come to terms with a realization that reality has to be understood in terms of its ontogeny, as well as its size or environment. The second phase would represent a relocation of organization analysis, or at least aspects of it, within a framework that would be much more explicitly political than the present one is. We already have Marglin's (1974) historical example; Sampson's (1976) analysis of the structural development of the oil industry is a study of contemporary organizations.

Organization and Control

The framework of control requires considerable development in organization analysis. Nonetheless, as this paper has sought to demonstrate, there is a substantial body of work that, while largely unfamiliar to organization theorists, is potentially fruitful for further theoretical construction and empirical work.

REFERENCES

Adam, Grygor
1975 "Multinational corporations and worldwide sourcing." In H. Radice (ed.), International Firms and Modern Imperialism: 89–104. Harmondsworth: Penguin.

Aglietta, Michel
1979 The Regulation of U.S. Capitalism. London: New Left Books.

Aldrich, Howard E.
1979 Organizations and Environments. Englewood Cliffs, NJ: Prentice-Hall.

Aronowitz, Stanley
1978 "Marx, Braverman, and the logic of capital." The Insurgent Sociologist, 8: 126–46.

Baldamus, W.
1979 The Structure of Sociological Inference. London: Martin Robertson.

Baran, Paul, and Paul Sweezy
1966 Monopoly Capital. New York: Monthly Review Press.

Barr, Kenneth
1979 "Long waves: A selective annotated bibliography." Review, 11: 675–718.

Braverman, Harry
1974 Labor and Monopoly Capital. New York: Monthly Review Press.

Brighton Labor Process Group
1977 "The capitalist labor process." Capital and Class, 1: 3–42.

Burawoy, Michael
1979 Manufacturing Consent: Changes in the Labor Process under Monopoly Capitalism. Chicago: University of Chicago Press.

Carchedi, Guglielmo
1977 On the Economic Identification of Social Classes. London: Routledge and Kegan Paul.

Castles, Stephen, and G. Kosack
1973 Immigrant Workers and Class Structures in Western Europe. London: Oxford University Press.

Chomsky, Noam
1968 Language and Mind. New York: Harcourt, Brace, Jovanovitch.

Clawson, Dan
1980 Bureaucracy and the Labor Process. New York: Monthly Review Press.

Clegg, Stewart
1975 Power, Rule and Domination: A Critical and Empirical Understanding of Power in Sociological Theory and Everyday Life. London: Routledge and Kegan Paul.
1977 "Power, organization theory, Marx and critique." In S. Clegg and D. Dunkerley (eds.), Critical Issues in Organizations: 21–40. London: Routledge and Kegan Paul.
1979 The Theory of Power and Organization. London: Routledge and Kegan Paul.

Clegg, Stewart, and David Dunkerley
1980 Organization, Class and Control. London: Routledge and Kegan Paul.

Coombes, Rod
1978 "Labor and monopoly capital." New Left Review. 107: 79–96.

Crawford, J.G., B.S. Inglis, R.J.L. Hawke, and N.S. Currie
1979 Study Group on Structural Adjustment. Report, Volume 1, March. Canberra: Australian Government Publishing Service.

Crozier, Michel
1964 The Bureaucratic Phenomenon. London: Tavistock.

Cutler, Anthony
1978 "The romance of 'labor'." Economy and Society, 7: 74–95.

Davis, Mike
1978 " 'Fordism' in crisis: A review of Michel Aglietta's Régulation et Crises: L'expérience des Etats-Unis." Review, 11: 207–269.

Edwards, Richard C.
1978 "The social relations of production at the point of production." The Insurgent Sociologist, 8: 109–125.
1979 Contested Terrain. New York: Basic Books.

Edwards, Richard C., Michael Reich, and Thomas E. Weisskopf
1972 The Capitalist System. Englewood Cliffs, NJ: Prentice-Hall.

Fox, Alan
1974 Beyond Contract: Work, Power and Trust Relations. London: Faber and Faber.

Friedman, Andrew
1977 "Responsible autonomy versus direct control over the labor process." Capital and Class, 1: 43–57.

Goodrich, Carter
1975 The Frontier of Control, reprint ed. London: Pluto Press.

Gorz, André
1972 "Technical intelligence and the capitalist division of labor." Telos, 12: 27–41.

Gramsci, Antonio
1971 Selections from the Prison Notebooks. Q. Hoare and G.N. Smith, eds. and trans. London: Lawrence and Wishart.

Habermas, Jurgen
1976 Legitimation Crisis. London: Heinemann.

Hickson, David J.
1966 "A convergence in organization theory." Administrative Science Quarterly, 11: 224–237.

Hickson, David J., C.R. Hinings, C.A. Lee, R.E. Schneck, and J.M. Pennings
1971 "A strategic contingencies theory of intra-organizational power." Administrative Science Quarterly 16: 216–229.

Hill, Stephen
1980 "Economic and industrial transformation: The waves of social consequence from technological change." In P. Boreham and G. Dow (eds.), Work and Inequality: Workers, Economic Crisis and the State. Melbourne: Macmillan.

Hinings, Christopher R., D.J. Hickson, J.M. Pennings, and R.E. Schneck
1974 "Structural conditions of intraorganizational power." Administrative Science Quarterly 9: 22–44.

Jacoby, R.
1976 "Review of H. Braverman, Labor and Monopoly Capital." Telos 29: 199–207.

Karpik, Lucien
1977 "Technological capitalism." In S. Clegg and D. Dunkerley (eds.), Critical Issues in Organizations: 41–71. London: Routledge and Kegan Paul

Lammers, Cornelis J., and David J. Hickson
1979 Organizations Alike and Unlike. London: Routledge and Kegan Paul.

Littler, Craig
1978 "Understanding Taylorism." British Journal of Sociology, 29: 185–202.

McCullough, Arthur, and Michael Shannon
1977 "Organizations and protection." In S. Clegg and D. Dunkerley (eds.), Critical Issues in Organizations: 72–85. London: Routledge and Kegan Paul.

Maier, C.S.
1970 "Between Taylorism and technocracy: European ideologies and the vision of productivity in the 1920s." Journal of Contemporary History, 5: 27–61.

Mandel, Ernest
1975 Late Capitalism. London: New Left Books.

Marceau, Jane, Alan B. Thomas, and Richard Whitley
1978 "Business and the state: Management education and business elites in France and Great Britain." In G. Littlejohn, B. Smart, J. Wakeford, and N. Yuval-Davis (eds.), Power and the State: 128–57. London: Croom Helm.

Marcuse, Herbert
1964 One Dimensional Man. London: Routledge and Kegan Paul.

Marglin, Steven A.
1974 "What do bosses do? — The origins and functions of hierarchy in capitalist production." Review of Radical Political Economics, 6: 60–112.

Marx, Karl
1976 Capital, vol. 1. F. Engels, ed. Harmondsworth, Penguin.

Mayo, Elton
1975 The Social Problems of an Industrial Civilization. London: Routledge and Kegan Paul.

O'Connor, James
1974 The Corporations and the State. New York: Harper Colophon.

Offe, Claus
1976 Industry and Inequality. London: Edward Arnold.

Palmer, Bryan
1975 "Class, conception and conflict: The thrust for efficiency, managerial views of labor and the working class rebellion, 1903–1922." Review of Radical Political Economy, 7: 31–49.

Perrow, Charles
1972 Complex Organizations: A Critical Essay. Glenview, IL: Scott, Foresman.

Polanyi, Karl
1957 The Great Transformation. Boston: Beacon.

Poulantzas, Nicos
1974 Classes in Contemporary Capitalism. London: New Left Books.

Rowthorn, Bob
1976 Review article: "Ernest Mandel's 'Late Capitalism'." New Left Review, 98: 59–83.

Salaman, Graeme
1979 Work Organization: Resistance and Control. London: Longman.

Sampson, Anthony
1976 The Seven Sisters. London: Coronet.

Silverman, David
1970 The Theory of Organizations. London: Heinemann.

Simon, Herbert A.
1952 "Decision-making and administrative organization." In R. K. Merton, A.P. Gray, B. Hockey, and H.C. Selvin (eds.), Reader in Bureaucracy: 185–194. New York: Free Press.

Sohn-Rethel, Alfred
1976 "The dual economics of transition." In CSE Pamphlet No. 1, The Labor Process and Class Strategies: 26–45. London: Stage 1.

Stark, David
1980 "Class struggle and the transformation of the labor process." Theory and Society, 9: 89–130.

Taylor, Frederick Winslow
1947 Scientific Management. New York: Harper and Row.

Vernon, Raymond
1973 Sovereignty at Bay: The Multinational Spread of U.S. Enterprise. Harmondsworth: Penguin.

Wallerstein, Immanuel
1974 The Modern World System: Capitalist Agriculture and the Origins of the European World Economy in the Sixteenth Century. London: Academic Press.

Weber, Max
1968 Economy and Society: An Outline of Interpretive Sociology. New York: Bedminster Press.

Weick, Karl E.
1969 The Social Psychology of Organizing. Reading, MA: Addison-Wesley.

Wheelwright, E.L.
1974 "International capitalism: The sorcerer's apprentice?" Radical Political Economy: Collected Essays: 35–46. Sydney, ANZ.

Part VII
Organizational Culture

In 1951, Elliott Jaques of the Tavistock Institute in London published a dissertation entitled *The Changing Culture of the Factory*, thereby setting in motion a trend in organization theory that was to bloom in the 1980s. His work, however, was dated earlier than organization theory as portrayed here, and I therefore claim that it was Edgar Schein's coining of the term 'corporate culture' that announced a new era of interest for culture in organizations. Schein's best-known book is *Organizational Culture and Leadership* from 1985,[8] but its intentions are clearly announced in the article reprinted here (Chapter 19). The popularity of organizational culture was such that Linda Smircich could already review the literature as early as 1983, noting that it had branched into several quite distinctive approaches (Chapter 20): the symbolist (cultural studies of organization, the most vital at present), the instrumentalist (culture as a control tool), and the anthropological (organizations as cultures). In the rush toward organizational culture, John Van Maanen and Stephen Barley (Chapter 21) attempted to keep interest in occupational culture alive, a move that gained importance with the increase of interest in such professions and new occupations as finance and information technology.

Note

8. San Francisco, CA: Jossey-Bass.

References

Jacques, E. (1951), *The Changing Culture of the Factory*, London: Tavistock.

[19]

Minerva, the Roman goddess of wisdom, is said to have sprung full-blown from the
forehead of Zeus. Similarly, an organization's culture begins life in
the head of its founder—springing from the founder's ideas
about truth, reality, and the way the world works.

The Role of the Founder
in Creating
Organizational Culture

Edgar H. Schein

How do the entrepreneur/founders of organizations create organizational cultures? And how can such cultures be analyzed? These questions are central to this article. First I will examine what organizational culture is, how the founder creates and embeds cultural elements, why it is likely that first-generation companies develop distinctive cultures, and what the implications are in making the transition from founders or owning families to "professional" managers.

The level of confusion over the term *organizational culture* requires some defini-

tions of terms at the outset. An organizational culture depends for its existence on a definable organization, in the sense of a number of people interacting with each other for the purpose of accomplishing some goal in their defined environment. An organization's founder simultaneously creates such a group and, by force of his or her personality, begins to shape the group's culture. But that new group's culture does not develop until it has overcome various crises of growth and survival, and has worked out solutions for coping with its external problems of adapta-

Organizational Dynamics, Summer 1983. © *1983, Periodicals Division,*
American Management Associations. All rights reserved. 0090–2616/83/0014–0013/$02.00/0

13

tion and its internal problems of creating a workable set of relationship rules.

Organizational culture, then, is the pattern of basic assumptions that a given group has invented, discovered, or developed in learning to cope with its problems of external adaptation and internal integration —a pattern of assumptions that has worked well enough to be considered valid and, therefore, to be taught to new members as the correct way to perceive, think, and feel in relation to those problems.

In terms of external survival problems, for example, I have heard these kinds of assumptions in first-generation companies:

> The way to decide on what products we will build is to see whether we ourselves like the product; if *we* like it, our customers will like it.

> The only way to build a successful business is to invest no more than 5 percent of your own money in it.

> The customer is the key to our success, so we must be totally dedicated to total customer service.

In terms of problems of internal integration the following examples apply:

> Ideas can come from anywhere in this organization, so we must maintain a climate of total openness.

> The only way to manage a growing business is to supervise every detail on a daily basis.

> The only way to manage a growing business is to hire good people, give them clear responsibility, tell them how they will be measured, and then leave them alone.

Several points should be noted about the definition and the examples. First, culture is not the overt behavior or visible artifacts one might observe on a visit to the company. It is not even the philosophy or value system that the founder may articulate or write down in various "charters." Rather, it is the assumptions that underlie the values and determine not only behavior patterns, but also such visible artifacts as architecture, office layout, dress codes, and so on. This

14

Edgar H. Schein *received his Ph.D. in social psychology from the Harvard Department of Social Relations in 1952. Following three years at the Walter Reed Institute of Research, he joined M.I.T.'s Sloan School, where he has been ever since. He is the author of a basic text entitled* Organizational Psychology *(Prentice-Hall, Inc., 1980), which is now in its third edition, the book* Process Consultation *(Addison-Wesley, 1969) and, most recently, the book* Career Dynamics *(Addison-Wesley, 1978). Currently Sloan Fellows Professor of Management at the Sloan School, he is pursuing research on the dynamics of organizational culture.*

distinction is important because founders bring many of these assumptions with them when the organization begins; their problem is how to articulate, teach, embed, and in other ways get their own assumptions across and working in the system.

Founders often start with a theory of how to succeed; they have a cultural paradigm in their heads, based on their experience in the culture in which they grew up. In the case of a founding *group*, the theory and paradigm arise from the way that group reaches consensus on their assumptions about how to view things. Here, the evolution of the culture is a multi-stage process reflecting the several stages of group formation. The ultimate organizational culture will always reflect the complex interaction between (1) the assumptions and theories that founders bring to the group initially and (2) what the group learns subsequently from its own experiences.

Figure 1
EXTERNAL AND INTERNAL PROBLEMS

Problems of External Adaptation and Survival

1. Developing consensus on the *primary task, core mission, or manifest and latent functions of the group* — for example, strategy.

2. Consensus on *goals*, such goals being the concrete reflection of the core mission.

3. Developing consensus on the *means to be used* in accomplishing the goals — for example, division of labor, organization structure, reward system, and so forth.

4. Developing consensus on the *criteria to be used in measuring how well the group is doing against its goals and targets* — for example, information and control systems.

5. Developing consensus on *remedial or repair strategies* as needed when the group is not accomplishing its goals.

Problems of Internal Integration

1. *Common language and conceptual categories.* If members cannot communicate with and understand each other, a group is impossible by definition.

2. Consensus on *group boundaries and criteria for inclusion and exclusion.* One of the most important areas of culture is the shared consensus on who is in, who is out, and by what criteria one determines membership.

3. Consensus on *criteria for the allocation of power and status.* Every organization must work out its pecking order and its rules for how one gets, maintains, and loses power. This area of consensus is crucial in helping members manage their own feelings of aggression.

4. Consensus on *criteria for intimacy, friendship, and love.* Every organization must work out its rules of the game for peer relationships, for relationships between the sexes, and for the manner in which openness and intimacy are to be handled in the context of managing the organization's tasks.

5. Consensus on *criteria for allocation of rewards and punishments.* Every group must know what its heroic and sinful behaviors are; what gets rewarded with property, status, and power; and what gets punished through the withdrawal of rewards and, ultimately, excommunication.

6. Consensus on *ideology and "religion."* Every organization, like every society, faces unexplainable events that must be given meaning so that members can respond to them and avoid the anxiety of dealing with the unexplainable and uncontrollable.

WHAT IS ORGANIZATIONAL CULTURE ABOUT?

Any new group has the problem of developing shared assumptions about the nature of the world in which it exists, how to survive in it, and how to manage and integrate internal relationships so that it can operate effectively and make life livable and comfortable for its members. These external and internal problems can be categorized as shown in Figure 1.

The external and internal problems are always intertwined and acting simultaneously. A group cannot solve its external survival problem without being integrated to some degree to permit concerted action, and it cannot integrate itself without some successful task accomplishment vis-à-vis its survival problem or primary task.

The model of organizational culture that then emerges is one of shared solutions to problems which work well enough to begin to be taken for granted — to the point where they drop out of awareness, become unconscious assumptions, and are taught to new members as a reality and as the correct way to view things. If one wants to identify the elements of a given culture, 15

Figure 2
Basic Underlying Assumptions Around Which Cultural Paradigms Form

1. *The organization's relationship to its environment.* Reflecting even more basic assumptions about the relationship of humanity to nature, one can assess whether the key members of the organization view the relationship as one of dominance, submission, harmonizing, finding an appropriate niche, and so on.

2. *The nature of reality and truth.* Here are the linguistic and behavioral rules that define what is real and what is not, what is a "fact," how truth is ultimately to be determined, and whether truth is "revealed" or "discovered"; basic concepts of time as linear or cyclical, monochronic or polychronic; basic concepts such as space as limited or infinite and property as communal or individual; and so forth.

3. *The nature of human nature.* What does it mean to be "human," and what attributes are considered intrinsic or ultimate? Is human nature good, evil, or neutral? Are human beings perfectible or not? Which is better, Theory X or Theory Y?

4. *The nature of human activity.* What is the "right" thing for human beings to do, on the basis of the above assumptions about reality, the environment, and human nature: to be active, passive, self-developmental, fatalistic, or what? What is work and what is play?

5. *The nature of human relationships.* What is considered to be the "right" way for people to relate to each other, to distribute power and love? Is life cooperative or competitive; individualistic, group collaborative, or communal; based on traditional lineal authority, law, or charisma; or what?

one can go down the list of issues and ask how the group views itself in relation to each of them: What does it see to be its core mission, its goals, the way to accomplish those goals, the measurement systems and procedures it uses, the way it remedies actions, its particular jargon and meaning system, the authority system, peer system, reward system, and ideology? One will find, when one does this, that there is in most cultures a deeper level of assumptions which ties together the various solutions to the various problems, and this deeper level deals with more ultimate questions. The real cultural essence, then, is what members of the organization assume about the issues shown in Figure 2.

In a fairly "mature" culture — that is, in a group that has a long and rich history — one will find that these assumptions are patterned and interrelated into a "cultural paradigm" that is the key to understanding how members of the group view the world. In an organization that is in the process of formation, the paradigm is more likely to be found only in the founder's head, but it is important to try to decipher it in order to understand the biases or directions in which the founder "pushes" or "pulls" the organization.

How Do Organizational Cultures Begin? The Role of the Founder

Groups and organizations do not form accidentally or spontaneously. They are usually created because someone takes a leadership role in seeing how the concerted action of a number of people could accomplish something that would be impossible through individual action alone. In the case of social movements or new religions, we have prophets, messiahs, and other kinds of charismatic leaders. Political groups or movements are started by leaders who sell new visions and new solutions. Firms are created by entrepreneurs who have a vision of how a concerted effort could create a new product or service in the marketplace. The process of culture formation in the organization begins with the founding of the group. How does this happen?

16

In any given firm the history will be somewhat different, but the essential steps are functionally equivalent:

1. A single person (founder) has an idea for a new enterprise.

2. A founding group is created on the basis of initial consensus that the idea is a good one: workable and worth running some risks for.

3. The founding group begins to act in concert to create the organization by raising funds, obtaining patents, incorporating, and so forth.

4. Others are brought into the group according to what the founder or founding group considers necessary, and the group begins to function, developing its own history.

In this process the founder will have a major impact on how the group solves its external survival and internal integration problems. Because the founder had the original idea, he or she will typically have biases on how to get the idea fulfilled —biases based on previous cultural experiences and personality traits. In my observation, entrepreneurs are very strong-minded about what to do and how to do it. Typically they already have strong assumptions about the nature of the world, the role their organization will play in that world, the nature of human nature, truth, relationships, time, and space.

Three Examples

Founder A, who built a large chain of supermarkets and department stores, was the dominant ideological force in the company until he died in his seventies. He assumed that his organization could be dominant in the market and that his primary mission was to supply his customers with a quality, reliable product. When A was operating only a corner store with his wife, he built customer relations through a credit policy that displayed trust in the customer, and he always

took products back if the customer was not satisfied. Further, he assumed that stores had to be attractive and spotless, and that the only way to ensure this was by close personal supervision. He would frequently show up at all his stores to check into small details. Since he assumed that only close supervision would teach subordinates the right skills, he expected all his store managers to be very visible and very much on top of their jobs.

A's theory about how to grow and win against his competition was to be innovative, so he encouraged his managers to try new approaches, to bring in consulting help, to engage in extensive training, and to feel free to experiment with new technologies. His view of truth and reality was to find it wherever one could and, therefore, to be open to one's environment and never take it for granted that one had all the answers. If new things worked, A encouraged their adoption.

Measuring results and fixing problems was, for A, an intensely personal matter. In addition to using traditional business measures, he went to the stores and, if he saw things not to his liking, immediately insisted that they be corrected. He trusted managers who operated on the basis of similar kinds of assumptions and clearly had favorites to whom he delegated more.

Authority in this organization remained very centralized; the ultimate source of power, the voting shares of stock, remained entirely in the family. A was interested in developing good managers throughout the organization, but he never assumed that sharing ownership through some kind of stock option plan would help in that process. In fact, he did not even share ownership with several key "lieutenants" who had been with the company through most of its life but were not in the family. They were well paid, but received no stock. As a result, peer relationships were officially defined as competitive. A liked managers to compete for slots and felt free to get rid of "losers."

A also introduced into the firm a number of family members who received favored treatment in the form of good developmental jobs that would test them for ultimate management potential. As the firm diversified, family members were made division heads even though they often had relatively little general management experience. Thus peer relationships were highly politicized. One had to know how to stay in favor, how to deal with family members, and how to maintain trust with nonfamily peers in the highly competitive environment.

A wanted open communication and high trust levels, but his own assumptions about the role of the family, the effect of ownership, and the correct way to manage were, to some degree, in conflict with each other, leading many of the members of the organization to deal with the conflicting signals by banding together to form a kind of counter-culture within the founding culture. They were more loyal to each other than to the company.

Without going into further detail, I want to note several points about the "formation" of this organization and its emerging culture. By definition, something can become part of the culture only if it works. A's theory and assumptions about how things "should be" worked, since his company grew and prospered. He personally received a great deal of reinforcement for his own assumptions, which undoubtedly gave him increased confidence that he had a correct view of the world. Throughout his lifetime he steadfastly adhered to the principles with which he started, and did everything in his power to get others to accept them as well. At the same time, however, A had to share concepts and assumptions with a great many other people. So as his company grew and learned from its own experience, A's as-

18

sumptions gradually had to be modified, or A had to withdraw from certain areas of running the business. For example, in their diversification efforts, the management bought several production units that would permit backward integration in a number of areas — but, because they recognized that they knew little about running factories, they brought in fairly strong, autonomous managers and left them alone.

A also had to learn that his assumptions did not always lead to clear signals. He thought he was adequately rewarding his best young general managers, but could not see that for some of them the political climate, the absence of stock options, and the arbitrary rewarding of family members made their own career progress too uncertain. Consequently, some of his best people left the company — a phenomenon that left A perplexed but unwilling to change his own assumptions in this area. As the company matured, many of these conflicts remained and many subcultures formed around groups of younger managers who were functionally or geographically insulated from the founder.

Founder B built a chain of financial service organizations using sophisticated financial analysis techniques in an urban area where insurance companies, mutual funds, and banks were only beginning to use these techniques. He was the conceptualizer and the salesman in putting together the ideas for these new organizations, but he put only a small percentage of the money up himself, working from a theory that if he could not convince investors that there was a market, then the idea was not sound. His initial assumption was that he did not know enough about the market to gamble with his own money — an assumption based on experience, according to a story he told about the one enterprise in which he had failed miserably. With this enterprise, he had trusted his own judgment on what customers would want, only to be proven totally wrong the hard way.

B did not want to invest himself heavily in his organizations, either financially or personally. Once he had put together a package, he tried to find people whom he trusted to administer it. These were usually people who, like himself, were fairly open in their approach to business and not too hung up on previous assumptions about how things should be done. One can infer that B's assumptions about concrete goals, the means to be used to achieve them, measurement criteria, and repair strategies were pragmatic: Have a clear concept of the mission, test it by selling it to investors, bring in good people who understand what the mission is, and then leave them alone to implement and run the organization, using only ultimate financial performance as a criterion.

B's assumptions about how to integrate a group were, in a sense, irrelevant since he did not inject himself very much into any of his enterprises. To determine the cultures of those enterprises, one had to study the managers put into key positions by B—matters that varied dramatically from one enterprise to the next. This short example illustrates that there is nothing automatic about an entrepreneur's process of inserting personal vision or style into his or her organization. The process depends very much on whether and how much that person wants to impose himself or herself.

Founder C, like A, was a much more dominant personality with a clear idea of how things should be. He and four others founded a manufacturing concern several years ago, one based on the founder's product idea along with a strong intuition that the market was ready for such a product. In this case, the founding group got together because they shared a concept of the core mission, but they found after a few years that the different members held very different assumptions about how to build an orga-

nization. These differences were sufficient to split the group apart and leave C in control of the young, rapidly growing company.

C held strong assumptions about the nature of the world—how one discovers truth and solves problems—and they were reflected in his management style. He believed that good ideas could come from any source; in particular, he believed that he himself was not wise enough to know what was true and right, but that if he heard an intelligent group of people debate an idea and examine it from all sides, he could judge accurately whether it was sound or not. He also knew that he could solve problems best in a group where many ideas were batted around and where there was a high level of mutual confrontation around those ideas. Ideas came from individuals, but the testing of ideas had to be done in a group.

C also believed very strongly that even if he knew what the correct course of action was, unless the parties whose support was critical to implementation were completely sold on the idea, they would either misunderstand or unwittingly sabotage the idea. Therefore, on any important decision, C insisted on a wide debate, many group meetings, and selling the idea down and laterally in the organization; only when it appeared that everyone understood and was committed would he agree to going ahead. C felt so strongly about this that he often held up important decisions even when he personally was already convinced of the course of action to take. He said that he did not want to be out there leading all by himself if he could not count on support from the troops; he cited past cases in which, thinking he had group support, he made a decision and, when it failed, found his key subordinates claiming that he had been alone in the decision. These experiences, he said, taught him to ensure commitment before going ahead on anything, even if doing so was time-consuming and frustrating.

19

While C's assumptions about how to make decisions led to a very group-oriented organization, his theory about how to manage led to a strong individuation process. C was convinced that the only way to manage was to give clear and simple individual responsibility and then to measure the person strictly on those responsibilities. Groups could help make decisions and obtain commitment, but they could not under any circumstance be responsible or accountable. So once a decision was made, it had to be carried out by individuals; if the decision was complex, involving a reorganization of functions, C always insisted that the new organization had to be clear and simple enough to permit the assignment of individual accountabilities.

C believed completely in a proactive model of man and in man's capacity to master nature; hence he expected of his subordinates that they would always be on top of their jobs. If a budget had been negotiated for a year, and if after three months the subordinate recognized that he would overrun the budget, C insisted that the subordinate make a clear decision either to find a way to stay within the budget or to renegotiate a larger budget. It was not acceptable to allow the overrun to occur without informing others and renegotiating, and it was not acceptable to be ignorant of the likelihood that there would be an overrun. The correct way to behave was always to know what was happening, always to be responsible for what was happening, and always to feel free to renegotiate previous agreements if they no longer made sense. C believed completely in open communications and the ability of people to reach reasonable decisions and compromises if they confronted their problems, figured out what they wanted to do, were willing to marshal arguments for their solution, and scrupulously honored any commitments they made.

20   On the interpersonal level, C as-

sumed "constructive intent" on the part of all members of the organization, a kind of rational loyalty to organizational goals and to shared commitments. This did not prevent people from competitively trying to get ahead—but playing politics, hiding information, blaming others, or failing to cooperate on agreed-upon plans were defined as sins. However, C's assumptions about the nature of truth and the need for every individual to keep thinking out what he or she thought was the correct thing to do in any given situation led to frequent interpersonal tension. In other words, the rule of honoring commitments and following through on consensually reached decisions was superseded by the rule of doing only what you believed sincerely to be the best thing to do in any given situation. Ideally, there would be time to challenge the original decision and renegotiate, but in practice time pressure was such that the subordinate, in doing what was believed to be best, often had to be insubordinate. Thus people in the organization frequently complained that decisions did not "stick," yet had to acknowledge that the reason they did not stick was that the assumption that one had to do the correct thing was even more important. Subordinates learned that insubordination was much less likely to be punished than doing something that the person knew to be wrong or stupid.

C clearly believed in the necessity of organization and hierarchy, but he did not trust the authority of position nearly so much as the authority of reason. Hence bosses were granted authority only to the extent that they could sell their decisions; as indicated above, insubordination was not only tolerated, but actively rewarded if it led to better outcomes. One could infer from watching this organization that it thrived on intelligent, assertive, individualistic people —and, indeed, the hiring policies reflected this bias.

So, over the years, the organization

C headed had a tendency to hire and keep the people who fit into the kind of management system I am describing. And those people who fit the founder's assumptions found themselves feeling increasingly like family members in that strong bonds of mutual support grew up among them, with C functioning symbolically as a kind of benign but demanding father figure. These familial feelings were very important, though quite implicit, because they gave subordinates a feeling of security that was needed to challenge each other and C when a course of action did not make sense.

The architecture and office layout in C's company reflected his assumptions about problem solving and human relationships. He insisted on open office landscaping; minimum status differentiation in terms of office size, location, and furnishings (in fact, people were free to decorate their offices any way they liked); open cafeterias instead of executive dining rooms; informal dress codes; first-come, first-serve systems for getting parking spaces; many conference rooms with attached kitchens to facilitate meetings and to keep people interacting with each other instead of going off for meals; and so forth.

In summary, C represents a case of an entrepreneur with a clear set of assumptions about how things should be, both in terms of the formal business arrangements and in terms of internal relationships in the organization—and these assumptions still reflect themselves clearly in the organization some years later.

Let us turn next to the question of how a strong founder goes about embedding his assumptions in the organization.

How Are Cultural Elements Embedded?

The basic process of embedding a cultural element—a given belief or assumption—is a

"teaching" process, but not necessarily an explicit one. The basic model of culture formation, it will be remembered, is that someone must propose a solution to a problem the group faces. Only if the group shares the perception that the solution is working will that element be adopted, and only if it continues to work will it come to be taken for granted and taught to newcomers. It goes without saying, therefore, that only elements that solve group problems will survive, but the previous issue of "embedding" is how a founder or leader gets the group to do things in a certain way in the first place, so that the question of whether it will work can be settled. In other words, embedding a cultural element in this context means only that the founder/leader has ways of getting the group to try out certain responses. There is no guarantee that those responses will, in fact, succeed in solving the group's ultimate problem. How do founder/leaders do this? I will describe a number of mechanisms ranging from very explicit teaching to very implicit messages of which even the founder may be unaware. These mechanisms are shown in Figure 3.

As the above case examples tried to show, the initial thrust of the messages sent is very much a function of the personality of the founder; some founders deliberately choose to build an organization that reflects their own personal biases while others create the basic organization but then turn it over to subordinates as soon as it has a life of its own. In both cases, the process of culture formation is complicated by the possibility that the founder is "conflicted," in the sense of having in his or her own personality several mutually contradictory assumptions.

The commonest case is probably that of the founder who states a philosophy of delegation but who retains tight control by feeling free to intervene, even in the smallest and most trivial decisions, as A did. Because the owner is granted the "right" to　21

Figure 3
How Is Culture Embedded and Transmitted?

Each of the mechanisms listed below is used by founders and key leaders to embed a value or assumption they hold, though the message may be very implicit in the sense that the leader is not aware of sending it. Leaders also may be conflicted, which leads to conflicting messages. A given mechanism may convey the message very explicitly, ambiguously, or totally implicitly. The mechanisms are listed below from more or less explicit to more or less implicit ones.

1. *Formal statements of organizational philosophy, charters, creeds, materials used for recruitment and selection, and socialization.*

2. *Design of physical spaces, facades, buildings.*

3. *Deliberate role modeling, teaching, and coaching by leaders.*

4. *Explicit reward and status system, promotion criteria.*

5. *Stories, legends, myths, and parables about key people and events.*

6. *What leaders pay attention to, measure, and control.*

7. *Leader reactions to critical incidents and organizational crises* (times when organizational survival is threatened, norms are unclear or are challenged, insubordination occurs, threatening or meaningless events occur, and so forth).

8. *How the organization is designed and structured.* (The design of work, who reports to whom, degree of decentralization, functional or other criteria for differentiation, and mechanisms used for integration carry implicit messages of what leaders assume and value.)

9. *Organizational systems and procedures.* (The types of information, control, and decision support systems in terms of categories of information, time cycles, who gets what information, and when and how performance appraisal and other review processes are conducted carry implicit messages of what leaders assume and value.)

10. *Criteria used for recruitment, selection, promotion, leveling off, retirement, and "excommunication" of people* (the implicit and possibly unconscious criteria that leaders use to determine who "fits" and who doesn't "fit" membership roles and key slots in the organization).

run his or her own company, subordinates will tolerate this kind of contradictory behavior and the organization's culture will develop complex assumptions about how one runs the organization "in spite of" or "around" the founder. If the founder's conflicts are severe to the point of interfering with the running of the organization, buffering layers of management may be built in or, in the extreme, the board of directors may have to find a way to move the founder out altogether.

The mechanisms listed in Figure 3 are not equally potent in practice, but they can reinforce each other to make the total message more potent than individual components. In my observation the most important or potent messages are role modeling by

leaders (item 3), what leaders pay attention to (item 6), and leader reactions to critical events (item 7). Only if we observe these leader actions can we begin to decipher how members of the organization "learned" the right and proper things to do, and what model of reality they were to adopt.

To give a few examples, A demonstrated his need to be involved in everything at a detailed level by frequent visits to stores and detailed inspections of what was going on in them. When he went on vacation, he called the office every single day at a set time and wanted to know in great detail what was going on. This behavior persisted into his period of semi-retirement, when he would still call *daily* from his retirement home, where he spent three winter months.

22

A's loyalty to his family was quite evident: He ignored bad business results if a family member was responsible, yet punished a non-family member involved in such results. If the family member was seriously damaging the business, A put a competent manager in under him, but did not always give that manager credit for subsequent good results. If things continued to go badly, A would finally remove the family member, but always with elaborate rationalizations to protect the family image. If challenged on this kind of blind loyalty, A would assert that owners had certain rights that could not be challenged. Insubordination from a family member was tolerated and excused, but the same kind of insubordination from a non-family member was severely punished.

In complete contrast, B tried to find competent general managers and turn a business over to them as quickly as he could. He involved himself only if he absolutely had to in order to save the business, and he pulled out of businesses as soon as they were stable and successful. B separated his family life completely from his business and had no assumptions about the rights of a family in a business. He wanted a good financial return so that he could make his family economically secure, but he seemed not to want his family involved in the businesses.

C, like B, was not interested in building the business on behalf of the family; his preoccupation with making sound decisions overrode all other concerns. Hence C set out to find the right kinds of managers and then "trained" them through the manner in which he reacted to situations. If managers displayed ignorance or lack of control of an area for which they were responsible, C would get publicly angry at them and accuse them of incompetence. If managers overran a budget or had too much inventory and did not inform C when this was first noticed, they would be publicly chided, whatever the reason was for the condition. If the manager tried to defend the situation by noting that it developed because of actions in another part of the same company, actions which C and others had agreed to, C would point out strongly that the manager should have brought that issue up much earlier and forced a rethinking or renegotiation right away. Thus C made it clear through his reactions that poor ultimate results could be excused, but not being on top of one's situation could never be excused.

C taught subordinates his theory about building commitment to a decision by systematically refusing to go along with something until he felt the commitment was there, and by punishing managers who acted impulsively or prematurely in areas where the support of others was critical. He thus set up a very complex situation for his subordinates by demanding on the one hand a strong individualistic orientation (embodied in official company creeds and public relations literature) and, on the other, strong rules of consensus and mutual commitment (embodied in organizational stories, the organization's design, and many of its systems and procedures).

The above examples highlighted the differences among the three founders to show the biases and unique features of the culture in their respective companies, but there were some common elements as well that need to be mentioned. All three founders assumed that the success of their business(es) hinged on meeting customer needs; their most severe outbursts at subordinates occurred when they learned that a customer had not been well treated. All of the official messages highlighted customer concern, and the reward and control systems focused heavily on such concerns. In the case of A, customer needs were even put ahead of the needs of the family; one way a family member could really get into trouble was to mess up a customer relationship.

All three founders, obsessed with   23

product quality, had a hard time seeing how some of their own managerial demands could undermine quality by forcing compromises. This point is important because in all the official messages, commitment to customers and product quality were uniformly emphasized—making one assume that this value was a clear priority. It was only when one looked at the inner workings of A's and C's organizations that one could see that other assumptions which they held created internal conflicts that were difficult to overcome—conflicts that introduced new cultural themes into the organizations.

In C's organization, for example, there was simultaneously a concern for customers and an arrogance toward customers. Many of the engineers involved in the original product designs had been successful in estimating what customers would really want—a success leading to their assumption that they understood customers well enough to continue to make product designs without having to pay too much attention to what sales and marketing were trying to tell them. C officially supported marketing as a concept, but his underlying assumption was similar to that of his engineers, that he really understood what his customers wanted; this led to a systematic ignoring of some inputs from sales and marketing.

As the company's operating environment changed, old assumptions about the company's role in that environment were no longer working. But neither C nor many of his original group had a paradigm that was clearly workable in the new situation, so a period of painful conflict and new learning arose. More and more customers and marketing people began to complain, yet some parts of the organization literally could not hear or deal with these complaints because of their belief in the superiority of their products and their own previous assumptions that they knew what customers wanted.

24   In summary, the mechanisms shown

in Figure 3 represent *all* of the possible ways in which founder messages get communicated and embedded, but they vary in potency. Indeed, they may often be found to conflict with each other—either because the founder is internally conflicted or because the environment is forcing changes in the original paradigm that lead different parts of the organization to have different assumptions about how to view things. Such conflicts often result because new, strong managers who are not part of the founding group begin to impose their own assumptions and theories. Let us look next at how these people may differ and the implications of such differences.

FOUNDER/OWNERS vs. "PROFESSIONAL MANAGERS"

Distinctive characteristics or "biases" introduced by the founder's assumptions are found in first-generation firms that are still heavily influenced by founders and in companies that continue to be run by family members. As noted above, such biases give the first-generation firm its distinctive character, and such biases are usually highly valued by first-generation employees because they are associated with the success of the enterprise. As the organization grows, as family members or non-family managers begin to introduce new assumptions, as environmental changes force new responses from the organization, the original assumptions begin to be strained. Employees begin to express concern that some of their "key" values will be lost or that the characteristics that made the company an exciting place to work are gradually disappearing.

Clear distinctions begin to be drawn between the founding family and the "professional" managers who begin to be brought into key positions. Such "professional" managers are usually identified as non-family and as non-owners and, therefore, as less "invested" in the company. Often they have been specifically educated to be managers rather than experts in whatever is the company's particular product or market. They are perceived, by virtue of these facts, as being less loyal to the original values and assumptions that guided the company, and as being more concerned with short-run financial performance. They are typically welcomed for bringing in much-needed organizational and functional skills, but they are often mistrusted because they are not loyal to the founding assumptions.

Though these perceptions have strong stereotypic components, it's possible to see that much of the stereotype is firmly based in reality if one examines a number of first-generation and family-owned companies. Founders and owners do have distinctive characteristics that derive partly from their personalities and partly from their structural position as owners. It is important to understand these characteristics if one is to explain how strongly held many of the values and assumptions of first-generation or family-owned companies are. Figure 4 examines the "stereotype" by polarizing the founder/owner and "professional" manager along a number of motivational, analytical, interpersonal, and structural dimensions.

The main thrust of the differences noted is that the founder/owner is seen as being more self-oriented, more willing to take risks and pursue non-economic objectives and, by virtue of being the founder/owner, more *able* to take risks and to pursue such objectives. Founder/owners are more often intuitive and holistic in their thinking, and they are able to take a long-range point of view because they are building their own identities through their enterprises. They are often more particularistic in their orientation, a characteristic that results in the building of more of a community in the early organizational stages. That is, the initial

founding group and the first generation of employees will know each other well and will operate more on personal acquaintance and trust than on formal principles, job descriptions, and rules.

The environment will often be more political than bureaucratic, and founder-value biases will be staunchly defended because they will form the basis for the group's initial identity. New members who don't fit this set of assumptions and values are likely to leave because they will be uncomfortable, or they will be ejected because their failure to confirm accepted patterns is seen as disruptive.

Founder/owners, by virtue of their position and personality, also tend to fulfill some *unique functions* in the early history of their organizations:

1. *Containing and absorbing anxiety and risk.* Because they are positionally more secure and personally more confident, owners more than managers absorb and contain the anxieties and risks that are inherent in creating, developing, and enlarging an organization. Thus in times of stress, owners play a special role in reassuring the organization that it will survive. They are the stakeholders; hence they do have the ultimate risk.

2. *Embedding non-economic assumptions and values.* Because of their willingness to absorb risk and their position as primary stakeholders, founder/owners are in a position to insist on doing things which may not be optimally efficient from a short-run point of view, but which reflect their own values and biases on how to build an effective organization and/or how to maximize the benefits to themselves and their families. Thus founder/owners often start with humanistic and social concerns that become reflected in organizational structure and process. Even when "participation," or "no layoffs," or other personnel practices such as putting marginally competent family

25

Figure 4

How Do Founder/Owners Differ from "Professional Managers"?

Motivation and Emotional Orientation

Entrepreneurs/founders/owners are . . .	*Professional managers are . . .*
Oriented toward creating, building.	Oriented toward consolidating, surviving, growing.
Achievement-oriented.	Power- and influence-oriented.
Self-oriented, worried about own image; need for "glory" high.	Organization-oriented, worried about company image.
Jealous of own prerogatives, need for autonomy high.	Interested in developing the organization and subordinates.
Loyal to own company, "local."	Loyal to profession of management, "cosmopolitan."
Willing and able to take moderate risks on own authority.	Able to take risks, but more cautious and in need of support.

Analytical Orientation

Primarily intuitive, trusting of own intuitions.	Primarily analytical, more cautious about intuitions.
Long-range time horizon.	Short-range time horizon.
Holistic; able to see total picture, patterns.	Specific; able to see details and their consequences.

Interpersonal Orientation

"Particularistic," in the sense of seeing individuals as individuals.	"Universalistic," in the sense of seeing individuals as members of categories like employees, customers, suppliers, and so on.
Personal, political, involved.	Impersonal, rational, uninvolved.
Centralist, autocratic.	Participative, delegation-oriented.
Family ties count.	Family ties are irrelevant.
Emotional, impatient, easily bored.	Unemotional, patient, persistent.

Structural/Positional Differences

Have the privileges and risks of ownership.	Have minimal ownership, hence fewer privileges and risks.
Have secure position by virtue of ownership.	Have less secure position, must constantly prove themselves.
Are generally highly visible and get close attention.	Are often invisible and do not get much attention.
Have the support of family members in the business.	Function alone or with the support of non-family members.
Have the obligation of dealing with family members and deciding on the priorities family issues should have relative to company issues.	Do not have to worry about family issues at all, which are by definition irrelevant.
Have weak bosses, Boards that are under their own control.	Have strong bosses, Boards that are not under their own control.

26

members into key slots are "inefficient," owners can insist that this is the only way to run the business and make that decision stick in ways that professional managers cannot.

3. *Stimulating innovation.* Because of their personal orientation and their secure position, owners are uniquely willing and able to try new innovations that are risky, often with no more than an intuition that things will improve. Because managers must document, justify, and plan much more carefully, they have less freedom to innovate.

As the organization ages and the founder becomes less of a personal force, there is a trend away from this community feeling toward more of a rational, bureaucratic type of organization dominated by general managers who may care less about the original assumptions and values, and who are not in a position to fulfill the unique functions mentioned above. This trend is often feared and lamented by first- and second-generation employees. If the founder introduces his or her own family into the organization, and if the family assumptions and values perpetuate those of the founder, the original community feeling may be successfully perpetuated. The original culture may then survive. But at some point there will be a complete transition to general management, and at that point it is not clear whether the founding assumptions survive, are metamorphosed into a new hybrid, or are displaced entirely by other assumptions more congruent with what general managers as an occupational group bring with them.

4. *Originating evolution through hybridization.* The founder is able to impose his or her assumptions on the first-generation employees, but these employees will, as they move up in the organization and become experienced managers, develop a range of new assumptions based on their own experience. These new assumptions will be congruent with some of the core assumptions of the original cultural paradigm, but

will add new elements learned from experience. Some of these new elements or new assumptions will solve problems better than the original ones because external and internal problems will have changed as the organization matured and grew. The founder often recognizes that these new assumptions are better solutions, and will delegate increasing amounts of authority to those managers who are the best "hybrids": those who maintain key old assumptions yet add relevant new ones.

The best example of such hybrid evolution comes from a company that was founded by a very free-wheeling, intuitive, pragmatic entrepreneur: "D" who, like C in the example above, believed strongly in individual creativity, a high degree of decentralization, high autonomy for each organizational unit, high internal competition for resources, and self-control mechanisms rather than tight, centralized organizational controls. As this company grew and prospered, coordinating so many autonomous units became increasingly difficult, and the frustration that resulted from internal competition made it increasingly expensive to maintain this form of organization.

Some managers in this company, notably those coming out of manufacturing, had always operated in a more disciplined, centralized manner — without, however, disagreeing with core assumptions about the need to maximize individual autonomy. But they had learned that in order to do certain kinds of manufacturing tasks, one had to impose some discipline and tight controls. As the price of autonomy and decentralization increased, D began to look increasingly to these manufacturing managers as potential occupants of key general management positions. Whether he was conscious of it or not, what he needed was senior general managers who still believed in the old system but who had, in addition, a new set of assumptions about how to run things that were more in   27 line with what the organization now needed. Some of the first-generation managers were quite nervous at seeing what they considered to be their "hardnosed" colleagues groomed as heirs apparent. Yet they were relieved that these potential successors were part of the original group rather than complete outsiders.

From a theoretical standpoint, evolution through hybrids is probably the only model of culture change that can work, because the original culture is based so heavily on community assumptions and values. Outsiders coming into such a community with new assumptions are likely to find the culture too strong to budge, so they either give up in frustration or find themselves ejected by the organization as being too foreign in orientation. What makes this scenario especially likely is the fact that the *distinctive* parts of the founding culture are often based on biases that are not economically justifiable in the short run.

As noted earlier, founders are especially likely to introduce humanistic, social service, and other non-economic assumptions into their paradigm of how an organization should look, and the general manager who is introduced from the outside often finds these assumptions to be the very thing that he or she wants to change in the attempt to "rationalize" the organization and make it more efficient. Indeed, that is often the reason the outsider is brought in. But if the current owners do not recognize the positive functions their culture plays, they run the risk of throwing out the baby with the bath water or, if the culture is strong, wasting their time because the outsider will not be able to change things anyway.

The ultimate dilemma for the first-generation organization with a strong founder-generated culture is how to make the transition to subsequent generations in such a manner that the organization remains adaptive to its changing external environment without destroying cultural elements

that have given it its uniqueness, and that have made life fulfilling in the internal environment. Such a transition cannot be made effectively if the succession problem is seen only in power or political terms. The thrust of this analysis is that the *culture* must be analyzed and understood, and that the founder/owners must have sufficient insight into their own culture to make an intelligent transition process possible.

ACKNOWLEDGMENTS AND SELECTED BIBLIOGRAPHY

The research on which this paper is based was partly sponsored by the Project on the Family Firm, Sloan School of Management, M.I.T., and by the Office of Naval Research, Organizational Effectiveness Research Programs, under Contract No. N00014-80-C-0905, NR 170-911.

The ideas explored here have been especially influenced by my colleague Richard Beckhard and by the various entrepreneurs with whom I have worked for many years in a consulting relationship. Their observations of themselves and their colleagues have proved to be an invaluable source of ideas and insights.

Earlier work along these lines has been incorporated into my book *Career Dynamics* (Addison-Wesley, 1978). Further explication of the ideas of an organizational culture can be found in Andrew M. Pettigrew's article "On Studying Organizational Cultures" (*Administrative Science Quarterly*, December 1979), Meryl Louis's article "A Cultural Perspective on Organizations" (*Human Systems Management*, 1981, 2, 246–258), and in H. Schwartz and S. M. Davis's "Matching Corporate Culture and Business Strategy" (*Organizational Dynamics*, Summer 1981).

The specific model of culture that I use was first published in my article "Does Japanese Management Style Have a Message for American Managers?" (*Sloan Management Review*, Fall 1981) and is currently being elaborated into a book on organizational culture.

[20]

Concepts of Culture and
Organizational Analysis

Linda Smircich

This paper examines the significance of the concept of
culture for organizational analysis. The intersection of culture theory and organization theory is evident in five current
research themes: comparative management, corporate culture, organizational cognition, organizational symbolism,
and unconscious processes and organization. Researchers
pursue these themes for different purposes and their work is
based on different assumptions about the nature of culture
and organization. The task of evaluating the power and
limitations of the concept of culture must be conducted
within this assumptive context. This review demonstrates
that the concept of culture takes organization analysis in
several different and promising directions.•

The concept of culture has been linked increasingly with the
study of organizations. With the recognition of the symbolic
aspects of organized settings have come calls for a cultural
perspective on organizations (Turner, 1971; Pondy and Mitroff,
1979; Pettigrew, 1979; Louis, 1980; Whorton and Worthley,
1981). Papers have appeared that treat management as symbolic activity (Peters, 1978; Pfeffer, 1981; Smircich and Morgan, 1982); while others have called attention to the power of
organizational symbolism, legends, stories, myths, and ceremonies (Mitroff and Kilmann, 1976; Dandridge, 1979; Dandridge, Mitroff, and Joyce, 1980; Wilkins and Martin, 1980;
Martin and Powers, 1983; Trice and Beyer, 1983). The idea that
business organizations have a cultural quality was recognized
recently by *Business Week* (1980) in the cover story, "Corporate Culture: The hard-to-change values that spell success or
failure." There is even a "Corporate Cultures" section in
Fortune Magazine (e.g., *Fortune Magazine,* March 22, 1982).

Culture may be an idea whose time has come; but what exactly
does a "cultural perspective" on organizations mean? The
culture concept has been borrowed from anthropology, where
there is no consensus on its meaning. It should be no surprise
that there is also variety in its application to organization studies.
How then may we critically evaluate the significance of the
concept of culture for the study of organization?

Such evaluation requires reflection on the ways the culture
concept informs us about organization. What aspects of the
phenomenon are illuminated or more explicitly revealed for
examination? What aspects are less likely to be attended to
because we link the terms organization and culture? This
special issue as a whole is concerned with these questions.

This paper in particular traces the ways culture has been
developed in organization studies: as a critical variable and as a
root metaphor. The paper summarizes the research agendas
that each of these perspectives entails. This review demonstrates that not only have organizational analysts held varying
conceptions of culture, but that these different conceptions
give rise to different research questions and interests. The
differences in approach to the organization-culture relationship
are derived from differences in the basic assumptions that
researchers make about both "organization" and "culture."
Thus, the task of evaluating the power and limitations of the
concept of culture must be conducted within this assumptive
context. Toward that end, this paper examines the assumptions
that underlie the different ways the concept of culture has been

© 1983 by Cornell University.
0001-8392/83/2803-0339/$00.75

•

Earlier versions of this paper were presented at the International Communication
Association/Speech Communication Association Conference on Interpretive Approaches to Organizational Communication, Alta, Utah, July 1981, and the Eastern
Academy of Management meetings, Baltimore, Maryland, May 1982. I would like to
express special appreciation to Mike
Pacanowsky and Linda Putnam for organizing the Interpretive Conference, which
provided the impetus as well as encouragement for the development of these
ideas. Thanks also to Gareth Morgan, Linda
Pike, Lou Pondy, and Karl Weick for their
various forms of inspiration.

used in organization studies. When the literature is regarded in this way, we see that the culture concept is highly suggestive and promising for many different ends that researchers pursue.

UNDERLYING ASSUMPTIONS AND METAPHORS

Several authors have addressed themselves to clarifying the range of assumptions that organization theorists bring to their subject (Ritzer, 1975; Burrell and Morgan, 1979; Morgan and Smircich, 1980; Van de Ven and Astley, 1981). In large measure, these authors agree that work in organization theory can be characterized by a range of assumptions about the ontological status of social reality — the objective-subjective question — and a range of assumptions about human nature — the determinist-voluntarist question. Researchers who maintain different positions on these questions approach the subject of organization in fundamentally different ways. Despite these basic differences, however, some have argued that *all* scientists create knowledge about the world through the drawing out of implications of different metaphoric insights for their subject of study (Pepper, 1942; Kaplan, 1964; Brown, 1977; Morgan, 1980). Others point out that the metaphoric process, seeing one thing in terms of another, is a fundamental aspect of human thought; it is how we come to know our world (Lakoff and Johnson, 1980). Perception and knowing are linked in an interpretive process that is metaphorically structured, allowing us to understand one domain of experience in terms of another (Koch and Deetz, 1981).

Throughout the development of administrative theory and practice, organization theorists and managers alike have used a variety of metaphors, or images, to bound, frame, and differentiate that category of experience referred to as (an) "organization." The metaphors of machine and organism have been used most frequently to facilitate understanding and communication about the complex phenomenon of organization (Pondy and Mitroff, 1979; Morgan, 1980; Koch and Deetz, 1981). For example, mechanical imagery undergirds the view of organizations as instruments for task accomplishment, consisting of multiple parts to be designed and meshed into fine-tuned efficiency. Such a conception of organizational experience can be found in one department head's desire to "have this department running smoothly like a well-oiled machine." Another widely elaborated conception is that of an organization as an organism. This notion underlies systems theory as applied to organizations (Trist and Bamforth, 1951; Burns and Stalker, 1961; Lawrence and Lorsch, 1967), where organizations are conceived as struggling for survival within a changing environment. Organizations are studied in terms of the way they manage interdependencies and exchanges across system boundaries.

Although metaphors from the physical world — organism and machine — are historically dominant, other metaphors, that are social, have also been used to elaborate aspects of organization (Morgan, 1980). For instance, we know that organizations are "theaters" for performance of roles, dramas, and scripts (Goffman, 1959; Mangham and Overington, 1983) and that organizations are "political arenas" oriented around the pursuit and display of power (Crozier, 1964; Pfeffer, 1981). Each of these metaphoric images focuses attention in selective ways

Concepts of Culture

and provides slightly different ways of knowing the phenomenon of organization (Morgan, 1980). The use of a particular metaphor is often not a conscious choice, nor made explicit, but can be inferred from the way the subject of organization is approached, by discerning the underlying assumptions that are made about the subject.

Recently Pinder and Bourgeois (1982) have cautioned organization scholars against the borrowing and unconsidered use of metaphors from other disciplines. Their concern is that, in so doing, organization scholars will be drawn far afield from that domain of experience they seek to know. To the extent that their argument can be read as a reminder for scholars to stay grounded in the experience of organization, it is well directed. To the extent that it seeks to discourage metaphorical thinking, it is misplaced. In fact, the term organization itself is a metaphor referring to the experience of collective coordination and orderliness. Meadows (1967: 82) has argued that organization theory is always rooted in the imagery of order and asserts that "the development of theories of organization is a history of the metaphor of orderliness."

Organization is a function of the problem of order and orderliness; similarly, conceptualizations of social organization have been a function of the conceptualizations of the problem of order and orderliness. Very early in human experience, order seems to have been a kind of inescapable and irretrievable empirical fact. The sun rises and sets; people are born and they die; the seasons come and go; and there is the procession of the stars. The spatial patterning and temporality of man's experience established an imagery of order, forming a backdrop to the drama of cosmos arising out of chaos. In the slow, incremental achievement of a substantial scientific stance with respect to the universe, there had been built into man's semiotic of experience and into his traditional pieties the unquestionable assumption that this is an orderly universe. (Meadows, 1967: 78)

Given the metaphorical nature of human knowledge, the suggestion that we in organization theory avoid metaphor misdirects our cautionary efforts. Rather than avoid metaphor, what we can aim for is critical examination of the ways in which our thinking is shaped and constrained by our choice of metaphors. This paper and this special issue are in line with that aim.

If, following Meadows, we see organization theory as dominated by the concern for the problem of social order, the current interest in the concept of culture is no surprise. In anthropology, culture is the foundational term through which the orderliness and patterning of much of our life experience is explained (Benedict, 1934). The same argument Meadows made about organization theory can be made about cultural anthropology. It, too, is inquiry into the phenomenon of social order. What we are seeing with the linking of culture and organization is the intersection of two sets of images of order: those associated with organization and those associated with culture.

The intersection of organization theory and culture theory is manifest in several "thematic" or content areas that are of interest to organization and management scholars, as shown in Figure 1. Different conceptions of organization and culture underlie research in these content areas: comparative management, corporate culture, organizational cognition, organizational symbolism, and unconscious processes and organization.[1] The variation in the ways the concept of culture is used by researchers interested in these different content areas can be traced directly to their different ways of conceiving "organization" and "culture." Their inquiry is guided by different metaphors and seeks different ends.

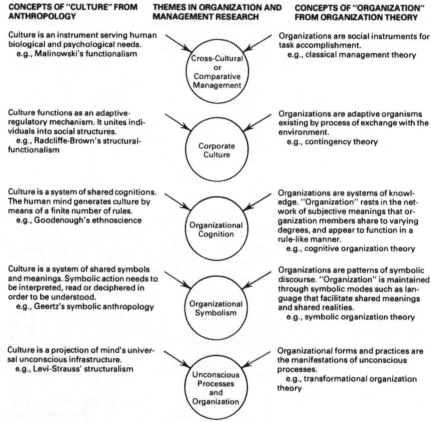

CONCEPTS OF "CULTURE" FROM ANTHROPOLOGY	THEMES IN ORGANIZATION AND MANAGEMENT RESEARCH	CONCEPTS OF "ORGANIZATION" FROM ORGANIZATION THEORY
Culture is an instrument serving human biological and psychological needs. e.g., Malinowski's functionalism	Cross-Cultural or Comparative Management	Organizations are social instruments for task accomplishment. e.g., classical management theory
Culture functions as an adaptive-regulatory mechanism. It unites individuals into social structures. e.g., Radcliffe-Brown's structural-functionalism	Corporate Culture	Organizations are adaptive organisms existing by process of exchange with the environment. e.g., contingency theory
Culture is a system of shared cognitions. The human mind generates culture by means of a finite number of rules. e.g., Goodenough's ethnoscience	Organizational Cognition	Organizations are systems of knowledge. "Organization" rests in the network of subjective meanings that organization members share to varying degrees, and appear to function in a rule-like manner. e.g., cognitive organization theory
Culture is a system of shared symbols and meanings. Symbolic action needs to be interpreted, read or deciphered in order to be understood. e.g., Geertz's symbolic anthropology	Organizational Symbolism	Organizations are patterns of symbolic discourse. "Organization" is maintained through symbolic modes such as language that facilitate shared meanings and shared realities. e.g., symbolic organization theory
Culture is a projection of mind's universal unconscious infrastructure. e.g., Levi-Strauss' structuralism	Unconscious Processes and Organization	Organizational forms and practices are the manifestations of unconscious processes. e.g., transformational organization theory

Figure 1. Intersections of culture theory and organization theory.

1

These themes are representative of current research trends in the organization and management literature and exemplify the continued interest of organization theorists in the problem of order. Themes that would flow from a Marxist or radical structuralist orientation are not shown here. They are much less well developed within organization and management theory because their fundamental problematic concerns questions of dominance and radical change. In this volume, Riley's paper on structuration is suggestive of that line of research.

The balance of the paper briefly summarizes five different programs of research that flow out of linking the terms culture and organization and examines their underlying assumptions and metaphors. In the first two, culture is either an independent or dependent, external or internal, organizational variable. In the final three, culture is not a variable at all, but is a root metaphor for conceptualizing organization. Each of these five represents a viable mode of inquiry. Considered together, they demonstrate that the promise of the concept of culture for the study of organization is varied and rich.

Concepts of Culture

CULTURE AND COMPARATIVE MANAGEMENT: CULTURE AS INDEPENDENT VARIABLE

The field of comparative management is concerned with variation in managerial and employee practices and attitudes across countries (Haire, Ghiselli, and Porter, 1966). In comparative management studies, culture is considered to be a background factor (almost synonymous with country), an explanatory variable (Ajiferuke and Boddewyn, 1970) or a broad framework (Cummings and Schmidt, 1972) influencing the development and reinforcement of beliefs. The literature can be segmented into that with a macro focus, examining the relationship between culture and organization structure, and that with a micro focus, investigating the similarities and differences in attitudes of managers of different cultures (Everett, Stening, and Longton, 1982).

This literature is extensive and has been subjected to several major reviews and critiques (e.g., Roberts, 1970; Bhagat and McQuaid, 1982). A brief sampling of the research, however, illustrates the trends in the work. For example, Harbison and Myers (1959) were concerned with variation in leadership beliefs, from authoritarian to participatory in countries with differing degrees of industrialization; Inzerilli and Laurent (1979) examined the conceptions of organization structure held by French and American managers; and Sekaran (1981) measured differences in the cognitive structuring of organizationally relevant variables of U.S. and Indian bank employees.

These works share a conception of the organization-culture relationship that is portrayed schematically in Figure 2. Culture is treated as an independent variable; it is imported into the organization through the membership (e.g., Fayerweather, 1959; Slocum, 1971). Its presence is believed to be revealed in the patterns of attitudes and actions of individual organization members. In practice, however, with the exception of Everett, Stening, and Longton (1982), most comparative management research leaves the concept of culture undeveloped (Bhagat and McQuaid, 1982).

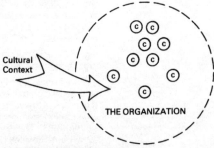

Cultural Context

THE ORGANIZATION

Figure 2. Culture and comparative management.

Characterized broadly, the research agenda deriving from this view is to chart the differences among cultures, locate clusters of similarities, and draw implications for organizational effectiveness. Some of the research may also have the less obvious intent of promoting particular values and ideologies (e.g., Harbison and Myers, 1959). The practical utility of such research would be seen most immediately for multinational organizations, and yet, because of the recognition of global interdependence, this research can be of widespread interest. One need only note the popularity of *Theory Z* (Ouchi, 1981) and *The Art of Japanese Management* (Pasquale and Athos, 1981) for confirmation.

CORPORATE CULTURE: CULTURE AS AN INTERNAL VARIABLE

A second major way that culture and organization are linked is that used by researchers who recognize that organizations are themselves culture-producing phenomena (Louis, 1980; Siehl and Martin, 1981; Deal and Kennedy, 1982; Tichy, 1982; Martin and Powers, 1983). Organizations are seen as social instruments that produce goods and services, and, as a by-product, they also produce distinctive cultural artifacts such as rituals, legends, and ceremonies. Although organizations are themselves embedded within a wider cultural context, the emphasis of researchers here is on socio-cultural qualities that develop within organizations. The degree to which researchers are concerned with linking these internal qualities to the wider cultural context varies greatly.

Research with this conception of culture is generally based on a systems theory framework. As such, it is concerned with articulating patterns of contingent relationships among collections of variables that appear to figure in organizational survival. Heretofore, typical variables considered in this research tradition were structure, size, technology, and leadership patterns (Woodward, 1965; Fiedler, 1967; Pugh and Hickson, 1976). Of late, more subjectivist variables, such as culture, have been introduced into the systems model, with the recognition that symbolic processes are occurring within organizations (Pfeffer, 1981; Meyer, 1981). Consistent with the systems theory framework, this research conceives of an organization as existing in a largely determinant relationship with its environment. The environment presents imperatives for behavior that managers may enact in their organizations through symbolic means (Pfeffer, 1981). The implication is that the symbolic or cultural dimension in some way contributes to the overall systemic balance and effectiveness of an organization. Several recent books argue that organizations with "strong" cultures are indeed apt to be more successful (Deal and Kennedy, 1982; Peters and Waterman, 1982).

Figure 3 illustrates schematically the relationship between organization and culture portrayed in this literature.

Culture is usually defined as social or normative glue that holds an organization together (Siehl and Martin, 1981; Tichy, 1982). It expresses the values or social ideals and the beliefs that organization members come to share (Louis, 1980; Siehl and Martin, 1981). These values or patterns of belief are manifested by symbolic devices such as myths (Boje, Fedor, and Rowland, 1982), rituals (Deal and Kennedy, 1982), stories (Mitroff and Kilmann, 1976), legends (Wilkins and Martin, 1980), and specialized language (Andrews and Hirsch, 1983).

Some of the earliest references to the concept of culture as an internal organizational variable are found in the literature of Organization Development (Jacques, 1952; Harrison, 1972).

Concepts of Culture

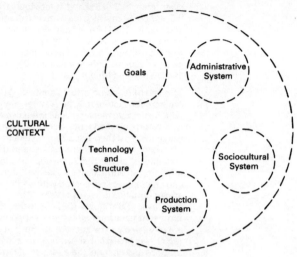

CULTURAL
CONTEXT

Figure 3. Culture and the systems theory framework.

Practitioners of OD are, for the most part, concerned with enhancing the adaptive mechanisms within organizations. OD interventions are often directed at the cultural subsystem to allow for the questioning of values and norms under which people operate (French and Bell, 1978). These activities then serve to make the culture more receptive to change, facilitating the realignment of the total organizational system into a more viable and satisfying configuration.

Recently, however, research efforts not explicitly concerned with planned change projects have focused on the normative and symbolic aspects of organizations. This stream of research acknowledges that subjective interpretive processes that may influence adaptability occur in organized settings, and it seeks to describe and predict the ways they are related to other outcomes such as turnover, absenteeism, and commitment. This research has investigated a variety of dimensions of organizational culture. For example, Schall (1981) studied the impact of the espoused corporate saga on the employees of a midwestern department store; Meyer (1981) revealed how managerial ideologies and organizational stories in hospitals served a structuring function; Kreps (1981) investigated folklore as a socializing tool; Martin and Powers (1983) examined the symbolic power of information; and Pfeffer (1981) proposed that management be considered as symbolic action. These researchers, and others, argue that cultural artifacts, and even the art of management itself, are powerful symbolic means of communication. They can be used to build organizational commitment, convey a philosophy of management, rationalize and legitimate activity, motivate personnel, and facilitate socialization.

This is only a sampling of the research on the various dimensions of organizational culture. As the number of studies increases, however, there is some convergence among them. Culture, conceived as shared key values and beliefs, fulfills several important functions. First, it conveys a sense of identity for organization members (Deal and Kennedy, 1982; Peters and Waterman, 1982). Second, it facilitates the generation of commitment to something larger than the self (Schall, 1981; Siehl and Martin, 1981; Peters and Waterman, 1982). Third, culture enhances social system stability (Louis, 1980; Kreps, 1981). And fourth, culture serves as a sense-making device that can guide and shape behavior (Louis, 1980; Meyer, 1981; Pfeffer, 1981; Siehl and Martin, 1981).

This line of research offers a tantalizing prospect — that organization culture may be another critical lever or key by which strategic managers can influence and direct the course of their organizations (Schwartz and Davis, 1981; Tichy, 1982). Given the less-then-hoped-for results from the wave of tools for strategic management that appeared in the sixties and seventies (Keichel, 1982), the idea of corporate culture is attracting an enthusiastic audience among those researchers and practitioners concerned with strategy formulation and implementation (*Business Week,* 1980; Quinn, 1980; Schwartz and Davis, 1981; Tichy, 1982; Salmans, 1983). The belief is that firms that have internal cultures supportive of their strategies are more likely to be successful. Research and popular books tend to emphasize that symbolic devices can be used to mobilize and channel the energies of organization members. The task awaiting individual managers is to find ways to use stories, legends, and other forms of symbolism in their unique situations, for their own particular ends (Peters, 1978). Managers will have plenty of assistance in this endeavor, because the marketing of "corporate culture" is already underway (Salmans, 1983).

Overall, the research agenda arising from the view that culture is an organizational variable is how to mold and shape internal culture in particular ways and how to change culture, consistent with managerial purposes.

Some, however, genuinely question whether organization culture is indeed manageable.[2] Much of the literature refers to *an* organization culture, appearing to lose sight of the great likelihood that there are multiple organization subcultures, or even countercultures, competing to define the nature of situations within organizational boundaries. The talk about corporate culture tends to be optimistic, even messianic, about top managers molding cultures to suit their strategic ends. The notion of "corporate culture" runs the risk of being as disappointing a managerial tool as the more technical and quantitative tools that were faddish in the 1970s. Those of a skeptical nature may also question the extent to which the term corporate culture refers to anything more than an ideology cultivated by management for the purpose of control and legitimation of activity.

Despite these questions, the idea of corporate culture arouses a great deal of interest among academics and practitioners. Perhaps because it is such a common-sense term, we all "know" what it means without much explanation (precisely why organization scholars should be cautious in using it). For academics, culture provides a conceptual bridge between micro and macro levels of analysis, as well as a bridge between organizational behavior and strategic management interests. For practitioners, it provides a less rationalistic way of under-

2
A public discussion of the question "Can organization culture be managed?" took place at a well-attended session of the Academy of Management national meetings in August 1982. Panelists were: Joanne Martin, William Starbuck, Noel Tichy, Caren Siehl, Craig Lundberg, and Peter Frost.

standing their organizational worlds, one closer to their lived experience.

CULTURE AS A VARIABLE: A COMPARISON

Although the themes of comparative management and corporate culture are distinct, they are in fact quite compatible with one another. They are both consistent with what has been called the functionalist paradigm (Burrell and Morgan, 1979), the system-structural view (Van de Ven and Astley, 1981), and the social factist paradigm (Ritzer, 1975). They are both derived from similar basic assumptions about the nature of the social world, of organizations, and of human nature.

Both assume that the social world expresses itself in terms of general and contingent relationships among its more stable and clear-cut elements, referred to as "variables" (Morgan and Smircich, 1980). Both approaches share the conception of organizations as organisms, existing within an environment that presents imperatives for behavior. In the first case, "culture" is part of the environment and is seen as a determining or imprinting force. In the second case, organizational culture is seen as a result of human enactment. In both approaches organizations and cultures are to be known through the study of patterns of relationships across and within boundaries. The desired outcomes of research into these patterns are statements of contingent relationships that will have applicability for those trying to manage organizations. Underlying the interests in comparative management and corporate culture is the search for predictable means for organizational control and improved means for organization management. Because both of these research approaches have these basic purposes, the issue of causality is of critical importance.

CULTURE AS A ROOT METAPHOR FOR CONCEPTUALIZING ORGANIZATION

The previous two ways the terms culture and organization are linked in the literature are consistent with the image of an organization as an organism. There are, of course, many other ways of conceiving of organizations, for example, as theaters (Goffman, 1959), texts (Ricoeur, 1971), and psychic prisons (Morgan, 1980).

Some theorists advance the view that organizations be understood *as* cultures. They leave behind the view that a culture is something an organization *has,* in favor of the view that a culture is something an organization *is* (Smircich, 1981). The use of culture as a root metaphor is quite different from drawing analogies between organizations and machines and organizations and organisms. It represents a shift from comparison with physical objects to comparison with another social phenomenon, an undertaking with greater room for ambiguity because of culture's nonconcrete status. Culture as a root metaphor for organizations goes beyond the instrumental view of organizations derived from the machine metaphor and beyond the adaptive view derived from the organismic metaphor. Culture as a root metaphor promotes a view of organizations as expressive forms, manifestations of human consciousness. Organizations are understood and analyzed not mainly in economic or material terms, but in terms of their expressive, ideational, and symbolic aspects. Characterized very broadly, the research agenda stemming from this perspective is to explore the phenomenon of organization as subjective experience and to investigate the patterns that make organized action possible.

The concept of culture as developed in anthropology serves as an epistemological device in much the same way as the organismic metaphor serves as a basis for the development of the systems theory perspective on organizations. As noted before, however, within anthropology, culture is conceptualized in diverse ways. When organization theorists develop a cultural analogy, they tend to elaborate a view of culture drawn from cognitive anthropology, symbolic anthropology, or, to a much lesser extent, structural anthropology and psychodynamic theories. In cognitive anthropology, culture consists of shared knowledge (Goodenough, 1971; Agar, 1982). In symbolic anthropology, culture is a system of shared meaning (Hallowell, 1955; Geertz, 1973). And according to structural anthropology and psychodynamics, culture is a manifestation and expression of the mind's unconscious operation (Rossi and O'Higgins, 1980).

These different conceptualizations of culture, drawn from modern anthropology, form the foundations for very different modes of organizational analysis. The research work stemming from these foundations will be considered below.

A Cognitive Perspective

According to the branch of cognitive anthropology referred to as ethnoscience (Goodenough, 1971), culture is a system of shared cognitions or a system of knowledge and beliefs (Rossi and O'Higgins, 1980). A culture is seen as "a unique system for perceiving and organizing material phenomena, things, events, behavior and emotions" (Goodenough, quoted in Rossi and O'Higgins, 1980: 63). Culture is generated by the human mind "by means of a finite number of rules or means of an unconscious logic" (Rossi and O'Higgins, 1980: 63–64). The task of the anthropologist who follows this perspective is to determine what the rules are, to find out how the members of a culture see and describe their world. In the field of communication studies, this same emphasis on understanding social interaction is pursued under the name of "rules theory" (Pearce, 1979; Shimanoff, 1980).

The work of Harris and Cronen (1979) is an excellent example of how the rules-theory perspective may be used for analyzing and evaluating organizations. They consider an organization as analogous to a culture, a particular structure of knowledge for knowing and acting. They propose that an organization culture may be represented as a "master contract" that includes the organization's self-image, as well as constitutive and regulative rules that organize beliefs and actions in light of the image. They assume that the master contract has developed out of ongoing interpersonal interaction and that it provides the context for further interaction. Their methodology examines the master contract/self-image and the degree of consensus on its constructs, assesses co-orientation (the extent to which members perceive others' construction of the organizational image accurately, so that they know how their behavior "counts" with others), and measures coordination (the extent to which mem-

Concepts of Culture

bers can organize the knowledge of the abstract image and constitutive rules into regulative rules that will be functional guides for cooperative action).

Harris and Cronen (1979) analyzed an academic department and reported significant differences between what members thought their coworkers would perceive as the actual and the ideal states of the organization and what members said was the ideal state. They revealed widespread misconceptions; for, in fact, individuals believed their organization was at its ideal state, but many did not realize their colleagues also believed so. We can only speculate about the energy drain that results from such misconceptions. Harris and Cronen did not say whether they fedback their analyses to the members of the organization for their validation or reaction. However, Harris and Cronen did offer an approach for generating knowledge that a group may use to alter its own functioning.

A cognitive perspective is increasingly being applied to the study of organizations (Argyris and Schon, 1978; Bougon, Weick, and Binkhorst, 1977; Harris and Cronen, 1979; Weick, 1979a, 1979b; Litterer and Young, 1981; Wacker, 1981; Ritti, 1982; Shrivastava and Mitroff, 1982; Bougon, 1983). These researchers may or may not use the term culture in their work. Their cognitive emphasis leads them to view organizations as networks of subjective meanings or shared frames of reference that organization members share to varying degrees and which, to an external observer, appear to function in a rule-like, or grammar-like manner. Some of these research efforts document how organization members conceive of themselves as a collectivity. They are also often diagnostic, in that they assess the extent to which there is a shared basis for action or grounds for conflict.

For example, Argyris and Schon (1978) referred to organizations as "cognitive enterprises." Their diagnostic methodology was a case-building approach in which organization members wrote scenarios that revealed the theories-in-use that guide their interaction. Argyris and Schon reported using their intervention strategy in different organization settings to generate maps that display the ways assumptions, beliefs, and norms trap people in counterproductive cycles of behavior.

Along similar lines, Wacker (1981) has proposed another methodology for assessing collective cognitive infrastructure based on the constructs organization members use to make sense of aspects of their organizational worlds. His method is adapted from Kelly's Repertory Grid, an instrument designed to elicit key elements in an individual's world and to chart the ways they are different from one another. Wacker suggested that the grid can be used for diagnosis and intervention.

Schall is developing a comprehensive strategy for discerning the normative communication rules in corporate settings.[3] Her work is explicitly interventionist. She engages organization members in cycles of data collection, interpretation, and reflection about how they enact their organizational realities. Schall suggests that uncovering the taken-for-granted rules that guide action could help organizations with employee selection, employee orientation, business strategizing, and change.

The understanding of organizations as cultures — structures of knowledge, cognitive enterprises, or master contracts — is

[3]
Personal communication. Maryan Schall is at the Department of Speech Communication, University of Minnesota, Minneapolis, MN.

strikingly similar to the notion of paradigm as it is applied in scientific communities. In other words, paradigms and cultures both refer to world views, organized patterns of thought with accompanying understanding of what constitutes adequate knowledge and legitimate activity (Benedict, 1934; Kuhn, 1962). Some theorists are finding the conceptualization of organizations as paradigms useful for thinking about the processes of strategic management and organization change (Sheldon, 1980; Litterer and Young, 1981; Pfeffer, 1981; Shrivastava and Mitroff, 1982; Smircich, 1983c).

For example, in their consulting work, Litterer and Young (1981) treat organizations as ideational systems. They identify three ideational patterns or paradigms — the entrepreneurial, the scientific, and the humanistic — which they suggest are common in American organizations. Their intervention approach is concerned with developing "managerial reflective skills," the ability of managers to examine, critique, and change their social ideational system, in a sense, to change paradigms.

The cognitive orientation to culture and organization is unified by these theorists' attention to the epistemological basis of social action, as well as by their search for a "grammar" to explain its patterning (e.g., Ritti, 1982; Shrivastava and Mitroff, 1982). A common underlying assumption of this work is that thought is linked to action. The major practical consequence of conceiving of organizations as socially sustained cognitive enterprises is the emphasis on mind and thought. Organization members are seen as thinking as well as behaving. This is hardly a startling view, and yet much organization research ignores the place of the human mind (Pondy and Boje, 1975). Viewing organizations as knowledge systems opens up new avenues for understanding the phenomenon of organized activity. Research questions take the form: What are the structures of knowledge in operation here? What are the "rules" or "scripts" that guide action? These questions are of practical concern to those who seek to understand, diagnose, and alter the way an organization is working.

A Symbolic Perspective

Anthropologists such as Hallowell (1955) and Geertz (1973) treat societies, or cultures, as systems of shared symbols and meanings. They see the anthropologist's task as interpreting the "themes" of culture — those postulates or understandings, declared or implicit, tacitly approved or openly prompted, that orient and stimulate social activity (Opler, 1945: 198). In order to explain the thematic systems of meaning underlying activity, anthropologists show the ways symbols are linked in meaningful relationship and demonstrate how they are related to the activities of the people in a setting.

When this symbolic perspective is applied to organizational analysis, an organization, like a culture, is conceived as a pattern of symbolic discourse. It thus needs interpreting (Manning, 1979), "reading" (Turner, 1983), or "deciphering" (Van Maanen, 1973), in order to be understood. To interpret an organization, a researcher focuses first on the way experience becomes meaningful for those in a setting. This is done by regard for the figure-ground relationships they maintain through their processes of attention, naming, and other patterns of action. The researcher may use several kinds of evidence to piece together

Concepts of Culture

a multifaceted and complex picture of the various kinds of symbol systems and their associated meanings. The researcher is also concerned with articulating the recurrent themes that represent the patterns in symbolic discourse and that specify the links among values, beliefs, and action in a setting. The themes, expressed in various symbolic modes, represent the heart of a symbolic analysis of an organization as culture (Smircich, 1983b).

Examples of this mode of research are Manning's (1979) study of the world of detectives, Smircich's (1983a) account of the organizational world of the executive staff of an insurance company, and the studies of police by Pacanowsky and Anderson (1981) and Van Maanen (1973, 1977). More specifically, Van Maanen was concerned with how people decipher organizations so that they can behave appropriately. This interest led him to focus on the process through which neophytes, in this case, police academy graduates, learned the meaning system maintained by their occupational group.

The focus of this form of organizational analysis is on how individuals interpret and understand their experience and how these interpretations and understandings relate to action. With this orientation, the very concept of organization is problematic, for the researcher seeks to examine the basic processes by which groups of people come to share interpretations and meanings for experience that allow the possibility of organized activity. The research agenda here is to document the creation and maintenance of organization through symbolic action.

By having this focus of interest, symbolic organization theorists have much in common with organizational leaders. Theorist and practitioner alike are concerned with such practical matters as how to create and maintain a sense of organization, and how to achieve common interpretations of situations so that coordinated action is possible. Some research work derived from this perspective in fact, offers the view that leadership can best be understood as the management of meaning and the shaping of interpretations (Peters, 1978; Smircich and Morgan, 1982).

Structural and Psychodynamic Perspectives

Culture may also be regarded as the expression of unconscious psychological processes. This view of culture forms the foundation of the structural anthropology of Levi-Strauss. It is also present in the work of organization theorists who are developing psychodynamic approaches to organizational analysis (e.g., Gemmill, 1982; Mitroff, 1982; McSwain and White, 1982; Walter, 1982). From this point of view, organizational forms and practices are understood as projections of unconscious processes and are analyzed with reference to the dynamic interplay between out-of-awareness processes and their conscious manifestation.

The structuralism of Levi-Strauss has had little development in organization theory. It assumes that the human mind has built-in constraints by which it structures psychic and physical content. Since we are unaware of this set of constraints or structures, they can be labeled the "unconscious infrastructure" (Rossi, 1974: 16–18). Culture displays the workings of the unconscious infrastructure; it reveals the form of the unconscious. From this perspective, the purpose of the study of culture is to reveal the hidden, universal dimensions of the human mind. The task of structural analysis is "to discover an order of relations that turns a set of bits, which have limited significance of their own, into an intelligible whole. This order may be termed 'the structure' " (Turner, 1977: 101).

According to Levi-Strauss, the 'structures' solve problems.

The "structures" that Levi-Strauss discusses typically solve "problems," problems with symbols, ideas or categories, problems with the application of these symbols, ideas and categories in the social world, and problems with the implications of the applications. The problem that kinship structures "solve," according to Levi-Strauss, is the problem of assuming that women "circulate" intergenerationally through the society. The solutions are arrangements of kinship categories and rules. The patterns that concern Levi-Strauss are patterns in variations between these arrangements. (Turner, 1977: 117)

If this approach to culture were applied to the study of organizations we could ask, What problems are solved by such persistent patterns in organizational arrangement as hierarchy? What do the patterns of organization reveal about the human mind?

From this perspective most organizational analysis would be criticized for being too limited in scope. Organizational research tends to deal only with the surface level "bits" that are, in fact, elements of the conscious models shared by organization participants and analysts. For example, the "formal structure" of the organization can be seen as an indigenous theory — a set of norms or rules that participants and researchers use to explain behavior in certain contexts (Turner, 1977). Behavior is explained, rationalized, and legitimized in terms of the formal organization structure. But formal structure is a myth.

Consider the parallel with the structural anthropologist who studies a primitive society. He or she would not be content to understand the significance of the members' behavior solely in the terms by which they make it accountable to themselves, the "native-view" perspective. To do so is to rely too heavily on the conscious attitude (McSwain and White, 1982) and rationalism (Walter, 1982). Structuralism and the psychodynamic models separate the experience of the phenomena from the underlying reality that gives rise to particular forms of social arrangements (Rossi, 1974). Thus the organization analyst guided by a structuralist or psychodynamic perspective would need to penetrate beneath the surface level of appearance and experience to uncover the objective foundations of social arrangements.

As of yet there are few organization analysts who are pursuing this task. Turner is one who attempts to apply an explicitly Levi-Strauss-type analysis to complex organizations — in one case, to understanding differences between bureaucratic and industrial arrangements (1977) and, in another case, to diagnosing organizational conflicts (1983). Mitroff (1982) draws on Jung's work on archetypes, rather than on Levi-Strauss' structuralism, yet he too is concerned with discovering structural patterns that link the unconscious human mind with its overt manifestations in social arrangements. McSwain and White (1982), Gemmill (1982), and Walter (1982) aim to understand organizational practices in terms of the transformation of unconscious energy into a variety of forms, e.g., lying, cheating,

Concepts of Culture

stealing, conflict, even the bureaucratic form. The organization theorists working from this psychodynamic perspective and contributing to the development of a transformational organization theory share a concern for reconstituting social science inquiry so that it embraces a more complex vision of human nature, one that integrates unconscious processes with the more obvious conscious processes (White and McSwain, 1983). Basic to this work is the belief in "the existence of a deep underlying structure built into the ordering capacities of the mind, and (the suggestion) that it is in these capacities in which the 'psychic unity of mankind' consists" (Turner, 1983).

CULTURE AS A ROOT METAPHOR: A COMPARISON

The cognitive, symbolic, structural, and psychodynamic perspectives on organization and culture have distinct foci of interest that lead scholars who hold these perspectives to ask different questions and to pursue their research programs in different ways. Some of this work is descriptive and documentary, some aims for social critique and reformation of social arrangements. Underlying these differences, however, is a mode of thought that sets these perspectives apart from those that treat culture as a variable. This mode of thought adopts the idea of culture as an epistemological device to frame the study of organization as social phenomenon. Although there may be different understandings of the specific nature of culture among cognitive, symbolic, structuralist, or psychodynamic theorists, by using culture as a root metaphor, they are all influenced to consider organization as a particular form of human expression. This is distinct from the views derived from the machine and organism metaphors, which encourage theorists to see organizations as purposeful instruments and adaptive mechanisms.

The mode of thought that underlies culture as a root metaphor gives the social world much less concrete status. The social world is not assumed to have an objective, independent existence that imposes itself on human beings. Instead, the social or organizational world exists only as a pattern of symbolic relationships and meanings sustained through the continued processes of human interaction. Social action is considered possible because of consensually determined meanings for experience that, to an external observer, may have the appearance of an independent rule-like existence.

The focus of attention of researchers here is also on language, symbols, myths, stories, and rituals, as in the culture-as-variable perspective discussed earlier. However, here these are not taken as cultural artifacts, but instead as generative processes that yield and shape meanings and that are fundamental to the very existence of organization. When culture is a root metaphor, the researcher's attention shifts from concerns about what do organizations accomplish and how may they accomplish it more efficiently, to how is organization accomplished and what does it mean to be organized?

CONCLUSION: TOWARD A CULTURAL ANALYSIS OF ORGANIZATION

In 1979, Pondy and Mitroff advocated that organization theory move "beyond open system models of organization" to a "cultural model" — a model that would be concerned with the higher mental functions of human behavior, such as language and the creation of meaning. Pondy and Mitroff were suggesting that the culture metaphor replace the open systems metaphor as an analytical framework in organization studies. Much of the research summarized in this paper and in this special issue stands as evidence that there is a trend in that direction. It is also apparent that the open systems analogy continues to be a dominant mode of thought in organization studies, but that now the idea of culture has been incorporated and given prominence as an internal variable as well as an environmental variable. Thus, not all of the research work mentioning culture refers to culture as a root metaphor.

Instead, we see that a variety of research agendas flow out of the linkage of different conceptions of culture and organization. These differences are highlighted in the five thematic areas of research representing various intersections of concepts of culture and organization. The insights that emerge from linking the two concepts are a function of the basic conceptions of culture and organization that the researcher brings to the inquiry situation. Thus the significance of culture for organization studies can only be considered against the broader backdrop of basic assumptions and purposes. When we question whether or not "a cultural framework" is a useful one, we need to ask more precisely, "Useful for whom and for what purpose?"

By considering together all the research efforts stemming from the linking of culture and organization, the differences in interests and purposes pursued by organization scholars are emphasized. Some researchers give high priority to the principles of prediction, generalizability, causality, and control; while others are concerned by what appear to them to be more fundamental issues of meaning and the processes by which organizational life is possible. Comparative management scholars seek to chart patterns of beliefs and attitudes, as well as managerial practices across countries. Those who research dimensions of corporate culture seek to delineate the ways these dimensions are interrelated and how they influence critical organizational processes and outcomes. Underlying both these areas of inquiry is the desire for statements of contingent relationships that will have applicability for those managing organizations. Cognitive organization theorists, on the other hand, consider organizations as systems of thought. Their interest is in charting the understandings or rules by which organization members achieve coordinated action in order to diagnose and intervene in organized settings. Symbolic organization theorists are concerned with interpreting or deciphering the patterns of symbolic action that create and maintain a sense of organization. They recognize that symbolic modes, such as language, facilitate shared realities, yet these realities are fleeting, always open to reinterpretation and renegotiation. Thus, for them, the very concept of organization is problematic. Organization theorists influenced by structural anthropology or psychodynamics seek to understand the ways in which organization forms and practices manifest unconscious processes. Their aim is to penetrate the surface level of appearance to uncover the workings of unconscious mind. The latter three research interests share a more subjective orientation to the study of organization. They have a common concern for studying the interactional dynamics that bring about organization.

Concepts of Culture

This paper has intended to clarify the differences in the ways the concepts of culture and organization have been linked, to illustrate the accompanying research agendas and to bring to the surface the underlying assumptions and purposes contained in those agendas. Despite the very real differences in research interest and purpose represented here, whether one treats culture as a background factor, an organizational variable, or as metaphor for conceptualizing organization, the idea of culture focuses attention on the expressive, nonrational qualities of the experience of organization. It legitimates attention to the subjective, interpretive aspects of organizational life.

A cultural analysis moves us in the direction of questioning taken-for-granted assumptions, raising issues of context and meaning, and bringing to the surface underlying values. The rational model of organization analysis is largely silent on these matters (Denhardt, 1981). Although organization scholars have already conducted much research on the values of individual managers, they have devoted much less energy to questioning the values embedded within modern corporate society and to examining the context in which corporate society is meaningful. A cultural mode of analysis encourages us to recognize that both the practice of organizational inquiry and the practice of corporate management are cultural forms, products of a particular sociohistorical context and embodying particular value commitments. In our present day these values are efficiency, orderliness, and even organization itself. Denhardt in *In the Shadow of Organization* (1981) noted that organization and administration studies tend to take as their task improving organizational efficiency rather than questioning the "ethic of organization" that has come to dominate modern life. Complex organization as a cultural form has enabled us to provide universal education, to eliminate deadly diseases such as polio and smallpox, and to explore outer space. Complex organization as a cultural form also facilitates environmental destruction and the possibility of nuclear annihilation. A cultural framework for analysis encourages us to see that an important role for both those who study and manage organizations is not to celebrate organization as a value, but to question the ends it serves.

Because we are of our own culture, it is difficult for us, researchers and managers alike, to both live in our cultural context and to question it. It is difficult to engage in contextual, reflexive management and research, with the requirement of examination and critique of one's own assumptions and values. It is difficult; but that is what a cultural framework for management and research urges us to do.

REFERENCES

Agar, Michael H.
1982 "Whatever happened to cognitive anthropology: A partial review." Human Organization, 41 (Spring): 82–86.

Ajiferuke, Musbau, and J. Boddewyn
1970 " 'Culture' and other explanatory variables in comparative management studies." Academy of Management Journal, 13: 153–163.

Andrews, John A. Y., and Paul M. Hirsch
1983 "Ambushes, shootouts, and knights of the roundtable: The language of corporate takeovers." In Louis R. Pondy, Peter Frost, Gareth Morgan, and Thomas Dandridge (eds.), Organizational Symbolism. Greenwich, CT: JAI Press (forthcoming).

Argyris, Chris, and Donald Schon
1978 Organizational Learning. Reading, MA: Addison-Wesley.

Benedict, Ruth
1934 Patterns of Culture. Boston: Houghton Mifflin.

Bhagat, Rabi S., and Sara J. McQuaid
1982 "Role of subjective culture in organizations: A review and directions for future research." Journal of Applied Psychology Monograph, 67: 653–685.

Boje, David M., Donald B. Fedor, and Kendrith M. Rowland
1982 "Myth making: A qualitative step in OD interventions." Journal of Applied Behavioral Science, 18: 17–28.

Bougon, Michel
1983 "Uncovering cognitive maps: The self-q technique." In Gareth Morgan (ed.), Beyond Method: Social Research Strategies. Beverly Hills, CA: Sage (forthcoming).

Bougon, Michel, Karl Weick, and Din Binkhorst
1977 "Cognition in organizations: An analysis of the Utrecht Jazz Orchestra." Administrative Science Quarterly, 22: 606–639.

Brown, Richard H.
1977 A Poetic for Sociology. Cambridge: Cambridge University Press.

Burns, Tom, and George M. Stalker
1961 The Management of Innovation. London: Tavistock.

Burrell, Gibson, and Gareth Morgan
1979 Sociological Paradigms and Organization Analysis. London: Heinemann.

Business Week
1980 "Corporate culture: The hard-to-change values that spell success or failure." October 27: 148–160.

Crozier, Michel
1964 The Bureaucratic Phenomenon. Chicago: University of Chicago Press.

Cummings, L. L., and Stuart M. Schmidt
1972 "Managerial attitudes of Greeks: The roles of culture and industrialization." Administrative Science Quarterly, 17: 265–272.

Dandridge, Thomas C.
1979 "Celebrations of corporate anniversaries: An example of modern organizational symbols." Working paper, State University of New York at Albany.

Dandridge, Thomas, Ian Mitroff, and William Joyce
1980 "Organizational symbolism: A topic to expand organizational analysis." Academy of Management Review, 5: 248–256.

Deal, Terrence E., and Allan A. Kennedy
1982 Corporate Cultures. Reading, MA: Addison-Wesley.

Denhardt, Robert B.
1981 In the Shadow of Organization. Lawrence, KS: Regents Press.

Everett, James E., Bruce W. Stening, and Peter A. Longton
1982 "Some evidence for an international managerial culture." Journal of Management Studies, 19: 153–162.

Fayerweather, John
1959 The Executive Overseas. Syracuse, NY: Syracuse University Press.

Fiedler, Fred E.
1967 A Theory of Leadership Effectiveness. New York: McGraw-Hill.

French, Wendell L., and Cecil H. Bell.
1978 Organization Development. Englewood Cliffffs, NJ: Prentice-Hall.

Gemmill, Gary
1982 "Unconscious processes: The black hole in group development." Paper presented at the Academy of Management Meetings, New York City, August.

Geertz, Clifford
1973 The Interpretation of Cultures. New York: Basic Books.

Goffman, Erving
1959 The Presentation of Self in Everyday Life. New York: Doubleday.

Goodenough, Ward H.
1971 Culture, Language and Society. Reading, MA: Addison-Wesley.

Haire, Mason, Edwin Ghiselli, and Lyman Porter
1966 Managerial Thinking: An International Study. New York: Wiley.

Hallowell, A. Irving
1955 Culture and Experience. Philadelphia: University of Pennsylvania Press.

Harbison, Frederick H., and Charles A. Myers
1959 Management in the Industrial World: An International Analysis. New York: McGraw-Hill.

Harris, Linda, and Vernon Cronen
1979 "A rules-based model for the analysis and evaluation of organizational communication." Communication Quarterly, Winter: 12–28.

Harrison, Roger
1972 "Understanding your organization's character." Harvard Business Review, 5(3): 119–128.

Inzerilli, G., and A. Laurent
1979 "The conception of organization structure — A comparative view." Paper presented at the Annual Meeting of the Academy of International Business.

Jacques, Elliot
1952 The Changing Culture of a Factory. New York: Dryden Press.

Kaplan, Abraham
1964 The Conduct of Inquiry. New York: Chandler.

Keichel, Walter
1982 "Corporate strategies under fire." Fortune, December 27: 35–39.

Koch, Susan, and Stanley Deetz
1981 "Metaphor analysis of social reality in organizations." Journal of Applied Communication Research, 9: 1–15.

Kreps, Gary
1981 "Organizational folklore: The packaging of company history at RCA." Paper presented at the ICA/SCA Conference on Interpretive Approaches to Organizational Communication, Alta, UT, July.

Kuhn, Thomas
1962 The Structure of Scientific Revolutions. Chicago: University of Chicago Press.

Lakoff, George, and Mark Johnson
1980 Metaphors We Live By. Chicago: University of Chicago Press.

Lawrence, Paul R., and Jay W. Lorsch
1967 Organization and Environment. Cambridge, MA: Harvard Graduate School of Business Administration.

Litterer, Joseph A., and Stanley Young
1981 "The development of managerial reflective skills." Proceedings, Northeast AIDS, April.

Louis, Meryl R.
1980 "A cultural perspective on organizations: The need for and consequences of viewing organizations as culture-bearing milieux." Paper presented at the National Academy of Management Meetings, Detroit, MI, August.

Mangham, Ian L., and M. A. Overington
1983 "Dramatism and the theatrical metaphor: Really playing at critical distances." In Gareth Morgan (ed.), Beyond Method: Social Research Strategies. Beverly Hills, CA: Sage (forthcoming).

Concepts of Culture

Manning, Peter K.
1979 "Metaphors of the field: Varieties of organizational discourse." Administrative Science Quarterly, 24: 660–671.

Martin, Joanne, and Melanie E. Powers
1983 "Truth or corporate propaganda: The value of a good war story." In Louis R. Pondy, Peter Frost, Gareth Morgan, and Thomas Dandridge (eds.), Organizational Symbolism. Greenwich, CT: JAI Press (forthcoming).

McSwain, Cynthia J., and Orion F. White, Jr.
1982 "The case for lying, cheating, and stealing — Organization development as an ethos model for management practice." Paper presented at the Academy of Management Meetings, New York City, August.

Meadows, Paul
1967 "The metaphors of order: Toward a taxonomy of organization theory." In Llewellyn Gross (ed.), Sociological Theory: Inquiries and Paradigms: 77–103. New York: Harper & Row.

Meyer, Alan
1981 "How ideologies supplant formal structures and shape responses to environments." Journal of Management Studies, 19: 45–61.

Mitroff, Ian I.
1982 "Stakeholders of the mind." Paper presented at the Academy of Management Meetings, New York City, August.

Mitroff, Ian I., and Ralph H. Kilmann
1976 "On organizational stories: An approach to the design and analysis of organizations through myths and stories." In Ralph H. Kilmann, Louis R. Pondy, and Dennis P. Slevin (eds.), The Management of Organization Design, 1: 189–207. New York: Elsevier-North Holland.

Morgan, Gareth
1980 "Paradigms, metaphors, and puzzle solving in organization theory." Administrative Science Quarterly, 25: 605–622.

Morgan, Gareth, and Linda Smircich
1980 "The case for qualitative research." Academy of Management Review, 5: 491–500.

Opler, Morris E.
1945 "Themes as dynamic forces in culture." American Journal of Sociology, 51: 198–206.

Ouchi, William G.
1981 Theory Z. Reading, MA: Addison-Wesley.

Pacanowsky, Michael, and J. A. Anderson
1981 "Cop talk and media use." Paper presented at the International Communication Association Convention, May.

Pasquale, Richard T., and Anthony G. Athos
1981 The Art of Japanese Management. New York: Warner.

Pearce, W. Barnett
1979 "The coordinated management of meaning: A rules-based theory of interpersonal communication." In G. R. Miller (ed.), Explorations in Interpersonal Communication: 225–240. Beverly Hills, CA: Sage.

Pepper, Stephen C.
1942 World Hypotheses. Berkeley, CA: University of California Press.

Peters, Thomas J.
1978 "Symbols, patterns and settings: An optimistic case for getting things done." Organizational Dynamics, 7: 3–23.

Peters, Thomas J., and Robert H. Waterman, Jr.
1982 In Search of Excellence. New York: Harper & Row.

Pettigrew, Andrew M.
1979 "On studying organizational cultures." Administrative Science Quarterly, 24: 570–581.

Pfeffer, Jeffrey
1981 "Management as symbolic action: The creation and maintenance of organizational paradigms." In Larry L. Cummings and Barry M. Staw (eds.), Research in Organizational Behavior, 3: 1–52. Greenwich, CT: JAI Press.

Pinder, Craig C., and V. Warren Bourgeois
1982 "Controlling tropes in administrative science." Administrative Science Quarterly, 27: 641–652.

Pondy, Louis R., and David M. Boje
1975 "Bringing mind back in: Paradigm development as a frontier problem in organization theory." Paper presented at the Annual Meetings of the American Sociological Association, San Francisco, August.

Pondy, Louis R., and Ian I. Mitroff
1979 "Beyond open system models of organization." In Larry L. Cummings and Barry M. Staw (eds.), Research in Organizational Behavior, 1: 3–39. Greenwich, CT: JAI Press.

Pugh, Derek S., and David J. Hickson
1976 Organization Structure in Its Context: The Aston Programme I. Farnborough, Hants: Saxon House/Lexington Books.

Quinn, J. Brian
1980 Strategies for Change. Homewood, IL: Richard D. Irwin.

Ricoeur, Paul
1971 "The mode of the text: Meaningful action considered as text." Social Research, 38: 529–562.

Ritti, Richard R.
1982 "The social bases of organizational knowledge." Working paper, The Pennsylvania State University.

Ritzer, George
1975 Sociology: A Multiple Paradigm Science. Boston: Allyn and Bacon.

Roberts, Karlene H.
1970 "On looking at an elephant: An evaluation of cross-cultural research related to organizations." Psychological Bulletin, 74: 327–350.

Rossi, Ino
1974 The Unconscious in Culture. New York: Dutton.

Rossi, Ino, and Edwin O'Higgins
1980 "The development of theories of culture." In Ino Rossi (ed.), People in Culture: 31–78. New York: Praeger.

Salmans, S.
1983 "New vogue: Company culture." New York Times, January 9: D1, D3.

Schall, Maryan S.
1981 "An exploration into a successful corporation's saga-vision and its rhetorical community." Paper presented at the ICA/SCA Conference on Interpretive Approaches to Organizational Communication, Alta, UT, July.

Schwartz, Howard, and Stanley Davis
1981 "Matching corporate culture and business strategy." Organizational Dynamics, Summer: 30–48.

Sekaran, Uma
1981 "Nomological networks and the understanding of organizations in different cultures." Proceedings of the Academy of Management: 54–58.

Sheldon, Alan
1980 "Organizational paradigms: A theory of organizational change." Organizational Dynamics, Winter: 61–80.

Shimanoff, S. B.
1980 Communication Rules: Theory and Practice. Beverly Hills, CA: Sage.

Shrivastava, Paul, and Ian Mitroff
1982 "Frames of reference managers use: A study in applied sociology of knowledge." Working paper, College of Business and Public Administration, New York University.

Siehl, Caren, and Joanne Martin
1981 "Learning organizational culture." Working paper, Graduate School of Business, Stanford University.

Slocum, John W.
1971 "A comparative study of the satisfaction of American and Mexican operatives." Academy of Management Journal, 14: 89–97.

Smircich, Linda
1981 "The concept of culture and organizational analysis." Paper presented at the ICA/SCA Conference on Interpretive Approaches to Organizational Communication, Alta, UT, July.
1983a "Organizations as shared meanings." In Louis R. Pondy, Peter Frost, Gareth Morgan, and Thomas Dandridge (eds.), Organizational Symbolism. Greenwich, CT: JAI Press (forthcoming).
1983b "Studying organizations as cultures." In Gareth Morgan (ed.), Beyond Method: Social Research Strategies. Beverly Hills, CA: Sage (forthcoming).

1983c "Implications of the interpretive perspective for management theory." In Linda Putnam and Michael Pacanowsky (eds.), Communication and Organization: An Interpretive Approach. Beverly Hills, CA: Sage (forthcoming).

Smircich, Linda, and Gareth Morgan
1982 "Leadership: The management of meaning." Journal of Applied Behavioral Science, 18(3): 257–273.

Tichy, Noel M.
1982 "Managing change strategically: The technical, political, and cultural keys." Organizational Dynamics, Autumn: 59–80.

Trice, Harrison M., and Janice M. Beyer
1983 "The ceremonial effect: Manifest function or latent dysfunction in the dynamic organization." Paper presented at the Conference on Myths, Symbols, and Folklore: Expanding the Analysis of Organizations. University of California at Los Angeles, March.

Trist, E. L., and K. W. Bamforth
1951 "Some social and psychological consequences of the longwall method of coal getting." Human Relations, 4: 3–38.

Turner, Barry A.
1971 Exploring the Industrial Subculture. London: Macmillan.

Turner, Stephen P.
1977 "Complex organizations as savage tribes." Journal for the Theory of Social Behavior, 7 (April): 99–125.
1983 "Studying organization through Levi-Strauss's structuralism." In Gareth Morgan (ed.), Beyond Method: Social Research Strategies. Beverly Hills, CA: Sage (forthcoming).

Van de Ven, Andrew H., and W. Graham Astley
1981 "Mapping the field to create a dynamic perspective on organization design and behavior." In Andrew H. Van de Ven and William F. Joyce (eds.), Perspectives on Organization Design and Behavior: 427–468. New York: Wiley.

Van Maanen, John
1973 "Observations on the making of policemen." Human Organization, 32: 407–418.
1977 "Experiencing organization." In John Van Maanen (ed.), Organizational Careers: Some New Perspectives: 15–45. New York: Wiley.

Wacker, Gerald
1981 "Toward a cognitive methodology of organizational assessment." Journal of Applied Behavioral Science, 17: 114–129.

Walter, Gordon A.
1982 "Beneath bureaucratic anarchies: The principle abyss." Paper presented at the Academy of Management Meetings, New York City, August.

Weick, Karl E.
1979a "Cognitive processes in organizations." In Larry L. Cummings and Barry M. Staw (eds.), Research in Organizational Behavior, 1: 41–74. Greenwich, CT: JAI Press.
1979b The Social Psychology of Organizing. Reading, MA: Addison-Wesley.

White, Orion F., Jr., and Cynthia J. McSwain
1983 "Transformational theory and organizational analysis. In Gareth Morgan (ed.), Beyond Method: Social Research Strategies. Beverly Hills, CA: Sage (forthcoming).

Whorton, Joseph W., and John A. Worthley
1981 "A perspective on the challenge of public management: Environmental paradox and organizational culture." Academy of Management Review, 6: 357–363.

Wilkins, Alan, and Joanne Martin
1980 "Organizational legends." Working paper, Graduate School of Business, Stanford University.

Woodward, Joan
1965 Industrial Organization: Theory and Practice. London: Oxford University Press.

[21]

OCCUPATIONAL COMMUNITIES:

CULTURE AND CONTROL IN

ORGANIZATIONS

John Van Maanen and Stephen R. Barley

ABSTRACT

One of the more persistent themes in sociology has been the presumed dichotomy between communal or colleagual and rational or administrative forms of work organization. While theories of organizations adopt the latter perspective, a conception of work organized in terms of occupational communities approximates the former. To this end, we define an occupational community as a group of people who consider themselves to be engaged in the same sort of work; whose identity is drawn from the work; who share with one another a set of values, norms and perspectives that apply to but extend beyond work related matters; and whose social relationships meld work and leisure.

The diverse origins of occupational communities are next discussed in relation to how physical and social conditions surrounding particular lines of work promote any or all of the definitional characteristics. Occupational communities are seen to create and sustain relatively unique work cultures consisting of, among other things, task rituals, standards for proper and improper behavior, work codes surrounding relatively routine practices and, for the membership at least, compelling accounts attesting to the logic and value of these rituals, standards and codes. We suggest that the quest for occupational self control provides the special motive for the development of occupational communities.

State support, an elaborate and advancing theoretical and procedural base to inform and mystify practice, and a relatively unorganized market in dire need of an occupational community's talents lend structural support to a community's quest for self control. We also suggest that the professions, when appropriately unpacked by speciality and interest, are best viewed as occupational communities and that they differ from other lines of work (and each other) only by virtue of the relative autonomy each is able to sustain within the political economy of a given society. Finally, the implications of occupational communities are explored in four domains of organizational research: careers, complexity, loyalty, and innovation.

Research in Organizational Behavior, vol. 6, pages 287–365
ISBN: 0-89232-351-5

To the study of human behavior in organizations, a field already choking on assorted paradigms, hypotheses, methods, variables, and other objects of intellectual passion, we offer in this essay even more conceptual paraphernalia. Specifically, we shall argue the utility of viewing behavior in organizations through an occupational rather than organizational lens. Considerable lip service has been paid to such a perspective by organizational theorists but, for a variety of reasons, focused and conceptually-driven research based on such a perspective has been notably absent in the organization behavior literature. This neglect has consequence, not the least of which is that organization researchers largely disregard the phenomenological boundaries recognized by members of particular work worlds. Descriptions of these intersubjective boundaries and the shared activities, social interactions, and common understandings established by those who fall within these boundaries are found, however, in the growing ethnographic records of contemporary work worlds. Such empirical materials represent lively, rich accounts of occupational ways of life; accounts we believe must be reckoned with if organizational theories are to locate and explain more of the behavioral variability of the workplace than has been the case to date.[1]

Consider, for example, the contrast between ethnographic writings about a person's work and career and the writings on the same topics found in the organization behavior literature.[2] The ethnographic versions feature closely detailed narratives of everyday work activities, first-hand accounts of observed events (routine and otherwise), free-flowing, lengthy descriptions of the various belief systems that appear to inform a person's selection of career and, perhaps all too frequently, precious little attempt to generalize across occupations or careers. The particular and occasionally unique things people do for a living are matters uncovered by ethnographers along with the meanings such activities hold for the people who do them. In the equally stylized organization behavior literature, the specifics of work and careers are glossed over while the aggregate and occasionally general ways people believe and behave in occupational settings are emphasized.

Such divergence is, of course, hardly surprising since the two genres differ in purpose, audience, format, and language. Yet, the dissimilarities between the two approaches are not simply matters of contrasting form or style, nor should the discrepancies be dismissed with the claim that variable-based research is somehow more objective or analytic than the context-sensitive ethnographic research and, therefore, less passionate, idiosyncratic, or biased. In our view, it remains noteworthy that "Charlie, the automobile repairman down at Joe's Garage" is, in the ethnographic writings, a "mechanic" and, in the organization behavior writings, an "employee."

We hold these genre disparities to be substantive, reflecting alternative and potentially conflicting models of how work is organized and interpreted. One perspective views a person's work from an organizational frame of reference and thus accentuates the meaning that such work has for others. The other approach employs an occupational perspective and concentrates upon the meaning of work for those who do it (Berger, 1964). Both perspectives operate as templates to select, mold, and present the subject in ways which transcend the obvious conceits of the genres. Several contrasting assumptions are at work when either framework is utilized.

From an organizational standpoint, most people are seen to regard their work careers largely in terms of movement (or lack thereof) within a set sequence of hierarchically ascending positions, each position offering more or less prestige, power, money, and other rewards. Observers employing an occupational perspective imply that persons weave their perspectives on work and career from the existing social, moral, physical, and intellectual character of the work itself. Individual assessments of work and career are cast in terms of one's getting better (or worse) at what one does, getting support (or interference) from others, exerting more (or less) influence over the nature of one's work, and so on. The two perspectives also differ on the importance of "work" as a concept for explaining social order. From the organizational perspective, a person's work is but a small part of the larger problems of coordination, authority, workflow, production method, or service design. Work is a concept subsidiary to the more abstract (but logically intertwined) relationships that are thought to engender the economic and social order of an organization or the society at large. From the occupational perspective, work and the groups that are inspired or flattened by it are themselves focal concepts for explaining social structure because they provide the basis of an occupationally stratified organization or society.

Contrasts such as these arise from placing differential emphasis on what Weber (1968:40) called the rational (associational or organizational) and traditional (communal or occupational) aspects of modern economy and society. For the most part, rational aspects have dominated organizational research and interest has been persistently directed toward the brisk correlates of organizational performance rather than the substantive nature of the work people perform during their working lives. Similarly, conflicts of interest in organizational settings have been examined almost exclusively by reference to vertical cleavages of authority or friction between functional units rather than by reference to clashes between organizational authorities and occupational interest groups.[3]

In this paper, we develop the notion of an occupational community as an alternative to an organizational frame of reference for understanding why it is that people behave as they do in the workplace. In essence, we want to develop a perspective that will prove valuable when regarding our hypothetical auto repairman as a "mechanic" rather than an "employee." Several analytic aims are served by this approach.

First, a focus on occupations preserves some of the existential, everyday reality of the firsthand experience of work. The fact that one works the swing shift in a cattle slaughterhouse as a hind-toe-remover is a rather straightforward descriptive statement. But, it is a statement that we belive conveys considerably more information than that conveyed by organizationally designed job descriptions of the sort seized upon by organizational researchers in their search for generality, such as unskilled laborer, machine operator, or assembly line worker. Social worlds coalesce around the objects produced and the services rendered by people at work. To focus on occupation, as the semantic tag tying together the bundle of tasks which constitute a given line of work, brings such social worlds and their many meanings to light.

Second, by examining the social worlds that coalesce around occupations, we broaden our understanding of social control in organizations. We take as axiomatic that the fundamental problem of organization—or, more properly, the management of organizations—is the control of the labor process. Occupational matters are undeniably central to this problem since all positions have histories marking their rise (and fall) in terms of the amount of self-control occupational members possess over the fruits and methods of their labors. The ongoing struggle of stable and shifting, formal and informal, large and small groups to develop and occupy some niche in the occupational structure of society is played out every day in organizations where rational or administrative principles of control (e.g., codification, standardization, hierarchical discipline, etc.) compete with traditional or communal principles of control (e.g., peer pressures, work ideologies, valued symbols, etc.).

Third, a focus upon work and occupation casts new light on problems of diversity and conflict in the workplace. From an administrative standpoint, "deviance" among organizational members is defined in terms of exceptions to managerial expectations. The sources of such deviance are typically ignored or muted since administrative solutions are sought in terms of correcting the "system" so that expectations can be met. That deviance is willful is a point often made in organizational studies, but seldom elaborated upon beyond bland reference to the ubiquitous "informal" groups contained within organizations. Even when deviance is treated seriously and in some depth by organizational theorists concerned with the individual orientations of organizational members toward their work, it is often treated as merely the result of non-work factors such as universal human needs ignored by the designers of work systems (Roethlisberger & Dickson, 1939); too rigorous, tight, punitive, or otherwise unenlightened management practices (McGregor, 1960; Argyris, 1964); narrow, standardized, efficiency-focused, mass production technologies (Blauner, 1964; Hackman & Oldman, 1979); subcultural, class-based norms imported into the workplace from outside (Katz, 1965; Dubin, 1956); situational opportunities seized upon by employees to improve earnings, thwart boredom, advance careers, or reduce risk (Dalton, 1969; Roy, 1960); and so on.

While these sources of informal adjustments or member deviance are undoubtedly present in all organizations, willful violation of managerial expectations may also correspond to a pervasive logic embedded within the historically developed practices of occupational members doing what they feel they must. Rather than a reflection of class interests or a knee-jerk response to flawed managerial schemes, organizational deviance may be proactive, not reactive. More important, it may also reflect the way a given line of work has come to be defined and practiced relatively independent of technology, managerial mistakes, or organization structure (Silverman, 1970). What is deviant organizationally may be occupationally correct (and vice-versa).[4] Aside from some of the early work conducted in the Tavistock sociotechnical traditions, organization theory rarely concerns itself with such contradictions (Trist & Bamforth, 1951; Rice, 1958).

Fourth, a focus on the common tasks, work schedules, job training, peer relations, career patterns, shared symbols, or any and all of the elements that comprise an occupation brings forth a concern regarding how a given line of work can be said to influence one's social conduct and identity, both in and out of the workplace. Goffman (1961a:87–88) makes this point nicely when he suggests: "A self (then) virtually awaits the individual entering a position; he needs only to conform to the pressures on him and he will find a 'me' ready-made for him. . . . being is doing." Although a position is organizationally created and sanctioned, the work that comprises such a position often has a history of its own and, therefore, a context that is not organizationally limited. Even rigidly defined positions are almost always more than most organization designers, authorities and, alas, researchers make them out to be (e.g., Roy, 1960). Some of these positions may offer an occupant far more than a job. Indeed, some may offer a rewarding and valued "me." The identity-bestowing characteristics of positions are, in short, frequently matters which are occupationally specific.

To develop an occupational perspective on concerns often considered organizational, we first identify and expand upon the notion of an "occupational community." Next, we suggest that occupational communities of all types are marked by distinctive work cultures promoting self control and collective autonomy for the membership. As a result, we take issue with the stance of many organization theorists who regard professional work as an occupational category clearly separable from other lines of work by describing, in comparative terms, some of the structural or external conditions that appear to foster self control. Following this discussion, we note how each of several long standing research domains within organizational studies—careers, conflict, loyalty, and innovation—can be enriched empirically and advanced conceptually by paying serious attention to the role occupational communities play within organizations.

ON THE NATURE OF OCCUPATIONAL COMMUNITIES

To know what dentistry, firefighting, accounting, or photography consists of and means to those who pursue it is to know the cognitive, social, and moral contours of the occupation. Of course, not all occupations can be said to possess decipherable contours, since the degree to which knowledge, practices, and values are shared among practitioners varies across occupations, across time, and across settings. However, some occupations display a rather remarkable stability in social space and time and, hence, can be decoded. It is for them that the idea of an occupational community is most relevant since it draws attention to those occupations that transmit a shared culture from generation to generation of participants.

The notion of an occupational community derives from two classical sociological premises. First is the contention that people bound together by common values, interests, and a sense of tradition, share bonds of solidarity or mutual regard and partake of a communal way of life that contrasts in idyllic ways with the competition, individualism, and rational calculation of self-interest associated with persons organized on utilitarian principles. The distinction between communal and utilitarian forms of human association and the consequences of the transformation of the former into the latter are issues that preoccupied social theorists of the late 19th and early 20th centuries. Comte, Weber, Durkheim, Tonñies, and Marx each sensed that Western civilization was undergoing a social upheaval brought about by industrialization of the economy and bureaucratization of the state. While disagreeing over the meaning of the transformation, all concurred that a shift from "gemeinshaft" to "gesellshaft" was irrevocable.[5]

The central dilemma spawned by such a transformation lies in the nature of the social contract: How can human relationships remain socially integrated and rewarding in and of themselves when they are based on principles of utilitarianism and rational calculation of self-interest? One answer claims that rational associations are themselves meritorious. Thus, Weber, while acutely aware that rational organization generates its own problems (notably, rigidity and narrowness of scope), put forth more persuasively than any of his contemporaries the special virtues of rational organization in his depiction of ideal state bureaucracies. The attributes of Weberian bureaucracy are well known: division of labor by specialization, qualification by examination, coordination by impersonal rules, and authority legitimated by hierarchical office. In comparison to other forms of state organization, Weber thought bureaucracy superior insofar as it sought, through rationalization, to eliminate advancement by patrimony or special interest, to eradicate encrusted traditions, and to promise collective achievement through the use of member expertise.

Durkheim (1933) was also relatively optimistic about the potential benefits of rational organization (particularly in his early writings). He claimed that gesellshaft relationships engender their own peculiar devices for moral integration since rational contracts presume trust and negotiated reciprocity. However, Durkheim, much like Weber, tempered his optimism with the proposition than only gemeinshaft-like relationships could ameliorate the anomic side effects of rational organization and the division of labor. Durkheim's prescription for maintaining the social fabric of community amplified the very cleavages born of the division of labor: The formation of occupational groups to serve as political entities as well as reference groups. We trace to Durkheim the second premise upon which the notion of occupational community rests: the idea that the work we do shapes the totality of our lives and, to a great extent, determines who we think we are.

> Besides the society of faith, of family, and of politics, there is one other . . . that of all workers of the same sort, in association, all who cooperate in the same function; that is, the occupational group or corporation. Identity of origin, culture, and occupation makes occupational activity the richest sort of material for a common life.
>
> Durkheim (1951:578)

> . . . this character of corporative organization comes from very general causes . . . When a certain number of individuals in the midst of a political society are found to have ideas, interests, sentiments, and occupations not shared by the rest of the population, it is inevitable that they will be attracted toward each other under the influence of these likenesses. They will seek each other out, enter into relations, associate, and thus little by little a restricted group, having its special characteristics, will be formed in the midst of the general society. But once the group is formed, a moral life appears naturally carrying the mark of the particular conditions in which it has developed. For it is impossible for men to live together, associating in industry, without acquiring a sentiment of the whole formed by their union, without attaching themselves to that whole, preoccupying themselves with its interests, and taking account of it in their conduct.
>
> Durkheim (1933:14)

The implication of Durkheim's remarks is that modern society is not only structured vertically by the rationality of industrial and state organization, but that it is also structured horizontally by occupational groupings. Although Durkheim proposed that occupations might provide the moral fabric for society, the so-called Chicago school of sociology showed empirically the diversity of this moral fabric.[6] For instance, the writings of Park and Burgess (1924), Hughes (1958, 1971), Becker (1963) and (especially) Becker et al. (1968), display the many moral, aesthetic, and social parameters of occupational groupings from the high status to low. In particular, Chicago School sociologists stress that the meaning of a line of work is socially constructed and validated in practice by members of an occupation; that an occupational career is decipherable only by reference to occupationally specific meanings; that occupations foster particular categorization schemes which structure work worlds as well as the larger social environment; and that work roles provide incumbents with a social identity and a code for conduct, both within and without the workplace.

The fusion of the community ideal, with the notion that one's work shapes one's life, finds expression in the vision of the artisan whose very being is inseparable from his means of livelihood and whose work suffuses every relationship with meaning. C. Wright Mills (1956:223) provides the example with his lyrical description of the craftsman.

> The craftsman's work is the mainspring of the only world he knows; he does not flee from work into a separate sphere of leisure . . . he brings to his non-working hours the values and qualities developed and employed in his working time. His idle conversation is shop talk; his friends follow the same line of work as he, and share a kinship of feeling and thought.

This blurring of the distinction between work and leisure, and the idea that certain kinds of work bind people together and help shape the course of their existence lies at the core of research ventures into occupational communities. For instance, working with high status occupations, Gertzl (1961:38) used the phrase "occupational community" to reflect the "pervasiveness of occupational identification and the convergence of informal friendship patterns and colleague relationships." Salaman (1974) elaborated upon the same theme when characterizing the work worlds of architects and railroaders. The term has also been used in the labor relations literature to describe relationships among union members or residents in towns where employment can be found in, or tightly bound to, only one line of work (Glaser, 1977; Hill, 1981).

The conception of occupational community developed here seeks to draw together much of this previous work. Our definition of an occupational community contains four elements. Each is separate analytically but interconnected empirically. By occupational community, we mean a group of people who consider themselves to be engaged in the same sort of work; who identify (more or less positively) with their work; who share a set of values, norms, and perspectives that apply to, but extend beyond, work related matters; and whose social relationships meld the realms of work and leisure.

Boundaries

In his critique of the concept of community, Gusfield (1975:31–32) cautions against operationally identifying communities on the basis of obvious or ascribed attributes of a group of individuals.[7] Two popular criteria for defining communities, inhabitance of common territory and possession of similar backgrounds, are especially misleading. Not only may the inhabitants of a small village be decisively divided into smaller groups that compete among themselves for resources, but persons with very diverse histories and traditions can attain a sense of solidarity (as did Jews of German and Russian origin who emigrated to the United States). Moreover, since human groups and relationships are multi-faceted, any number of attributes can be invented or discovered along which members can be compared and contrasted. Consequently, even if members are alike in some respect, there is no guarantee that the respect is relevant. More crucial parameters for identifying communities are the social dimensions used by members themselves for recognizing one another, the social limits of such bonds, and situational factors which amplify or diminish the perceived common identity. Gusfield (1975:33) writes that "the concept of community is part of a system of accounts used by members and observers as a way of explaining or justifying the member's behavior. It is the criteria of action . . . rather than the physical arena within which action occurs . . . it is the behavior governed by criteria of common belonging rather than mutual interest."

Following Gusfield's idea that "consciousness of kind" is the fundamental basis for a community, we submit that the relevant boundaries of an occupational community are those set by the members themselves. Hence, the first attribute of an occupational community is that it is composed of people who consider themselves "to be" members of the same occupation rather than people who "are" members of the same occupation. This distinction relies solely upon internal rather than external accounts and is of theoretical and methodological significance.[8]

The social organization of an occupation as seen by insiders is typically quite different from that seen by outsiders. Insiders may group themselves along connotative dimensions that escape the uninitiated and these connotative dimensions may lead some members to separate themselves from others who do denotatively similar work. This point, well established in cognitive anthropology (Goodenough, 1970; Spradley, 1979), is crucial when empirical work turns toward intensive occupational study because official occupational titles provide only a dim suggestion of where community boundaries may lie. Occupational studies that rely on Census Bureau classifications are obviously well outside our definitional limits. "Professional, technical and kindred" covers authors, draftsmen, strip tease artists and accountants; "managers, officials and proprietors" embraces political appointees, bank officials, taco vendors and chief executive officers.

Nor are commonsensical and conventionally applied occupational labels particularly helpful. Conventional labels typically represent the theoretical limit of an occupational community. Within this boundary, socially significant types (i.e., of dentists, of firefighters, of accountants, etc.) are sure to exist which are, for all practical purposes, mutually exclusive and quite distinct in the minds of the insiders. When studying occupational communities, it is to the ethnographic record a researcher must go.

Commerical fishing provides a useful example because within its boundaries are found several rather distinct occupational communities. "Traditional fishermen" recognize differences between themselves and "nontraditional fishermen" such as "educated fishermen," "part-timers," and "outlaw fishermen" (Miller & Van Maanen, 1982). Even more important are distinctions made within types. Thus, in the port of Gloucester, Massachusetts, traditional fishermen divide themselves into two groups, Guineas and Greasers.[9] Each group represents an identifiable and self-referential occupational community. Though members of both groups call themselves fishermen and exemplify the traditional approach to the trade, the two groups neither work together nor associate with one another outside of work. Both the social idealization and the practical realization of a fishing career are quite different within each group.

More familiar examples are easily located within academic settings. Consider the sub-worlds to be discovered within scholarly disciplines as catalogued by Crane's (1971) insightful mapping of "invisible colleges." Consider also the two sociologies so elegantly portrayed by Dawe (1980). In the United States, social theorists of both symbolic interactionist and structural-functional bent certainly consider themselves sociologists. Yet, the members of each theory group rarely cite work done by members of the other group (except as targets for attack), almost never collaborate on joint research projects, and interact professionally only with some difficulty. When one considers the research programs advocated in each camp, the inescapable conclusion is that whatever a symbolic interactionist is, a structural functionist is not.

The failure of well-known occupational labels to identify the bounds of

an occupational community is also aggravated by the fact that many occupations are effectively hidden from public view. Given the indefinite
number of jobs that exist and their respective distance from social researchers, superficial occupational descriptions are the norm in work
studies, not the exception. Abstractions such as "unskilled labor," "semi-
skilled labor," "manager," and even "engineer," are merely linguistic
proxies for an uncharted population of distinct occupational pursuits. Few
of us would guess that petroleum landmen share a particularly strong
occupational community because few of us would even know that petroleum landmen exist, and we certainly would not know what they do
(Bryant, 1972a).

Obscurity is not the only blinder. A greater myopia is the presumption
that our categories are actually descriptive. The muddle of research on
cosmopolitan and local orientations of so-called professionals is, in part,
the outcome of inadequately specified occupational boundaries or limits.
Not only have researchers in this domain confused "industrial scientist"
with "industrial engineer" (Glaser, 1964; Ritti, 1968), they have also failed
to recognize that worlds of engineering are differentiated by specialties
as well as by differences in the scope, type, and intent of the work that
passes as engineering in industry (Allen, 1977; Bailyn, 1980). Engineers
themselves are often unable to say what engineers do except within the
well defined setting of some company (Becker & Carper, 1956).

Abstract aggregation serves as ideology. It allows stereotypes to mas-
querade as knowledgeable descriptions. A classic example is the uncritical
acceptance of the proposition that workers in "unskilled" and "semi-
skilled" occupations lack careers or career ladders. Since some research
has shown that some "unskilled" workers (in some occupations, in some
periods, in some industries) are unlikely to follow or hope for an orderly
progression of jobs (Chinoy, 1955; Wilensky, 1961; Beynon & Blackburn,
1972), researchers extend the attribute of "career-less-ness" to an undifferentiated mass of nominally unskilled workers. This uncritical generalizing of results proceeds by reducing a heterogeneous population to
homogeneity and by discounting the probability that occupational life is
shaped by specific contexts of work. More insidiously, generalizing across
aggregates discourages particularistic research which might surface conditions under which the generalizations do not hold. Thus, so-called anomalies, such as the existence of career paths for laborers on pipeline
construction crews (Graves, 1958), for janitors in urban communities
(Gold, 1964), for steelworkers in South Chicago (Kornblum, 1974), or for
poker players in California gambling establishments (Hayano, 1982) are
unlikely to be discovered, or, when discovered, discounted as mere exceptions to the general rule.

Adequate delineation of the boundaries of occupational communities requires research strategies open to the discovery of socially meaningful work groups and methodologies that resonate to the inner cleavages of work worlds. In lieu of sufficiently detailed and phenomenologically sensitive taxonomies of occupational groupings, researchers face a dual task: the actual discovery of existing occupational communities and the depiction of the dimensions along which they are formed. The two tasks must proceed simultaneously since delimiting boundaries entails knowing the social criteria that generate them.[10]

One final point regarding boundaries concerns the territorial or geographic dispersion of the membership of an occupational community. Geographic proximity or common territory are, to many, natural indicators of community and, indeed, propinquity undergirds the use of the term "occupational community" by those researchers who employ it as a label for occupationally homogeneous towns or villages (Hill, 1981). Our use of the phrase, however, does not presume that members of an occupational community necessarily live or work near one another. Propinquity is then an attribute along which occupational communities vary. Certainly, propinquity may hasten and otherwise contribute to the development and maintenance of an occupational community, but it is not itself a definitional matter. Whether a particular community is geographically dispersed or clustered is an empirical question to be answered as communities are identified and analyzed.

Social Identity

The second definitional feature of an occupational community is that members derive valued identities or self-images directly from their occupational roles. In brief, individuals, from our perspective, carry social selves, each constructed and reconstructed in daily interaction with others as people learn to view themselves from the point of view of others (Mead, 1930; Blumer, 1969; Van Maanen, 1979). To be sure, these social selves are contextually tied, but, as they are refined and confirmed as more or less impressive and serviceable across recurrent situations, they typically enable a person to present a reasonably comfortable, consistent, and, with occasional lapses, socially acceptable image to others (Goffman, 1959).

Some social selves are, of course, more central to one's sense of identity than others. The more central the social self, the less easily modified and the more omnipresent it is in everyday interaction (Schein, 1971). In occupational communities, the social identities assumed by most members include, in a prominent position, one based upon the kind of work they do and, as such, it is often quite central in their presentations of self to others (particularly to those outside the community) in everyday life. In this sense, a person may be, among other things, a guinea fisherman, a

Catholic, and an employee for Peter Pan. Another may be a street cop, a jogger, and a mother. Individuals do not necessarily order the importance and value of such presentations (they are all important and valuable). Without question, social identities are sensitive to and reflective of the social situations to which an individual is party. But, for members of occupational communities at least, occupational identities are typically presented to others with some pride and are not identities easily discarded for they are central to an individual's self-image (Van Maanen, 1979).

Indirect evidence of identification with an occupation is demonstrated by distinctive accouterments, costumes, and jargon. Members of fishing communities wear particular types of baseball caps to tell other fishermen what port they are from and what their involvement with fishing is likely to be (Miller & Van Maanen, 1982). Police officers carry courtesy cards, off-duty revolvers, and wallet badges. The unique properties of each convey significant clues to other officers as to where the owner stands in the community (Van Maanen, 1974; Rubinstein, 1973). Bawdy urban procurers are known to drive automobiles of distinctive style and color called "pimpmobiles" (James, 1972). Electricians recognize other electricians by the color of their overalls and by the shoes they wear (Reimer, 1977). And, one needs only to catch snippets of conversation among members of an occupational community to appreciate the role special language plays (e.g., "We apprehended that dirtbag on a stand-up just next to my duck pond on 3rd and Main").

These visible identification devices serve as "tie-signs" that establish cognitive and socially verified links between person and occupation (Goffman, 1971: 194–5). More fundamentally, they represent only the most obvious of a multitude of signs that comprise a complex system of codes which enable the members of an occupation to communicate to one another an occupationally specific view of their work world. Although languages are the most versatile of all codes and may call attention to themselves when they take the form of jargon and argot, any object, event, or phenomenon becomes a part of a code, a sign, when it signifies something to someone (Pierce, 1958; Barthes, 1964). Since signs and codes are established by the conventions of a particular group and are imparted by socialization practices, any given entity can potentially carry many connotations and denotations (Hawkes, 1977; Eco, 1976). The loose and arbitrary coupling between vehicle and content implies that a particular word, object, or event can signify different meanings for people who employ different codes.

We typically assume that specialists know more than laymen because of the knowledge presumably gained by extensive training. But, differences in understanding are qualitative as well as quantitative. Expertise arises, in part, because experts and laymen employ different codes for interpreting events. Where a frustrated parent sees only an incorrigible child, the psychotherapist sees vestiges of an unresolved Oedipal conflict. Where a puzzled automobile owner hears but a strange puttering, the mechanic recognizes a missing cylinder or worn points. Becoming a member of an occupation always entails learning a set of codes that can be used to construct meaningful interpretations of persons, events, and objects commonly encountered in the occupational world.

The more pervasive, esoteric and numerous the codes employed by members of an occupation, the more likely the occupation engenders identity because the confluence of codes overdetermines a perspective on reality and overrides the plausibility of naive interpretations of the same matter (Barley, 1983). Even when on vacation, police officers see cues of wrongdoing and danger in everyday settings. Funeral directors, when out on the town, continue to monitor their demeanor (Habenstein, 1962). Psychiatrists in training practice their trade by staying diagnostically alert to the emotional and mental states of their friends and acquaintances (Light, 1980). When codes of an occupation generate such an all-bracing orientation, an occupational community is likely to be found.

The possession and use of pervasive and peculiar codes is but one factor that encourages positive identification with an occupation. Occupational identities are also fostered by high involvement in the work itself. In a study of the work worlds of graduate engineers, Lynch and Bailyn (1980) note that involvement in work implies something quite different than simply seeking or drawing satisfaction from work. Involvement implies, among other things, absorption in the symbolic nature of work so that work takes on a special significance and sets the involved apart from others who do not pursue the same livelihood in the same fashion. The sense of being apart and different underlies the development of a shared identity. Discussing the concept of community, Weber (1968: 42–43) insisted that "consciousness of kind" arises structurally and only in conjunction with "consciousness of difference."

> "A common language, which arises from a similarity of tradition through the family and surrounding the social environment, facilitates mutual understanding. . . . but, taken by itself, it is not sufficient to constitute a communal relationship. . . . it is only with the emergence of a consciousness of difference from third persons who speak a different language that the fact that two persons speak the same language and, in that respect, share a common situation, can lead them to a feeling of community and to modes of social organization consciously based on the sharing of the common language."

Ethnographically detailed research on occupations describe several factors that appear to compel special involvement with work as well as a sense of commonality and uniqueness among the members of an occupation. Danger ranks high on this list. For example, Haas (1977) documents the cameraderie, mutual regard, and intense involvement among high-steel ironworkers and attributes much of this to the constant, eminent peril that comes with working on open girders hundreds of feet above the ground. Danger also invites work involvement and a sense of fraternity among police officers and fishermen where the consequences of one simple mistake may be severe (Van Maanen, 1980b). Recognition that one's work entails danger heightens the contrast between one's own work and the safer work of others, and encourages comparison of self with those who share one's work situation. Attitudes, behavior, and self-images for coping physically and psychologically with threat become part of an occupational role appreciated best, it is thought, only by one's fellow workers. Danger spawns an insider-outsider dichotomy characteristic of communal identities (Becker, 1963; Gusfield, 1975).

A second factor encouraging involvement and identification with one's occupation occurs when members of an occupation possess (or, more properly, believe they possess) certain esoteric, scarce, socially valued, and unique abilities. Skilled tradesmen occupy separate subworlds in the construction industry because mastery of their craft licenses them (as does the state and the occupational association) to make autonomous, specialized, minute-by-minute decisions (Stinchcombe, 1959). Thus carpenters raise roofbeams and plumbers attend sinks and toilets in rather splendid isolation, despite the often frantic coordinating attempts of contractors.

The crafts and trades are often held forth as the last vestiges of occupations that encourage a sense of identity and community. But, according to the deskilling argument, technological innovations such as the numerical machine tool (Braverman, 1974; Noble, 1977) and bureaucratic controls (Johnson, 1972; Edwards, 1979) increasingly promote and permit the encoding of the craftsman's expertise and the subsequent partitioning and rationalization of trade work. A careful and detailed look at the systematic and disturbingly unilateral dismantling of several occupational communities of craftsmen in the steel industry by cost-conscious managers is provided by Stone (1979) and given theoretical meaning by Marglin (1974).

While managerially-sponsored technology may deskill some occupations, technological innovation in other settings may generate occupational communities whose members possess new forms of esoteric skill. Pettigrew's (1973) study of the installation of computers into a Scottish firm underscores the power computer programmers and systems analysts derive from their knowledge of the machine and its language. For a number of years, the programmers in Pettigrew's firm were allowed to develop work identities, a community, and customs that clashed with the managerial, staff, and production cultures in the organization simply because the programmers controlled scarce and impenetrable knowledge. Similarly, new radiological technologies, such as ultrasound, create a community of radiologists and radiological technicians who are the only individuals in the hospital capable of interpreting the meanings of images that appear to be just noise to consulting physicians. Command of such expertise has led some radiologists to assert with more than a little enthusiasm that radiology has become a crucial link in the hospital's delivery of services (Barley, forthcoming).

Rather than claim progressive deskilling and the general demise of all occupational identities and communities, a theory of occupational change modeled after the notion of speciation provides a more plausible view. As the technical expertise of some occupations becomes codified, disseminated, partitioned, grasped by outsiders, normalized and demystified, the occupational community wanes. But, at the same time, new forms of technical expertise and new occupations may arise in the wake of the old, thus creating new occupational communities. A population of occupations in a state of ebb and flow may more accurately depict historical experience. As the knowledge of computer programming becomes more widespread and uncoupled from knowledge of mathematics, programming becomes far less esoteric. At the same time, however, a new occupational identity arises to deal with the remaining indeterminacies programming entails, the systems analyst (Pettigrew, 1973). Consequently, to the degree that those pursuing a line of work manage to maintain control over a scarce set of abilities or to develop an expanded knowledge base which only they can apply, occupational identities are likely to be sustained over time, if not enhanced. These are topics we will return to in following sections for they bear directly on the definitional questions surrounding the nature of what is (and what is not) usually called professional work.

Claimed responsibility for others is a third factor promoting identification with and involvement in a line of work. The "hogsheads" (locomotive engineers) studied by Gamst (1980) believe they perform especially important work which sets them apart from other workers because the safety of the train, its passengers, and its cargo depend on their performance. Air traffic controllers, police officers, taxi drivers, nurses, and emergency medical technicians, all extoll the virtues of service as an occupational creed. In some cases, there accrues a certain reverence, awe, and prestige for those in occupations granted life-and-death responsibilities over others. Even when responsibilities are not so weighty or visible in the public eye, members of the occupation may still attempt to manufacture and maintain a sense of occupational honor through doing the public good (Hughes, 1958). Garbage collectors develop an ideology around the public health functions of their work which, in turn, may (but usually does not) provide a respectable basis for adopting the identity of sanitation worker (Lasson, 1971). When one believes that one holds a symbolic trust, identification with an occupation is facilitated.

In essence, the confrontation of danger in one's work, the possession of esoteric skills, and the belief that one does special and socially significant work provide conditions which encourage the perception that oneself and one's colleagues are somehow different from the rest of the working population. Common skills, common risks, and common adventures form the basis for a communal identity by promoting interaction with those others who "know the score" and thereby increase the probability that members of such occupations will consider themselves to be unique.

Reference Group

To maintain a social identity, support and confirmation from others is required (Mead, 1930; Goffman, 1959). The third defining feature of an occupational community is that members take other members as their primary reference group such that the membership comes to share a distinct pattern of values, beliefs, norms, and interpretations for judging the appropriateness of one another's actions and reactions.[11] This would include moral standards surrounding what work is to be considered good and bad, what work is "real work" and, therefore, in contrast to "shit work," what formal and contextual rules of conduct are to be enforced, what linguistic categories are to be used in partitioning the world, and so forth. To say an occupational community provides members with a value system is to say that members make use of a collective perspective in everyday matters, that they evaluate themselves in its light, and that such a perspective carries over to matters falling outside the realm of work itself.

Several conditions appear to foster the adoption of shared occupational values. First, when an occupation is stigmatized or viewed by outsiders as marginal in society, members will turn to one another for aid and comfort and, through such interaction, sustain a view of the world that justifies and vindicates itself as a defense against outsiders. Street sweepers in India are avoided by members of higher castes because the work they do is considered polluting. Yet, sweepers who live together in closed communities in Benares share a value system that partially compensates for the low social status of their work by positing that the very attributes feared by higher castes are, in fact, qualities to be appreciated (Searle-Chaterjee, 1979). Sweepers are likely to flaunt their untouchable status and wield it as a collective political and social weapon for securing autonomy and other occupational rewards incommensurate with their caste's status.

The solidarity of marginal or stigmatized occupations is by no means confined to societies with rigid caste systems. Becker's (1951) jazz musicians come to respect only the judgements, tastes, and perspectives of like-minded musicians. These values are predicated upon, and, at the same time create, the musicians' view of themselves as different from the "square" majority. Such aloofness and self-sealing interaction loops are also found in the high status occupations whose members are celebrated rather than stigmatized. In some cases, outsiders may even consider the occupation to be inspirational as seems to be the case with medicine and the clergy. However, we must note that the celebrated status of such occupations is contingent upon more than the presumed social problems addressed or socially valued work performed by occupational members since the celebration is both cultivated and protected by occupational members. Physicians have long sought, for example, to build and maintain a view of themselves as knights in the battle against pestilence. The current attack upon medical prestige and practice takes shape through the attempted destruction of the "myth of the healer" as promulgated by medical interest groups (e.g., Illich, 1976).

Occupations that penetrate multiple aspects of a person's life also create conditions favorable to taking members of the occupation as one's primary reference group. To maintain a career in some occupations requires adopting a particular style of life. For example, funeral directors with neighborhood-based practices understand that their work dictates the modeling of certain community and religious standards. Since advertising is considered inappropriate by local funeral directors, they rely upon their community involvement and reputation to attract clientele. Under the theory that certain kinds of behavior might offend potential clients, funeral directors present themselves with heightened personal reserve and the sort of social conservatism respectful of local traditions (Habenstein, 1962). Consequently, certain forms of public behavior, for instance, drunkenness, boisterousness, or even the relative luxury of not attending religious services regularly, are taboo not only for the funeral director but often also for his family. Moreover, the practices of providing twenty-four hour availability and living in the funeral home are widespread across the membership of the occupation. These features act as common denominators that foster a shared world view for interpreting the occupational experience (Barley, 1980). Such social conditions suggest funeral directing's similarity to other occupations whose members are required to be constantly "on" (e.g., entertainers, priests, presidents, and, arguably, college professors in small towns). Only others who face the same demands can constitute a reference group able to bolster performances and sustain the centrality of the role to the membership (Messinger et al., 1962).

Rigorous socialization is a third condition that influences members to adopt the standards of the occupational group. The ordeal-like atmosphere of the police academy draws individuals together for mutual support and creates a recruit culture within which novice police officers can interpret their experiences in ways shared by others (Van Maanen, 1973). Various occupations utilize different socialization practices, but, in general, the more harsh, formal, lengthy, and isolated the process, the more uncertain the outcome, and, the more controlled the aspirant by the social pressure of peers, the more similar the values adopted by those who pass into the occupation (Van Maanen & Schein, 1979). Elite professional schools are obvious exemplars in this regard.

Social Relations

The fourth and final attribute of an occupational community to be singled out is the blurring of the distinction between work and leisure activities within occupational communities. The melding of work and leisure may come about when leisure activities are connected to one's work or when there is extensive overlap between work and social relationships. In some occupational communities, specific leisure pursuits themselves are linked to the occupation. The connection may either be simple and intuitively obvious, or unexpected, but nonetheless regular. Both Salaman (1974) and Gamst (1980) provide examples of unsurprising links when they note that many railroaders include among their hobbies the building of model trains which are displayed to one another during recreational hours. An unexpected link is found in the case of early nineteenth century loom-weavers in London who were also widely known as botanists and entomologists, and who established a number of floricultural, historical, and mathematical societies (Braverman, 1974).

The point here lies not in the substantive nature of the tie between work and leisure, but rather in the tight network of social relations created when members of an occupation seek, for whatever reasons (e.g., pleasure, anxiety reduction, opportunistic advantage, etc.), close relationships with one another outside the workplace. As with the other defining characteristics, several conditions appear to favor the overlapping of work and social relations.

First is the degree to which members of an occupation are geographically or organizationally clustered. While physical proximity is neither a necessary nor sufficient condition for the formation of an occupational community, proximity nevertheless promotes and eases social interaction. Fishermen, police officers, prison guards and lumberjacks, for example, must work closely together and temporal considerations require them to live relatively near where they work. Neiderhoffer and Neiderhoffer (1968) report that the residences of members of some police departments are so geographically congregated that certain neighborhoods gain reputations for attracting only the police as homeowners. When the materials and resources with which an occupation operates are localized or when the majority of the residents of a vicinity are employed in the same line of work, overlap between work and social relationships becomes almost inevitable as is the case for coal miners in West Virginia or dockers in Hull, England (Hill, 1981). A similar phenomenon is apparently found among computer engineers in California's Silicon Valley and in the Boston suburbs along Route 128 (*Los Angeles Times*, July 12, 1982).

The melding of work and social relationships is also encouraged by occupations whose characteristics restrict their members' social relations. Shift work, night work, extensive travel, isolated postings, long periods of work-induced isolation followed by extended periods of leisure, all tend to mitigate opportunities for establishing friendships outside of work. Such restrictions alter time schedules so that members of the occupation are out of sync with the rhythm of a "normal" work week and must structure leisure time in ways that are at odds with the repose times of the majority of other employed persons. Cottrell (1938) and Salaman (1974) document how the enslavement of railroaders to precise time schedules, federal regulations on work hours, and variable shift work precludes the possibility of their participation in typical community and family activities. Another example of how work shapes social relations is found among New York City firefighters, many of whom frequently spend large portions of their off-duty time at station houses chatting with on-duty colleagues (Smith, 1972).

Third, occupations that are kin-based and entered by virtue of birth lead to an extensive overlap among social and work relations. Commercial fishing is an occupation where sons typically follow fathers into the line of work and all family members are, to a large degree, caught in its net (Miller & Van Maanen, 1982). One New England fisherman, when asked how he decided to enter the occupation, replied quite succinctly (and with some bemusement), "I'm a fisherman until I prove that I'm not." Funeral directing is another occupation sharing this kin-based recruitment pattern (Barley, 1980).

A final condition favorable to an overlap between work and social relationships arises through a sort of occupational intrusion into all aspects of a person's life. To paraphrase Goffman (1961), some occupations are "total work institutions." The lives of fighter pilots, submariners, intelligence officers, as well as most military personnel and their spouses come immediately to mind. Stationed on bases and encouraged to socialize only with other colleagues (of similar rank and function), occupational communities are created almost by fiat (Janowitz, 1960). But, the military is not the only example of the total work institution. Bryant (1972b) notes that carnival personnel are likely to work, eat, sleep, relax, fight, and travel with one another. Carnival people are also quite likely to intermarry and to provide collectively for on-the-road education of their children. Less exotic examples are trained counselors who hold full time, live-in positions in college residence halls. In situations where the college provides the counselors with room, board, and recreation as well as work, the counselors are most likely to establish social relations mainly with fellow counselors (Barley, 1979). In short, those who live within an occupational embrace find their work and leisure pursuits mixed in many ways and mixed so that where one ends and the other begins is a matter of some ambiguity (Kanter, 1977).

OCCUPATIONAL COMMUNITIES AS WORK CULTURES

Any outsider who observes naturally occurring conversation among self-defined members of an occupational community would quickly discover that members who have not previously met and who are of different ages, geographic regions, sexes, ethnic origins, or educational backgrounds are able to converse over a wide range of topics indecipherable by outsiders. Such is the manifestation of a shared culture. When, for example, a police officer remarks to another officer, "We didn't do any police work tonight, wrote a couple of movers and watched Stripes jump another one of our fucking calls," that officer makes substantial use of cultural materials which a listener who is familiar with such materials must make use of when assigning meaning to the remark. A description of the knowledge necessary to understand such an interaction would represent, then, a partial description of the culture. Such knowledge can never be fully explicated, in part, because it is inextricably tied to the context which gives rise to its use and, in part, because even the most astute of cultural members know that such knowledge is continually in flux and thus more than an occasional problem for cultural members themselves. From this standpoint, culture is as much a dynamic, evolving way of thinking and doing as it is a stable set of thoughts and actions.

This is not to say, however, that culture is just another variable. Culture is not something a group possesses more or less of at any given time; it is something it is. When cultures are described, meanings are central, not frequencies.[12] This is a cognitive, ideational view of culture that emphasizes, by definition, "the things a person must know to be a member of a given group" (Goodenough, 1970; 41). In occupational communities these "things" include decoding schemes for assigning meaning to the various practical routines which members engage in during the workday, as well as the typical objects, persons, places, times, and relations members encounter at work (and, often, beyond). At a deeper, interpretive level, these surface manifestations of culture reflect integrative themes or ordering assumptions held by the membership which provide for some commonality and connection across specific domains of thought and action (Geertz, 1973). In the police world, for example, an "asshole" is a technical term used by officers to signify those citizens believed to be out to provoke and embarrass the police in routine social interaction (Van Maanen, 1978). The use of such a term (and others of like ilk) is premised upon the police officers' taken-for-granted assumptions regarding just what is and is not proper and orderly social interaction with members of the public (i.e., an interaction initiated, directed, and terminated by the police, not the citizen). Cultures vary, therefore, on the basis of differing meaning systems. To compare cultures is to compare codes and assumptions which give rise to behavioral and cognitive diversity.

Occupational communities, as we have suggested, transmit to new members shared occupational practices, values, vocabularies, and identities. More to the point, such cultural transmission transcends specific organizational settings since members who are widely dispersed and unfamiliar with one another display similar understandings and attitudes toward the work they do. Although, as we will discuss, occupational communities penetrate and are certainly penetrated in various ways by employing organizations, they are to be sharply distinguished from other work cultures—such as the much discussed organizational ones—on several grounds.[13]

Members of occupational communities are favorably oriented toward their jobs and careers. To them, work is more than merely "making a living;' it is a source of meaning and value. The secretaries and office workers studied by Benet (1972) certainly possess both an identity and a distinct work culture within the confines of their employing organization, but neither do they value the identity nor is the culture much more than a set of responses to specific managerial practices of the office. It is a "culture of resistance" based upon opposition to subordinate position and status within a given organization. Our hypothetical "hind-toe-removers" presumably check their social identities and cultures of reference at the gate when entering the slaughterhouse in the morning and pick them up again when leaving in the evening. While they may partake of a work or organization culture while on the job, the centrality of that

culture to their life outside the workplace is minimal. There are social
identities (held at a distance) involved here, but the flow of identities and
interests is from outside into the workplace. For those in occupational
communities, the flow is reversed.[14]

Individual status within occupational communities is, in the abstract,
based on displayed skill and performance of those tasks most members
consider essential to the occupation. Member judgements on such matters
are based on historically developed standards which represent definitions
of proper (and, by implication, improper) occupational practice. In this
sense, a "culture of achievement" exists in occupational communities,
not a "culture of advancement" so often reported in studies of organizations and their managers (e.g., Dalton, 1959). Segmentation and specialization are, to be sure, found in occupational communities, as are
hierarchies, but whatever segmentation, specialization, or hierarchical
distinctions are to be found have origins within, not without, the community and, therefore, reflect the performance standards of the membership. In the ideal, only the members dictate how their labor is to be
organized.

To the extent that the occupation and the bundle of tasks and interactions it involves are matters held in high regard by members of occupational communities, one would expect the membership to lay claim to
control the work they do. In essence, occupational communities are premised upon the belief that only the membership possesses the proper knowledge, skills, and orientations necessary to make decisions as to how the
work is to be performed and evaluated. Here lies the core of the matter,
for it is obvious some occupational communities (notably the so-called
free professions and, to a lesser extent, the established trade associations
and unions) have been more successful than others in creating, maintaining, and protecting a distinctive and relatively autonomous culture.
Self-control of occupational matters is then the key variable upon which
distinctions among occupational communities are to be made. Self-control
refers to the occupational community's ability to dictate who will and will
not be a member, as well as how the content and conduct of a member's
work will be assessed. The grounds upon which such self-control is based
are numerous, complicated, and constantly problematic for the membership. Four particularly crucial (yet relatively general) obstacles to occupational self-control are evident.[15]

Service to Management

If service to organizational officials who are not occupational community members is a condition of employment, occupational self control
decreases. Self-employment or employment within an occupationally-

based organization such as is found in certain legal practices, trade unions, public service agencies, and medical groups increases occupational self-control. The matter is not, however, quite so straightforward. For example, many studies have noted that management goals are not necessarily exclusive of those rooted in an occupation (e.g., Montagna, 1973; Schreisheim, et al., 1977). To wit, certain kinds of engineers often discover that their collective aims and identities can be satisfied only within large, heteronomous organizations where sufficient resources to pursue occupationally-valued ends are to be found (Scott, 1965; Harlow, 1973; Brown, 1981). Many public service organizations, such as hospitals, maintain separate administrative and occupational hierarchies thus allowing occupational values to be served alongside organizational ones (Freidson, 1970). In both cases, members of the respective occupational communities retain substantial self control over their work, even though many of them are located well down the formal chain of command in the organization.

From this perspective, self control is problematic to members of an occupational community only when organizational officials seek to impose certain "outsider" standards, goals, work tasks, evaluative schemes, and so forth upon the membership. In and of itself, hierarchy is not an issue. It is the use of hierarchical authority to direct member activities in ways the membership considers untoward that presents the problem and threat to self control. Such a threat and its realization may vary, of course, by the organizational position held by an occupational community member. For example, there is apparently substantial autonomy for many senior accountants in business corporations. For these highly placed accountants, occupational values and standards play a large role in their everyday activities (and may influence even the direction of the firm itself). But, much less autonomy exists for accountants at the junior and lower levels of the same corporations who may, to their chagrin, find themselves performing organizationally dictated, highly regimented bookkeeping functions which provide little opportunity to exercise valued occupational skills (Montagna, 1973). Such tasks are held in low regard, perhaps contempt, by community members, even though, within an administrative frame of reference, the performance of such tasks provides an important service to management.

More generally, self control for employees within any organization varies by employment opportunities elsewhere (Hirschman, 1970). For members of occupational communities, opportunities to engage in solo practice or in highly specializaed organizations promoting occupational interests are no doubt important conditions that help sustain the very norms and identities which constitute the community. Such opportunities provide an exit option to members who are displeased with the way their skills are being utilized by an organization. The more limited such opportunities, the more community members must bend their occupational standards to organizational interests and whims.

Finally, we must note that loyalty and tenure considerations may dampen the value of self control for members of organizational communities who remain in a given organization for long periods of time. External labor value typically decreases with age (e.g., Bloch & Kuskin, 1978). Thus occupational mobility of the sort requiring organizational shifts may be restricted to younger, more recently trained, and (perhaps most crucially) cheaper members of the community (Pfeffer, 1983). The so-called "golden handcuffs" associated with many long tenure organizational careers represent telling examples in this regard. The point here is that such handcuffs signify ties to an organization and its managerially-designed reward systems rather than ties to an occupation and its member-designed reward systems. To the degree that service to management provides unique and valued rewards that are believed to surpass those obtainable through service to the occupation, the importance of self control to occupational members will undoubtedly lessen.

Theory and Procedure in Occupational Practice

If an occupational community is able to maintain a relative monopoly over its theory and procedures, self control will be maintained. If other groups secure access to such knowledge, self control is reduced (Child & Fulk, 1982). Both theory and procedure have explicit (i.e., cognitive) and implicit (i.e., skill) components. These components and their interaction are vital elements when accounting for the mandate occupational communities are able to manufacture and sustain within a society as well as within an organization.

The cognitive base of an occupation represents declarative sorts of knowledge such as facts, descriptions, and technologies. Since declarative knowledge is rule-based, it can be transmitted by word of mouth or by print. Although it may be complex, scientific in origin, and take years to master, it is, in principles, subject to codification. In contrast, skill is fluid and, to outsiders at least, mysterious. Skill is akin to what is called "know-how" and is represented by what acknowledged experts in all fields are demonstrably able to do but are often unable or unwilling to precisely describe (Roberts et al., 1966). For example, cab drivers in Boston know that direct traffic has the right of way over vehicles making left-hand turns in an intersection. This is a cognitive or declarative matter. But, these cab drivers also know when there is just enough time for them to "safely" make left-hand turns before the next approaching car enter the collision zone. That cab drivers skirt collisions in most instances is a result of perceptual understanding, aggressive motor behaviors, and probably sheer nerve, all of which are learned by experience. Such skill defies description by general rule. To build on Polanyi's (1966:4) much quoted line, cab drivers "know more than they can (or will) tell."[16]

This distinction is helpful when considering how occupational self-control is amplified or reduced. On one hand, the larger the cognitive component and the more rapid the rate at which it grows, the more likely occupational self-control will be sustained. On the other hand, the cognitive component is, in the ideal, available to others since it can be codified (Child & Fulk, 1982). The recent spate of books on do-it-yourself divorce, the at-home pregnancy test, the design-your-own home handbook, or complete-idiot's-guide to television repair are all mundane examples of domains in which occupational communities have potentially lost a degree of self-control. Perhaps more seriously, Oppenheimer (1973) and Haug (1975, 1977) have claimed that computer technology is hastening the "proletarianization of the professions" since it enables non-experts to utilize expert techniques by virtue of electronic storage and retrieval of professional routines. Hence, the central question in terms of self-control over the cognitive component of occupational practice concerns the pace at which new knowledge is being acquired and monopolized by community members relative to the rate at which old knowledge is being standardized and dispersed.

Regarding the procedural knowledge contained within an occupational community, self-control can be threatened by damaging public disclosures which reveal practices most members would prefer to keep private. Boston taxi drivers notwithstanding, demystification of certain occupational practices is always possible and various forms of muckraking can be of serious consequence. The threat is even more serious when an occupation is shown to have claimed skill when, in fact, little skill has been exercised (or, perhaps, even needed). For example, proposals for Civilian Review Boards seem to follow police scandals, and political intrusions into welfare agencies are apparently generated whenever documented claims reveal a large number of "welfare cheats." To the degree an occupational community is able to conduct its business in private, train and license its members relatively free from the scrutiny of audiences not of its choosing, and maintain the strong loyalties of its members so that even the disenchanted are unlikely to speak publicly, its sacred procedural knowledge is relatively secure. But, like Toto pulling on the Wizard of Oz's curtain, when "know-how" is made public, the show may be damaged. All occupational communities rely on ill-defined procedures and techniques as the sort of mystical heart of the practice, a heart that, to keep beating, must remain protected.

The two knowledge forms of an occupational community are linked together in intriguing ways. Typically, the greater the cognitive base, the more skill required to put such cognitive matters into practice and the more distant both become to lay actors outside the community. Thus, even if non-members become users of well developed occupational practices, they may still turn to a community member at some point, if only for simple assurance that their use has been proper and in accord with community standards. Thus, even when not legally required to do so, some highly skilled do-it-yourself home builders turn to professional contractors to inspect the results of their work (Glaser, 1972). In this sense, the demand for cognitive or technical knowledge may decrease, but the occupational community remains unaffected because the demand for skill and the judgemental prerogatives associated with recognized procedural knowledge remain fixed. Transactions in such instances are based on the provision of sanctioning evaluations rather than the provision of direct labor. In this manner, the uncertainty and indeterminacy surrounding "know-how" protects occupational self-control.

Market Structure

All else being equal (certainly the exception in social life), the more visible, organized, and homogeneous the market to which an occupational community is linked, the less self-control will be held by that community. The more isolated, individualized, and heterogeneous the market, the greater the self-control. Submissiveness of client or consumer groups is a central characteristic of many occupational communities which have developed strong self-control mandates. The patient vis-à-vis the doctor (Freidson, 1970), the accused vis-à-vis the public defender (Sudnow, 1965), the bereaved vis-à-vis the funeral director (Mitford, 1969) all stand as good examples. Far less self-control is found among commercial fishermen operating within monopsonistic markets comprised of a few large fish buyers (Van Maanen, et al., 1982). Teachers possess relatively less self-control when employed by homogeneous rather than heterogeneous school districts (Lortie, 1974).

There are, of course, some ironies involved with this relationship. One concerns the asymmetry of authority between an occupation and its marketplace. The more direct and transparent the occupational community's effect on consumers or clients, the more likely those consumer or clients will themselves organize as a means of mediating such effects (Child & Fulk, 1982). The growing movement toward socialized medicine and legislation establishing health service organizations represent good examples in this regard, for both developments attempt to limit the autonomy of physicians and hospitals. The dialectic is also amplified because as client submissiveness declines. members of an occupational community may further solidify behind a common front. A sort of "us-versus-them" stance is one result and a struggle for control ensues. Again, medicine provides the case in point. Where consumers or clients have no alternatives to highly valued products or services, the struggle is likely to be lengthy and highly charged.

State Control

Occupational self-control varies directly with the degree to which the state sanctions such control. Self-control of an occupation is sought in part because members deem it just, and in part because it serves the cause of upward social mobility for the occupational community as a whole. Occupational communities lobby directly and indirectly to gain control of relevant market segments via state intervention. The state intervenes in matters of vital interest to an occupation. Consider the funding of training programs, the limitations set upon the size of an occupational community, work and safety standards, the providing of direct employment in the public sector, the setting (or not setting) of cost and price guidelines for products and services, the provision of payments for occupational work, and numerous other interventions as examples of state-directed activities that significantly influence the amount of self-control available to members of an occupational community. Mystique may erode, clients may revolt, cognitive dimensions of practice may be codified and widely distributed, and organizational managers and owners may be the prime beneficiaries of occupationally-produced goods or services, but if the state chooses to protect an occupational community by granting it, in effect, a legal monopoly on practice, self-control will stubbornly persist. The traditional professions of law and medicine are reminders of just how crucial a role the state plays in providing for occupational self-control (Johnson, 1972). In effect, the distinction of having an occupation rather than having a job or position is that those with an occupation potentially can call on sources of legitimacy for their work performances other than those offered by the employing organization. When these sources are backed up and certified by the state, legitimacy and self-control are virtually synonymous.

CAREERS OF OCCUPATIONAL COMMUNITIES

We have argued thus far that occupational communities represent bounded work cultures populated by people who share similar identities and values that transcend specific organizational settings. Moreover, self-control is a prominent cultural theme in all occupational communities, although its realization is highly problematic. Occupational communities vary with respect to how much self-control they have been able to carve out. The more self-control possessed by an occupational community, the more distinct and self-perpetuating its culture. Although occupational communities hermetically sealed off from a society would be impossible to find, occupational communities can be arrayed on a continuum of self-control. The differing values, practices, ideologies, and selected identities associated with each represent strategic choices exercised within a community as to how best to present itself and exert occupational control.

Much historical and sociological work documents the rise and fall of occupations, the sources of prestige and status among occupations, and changes in the occupational structure within a society.[17] This work highlights how occupations have gained varying degrees of self-control. Unionization and professionalization are prominent strategies in this regard since each presumably promotes the interests of the collective over time. They are bootstrapping tactics used by some occupational communities (sometimes simultaneously, sometimes separately) to enhance the collective career of the membership (Van Maanen, 1976).

Unionization is a means of modifying and reducing the degree to which members of an occupation employed in organizational contexts are directed and controlled by the non-occupational members of an organization. Although unionization is frequently associated with an ideology stressing occupational control over the work its members perform, this ideology must not be accepted uncritically. Unions are hardly identical in either form or function. For example, in the United States at least, unionization trends has been toward consolidated unions, such as the United Auto Workers, which claim to speak for a diversity of occupational groups. Such diversity may well interfere with the interests of distinct occupational communities contained within umbrella-like unions.

On the other hand, some unions, such as the International Typographical Union or the United Mine Workers, appear to be organized as occupational associations whose members share similar occupational interests. Thus, the more similar the tasks performed by union members, the more likely the union itself promotes the special concerns of an occupational community, including self-control. To paraphrase Hirschman's (1971) catchy terms, such unions offer to members of occupational communities "voice" rather than "exit" as a way of influencing where, when, how, for whom, and for what rewards their work is to be provided. Once unionization is itself achieved, it may become the means by which the community can monopolize and protect areas of expertise, control its labor market, and attain upward social mobility. This is, at least, the promise, if not the reality, of most single-occupation unionization campaigns.

More generally, the primary mission of unions concerns the well-being of its membership. As institutionalized through collective bargaining in the United States, unions are involved in determining the terms and conditions of employment which bear on job satisfaction (Dunlop, 1958). When these terms are defined to include policies governing the content and quality of products and services provided by the members of an occupational community as well as the more traditional bread-and-butter issues, then the union is essentially involved in promoting the occupational norms and mission within the society. When successful, the career of the community is itself furthered. Consider, for example, the potential status and position of American auto workers were they able to bargain with management over the poor quality of American cars. Hence, we are suggesting, along with Haug and Sussman (1973), that the presumed antithesis between normative commitments to service or quality and the so-called bread-and-butter functions of labor unions are largely a fiction (even though, in practice, the bread-and-butter concerns are often traded off against normative concerns).

Professionalization is a process serving goals similar to those of unionization. The traditional, and what Turner and Hodge (1970) have called the "formal organization" approach to the study of the professions, holds that professions are somehow quite different from other occupations.[18] Typically, advocates of this approach propose a set of attributes or traits which define the difference (Carr-Sanders & Wilson, 1933; Greenwood, 1957; Vollmer & Mills, 1966). Though the trait lists vary by author, four attributes found on all lists are: (1) possession of a substantive body of knowledge imparted to novices through systematic training; (2) formation of an occupational association which certifies practitioners; (3) societal recognition of the occupation's authority and (4) a service orientation articulated by a code of ethics.

The critique of a separate sociology of the professions has been intensified of late and it is one of some strength (Johnson, 1972; Roth, 1974; Larson, 1977; Klegon, 1979). In essence, the trait approach to the professions has been examined closely and comes up wanting. From the vantage point of the critique, professions are not distinct because of the sterling personal qualities of their membership or the attributes of the work their members perform, but because of the success those self-defined professionals have had in claiming occupational self-control. For example, Johnson (1972) holds that the professions represent a peculiar form of social control in which the producers define the needs of the consumers. Larson (1977) argues that a profession is merely the end state in a process of upward social mobility for a collective wherein the producers eventually come to monopolize the market for their expertise. Freidson (1970) bluntly suggests that a profession contrasts to other occupations only in that it has been given the right by the state to control its own work. Moreover, the critics note that trait approaches to the professions must take for granted the separate and distinct status of a particular line of work since, by definition, such approaches seek to uncover features of the work (or its membership) which will justify the ascribed, yet unquestioned, status. Wittingly or unwittingly, such approaches and the self-referential tropes they employ provide symbolic support for professional uniqueness, an argument which clearly furthers the self-interest of any line of work called professional (Roth, 1974; Whittington, 1982).

Even more crucially, the list of traits which comprise the ideal type of profession have been shown to be empirically suspect. For example, even in the most revered of professions, medicine, recent research questions the effectiveness and even existence of colleagual control (Millman, 1979; Bosk, 1979). Other studies suggest that the attributed characteristics of the clientele are at least as significant in terms of treatment as any universalistic or scientific methods of diagnosis and therapy (Freidson, 1970; Bucher & Strauss, 1961). Altruistic norms of public service have also been severely questioned when examinations of pay schedules, geographical distribution of licensed physicians, or medical review practices dealing with surgical mistakes have been undertaken (Glaser, 1970; Garfield, 1970; Millman, 1979). At best, trait theories such as those surrounding the definition of medicine as a profession suggest not what the profession is, but what it pretends to be (Hughes, 1951).

When researchers examine what professionals actually do in everyday life to negotiate and sustain their special positions, a rather different perspective emerges. We find that the normative attributes are important to professional practice and practitioners, but they are important because they are used (with more or less success) as arguments and accounts to legitimize professional self-control.[19] Like members of many other occupations, those considered professionals have sought to free themselves from administrative control, to secure the sanctity of their theory and procedures, and to control the market structure they face so as to secure occupational autonomy. If the professions can be set apart from other occupational groups it is because their vaunted autonomy is ultimately secured by the grace of the state, a grace which requires massive and continual nurturing and monitoring through legal and political processes. From this standpoint, professions exercise self-control largely because of their state-protected monopoly on conditions of practice, the knowledge upon which such practice rests, and the right to control entrance to and exit from the profession.

Even with state support, the maintenance of market control is not to be blindly assumed. For example, demand itself must be generated and sustained. Further challenges may arise when the consumers of the service attempt to counterbalance monopolistic authority over the delivery of services. Moreover, when a profession's performance no longer meets the values and needs of the society that suffers it, the demise of that profession is but a matter of time (Bledstein, 1976). This is merely to say that social change has numerous implications, some of them of enormous impact, upon professional status and practice within a society. Successful revolutionaries who initiate their regimes by exporting (or worse) the lawyers of the old order provide a pointed reminder of just how dependent the professions are upon the good will and tolerance of the society of which they are a part.

Even within the professions, challenges to occupational self-control will appear as new specialties are created alongside the old. As Freidson (1970) points out, there is a continuous process of occupational differentiation within all professions. At any given time, wide discrepancies of status and rewards exist such that any one profession (even with its institutional support systems, its self-administered code of ethics, and its professional schools and associations) is a mix of many occupations and occupational communities. As new technologies and approaches evolve, new groups of practitioners who understand and promote the innovations arise to challenge the authority and control of the communities within whose domain the service previously lay. Again, medicine provides an example with its enormous number of specialties and keen competition among them for clients and intra-professional status. Bucher and Strauss (1961) provide the key words: "Professions are loose amalgamations of diverse segments pursuing different manners, and more or less held together under a common name in a particular period of history."

Three points are to be drawn from our discussion thus far. First, a profession is not an occupational community per se, although some of its subdivisional units or specialties may be. Second, and far more important, the professions are not to be considered as a class apart from other occupations. The notion of a profession is one of those seemingly natural concepts fraught with unexamined ideological baggage that has penetrated much organizational and occupational research. Too often researchers simply accept a profession's own definition and image of itself without examining what uses are to be found behind such definitions and images. Third and finally, the process of professionalization must be understood as but one path by which occupational communities may gain self-control. There are no fundamental distinctions to be found between a profession and an occupation which are inherent in the work itself.

These points suggest that both professionalization and unionization can be considered strategies for advancing the collective career of an occupational community (or a collection of related communities). The difference between unionization and professionalization is, therefore, one of means, not ends. The distinction between the two strategies hinges, first, upon the degree to which an occupation attempts to trade on its special knowledge and, second, the degree to which an occupation faces organized opposition when attempting to assert its independence and establish the legitimacy of self-control. The values and ideologies supporting each process reflect choices about how occupational self-control can best be gained and guarded rather than any deep discontinuities of purpose.

An example of the similarities and the differences between these two processes is provided by the so-called "New Unionism" or "Professional Unions" (Jessup, 1978). Such hybrid associations have developed in the wake of what Mechanic (1976) calls the "bureaucratization of the professional." Particularly in public services, members of relatively high-status occupational communities have tried to unionize as a way of confronting managerial decrees seen to violate member standards of proper conduct (Fielding & Portman, 1980). While relatively narrow economic self interest are most certainly relevant, control over the work itself is nonetheless also a prominent objective for members of professional unions. For example, after citing the slogan "social work, not paperwork," one nationally prominent arbitrator observed in a somewhat shocked, if not outraged fashion: "What is really happening in public service is that the sovereignty argument has now been transferred to the scope of bargaining questions" (Rock, 1968, quoted in Mendes, 1982).[20]

Unionization or professionalization are, of course, not always achieved. As the bloody history of organized labor in the United States makes clear, the processes are political and full of uncertainty and strife. Professionalization, when realized, is perhaps the more powerful and convincing form of self-control in this country since groups opposing professionalization tend (historically) to be relatively unorganized and of lesser status than those comprising the occupational community seeking the professional label and its symbolic protection. Professionalization may also be a somewhat cleaner, less visible struggle, fought mainly by mannered proxies on the floors of courtrooms and government agencies rather than by angry members of an occupation on the docks or in the mines. Moreover, conventional use of the professional label in the United States usually connotes "sacred" attributes such as rationality, public service, and disinterest rather than "profane" attributes such as economic expediency, corruption, and self-interest often associated with the term "union" in this society (Hill, 1981).[21]

In this regard, it is interesting to examine strategies utilized by some occupational communities currently attempting to convince relevant audiences that its members should be accorded professional status. As we have previously argued, the so-called traits of a profession provide resources for such purposes. However, it appears that new traits are also being added to the old list. One new trait, stress, is worth considering in some detail since it currently seems to be achieving some notoriety as a mark of occupational status and, therefore, serves nicely as an example of how any given trait can be used to further occupational ends.

The notion of job stress, particularly when used in the context of public service jobs, is a perfect vehicle to convey the symbolic virtues of an occupation not yet recognized as professional. Good examples of occupations that have strategically embraced stress include: police service, nursing, air traffic controlling, public school teaching, firefighting, and social work. While Merton's (1949) notion of "sociological ambivalence" and Goode's (1960) idea of "role strain" are of some merit in understanding the sociological sources of stress, they are less valuable in understanding the occupational practice of making stress claims. Terry (1981b), in an examination of selected occupational literatures, found nearly ten times the number of articles dealing with job stress in police and nursing periodicals than in comparative periodicals of law and medicine.[22] Since stress in all these occupations is said to arise largely from the responsibility occupational members carry for alleviating other people's misery, the question must be raised as to why the nurses and the police are claiming stress and the doctors and lawyers are not. Both occupational pairs work in similar domains with similar clients. If anything, doctors and lawyers carry more of a burden for the fate of their clients than do nurses or police officers. Were stress keyed only to the work performed by occupational members, a reversal of such claims would be expected. It appears then, that stress is relatively more important (and useful) to the bootstrapping occupations than to those occupations already established at the top of the reward and recognition ladder.

Empirical investigations of claims of occupational stress lend credence to its largely symbolic nature for one finds little systematic evidence to document the alleged consequences of stress. For example, in the police world, the results of stress are thought to be job dissatisfaction, chronic alcoholism, high divorce rates, suicide, and a veritable laundry list of mild to serious physiological ailments. But, as Terry (1981a) shows, these claims have been highly exaggerated. Turnover in police agencies is quite low and police officers do not display high levels of job dissatisfaction; cardiovascular disease is high, but lower than the incidence rate among music teachers, transportation workers, cooks, and firefighters; divorce is lower than the national average, as is (in most cities) police suicide; alcoholism does not seem to be out of line with other occupational groups of comparable economic and social standing. Most important perhaps is the fact that any and all stress claims made by the police are notoriously difficult to document.

Whether or not stress (and its consequences) is an objective condition of the work in these ambitious occupational communities is, for our purposes, less important than its presence or absence in public discourse and its conscious employment as a means of achieving occupational goals including greater self-control. We are not suggesting, however, that by emphasizing stress an occupation will magically be granted greater reward, recognition, and self-control. Stress may, in fact, be more important internally as a way of sharing common problems and increasing the sense of fellowship among members. Externally, stress stands as an indicator of a larger family of occupational claims (e.g., service goals, responsibility for other people's problems, personal sacrifice, bureaucratic interference or indifference) residing under the sacred canopy of "being called to a set of higher ideals." Such a canopy cannot be conjured up on claims alone. As Hughes (1958) and many others have pointed out, there also needs to be widespread agreement among the public regarding the importance of the occupational service, some consensus surrounding the validity of the occupation's claim to be able to provide such a service, and, perhaps most importantly, no real or perceived alternative sources for the performance of the service. These are indeed powerful constraints and, as the police and other public servants—such as those who once served in the now-defunct Association of Air Traffic Controllers—have discovered, they are not easily bypassed.

CAREERS IN OCCUPATIONAL COMMUNITIES

Although the careers of individual members of occupational communities are clearly affected by the fortunes of the community within the larger occupational structure of society, individual careers are also based upon processes of attainment existing within the communities themselves. In this section, we are concerned with individual careers as they are played out within specific occupational boundaries, holding at bay, for the moment, the question of just how occupational communities themselves fare within organizational marketplaces.

The idea of a career necessarily imputes coherence and order to a sequence of experiences, roles, statuses, or jobs. Attributions of coherence underlie every formal definition of a career that makes of it something more than a job history (e.g., Becker & Strauss, 1956:253; Glaser, 1968:1; Wilensky, 1961:251; Goffman, 1961b:128, Slocum, 1966:5; Hall, 1976:3). But, since work careers are constructed from contextual and historical particulars, the particulars attain coherence only when viewed against some backdrop or setting. Beyond the conspicuous setting of an organization, careers can be played out against such backdrops as an occupation (Hughes, 1958), a family life cycle (Schein, 1978), a social category or label (Goffman, 1961; Becker, 1963), an internal standard such as a "career anchor'' (Schein, 1978), and so forth. These backdrops not only direct and constrain the visible path of a person's "external" career, they also provide tasks, colleagues, symbols, and ideologies that influence the individual's subjective construction of an "internal" career—the meaning a person attributes to the sequence of work-related experiences that comprise the career.[23]

The indispensability of understanding the context within which a person's career is played out is underscored by two frequently-made academic points (academic in the sense that they are points alarmingly overlooked when career research is undertaken). First, the career setting noticed by the observer may not be the one used by the person in the career. It is not, for example, readily apparent that all who work in an organization consider their careers in organizational terms. Industrial scientists are certainly employed in organizational contexts, but they may well measure their careers against the backdrop of their specialties (Marcson, 1960; Kornhauser, 1962; Ritti, 1968). Academics, too, belong to organizations, but evidence suggests that some see themselves in the context of their scholarly fields (Caplow & McGee, 1958; Gouldner, 1957). Second, when constructing careers, people may make use of several backdrops, sometimes simultaneously and sometimes sequentially (Van Maanen, 1980a; Kanter, 1979).

Recent career research and theory is tied to the experiences of people occupying a relatively small set of organizationally-defined positions (Sonnenfeld & Kotter, 1982). In particular, managers and administrators receive most of the attention. These positions carry career lines defined largely in terms of hierarchical advancement. In fact, many current terms and descriptive cliches found in discussions of careers only make sense when the relevance of an organization's hierarchy is presumed. "Plateauing," "up or out," "demotion," "lateral move," "fast track," and "career ladder" are understandable only when juxtaposed to the vertical dimension of organizations. But, if one is to regard U.S. Department of Labor Statistics (1980) as an authoritative source, only 12 percent of the labor force is counted as currently occupying managerial or administrative posts.

What is troubling about considering vertical mobility within an organization to be the centerpiece of career research is the accompanying tendency to deny careers to be a substantial portion of the working population. Consider the following examples:

> With reference to occupational careers in organizations, the theoretical model involves entry into a position that requires the performance of occupational duties at the lowest rung of the occupational ladder. This is followed by a sequence of promotions into higher-level positions within an organization, leading eventually to the pinnacle, and finally to retirement. Although this generalized model calls for upward

progression from the bottom to the top, we know that not every entrant moves through all these steps. There are thus varying degrees of conformity to the model . . .

(Slocum, 1966:5)

Occupational careers that conform reasonably well to the model are restricted to professionals, managers, skilled craftsmen and a few others . . . this does not mean the concept of career has no relevance for the study of other occupations. However, it has little utility for the study of unskilled occupations or others that do not provide differentiated steps or grades.

(Slocum, 1966:226)

Individuals may work at a series of activities during their lives, but with no perception that they follow a career path. We might speak of the career of a dentist or an accountant, but we would hardly speak of the career of a dishwasher or a hospital orderly. Unless the person and the containing social structure see some relation between the activities, there is no career.

(Braude, 1975:112)

One wonders if it would not be more appropriate for Slocum and Braude to question their models than to default an unknown but obviously large percentage of the working population from the universe of career holders.[24] A key to how career theorists circumscribe career's domain of reference lies in what Braude calls the "containing social structure." We suppose what is meant by this term is something akin to an organization or a set of reasonably high(er) status actors (managers) who are deemed fit to "see some relation between the activities" and "the career." If we accept an upwardly mobile, white collar, organizational model of the career, then it is true that few people will have careers simply because most people work at the base of organizational pyramids. Given that positions decrease as one ascends a pyramid, even if we are willing to grant the liberal assumption that promotions are handed out randomly, the probability of a person being promoted decreases rapidly the closer that person is to the pyramid's base. Rosenbaum (1979) estimates the probability that non-management personnel will be promoted in a large utility company peaks at age 35 at one in five. Afterwards, the probability of promotion decreases exponentially.

An organizational model of career may simply be inappropriate for the majority of the labor force. An alternative model would be to consider the "containing social structure" of a career to be the social context which the worker considers most proximal. Hence, a career's backdrop is the standard by which the career holder measures the career, not the standard of the observer. Although potential contexts for constructing a career are probably numerous and certainly particularistic, consider how careers might be constructed within the context of an occupational community.

One striking feature associated with the work-specific illustrations we have thus far emphasized as more or less meeting the definitional requirements of an occupational community is that for many of them there are few hierarchical levels or offices of authority to which members might aspire. Although crew members may specialize in particular tasks, traditional fishermen are, with the exception of the captain of a boat and perhaps his eldest son, of essentially equal status (Miller & Van Maanen, 1982).[26] Musicians in orchestras may change chairs or join a major symphony, but their movement is across lines of skill and prestige and does not entail the formal accrual of power and authority over others in the occupational line (Faulkner, 1974). The careers of police officers are relatively flat. Only a very few patrol officers reach the rank of sergeant during their police careers, and those who do find themselves distrusted and considered outside the occupational community comprised of their former colleagues (Van Maanen, forthcoming). The tag "steady state" career used by Driver (1981:9–10) nicely captures some key elements of work careers in occupational communities:

> The steady state concept refers to a view of careers in which one makes an early commitment to a field and holds it for life. There may be minor changes . . . and inner growth of competence in one's field leading to some upward movement, but the essential thing is a fixed identity within a field.

Schein's (1971, 1978) model of an organization provides a dimension of particular interest when careers in occupational communities are examined. Though originally applied to the task of describing organizational careers, the model is applicable to many social settings (Van Maanen & Schein, 1979). The model uses three dimensions to describe a person's location in an organization. The three dimensions are hierarchy, function, and inclusion.[25] When considering occupational communities, of most interest is the third dimension, inclusion.[26]

Persons who move toward greater inclusion gain centrality within the network of community members. They may attain special privileges, increased rewards, become privy to secrets about "how things really work," and gain heightened respect from community members. Individuals who have achieved visible centrality in the community are often identified by the labels or folk types used by members to note occupational wisdom. The "sage," "pro," "guru," "old hand," and legendary "old timer" are stereotypes in this regard. As these social types suggest, centrality can carry prestige, honor, knowledge, and power.

Penetration toward a more central position in an occupation involves one or more of what Glaser and Strauss (1971) call "status passages." All occupations provide for a period of training and testing during which neophytes are taught (and usually learn) the "rules of the game" while their willingness to play by these rules is scrutinized by their more experienced workmates (Van Maanen, 1980a). For example, newcomers may be assigned "dirty work" as a way of having their mettle tested to reveal any character flaws, or as a way of testing their commitment to the occupation or work group. The period of testing and training may be informal and unplanned or highly structured and formalized. Both can be rigorous. Haas (1977) offers a witty account of how high-steel workers are informally taught to maintain a front of fearlessness while remaining keenly aware of the danger of the work. The testing process includes "binging," a barrage of barbed and crude insults slung at recruits by veteran ironworkers as a way of ascertaining the emotional calm and physical dexterity of novices on high steel.

Psychiatrists, during the early phases of training, are assigned the so-called hopeless cases as a way of "socializing them to failure", according to Light (1980). Other apprenticeship periods may compel the green recruit to do distasteful service as the butt of community pranks or as the unwitting scapegoat for mistakses made by others. Whenever special skills and complex role behaviors are central components of occupational responsibility, relatively intense induction programs are likely to be present (whether by design or accident). It makes little difference how special and complex such role behaviors are relative to others or how central such behaviors are in the actual occupational scheme of things; what is crucial is that members consider them to be special, complex, and central.

Beyond the status passages that occur during the early periods of occupational learning, we find ourselves in poorly charted domains.[27] Precisely what steps lead to more or less centrality in occupational communities are unclear. Some occupational communities such as certain medical specialties, legal practices, and craft associations, have well formulated boundaries through which members pass as they move toward the inner circles. Some occupational communities are premised on a sort of downward slide where members enter (or achieve at a very early phase) centerstage, obtaining a more central position in the occupation than they will every again occupy. Modeling, prostitution, and professional athletics provide worhty examples in this regard. In other occupational communities, the transitions in or out may be smooth, occurring in nearly invisible ways.

Since any of these alternatives are feasible, the pattern holding for a given occupational community is an empirical matter on which data are scarce. It is possible, however, to extract from the literature on work and occupations at least three domains of involvement through which members of an occupational community conceivably attain centrality as seniority and work experience accumulate. The three domains are: the work itself; the setting(s) in which the work is performed; and the network of social relations which surround the work. Consider each in turn.

The Work Itself.   Members of some occupational communities attain centrality by acquiring reputations for expertise. Such recognition may accompany the invention or mastery of more advanced technique, knowledge, and skill; the accumulation of experience with a variety of work situations and the acquisition of a repository of occupational wisdom; or, the development of finesse, flair, or style in one's work. Renowned craftsmen are known for their subtlety and refinement of technique. Police detectives acquire centrality among fellow sleuths as they build widespread informant networks, develop interrogation tactics and theories, and, to a much smaller degree, master fingerprinting and ballistics testing (Saunders, 1977). Academics gain recognition by accumulating lists of publications and achieve acclaim when they are seen to advance technique or pose new paths of inquiry (Crane, 1972). Senior electricians carry devices and tools which signify their ability to handle jobs seldom entrusted to more inexperienced colleagues (Reimer, 1977).

The Work Setting.   Within some occupational communities, centrality may be attached to working in particular settings. Gold (1964) notes that janitors gain recognition from peers by becoming custodians in upper-middle class apartment buildings where the pay is only slightly higher, but the probability of servicing "good tenants" is greater. Hockey players move to the center of their occupation when they move from the minors to the majors (Faulkner, 1974) and jazz musicians have made it when they find gigs before more appreciative audiences (Becker, 1951). The notion of the "big leagues" underlies this sort of movement, as when a newspaper reporter working on a small, insignificant, local paper yearns to become a reporter for the *New York Times*. Deep sea fishermen, like bears that go over mountains, long to work better waters where more lucrative fishing holes are though to be found (Zulaida, 1981). One should note that in each case the work remains essentially the same, but the characteristics of the setting change.

The Social Network.   Finally, centrality may be gained by strategic expansion or revision in one's network of acquaintances. With whom one works and who one knows become dimensions upon which careers may rest. Any doctoral student will verify that the reputation of the faculty represents a special catapult for launching a career in academia. To be allowed to stand on the bridge with the captain during a fishing trip taps a fisherman for initiation into the intricate and well-guarded secrets of captain's work and signals to the crew the fisherman's probable succession to the helm. Faulkner (1982) provides a most useful example of an occupational career highly dependent upon one's position in a given social network. The context is the movie business and Faulkner's analysis shows that film composers move to the inner core of their occupation (where work is plentiful and prestigious) only as they become connected to certain film producers, directors, and agents. The network that counts in Hollywood is the one linking high status members across occupational communities since only a few members of each community handle most of the industry's work. The vast majority of members in a given community compete among themselves for the little work that remains. The career rule is simple: Central and successful producers work only with central and successful film composers. Career opportunities in other occupational communities may be similar if they are constructed on the sort of project-by-project (or job-by-job) basis as typified by film composers. Unlike organizational careers based on promotions which create opportunities for others in the organization, an "opening" for a film composer has little effect on other film composers outside the charmed circle. Only by entering the circle can skill and talent be displayed.

In occupational communities where the work is spread more evenly across the membership, the opportunity to move toward a more central position is enhanced. Of importance always is the chance to exhibit skills highly valued by colleagues and these chances may have their own distribution of occurrence, little affected by the membership. For example, to maintain one's calm and mannered indifference while handling the wheel of a prowl car in a high speed chase serves to increase a street cop's prestige among his colleagues, many of whom are listening intently to the communication stream occurring between dispatch and the involved officer. Any hint of terror or the losing of one's cool are sure to be noted by others. The killing of the proverbial "fleeing felon" can also enhance the patrol officer's reputation (Van Maanen, 1980b). Among tradesmen and construction workers, those with quick situational wit are often at the hub of the work group (Riemer, 1977). Such displays of situational talent and the stories that become associated with them can ennoble (or embarrass) occupational members, moving them toward the center (or periphery) of their fellow workers.

The observation that occupational careers may be tied to colleagual relations, settings, or the work itself is primarily an analytic convenience. The three spheres are closely interconnected and relative success in one usually brings success in the others. But, by considering each spere in turn, we have tried to emphasize the importance of performance when considering career movement in occupational communities. Whereas orgnizational careers of the sort premised on what White (1970) calls "vacancy chains" (openings move down as people move up) shuffle people continually across varied work roles, occupational careers contain less role variability across moves. Moreover, individual moves by a member within the community may have little or no effect on other members except to the extent that such moves increase or diminish the status of the collective as a whole, vis-a-vis outsiders.

Role Performance

In essence, careers in occupational communities are based upon what any given member's activities say to other members. Role performances (in both the theatrical and accomplishment senses) in occupational communities have strong communicative powers by which members, through their daily actions, carve out and display a central or peripheral (but unique) position within the membership. Three domains of role performance in occupational communities deserve comment for they reflect directly upon the knowledge base of the occupation discussed previously in the context of occupational self-control.

Knowledge. First, for a would-be member contemplating membership in an occupational community, knowledge must be acquired. Learning, socialization, practicing, training, feedback, testing, memorizing, and so forth are all involved, but the nature of these acquisition and transmission mechanisms varies across communities. What doesn't vary is the fact that recruits must master the substantive core of the occupation. Police officers must learn the laws they are charged with enforcing, dentists must learn the procedures they will use, pilots must learn how to read instrument panels and communicate with control towers. Such learning constitutes the dues to be paid before one earns the right to claim membership in an occupational community. By and large, such learning serves only to distinguish the initiated from the uninitiated.

Application. The second crucial aspect of role performance is the application of basic knowledge and skill to the continuously varying work members must, in an everyday sense, perform. To know the law is not to know when its use will be considered appropriate or inappropriate by other members. Situational features of the work become important and the initiated must begin learning routine and contextual applications. Skill and knowledge acquisition give way to the learning of task rituals where particular practices for getting the job done become taken for granted. Members of occupational communities utilize conventionalized, practical methods to accomplish much of what they do, and it is on the use of such rituals that members can assess one another in terms of proper role performance. Police officers have practical methods to issue tickets and make departmentally-defined quotas (Van Maanen, 1974). Welfare workers possess informal techniques for satisfying formal record-keeping demands

(Zimmerman, 1969). Public defenders have collective rules of thumb to guide their handling of individual cases (Sudnow, 1965). The point here is that these learned rituals are applied to tasks viewed as important because in the work world they are unavoidable and frequent. Such activity can be and is organized routinely with a purpose and significance for occupational members that transcends externally imposed standards such as managerial notions of efficiency or productivity and internally valued claims such as quality service or humane treatment. The routine properties of the gynecological exam by which doctors and nurses defuse their potentially embarassing probes into the body of a patient by use of strategically placed garments, ritualized humor, speedy procedures, and a most restricted sociability with the probed provide another superb exhibit of such task rituals (Emerson, 1969).[28]

Innovation.   The third role performance feature of concern to occupational members involves the discarding of set skills and practical routines. Testing or breaking rules may secure a central position in the community for members who can accomplish valued occupational goals in new and untried ways. Schein (1971) uses the phrase "content innovations" to distinguish such actions. Working at the margin on different, perhaps difficult ventures, using resources in innovative ways, dealing smoothly with crises, pushing performance successfully to the limits of personal safety are the matters by which reputations are made. Members who work by design or accident at these margins, and who avoid failure where neither traditional occupational skills nor task rituals offer any predictable formulas for success, are quite likely to be the heroes of the occupation (Klapp, 1962). Such performances become displays of the "right stuff" of which stories are told and legends are made. The potential for stylish, episodic rule-breaking available to the membership transforms mundane, typically uneventful occupational life into a source of passion and drive. Simply to listen to carpenters talking about the successful completion of tough jobs, to cops on the raw details of how they handled a family fight, or to fishermen on the nature of storms endured, is to hear vivid testimony on what is, and what is not, central in their respective communities.

Individual careers in occupational communities are matters measured by centrality and work performance. Centrality may be achieved in a variety of ways, of course, but the more spectacular careers will almost invariably entail the violation of social conventions, accepted knowledge, or the received wisdoms of the trade. Such violations also have the potential to transform the occupational community itself in certain ways through the vivid demonstrations of new ways of seeing and doing things.

When such transformations occur, "role innovation" is achieved and occupational goals themselves are altered (Schein, 1971). In such a fashion, an occupational community itself may gain (or lose) status.

It is true, too, that in other occupational communities the technical, social, or moral innovators may never achieve centrality. The central positions may be reserved only for those members who best exhibit and articulate the community's traditional values, norms, and perspectives. Innovators may be widely recognized and perhaps consulted by core members, but they may not be accorded great honor, respect, or position. Nor is centrality, when ahieved, necessarily enduring or obvious. There are no doubt many members who are, in fact, central in occupational communities but who do not feel special, rewarded, or even successful within their individual lines of work. Caplow and McGee (1956) report on a number of academics who, even though widely cited within their disciplines, consider their work and careers to be "trivial," "unrecognized;" "stalled," "cannibalized," and so forth. This seems indeed to be a major problem for those seeking careers in occupational communities generally since the basis upon which one can assess the "success" of one's career is multidimensional, shifting, uncertain, and, more often than not, tied to the career of the occupation itself.

Finally, we must again note that individual careers in occupational communities are premised on the existence of some niche carved out in the occupational structure of society that is more or less controlled by fellow occupational members. Clearly, such a niche is not always to be found, nor is such a niche always secure since there are other social processes at work in occupational settings which attempt to deny or strip away such self-control. Organization, technological change, bureaucratization, standardization, formalization, are all processes of concern to those who seek to follow an occupational career. These processes potentially subject members to authority and discipline coming from outside the community boundaries. Braverman's (1974) analysis of deskilling is useful in this regard for it provides considerable insight into the demise of some occupational communities (and, perhaps, some not-too-subtle indicators as to why some occupational communities never emerge). In brief, Braverman shows how occupational members lose control of the labor process as job skills and knowledge become codified and standardized. By gathering, formulating, and systematizing the skills and traditions of certain crafts, managers of organizations are able to separate the conception and execution of work projects under their authority. No longer in sole possession of technique, occupational communities subjected to substantial rationalization lose their basis for market control and power (Giddens, 1973).[29] Such processes potentially affect the careers of all members of occupational communities, particularly those whose skills are employed exclusively in organizational contexts. It is to selected aspects of these organizational matters that we now turn.

OCCUPATIONAL COMMUNITIES AND ORGANIZATION

Three generic types of interlocking relationships between occupational communities and organizations are possible. First, an occupational community may itself be organized to promote member interests and self-control. Typically, such organizations do not employ but rather enroll practitioners of a given occupation. Occupations organize in voluntary or compulsory associations in order to secure more favorable conditions for the membership (e.g., to secure useful legislation, to control entrance to the occupation, to set standards of work, etc.). Of course, forms of occupational organization vary across a broad range, from unions to professional societies, from informal coalitions to formal interest groups employing many lobbyists, and so on. Forms of association within an occupation differ also. For example, fishermen in several New England ports have organized cooperatives to obtain supplies more cheaply and market fish more effectively than they were previously able to do. Fishermen in other ports have organized unions in an effort to mediate the influence of large, powerful fishbuyers (Van Maanen, Miller & Johnson, 1982). While the formation of an association of some type is usually the first step toward legal control of work through professionalization of unionization (Caplow, 1954; Bledstein, 1976), the motive for formation need not always be economic. As many academic specialties have done, geographically dispersed occupational communities may develop societies simply to foster communication among members. Although the formation of an association entails the creation of positions to which members may aspire, these offices are sometimes best construed as structured paths for attaining centrality or for bestowing prestige on central members within the community since they may not provide much in the way of material rewards or grant much power (other than symbolic) to direct, supervise or dictate members' occupational endeavors. In other cases, these offices carry considerable authority and provide rewards that go well beyond the purely symbolic. Careers for aspiring or designated leaders in these occupational communities are then available (although they are usually few in number).

Second, an organization may employ only members of a given occupational community so that the organiztion itself provides a locale for the activities of an occupation. Some medical research laboratories, law firms, consulting firms, fire departments, and academic departments exemplify such confluence of organizational and occupational interests. Glaser (1964) notes that within research and development laboratories where recognition for scientific achievement is the primary means of career advancement, the achievements and perspectives that lead scientists to greater centrality in their occupational communities also lead to vertically-ascending organizational careers. Bailyn (1982) has recently commented upon the ironies and contradictions of such careers since considerable personal ambivalence and role strain seem to be associated with hierarchically-graded occupational careers. Research-centered universities encourage professors' deep involvement in occupational communities, but such involvement does not preclude organizational advancement and, in fact, may encourage it, to the possible distress of the professors who no longer profess (Schein, 1978). For many people in these settings, the organization may be of only secondary importance, but, nonetheless, its value (and its demands) cannot be ignored because it provides scarce resources necessary for pursuing occupational interests; resources which may not be available elsewhere.

Bureaucratic growth, in particular, seems to create problems for occupationally-based organizations. Administrative concerns such as efficiency, quality control, specialization, and productivity tend to increase in salience, thus potentially driving out occupationally-based traditions and interests. Displacement of goals is the classic phrase used to describe situations where fundamental occupational objectives appear thwarted by administrative demands (Merton, 1949; Blau, 1955). In welfare agencies, for instance, occupational members at the bottom of the organization often believe that members at the top prohibit or at least divert them from accomplishing their "real work," the work which presumably led all of them into the occupation in the first place. From the caseworker's perspective, managerial demands for "people processing" and properly documenting the eligibility of welfare clients eliminate any opportunity to really help people in need (Lipsky, 1979). Even though most administrators began their careers as welfare workers and may well continue to consider themselves members of the occupational community, the practical demands of general administration eclipse occupationally-relevant goals. Thus, even in single service organizations, where all members at least nominally share membership in the same occupational community, across-rank conflict is seldom absent.

Third and finally are those settings where organizations employ members of existing occupational communities, (or, through employment, create an occupational community) but where the membership in the community and the organization is not co-extensive. Incomplete overlap between an occupational community and an employing organization is, without question, the most frequent form of relationship between the two and represents the critical intersection of potentially competing work systems. As we noted earlier, when occupational communities are nested within heteronomous organizations, it is generally more difficult for the local membership to maintain occupational standards of work and also more difficult for the membership to prevent non-occupational members from performing work which lies within the occupation's traditional domain. From this perspective, understanding organizations very much involves understanding how members of occupational communities cope with, negotiate, and otherwise deal with organizational demands (i.e., Schein, 1972). How organizations are, in part, shaped by virtue of the occupational communities employed within them is the subject of the following discussion as we examine some rather familiar streams of organization theory in light of the occupational community framework presented in this paper.

Organizational Complexity and Managerial Control

Organization theory offers two complementary structural explanations for the complexity of organizations and for conflict within them. On one hand, an organization grows complex as tiers of subordination multiply, lengthening the chain of command. The greater the number of levels in a hierarchy, the more likely it is that messages will be distorted as they pass from stratum to stratum. To the degree that each level evolves its own peculiar tasks and sets of problems, the probability of conflicts of interest between levels increases since each may project different objectives for the organization. On the other hand, organizational complexity also increases as the number of departments and divisions within the organization multiply. Since each functional area tends to develop its own language, norms, time-horizons, and perspectives on the organization's mission, when forced to compete for resources or to cooperate on joint ventures, departments are likely to vie for the privilege of defining the situation (e.g., Lawrence & Lorsch, 1967; Thompson, 1967).

The problem with using horizontal and vertical differentiation to describe complexity is not that they are inaccurate, but rather that they do not go far enough. Ironically, their limitations arise from their virtues. Hierarchical and functional lines of demarcation are both theoretically parsimonious and methodologically elegant and they both correspond to the ways organizations formally depict themselves (Bittner, 1965). Consequently, researchers can identify presumably conflicting groups and perspectives by quick reference to the table of organization. They can construct simple empirical indices of structural complexity by counting hierarchical levels or functionally distinct groups, measuring spans of supervisory control, calculating staff-to-line ratios, and so forth, but as descriptions of an organization's social structure, hierarchy and function, as detailed by the official table, underestimate the extent and ambiguity of an organization's complexity along several lines.

First, departmental or divisional demarcations entail a level of analysis that hides potential interest groups and unrealistically homogenizes functional areas. Departments are often composed of smaller groups which may or may not be formally designated, but whose interests nevertheless clash. Divisions of student affairs in universities are typically composed of several departments such as counseling services, student unions, and housing or residence life. On some issues (budgeting for example) each department acts as a unified interest group. On other issues, segmentation within departments is quite visible. Housing departments, for instance, employ some personnel who are oriented primarily toward maintenance of the physical plant and others who view themselves as student personnel workers. While the two are grouped together in an administrative unit, those concerned with the physical plant are often at odds with their student personnel colleagues on specific issues such as how to handle students who damage university property, or over what constitutes an adequate room painting policy (Barley, 1979). Functional areas often contain a plurality of interest groups who coalesce as a unified entity only on rare occasions.

Second, relevant groupings in organizations crosscut both divisional and hierarchical lines. To again take Barley's (1979) example, because student personnel workers are trained as counselors, they often align themselves with counseling service personnel, thereby forming a coalition of peers that blurs, if not erases, functional boundaries. Nor are hierarchical lines of demarcation sacrosanct. Even in the quasi-military context of police agencies, supervisory personnel frequently side with the supervised rather than with each other or with higher officials in the agency on matters such as work pacing, scheduling, discipline, and productivity (Van Maanen, 1983).[30]

Finally, as our lengthy discussion of occupational communities suggests, some members of an organization align themselves with groups external to the organization and thereby possess a potentially useful resource to both support and oppose specific organizational policies and practices. Organizational development personnel, for example, marshall forth the wisdom of their occupational peers when recommending particular actions to decision makers of the firms for which they work (Klein, 1976). More familiar perhaps is the potential conflict existing when organizations employ individuals with even stronger occupational identities. Clinicians in university medical clinics emphasize the confidential nature of therapist-client relations as do therapists in other settings. Although the clinical value system generally coexists peacefully with the interests of other groups in the university, on occasion the clinician's vow of confidentiality conflicts with the demands of administrative personnel. For example, when a client has been referred for disruptive behavior, the clinician may become privy to information of interest to administrators who might prefer to take punitive or legal action against the student. In such cases, administrators and clinicians are thrown into conflict because the latter's insistence upon inviolate confidentiality thwarts speedy disciplinary action on the part of the former (Barley, 1979).

Such altogether transparent observations bring us back to the view that organizations are most accurately viewed as complicated sets of sometimes issue-specific coalitions, each exhibiting varying degrees of stability and overlapping memberships (March & Simon, 1962; Bacharach & Lawler, 1980). Formal indices of potential coalitions, such as hierarchical and functional differentiation, may provide clues to the relevant lines of conflict, but from an insider's point of view they portray only the tip of the iceberg. A more veridical approach would be to identify groups based upon the distinctions organizational members make among themselves. Member-relevant distinctions would be based upon dimensions of perceived commonality as well as upon the particular circumstances that make perceived commonality salient by setting one group against another. Since specific members of an organization can draw upon numerous social statuses and roles for referencing and identifying themselves, a plurality of overlapping groups is possible. Within organizations, potential bases for forming coalitions include proximity of work station, shift, perceived career potential, gender, education, friendship, and similarity of work. When this last factor—similarity of work—is descriptively relevant and the observed coalition formed in its shadow demonstrates a unity of purpose and structural stability over time and across a wide range of potentially divisive organizational controversies, the coalition represents a local manifestation of an occupational community. Such coalitions will be tenacious and, as we have suggested, not easily managed by those who fall outside its membershi boundaries.

Occupational communities promote self-serving interpretations of the nature and relevance of their work in the organization as a means of generating control over that work. Moreover, occupational communities represent relatively well integrated social systems. To the extent occupational communities succeed in convincing themselves and other that they solely command the expertise necessary to execute and evaluate their work, they gain autonomy and discretion. Hence, internally, occupational communities are tightly coupled systems but may be only loosely coupled to the larger organization (Weick, 1976, 1979).[31]

From this standpoint, many organizations more closely resemble tribal federations or fiefdoms than they do computing machines. Such organization has value even though the links between any two subsystems are highly problematic. Weick (1979) in particular has been persuasive when pointing to the virtues of increased complexity (caused, in part, by loose-coupling) such as a reduced responsiveness to external pressures or uncertainties and the greater variability of an organization's output. Several conditions relevant to our concern with occupational communities appear to foster loose-coupling in organizations.

First, geographically dispersed occupational communities that enjoy social and legal recognition and whose skills are in high demand can, with some impunity, resist managerial requests. The occupational community need not be a large component of the organization nor be seen as particularly crucial to the organization's mandate to secure and protect its relative autonomy. In some cases, such communities exercise considerable influence over the direction of the organization itself as its members assume high positions in the organization. Second, the numerical strength of an occupational community in an organization may promote loose-coupling since relative numerical superiority provides a political base in the organization for resisting administrative control. Third, an occupational community located at a critical juncture in the flow of an organization's work may foster loose-coupling. The mechanics studied by Crozier (1964) countered both managerial and production worker appeals to alter their occupational habits largely because their ever-reluctant services were considered by management and worker alike to be too vital to organizational functioning to risk confrontations. Fourth, scarcity of expertise, maintained in part by an occupational community through its monopoly of technique and knowledge, promotes loose-coupling in organizations. Since alternative sources of expertise are not readily available, management must take care not to offend the source it has, and thus may grant them relatively high amounts of autonomy. Organizations highly dependent upon new knowledge and proprietary technologies may find they are more successful buying such knowledge and granting its holders liberty than by trying to develop it internally under managerial direction.

These sources of complexity and loose-coupling are, by and large, structural matters. Complexity, however, also arises and is sustained by the very practices that make an occupational community distinct no matter what structural supports are to be located within the organization. Consider the role that codes and languages play in an organizational life. When occupational members employ community-based codes for interpreting and communicating the meaning of work-related events, it is difficult for outsiders to penetrate the codes in order to know what is really going on. Since codes allow their users to segment a flow of events, they provide members of an occupational community with more than a degree of freedom to reconstruct the meaning of events. Such transformations loosen the theoretical bonds between stimulus and response and allow members of occupational communities to perform their work relatively free from the influence of outsider demands (Manning, 1979). Moreover, since occupational codes appear mysterious, esoteric, and vaguely intimidating to those not well versed and practiced in their use, the understanding of certain phenomena may appear to be impenetrable to those outside the occupation. Certainly in the past and, to a lesser extent, currently, computer programmers and systems analysts have been able to secure a certain amount of occupational autonomy within some organizations because, in part, their languages are indecipherable by those not introduced to the mysteries of the occupational community and because, in further part, the codes blind members to the realities of other work groups (Haug, 1973).

All of this is not to say that complexity and conflicting sources of authority are welcomed by organizational managers. Loose-coupling is hardly embraced enthusiastically by administrators and others who must worry about coordination and control across their organization. The image and its referents are in high contrast to the ideal managerial organization whose well-lubricated parts are interdependent and mutually responsive. From this standpoint, it is easy to understand why so many organizational intervention techniques (e.g., participatory management, team building, goal setting, management-by-objectives, project and matrix supervision, etc.) aim to bolster the lagging integration and responsiveness among groups within an organization. More to the point, however, the decline of many occupational communities suggests that organizational principles of control are hardly on the defensive although, as we have tried to point out by emphasizing the diverse orientations of organizational members toward their work, the use of such principles is far more problematic than commonly conveyed. Two very general strategies for tightening organizations merit discussion. Each directly influences the very existence of an occupational community.

Fragmentation of work through its subdivision into component parts represents the most powerful method of increasing managerial control of the labor process and, by implication, of occupational communities. The celebrated robot is, of course, the perfect employee for it entails no mystery, possesses no loyalties, and seeks no exclusiveness. It is the ideal command-based work system. The application of tacit skill and judgement in the performance of work tasks is obviously ruled out. But the tasks that are programmed will be accomplished without ritual or exception. In the absence of robots, highly rationalized, minutely designed and carefully monitored work processes serve the same goals. Since control by fragmentation and standardization has been a centerpiece of organizational writings after Frederick Taylor established his devilish pact with Schmidt, the pig-iron loader, we will not comment further except to note the occasional irony presented by control systems that become so complex themselves that they increase the very problems they were designed to prevent. Gouldner's (1954) justly famous "vicious cycle of rules" is a case in point.[32]

Hierarchical control is the second managerial strategy of relevance to this discussion. To the degree that coercive authority and the application of discipline in the workplace is required, hierarchical control can quickly get out of hand since strong cultures of resistance can be expected to develop (Etzioni, 1964). Authority, in all its guises, is most effective when those to whom it is directed are favorably disposed to obey. When the orientation of organizational members is to the organization as represented by higher authorities in the workplace rather than to the occupation as represented by skillful practitioners who may or may not be higher authorities in the organization, control and direction of the labor process is eased. The Weberian solution to this problem is to provide careers for employees in such a way that their loyalty and effort become tied to organizational matters, not occupational ones. Edwards (1979:134) offers some thought-provoking evidence regarding the degree to which such a strategy has been employed in some organizations.

> With eighteen different job families, three hundred job titles and fourteen different pay grades, not to mention the dichotomy between salaried and hourly workers, it might appear that Polaroid had gone far enough in dividing and redividing its workers. Not so. Each job is now further positioned along the pay scale so that for any given job . . . seven distinct pay steps are possible, from entry level through 5 percent increments to top pay for the job . . . taking just the job titles and pay steps and ignoring the job families classification, Polaroid has created roughly 2,100 (300 times 7) individual slots for its 6,397 hourly workers.

One must pause for a moment at such categorization. Finely graded job structures represent the stuff of which organizational careers are made. The differences in positional characteristics hardly noticeable to the outsider often provide enormous incentive value to employees eager for advancement (Kanter, 1979). An "Assistant Professor, Step Two" may not appear different than an "Associate Professor, Step Three" to the outsider, but, to insiders, the differences are sure to be noticed and felt. Such tightening creates internally contrived images of mobility and, at times, prevents organizational participants from seeing the similarity of their position to others both inside and outside the organization (Jermier, 1982). Organizational careers, when used by employees as the measure of vocational success, serve to break up occupational communities and, in general, to increase compliance with managerial directives. One study suggests that in the higher circles of management the fundamental criteria used in the promotion of subordinates is their "orientation to advancement" as read by superiors (Sofer, 1970).[33]

In sum, complexity can be seen to be furthered both by the presence of occupational communities in organizations and by the efforts of management to drive them out or, at least, reduce their influence. Managerial control, however, is always problematic. Its effectiveness waxes and wanes over historical periods and varies across organizational and occupational contexts. We do not propose any general formula by which complexity can be predicted or control fully understood. These are highly uncertain issues. But we can say that to examine complexity and control in organizations as if the orientations of the membership to their work and occupation were unimportant would be folly. It is to these orientations we now move.

Organizational Loyalty and Work Careers

For members of occupational communities, employment in heteronomous organizations involves concomitant membership in two social systems of work. Such dual membership may generate an ever-present tension as an employee attempts to pursue simultaneously both an organizational and an occupational career, each of which may proceed in quite different directions and demand different loyalties. The issue for the person, the occupational community, and the organization as well, is which of the two social systems (if either) will achieve relative ascendancy in the person's vocational scheme of things.

Loyalty splits between an occupation and an organization and the dilemma of choosing between an occupational or organizational career resemble issues addressed by research on the "local" and "cosmopolitan" orientations of organizational members. Despite the fact that the local-cosmopolitan literature intends to illuminate the sources and consequences of the conflict between occupational and organizational loyalty, this literature has historically lacked coherence, displayed a rather shoddy methodology, failed to clarify its concepts, and, over the years, generated a muddle of contradictions (Grimes & Berger, 1970).[34] A good part of the problem is that the concept of "professional" undergirds research conceptualizations of the occupations thus far studied. By framing the debate in terms of an individual's orientation to occupational communities and to employing organizations, some of the pitfalls may be avoided while retaining the basic insights of the original theory.

Gouldner (1957, 1958) adopted the terms "local" and "cosmopolitan" from Merton (1949) who originally used them to differentiate between community leaders whose influence arises from contacts and accomplishments within the community (locals) and those whose influence arises from contacts and accomplishments beyond the community (cosmopolitans). Gouldner's intent was to distinguish between individuals whose loyalty and careers were tied to their employing organization and those whose careers and loyalty were focused on their occupational groups (Gouldner, 1957:288–89). Since Gouldner studied college faculty and administrators, the correspondence between local and organizational orientations and between cosmopolitan and occupational (or disciplinary) orientations was more or less acceptable, at least for academics in disciplines given to publication and research. Yet, once the concepts were extended beyond the academic setting to other occupational groups, discrepancies between predictions and results began to accumulate.

Consider several telling examples. In the Bennis et al. (1958) study of an outpatient clinic, "cosmopolitan nurses" were defined as those who sought professional careers by remaining tied to nursing work and "local nurses" were defined as those who sought administrative careers within the hospital by rising in the ranks of the nursing hierarchy. The researchers found, to their apparent surprise, that cosmopolitan nurses were more loyal to their work groups then local nurses. The results were contrary to the predictions flowing from the theory that guided the research. Similarly, studies of engineers employed in heteronomous organizations suggest that most engineers are local in orientation, yet local engineers, like their cosmopolitan colleagues, personify the values of technical excellence. Research on engineering occupations has yet to demonstrate any consistent differences between the two orientations in terms of work values, technical knowledge, commitment to keeping abreast of the field, conference attendance, or even journals that (presumably) are read (Kornhauser, 1962; Ritti, 1968; Goldberg, 1976).

Currently there are no general results to be found in the empirical literature devoted to exploring the local-cosmopolitan distinction (as defined operationally by the administrative-professional career orientations of organizational participants). The research indicates only that conflict is not always indicated by the findings and there is high variability in the types of relationships that exist between different occupational groups and the organizations in which they are employed (e.g., Hall & Lawler, 1970; Satow, 1975; Tuma & Grimes, 1981). Yet, since these studies are not comparative, the systematic basis for such variability has not been pursued and what is being "discovered" (and rediscovered) is that in specific circumstances members of this-or-that occupational group will adapt to organizational life and not experience the presumed inevitable conflict. The conceptual underpinnings of the theory are then left in place while, paradoxically, empirical work raises fundamental questions about the usefulness of the theory.

One problem with using the local-cosmopolitan or administrative-professional distinctions to differentiate the occupationally and the organizationally loyal is the assumption that an occupational orientation is based on a reference group external to the employing organization.[35] Although external reference groups may exist for members of some occupations such as tradesmen, academics, or industrial scientists, people in many lines of work do not know people who do denotatively similar work in other settings. Police officers, teachers, and fishermen know there are other police officers, teachers, and fishermen in other work settings, but they may not personally know them or interact with them on more than a sporadic or episodic basis. In many lines of work there are no annual meetings to attend, trade journals to read, or frequent opportunities available to meet colleagues outside the workplace who are not also members of one's employing organization.

What is crucial for the development of an occupational community is not, however, the presence of an extended work group, but rather that, through socialization, an occupation's value system comes to shape a person's work perspectives and self concepts—work perspectives and self–concepts that are supported over time in a person's daily interactions. Hence, one may be occupationally oriented but local. The concept of an occupational community does not assume that the occupational group of reference necessarily extends beyond an organization. Since the concept is defined phenomenologically, the researcher must first assess the community's interactive borders as they are perceived by members. Only when such an analysis reveals that an occupational community is organizationally extended in the experience of the membership will occupational loyalty be congruent with a cosmopolitan orientation. When the occupational community is clustered within the organization, people may choose an occupational over an organizational orientation and yet, like nurses and perhaps engineers, be local in their orientation.

When occupational communities do not extend beyond the organization, several conditions appear to influence personal loyalties. Promotion opportunities seem to be particularly salient (Sykes, 1965; Kanter, 1979). If the occupational community is small and the chance for promotion within the organization reasonably good, then organizational careers are likely to prove seductive, particularly if the occupational community lacks power by virtue of its peripheral position in the workflow or by its inability to provide scarce resources in high organizational demand. Social scientists in technically-driven universities provide a convenient (if biased) example in this regard. However, if the organization does not itself offer much opportunity for advancement, or if the occupational community comprises a large proportion or powerful segment of the organization's membership, then individuals may be more inclined to choose careers in the occupational community. Such a choice might appear as a "plateau" from the perspective of an organizationally grounded theory of career. But, from the perspective of the membership within an occupational community, the choice carries no negative connotations. It is, of course, sometimes the case that to be called "a real pro" implies that one will never be anything else.

Often the loyalty issues are not apparent until organization or occupational shifts have been undertaken (Lieberman, 1956; Schein, 1978). Thus, when individuals are shifted from one functional area to another or when hierarchical movement occurs within an organization, exit from the occupational community may be forced upon persons more or less against their will. Becker and Strauss (1956) have suggested that many, if not most, passages in the workplace induce problems of loyalty for the person undergoing the transition. When a member of an occupational community accepts a supervisory position or shifts to another department, members left behind may feel the person is "no longer one of us." A new organizational role may also demand the development of new skills because different problems are faced and, in learning these skills, an entirely new set of colleagues is encountered. In cases where major shifts of perspective are to be expected when moving up and away from one's occupational community, strong prohibitions may exist among the membership to discourage such movement, even when some members are favorably disposed toward an organizational career.

For example, Manning (1977) documents how an occupational community of police officers protected its members from the scrutiny of organizational authorities. Among members of this police community, to become a sergeant was to betray the very trust upon which the community rested. Promotion-seeking itself may estrange individuals from colleagues by requiring the promotion seeker to act in ways regarded as inappropriate by members. Van Maanen (1983) observed in another police community that even to talk about one's desire for upward mobility in the organization was to invite the ridicule of one's colleagues. Not only were such aspirations seen as foolishly optimistic, higher rank itself was seen by patrol officers to offer only the paperwork headaches that come with virulent forms of memo madness. The power of such shaming tactics should not be disregarded by students of organizational careers, Shaming may be directed at the most central and skilled members of the community, leaving only the most peripheral members free from its influence. The pool of those available for administrative or organizational careers may then be comprised largely of the least respected and least skilled members of an occupational community. Deans who are not thought by the professoriate to be "real scholars" come to mind in this regard, as are doctors-turned-hospital-administrators who, when evaluated by the medical staff, are held in low regard for "never having really practiced."

It appears that a paradox occurs when particularly strong occupational communities are enclosed within an organization. In such cases, organizational loyalty is negatively correlated with occupational loyalty. But, since the community is bounded by the organization itself, committed members will be reluctant to leave. Leaving would demand exiting the occupational community. Hence, occupational loyalty would be negatively correlated with turnover. Considering these relationships together, organizational loyalty appears positively associated with turnover insofar as the relation is premised upon the existence of an occupational community within the organization. Just such a situation seems to exist in police agencies where patrol officers most desirous of a managerial career and most committed to the organization are typically the least satisfied and most estranged from the patrol officer community (Van Maanen, 1975). Such members are also the most likely to "turnover" since promotion is both quite slow and (seemingly) capricious in police agencies. Occupational communities profit by this paradox since those least attracted and attractive to the membership are also the most likely to depart.

Although dual membership in an occupational community and an organization engenders conflicts of loyalty, researchers must not assume that the issue of loyalty is always in the foreground or that the choice of an organizational career automatically alienates a member from others who continue to follow the occupation. Conflicts of loyalty are typically contextual and issue-specific. While many patrol officers do not desire the sergeant rank, many engineers do aspire to supervisory positions. Patrol officers often feel making rank reduces their ability to control what they do while engineers often believe making rank will help them achieve such control (Van Maanen, 1983; Goldner & Ritti, 1967). Clearly, to study occupational-organizational tensions and differentiate in any meaningful way between the occupationally and organizationally loyal is also to study the moral, social, and cognitive contours of occupational communities. As several decades of research suggest, much variability is sure to be found.

Innovation, Technology, and Managerial Control

The fertility of occupational communities for the creation and introduction of work-oriented innovations is equivocal. On one hand, to the degree that an occupational community represents a traditional social system that claims sole propriety over the jurisdiction of its work, resistance may be expected to any form of organizational or technological change which would threaten the community's sovereignty in its work domain. Certainly organizational interventions designed to increase the community's responsiveness and integration within the organization will be dismissed as attempts to destroy the autonomy of the occupational community. Technological innovations which are interpreted as potentially deskilling or which might disrupt the social structure and prestige of the community as it is currently organized will be resisted and, if possible, sabotaged.[35] For example, spotters in the Israeli artillery have traditionally prided themselves on their ability to relay accurate and timely coordinates over a field radio to soldiers in the batteries. However, since the radio is a public medium, many spotters gain notoriety for their airwave antics and personae as well as for their military acumen. After the last war with Egypt, the Israeli command installed computerized radio transmitters in spotters' halftracks. The computers were intended to enhance the spotter's efficiency since a spotter could now enter the coordinates directly into the computer and relay them into another computer attached to a fieldpiece by the mere push of a button. Needless to say, faced with the loss of potential status, many spotters gutted or otherwise disengaged the electronic equipment and continued to broadcast live. Of course, housings were discreetly left mounted and intact in case officers happened to inspect the operation. (Kunda, 1982).

On the other hand, since members of an occupational community identify with their work and with their skill and expertise, innovations which come from within the community may very well be encouraged and embraced. Skilled craftsmen and machinists who design new tools that allow easier, more precise, and perhaps speedier, work as well as computer programmers who constantly seek more elegant algorithms provide examples of innovations that serve to advance one's standing in the occupation by providing benefits to all members. Perhaps the best indicator of a community's response to innovation is whether or not the innovation comes from within the community and whether or not it will remain under the community's control.

It is worth noting too, that some occupational communities are apparently quick to adopt technological innovations, even those characterized by the membership as ''not invented here.'' Yet, the evidence does not suggest that the adopted innovations necessarily improve the community's ability to conduct its work effectively or efficiently. There is no functional imperative that works in this domain. Police agencies are notorious consumers of new technology and police officers of all ranks take pride in sporting the newest electronic gadgets, the latest model cars, the most powerful weapons, and so forth. But, despite the rising sophistication of crime–fighting technology, there is absolutely no evidence that the ability of the police to detect and deter crime has improved (Wilson & Kelling, 1982). There is even a hint that this rising sophistication has impaired their ability (Manning, 1979).

Of course, some technological innovations have not been adopted so enthusiastically by the police. Electronic scanners that make possible continuous monitoring of patrol car activities are one such innovation that has stirred up considerable controversy within police agencies. Consider also that when two-way radios were first being installed in patrol cars, replacing the fixed-post telephone systems of communication, many radios were reported lost, stolen, broken, jammed, or otherwise tampered with by "unknown persons" (Rubinstein, 1973). Similar reports are heard today with even the most foolproof communication systems wherein dispatchers are unable to establish the whereabouts of errant squad cars due to [claimed] static, low-flying objects, or black holes in the airwaves.[37]

As a general rule, the more technologically or methodologically sophisticated an occupational community becomes, the more splintered and fragmented its membership—becoming, at times, many little occupational communities rather than one. Social scientists developed statistical routines to aid in the interpretation of collected data. Over the years, small pockets of statisticians have penetrated each of the social sciences. The more refined and powerful the analytic techniques, the fewer the number of occupational community members familiar and comfortable with their use (Daft, 1980). Such splintering heightens the possibilities for organizational control since managers may argue that only occupational members with particular (rather than general) skills are to be employed. Some members benefit, others may vanish and a wedge is driven into the community. In occupational communities where the knowledge base and technical skills are rapidly advancing, cohort splintering may be prominent. New members possess more recent knowledge and hence may be of more value to organizations (and perhaps to the occupational community as well) than the older members. The wedge is driven further because there are usually economic incentives to be found when purchasing young talent rather than buying, retaining, or upgrading old talent.

The ambivalence of some occupational communities toward innovation is hardly surprising given that their own demise may be forthcoming. Nor is the glee and eager pursuit of innovation among managerial bodies difficult to understand since innovation may be as valuable in terms of controlling the membership of an organization as it is for whatever reputed gains in productivity or efficiency are to be claimed for its implementation. Office automation and the computerization of newspaper printing are good examples in this regard (Champion, 1967; Wallace & Kallenberg, 1982). In both spheres, technological innovation has central-relevant implications since it has enlarged the prerogatives of management and diminished craft practices and judgemental tasks required of both secretaries and newspaper printers.

Where the knowledge base and skill levels contained within an occupational community remain relatively stable, danger to the community from lack of innovation may develop. Accounting provides an interesting case for it appears that the mystique and exclusivity once associated with the black (and white) arts of accounting have significantly eroded as knowledge of accounting principles and financial management techniques have become less arcane and more dispersed throughout an organization. The new technology surrounding computer programming, making the use of computing machines far more accessible to those untrained in information processing, represents another erosion of a formerly glamorous occupational community (Kraft, 1979).

This is not to say that increases in information or new technologies always disrupt and reorder the status and power of occupational communities. Certainly knowing the technology does not allow an analyst to predict what forms of social organization will develop to surround it as the comparative industrial experience of Britain and Japan all too pointedly testify (Dore, 1973). The claim that new technologies inevitably fragment work and deskill people will not hold across the board. Some technologies, as we have suggested, conceivably create occupational communities where none existed before, or empower existing communities. New diagnostic devices such as head and body scanners (CATscans) now used in some radiology departments of large hospitals seem to bolster the technicians' sense of work community and give them occupational clout because, within a given hospital, they are among the only skilled and practiced interpreters of the output created by the new machines (Barley, forthcoming).

In sum, occupational communities are bound to rise and fall with social and technological innovation, but the precise path such a rise and fall may take and the ripple effects it will have on organizational matters are quite difficult to reckon with in the abstract. We do not share the Marxist gloom that craft skills and communal occupational ties are always destroyed by the advance of technology in capitalistic societies. Nor are we convinced by the more sanguine predictions made by those enamored with technology of the new freedoms and work communities to be encouraged. Historical, longitudinal, comparative studies are required and there are precious few such studies currently available in the organizational literature to be able to say much about what theories will or will not be generally useful in this area.

SOME CLOSING COMMENTS

We had two purposes in mind while constructing this essay. First, we wanted to convey a set of ideas for understanding work and work organizations that might complement those ideas currently in fashion within organization theory. In particular, we have tried to show how the concept of an occupational community might provide greater insight into the way careers are understood by people, the way complexity is managed and magnified, the way occupational loyalty is played out in organizations, and so forth. Our first intent then was to complicate organizational theorizing by suggesting how some of the "blooming, buzzing, confusion" of phenomenological approaches to the study of work worlds can be captured by our theories.

Our second purpose was more rhetorical and informed by some structural observations. Here we wanted to convey a sense of disenchantment with handed-down organization theory emphasizing harmony and cooperation in the workplace. Too often organizational research represents a sort of effete innocence which speaks of attitudes, values, supervision, structure, goals, rules, ethos, culture, and communication, but not of conflict and power. To this end, we have tried in our essay to dismantle some of the seeming neutrality surrounding organization studies by emphasizing the political and economic roots of occupational self-control, by questioning the assumed traits of service and knowledge so often considered definitional when professions are studied and, in general, by presenting alternative sources of workplace authority. Our second intent then was to open up organizational theorizing in a manner that would allow some of these broader and ideologically sensitive matters to be addressed.

Whether or not such purposes have been served well or poorly is not ours to say. What we can do in these few remaining pages, however, is to briefly review our main points and then make a few suggestions as to why and where we think these points are particularly relevant.

We began by noting that a persistent theme in the sociological literature is the presumed dichotomy between communal or colleagual and rational or administrative forms of work organization. Occupational communities, we argued, approximate the former and must be defined in terms of member-perceived boundaries. Within such boundaries, members of occupational communities claim a distinctive and valued social identity, share a common perspective toward the mission and practices of the occupation, and take part in a sort of interactive fellowship that transcends the workplace.

The diverse origins of occupational communities were discussed in terms of how certain physical and social conditions surrounding particular lines of work might promote any or all of these definitional characteristics. Occupational communities were seen to create and sustain relatively unique work cultures consisting of, among other things, task rituals, standards for proper and improper behavior, work codes which surround relatively routine practices and, for the membership at least, compelling accounts attesting to the logic and value of these rituals, standards and codes. The difficult but persistent quest for occupational self-control represented the single universal in our scheme. Although this quest has a Sysiphus-like character for all occupational communities, some have developed and maintain considerable structural advantages such as state support, an elaborate and advancing theoretical and procedural base to inform (and mystify) practice, and a relatively unorganized market in dire need of an occupational community's talents. We then suggested that the professions, when appropriately unpacked by specialty and interest, were best viewed as occupational communities, and that they differ from other lines of work (and each other) only by virtue of the relative autonomy each is able to sustain within the political economy of a given society. Finally, we catalogued a few of the implications the study of occupational communities posed for certain domains of organization research. Careers (individual and collective), complexity, loyalty, and innovation were areas given special attention.

By and large, throughout this paper we have taken organization behavior researchers to task for paying inordinate attention to the way managers attempt to control the labor process in organizations, and not enough attention to the ways those who are managed also attempt to control their labor. Along with Kerr (1977), we think theories of organization behavior exaggerate the role formal leadership plays as a control device in organizations by too often failing to consider the nature and source of employee work orientations. Diversity is masked and only the most visible tip of the control structure is apparent when the research focus is upon hierarchy and workflow. One (and we emphasize one) way to redirect attention is through the study of occupational communities. The standards of evaluation, grounds for respect, and sources of ambition vary across occupational communities, yet we currently know very little about the conditions under which such variance is to be expected. A fruitful and ongoing research rask, then, is to add to the ethnographic record of occupational communities, particularly those that appear to be located in organizational contexts.

Longitudinal studies of selected occupations are also needed. Communities rise and fall with social and economic change. The organizational implications of such shifts are more or less unknown. There may be some urgency to this task since many occupations are changing rapidly in the face of new technologies designed to alter work practices. The increased codification of occupational knowledge carries with it the distinct potential for allowing persons outside an occupational community to perform tasks previously reserved for the membership. Computer-based diagnostic routines, for example, make it possible for technicians to perform certain medical examinations without a doctor's presence. While some of these tasks may seem trivial and unrelated to the "real work" of a given occupation, over time the inroads made by outsiders may well loosen occupational monopolies, demystify practice, and increase the amount of administrative control exercised over occupational members. Such a theme is becoming prominent in sociological circles where, within a decade, the happy concern for the "professionalization of everyone" (Wilensky, 1964) has become a sour concern for the "deprofessionalization of everyone" (Haug, 1975).

A focus on occupational communities offers new directions for research on organizational careers and socialization practices. Interorganizational career studies is one area to be developed (Faulkner, 1982). Skill acquisition and the learning of specific work routines and practices is another. While new entrants are socialized into the mores of a company, for example, they are also absorbing from colleagues and others the accumulated wisdom of an occupation, say, management. Such enculturation often transcends the organization's learning requirements and provides continuity (or lack thereof) with the lessons learned during anticipatory socialization undergone in educational institutions. To focus on occupational careers may also become less a matter of choice than a requirement. The sluggish economy with no surge in sight and the apparently common situation of declining opportunity in many, if not most, Western industries suggests a need to place more emphasis upon how to generate increases in both the quantity and, perhaps more importantly, the quality of goods and services produced by our major work institutions. This must be done without appeal for massive infusions of additional capital which, in all probability, will be in short supply. We believe members of occupational communities have much to tell us in this regard.

Dedication to high standards of work performance and craft excellence are not matters easily promoted from outside an occupational community. Ways must be found, therefore, to preserve and encourage such dedication. At the same time, we need to more carefully examine the social (and ideological) mechanisms of accommodation to stable, "plateaued" organizational careers. A concern for how people draw meaning and value from what to some are "stalled" or "flattened" careers will have considerable practical importance. Bailyn (1982) makes this same point more forcefully in the context of how different career paths influence men and women in their relations outside the workplace. Ways which protect and expand the influence of occupational communities within organizations may become as interesting to researchers (and managers) as the ways that destroy them are now.

All this is not to suggest that the study of those whose work histories are punctuated by disorderly and rapid shifts among jobs and occupations is to be foregone. An occupational community can be understood only by knowing what it is not. Discretion over the methods, pace, schedule, and outcome of one's work is the ambition of occupational communities but it is an ambition not often achieved and, even when achieved, it can be grasped only tentatively. Historical studies promise to untangle some of the knots which presently restrict understanding occupational communities by depicting the origins of such communities within the larger society (e.g., Larson, 1977; Edwards, 1979). An important feature of this work is that it also reveals organizational control principles. Occupational communities are, by and large, those work domains where member identities and work practices have not been fragmented into organizationally-defined positions by highly detailed job descriptions, where work performance is not ultimately judged by a management cadre, and where entrance to and exit from the occupation is not controlled by any one heteronomous organization. These are, of course, matters of degree but, as principles of occupational authority and control, they contrast to those prevalent in management textbooks. An historical study awakens us to some fundamental constraints on management influence that go far beyond the much-discussed limitations of improper spans of control, poor supervisory style, insensitive task design, or inadequate goal setting procedures.

One final caveat. We think the study of occupational communities vital to a concern for what people at work do all day (or would like to do). Organization theory has had relatively little to say about the things people actually do at work (although much to say about what others think they should be doing). We are just now learning, for instance, that middle and high level executives do not spend much time thinking or planning about what strategic options are available to their firms or departments. Evidence suggests they may not think or plan much at all, since they are busily rushing about answering phones, attending meetings, and engaging in brief encounters of the short kind (Stewart, 1968; Mintzberg, 1973; Feldman, 1982). Strategic decisions, then, are more or less backed into, and justified retrospectively with little, if any, foresight. Many organizations seem to move more from drift than design based on, in Weick's (1982) marvelous phrase, "the presumption of managerial logic." Certainly at lower levels of organizations the disparity between depictions and predictions (both manager and researcher) of what people do all day and descriptions and accounts (both member and researcher) of what people, in fact, do all day is equally disturbing and upsetting of received theories of organizational behavior (Van Maanen, 1981). Studies of occupational communities, by forcing the analyst to move inside them to discover member understandings of the work they do, give license to explore the practical and moral contours of work worlds against which organization theories can be assessed. With this remark, we are back to where we began and can wonder again in print whether it makes more or less sense to view Charlie, our hypothetical auto repairman down at Joe's Garage, as a "mechanic" or as an "employee." We suspect that for Charlie the former matters and not the latter, although that answer must not be assumed.

ACKNOWLEDGMENTS

A dim and most abbreviated version of this paper was first presented at the ORSA/TIMS National Meetings, Colorado Springs, November 11, 1980, under the title "Careers in occupational communities: On being what you do." We have extensively revised that paper (several times), sometimes deleting, but mostly adding, materials we felt appropriate. Critical readers of note include Lotte Bailyn, L. L. Cummings, Deborah Kolb, Peter K. Manning, Edgar H. Schein, and Barry Staw. They are not to be blamed for whatever substantive or judgemental errors are contained in this paper. They tried to warn us. Partial support for the writing was provided by: Chief of Naval Research, Psychological Services Division (Code 453), Organizational Effectiveness Research Programs, Office of Naval Research, Arlington, Virginia, 22217; under Contract Number N00014-80-C-0905; NR 170-911.

NOTES

1. A sociology of knowledge perspective informs the way we handle the various work ethnographies (Berger and Luckman, 1966; Schutz and Luckman, 1973). Such an approach emphasizes the many ways people make sense of their lives and find meaning in work. A sociology of knowledge perspective also encourages the enlargement of our field of study by suggesting that people draw meaning and worth from endeavors beyond those traditionally studied by organizational researchers. Streetcorner hustlers, carnival workers, organic farmers, dishwashers, drug dealers, gamblers, fishermen, street sweepers, and housewives all work and, for the most part, define what they do as work. Such activities are rarely part of the popular conception of "real work" in this society, yet, for those involved, such activities are, indisputably, work. We follow Polanyi (1958) in this regard and take the view that any activity used to make a living is to be treated as work and, as such, treated as an occupation. Miller (1981) provides an excellent introduction to this approach.

2. For examples of the best in the genres, we would suggest, in the ethnographic writings: Millman's (1977) examination of the wonderful world of surgery, Willis's (1977) care-

fully detailed analysis of how working class youngsters get working class jobs, and much of the qualitative materials appearing in the journal *Urban Life*. In the organization behavior writings, Pfeffer's (1981) analysis of the sources and uses of power in organizations comes to mind as does Weick's (1979) highly charged writings on social systems and virtually all that appears in *Administrative Science Quarterly*. To bring these two literatures to bear on one another is an important task.

3.   An exception to this general rule is found in studies of labor-management relations. Historically, the so-called institutional school emphasized participant-observation studies of work life and suggested that the roots of labor-management conflict are found in the expropriation of labor value by management (Hill, 1981). More recently, however, the institutional approach has lost ground (at least in the United States), replaced by the more sanguine view of work organization as a "system" by which divergent interests are brought into line through such mechanisms as collective bargaining, strikes, grievance procedures, and so on (Dunlop, 1958). Studies in this newer tradition take a variable approach, emphasizing large samples and sophisticated, quasi-experimental, statistical research designs in the apparent hope of uncovering the correlates of various dispute settlement patterns. As a result, the industrial relations literature and the organization behavior literature have begun to very much resemble one another (e.g., Kochan, 1980; Bacharach and Lawler, 1980). When labor-management clashes are unavoidable, such impasse is seen in terms of the divergent interest of unions (composed of a federation of occupations) and organizations (composed of managers representing de facto ownership). Rarely, then, do the thwarted but specified occupational interests of workers (or managers) enter into the analysis of union-management relations. Braverman's (1974) work represents a break from U.S. traditions, but such work has yet to become the research norm. A good review of these traditions and an overview of what, in England, has become the "New Industrial Relations" is provided by Hill (1981).

4.   This conceptual situation is, in part, an artifact of viewing work organizations as systems for the achievement of goals (Bernard, 1938). Such a view emphasizes cooperation and anything seen to disrupt goal achievement is, by definition, dysfunctional and deviant. Behavior is viewed according to plan and is of note only when it is out of line. Key figures in the control scheme are supervisors who keep the enterprise "on track" by providing "negative feedback" to correct deviations. The so-called natural or taken-for-granted condition is the existing set of organizational relations and goals to which organizational members are to attach themselves. When they do not, moral or ethical questions are entertained, thus making any demonstrated lack of attachment deviant. The failure of researchers to appreciate value diversity, particularly in regard to worker resistance to dissatisfying work roles and goals, is a failure we would like very much to correct. This point has been a key notion in the so-called Critical Theory approach to organizational theorizing and is made powerfully by Clegg and Dunkerley (1980). A brief discussion of the role critical theory might play within an interpretive and phenomenological framework is provided by Van Maanen (1981).

5.   The two forms of social organization were given different names by various theorists. Weber (1968) wrote of the "communal" and the "associative." Durkheim (1933) contrasted "mechanistic" with "organic" solidarity. Tönnies (1957) used "gemeinshaft" and "gesselshaft" which, according to Gusfield (1975) are the terms most frequently adopted by sociologists.

6.   On the Chicago School's contribution to an understanding of modern life, see both Faris's (1979) social history and Rock's (1979) intellectual history. The theoretical perspective most frequently associated with Chicago School sociology is symbolic interactionism of which Blumer's (1969) description is authoritative.

7.   Gusfield's caution and preference for phenomenologically sensitive depictions of the boundaries of a community echo those of Weber (1968:42):

"It is by no means true that the existence of common qualities, a common situation, or common modes of behavior imply the existence of a communal social relationship. Thus, for instance, the possession of a common biological inheritance by virtue of which persons are classified as belonging to the same 'race,' naturally implies no sort of communal social relationship between them. By restrictions on social intercourse and on marriage, persons may find themselves in a similar situation, a situation of isolation from the environment that imposes these distinctions. But, even if they all react to this situation in the same way, this does not constitute a communal relationship. The latter does not even exist if they have a common 'feeling' about this situation and its consequences. It is only when this feeling leads to a mutual orientation of their behavior to each other that a social relationship arises between them rather than of each to the environment. Furthermore, it is only so far as this relationship involves feelings of belonging together that it is a 'communal' relationship."

8. The distinction used by Harris (1968, 1975) between "emic" and "etic" modes of analysis is useful in this regard. Emic study attempts to understand and describe the world from the perspective of those who are studied. Etic study attempts to understand and describe the world scientifically, using variables which pattern behavior in ways typically hidden from those who are studied. Though we perhaps err in the direction of run-on emics when depicting work worlds (in part, a reaction to the abstract and rather dull organizational theorizing currently in vogue), the interplay between the two is very much our concern in this paper.

9. "Guinea" is a term used by fishermen in Gloucester to identify Italian fishermen, typically Sicilian, who have more or less adopted American customs and mores. "Greaser" is a term used by Guineas to refer to recent immigrants, also typically Sicilians, who have not yet become acculturated to the larger American scene. Greasers are thought to cling stubbornly to their native language and the ways of the old country (Miller and Van Maanen, 1979).

10. Joining network analysis with interview or ethnographic techniques offers a promising methodological strategy in this regard. Network models operate on observed or self-reported connections (e.g., exchanges, communications, acquaintances, etc.) among members of a given population. The meaning of such networks to members, as well as the grounds upon which such networks are built and change are, however, matters not so easily mapped since they require sensible qualitative study. Usually, one method or the other is employed in social research, but rarely both. The result is an elegant network model whose meaning to those modelled is quite unclear; . . . or, a rich account of the meanings members provide to their world whose empirical references (and connections) are left largely unchecked. A recent exception to this rule is Faulkner's (1982) inventive melding of the two approaches. Granovetter (1974) provides an early example.

11. By reference groups, we follow Shibutani's (1962:132) lead: "[The] group whose presumed perspective is used by an actor as the frame of reference in the organization of his perceptual field. . . . A reference group is an audience consisting of real or imaginary personifications, to whom certain values are imputed. It is an audience before whom a person tries to maintain or enhance his standing." It is hard to improve on this definition.

12. Culture, from this standpoint, is not strong or weak any more than it is good or bad. It simply is. Any two cultures will, of course, contrast but it takes an outsider to provide the dimensions of contrast and, as we suggest in this paper, such dimensions may or may not be of relevance to cultural members. On alternative perspectives on culture, Sanday's (1979) review of ethnographic paradigms has direct relevance to organizational and occupational research.

13. Occupational cultures may, of course, reside more or less peacefully within (and as part of) organizational cultures, may exist alongside and in opposition to them, may be

buried by them, or may even contain them. Within organizations, occupational cultures are subcultures harboring segments of relative diversity within a generally approved organization plan; alongside organizations, occupational cultures compete with the plan, offering to its membership alternative goals; when buried by organizations, occupational cultures cease to exist; and, when containing organizations, the occupational and organization cultures are one and the same. This crude taxonomy, discussed in more depth later in the paper, only begins to suggest the kinds of interactions possible. The main point is, however, the need to explain each rather than assume the priority of one over the other. Schein's (forthcoming) analysis of organizational culture is sensitive to these issues, unlike other ventures into this domain where culture is treated too often as an undifferentiated organizational variable subject to varying degrees of managerial control (Schwartz and Davis, 1981; Deal and Kennedy, 1982). In such a fashion, culture becomes merely another roadside attraction in the study of organizations, something to be attended to or not, based on an analyst's preference.

   14.   Goffman's (1961a) version of role distance is of obvious relevance here as are some of the empirical materials on the role working class cultures play inside some organizations, such as Katz (1965), Shostack (1969), Ferree (1976), and Foner (1976). Much of this material suggests that the less control people have over the pace, methods, outputs of work, the more likely they are to smuggle in interests and identities relevant outside the workplace. As noted in the text, in occupational communities the flow of interests and identities goes the other way.

   15.   The materials in this section draw on work highly critical of research treating the professions as homogeneous social groups whose members are united by common expertise and a calling to service (e.g., Johnson, 1972; Roth, 1974; Larson, 1977; Bledstein, 1976). As noted later in the text, professions are best regarded as loose federations of multiple groups, some of which may be occupational communities, forming around special interests, ideologies, and skills (Bucher and Strauss, 1961). The structural conditions allowing an occupational group self-control more or less are derived from Child and Fulk's (1982) first-rate comparative analysis of the professions' control of occupations. We think these dimensions have a more general worth and thus have followed their lead in this section.

   16.   We turn back to this topic later in the paper when discussing occupational careers. There we will argue that the cognitive learning associated with an occupational role precedes the learning of skills and that the difference is reflected in the popular conceptions of "knowing" and "know-how." The latter, in terms of establishing an occupational niche, is far more important than the former.

   17.   Caplow (1954) still provides the sociological primer on these matters; the examples may be dated, but the ideas are not. Bensman and Lilienfeld (1973) provide a useful reading of the historical sources of meaning in work. Recent writings tend toward the more specific and, hence, occupationally unique histories such as Noble's (1979) look at engineers in America or Miller's (1977) comparative treatment of cops and bobbies.

   18.   Turner and Hodge (1970) also point to a second approach to the professions which they call the "community approach." This approach emphasizes social characteristics, in particular the attitudes and values of those certified to practice the profession (Goode, 1957). We fall closer to the community approach but do not feel it is useful, as discussed in the following section, to sharply distinguish the professions as unique occupational communities.

   19.   Lyman and Scott (1970) on "accounts" and Hewitt and Stokes (1975) on "disclaimers" are mandatory reading on this matter. Both owe debts to Mills (1940) "vocabulary of motives" idea. Bringing this line of thought to organizational theorizing is Starbuck (1982) in his examination of organizational ideologies.

   20.   The classic case of occupational control via union activity is, of course, the now woefully out-of-date Lipset *et al.* (1956) study of the typographical union. Currently, the battle of occupational self-control through unionization seems most visible in the public

services—particularly in teaching (e.g., Cole, 1969) and policing (e.g., Long and Fenulli, 1974). Freidson's (1973) reader is good on the issues raised by occupational communities in public organizations as is a recent article by Ponak (1981).

21.   Bledstein (1976) is good on this point, taking care to note the special and elite connotations the term "professional" holds for Americans in contrast to the equally special but low connotations carried by the union-member tag. Larry Cummings (personal communication) suggests that unionization of an occupational group may actually lower the occupation's social status. For example, faculty unionization may lower the status of an institution's faculty in the eyes of the general public. While data are scarce on these matters, similar propositions seem not to hold in Western Europe where union membership neither symbolizes the vulgar pursuit of filthy lucre, nor conveys relatively low social standing. Unlike Europe, in the United States union membership as a proportion of the workforce has been on a downward slide for some time (Edwards, 1979:202). Certainly this suggests the diminished appeal of unions in the U.S., but the reasons underlying such trends are no doubt far more complicated than by what can be slipped in under the social status argument.

22.   Representative writings on occupation stress (and its popular semantic referent, "burnout") in the human service industry include Paine (ed.) (1982), and Cherniss (1980). Perhaps one reason behind the disproportionate attention given to stress in the bootstrapping versus elite occupations is that the elite are well compensated for their efforts and are relatively more distant from the carriers and substance of "other people's misery." Were the elite trades such as law and medicine to claim "burnout," the public might well begin to question the practical premises upon which these occupations are based (i.e., that they do what they claim to do and the practitioners are well qualified and screened to do it). Aside from more money, one solution to stress, infrequently mentioned in the literature of course, is for an occupational community to somehow generate a "better class" of clients which, empirical evidence suggests, also leads to heightened professional standing (Freidson, 1970).

23.   The terms "external" and "internal" career are found in Van Maanen, Schein, and Bailyn (1977). The phrase "external career" refers to the path and sequence of positions and roles that constitute a career in an organization or occupation. "Internal career" connotes the meaning career related roles and experiences have for an individual. See Van Maanen (1977) for an elaboration of how internal careers are constructed.

24.   The use of "career" to refer to advancement within a sequence of hierarchically arranged positions no doubt reflects the use of the term in everyday language. We are suggesting, however, that popular discourse may not be the best guide for the definition of a concept thought to have theoretical value. Indeed, we are arguing that, as an analytic construct, the term "career" needs to be broadened beyond its colloquial connotation. Lotte Bailyn (personal communication) argues that to achieve such aims we may need to invent a new term devoid of an implied escalator clause. We tentatively agree, but are waiting for inspiration.

25.   Although the least studied of Schein's (1971) three dimensions, some recent work has been devoted to formalizing the inclusionary or centrality dimension. Van Maanen (1980a) notes that movement along this dimension can be seen in terms of rule learning, rule use, rule breaking, rules about rule breaking, and so on. Gregory (1980) provides a taxonomy of organizational inclusion that is sensitive to cross-cultural contexts.

26.   The rigid separation between captain and crew seems, in the United States at least, to be less prominent than sea stories would have us believe. In particular, the increasing geographic mobility of fishermen, along with the diminishing (regulated) lengths of fishing seasons, has created a situation where many fishermen jump from port to port throughout the year. These so-called flying fishermen not only fish different species in different ports in different seasons of the year, they often do so in different occupational roles. Thus, a

skipper on a salmon vessel may also be an engineer on a tuna boat and a deckhand on a groundfish dragger. With such movement has come greater egalitarianism among fishermen. For a descriptive treatment of the causes and consequences of this relatively recent phenomena, see Van Maanen, Miller, and Johnson (1982).

27. We must note that the phrase "early periods of occupational learning" is a relative one. Some occupations require apprenticeships that extend over very long periods of time. Trades such as masonry are excellent examples where one passes from laborer or helper, to apprentice, to journeyman, and, finally to craftsman. The trek takes many years. Consider, also, psychiatrists, who may be well into their mid- to late-thirties before fully shedding the student role. Greer (1972) provides a nice set of examples of varying forms of apprenticeship.

28. On the matters of practical reasoning and task rituals, ethnomethodologists have much to say as Garfinkel's (1967) classic analysis of "good reasons for bad organizational records" demonstrates. From this perspective, Kolb (forthcoming) provides a marvelous example of how the members of one relatively tight occupational community (federal mediators) routinely orchestrate work matters in ways that dramatically contrast to those rituals adopted by another, relatively similar, occupational community (state mediators).

29. This process is, at least according to Marxist scholars, in no way a natural or evolutionary one. Deskilling proceeds through the conscious design of management rather than being merely a technical requirement of the production of particular goods and services (Braverman, 1974). We tend to agree but hasten to add, as does Giddens (1973), that class determinism is as equally full of dogma and unsupported contention as the technological determinism it seeks to replace.

30. Our discussion of coalitions parallels Dalton's (1959:57–65) more refined consideration of clique-formation in management circles. In Dalton's scheme, three general types of cliques can be identified: vertical, horizontal, and random. Vertical cliques subdivide into the symbiotic varieties where exchanges between higher level and lower level members of the organization are more or less balanced and the parasitic varieties where lower level members receive more than they give. Horizontal cliques are distinguished by their defensive or aggressive stance vis-a-vis general organizational policies. Random cliques are those based strictly on friendship and social satisfaction without conscious consideration of organizational policy or work goals. Occupational communities, if viewed as cliques inside an organization, would typically fall into Dalton's horizontal-aggressive classification when not faced with immediate threat. But, occupational communities, in our view, are much more than cliques since: (1) their formation rests on matters not organizationally specific; (2) the ties binding the membership are long lasting, potentially binding across the working lives of the members; and (3) though they may perform some of the same functions cliques in organizations do, such as bridging the official and unofficial goals of organizational members, their substantive concern for occupational self-control will invariably transcend issue-specific organizational concerns.

31. The essence of loose-coupling, as used in the organization literature, is that the stimulus-response links between any two subsystems are unpredictable (Glassman, 1973; Weick, 1976). A very nice, highly detailed illustration of equivocal and tentative links is provided in Manning's (forthcoming) analysis of police communication systems where the subsystems of dispatch and patrol are shown to be loosely-coupled for a variety of structural and phenomenological reasons. Attempts to tighten the links between the two by police administrators have repeatedly met with failure.

32. Gouldner's (1954) "vicious cycle" emerged from a study of underground miners who, prior to a personnel switch in management, possessed considerable work autonomy. When new management moved to call in some of this autonomy by formulating a set of new work rules, the miners reacted by claiming new ares of autonomy which brought forth more rules from management, and so on. A related point, well made by Douglas (1970), is that formal rules indicate deviance: the more rules, typically, the more rules, typically, the more

and more widespread the deviance. That the two play off each other is Gouldner's (1954) original point.

33. The irony should not be lost. What Sofer's (1970) work suggests is that promotion is based, in part, on one's "desire for promotion." A self-sealing cycle may be created in which ambition is valued for ambition's sake, driving out even the most sincere efforts to pin promotions upon demonstrated performance at a given level. Part of the problem is, no doubt, the ambiguity surrounding the assessment of managerial work so the search for promotional criteria leads back to such personal attributions as ambition, desire, drive, strength, will, and so forth Apparently, the situation in many American firms is that, in the absence of performance indicators, striving will do. Sennett (1977) provides interesting commentary on these matters, updating the master work in the field of organization men by Whyte (1956).

34. Despite this list of four deadly sins, research in the area is by no means dead. Recent work is still attempting to clarify the meaning of "local" and "cosmopolitan." Several studies proceed by factor analysis of items drawn from Gouldner's original questionnaire or from a questionnaire developed by Goldberg, *et al.* (1965). For example, Berger and Grimes (1973), Flago and Brumbaugh (1974), and Tuma and Grimes (1981) all show that localism and cosmopolitanism are independent dimensions rather than bi-polar, and that each are aggregate concepts "tapping" any number of underlying concepts. Whether or not such studies, in fact, clarify the meaning of local and cosmopolitan is, in our view, most uncertain.

35. This assumption derives directly from Gouldner's (1957:290) original paper where he notes "cosmopolitans are oriented to outer reference groups whereas locals use an inner reference group."

36. Lest we be accused of being Luddites in this regard, we must specify our context. In some areas, notably communication systems through which stolen cars and property can be traced, technology has increased the police's ability to at least detect, if not deter, crime. In other areas, such as the use of automobile patrol units in high population density neighborhoods, technology has impaired police functioning since they have lost touch with their clientele whose cooperation is essential for detecting some crimes, particularly street crimes. The ambiguity of technology in the context of police work is a point well covered by Manning (1981; forthcoming).

37. Again, Manning (1981) provides the empirical materials in his police communication work. The point not made explicitly in the text is that the presence of static, low flying objects, and black holes serves a purpose for patrol officers who are busy at times with matters from which they do not wish to be distracted. Not wanting to be bothered by intrusive dispatchers who may try to whisk them away on other, less desirable, missions of mercy such as locating barking dogs or calming belligerent drunks, patrol officers simply fail to respond to dispatch, claiming later, if the matter arises, that they never heard the command or request. While sophisticated equipment allows dispatchers to efficiently send a message with very little noise, they must still rely on human contact to discover that their message has been received. This stands almost as a textbook example of a loosely-coupled system masquerading as a tightly-coupled one.

REFERENCES

Allen, T. *Managing the flow of technology*. Cambridge, MA: MIT Press, 1977.
Argyris, C. *Integrating the individual and the organization*. New York: Wiley, 1964.
Bacharach, S. B., and Lawler, E. J. *Power and politics in organizations*. San Francisco: Jossey Bass, 1980.
Bailyn, L. *Living with technology*. Cambridge, MA: MIT Press, 1980.

Bailyn, L. *Work and family: Testing the assumptions*. Paper presented at the Academy of
    Management Annual Meetings, New York, 1982.
Barley, S. *The student life office: A case study*. Unpublished manuscript, Cornell University.
    1979.
Barley, S. *Taking the burdens: The strategic role of the funeral director*. Working paper
    No. 1129-80, Sloan School of Management, MIT, 1980.
Barley, S. The semiotics of funeral work. *Urban Life*, 1983, *12*, 3–33.
Barley, S. The professional, the semi-professional, and the machine: A study of the intro-
    duction of new imaging modalities into three radiology departments, (PhD dissertation)
    MIT, forthcoming.
Barthes, R. *Elements of semiology*. Boston: Beacon Press, 1967.
Becker, H. S. The professional dance musician and His audience. *American Journal of
    Sociology*, 1951, *57*, 136–144.
Becker, H. S. *Outsiders: studies in the sociology of deviance*. New York: Free Press, 1963.
Becker, H. S. and Carper, J. The elements of identification with an occupation. *American
    Sociological Review*, 1956, *21*, 341–48.
Becker, H. S. and Strauss, A. Career, personality, and adult socialization. *American Journal
    of Sociology*, 1956, *62*, 253–263.
Becker, H. S., Geer, B., Riesman, D. & R. Weiss. *Institutions and the person*. Chicago:
    Aldine, 1968.
Benet, M. K. *The secretarial ghetto*. New York: McGraw-Hill, 1972.
Bennis, W. G., Berkowitz, N., Affinito, M., & M. Malone. Reference groups and loyalties
    in the outpatient department. *Administrative Science Quarterly*, 1958, *2*, 481–500.
Bensman, J. & Lilienfeld R. *Craft and consciousness*. New York: Harper and Row, 1973.
Bernard, C. I. *The functions of the executive*. Cambridge, MA: Harvard University Press,
    1938.
Berger, P. L. *The human shape of work*. South Bend, IN: Gateway, 1964.
Berger, P. L. & Luckman, T. *The social construction of reality*. New York: Doubleday,
    1966.
Berger, R. R. & Grimes, A. J. Cosmopolitan and local: A factor analysis of the construct.
    Administrative Science Quarterly, 1973, *18*, 223–235.
Beynon, H. 1973, & Blackburn, R. M. *Perceptions of work: variations within a factory*.
    Cambridge: Cambridge University Press, 1972.
Bittner, E. The concept of organization. *Social Research*, 1965, *32*, 239–255.
Blau, P. K. *The dynamics of bureaucracy*. Chicago: University of Chicago Press, 1955.
Blauner, R. *Alienation and freedom*. Chicago: University of Chicago Press, 1964.
Bledstein, B. J. *The culture of professionalism*. New York: Norton, 1976.
Bloch, F. E. & Kuskin, M. S. Wage determination in the union and non-union sectors.
    Industrial and Labor Relations Review, 1978, *31*, 183–192. (no. 28)
Blumer, H. 1978, *Symbolic interactionism*. Englewood Cliffs, NJ: Prentice-Hall, 1969.
Bosk, C. L. *Forgive and remember: managing medical failure*. Chicago: University of Chi-
    cago Press, 1979.
Braude, L. *Work and workers: A sociological analysis*. New York: Praeger Publishers, 1975.
Braverman, H. *Labor and monopoly capital*. New York: Monthly Review Press, 1974.
Brown, A. J. *The structure of career opportunities in organizations* (General Series Dis-
    cussion Paper #95). Coventry, England: Centre for Industrial Economic and Business
    Research, University of Warwick, 1981.
Bryant, C. D. Petroleum Landmen: Brothers in the 'Oil Fraternity'. In C. D. Bryant (Ed.),
    The Social Dimensions of Work. Englewood Cliffs, NJ: Prentice-Hall, 1972a.
Bryant, C. D. Sawdust in their shoes: The carnival as a neglected complex organization and
    work culture. In C. D. Bryant (Ed.), *The Social Dimensions of Work*. Englewood Cliffs,
    N.J.: Prentice-Hall, 1972b.

Bucher, R. & Strauss, A. Professions in Process. *American Journal of Sociology*, 1961, *66*, 325–334.

Caplow, T. *The Sociology of Work*. New York: McGraw Hill, 1954.

Caplow, T. & McGee, R. J. *The academic marketplace*. New York: Basic, 1958.

Carr-Sanders, A. M. & Wilson, P. A. *The professions*. Oxford: Clarendon, 1933.

Cherniss, C. *Staff burnout: Job stress in the human services* (Volume 2.). Beverly Hills, CA: Sage, 1980.

Child, J. & Fulk, J. Maintenance of occupational control: The case of professions. *Work and Occupations*, 1982, *9*, 155–192.

Chinoy, E. *Automobile workers and the american dream*. New York: Doubleday, 1955.

Clegg, S. & Dunkerly, D. *Organization, class, and control*. London: Routledge and Kegan-Paul, 1980.

Cole, S. *The unionization of teachers: A case study of the UFT*. New York: Praeger, 1980.

Cottrell, W. F. Of time and the railroader. *American Sociological Review*, 1934, *4*, 190–198.

Crane, D. *Invisible colleges: diffusion of knowledge in scientific communities*. Chicago: University of Chicao Press, 1972.

Crozier, M. *The bureaucratic phenomenon*. London: Tavistock, 1964.

Daft, R. L. The evolution of organizational analysis in ASQ: 1959–1979. *Administrative Science Quarterly*, 1980, *25*, 623–636.

Dalton, M. *Men who manage*. New York: Wiley, 1959.

Dawe, A. *The two sociologists*. London: Longmans, 1980.

Deal, T. and A. Kennedy (1982) *Corporate Cultures: The Rites and Rituals of Corporate Life*, Reading, MA: Addison-Wesley.

Dore, R. P. *British factory—Japanese factory*. Berkeley: University of California Press, 1973.

Douglas, J. D. (Ed.). *Understanding everyday life*. Chicago: Aldine, 1970.

Driver, M. J. Career concepts and organizational change. In C. B. Derr (Ed.), *Work family and career: New frontiers in theory and research*. New York: Praeger, 1980.

Dubin, R. Industrial workers' worlds. *Social Problems*, 1956, *3*, 131–142.

Dunlop, J. *Industrial relations systems*. Carbondale, IL: Southern Illinois University Press, 1958.

Durkheim, E. [*The division of labor in society*] (G. Simpson, trans.) New York: Free Press, 1933. (Originally published, 1893.)

Durkheim, E. [*Suicide*] (J. A. Spaulding and G. Simpson trans.) Glencoe, IL: Free Press, 1951. (Originally published, 1897.)

Eco. *A theory of semiotics*. Bloomington: Indiana, 1976.

Edwards, R. *Contested terrain*. New York: Basic, 1979.

Emerson, J. Behavior in public places: sustaining definitions of reality in gynecological examinations. In H. P. Dreitzel (Ed.), *Recent sociology*. New York: Macmillan, 1970.

Faris, R. E. L. *Chicago sociology, 1920–1932*. Chicago: University of Chicago Press, 1979.

Faulkner, R. R. Coming of age in organizations: A comparative study of career contingencies and adult socialization. *Sociology of Work and Occupations*, 1974, *1*, 131–173.

Faulkner, R. R. *Music on demand*. Philadelphia: Trans-action Books, 1982.

Feldman, S. P. *The culture of monopoly management: An interpretive study in an american utility*. Unpublished Ph.D. Dissertation, University of Pennsylvania, 1982.

Ferree, M. M. Working-class jobs: Housework and paid work as sources of satisfaction. *Social Problems*, 1976, *23*, 431–441.

Fielding, A. G. & Portwood, D. Professions and the state: Towards a typology of bureaucratic professions. *Sociological Review*, 1980, *28*, 1, 23–53.

Flango, V. E. & Brumbaugh, R. B. The dimensionality of the cosmopolitan-local construct. *Administrative Science Quarterly*, 1974, *19*, 198–210.

Foner, P. S. *Factory girls*. Urbana, IL: University of Illinois Press, 1977.

Freidson, E. *Professional dominance: The social structure of medical care*. New York: Atherton Press, 1970.

Freidson, E. (Ed.). *The professions and their prospects*. Beverly Hills, CA: Sage, 1973.

Gamst, F. C. *The hogshead*. New York: Holt, Rinehart, and Winston, 1980.

Garfield, S. R. The delivery of medical care. *Scientific American*, 1970, *222*, 15–23.

Garfinkel, H. *Studies in ethnomethodology*. Englewood Cliffs, NJ: Prentice-Hall, 1967.

Geertz, C. *The Interpretation of Culture*. New York: Basic, 1973.

Gertzl, B. G. Determinants of occupational community in high status occupations. *Sociological Quarterly*, 1961, *2*, 37–40.

Giddens, A. *The class structure of the advanced societies*. London: Hutchinson, 1973.

Glaser, B. G. *Organizational scientists*. Indianapolis: Bobbs-Merrill, 1964.

Glaser, B. G. (Ed.). *Organizational careers: A sourcebook for theory*. Chicago: Aldine, 1968.

Glaser, B. G. & Strauss, A. *Status passages*. Chicago: Aldine, 1971.

Glaser, B. G. *Expert versus laymen: A study of the patsy and the subcontractor*. Mill Valley California: The Sociology Press, 1972.

Glaser, W. A. *Paying the doctor: systems of remuneration and their effects*. Baltimore: Johns Hopkins Press, 1970.

Goffman, E. *The presentation of self in everyday life*. Garden City, NY: Anchor, 1959.

Goffman, E. *Encounters*. Indianapolis: Bobbs-Merrill, 1961a.

Goffman, E. The moral career of a mental patient. *Asylums*. New York: Anchor, 1961b.

Goffman, E. *Frame analysis*. New York: Harper and Row, 1974.

Gold, R. L. In the basement: The apartment building janitor. In P. L. Berger (Ed.), *The Human Shape of Work*. South Bend IN: Gateway, 1964.

Goldberg, L. C., Baker, E. & Rubenstein, A. H. Local-cosmopolitan: Unidimensional or multidimensional. *American Journal of Sociology*, 1965, *2*, 704–710.

Goldner, F. H. & Ritti, R. R. Professionalization as career immobility. *American Journal of Sociology*, 1967, *72*, 489–502.

Goode, W. J. A theory of role-strain. *American Sociological Review*, 1960, *25*, 483–496.

Goode, W. Community within a community. *American Sociological Review*, 1957, *22*, 194–200.

Goodenough, W. *Description and comparison in cultural anthropology*. Chicago: Aldine, 1970.

Gouldner, A. Cosmopolitans and locals: toward an analysis of latent social roles. *Administrative Science Quarterly*, 1957, *2*, 281–306.

Granovetter, M. S. *Getting a job: A study of contacts and careers*. Cambridge, MA: Harvard University Press, 1974.

Graves, B. Breaking out: An apprenticeship system among pipeline construction workers. *Human Organization*, 1958, *17*, 9–13.

Greenwood, E. Attributes of a Profession. *Social Work*, 1957, *2*, 45–55.

Greer, B. (Ed.). *Learning to work*. Beverly Hills, CA: Sage, 1972.

Gregory, K. L. Work organizations and careers: A theoretical framework for anthropologists and three cross-cultural applications. Unpublished paper, Department of Anthropology, Northwestern University, 1980.

Grimes, A. J. & Berger, P. K. Cosmopolitan-local: evaluation of the construct. *Administrative Science Quarterly*, 1970, *15*, 407–416.

Gusfield, J. R. *Community: A critical response*. New York: Harper and Row, 1975.

Haas, J. Learning real feelings: A study of high steel ironworkers reactions to fear and danger. *Sociology of Work and Occupations*, 1977, *4*, 147–171.

Habenstein, R. W. Sociology of occupations: The case of the american funeral director. In A. Rose (Ed.), *Human Behavior and Social Processes*. Boston: Houghton Mifflin, 1962.

Hackman, J. R. & Oldham, G. R. *Work redesign*. Reading, MA: Addison-Wesley, 1979.

Hall, D. T. *Careers in organizations*. Pacific Palisades, CA: Goodyear, 1976.

Hall, D. J. & Lawler, E. E. Job characteristics and pressures and the organizational integration of professionals. *Administration Science Quarterly*, 1970, *57* (3), 271–281.

Harlow, D. Professional employees' preference for upward mobility. *Journal of Applied Psychology*, 1973, *57* (2), 137–141.

Harris, M. *The rise of anthropological theory*. New York: T. Y. Crowell, 1968.

Harris, M. Why a perfect knowledge of all the rules that one must know in order to act like a native cannot lead to a knowledge of how natives act. *Journal of Anthropological Research*, 1975, *30*, 5–22.

Haug, M. The deprofessionalization of everyone. *Social Focus*, 1975, *8*, 197–213.

Haug, M. Computer technology and the obsolescence of the concept of profession. In M. R. Haug and J. Dofny (Eds.), *Work and Technology*. Beverly Hills: Sage, 1977.

Haug, M. R. & Sussman, M. B. Professionalization and unionism: A jurisdictional dispute? In E. Freidson (Ed.), *The Professions and their Prospects*. Beverly Hills, CA: Sage, 1973.

Hawkes, T. *Structuralism and semiotics*. Berkeley: University of California Press, 1977.

Hayano, D. *Poker faces: The life and work of professional card players*. Berkeley: University of California Press, 1982.

Hewitt, J. W. & Stokes, R. Disclaimers. *American Sociological Review*, 1975, *40* (1), 1–11.

Hill, S. *Competition and control at work: The new industrial sociology*. Cambridge, MA: MIT Press, 1981.

Hirschman, A. O. *Exit, voice and loyalty: Responses to decline in firms, organizations, and states*. Cambridge, MA: Harvard University Press, 1970.

Hughes, E. C. Work and self. In J. Rohrer and M. Sherif (Eds.), *Social Psychology at the Crossroads*. New York: Harper and Row, 1951.

Hughes, E. C. *Men and their work*. Glencoe, IL: Free Press, 1958.

Hughes, E. C. *The sociological eye: Selected papers on work, self, and the study of society*. Chicago: Aldine, 1971.

Illich, I. *Medical nemesis*. New York: Pantheon, 1976.

James, J. On the block. *Urban Anthropology*, 1972, *4*, 125–140.

Janowitz, M. *The professional soldier*. Glencoe, IL: Free Press, 1960.

Jermier, J. J. Labor process control in modern organizations. Unpublished paper, Department of Management and Administrative Sciences, University of Florida, 1982.

Jessup, D. K. Teacher unionization: A reassessment of rank and file motivation. *Sociology of Education*, 1978, *51*, 41–55.

Johnson, T. J. *Professions and power*. London: Macmillan, 1972.

Kanter, R. M. *Men and women of the corporation*. New York. Basic, 1979.

Katz, F. Explaining autonomy in formal work groups in complex organizations. *Administrative Science Quarterly*, 1965, *10*, 204–223.

Kerr, S. Substitutes for leadership: Some implications for organizational design. *Organization and Administrative Sciences*, 1977, *8*, 135–146.

Klapp, O. E. *Heroes, villains, and fools*. Englewood Cliffs, NJ: Prentice-Hall, 1962.

Klegon, D. The sociology of the professions: An emerging Perspective. *Sociology of Work and Occupations*, 1979, *5* (3), 276–292.

Klein, L. *A social scientist in industry*. London: Gower Press, 1976.

Kochan, T. A. *Collective bargaining and industrial relations*. Homewood, IL: Richard D. Irwin, 1980.

Kolb, D. *The Mediators*. Cambridge, MA: MIT Press, forthcoming.

Kornblum, W. *Blue collar community*. Chicago: University of Chicago Press, 1974.

Kornhauser, W. *Scientists in industry: Conflict and accommodation*. Berkeley: University of California Press, 1962.

Kraft, P. The routinization of computer programming. *Sociology of Work and Occupations*, 1979, *6* (2), 139–155.

Kunda, Gideon. Personal communication. MIT, 1982.

Larson, M. S. *The rise of professionalism*. Berkeley: University of California Press, 1977.

Lasson, K. *The workers: Portraits of nine american jobholders*. New York: Grossman, 1971.

Lawrence, P. R. & Lorsch, J. W. *Organization and environment*. Cambridge, MA: Harvard University Press, 1967.

Lieberman, S. The effects of changes in role on the attitudes of role occupants. *Human Relations*, 1956, *9*, 385–402.

Light, D. *Becoming psychiatrists*. New York: Norton, 1980.

Lipset, S. M., Trow, M. & Coleman, J. *Union democracy*. New York: Free Press, 1956.

Lipsky, M. *Street level bureaucracy*. New York: Sage, 1980.

Long, G. & Feuille, P. Final offer arbitration: Sudden death in eugene. *Industrial and Labor Relations Review*, 1974, *27*, 186–203.

Lortie, D. C. *Schoolteacher*. Chicago: University of Chicago Press, 1975.

Lyman, S. & Scott, M. *A Sociology of the absurd*. New York: Meredith, 1970.

Lynch, J. T. & Bailyn, L. *Engineering as a lifelong career*. Unpublished paper, Sloan School of Management, MIT, 1980.

Manning, P. K. *Police work: The social organization of policing*. Cambridge, MA: MIT Press, 1977.

Manning, P. K. *Crime and technology: The role of scientic research and technology in crime control*. Paper prepared for the National Science Foundation Science and Technology Project, Washington, D. C., 1979.

Manning, P. K. *Producing drama: Symbolic communication and the police*. Unpublished paper, Wolfson College, Oxford University, 1981.

Manning, P. K. Organization control and semiotics. In M. Punch (Ed.), *Control in Police Organization*. Cambridge, MA: MIT Press, 1983.

March, J. G. & Simon, H. A. *Organizations*. New York: Wiley, 1958.

Marcson, S. *The scientist in american industry*. New York: Harper and Row, 1960.

Marglin, S. A. What do bosses do: The origins and functions of hierarchy in capitalist production. *Review of Radical Political Economics*, 1974 *6*, 60–112.

McGregor, D. *The human side of enterprise*. New York: McGraw-Hill, 1960.

Mead, G. H. *Mind, self, and society*. Chicago: University of Chicago Press, 1930.

Mechanic, D. *The growth of bureaucratic medicine*. New York: Wiley, 1976.

Mendes, R. H. P. *Sociological ambivalence, role strain, and the professional union*. Unpublished paper, Department of Sociology, Brooklyn College, 1982.

Merton, R. K. Patterns of influence: A study of interpersonal influence and of communications behavior in a local community. In P. F. Lazarsfeld and F. Stanton (Eds.), *Communications Research 1948–49*. New York: Harper, 1949.

Messinger, S. L., Sampson, H. & Towne, P. D. Life as theatre: Some notes on the dramaturgic approach to social reality. *Sociometry*, 1962, *25*, 98–110.

Midford, J. *The American way of death*. New York: Simon & Shuster, 1963.

Miller, G. *It's a living: Work in modern society*. New York: St. Martin's Press, 1981.

Miller, M. & Van Maanen, J. Boats don't fish, people do: Some ethnographic notes on federal management of fisheries. *Human Organizations*, 1979, *38*, 377–385.

Miller, M. & Van Maanen, J. Getting into fishing: Social identities of fishermen. *Urban Life*, 1982, *11*, (1), 27–54.

Miller, W. *Cops and bobbies*. Chicago: University of Chicago Press, 1977.

Millman, M. *The unkindest cut: Life in the backrooms of medicine*. New York: Morrow Quill, 1977.

Mills, C. W. Situated actions and vocabularies of motive. *American Sociological Review*, 1940, *5*, 904–913.

Mills, C. W. *White Collar*. New York: Oxford University Press, 1956.

Mintzberg, H. *The nature of managerial work*. Englewood Cliffs, NJ: Prentice-Hall, 1973

Montagna, P. D. The public accounting profession: Organization ideology and social power. In E. Freidson (Ed.), *The Professions and Their Prospects*. Beverly Hills, CA: Sage, 1973.

Niederhoffer, A. & Niederhoffer, E. *The police family*. Lexington, MA: D.C. Heath, 1978.

Noble, D. F. *America by design*. New York: Oxford University Press, 1977.

Oppenheimer, M. The proletarianization of the professional. *Sociological Review Monograph*, 1973, *20*, 213–227.

Paine, W. S. (Ed.). *Job stress and burnout*. Beverly Hills, CA: Sage, 1982.

Park, R. E. & Burgess, E. W. *Introduction to the science of sociology*. Chicago: University of Chicago Press, 1924.

Peirce, C. S. *Collected Papers of Charles Sanders Peirce*. Cambridge, MA: Harvard University Press, 1931–1958.

Pettigrew, A. M. *The politics of organizational decision making*. London: Tavistock, 1973.

Pfeffer, J. Organizational demography. In L. L. Cummings and Barry M. Staw (Eds.), *Research in Organizational Behavior*, Vol. 5. Greenwich, CT: JAI Press, 1983.

Polanyi, M. *Personal knowledge: Towards a post-critical philosophy*. Chicago: University of Chicago, 1958.

Polanyi, M. *The tacit dimension*. Garden City, NJ: Doubleday, 1966.

Ponok, A. M. Unionized professionals and the scope of bargaining. *Industrial and Labor Relations Review*, 1981, *34*, 396–407.

Reimer, J. Becoming a journeyman electrician. *Sociology of Work and Occupations* 1977, *4*, 87–98.

Rice, A. K. *Productivity and social organization: The ahmedabad experiment*. London: Tavistock, 1958.

Roberts, J. M., Thompson, W. E. & Sutton-Smith B. Expressive self-testing in driving. *Human Organization*, *25*, 54–63.

Rock, P. *The Making of Symbolic Interactionism*, Totona, NJ: Rowman and Littlefield.

Ritti, R. Work goals of scientists and engineers. *Industrial Relations*, 1968, *7*, 118–131.

Roethlisberger, F. J. & Dickson, W. J. *Management and the worker*. Cambridge MA: Harvard University Press, 1939.

Rosenbaum, J. E. Organizational career mobility: promotion chances in a corporation during periods of growth and contraction. *American Journal of Sociology*, 1979, *85*, 21–48.

Roth, J. A. Professionalism: The sociologist's decoy. *Sociology of Work and Occupations*, 1974, *1*, 6–23.

Roy, D. Banana time: Job satisfaction and informal interaction. *Human Organization*, 1960, *18*, 158–168.

Rubinstein, J. *City Police*. New York: Farrar, Straus & Jeroux, 1973.

Salaman, G. *Community and occupation*. London: Cambridge university press, 1974.

Sanday, P. R. The ethnographic paradigm(s). *Administrative Science Quarterly*, 1979, *24*, 527–538.

Sanders, W. B. *Detective work*. New York: Free Press, 1977.

Satow, R. L. Value-rational authority and professional organizations. *Administrative Science Quarterly*, 1975, *20* (4), 526–531.

Schein, E. H. The individual, the organization, and the career: A conceptual scheme. *Journal of Applied Behavioral Science*, 1971, 7, 401–426.

Schein, E. H. *Professional education: Some new directions*. New York: McGraw-Hill, 1972.

Schein, E. H. *Career dynamics: Matching individual and organizational needs*. Reading, MA: Addison-Wesley, 1978.

Schriesheim, J. M., Von Glinow, A. Kerr, S. Professionals in bureaucracies: A structural alternative. In P. Nystrom and W. Starbuck (Eds.), *Prescriptive Models of Organizations.* New York: North-Holland, 1977.

Schutz, A. & Luckmann, T. [*The Structure of the Life-World*] (R. M. Zaner and H. T. Engelhardt, Jr. trans.) Evanston, IL: Northwestern University Press, 1973.

Schwartz, H. & Davis, S. M. Matching corporate culture and business strategy. *Organizational Dynamics,* 1981, pp. 30–48.

Scott, W. R. Reactions to supervision in a heteronomous professional organization. *Administrative Science Quarterly,* 1965, *10,* 65–81.

Searle-Chatterjee, M. The polluted identity of work: A study of benares sweepers. In S. Waldman (Ed.), *Social Anthropology of Work.* New York: Academic Press, 1979.

Sennett, R. *The Fall of Public Man.* New York: Knopf, 1977.

Shibutani, T. Reference groups and social control. In A. Rose (Ed.), *Human Behavior and Social Processes, An Interactionist Approach.* Boston: Houghton Mifflin, 1962.

Shostak, A. B. *Blue collar life.* New York: Random House, 1969.

Silverman, D. *The theory of organizations.* New York: Basic, 1970.

Slocum, W. L. *Occupational careers: A sociological perspective.* Chicago: Aldine, 1966.

Smith, D. *Report from engine company eight two.* New York: Dutton, 1972.

Sofer, C. *Men at mid-career.* Cambridge: Cambridge University Press, 1970.

Sonnenfeld, J. & Kotter, J. P. The maturation of career theory. *Human Relations,* 1982, *35* (1), 19–46.

Spradley, J. *The ethnographic interview.* New York: Holt, Rinehart, and Winston, 1979.

Starbuck, W. J. Congealing oil: Ideologies to justify acting ideologies out. *Journal of Management Studies,* 1982, *19,* (1), 3–28.

Stewart, R. The manager's job: Discretion vs. demand. *Organizational Dynamics: Managers and Their Jobs.* London: Macmillan, 1968.

Stinchcombe, A. Bureaucratic and craft administration of production: A comparative study. *Administrative Science Quarterly, 1959, 4,* 168–187.

Stone, K. The origins of job structures in the steel industry. *Review of Radical Political Economics,* 1974, *6,* 61–97.

Strauss, G. Union government in the U.S.: Research past and future. *Industrial Relations,* 1977, *16,* 215–242.

Sudnow, D. Normal crimes: Sociological features of the penal code in a public defender office. *Social Forces,* 1965, *12,* 25–76.

Sykes, A. J. M. Some differences in the attitudes of clerical and manual workers. *Sociological Review,* 1965, *13,* 297–310.

Terry, W. C. Police stress: The empirical evidence. *The Journal of Police Science and Administration,* 1981a, *9,* (1), 61–75.

Terry, W. C. *Police Stress as a professional self-image.* Unpublished paper, Department of Sociology, University of Florida, 1981b.

Thompson, J. D. *Organizations in action.* New York: McGraw Hill, 1967.

Tonñies, F. [*Community and Society*] (C. P. Loomis, trans.) East Lansing, MI: Michigan State University Press, 1957. (Originally published, 1887.)

Trist, E. L. & Bamforth, L. K. Some social and psychological consequences of the long-wall method of coal getting. *Human Relations,* 1951, *4,* 1–38.

Tuma, N. B. & Grimes, A. J. A comparison of models of role orientations of professionals in a research-oriented university. *Administrative Science Quarterly,* 1981, *26,* 187–206.

Turner, C. & Hodge, M. N. Occupations and professions. In J. A. Jackson (Ed.), *Professions and Professionalization.* Cambridge: Cambridge University Press, 1970.

Valentine, C. A. *Culture and poverty.* Chicago: University of Chicago Press, 1968.

Van Maanen, J. Observations on the making of policemen. *Human Organization,* 1973, *32,* 407–418.

Van Maanen, J. Working the street: A developmental view of police behavior. In H. Jacob (Ed.), *The Potential for Reform of Criminal Justice*. Beverly Hills, CA: Sage, 1974.

Van Maanen, J. Police Socialization. *Administraive Science Quarterly*, 1975, *20* (3), 207–228.

Van Maanen, J. Breaking-in: Socialization to work. In R. Dubin (Ed.), *Handbook of Work, Organization and Society*. Chicago: Rand McNally, 1976.

Van Maanen, J. Experiencing organizations: Notes on the meaning of careers and socialization. In J. Van Maanen (Ed.), *Organizational Careers: Some New Perspectives*. New York: Wiley, 1977.

Van Maanen, J. The Self, the situation, and the rules of interpersonal relations. In W. Bennis, J. Van Maanen, E. H. Schein, and F. G. Steel, *Essays in Interpersonal Dynamics*. Homewood, IL: Dorsey Press, 1979.

Van Maanen, J. Career Games. In C. B. Derr, (Ed.), *Work, Family, and the Career*. New York: Praeger, 1980a.

Van Maanen, J. Beyond account: The personal impact of police shootings. *The Annals of the American Academy of Political and Social Science*, 1980b, *451* (3), 145–156.

Van Maanen, J. *Some thoughts (and afterthoughts) on context, interpretation, and organization theory*. Paper presented at Academy of Mangement Annual Meetings, San Diego, CA, 1981.

Van Maanen, J. The boss: A portrait of the american police sergeant at work. In M. Punch (Ed.), *Control in Police Organization*. Cambridge, MA: MIT Press, 1983.

Van Maanen, J. & Schein, E. H. Toward a theory of organizational socialization. In B. Staw (Ed.), *Research in Organizational Behavior*. Greenwich, CT: JAI Press, 1979.

Van Maanen, Miller, J. M. & Johnson, J. C. An occupation in transition: traditional and modern forms of commercial fishing. *Work and Occupations*, 1982, *9*, 193–216.

Van Maanen, J., Schein, E. H. & Bailyn, L. The shape of things to come. In L. W. Porter et al. (Eds.), *Perspectives on Behavior in Organizations*. New York: McGraw Hill, 1977.

Vollmer, H. M. & Mills, D. L. *Professionalization*. Englewood Cliffs, NJ: Prentice Hall, 1966.

Weber, M. [*Economy and society*] (G. Ruth and C. Wittich, Eds.) Berkeley, CA: University of California Press, 1968. (Originally published, 1922.)

Weick, K. *The Social Psychology of Organizing*. Reading, MA: Addison Wesley, 1979.

Weick, K. *The presumption of managerial logic*. Unpublished paper, Department of Business Administration, Cornell University, 1982.

White, H. C. *Chains of opportunity*. Cambridge, MA: Harvard University Press, 1970.

Whittington, B. *The Fall and Rise of Trait Theories of the Professions*. Unpublished paper, Graduate School of Management, University of California at Irvine, CA, 1981.

Willis, P. *Learning to labor*. New York: Columbia University Press, 1977.

Wilson, J. Q. Kelling, G. L. Broken windows: The police and neighborhood safety. *The Atlantic Monthly*, March 1982, pp. 29–38.

Whyte, W. H. *The Organization Man*. New York: Simon and Schuster, 1956.

Wilensky, H. L. Orderly careers and social participation: The impact of work history on social integration in the middle mass. *American Sociological Review*, 1961, *26*, 251–539.

Wilensky, H. L. The professionalization of everyone? *American Journal of Sociology*, 1964, *70*, 137–158.

Zimmerman, D. H. Record keeping and the intake process in a public welfare organization. In S. Wheeler (Ed.), *On Record*. New York: Russell Sage Foundation, 1969.

Zulaida, J. *Terranova: The ethos and luck of deep sea fishermen*. Philadelphia: Institute for the Study of Human Issues, 1981.

Name Index